T5-AXM-987

Expositions of the Psalms

THE WORKS OF SAINT AUGUSTINE

A Translation for the 21st Century

Part III – Books

Volume 16:

Expositions of the Psalms

33-50

THE WORKS OF SAINT AUGUSTINE
A Translation for the 21st Century

Expositions of the Psalms

33-50

III/16

translation and notes by
Maria Boulding, O.S.B.

editor
John E. Rotelle, O.S.A.

New City Press
Hyde Park, New York

Published in the United States by New City Press
202 Cardinal Rd., Hyde Park, New York 12538

Cover picture (paperback): A Person in Prayer Calls Upon the Lord; Exaudi, Domine, vocem meam, etc., by Pellegrino di Mariano (1460), from the Gradual of the Choir Books of the Augustinian Monastery of Lecceto (Siena), Italy.

Library of Congress Cataloging-in-Publication Data:

Augustine, Saint, Bishop of Hippo.
The works of Saint Augustine.
"Augustinian Heritage Institute"
Includes bibliographical references and indexes.
Contents: — pt. 3, v .15. Expositions of the Psalms, 1-32
—pt. 3, v. 1. Sermons on the Old Testament, 1-19.
— pt. 3, v. 2. Sermons on the Old Testament, 20-50 — [et al.] — pt. 3, v. 10 Sermons on various subjects, 341-400.
1. Theology — Early church, ca. 30-600. I. Hill, Edmund. II. Rotelle, John E. III. Augustinian Heritage Institute. IV. Title.
BR65.A5E53 1990 270.2 89-28878
ISBN 1-56548-055-4 (series)
ISBN 1-56548-147-X (pt. 3, v. 16)
ISBN 1-56548-146-1 (pt. 3, v. 16: pbk.)

We are indebted to Brepols Publishers, Turnholt, Belgium,for their use of the Latin critical text of *Enarrationes in Psalmos I-CL,* ed. D. Eligius Dekkers, O.S.B. et Johannes Fraipont, *Corpus Christianorum Latinorum* XXXVIII-XL (Turnholt, 1946) 1-2196.

Nihil Obstat: John E. Rotelle, O.S.A., S.T.L., Censor Deputatus
Imprimatur: + Patrick Sheridan, D.D., Vicar General
Archdiocese of New York, July 22, 1999

The *Nihil Obstat* and *Imprimatur* are official declarations that a book or pamphlet is free of doctrinal or moral error. No implication is contained therein that those who have granted the *Nihil Obstat* and *Imprimatur* agree with the contents, opinions or statements expressed.

Printed in the United States of America

Contents

Exposition 1 of Psalm 33 13

Introduction: knock, and it shall be opened to you — 13; He begins to expound the title: David before Abimelech/Achis — 13; Why has the name been changed? — 15; Christ cut down the devil by humility — 16; Melchizedek's sacrifice — 16; The Word makes himself assimilable to mortals — 17; He turned from the Jews to the Gentiles — 18; The scandal of the Eucharist — 19; The tender affection of Christ — 20; The drum — 21; Eucharist and humility — 21; Childlike words concealing strength — 22; Conclusion — 22

Exposition 2 of Psalm 33 23

Introduction: yesterday's promise is to be kept today — 23; Verse 1. Recapitulation of yesterday's findings — 23; Verse 2. It takes humility to bless the Lord all the time — 25; Verse 3. The Lord's donkey — 26; Verse 4. No jealousy among God's lovers — 27; Christ crucified and the Donatist schism — 28; Verse 5. Spring-clean your heart — 29; Verse 6. Drawing near to the Light — 31; Verses 7-8. Rescue for the poor — 32; Verse 9. Parallels: David and Christ, Achis and the incredulous Jews — 33; Verses 10-11. Being rich in the Lord — 34; Verse 12. Christ the teacher — 36; Verse 13. Longing for "good days" — 36; Verse 14. You cannot have it both ways — 37; Verse 15. The search for peace — 38; Verse 16. Cruel to be kind — 39; Verse 17. God watches the wicked equally — 39; Verse 18. Being heard in the furnace of persecution — 40; Verses 19-20. The troubles of the just — 40; Verse 21. Bones are safeguarded — 41; Verse 22. The last end of the wicked — 42; Verses 22-23. But not all kinds of sinners — 43

Exposition 1 of Psalm 34 45

Introduction: Christ, strong of hand and object of our desire, is speaking — 45; Verses 1-2. The armor of God — 46; Verse 3. God our ally in the fight against dark forces — 47; Verse 4. "I am your salvation" — 48; Verses 5-6. Dark and slippery paths for the wicked — 52; Verses 7-8. The trap springs back on the setter — 52; Verse 9. God offers you himself — 54; Verse 10. Christ's bones cry out in praise — 55

Exposition 2 of Psalm 34 59

Introduction: Christ and the Church, one body, one voice — 59; Verses 11-12. In what sense was Christ ignorant? — 60; Verse 13. Sackcloth, fasting and prayer, as interpreted of Christ — 61; Verse 14. Being near to God, or far from him — 64; Verse 15. Blessed are the mourners — 66; Verse 16. Persecution, past and present — 66; Verse 17. Why help is delayed — 66; Verse 18. Praise from the "weighty people" — 67; Verses 19-21. Christ and those who tried to trap him — 67; Verse 22. God's silence — 68; Verses 23-24. The cause, not the pain, makes the martyr — 69; Verses 24-26. Swallowing the wicked — 70; Verses 27-28. How to praise God all day long — 70

Exposition of Psalm 35 72

Verse 1. Willful lack of understanding — 72; God is present within — 73; Verses 3-4. Dishonest searching — 73; Verse 5. Inner peace — 74; Who wins the battle? — 76; Verse 6. God's good gifts, temporal and eternal — 77; Verse 7. God's true and humble mountains — 79; The depths of sin and judgment — 81; Verses 7-8. God's kindness to humans and animals — 82; Becoming "sons of men" — 83; Verse 9. Thirsting for a reality beyond description — 85; Verse 10. Fountain and light — 86; Verse 11. Conformity with God's will — 86; Verse 12. Beware of the foot of pride — 87; Verse 13. Watching the tempter's head — 88

Exposition 1 of Psalm 36 90

Ignorance about the last day — 90; One is taken, another left — 92; Verses 1-2. Why do the wicked flourish? — 93; Verses 3-4. The wealth of the Lord's land — 94; The pleas of the flesh and of the heart — 95; Verses 5-6. Darkness will give way to light — 95; Verses 7-9. Curb your resentment if you want to see straight — 97; Verse 10. Time passes swiftly, though to the sick it seems long — 98; Sinners have their uses — 100; Verse 11. Peace and innocence — 101

Exposition 2 of Psalm 36. 103

Introduction: two different types of people — 103; Verses 12-13. The sinner's day is coming — 104; Verses 14-16. The persecutor shoots himself in the foot — 105; Verse 17. By word and example the Lord strengthens the righteous — 106; Paul: persecutor, converted, sufferer, strengthened by the Lord — 107; Verse 18. The vision of God is promised to us — 108; Verse 19. A hope that does not deceive — 110; Verse 20. No place for the sinner to call home — 110; Two roving Donatists — 111; Evanescent grandeur — 112; Verse 21. Ingratitude contrasted with generosity — 113; Verse 22. Cursers become blessers — 114; Verse 23. Following Christ — 115; Verse 24. Whatever you may suffer, Christ suffered before you — 116; The Donatists are in the same tradition of lying — 117; The Donatists repaid in their own coin: a historical parallel — 118; The historical parallel pursued, Primian and Caecilian — 126; Priority in time versus preponderance of numbers — 126; Another argument: a condemned person cannot sit as judge — 127; Divergences between Primian's case and Caecilian's — 127; The numbers game again — 128

Exposition 3 of Psalm 36. 129

Verse 25. Does it match experience? — 129; Spiritual paralysis — 130; Letting the paralytic down through the roof — 130; The Church's long memory — 131; Chewing on God's bread — 132; Verse 26. Lending to God — 132; Blessed sowing — 134; Verse 27. Avoid evil but also do good — 135; Verse 28. Hidden and visible judgment — 136; Verse 29. The land of the living — 137; Verses 30-32. The security of the just — 138; Verse 33. The persecutor's dominance is illusory — 138; Verses 34-36. The rapid disappearance of the ungodly — 140; Verses 37-38. Innocence, a straight eye, and a promised future — 141; Verses 39-40. The final discrimination — 142; Conclusion: Donatist onslaughts — 142; Augustine's past life, target of Donatist attacks — 143; Keep to the point: what matters is the truth — 144

Exposition of Psalm 37. 146

Introduction: this psalm could belong to the Canaanite woman — 146; Verse 1. Wistfully remembering the Sabbath rest — 146; Verses 2-3. Chastened by fire — 147; Verse 4. True health is reserved for the future — 148; The voice of the Head, the voice of his body: two in one flesh — 150; Verse 5. A weight on one's head — 152; Verse 6. The smell of sin — 152; Verse 7. Curvature of the heart — 153; Verse 8. Fantasies will be superseded by the vision of truth — 154; Verse 9. Homesickness — 155; The groaning heart — 156; Verse 10. Continuing desire is unceasing prayer — 156; Verse 11. Turmoil of the heart and spiritual blindness — 157; Verse 12. The Head speaks of his sufferings, which are also ours — 158; Who is near, who far? — 159; Verse 13. Seeking Christ's life — 160; Verses 14-15. The Lord's silence under attack — 161; Verse 16. Trust God when you have no human advocate — 162; Verse 17. Gloating enemies — 162; Verse 18. Scourging — 163; Verses 18-19. The proper motive for grief — 163; Verse 20. My enemies are alive and well — 164; Verse 21. The accursed upon the tree — 165; Verse 22. The person of the sinner is transfigured into Christ — 166; Verse 23. The denarius of eternal life — 166

Exposition of Psalm 38. 168

Verse 1. Learning to leap — 168; Verse 2. No one avoids all faults in speaking; the hearers must take it in good part — 170; Verse 3. Woe betide a preacher who falls silent — 172; Verses 4-5. Longing for the goal — 173; Time, the dimension of contingent being — 176; What I have and what I lack — 178; Verse 6. The passage from the old to the new — 178; Emptiness all round — 180; Verse 7. For whom are you amassing your wealth? — 181; There is a safer place to store it — 182; Verse 8. Still waiting — 184; Verse 9. Perfection through knowing one's imperfection — 185; On show before mortals and angels — 186; Verses 10-11. Struck dumb — 187; Verse 12. Salutary correction — 187; Experienced weakness leads to humility — 188; Only death is certain — 190; Verse 13. Weeping for the distant prospect — 190; No security of tenure — 191; Verse 14. The goal of true being — 192

Exposition of Psalm 39. 194

Persecution, overt and insidious — 194; Verses 2-3. Waiting for the Lord — 196; Verse 4. Out of the mud — 197; A hymn of praise, but for our benefit, not God's — 199; Christ's voice in the song of his members — 200; Leaders and followers — 201; Verse 5. Steer clear of the broad road — 202; Fanatical addiction — 203; Verse 6. There are better shows in God's Church — 204; Verse 7. The course of love — 207; Sacrifice, old and new — 207; Verse 8. The mark of Cain — 208; Verse 9. Christ's obedience — 210; Verse 10. The mouth speaks the heart's thoughts. The repentant thief — 210; Neither fear nor falsehood — 211; Verse 11. Speaking the truth under threat — 212; Christ is truth and salvation —

213; Mercy now, justice later — 213; Verses 12-13. The near mercy — 214; The cure for spiritual blindness — 215; Small sins are very numerous — 216; Verses 13-14. Hearty incomprehension — 216; Verse 15. Seeking Christ's soul/life — 217; The place for followers is behind the Lord — 217; Verses 16-17. Open malevolence and false flattery — 218; Verse 18. God's care for his poor — 220; The prayer of one single poor man, Christ and his members — 221

Exposition of Psalm 40. 224

Christ, leader of martyrs — 224; Verse 2. Christ the poor man — 226; Christ, divine and human, rich and poor — 226; Verse 3. Eternal life and temporal help are both God's gift — 227; The devil revises his tactics — 228; Verse 4. The uncomfortable bed — 230; Verse 5. Confession of sin—Christ's words? — 231; Verse 6. Already expounded — 232; Verse 7. Spies within who spread slander abroad — 232; What counts is the intention behind the words — 233; Verse 9. Eve is created from Adam's sleep — 234; Verse 10. How could Jesus have trusted Judas? — 235; Verse 11. The green wood did not burn — 236; Verse 12. The killers' glee was premature — 237; Verses 13-14. The Christian case against the pagans is proved from the Jewish scriptures — 237

Exposition of Psalm 41. 239

Introduction: longing on both sides — 239; Verse 1. Understanding offered to the "children of Korah" — 240; Verse 2. Deer kill snakes, and then feel thirstier — 241; Kindly arrangements among deer — 242; Verse 3. The longing is intensified by waiting — 242; Verse 4. A diet of tears — 243; Where is your God? The search through creatures and in oneself — 244; Verse 5. The soul is poured out above itself — 245; In the admirable tabernacle he catches the sound of another festival — 246; Verse 6. Subsequent sadness — 248; Verse 7. Hope and salvation — 249; Turn away from yourself — 249; Verse 8. The human heart is a great deep — 251; The depth of God's judgments — 252; Waves and breakers — 253; Verse 9. Gather the word while you can — 253; Verses 9-10. The inner prayer: "Why have you forgotten me?" — 254; Verses 10-11. Even my bones are broken — 254; Verses 11-12. Where is your God? — 255

Exposition of Psalm 42. 256

The song of Christ's body — 256; A common lot for all, but different desires — 256; Verse 2. The cause of your sorrow — 257; Verse 3. Light and truth; the mountain and the tent — 258; Verse 4. God is praised with both lyre and psaltery — 259; Verse 5. The higher part of the mind converses with its soul — 261; You cannot be wholly free from sin — 262; Fasting, almsgiving and prayer — 263

Exposition of Psalm 43. 265

Verse 1. Why God's favor seems to be withdrawn — 265; Verses 2-3. Contrast: then and now — 266; Verse 4. Strength comes from God's presence — 267; Verse 5. God yesterday, tomorrow and today — 268; Verses 6-7. Hope for the future too — 268; Verse 8. Future salvation is as sure as though already past — 269; Verse 9. Definitely a future prospect — 270; Verses 10-11. Present failure — 270; Verses 12-13. Disaster — 271; Verses

14-15. The example of the cross — 271; Verses 16-17. Disinterested love: further understanding — 272; Verses 18-20. The hard way — 274; Verses 21-22. God knows our hearts, though we may not — 275; Verse 23. Arise, Lord! — 277; Verses 24-25. Ultimate humiliation — 277; Another interpretation: those who fail — 278; Verse 26. Unmerited help — 279

Exposition of Psalm 44. 280

Verse 1. Childish mockery of a bald man — 280; The world has changed, and so have we — 281; The Word weds the Church; the Bridegroom's beauty — 282; Verse 2. The Father speaks — 284; Verse 3. The Bridegroom brings grace — 286; An alternative interpretation: the psalmist has spoken throughout — 288; Verse 4. The sword of division — 289; The sacredness of the thigh — 291; Verse 5. Gentleness and power — 292; Verse 6. Christ's piercing shafts — 293; Verse 7. The straight ruler — 294; Verse 8. Attend to your sins before God does — 295; God's anointing of God — 296; Jacob's anointed stone and Jacob's ladder — 297; Verse 9. The scent of Christ — 299; Verse 10. The apostles' daughters — 300; The queen's apparel — 302; Verse 11. The admonition to the bride — 302; Verse 12. Her beauty is the king's gift — 304; Verse 13. The homage of the Gentiles and of the rich — 304; Verses 14-15. Inner beauty — 306; Verse 16. The joyful entry of the virgins — 307; Verse 17. Sons to take the place of fathers for the Church — 307; Verse 18. The city of God — 308

Exposition of Psalm 45. 310

Verse 1. Christ's cross unlocks mysteries — 310; Verse 2. Insecure refuges, and the worst tribulations — 311; The remedy — 313; Verse 3. Christ stills the storm — 314; The mountains move — 314; Verse 4. The apostles raise a storm — 315; Verse 5. The river of the Holy Spirit — 316; Verse 6. Divine indwelling — 317; Verse 7. The rain of salvation — 317; Verse 8. God undertakes to support us — 319; Verse 9. The stone that grew into a mountain — 319; Verse 10. Banishment of war, and of weapons — 321; Verse 11. Be still and see — 322; Christ's triumph among both Gentiles and Jews — 323

Exposition of Psalm 46. 324

One truth, varied expressions — 324; Verse 1. The children of Korah — 324; Verse 2. The joy of the Gentiles — 326; Verse 3. King of the Jews, and of all the earth — 326; Verse 4. Worldwide sovereignty? — 327; Verse 5. Jacob and Esau — 328; Verse 6. Joy at Christ's ascension — 329; Verse 7. Christ is God from eternity — 330; Verse 8. The universal God — 330; Verse 9. The Lord's enthronement in the souls of the just — 331; Verse 10. Abraham's progeny — 332; The centurion — 333; The high and mighty — 334

Exposition of Psalm 47. 335

Verse 1. The second day of creation: the Church — 335; Verse 2. The city and the mountain — 336; Verse 3. The "companions of the north" join with Zion — 337; Verse 4. Sheer grace — 339; Verses 5-7. The King and the kings — 340; Verse 8. The destruction of the proud ships — 341; Verse 9. The Church contemplates prophecies fulfilled — 342; Verse 10. A mixed crowd in the Church — 343; How many will be saved? — 344; Verse 11. God is praised not in a sect, but worldwide — 345; Verse 12. The discerning winnower — 346; Verses 13-14. The strength of charity — 347; Verse 15. This is our God — 348

Exposition 1 of Psalm 48. 350

Introduction: Trying to bend God to our perverse desires — 350; Verse 2. Two ways of listening, two ways of dwelling — 351; Verse 3. Rich and poor listeners — 352; Verses 4-5. Practicing what we preach — 354; Verse 6. The serpent at our heels — 356; Verses 7-8. Reliance on Christ, our brother — 357; Verses 8-9. Making a good investment — 358; Verses 9-10. Reversal of fortunes after this life — 359; Verse 11. Death and eternal life — 360; Prudent use of riches — 361; Who are the strangers? — 362; Verse 12. The dead are not helped by feasts at their tombs — 364; Verses 13-14. Loss of insight, and hypocrisy — 365

Exposition 2 of Psalm 48. 367

Verse 14, continued. Yesterday's conclusion recalled — 367; Verse 15. Shepherded by death — 368; Night and daybreak, winter and summer, trees and grass — 369; Verse 16. "As if . . ." — 372; Verse 17. Do not lose your nerve — 373; Verses 17-18. Dying in style — 374; Verse 19. Teeth on edge — 375; Mercenary praise — 376; Verses 20-21. Wicked and righteous lines of descent — 378

Exposition of Psalm 49. 380

Verse 1. Christ calls — 380; The truly deified and the false gods — 380; Christ's universal lordship — 382; Verse 2. "Beginning from Jerusalem" — 383; Verse 3. Hidden and silent now, Christ will be manifest later as judge — 385; The fire of judgment — 386; Will there be enough thrones? — 388; Verse 4. "Heaven" is Christ's partner as he sorts out the earth — 391; Verse 5. Mercy is better than sacrifices — 393; Verse 6. Infallible discernment — 393; Verse 7. He is God, and your God — 394; Verse 8. Genuine sacrifice — 395; Verse 9. The old sacrifices are superseded — 396; Verse 10. All animals, wild and tame, are God's — 396; Verse 11. God's knowledge of creatures — 397; Verses 12-13. God is not hungry — 398; Verse 14. The sacrifice of praise — 399; Verse 15. Longing for heaven is painful — 400; Verse 16. Preachers, beware! — 401; Verses 17-18. Contempt for God's words; complicity in sin — 403; Verse 19. More collusion with evildoing — 403; Verse 20. Further charges: slandering a brother and scandalizing the weak — 404; Verse 21. You should be like God; do not try to make him like you — 405; Verse 22. The lion — 406; Verse 23. Who offers the sacrifice of praise? — 407; Discovering Christ as God's salvation — 408

Exposition of Psalm 50. 410

Introduction: pray for the absentees — 410; Verses 1-2. David's adultery — 411; The prospect of pardon — 413; Verse 3. Mercy for witting and unwitting transgressions — 414; Verse 4. Mercy does not nullify justice — 414; Verse 5. Nathan's parable; the adulteress and Christ — 415; Verse 6. The sinless Christ, himself judged, alone judges justly — 416; Verse 7. Original sin — 418; Verse 8. Repentance entails a risk — 419; Verse 9. Hyssop — 420; Verse 10. The humility of one who listens — 421; Verse 11. "Look away from my sins" — 422; Verse 12. David's patience in adversity — 423; Verses 13-14. The Holy Spirit — 424; Verse 15. An ex-sinner teaches sinners — 425; Verse 16. The prospect of ultimate incorruptibility — 426; Verses 17-19. Praise and true sacrifice — 427; Verse 20. Zion the lookout post, Jerusalem the vision of peace — 428; Verse 21. God's fire — 428; Concluding exhortations on family discipline — 429

Index of Scripture 431

Index 439

Exposition 1 of Psalm 33

First Sermon

Introduction: knock, and it shall be opened to you

1. There seems to be nothing in the text of this psalm that is obscure or needs explanation, but its title calls for careful attention and invites us to knock on its door. And since in this psalm we find it written that anyone who hopes in the Lord is blessed, let us all hope that when we knock he will open to us.[1] He would not have exhorted us to knock unless he were willing to open the door to us when we do. It sometimes happens that someone who had decided to keep his door shut is nevertheless so wearied by repeated knocking that he changes his mind, gets up, and opens, so that he may not have to put up with the persistent caller any longer;[2] have we then not much better reason to hope that God will quickly open to us, when he himself has commanded, *Knock, and the door will be opened to you* (Mt 7:7)? With all the earnestness of my heart that is what I am doing now, knocking at the door of the Lord God, asking him graciously to reveal this mystery to us; and I beg you too, beloved,[3] to join me in knocking, with the intention of listening and in a spirit of humble readiness to pray for me; for we must admit that it is a deep and vast mystery we have here.

He begins to expound the title: David before Abimelech/Achis

2. This is how the title reads: *A psalm of David, when he altered his behavior in the presence of Abimelech, and forsook him, and went away*. We need to look through what scripture relates about David's exploits to find out when this happened, as we did when examining the title of another psalm, *when David was in flight from the face of Abessalon, his son* (Ps 3:1). In that connection we read in the Books of Kings[4] how David was on the run from his son Abessalon. This is something that really happened, and what happened has been written down; so that although the title of that psalm was assigned very mysteriously, it was, all the same, derived from an event that really occurred.[5]

---

1. See Mt 7:7-8.
2. See Lk 11:8.
3. *Caritas vestra.*
4. Second Book of Samuel in our usage. "Abessalon" is the reading of the best manuscripts.
5. See 2 Sm 15:14.

I think the position is the same with our present psalm, and that we shall find this episode, that *David altered his behavior in the presence of Abimelech, and forsook him, and went away*, also recorded in the Books of Kings,[6] where everything about David's exploits is told. We do not find this story precisely, but we do find an event from which the story seems to be derived. Scripture records that when David was fleeing from his persecutor, Saul, he took refuge with Achis, King of Gath;[7] this man was king of a territory bordering on that of the Judeans. There David lay low to escape Saul's hostility. But the memory of David's triumph was still fresh, the triumph that had earned him hatred for the good he had done in killing Goliath, and winning both honor and safety for kingdom and king in a single fight.[8] While Goliath was uttering his taunts Saul had seethed with rage, but as soon as Goliath had been overthrown Saul's attitude changed into enmity for the man whose hand had slain his foe, and he became jealous of David's reputation. This was more especially the case because the people were ecstatic with joy, and the women danced and sang of David's prowess, crying that Saul had slain thousands, but David tens of thousands.[9] As a result Saul was very upset, because this boy was beginning to acquire higher renown than himself through one fight, and was being exalted above the king in the praises sung by all. As Saul fell prey to sickly malice and worldly pride, he began to be jealous of David and to hound him. This was when David took refuge with the King of Gath, as I have said. This king's name was Achis.

But the attendants of Achis pointed out to him that the fugitive he was sheltering could be none other than the man who had won great glory among the Judeans. They said to him, *Isn't this David, the man to whom the chorus of Israelite women sang, "Saul has slain thousands, and David tens of thousands"?* (1 Sm 21:11). Now if that reputation had begun to arouse Saul to jealous hatred, did not David have reason to fear that this other king, with whom he had sought refuge, might be minded to treat him badly? David could be an enemy on his very doorstep if he let him live, or so the king might think. So scripture tells us, *David was afraid of him as well, and altered his behavior in front of them all, affecting madness. He drummed on the doors into the city and was carried in his own hands, and fell down outside on the threshold, as saliva dribbled down his beard*. The king in whose country he was hiding saw him and demanded of his attendants, *What have you brought this madman to me for? Do you think I want him in my house?* (1 Sm 21:12-15). The king threw him out and banished him, and so David departed unharmed, thanks to this feigned insanity.

6. Samuel.
7. See 1 Sm 21:10-15.
8. See Sm 17:41-54.
9. See 1 Sm 18:7.

It is because of the pretended insanity that the title of our psalm seems to relate to this story: *A psalm of David, when he altered his behavior in the presence of Abimelech, and forsook him, and went away*. In the story it was Achis, not Abimelech, but the only disagreement is in the name, for the event has been described in the psalm's title in almost the same words as in the Book of Kings. This fact should prompt us to seek more carefully the mysterious reason[10] for the change of name. Clearly it has been changed; but not without reason. It signifies something. The episode was recalled, yet the name was altered, and there must be some reason for this.

Why has the name been changed?

3. The profundity of these mysteries must be obvious to you, brothers and sisters. If it was no mystery that Goliath was killed by a mere boy, then neither was it a mystery that David altered his bearing, and feigned madness, and drummed on the door, and fell down at the city gates and on the threshold, and that saliva trickled down his beard. How is it possible that all this had no significance? The apostle tells us plainly, *All these things happened to them, but with symbolic import, for they are written down as a rebuke to us, upon whom the climax of the ages has come* (1 Cor 10:11). Did the manna signify nothing, the manna of which the apostle said, *They ate spiritual food* (1 Cor 10:3)? What of the parting of the sea, and the leading of the people safely through it so that they might escape from Pharaoh's persecution—did that mean nothing, when the apostle declares, *I would not have you ignorant, brothers and sisters, that all our ancestors walked under the cloud, and all crossed the sea, and all were through Moses baptized in cloud and sea* (1 Cor 10:1-2)? What about the rock that was struck, so that water gushed out—is that void of significance, in view of the apostle's statement that *the rock was Christ* (1 Cor 10:4)? Do all these things, historical events as they were, have no further meaning? Finally, think of Abraham's two sons, born in the natural way, yet called by the apostle figures of the two covenants, old and new. *These are two covenants, allegorically prefigured*, he says (Gal 4:24). If all these signify nothing, in spite of the statement backed by apostolic authority that they happened as mysterious types of what was to come, then we are right to think that what I read to you just now about David from the Book of Kings had no further meaning either. Nor, consequently, is there any significance in the change of name when the psalm says, *In the presence of Abimelech*.

10. *Sacramentum*.

Christ cut down the devil by humility

4. Let me have your attention now, please. Everything that I have been saying has been said as from a knocking hand; the door has not been opened yet. I was knocking while I said it, you were knocking as you listened; now let us all persevere in knocking and praying that the Lord may open to us. We have an interpretation of the Hebrew names, for there has been no lack of learned men[11] to translate these names from Hebrew into Greek, and thence into Latin. If we look up these names we find that Abimelech means "My father's kingdom" and Achis "How can this be?" Let us consider the names carefully, for perhaps the door is beginning to open for us. If you ask, "What does Achis mean?" you are told it means, "How can this be?" But "How can this be" is what a person says who is bewildered, and cannot understand. Abimelech means "my father's kingdom," and David means "strong of hand." David represented Christ, as Goliath represented the devil, and when David laid Goliath low he prefigured Christ, who crushed the devil. But what is Christ, who cut down the devil? He is humility, the humility that slew pride. So when I say, "Christ," my brothers and sisters, I am drawing attention most especially to his humility. It was by humility that he opened a way for us. We had wandered far from God by pride, and could not find our way back except through humility; yet we had no model of humility to hold before us and imitate. The whole mortal race of humans had swollen with pride. Even if someone of humble spirit did emerge, such as the prophets and patriarchs, humankind disdained to imitate humble humans. To overcome their unwillingness to do so, God himself became humble, so that at any rate human pride would not disdain to follow in the footsteps of God.

Melchizedek's sacrifice

5. As you know, the Jews of old offered sacrifices proper to the order of Aaron, using animals as victims. This was a mysterious prophetic sign. The sacrifice of the Lord's body and blood had not yet been offered; the faithful know about this, as do all who have read the gospel, and this sacrifice is now widespread throughout the world. Keep both kinds of sacrifice before your mind's eye, the one after the order of Aaron, the other after the order of Melchizedek; for scripture says, *The Lord has sworn, and will not revoke it: you are a priest for ever, after the order of Melchizedek* (Ps 109(110):4). Now of whom is this said, *You are a priest for ever, after the order of Melchizedek*? Of our Lord Jesus Christ. Who was Melchizedek? He was King of Salem. Salem was the ancient city, but the city in the same place in later days was called Jerusalem, according to the experts. So before ever the Jews established their

---

11. Such as Jerome.

kingdom the priest Melchizedek was there, and Genesis describes him as a priest of God Most High.[12] On the occasion when Abraham delivered Lot from the power of his enemies, Melchizedek met him. Abraham had struck down Lot's captors and set his kinsman free, and it was after this rescue that Melchizedek came out to meet him. So great was Melchizedek that he could confer a blessing on Abraham. He set forth bread and wine, and blessed Abraham; and Abraham gave him tithes. Consider what he set forth, and who the man was to whom he gave his blessing. Then, later on, scripture says to someone, *You are a priest for ever, after the order of Melchizedek.* David said this in spirit[13] long after Abraham's day, yet Melchizedek was Abraham's contemporary. To whom, then, does the prophecy refer, *you are a priest for ever, after the order of Melchizedek*? To whom else, but the one whose sacrifice is known to you?

The Word makes himself assimilable to mortals

6. The sacrifice of Aaron was therefore superseded, and the sacrifice according to the order of Melchizedek came into being. To this end, someone *altered his behavior.* Who is this someone? Let him not be just "someone," for our Lord Jesus Christ is known to us.[14] He willed us to find salvation in his body and blood. But how could he make his body and blood available to us? Through his humility; for if he had not been humble, he could not have been eaten and drunk. Contemplate his lofty divinity: *in the beginning was the Word, and the Word was with God; he was God* (Jn 1:1). That is eternal food. The angels eat it, the celestial powers eat it, the blessed spirits eat it, and in eating they are totally satisfied, yet this food that fills them and gives them joy remains undiminished. What human being could aspire to that food? Where could a human heart be found fit to eat food like that?

It was necessary for that banquet to be converted into milk if it was to become available to little ones. But how does food become milk? How can food be turned into milk, except by being passed through flesh? This is what a mother does. What the mother eats the baby eats too, but since the baby is unable to digest bread, the mother turns the bread into her own flesh, and through the humility of the breast and its supply of milk she feeds her baby with the same bread. How then does the Wisdom of God feed us with that supernal bread? *The Word was made flesh, and dwelt among us* (Jn 1:14). Think of the humility of it: humans have eaten the bread of angels, as scripture says: *He gave them bread from heaven; mortals ate the bread of angels* (Ps 77(78):24-25). The eternal

12. See Gn 14:18.
13. Or "in the Spirit."
14. A variant in punctuation, supported by some witnesses, translates as "Who is this someone? A Someone well known, for our Lord Jesus Christ is known to us."

Word on whom the angels feed, the Word who is equal to the Father, this Word human beings have eaten. He who, *being in the form of God, deemed it no robbery to be God's equal*, he on whom the angels feed to their total satisfaction, *emptied himself and took on the form of a slave. Bearing the human likeness, sharing the human lot, he humbled himself and was made obedient to the point of death, even death on a cross* (Phil 2:6-8), so that from the cross the Lord's flesh and blood might be delivered to us today as the new sacrifice. This was because *he altered his behavior in the presence of Abimelech*, that is, in the presence of "his father's kingdom," for "my father's kingdom" was the kingdom of the Jews. In what sense could that be called his father's kingdom? In that it was David's kingdom, Abraham's kingdom. The kingdom of God the Father is the Church, rather than the Jewish people; but with regard to Christ's human descent the people of Israel was "his father's kingdom." It was said of him, *The Lord God will give him the throne of his father, David* (Lk 1:32). This proves that according to carnal descent David was the father of our Lord, though in his divinity Christ was not David's son but David's Lord. The Jews were familiar with Christ in the flesh, but had no knowledge of his divinity. Accordingly he put to them the question, *What do you think of Christ? Whose son is he? They replied, "David's." Jesus said to them, Then how is it that David in spirit calls him "Lord," saying, The Lord said to my Lord, "Sit at my right hand, until I make your enemies into your footstool"? If David in the spirit calls him "Lord," how can he be David's son? And they had no answer to give him* (Mt 22:42-46), because all they knew of Christ was what they could see in him with their eyes, not what was to be understood with the heart. If only they had had eyes within as they had eyes without, they would have recognized David's son from what they saw outwardly, but from what they understood inwardly they would have recognized him as David's Lord.

He turned from the Jews to the Gentiles

7. So *he altered his behavior in the presence of Abimelech*. What does *in the presence of Abimelech* mean? In the presence of his father's kingdom. And what does that mean? In the presence of the Jews. *And he forsook him and went away.* Whom did he forsake? He forsook the Jewish people, and went away. Look for Christ today among the Jews, and you do not find him. Why did he forsake them and go away? Because although he *altered his behavior* they clung to the old sacrifice after the order of Aaron, and did not grasp the sacrifice according to the order of Melchizedek; so they lost Christ, and the Gentiles came to possess him, even though he had not previously sent any preachers to them. He had sent plenty of preachers to the Israelites: David himself, and Abraham, Isaac and Jacob, Isaiah, Jeremiah and the other prophets. All these he had sent, but in spite

of it few had come to know him, or at any rate few in comparison with those who were lost, for they were many. We read of thousands. Scripture says, *A remnant shall be saved* (Rom 9:27);[15] but if you look for Christians today among the circumcised, you find none. Earlier in the Christian era, not so long ago, there were many thousands of Christians from the circumcised, but if you look for them now you will not find them; and it is with good reason that you find none, for Christ *altered his behavior in the presence of Abimelech, and forsook them and went away.*

But it was in the presence of Achis that David altered his behavior, and forsook him and went away. The names were changed deliberately, to alert us to the mystery this change signified. Otherwise we might have thought that what the psalm recalled and related was nothing more than the event recounted in the Books of Kings; then we would not have sought out any prefiguration of future happenings, but read it simply as the story of past events. But the names are changed, and what does this tell you? That there is something still closed here. Knock then. Do not remain stuck in the letter, for the letter is death-dealing,[16] but desire the spiritual meaning, for the Spirit gives life, and spiritual understanding saves the believer.

The scandal of the eucharist

8. Listen now, brothers and sisters, to how he forsook King Achis. I have told you that the name Achis means "How can this be?" Now recall the occasion in the gospel when our Lord Jesus Christ was speaking about his body, and said, *Unless you eat my flesh and drink my blood, you will not have life in you, for my flesh really is food, and my blood really is drink* (Jn 6:54.56). The disciples who were following him were appalled, and shuddered at what he said. They did not understand it, and thought the Lord was making some dreadful proposal: that they were to eat that flesh of his that they could see, and drink the blood. They could not bear it, and it was as though they were asking, "How can this be?" Their mistake, their ignorance, their stupidity, were prefigured in King Achis, for when someone asks, "How can this be?" it indicates a lack of understanding, and where there is no understanding, there is the darkness of ignorance. So ignorance, like King Achis, held sway over them; over them the kingdom of error held sway. But Christ went on, saying, *Unless you eat my flesh and drink my blood. . . .* He had "altered his behavior," and so the notion of giving his flesh to people to eat, and his blood to drink, seemed to them dementia, insanity. David likewise seemed insane to Achis, who protested, "You have brought a madman into my house." Indeed, does it not sound like insanity to say, "Eat my flesh,

15. See Is 10:22.
16. See 2 Cor 3:6.

drink my blood"? Yet here is Christ saying, *Unless you eat my flesh and drink my blood, you will not have life in you.* He seems to be mad. But it is to King Achis that he seems to be mad, that is, to the stupid and ignorant. Accordingly he forsakes them and goes away; understanding has fled from their hearts, so that they cannot comprehend him. What had they to say? *"How can this be?"* which is what the name Achis means. They objected, *"How can this man give us his flesh to eat?"* (Jn 6:53). They thought the Lord was a madman, that he did not know what he was saying, that he was raving. But he knew very well what he was saying by this alteration in his behavior; by making use of apparent madness and insanity he was proclaiming his sacraments, so he affected madness, and drummed on the doors into the city.

The tender affection of Christ

9. We must inquire next the meaning of the phrases, "he affected," and "he drummed on the doors into the city." Moreover it was not without some good reason that scripture said, *He fell down outside on the threshold, and saliva trickled down his beard.* No, it was by no means without good reason. A somewhat long-winded explanation will not seem burdensome to us if it rewards us with insight. Now you are aware, brothers and sisters, that the Jews, in whose presence he altered his behavior, whom he forsook when he went away, are having a holiday today.[17] They have lost Christ; he has left them and gone away, so their holiday is an empty one. But we enjoy a fruitful holiday, with the opportunity to understand Christ who left them and came to us. Nothing in all this is without purpose, even in David's crazy behavior, where he is said to have *affected madness, and drummed on the doors into the city; he was carried in his own hands, and fell down outside on the threshold, and saliva dribbled down his beard.* We are told that he *affected madness*; what does *affected* suggest? He had affection. But what is it to have affection, or be affectionate? He had compassion on our infirmities; that was why he willed to assume that very flesh in which he could slay death. He had compassion on us; it is saying that he had tender affection for us. The apostle rebukes people who are hard-hearted and without affection. Censuring some people of this type, he says they are *without affection, devoid of mercy* (Rom 1:31). Where there is affection, there will mercy be. Where did we find mercy? In him who was merciful to us from above. If he had been unwilling to empty himself, and had chosen rather to remain where he is—eternal, and equal to the Father—we would have remained in eternal death; but in order to free us from that eternal death into which the sin of pride had plunged us, he humbled himself, and became obedient unto death, even the

17. The sermon was preached on a Saturday, as is clear from its closing words.

death of the cross. This is where his affection for us took him, as far as dying on the cross.

The drum

Now when someone is crucified, he is stretched out on a wooden instrument. But when you want to make a drum, you stretch out flesh—skin, that is—over a wooden frame. This is why scripture has it that *he drummed*; it means that he was crucified, he was stretched out on a wooden frame. *He affected*: that is, he felt affectionate tenderness for us, even to the point of laying down his life for his sheep.[18] And *he drummed*. How? *At the doors into the city*. This door is the one that is opened to us so that we may believe in God. We had closed our doors against Christ, and opened them to the devil; our hearts were closed against eternal life. But because we humans had our hearts shut against eternal life and could not see that Word on whom the angels gaze, our Lord God himself opened the hearts of mortals; he drummed on the doors of the city.

Eucharist and humility

10. *And he was carried in his own hands*. How on earth are we to understand this, my brothers and sisters, how is it humanly possible? How can someone be carried in his own hands? A person can be carried in the hands of others, but not in his own. Well, we have no way of knowing what it literally means in David's case; but we can make sense of it with regard to Christ. Christ was being carried in his own hands when he handed over his body, saying, *This is my body* (Mt 26:26); for he was holding that very body in his hands as he spoke. Such is the humility of our Lord Jesus Christ, and this humility is what he recommends to us most strongly. He exhorts us to practice it too, brothers and sisters, so that by imitating his humility we may have life. By holding fast to Christ's humility we can strike down Goliath and conquer our pride. *He fell down outside on the threshold*. What does that signify, *he fell down*? He threw himself down into humility. But why *on the threshold*? At the place where we make our entrance into faith, that entrance that admits us to salvation. There is no way in except through this preliminary faith, as the Song of Songs declares, *You will come and pass through, beginning from faith* (Sg 4:8, LXX). We too shall come, and see him face to face, as scripture promises: *Dearly beloved, we are children of God already, but what we shall be has not yet appeared. We know that when he appears, we shall be like him, because we shall see him as he is* (1 Jn 3:2). When shall we see him? When all these other things have passed away. Listen to a similar testimony from the apostle Paul: *Now we see a tantalizing reflection in a*

18. See Jn 10:15.

mirror, but then face to face (1 Cor 13:12). Until we come to see the Word face to face, as the angels see him, we still need the threshold where the Lord fell down, humbling himself even to death.

Childlike words concealing strength

11. What significance is there in *the saliva dribbled down his beard*? This is part of the way in which he *altered his behavior in the presence of Abimelech* (or Achis); and then *he forsook him and went away*. He forsook those who did not understand. And to whom did he go? To the Gentiles. Let us then try to understand what they found incomprehensible. Saliva dribbled down David's beard; what is saliva? It represents the babbling of infants, for babies do plenty of dribbling. And were these words not like baby-talk: "Eat my flesh, drink my blood"? Yet these infantile words masked virile strength, for virile strength[19] is symbolized by the beard. So then, what else does saliva dribbling down his beard represent, but the weak words that concealed his strength?

Conclusion

I think you have understood the title of this psalm now, holy brethren.[20] If we were to attempt to explain the psalm itself now, there would be a risk that what you have heard might slip your memories. But tomorrow is Sunday, when we owe you a sermon, so let us put the rest off till then, so that you may be ready to listen to the text of the psalm with fresh enjoyment. We shall have dealt with the title, in the name of our Lord Jesus Christ.

19. *Virtus.*
20. *Sanctitas vestra.*

Exposition 2 of Psalm 33

Second Sermon

Introduction: yesterday's promise is to be kept today

1. Those of you who were here yesterday will no doubt remember that we made you a promise; it is time now to keep it in the name of the Lord. He inspired us to promise, and he will enable us to pay our debt, though we remain always in debt to charity. Charity is the kind of thing that is always being paid out, yet always still owing, as the apostle suggests: *Be in no one's debt, apart from owing love to each other* (Rom 13:8). Yesterday we explained the title of this psalm, and the discussion detained us for rather a long time; so we therefore deferred the explanation of the text. So now let us listen to what the Holy Spirit has said through the mouth of the holy prophet in the rest of the psalm, and see if it fits in with the title we dealt with yesterday. There are some of you who were not here yesterday but may feel they have a right to know what we discussed then; but if we took all that time over again to recall it, we would sell short the others among you, to whom we are still in debt. We will summarize it briefly, therefore, in the hope that those who are present today but were absent yesterday may make the best sense of it they can. If anything in this summary suggests to them that they ought to explore some point more thoroughly, they will find me ready to listen in Christ's name at other times, so that we may not be further delayed now.

Verse 1. Recapitulation of yesterday's findings

2. We explained that the Book of Kings[1] records how David, while on the run from Saul, wanted to lie low in the territory of a king of Gath, named Achis. But his fame had reached even here, and David was afraid that the king of the place might out of spite contrive to do him harm, so he feigned insanity and, as we read, acted as though he was crazy: *he altered his behavior, and affected madness. He drummed on the doors into the city and was carried in his own hands, and fell down outside on the threshold. And King Achis demanded, "What have you brought this madman to me for? Do you think I want him in my house?"* (1 Sm 21:12-15). So David left him, so that the prophecy written here in our psalm might be fulfilled: *he altered his behavior, and forsook him and went*

1. 1 Samuel in our usage.

away. But the person he forsook was Achis, whereas what we find in the title of the psalm is, *he altered his behavior in the presence of Abimelech, and forsook him and went away*. I told you that the name was changed to indicate that there is some mystery[2] here. If the title of the psalm had taken over the original name unchanged, it might have seemed that we had only a piece of narrative, not a mysterious prophecy. In fact both names have profoundly mysterious significance. Achis is interpreted to mean, "How can this be?" Abimelech means, "My father's kingdom." The phrase, "How can this be?" signifies ignorance; it looks like the question of someone who is bewildered and does not understand. In the interpretation of the name Abimelech we find the kingdom of the Jews, for from Christ's standpoint this kingdom could be called, "My father's kingdom," since according to carnal descent David was the ancestor of Christ, and David's sovereignty was over the Jewish people. It was, therefore, in the presence of his father's kingdom that Christ *altered his behavior, and forsook him and went away*, because there among the Jews the sacrifice according to the order of Aaron's priesthood persisted, while Christ later instituted that sacrifice according to the order of Melchizedek in which his own body and blood are offered. He thus altered his appearance and behavior in respect of the priesthood, and abandoned the Jewish people, and came to the Gentiles.

In the light of this, what is the meaning of *he affected*? It means he was full of affection. What could ever be as full of affection as is the mercy of our Lord Jesus Christ, who in consideration of our infirmity accepted temporal death amid such violence and degradation, to free us from everlasting death? *He drummed* because a drum can be made only by stretching a skin across a wooden frame, so David's drumming was a prediction that Christ was to be crucified. *He drummed on the doors into the city*; and what else are *the doors into the city* but our hearts, which we had shut against Christ? But from the drum of his cross he opened the hearts of us mortals. *He was carried in his own hands*; how was this possible? Because when he entrusted to us his very body and blood, he took into his hands what the faithful know about,[3] and so in a sense he was carrying himself when he said, *This is my body*. Scripture then relates that David *fell down outside on the threshold*, which signifies that Christ humbled himself by descending even to that doorway which is our entrance into faith. The beginning of faith is like a doorway which the Church must pass through on the way to vision, for while we go on believing what we do not see we are being made ready to enjoy what we believe, once we come to see God face to face.

2. *Sacramentum*.
3. A reference to the "Discipline of the Secret," whereby some of the most sacred aspects of the Christian faith were concealed from pagans and catechumens. Its existence is attested from the second century, and it had special point during times of persecution. By Augustine's day it was obsolescent, though he sometimes makes a formal gesture toward it, as here; by the sixth century it had virtually disappeared.

So much for the title of the psalm. We have summarized its contents briefly; now let us hear what this affectionate drummer at the door of the city has to say.

Verse 2. It takes humility to bless the Lord all the time

3. *I will bless the Lord, at all times; his praise shall be in my mouth always.* Christ says this, so let every Christian say it too, because each Christian is part of Christ's body, and Christ is human to the end that every Christian who says, *I will bless the Lord,* may be an angel.[4] When are you to *bless the Lord*? When he showers blessings on you? When earthly goods are plentiful? When you have a plethora of grain, oil, wine, gold, silver, slaves, livestock; while your mortal body remains healthy, uninjured and free from disease; while everything that is born on your estate is growing well, and nothing is snatched away by untimely death; while every kind of happiness floods your home, and you have all you want in profusion? Is it only then that you are to bless the Lord? No, but *at all times*. So you are to bless him equally when from time to time, or because the Lord God wishes to discipline you, these good things let you down or are taken from you, when there are fewer births or the already-born slip away. These things happen, and their consequence is poverty, need, hardship, disappointment and temptation. But you sang, *I will bless the Lord at all times; his praise shall be in my mouth always*, so when the Lord gives you these good things, bless him, and when he takes them away, bless him. He it is who gives, and he it is who takes away, but he does not take himself away from anyone who blesses him.

4. Who is the person who blesses the Lord at all times? Who but the one who is humble of heart? Our Lord taught us this humility through his body and blood, because in handing over his body and blood to us he also handed over his humility. This is apparent in an episode we have left out, recorded in the story of David's feigned madness: *saliva dribbled down his beard.* While the lesson from the apostle was being read, you heard about this saliva—saliva, yes, but dribbling down a beard. "Saliva?" I heard someone say. "When did we hear anything about that?" Just now, when the apostle was saying, *The Jews demand signs, and the Greeks seek wisdom; but we preach Christ crucified* (that was when he was drumming), *to Jews a stumbling-block and to Gentiles folly; but to those who are called, both Jews and Greeks, a Christ who is the power of God and the wisdom of God. For the foolishness of God is wiser than mortals, and the weakness of God is stronger than mortals* (1 Cor 1:22-25). Saliva is a symbol of foolishness and a token of weakness. But if God's foolishness is wiser than that

4. An unusual statement, but prompted here perhaps by the context (praising God), and comparable to his reflections on happiness and the perfectibility of human nature in his Exposition 3 of Psalm 32, 16. Compare also his allusion to Mt 22:30 and Mt 18:10 in section 9 below.

of human beings, and God's weakness stronger than that of humans, then God's foolishness and weakness must not offend you like saliva. They dribble down the beard, and if you will give me your attention I will tell you why. Just as saliva is a sign of weakness, so a beard indicates manly strength.[5] So Christ screened his strength behind the weakness of his body. What showed was a weakness like saliva, but divine strength was concealed behind it, inner strength symbolized by the beard.

This is how humility is enjoined on us. Be humble if you wish to bless the Lord at all times, with his praise in your mouth always. Job blessed the Lord, but not only when everything lay before him in abundance, making him rich and happy, as we read—rich in cattle and servants, owner of a fine house, happy in his children and all his possessions. All at once his whole fortune was swept away, but he reacted as this psalm instructs us to do. *The Lord gave, and the Lord has taken away*, he said. *This has happened as the Lord willed: may the Lord's name be blessed* (Jb 1:21). There you have an instance of someone blessing the Lord at all times.

Verse 3. The Lord's donkey

5. What prompts a person to bless the Lord at all times? Being humble. What does being humble consist in? Being unwilling to be praised in yourself. Any of us who want to be praised in ourselves are proud; but whoever is not proud is humble. So you don't want to be proud? All right: in order to be humble, make the words of this psalm your own: *In the Lord shall my soul be praised; let the gentle*[6] *hear it and rejoice*. Those who do not want to be praised in the Lord are not gentle; they are savage, rough, arrogant and proud. The Lord wants gentle, compliant animals for his use; so you be the Lord's beast; be gentle, I mean. He sits on you, he himself controls you. Do not fear that you may stumble or fall headlong. Weakness is characteristic of you, certainly, but think who your rider is. Donkey's colt you may be, but you are carrying Christ. Remember how even he approached the city mounted on the foal of a donkey, and that beast was gentle and meek. Was it the animal that was being praised? Was the shout, *Hosanna, Son of David! Blessed is he who is coming in the name of the Lord!* (Mt 21:9) addressed to the donkey? The colt was carrying him, but the rider was being praised by those who went ahead and those who followed. Perhaps the animal was saying, *In the Lord shall my soul be praised; let the gentle hear it and rejoice*? No, brothers and sisters, the donkey never said it, but let the race that imitates that animal say it, if it wishes to carry its Lord.

5. *Virtus*.
6. *Mansueti*, literally "tamed." The word is represented by "meek" in older biblical translations.

Perhaps this race is angry with me for comparing it to the donkey's colt on which the Lord sat? Proud and arrogant folk will say, "Listen to that! He thinks we're donkeys!" But anyone who feels like objecting should try to be the Lord's donkey, and try not to be like a horse or a mule that cannot understand; for you are familiar with another psalm that says, *Do not be like a horse or a mule, devoid of understanding* (Ps 31(32):9). Horses and mules sometimes rear up fiercely and throw their riders. They are broken in with bridle, bit and beatings, until they learn to be submissive and carry their masters. But as for you, take care to be meek and submissive before your mouth is bruised with a bit. Carry your Lord. Do not hope to be praised in yourself, but let him who rides you be praised, and say, *In the Lord shall my soul be praised; let the gentle hear it and rejoice*. When those who are not gentle hear it, it provokes them not to joy but to anger; and it is these same people who complain about our calling them donkeys. Let those who are truly meek humble themselves to hear, and to become this meek animal about whom they are hearing.

Verse 4. No jealousy among God's lovers

6. The psalm continues, *Magnify the Lord along with me*. Who is the speaker, who is encouraging us to join him in magnifying the Lord? My brothers and sisters, every one of us who is in the body of Christ should bend his or her efforts to encourage others to magnify the Lord with us. For whoever this member of Christ is, he or she loves the Lord. Loves him—but how? In such a way that we are not jealous of our fellow-lovers. With carnal love it is different. The love of a carnally-minded person is inevitably accompanied by baneful jealousy; if he manages to see naked a woman whom he has desired lustfully, does he want someone else to see her too? Chastity is preserved only if the sole person who sees her is he who has a right to, if no one does.

With the Wisdom of God it is not so. We shall see her face to face; we shall all see her, and none of us will be jealous. She shows herself to all, and for all she is inviolate and chaste. Her lovers are changed into her likeness; she is not changed into theirs. She is Truth, she is God. You have never heard of our God being changed, have you, brothers and sisters? Truth is nobler than all else, Truth is the Word of God, the Wisdom of God, through whom all things were made; and God has his lovers. One such lover invites us, *Magnify the Lord along with me*. I don't want to be the only one magnifying the Lord, I don't want to be his only lover, I don't want to embrace him all by myself. It is not as though there will be no room for any others to put their hands, if I am embracing him. God's Wisdom is so wide that all souls can embrace and enjoy her. How can I make it clearer, brothers and sisters? Should they not blush, the people who so love God as to be jealous of others? Dissolute folk love a charioteer, and anyone who is enamored of a charioteer or a hunter of wild animals in the arena wants the whole populace to share his fervor. He begs them to join him in his infatuation: Come on, love that actor with me, or that chorus girl, or some disgraceful amusement. He shouts to the crowd, urging them to join him in his debased love. And is a Christian too shy to shout to others in church to love the truth of God along with him?

Stir up this love in yourselves, my brothers and sisters, and shout to every one of your friends and relatives, *Magnify the Lord along with me!* Let this love burn in you. Why else are these verses of the psalm recited to you, and expounded? If you love God, seize all your kinsfolk and drag them along to the love of God, and all your household. If the body of Christ is dear to you, if you love the unity of the Church, seize them all and bring them along to enjoy it; say to them, *Magnify the Lord with me!*

Christ crucified and the Donatist schism

7. *And let us exalt his name together.*[7] Why does it say, *Let us exalt his name together*? Because it means "in unity"; many codices indeed have *Magnify the Lord along with me, and let us exalt his name in unity.*[8] So whether we read *together* or *in unity* it means the same. Seize all those you can, then; seize them—by exhortation, by bringing them along bodily,[9] by questioning and disputing and putting sound arguments before them (though gently and with kindness); seize them and drag them to love, so that if they magnify the Lord they may do so to promote unity. If the Donatist sect thinks it is magnifying the Lord, has it any reason to be offended if the whole world does so? Brothers and sisters, it is our job to say to the Donatists, *Magnify the Lord with me; and let us exalt his name in unity*. Why do you want to magnify him by amputation? He is one, so why do you try to create two peoples for God? Why seek to dismember the body of Christ? We hold it as certain that the drumming means that he hung on the cross, and that while he was hanging on the cross he breathed forth his spirit. When the men who had crucified him came and found he had already expired, they did not break his legs, though they did break the legs of the thieves who were still alive on their crosses, so that through the pain of it they might be delivered from their agony by a speedy death. This was customarily done to crucified persons. The executioner arrived, and found that the Lord had quietly surrendered his spirit, for he had said himself, *I have the power to lay down my life* (Jn 10:18). For whom did he lay it down? For his entire people, for the whole of his body. The executioner arrived, then, and did not break Christ's legs; Donatus arrived, and tore Christ's Church apart. Christ's body is whole and

7. *In idipsum.*
8. *In unum.*
9. *Portando*, literally "by carrying." Some witnesses have *operando*, "by working at it."

complete on the cross in the hands of his persecutors, but in the hands of Christians his body, the Church, is not whole.

With this in mind, brothers and sisters, let us shout and wail with all our might, *Magnify the Lord along with me, and let us exalt his name in unity*. It is the Church that is shouting to them; the voice is the Church's voice, crying out to those who have cut themselves off. How did this severance come about? Through their pride. But Christ teaches humility when he entrusts his body and blood to us. This is what we have been telling you, holy brethren;[10] it is acted out and celebrated in the present psalm, where the body and blood of Christ are brought before us, and with them Christ's humility, the humble state he graciously accepted for our sake.

Verse 5. Spring-clean your heart

8. *I sought the Lord, and he hearkened to me*. Where did the Lord hearken? Within. And where does he give you what you ask? Within. There you pray, there you are heard, there you are made happy. You prayed, your prayer was heard, you are happy; yet a person standing beside you knows nothing about it, because the whole transaction took place in a hidden way, as the Lord commanded in the gospel: *Go into your private room, shut your door, and pray in secret, and your Father who sees in secret will give you your reward* (Mt 6:6). Entering your private room means entering your heart. Blessed are those who enjoy entering their hearts, and find nothing unpleasant there.

Pay careful attention to this point, holy brethren.[11] Men who have cross-grained wives are reluctant to go home; think how they go off to the forum and enjoy themselves there. As the time approaches when they must go home they come over all depressed, because they know they will go home to find weariness, grumbling, bitter exchanges and everything upset, for a home cannot be tranquilly ordered if there is no peace between husband and wife. The husband prefers to wander about out of doors. Those men are miserable who are afraid that if they return to their own four walls they will be upset by domestic disharmony; how much more miserable then are they who are unwilling to return to their own consciences, lest they be upset there by their accusing sins!

Do all you can to make your home-coming to your own heart pleasant. Clean it, because the clean of heart are blessed, and they will see God.[12] Take the filth of disordered desires outside; get rid of the dirt of avarice and poisonous superstitions, banish profanities and evil thoughts. As for hatred—and I do not mean only hatred of your friend, but even of your enemy—rid your heart of every trace

10. *Sanctitati vestrae.*
11. *Sanctitas vestra.*
12. See Mt 5:8.

of it. Then enter your heart, and you will enjoy being there. When you begin to enjoy it, the very cleanliness of your heart will be a delight to you and make you want to pray. You know how it is if you go into some place where there is silence and an atmosphere of peace, a clean place. You say, "Let's pray here." The harmony of the place delights you, and you are ready to believe that God will hear you there. If the cleanliness of a visible place is so delightful to you, why does the uncleanness of your heart not offend you? In you go! Clean up everything, then lift your eyes to God and he will immediately hearken to you. Cry out to him, *I sought the Lord and he hearkened to me, and rescued me from all my troubles*. Troubles? Yes, because when you have been enlightened[13] and have begun to live with a good conscience in this world, troubles remain. Some weakness remains in you until death is swallowed up in victory and this mortality of ours is clothed with immortality.[14] Inevitably you will feel the lash in this world; you are bound to suffer some temptations and sinful urges. God will cleanse it all and rescue you from every trouble. Seek him.

9. *I sought the Lord and he hearkened to me*. Those whose prayer is not heard are the people who are not seeking the Lord. Notice this point, holy brethren:[15] the psalmist does not say, "I sought gold from the Lord, and he hearkened to me," or "I sought long life from the Lord, and he hearkened to me," or "I sought this advantage or that from the Lord, and he hearkened to me." It is one thing to seek some favor from the Lord, quite another to seek the Lord himself. The psalm says, *I sought the Lord, and he hearkened to me*. Now, what about you? When you pray, "Please God, kill that enemy of mine," you are not seeking the Lord, but setting yourself up as judge over your enemy and trying to make your God into an inquisitor.[16] How do you know that the person whose death you are seeking is not better than you? Perhaps the very fact that he or she is not seeking your death proves it! Do not seek any extraneous thing from the Lord, but seek the Lord himself. He will hearken to you, and even while you are still speaking he will say, *Here I am.*[17] What does this *Here I am* suggest? "Look, I am present; what do you want? What are you asking of me? Whatever I give you, it will be of far less worth than myself. Have me, have me myself, enjoy me, embrace me. You can't yet do so with your whole self, but lay hold on me by faith and you will remain united to me, dwelling in me." This is what God tells you. "And I will lift from your shoulders those other burdens, so that you may cleave to me with your whole being when I change your mortal state into immortality, and then you will

13. Perhaps a reference to baptism, often called "Illumination."
14. See 1 Cor 15:54.
15. *Sanctitas vestra*.
16. *Quaestionarium*. The *quaestionarius* was an officer who interrogated witnesses, often (especially in the case of slaves) under torture. Hence the connotation of "executioner" in the Acts of the martyrs, and in the present passage.
17. Probably a conflation of Is 65:24 and 52:6.

be equal to my angels and see my face everlastingly,[18] and be full of joy, a joy of which no one will ever rob you."[19] Such will be God's promises if you have sought the Lord, and he has hearkened to you, and rescued you from all your troubles.

Verse 6. Drawing near to the Light

10. We pointed out to you not long ago who it is who is encouraging us, this lover who does not want to be the only one embracing what he loves. Now he invites us, *Draw near to him and receive his light*. He is talking about something he knows from experience. What has he to tell us, this spiritual person, this member of Christ's body? Or perhaps it is our Lord Jesus Christ himself according to the flesh, as the Head exhorting his own members. What does he say? *Draw near to him and receive his light*. Or perhaps it would be better to take it as some spiritual Christian inviting us to draw near to our Lord Jesus Christ himself. But we are to draw near to him in order to be illumined, not like the Jews, who approached him only to be plunged into darkness. They drew near to crucify him; we must draw near to receive his body and blood. They were plunged into darkness in the presence of the Crucified; we are illumined by eating and drinking the Crucified. *Draw near to him and receive his light*: the invitation is addressed to the Gentiles. Amid Jews who gazed savagely at him the crucified Christ was raised up; the Gentiles were not there to see. But now they who were in darkness have drawn near, and those who did not see have been illumined. How do the Gentiles draw near? By following him with their faith, longing for him with their hearts, and running to him with their charity. Your feet are your charity. Make sure you have two feet; don't be lame. Two feet? Yes, the paired commandments of love, love of God and love of your neighbor. Run toward God on these feet, draw near to him, for he himself has incited you to run, and has himself scattered his light to enable you to follow him magnificently, with godlike speed.[20]

And then you shall not be put out of countenance. This is the next promise. *Draw near to him and receive his light, and then you shall not be put out of countenance*. The only red faces are those of the proud. Why is that? Because proud persons aspire to be high and mighty, and when they encounter insults, or ignominy, or make some *faux pas*, or suffer some affliction, they are put out of countenance. But you need not be afraid; simply draw near to God, and there will be no shamefacedness for you. Your enemy may score off you, and in the eyes of the world he will seem to have demonstrated his superiority; but in God's eyes

18. Compare Mt 22:30 with Mt 18:10.
19. See Jn 16:22.
20. Variant: ". . . his light. Then in a magnificent and godlike way he continues . . ." (with reference to the following clause).

you are superior to him. "I have caught that fellow, I have tied him up, I have killed him." They think they have come out on top, people who talk like this. How superior the Jews thought themselves when they were slapping the Lord, spitting in his face, hitting him over the head with a cane, crowning him with thorns and garbing him with ignominy! How obviously they seemed to have the upper hand! And he seemed so much lower, he who was falling down outside on the threshold. But he was not put to shame. He was the true Light, who illumines everyone coming into the world.[21] As that Light cannot be extinguished, so he does not allow anyone whom he has illumined to be extinguished either. So *draw near to him and receive his light, and you shall not be put out of countenance.*

Verses 7-8. Rescue for the poor

11. Perhaps someone may object, "How can I draw near to him? I am laden with grave offenses, burdened with serious sins. The foulest crimes raise their clamor from my conscience. How can I dare to approach God?" How? Quite easily, if you have first humbled yourself in repentance. "But I am ashamed to repent," you answer. Well then, draw near to him and you will be illumined, and then your face will not be forced to blush with shame. Think it through. If the fear of being put to shame deters you from repentance, but repentance causes you to draw near to God, do you not see that you are wearing your punishment on your face? Your face has gone red because it has not drawn near to God, and the reason it has not drawn near to him is that it is unwilling to repent! The prophet bears witness that *this poor man cried out, and the Lord hearkened.* He is teaching you how to win a hearing. You see why you are not listened to: you are too rich. Perhaps you have often cried out and you were not heard; now you know why. *This poor man cried out, and the Lord hearkened.* Cry out in poverty, cry as a poor person, and the Lord will listen. "But how am I to cry out as a poor person?" Cry to him in such a way that even if you have possessions, you do not trust in your own resources, cry to him in a frame of mind that understands your need, cry to him in the knowledge that you will always be a pauper as long as you do not possess him who makes you rich. How did the Lord hearken to this poor person? He *saved him from all his troubles.*[22] And how does he save him from all these troubles? *The Lord's angel will send in his forces around those who fear him, and will deliver them.* This is the true reading, brothers and sisters. Certain manuscripts have *to those who fear him the Lord will send his angel, and will deliver them*, but the correct one is as I have said, *the Lord's angel will send in his forces.* Whom did it mean by this angel of the Lord, who will send in his forces

21. See Jn 1:9.
22. Variant: "will save him."

around those who fear him, and deliver them? Our Lord Jesus Christ himself is called in prophecy the Angel of Great Counsel, the messenger who brings news of the great plan.[23] This is the name the prophets gave him. This Angel of Great Counsel, this Messenger, will send in his forces around those who fear him, and will deliver them. Don't be concerned that he may miss you; as long as you fear the Lord, the Angel who is to send in his forces will know where to find you, wherever you are, and he will deliver you.

Verse 9. Parallels: David and Christ, Achis and the incredulous Jews

12. The psalmist wants to speak openly now about the sacrament that the Lord held in his hands. *Taste and see how sweet the Lord is.*[24] The psalm is opening its meaning to you now, surely? It shows you that the feigned insanity and persistent madness of David was a sane insanity, a sober intoxication, for he was prefiguring something.[25] Like King Achis[26] the Jews replied, "How can this be?" when the Lord kept telling them, *Unless you eat my flesh and drink my blood, you will not have life in you* (Jn 6:54). King Achis, who stands for error and ignorance, was sovereign in them as they objected, *How can this man give us his flesh to eat?* (Jn 6:53). If you do not know, taste and see how sweet the Lord is; but if you do not understand this, you are King Achis. David will alter his behavior and withdraw from you; he will forsake you and go away.

13. *Blessed is the man who trusts in him.* We do not need to spend much time explaining that, I think. Whoever does not trust in the Lord is in a wretched state. But who are they who do not trust in the Lord? Those who trust in themselves. Sometimes, brothers and sisters, there is an even worse condition: think now. There are some who do not even trust in themselves, but put their trust in other people. "I'm all right, I'm under the protection of Gaius Seius;[27] you can't touch me," and the person mentioned may be already dead. Or they will say in this city, "I'm all right, I'm under the protection of So-and-So," who may well have died somewhere else. How ready people are to talk like this, but not to say, "I trust in God, and he will not let you hurt me." Nor do they say, "I trust in my God, because even if he does give you some license to harm my property, he will give you no power over my soul." But when foolish people declare, "I'm safe[28] under So-and-So's protection," what they want is not really salvation, and they put an unfair burden on those to whom they look for safety.

23. See Is 9:6, LXX.
24. Variant: "that the Lord is sweet."
25. Variant preferred by the CCL editors of the Latin text: " . . . prefiguring the sacrament of the Lord."
26. Variant: "Like those miserable people around King Achis."
27. Mentioned also in Tertullian's *Apol.* 3,1,3; 48,1,8; and by Augustine in his Exposition of Psalm 140, 17.
28. *Salva salute illius*: safety or salvation.

Verses 10-11. Being rich in the Lord

14. *Fear the Lord, you his saints, for they who fear him lack for nothing.* There are plenty of people who hesitate to fear the Lord, because they think they may go hungry if they do. They are told, "Do not cheat." And they protest, "How am I to eat, then? Handicrafts need a little dishonesty to succeed, and business cannot flourish without fraud." But God punishes fraud. Fear God. "But if I fear God, I will not have enough to live on." *Fear the Lord, you his saints, for they who fear him lack for nothing*. To the anxious, to any who suspect that by fearing the Lord they will lose their superfluity, he promises ample resources. The Lord took care of you when you despised him; is he likely to abandon you when you fear him? Put your mind to it, and do not object, "That other fellow is rich, and I am poor; I fear the Lord, but look how much wealth he has amassed by not fearing him, while I through fearing him have been stripped of everything." Look at the next line: *the rich have been in need and have gone hungry, but those who seek the Lord will not be deprived of any good thing*. If you take this literally, it will look like a fallacy, for you see around you plenty of rich, unjust people who die amid their riches. They were not reduced to poverty in their lifetime. You watch them growing old and reaching the last days of their lives amid vast wealth; you see a funeral conducted for them with great pomp and no expense spared; you watch a rich man being carried to the grave as a rich man still, one who breathed his last in an ivory bed with his relatives and domestics weeping round him. And if by any chance you know something of his sins and shameful deeds, you say to yourself, "I know what great sins that man committed, yet here he is surviving into old age, dying in his own bed, carried to the grave by his kinsfolk, honored by so ostentatious a funeral. I know what he did; so scripture has misled me, it has hoodwinked me in that verse where I hear (and have even sung myself), *the rich have been in need and have gone hungry*. When did he ever feel the pinch? When did he go hungry? *Those who seek the Lord will not be deprived of any good thing*, says the psalm. Yet every day I get up and go to church, every day I bend the knee, every day I seek the Lord, and I have nothing good to show for it. As for him, he did not seek the Lord, yet he dies surrounded by good things."

If we entertain thoughts like these we are in danger of being throttled by the noose of scandal. We are seeking on earth food that will perish, and not seeking the true recompense in heaven. We are putting our head into the devil's noose; it tightens round our throat and the devil holds us enslaved to wrongdoing; and then we imitate that rich man whose death amid such wealth we have been observing.

15. Clearly the psalm cannot be interpreted in that way. "How am I to understand it, then?" It refers to the good things of the spirit. "But what are they?" They are seen not with the eyes but with the heart. "I don't see them." Anyone

who is in love sees them. "I can't see righteousness;[29] it's not gold, it's not silver." If it were gold, you would see it, but because it is faith,[30] you don't see it. But let me ask you this: if you can't see faith, why is a faithful servant precious to you? Put the question to yourself: what kind of servant do you regard as worthy of your love? Perhaps you have a good-looking slave, very tall and well-built, but he is a thief, a bad character, deceitful. And you have another slave, perhaps, who is short, disfigured in the face, repulsive in color, but he is faithful, thrifty and sober. Think about it: which of the two do you rate more highly? If you consult your bodily eyes, the handsome, dishonest fellow will come out on top; if you go by what the eyes of your heart tell you, the ugly but faithful slave wins. So, you see, what you want others to show toward you—faithfulness—you must show to them. Why do you rejoice over the person who deals with you faithfully, and praise him for good qualities which cannot be seen except with the vision of the heart? Apply it to yourself now: when you have been filled to the brim with spiritual wealth, will you be poor?[31] Was that other man we were speaking about rich because he had a bed made of ivory, and you poor when the bedroom of your heart is full of such precious jewels of virtue—jewels of justice, truth, charity, faith, patience and endurance? If you have riches, unwrap them, and compare them with the worldly riches of the affluent. That other man found valuable mules, say, on the market, and bought them. If you found faith on sale, what a sum you would be willing to hand over! Yet God wants you to have it free, and can you still be ungrateful? Those rich folk are truly in need, they really are badly off; and what is worse, they are in need of bread. I don't mean that they are in need of gold and silver (though in fact they think they are. What a lot someone like that had, yet did it satisfy him? He did die needy then, in that he wanted to get more than was in his grasp already). Yes, as I was saying, they are in need even of bread. Why are they in need of bread? If you do not understand what "bread" means, listen to the Lord's words: *I am the living bread which has come down from heaven* (Jn 6:41), and again, *Blessed are those who hunger and thirst for righteousness, for they shall be satisfied* (Mt 5:6). The psalm is right: *those who seek the Lord will not be deprived of any good thing*; but we have explained what kind of good thing is meant.

29. Variant: "Anyone in love sees righteousness. 'I can't.' "
30. In this paragraph Augustine uses the Latin word *fides* to cover both "faithfulness" (as in the case of the two slaves he contrasts, and of honest dealings with one's neighbor) and "faith" (more appropriate where he says that God gives it "free").
31. Variant: " . . . deals with you faithfully, and praise him? Apply it to yourself now: when you have been filled brimful with good qualities which cannot be seen except with the vision of the heart, will you be poor?"

Verse 12. Christ the teacher

16. *Come, children, and hear me; I will teach you the fear of the Lord.* You think I am saying this, brothers and sisters; but no, think rather that David is saying it, think it is the apostle saying it; best of all that it is our Lord Jesus Christ himself who is saying, *Come, children, and hear me.* Let us all listen to him together; and you listen to him speaking through me, for he wants to teach us. He who is humble, who drums, who has affection for us,[32] wants to teach us. And what does he say? *Come, children, and hear me; I will teach you the fear of the Lord.* Let him teach us, then, and let us yield our ears to him, let us yield our hearts. We must not open our bodily ears while keeping our hearts closed; rather we must do as he commanded in the gospel: *Let anyone who has ears for hearing, listen* (Mt 11:15). Surely all of us would want to hear Christ teaching us through the prophet?[33]

Verse 13. Longing for "good days"

17. *Is there anyone who wants life, and loves to see good days?* It is a question. And will not every one of you reply, "Yes, I do!" Can there be anyone among you who does not love life, who does not want life, and does not love to see good days? Do you not grumble every day, "How long do we have to put up with this? Things get worse and worse by the day. Our parents had happier days, things were better in their time." Oh, come on! If you questioned those parents of yours, they would moan to you about their days in just the same way: "Our ancestors were happy, but we are in a wretched state. There was that fellow who bossed us, and we used to think that when he died we would get some relief, but things went from bad to worse. O God, show us good days!" *Is there anyone who wants life, and loves to see good days?* Let such a person not look for good days here. He or she is looking for a good thing, but not in the place where it belongs. Suppose you were in search of some good man in a country where he did not live. Someone might say to you, "He is a fine man, the one you are looking for, a great man. Go on looking for him, but not here. You are wasting your time looking for him here; you will never find him."

So you are looking for good days. Let us all look for them together, but not here. "But our ancestors had them," you say. Did they? You are wrong! All of them had a hard time here. Read the scriptures, for the Lord's purpose in causing them to be written was that we might find comfort there. In Elijah's time there was a famine, and our forebears had to endure it.[34] The heads of dead animals

32. See Augustine's earlier play on *affecto*, to "affect" (madness), or to "have affection for," paragraph 2 above.
33. Variant: "Which of us is able to hear . . . ?"
34. See 1 Kgs 17-18.

were being sold for gold; people killed their own relatives and ate them. Two women made a pact that they would kill their children and eat them; one killed her son, and both of them ate him; then the other refused to kill hers, and the one who had been the first to kill her son demanded that she should, and the rumor of their dreadful quarrel reached the ears of the king. They betook themselves to the king, still arguing over the slaughter of their sons.[35] God forbid that we should ever resort to such food. There are always evil days in this world, but always good days in God. Abraham enjoyed good days, but only within his own heart; he had bad days when a famine forced him to migrate in search of food.[36] But everyone else had to search too. What about Paul: did he have good days, he who had *often gone without food, and endured cold and exposure* (2 Cor 11:27)? But the servants have no right to be discontented; even the Lord did not have good days in this world. He endured insults, injuries, the cross and many a hardship.

Verse 14. You cannot have it both ways

18. Let no Christian complain, but let us remember in whose footsteps we are walking. Let any Christian who loves good days listen to our Teacher, who bids us, *Come, children, and hear me; I will teach you the fear of the Lord*. What do you want? "Life and good days." Very well, listen, and then get on with it: *Restrain your tongue from evil*. Do just that. "But I don't want to," some miserable objector replies. "I don't want to restrain my tongue from evil, but I do want life, and good days to enjoy." If your gardener were to say to you, "I am going to lay this vineyard waste, and I expect you to pay me. You hired me for the vineyard, to trim and prune it. I'm cutting away all the useful wood, and chopping down the very trunks of the vines to make sure you get no crop here; and when I've finished, you can pay me for my labor." Would you not say he was crazy? Wouldn't you throw him out of your employment before he could take hold of the sickle? But that is what people are like who want to do wrong, and perjure themselves, and blaspheme against God, and grumble, and defraud others, and get drunk, and drag other people off to court, and commit adultery, and tie lucky charms onto themselves, and consult diviners, and still see good days. To anyone like this it must be said, You cannot look for a good reward while you are doing bad things. You may be unjust, but will God be unjust too? "What am I to do, then?" Well, what do you want? "I want life, I want good days." Then *restrain your tongue from evil, and your lips from guileful speech*. Speak deceitfully to no one, lie to no one.

35. See 2 Kgs 6:25-30.
36. See Gn 12:10; 26:1.

Verse 15. The search for peace

19. What does the next line imply: *turn away from evil*? It is not much to ask that you refrain from hurting anyone, that you kill no one, and do not steal, or commit adultery, or defraud anyone, or give false testimony. *Turn away from evil*; and when you have turned away from it, you say, "Now I'm safe, I've done it all perfectly, so I will have life, I will see good days." But you need to do more than turning away from evil, you must also *do good*. It is not enough to refrain from stripping someone, you must clothe the naked. If you have not despoiled anyone, you have turned away from evil, but you will only have done good when you have welcomed the traveler into your home. Turn away from evil, yes, but in order to do good.

Seek peace and pursue it. Scripture does not promise you that you will have peace here; seek it, pursue it. "Where shall I pursue it to?" To the place where it has gone ahead. The Lord is our peace;[37] he has risen and ascended into heaven. *Seek peace and pursue it*, because when you too have risen from the dead, the mortal part of you will be transformed, and you will embrace peace, there where no one will trouble you. Perfect peace is found where you will never be hungry. Here on earth bread pacifies you; take bread away, and feel what a war rages in your belly! The righteous themselves groan here below, brothers and sisters, to make it clear to you that we seek peace here, but will obtain it only at the end. Yet we do have peace in some degree here, in order that we may deserve to have it totally there. Why do I say, "in some degree"? Let us be of one heart here, let us love our neighbor as ourselves. Love your brother and sister as you love yourself, and have peace with them.

It is impossible, though, for disputes never to arise. They have broken out between brethren, even between saints, between Barnabas and Paul,[38] but not so as to destroy the unity of hearts, not so as to kill charity. You are sometimes at odds even with yourself, yet you do not hate yourself. Anyone who is sorry for having done something is picking a quarrel with himself or herself. Such a person has sinned, he comes back, he is angry with himself for what he did, for the sin he committed. So he is quarrelling with himself, but this kind of quarrel leads to harmony. If you want an example of a just person having an argument with himself, think of another psalm: *Why are you sorrowful, O my soul; why do you disquiet me? Hope in the Lord, for I will still confess to him* (Ps 42(43):5). If the speaker says to his soul, *Why do you disquiet me?* it is obvious that his soul is troubling him. Perhaps he wanted to suffer for Christ, but his soul was very upset about it. Clearly a person who knew this and kept on saying, *Why are you sorrowful, O my soul; why do you disquiet me?* was not yet at peace with

37. See Eph 2:14.
38. See Acts 15:39.

himself; but he was clinging to Christ in his mind, willing his soul to follow him and disquiet him no longer.[39] Seek peace, then, brothers and sisters. The Lord said, *These things I tell you, that in me you may have peace. I do not promise you peace in this world.*[40] In this life there is no true peace, no tranquillity. We are promised the joy of immortality and fellowship with the angels. But anyone who has not sought it here will not find it on arriving there.

Verse 16. Cruel to be kind

20. *The eyes of the Lord are upon the righteous.* Don't worry, go on trying; the Lord's eyes are on you. *And his ears are open to their prayers.* What more could you wish? If in some great house the master did not hear the complaints of a servant, the servant would protest, "What a lot we have to put up with here, and nobody listens to us!" You cannot say that of God—"What a lot I have to put up with, and nobody listens to me"—now can you? Perhaps you may say, "But if he heard me he would take my trouble away; I appeal to him, but I still have the trouble." Just hold steady and keep to his ways, and when you are in trouble he hears you. But he is a physician, and there is still some diseased tissue in you. You cry out, but he goes on cutting, and he does not stay his hand until he has done all the cutting he knows to be necessary. In fact it is a cruel doctor who listens to the patient's cries, and leaves the festering wound untouched. And think how mothers rub their children down vigorously in the bath, for their own good. The little ones cry out in their mothers' hands, don't they? Does that mean the mothers are cruel in not sparing them, in ignoring their tears? Are they not really full of tender love? All the same, the children cry, and they are not let off. So too our God is full of charity, but he seems to be deaf to our entreaty because he means to heal us and spare us for all eternity.

Verse 17. God watches the wicked equally

21. *The eyes of the Lord are upon the righteous, and his ears are open to their prayers.* Possibly the wrongdoers may say, "That's all right, then. I can do wicked deeds, because the Lord's eyes are not on me. God focuses on the righteous, and does not watch me. So I can do anything I like without worrying." But the Holy Spirit, aware of these human delusions, immediately added a warning, *the eyes of the Lord are upon the righteous, and his ears are open to*

---

39. This evocation of a divided self resembles passages in Augustine's *Confessions*, where in a similar context of grief he is dragging his soul along: "I questioned my soul, demanding why it was sorrowful and why it so disquieted me, but it had no answer. If I bade it, 'Trust in God,' it rightly disobeyed me. . . . Within me I was carrying a tattered, bleeding soul that did not want me to carry it, yet I could find no place to lay it down. . . . " (*Conf.* IV,4,9; IV,7,12).

40. See Jn 16:33; 14:27.

their prayers; but the Lord frowns on evildoers, to blot out their memory from the earth.

Verse 18. Being heard in the furnace of persecution

22. *The righteous cried out, and the Lord hearkened to them, and rescued them from all their distress.* The three young men were righteous. They cried to the Lord in the furnace, and as they praised him the fire cooled down. The flame could not touch these innocent, just youths, or do them any harm as they praised God, and he rescued them from burning.[41] Someone will object, "Sure enough, they were truly righteous and they were heard, just as the psalm says: *the righteous cried out, and the Lord hearkened to them, and rescued them from all their distress.* But what about me? I cried to him and he did not rescue me; so either I am not righteous, or I am not following his instructions, or perhaps he can't see me." Do not be afraid, just do what he orders; and if he does not rescue you in bodily fashion he will rescue you spiritually. He pulled the three youths clear of the flames, but did he pull the Maccabees out of their fire?[42] Did not the one group sing hymns in the fire, and the other group die in it? Is not the God of the three youths the God of the Maccabees as well? The first he rescued, the second he did not rescue, or, more truly, he rescued both; but he delivered the three youths in a way that dumbfounded those who could think no further than the body, while he delivered the Maccabees in such a way that their persecutors would be consigned to still greater torments, even as they thought they had crushed God's martyrs. God also rescued Peter when the angel came to him as he lay in fetters, and said to him, *Get up and leave* (Acts 12:7); the fetters were suddenly loosened, Peter followed the angel, and so God delivered him. But he did not rescue Peter from the cross: does that mean that Peter had meanwhile lost his righteousness? But did God really not deliver him from the cross? Deliver him he certainly did; would Peter have been allowed to live so long, only to deteriorate into unrighteousness? Perhaps God heard him at that later time even more surely, because this time he truly did deliver him from all his pains. When Peter was rescued the first time, what a lot of suffering still lay ahead of him! But at this later time God sent him to a place where he would never suffer again.

Verses 19-20. The troubles of the just

23. *The Lord is close to those who have bruised their hearts, and he will save those of humble spirit.* God is on high, but a Christian's business is to be lowly. If Christians want the Most High God to be near them, they must be humbly

41. See Dn 3:49-50.
42. See 2 Mac 7.

abased. These are great mysteries, brothers and sisters. God is above all things; if you lift yourself up, you do not touch him, but if you humble yourself, he comes down to you. *Many are the troubles of the righteous.* Does he tell us, "Christians ought to be righteous, and listen to my word, because that way they will have no troubles to put up with"? Not at all. *Many are the troubles of the righteous.* It is the other way round; the more unrighteous people are, the fewer troubles they have, while those who are righteous have plenty. Yet after only a few tribulations, or even none at all, the wicked will be consigned to trouble everlasting, while the righteous, after many troubles, will arrive at everlasting peace, where they will suffer no kind of evil ever again. *Many are the troubles of the righteous, but from them all the Lord will rescue them.*

Verse 21. Bones are safeguarded

24. *The Lord guards all their bones: not one will be broken.* We certainly must not take this in a material sense, my brothers and sisters. The "bones" are the firm supports of the faithful. In our bodies the bones provide strong support, and in the same way faith provides firm support in the heart of a Christian; and endurance born of faith is like a spiritual skeleton. These are the bones which cannot be broken. *The Lord guards all their bones: not one will be broken.*

It may be that when the psalm made this prophecy it had our Lord Jesus Christ in view. The Lord guards all the bones of his Son, and not a single one of them shall be broken. Another passage also speaks prophetically about him, where the Israelites are directed to slay a lamb, but *you shall not break any of its bones* (Ex 12:46). The prophecy was fulfilled in our Lord, because as he hung on the cross he expired before the soldiers arrived; they found his body already lifeless, so they had no wish to break his legs; thus the scripture was fulfilled.[43]

But the promise was made to all Christians: *the Lord guards all their bones; not one will be broken.* Now consider, brothers and sisters: does this mean that if we see holy people suffering—perhaps undergoing surgery, or mangled by a persecutor—in such a way that their bones are fractured, we should say, "These cannot have been righteous people, because the Lord made this promise to his righteous servants, *the Lord guards their bones; not one shall be broken*?" Certainly not. Would you like me to prove to you that the prophecy relates to a different kind of bones, to the qualities we have called the strong supports of faith, namely patient endurance and long-suffering in all troubles? These are the bones that remain unbroken. Listen, and I will show you how the proof is contained within the same story of the Lord's passion. The Lord was crucified in the central position, flanked by two robbers. One of them railed at him, the other believed; one was damned, the other justified; one had his punishment both here

43. See Jn 19:33.

and hereafter, but to the other the Lord said, *Truly I tell you, today you will be with me in paradise* (Lk 23:43). Yet when the soldiers came they did not break our Lord's bones, but they did break those of the robbers;[44] and so both of them had their bones broken, the one who believed just as much as the one who blasphemed. What had become of the promise in scripture, *the Lord guards all their bones; not one shall be broken*? Had he no power to guard intact the bones of the man to whom he said, *Today you will be with me in paradise*? The Lord answers your question: "Indeed I did guard them, for the strong support of his faith could not be broken by the blows that smashed his legs."

Verse 22. The last end of the wicked

25. *Very wretched is the death of sinners.* Let me have your attention, brothers and sisters. Think about what we have been saying. It is true that the Lord is great, and that his mercy is great; indeed it is true, for he gave us as our food that body in which he suffered so intensely, and his blood as our drink. What is his view of people who think, wrongly, along these lines: "That man died hard, he was devoured by beasts. He cannot have lived righteously; that must be why he had such a painful death, because he would not have perished like that if he had been a good man"? So you think, do you, that someone else must have been righteous, because he dies at home, in his own bed? "Well," you reply, "it does puzzle me, I admit, because I know about his sins and crimes, yet he had a good death in his own home, in familiar surroundings, with no injuries picked up in his travels, and none even in old age." But listen: *very wretched is the death of sinners*. What looks like a good death to you would seem very dreadful if you could see the inner side of it. Outwardly you see him lying in bed, but do you see the inner reality, as he is dragged off to hell? Listen, brothers and sisters, to what this very wretched death of sinners is, and look to the gospel for an example of it. There were in our Lord's day two men,[45] one of whom was rich and clad in purple and fine linen, and feasted splendidly every day. The other was a pauper who lay at the rich man's gate covered with sores. The dogs came and licked his sores, and the poor man longed to satisfy his hunger with crumbs that fell from the rich man's table. Now it happened that the poor man died; he was a righteous man, and he was transported by angels to Abraham's embrace.[46] If anyone had seen his body lying there at the rich man's gate, with no one to bury it, what a lot the passer-by might have read into that! "I hope my enemy meets his end like that," the onlooker might have said, "and that other fellow too, who makes my life a misery. I'd like to see him reduced to this!" The body is insulted

44. See Jn 19:32.
45. Or, "There were two men in this world, one of . . ."
46. See Lk 16:19-31.

with spittle,[47] and its wounds stink, yet the man himself lies peacefully in the arms of Abraham. If we are Christians, let us believe it; if we do not believe it, brothers and sisters, let none of us pretend to be Christians. Faith leads us all the way. As the Lord described things, so they are. If you take what an astrologer[48] tells you as the truth, can you think that when Christ tells you something, it is false? What kind of death did the rich man die? What an impressive death it could have been, amid purple and fine linen, what a sumptuous death, what a showy one! And what kind of funeral would he have been given, what a weight of spices would have been used to bury the corpse! And yet, tormented in hell, he longed for a drop of water to trickle onto his burning tongue from the finger of the despised poor man, but he did not get it. Learn from this example what the psalm means by saying, *Very wretched is the death of sinners*. Do not put your questions to beds draped with costly coverings, or flesh muffled up in rich clothes, or mourners with their extravagant laments, or a weeping family, or a crowd of flunkeys before and behind when the corpse is taken out for burial, or monuments marble and gilded. If you put your questions to these, they tell you lies, for many people there are who have not merely sinned in small matters but have been thoroughly wicked, who yet have had a plush death like this, who have been judged worthy of being mourned, embalmed, clothed, carried in procession to the grave and buried in no other fashion than this. Put your questions rather to the gospel, and it will reveal to your faith the soul of the rich man burning in torments, helped not a whit by the honors and obsequies that the vanity of the living has lavished on his dead body.

Verses 22-23. But not all kinds of sinners

26. But there are many different kinds of sinners, and it is difficult, perhaps impossible in this life, not to be a sinner; and therefore the psalm immediately makes clear what kind of sinners come to this very wretched death. *And those who hate the just one will offend*. Who is this "just one," if not he who justifies the godless?[49] Who else is this just one, but our Lord Jesus Christ, who is also the propitiatory offering for our sins?[50] Those who hate him therefore do meet that most wretched death, because all who are not reconciled to our God through him die in their sins. But *the Lord will redeem the souls of his servants*. Whether we think of a wretched death or a fine death, it is in terms of the soul that we must

---

47. Literally "cursed with spittle," *exsecratur . . . sputo*; but the CCL editors suggest *excreatur . . . sputo*, "coughed at with spittle" or simply "spat on."
48. *Mathematicus*. The term was originally applied to anyone who made mathematical calculations about astronomy; but it became debased and was used for one who superstitiously traced the causes of human actions in the stars, an astrologer.
49. See Rom 4:5.
50. See 1 Jn 2:2.

appraise it, not of the body and the insults or honors heaped on it, where human onlookers see. *And none who trust in him will offend.* This is the measure of righteousness for human beings, that though in our mortal life, however much progress we may have made, we cannot be without sin, at least in this regard we do not offend, that we go on trusting in him; for in him is the forgiveness of our offenses. Amen.

Exposition 1 of Psalm 34

First Sermon, at Thagaste[1]

Introduction: Christ, strong of hand and object of our desire, is speaking

1. You know, beloved brethren,[2] that my brother-bishops have laid on me the task of expounding this psalm. Their wish is that we should all hear something about it; for we are indeed all listening to Christ. We all learn from him, and in his school all of us together are students. The title need not delay us, because it is short and not difficult to understand, especially for those nurtured in God's Church. The title is, *For David himself.* This psalm, therefore, is for David, and the name "David" means "strong of hand," or "desirable." The psalm is for him who is both strong-handed and desirable, who conquered our death and promised us life. His strength of hand is proved in his defeat of our death, his desirability in his promise of eternal life. What could be stronger than the hand that touched the bier, and caused the dead man to arise?[3] And what stronger than a hand that conquered the world, not mail-clad but nailed to wood? But who is more desirable than he for whom the martyrs longed to die that they might reach him, even though they could not see him? This psalm is his. Let our hearts sing it to him, let our tongues sing it tunefully to him, and let us depend on him to provide us with what we may fittingly sing. No one sings anything to him that is worthy, unless he has first given it. What we sing today has come to us through the prophet at the prompting of Christ's Spirit, and in its words we recognize both ourselves and him. I say, "both ourselves and him," and this is in no way derogatory to him, for even from heaven he cried, *Why are you persecuting me?* (Acts 9:4), though no one was touching him; we only were toiling away on earth.

In view of this we are right to listen to his voice, knowing that it is sometimes the voice of his body, sometimes that of the Head.[4] This psalm in particular invokes God's help against enemies amid the tribulations of this world; and it is undoubtedly Christ who is praying, for once the Head was beset by tribulation, and now it is his body. Nonetheless through these tribulations he gives eternal life to all his members, and in promising it he has made himself desirable to us.

---

1. Augustine's birthplace. The sermon is possibly to be assigned to the year 414.
2. *Caritas vestra.*
3. See Lk 7:14.
4. Augustine's most fundamental conviction about the psalms.

Verses 1-2. The armor of God

2. *Judge those who do me harm, Lord, and assail those who assail me*, says the psalm. If God is fighting for us, who can stand against us?[5] And what does God use to give us this aid? *Grasp your shield and buckler, and arise to help me.* A wonderful sight this is, to see God armed in your cause! And what is his shield? What kind of weaponry does he favor? The same psalmist says elsewhere, *Lord, you have encompassed us as with the shield of your good will* (Ps 5:13(12)). His weapons, the weapons he employs not only to defend us but also to attack our enemy, will be nothing else but ourselves, if we are making good progress; for just as we arm ourselves with what we receive from him, so he arms himself with us. The difference is, though, that he arms himself with those he has made, while we are armed with what we have been given by him who made us. The apostle somewhere enumerates our pieces of armor, speaking of the shield of faith, the helmet of salvation, and the sword of the Spirit, which is the word of God.[6] With these weapons God has equipped us. They are glorious weapons that have never known defeat, invincible and splendid; but spiritual and invisible arms, of course, since it is invisible enemies that we have to fight. When you can see your enemy, it is visible arms you need. We are armed with faith in realities we cannot see, and we overthrow enemies we cannot see either.

All the same, dear friends, you must not think these weapons are such that what is a shield will always be a shield, or that a helmet will always be a helmet, or cuirass always a cuirass. This is true even in the case of material arms, iron though they are. What has been made can be recast into something else; a sword, for instance, might be converted into an axe. We find the same apostle speaking in one place of the cuirass of faith,[7] in another place of the shield of faith. The same faith, then, can be both cuirass and shield. It is a shield because it catches the spears of the enemy and turns them aside, but a cuirass because it prevents any weapon from penetrating your body.

Such are our arms; now what about God's? We read in scripture, *Deliver my soul from the wicked, your sword from the enemies of your hand* (Ps 16(17):13-14). In the first half of this verse he says, *from the wicked*, in the second, *from the enemies*; and correspondingly where the first half has *my soul*, the second has *your sword*; so he is calling his own soul God's sword. *Deliver my soul from the wicked*, he says, *your sword from the enemies of your hand.* You grasp my soul, and topple my enemies with it. And what is our soul? A splendid weapon it may be, long, sharp, oiled, and coruscating with the light of wisdom as it is brandished. But what is this soul of ours worth, what is it capable of, unless God holds it and fights with it? Any sword, however beautifully made, lies idle if

5. See Rom 8:31.
6. See Eph 6:16-17.
7. See 1 Th 5:8.

there is no warrior to take it up. We said just now that in the case of our own weaponry we should not take things to be so fixed that one thing cannot be turned into something else; and we find the same to be true of God's arms. The psalm called a righteous person's soul God's sword, but the righteous soul is said elsewhere to be God's throne, the throne of Wisdom. So God does whatever he wishes with our soul. Since it is in his hand, it is his to use as he will.

3. May God arise, then, as we have begged him to, and seize his weapons, and bestir himself to help us. In another text we are told by the same voice why he needs to arise: *Arise! Why do you sleep, O Lord?* (Ps 43(44):23). When he is said to be sleeping it is really we who are asleep, and when he is said to arise it is we who are awakened. Our Lord was asleep in a boat, and the boat was tossed about because Jesus was sleeping; if Jesus had been on watch there, the boat would have been steady. Your boat is your heart; Jesus in the boat represents faith in your heart. If you remember your faith, your heart is not tossed to and fro; but if you forget your faith, Christ goes to sleep, and then look what a shipwreck there is. Do all you can to rouse him if he is asleep; say to him, "Wake up, Lord, we are sinking!";[8] arouse him so that he can rebuke the winds and bring tranquillity to your heart, for if Christ—your faith, I mean—is on the watch in your heart, all temptations will die away, or at any rate lose their force. What does *arise* mean? Make yourself known, show yourself, make your presence felt. *Arise to help me.*

Verse 3. God our ally in the fight against dark forces

4. *Loose your sword and make an end of those who persecute me.* Who are your persecutors? Your neighbor, perhaps, or someone you have hurt or treated unjustly, or someone who plans to rob you of your property, or against whom you have stood up for the truth, or whose sin you rebuke, or some person of disreputable life who is offended by the honorable way you live. These are our enemies, to be sure, and they do persecute us; but we are taught to recognize other enemies too, against whom we are waging invisible warfare. The apostle warns us about them: *It is not against flesh and blood that you have to struggle—not against human adversaries, that is, whom you can see—but against principalities and powers and the rulers of this world of darkness* (Eph 6:12). In saying, *the rulers of this world*, he obviously meant the devil and his angels; but he had to make sure that no one would misunderstand, and think he meant that this world is ruled by the devil and his subject-demons. This visible fabric is called "the world," and the same term, "world," can mean sinners, or those in love with the world, the people of whom it was said, *The world did not know him* (Jn 1:10), and again, *The whole world is in the power of the evil one* (1 Jn 5:19). So the apostle made clear whom he meant by world-rulers by speci-

8. See Mt 8:25.

fying *this world of darkness*: "I mean the world-rulers of darkness," he implies. And he goes further, to make us understand the meaning of this reference to darkness. Who are the dark subjects ruled by the devil and his angels? All unbelievers, all the wicked, of whom it was said, *The Light shines in the darkness, and the darkness has never been able to master it* (Jn 1:5). But what has this same apostle to say to the many believers who have been drawn from their number? *You were darkness once, but now you are light in the Lord* (Eph 5:8). Do you want to be ruled by the devil? No? Move into the light, then. And how will you be able to move into the light, unless the Lord looses his sword to deliver you from your enemies and persecutors? How does he loose his sword? Well, we have already heard what his sword is: it is the soul of a righteous person. Only let the just increase in numbers and his sword is loosed, and your enemies are dispatched. But the apostle has a warning to add: we must live righteous lives if this sword is to be unsheathed, so he tells us to live in such a way *that our adversary may respect us, finding nothing derogatory to say of us* (Ti 2:8). An end is made of him, because he can find nothing to allege against the saints.

5. But how will they become righteous? What do our persecuting enemies say? And our invisible enemies, what do they say? Have they no answer? Oh, yes, they have. These unseen enemies have a favorite suggestion to make to the human heart: God is not our ally.[9] They mean us to look for other sources of help, and to find them useless, and so be taken prisoner by themselves, our enemies. These are the hints they drop; but we must be assiduously vigilant against their suggestions, which are shown up in another psalm: *many rise up against me; many say to my soul, "He can find no salvation in his God"* (Ps 3:2-3(1-2)). How does our present psalm rebut these insinuations? *Say to my soul, "I am your salvation."* If you have said to my soul, *I am your salvation*, it will live righteously, so that I may seek no ally but you.

Verse 4. "I am your salvation"

6. Now, what comes next? *Let them be confounded and awed, who seek my soul*, for they seek it to destroy it. If only they would seek it to good purpose! In another psalm people are reproached because they did not seek his soul: *No chance of flight is open to me, yet there is no one to seek my soul* (Ps 141:5(142:6))—to care for it, he means. Is not the speaker here the same man of whom it was said so long ago in prophecy, *They dug holes in my hands and my feet, and numbered all my bones. They looked on and watched me, they shared out my garments among*

9. A different punctuation in some manuscripts yields the meaning: " . . . no answer? And those unseen ones? What do our enemies say? Nothing so insistently as that God is not our ally."

them, and cast lots for my tunic (Ps 21:17-19(22:16-18))?[10] These very things were happening before their eyes, yet there was no one to care for his soul.

Let us all call upon him, brothers and sisters, to say to our soul, *I am your salvation*, and to open our spiritual ears so that we may hear him saying, *I am your salvation*. He says it, but some of us are getting deaf, so that when we find ourselves in trouble we prefer to listen to the enemies that harry us. If something needful is missing, if the soul is hard pressed, or feeling the pinch in temporal matters, it is likely to seek help from the demons, tempted to consult persons demoniacally inspired and have recourse to soothsayers. Those invisible enemies, the persecutors, have approached this soul, invaded it, attacked, captured and conquered it, telling their captive that *he can find no salvation in his God*. This soul has been too deaf to hear the voice that assured it, *I am your salvation*.

Say to my soul, "I am your salvation," so that *they may be confounded and awed, who seek my soul*, this soul to which you say, *I am your salvation*. I will listen, then, to him who says to me, *I am your salvation*. I will seek no salvation[11] other than the Lord my God. If salvation is offered to me by any creature, it comes from God; if I lift my eyes to the mountains, whence aid may come to me, it is not from the mountains that it comes but from the Lord who made heaven and earth (see Ps 120(121):1-2). Even in your temporal problems it is God who helps you through human agency, for he is your salvation. Or perhaps God comes to your help through an angel; all the same, he himself is your salvation. All things are subject to him, and he undoubtedly supports our temporal life, differently in the case of each person; but eternal life he gives only from himself. When you are in a tight place your hand may not find what you seek, but he is at hand whom you seek.[12] Seek him who can never leave you in the lurch. His gifts may be withdrawn from you, but is the Giver withdrawn? What he once gave you he may give back again; are you going to reckon them riches when you get them back, and not look on him as your riches, who took them away to test you, and returns them to you for your comforting? He does indeed comfort us when we have these things that we need. He gives them to us as comforts along our way, but we must understand the way aright. Your entire life, and all the things you use in this life, should seem to you like a hostelry to a traveler, not a house for someone who means to settle down there. Remember that though you have covered part of your journey, some still remains, and that you have turned aside for quiet, not to quit.[13]

10. Variant: ". . . no one to seek, that is, to ask, Who is he who is crucified? Surely he who says, *They dug* . . . ."
11. *Salutem*; here and in the following sentence the word has a broader meaning than "salvation," connoting also "safety," "health," etc.
12. *Non subest quod quaeris, sed adest quem quaeris.*
13. *Ad refectionem, non ad defectionem.*

7. There are people who say, "God is good, great, supreme, invisible, eternal, incorruptible. He is to give us eternal life, and the incorruptibility that belongs to the life of resurrection; he has promised this. But secular and temporal interests are the province of demons, of the powers that rule this dark world." In saying this they become affectionately attached to these things, and dismiss God as though he had no concern with them; and they attempt by illicit sacrifices, or various charms, or some sort of inducement forbidden to human beings, to provide for their temporal needs—money, a wife, children, and all the other things they want, either as comforts for this life as it slips away, or to slow its onward march.

Divine providence was on the watch, though, to counter this view. God wished to show that all these things belong to him and are within his domain, not only the eternal happiness he has promised us for the future, but also the temporal goods he gives on earth to whomsoever he wills, and whenever he judges it to be expedient, well knowing to whom he gives and from whom he withholds them, like a physician dispensing medication, who knows the patient's illness better than the patient does. Since God wished to show us this he made a distinction between the eras of Old and New Testament. In the Old Testament his promises bear on temporal goods; in the New he promises the kingdom of heaven. There are plenty of precepts concerned with worshiping God and leading a good life which are the same in both the one and the other, but his promise differs between the two dispensations. Therefore while the order of the one who commands and the obedience of the one who serves are the same in both instances, the reward seems not to be. On God's people the commandments were laid "so that you may receive the land of promise, and set up your kingdom there, and overcome your enemies, and not be subjugated by them, and possess all you need in abundance, and procreate children." These are earthly promises, yet figurative also. Imagine that some people received these things just as they were promised; and indeed many did so receive them. The land was given to the Israelites, they were given riches, sons were granted to sterile women—even to old crones who besought God and relied on him alone, refusing to look elsewhere for help even for this. They heard the Lord's voice in their hearts, *I am your salvation*. If he avails for eternal rewards, why not for temporal as well?

God proves this in the case of the holy man, Job. Even the devil has no power to take his property away from him, except when he has received it from that almighty power. He could envy the holy man, but could he do him any harm? No. He could accuse him, but could he get him condemned? Was he able to take anything away from him, to hurt a fingernail or a hair, without first saying to God, *Stretch out your hand* (Jb 1:11)? What does that mean, *Stretch out your hand*? "Give me the power." He received it. He did the tempting, and tempted Job was indeed, but the tempted man emerged victorious and the tempter was vanquished. God had allowed the devil to take Job's goods away, but he had not inwardly abandoned his servant, and out of his servant's soul he fashioned for himself a sword to defeat the devil. What does this signify? I am talking about the human race as a whole. Humankind was conquered in paradise, but conqueror on this dungheap. There a man was worsted by the devil through a woman, here he gets the better of both the devil and a woman. *You have spoken like the silly woman you are*, he says. *If we have received good things from the Lord's hands, should we not endure the bad too?* (Jb 2:10) How well he had heard, *I am your salvation*!

8. *Let them be confounded and awed, who seek my soul.* These are human persons, remember, and the Lord tells us, *Pray for your enemies.*[14] But this petition in the psalm is really a prophecy. Requests phrased as desires are explained when we understand that prophecy is involved. If a psalm says, "May this and that happen," it is the same as saying, "This and that are to happen." Similarly you must understand this verse as a prophetic statement: *Let them be confounded and awed, who seek my soul.* What does *let them be confounded and awed* mean? Simply that they will be confounded and awed. And that is what happened. Many people were confounded for their own good, many were so awed by the persecution of Christ that they crossed over into the fellowship of his members with heartfelt devotion; and this would not have come about had they not first been confounded and awed. In this sense the psalmist hoped for what would benefit them.

But there are two kinds of people who are overcome, because there are two ways of being overcome. Either they are overcome in order to be converted to Christ, or they are overcome to be condemned by Christ. The present passage in our psalm points out the difference between the two kinds; its explanation is obscure, admittedly, but calls for a perceptive listener. You can take the petition, *Let them be confounded and awed, who seek my soul*, to apply to people who are converted. But it goes on, *Let them be thrust back*; in other words, let them not go ahead, but follow behind, let them not give advice, but take it. Peter wanted to go ahead of the Lord when the Lord was foretelling his passion; he wanted to give the Lord what he thought was salutary advice, the sick man giving salutary advice to the Savior! And what did he tell the Lord, who was asserting the truth about his future suffering? *Far be it from you, Lord*; show yourself some kindness; *this will not happen.* And what was the Lord's answer? *Get behind me, Satan* (Mt 16:22,23). If you rush ahead, you are a Satan; if you follow, you will be my disciple. To such people the next line applies: *Let them be thrust back and confounded, those who have evil designs on me*; for when they begin to follow behind, they will have no evil designs, but will desire only my good.

14. See Mt 5:44.

Verses 5-6. Dark and slippery paths for the wicked

9. What about others? It is not everyone who is overcome in such a fashion as to be converted and brought to faith; there are many who remain fixed in their obduracy, and many who harbor in their hearts those spirits who want the front position. They may not thrust themselves forward, but they are fertile, and when they have found a suitable place they beget progeny. What has the next verse of our psalm to say about such people? *May they become like dust before the wind.* As another psalm has it, *The ungodly are like dust which the wind sweeps away from the face of the earth* (Ps 1:4). The wind is temptation, and the dust is wicked people. When temptation blows hard the dust is whirled away; it cannot hold its ground or resist. *May they become like dust before the wind, with an angel of the Lord to harass them. May their path be dark and slippery.* What a daunting path! Darkness alone is enough to frighten anyone. And everyone is anxious on a slippery surface. But with both together, in darkness and on slippery ground, how can you walk at all? Where will you find firm footing? These two evils are the great scourges of humankind: the darkness of ignorance and the slipperiness of sensuality. *May their path be dark and slippery, with an angel of the Lord to harass them*, so that they cannot stand upright. If anyone finds himself or herself in a dark and slippery spot, with the likelihood of falling if even a foot is shifted, and with no light to see where any foot could be safely placed, the best thing that person can do may perhaps be to wait for dawn. But there is the angel of the Lord to harass the wicked.

The psalmist has not been praying for these calamities to occur, but foretelling that they will. And even though, speaking by God's Spirit, he has cast them in the form of a petition, he does so in the same way that God fulfills the prophecy; for God acts with unerring judgment, a judgment good, just, holy and calm; he is not discomposed by anger, or by bitter jealousy, or by any urge to vent his animosity. His intention is solely justice, in the due punishment of vices. However, this is still a prophecy.

Verses 7-8. The trap springs back on the setter

10. Why such severe punishment? What has merited it? The next verse tells us why they have deserved it: *Because without provocation they hid their foul trap*[15] *for me.* Look to our Head for the interpretation of this, for this is what the Jews did to him. They laid their foul trap. For whom did they conceal it? For the one who was all the while seeing the hearts of those who hid it. Nonetheless he lived among them in the guise of an ignorant man liable to be duped, even though they were themselves hoodwinked by their belief that he was duped. His reason

15. Literally "mousetrap" here and in the following lines.

for pretending to be deceived while he lived among them was that we would be obliged to live among similar folk in such a way that we undoubtedly would be duped. Christ saw his betrayer all along, and chose him as all the more necessary to the work in hand. It is true that through the traitor's evil deed Christ effected great good, yet the traitor was chosen as one of the Twelve, so that not even that small group of twelve should be free from a bad element. This was to give us an example of patience, since it would be necessary for us to live among bad people, necessary for us to endure those who do evil, wittingly or unwittingly. Christ provided you with this example of patience so that you may not lose heart when you find yourself living among scoundrels. And if Christ's college of twelve did not lose heart, how much more steadfast ought we to be, now that all that was foretold about the mingling of good and evil is being played out in the great Church? That little college never saw the fulfillment of the promise made to Abraham, nor the threshing-floor from which would come the great heap to fill the barn. Have we not better reason, then, to put up with the chaff now, while the threshing is under way, until the final winnowing gets rid of it? The fate you have heard about awaits the wicked.

11. What is to be done to them? *Without provocation they hid their foul trap for me*. Why does he say, *Without provocation*? Because the people who did it were those to whom I have done no evil, whom I have in no way harmed. *With empty accusations they reproached my soul.* Why *empty*? Because they were accusing me falsely, offering no proof at all. *May the trap they do not suspect spring shut on them.* That is a splendid punishment, and supremely just. They hid their trap so that I would not suspect it; now let the trap they do not suspect spring shut on them. I am aware of their trap; but what kind of trap will catch them? A trap of which they are unaware. Let us listen carefully; perhaps he is going to tell us about this trap. *May the trap they do not suspect spring shut on them.* Should we take it to mean that they hid one trap, and a different one will ensnare them? No. What then? Everyone is entangled by the fine hairs of his or her own sins.[16] Sinners are deluded by the very schemes with which they try to delude others. They will be hurt by the same device with which they tried to hurt their victims. This is why the psalm continues, *And may the snare they have concealed grip them.* It is like the case of someone who prepared a poisoned drink for someone else, and then absent-mindedly drains it himself; or as though someone dug a pit, hoping that his enemy would fall into it in the dark, but then forgot that he had dug it and went that way himself first, and fell into it.

I want to stress this, my brothers and sisters. Take it to heart, be very sure of it and believe it—or if you are endowed with better insight and prudence, see the truth of it for yourselves—there is no one who does evil without first of all doing mischief to himself. Think of the evil person's malice as a fire. Now suppose you

16. See Prv 5:22.

want to burn something. You have to apply some smoldering object to it, and unless this is alight, what you want to burn will not catch. So you take a glowing twig to use like a little torch, and apply it to what you want to burn. This twig you are using must be on fire first, mustn't it, if you are going to set the other thing on fire? So with malice: it comes from yourself, and whom does it destroy first? Yourself. And if it injures the twig that carries it, does it not also injure the place where the twig was rooted? What I am saying is that it is possible for your malice not to hurt someone else, but it cannot do otherwise than hurt you. What injury was done to the holy man Job, of whom we spoke earlier? Another psalm makes the same point: *like a sharp razor you worked your guile* (Ps 51:4(52:2)). What is a sharp razor used for? For cutting away hairs, unwanted things. So what are you doing to the person you want to harm? If the one you mean to harm is likewise malicious and wants to harm you, it is not your malice that will hurt that person, but his or her own. If, however, that other person's heart is free from malice, and surrendered to the voice which says, *I am your salvation*, then you may slash at him outwardly, but you will not touch his inner self. All the same, since your malice springs from your inner self, it renders you worthless first of all. You are rotten inside. From that corruption the maggot has crawled out, and it has left nothing sound within you. *May the snare they have concealed grip them, and may they fall into the same trap*. Perhaps when you heard a little while ago, *May the trap they do not suspect spring shut on them*, you thought it meant some other trap, something hidden that they could not avoid? Not so. What trap, then? The same iniquity, the very same, that they hid to catch me. This was what happened to the Jews, wasn't it? The Lord defeated their iniquity, but by their iniquity they were themselves defeated. He rose from the dead for us, but they were left to themselves to die.

Verse 9. God offers you himself

12. The foregoing verses have been concerned with those who want to injure me; now what about me? *But my soul will rejoice*[17] *in the Lord*, in him from whom it heard the promise, *I am your salvation*. My soul seeks no other wealth, nor does it seek to wallow in pleasures or earthly goods; it loves its true Bridegroom without looking to any reward, nor desiring to receive from him any delight save that of keeping before its eyes him alone in whom it may find all delight. What better thing than God shall be given to me? God loves me; God loves you.[18] Look, he has made you an offer: ask whatever you will. If the emperor were to say to you, "Ask whatever you will," you would be blurting out

17. Variant: "has rejoiced."
18. Variant: "What is better than God? Someone says to me, God loves me, God loves you."

a mouthful of requests for the office of tribune or lordly rank.[19] What splendid possibilities you would pass in review, things you could ask for yourself and distribute to others! But when God invites you, "Ask what you will," what request will you make? Cudgel your brains, out with your greed, stretch it as far as you possibly can, widen your desire. It is not just any ordinary person but almighty God who has said to you, "Ask what you will." If possessions mean a lot to you, you will be desiring the whole world, so that all those who are born will be your tenants or your servants. Then what next, once you own the whole earth? You will be asking for the sea, even though you will be unable to live in it. In this display of greed the fishes will outdo you. But perhaps you will own the islands. Go higher though; this is not enough. Ask for the air as well, even though you cannot fly; lift your longing even to the sky, say that the sun is yours, and the moon and the stars, because he who made all things has said to you, "Ask whatever you will." Nothing more precious will you find, though, nothing better, than him who made them all. Ask for him who made them; in him and from him you will have everything he has made. They are all precious because they are all beautiful, but what is more beautiful than he? They are strong, but what is stronger than he? And what he wants most of all to give you is himself. If you have discovered anything better, ask for it. But if you do ask for anything else, you will be insulting him and inflicting loss on yourself, because you will be esteeming something he has made more highly than its Maker, even though the Maker wants to give you himself. A soul in love with him like this said, *You are the portion allotted to me, O Lord* (Ps 118(119):57; compare Ps 72(73):26). Let others choose for themselves what they want as their possessions, let them share things out and allot themselves what they will; but you are my allotted portion, you I have chosen for myself. Another psalm says, *The Lord is my portion and my inheritance* (Ps 15(16):5). Let him possess you so that you may possess him; you will be his estate, you will be his home. He possesses you to enrich you; he is possessed by you to enrich you. Do you confer any benefit on him? No, says that other psalm: *I said to the Lord, You are my God, because you have no need of any good things from me* (Ps 15(16):2). *But my soul will rejoice in the Lord, and find delight in his salvation*. God's salvation is Christ himself, for scripture says, *My eyes have seen your salvation* (Lk 2:30).

Verse 10. Christ's bones cry out in praise

13. *All my bones will say, "Lord, who is like you?"* Who could comment worthily on these words? I think they should simply be read out, not explained. Why seek this thing, that thing? What can be compared to your God? Him you

---

19. *Tribunatus comitivasque*, the dignity or rank of chief officers. But the CCL editors of the Latin text amend to *comitatusve*, "or retinues/escorts."

have before you. *All my bones will say, "Lord, who is like you?"* The wicked have told me titillating tales, but they have nothing to do with your law, O Lord.[20] There have been persecutors who insisted, "Worship Saturn, worship Mercury," "No," says the psalmist, "I do not pay homage to idols. *Lord, who is like you?* They have eyes, but do not see, and ears, but do not hear.[21] *Lord, who is like you*, who made the eye for seeing and the ear for hearing? I do not worship idols that were made by a craftsman." "Worship a tree, and a mountain, then; did a craftsman make them?" The psalmist answers, "*Lord, who is like you?* Earthly realities are being pointed out to me, but you are the earth's Creator." Perhaps now they turn to a higher creature, and say to me, "Worship the moon, worship that sun which uses its radiance like a mighty lamp in heaven to give us the day." And here I say without hesitation, "*Lord, who is like you?* You made the moon and the stars, you enkindled the sun to provide daylight, you deployed the heavens. And many invisible beings there are, better still than these." So perhaps I shall be told, "Worship the angels, then, adore the angels." And I shall answer, "*Lord, who is like you?* Even the angels are your creation. The angels are nothing, except by virtue of seeing you. It is better for me in their company to possess you, than by adoring them to fall away from you."

14. *All my bones will say, "Lord, who is like you?"* O body of Christ, O holy Church, let all your bones cry, *Lord, who is like you?* Even if your flesh has succumbed to persecution, let the bones say, *Lord, who is like you?* For it was said of the righteous, *The Lord loves all their bones: not one will be broken.*[22] How many righteous people did have their bones broken under persecution! Nonetheless we must remember that a person who is righteous through faith has life, and it is Christ who makes righteous one who has been godless.[23] And how does he make someone righteous? Through that person's believing and confessing. It is written, *The faith that issues in righteousness is in the heart, and the confession that leads to salvation is made with the lips* (Rom 10:10). This is why the robber who had been dragged from his crime to the judge, and from the judge to the cross, was in spite of everything made righteous on the cross; he believed in his heart and confessed with his lips. The Lord could not have promised to one who was still unrighteous and not yet justified, *Today you will be with me in paradise* (Lk 23:43). Yet, for all that, the robber's bones were broken. When the time came for the bodies to be taken down because of the nearness of the Sabbath, the Lord was found to be already dead, so his bones were not shat-

20. Compare Ps 118(119):85, and Augustine's use of this line in the vision of Continence at the crisis of his conversion, *Conf.* VIII,11,27.
21. See Ps 113B(115):5,6.
22. Ps 33:21(34:20). The preferred reading here is *diligit*, "loves," though a few lines further on Augustine reads *custodit*, "guards," as he also does when commenting on Ps 33 (Exp. 2, 24). His treatment of the theme of bones here recalls that in the preceding Exposition.
23. See Rom 1:17; 4:5.

tered. But the others were still alive, and since it was necessary for them to be taken down soon, their legs were broken, so that the pain might finish them off and they could then be buried. Do we read that the bones of only one robber were broken, that one who persisted in his impiety even on the cross, and not those of the one who had in his heart the faith that issued in righteousness, and made with his lips the confession that led to salvation? No, that was not the way of it. So what had become of the pledge, *the Lord guards all their bones, not one will be broken*? It must mean that the bones are all the righteous people in the body of the Lord, the steadfast of heart, the valiant, the people who do not give way and consent to do wrong, however fierce the persecutions and temptations. And when did they get the chance to show they would yield to no temptations? When the persecutors said, "Look, this is god, look how wonderful he is! Let him come and bind up your wounds.[24] Up there on the mountain there is a powerful priest. This may be why you are poor: the god is not helping you. Put your petitions to him and he will. Or perhaps you are ill because you are not his suppliant; be his suppliant, then, and you will get better. Or again your childless state is due to your not paying cult to him: present your request to him and you will have children." But the believer who is numbered among the bones in the Lord's body rejects these suggestions and says, "*Lord, who is like you?* If it is your will, give me what I seek in this life; and if it is not your will, be yourself my life, you whom I ever seek. Shall I be able to hold up my head as I depart this life, if I have worshiped another god and offended you? I may die tomorrow, and then how will I face you?" God's mercy is very great; he has taught us how to live rightly and has hidden from us when our last day will be, the day when we shall die, to ensure that we make no promises to ourselves about our future. I do something today, while I am alive; tomorrow I may not be able to do it. What if tomorrow dawns and you are not here? Say then, you who are among Christ's bones, *Lord, who is like you? All my bones will say, "Lord, who is like you?"*

15. *Lord, who is like you, who pluck the helpless out of the hand of the stronger, the poor man from those who would snatch him away?* We have read the psalm to this point today, and this as much as we can deal with. I don't want you to get bored with what has been said already, because there are other things I want to tell you as well. So let just these words bring us to a close today: *you pluck the helpless out of the hand of the stronger*. Who is it who plucks him out? The strong-handed one, surely; our David will pluck the helpless person out of the hand of the stronger foe. When the devil captured you he proved the stronger; he overcame you because you consented. But what did the strong-handed champion do? No one forces an entrance into a strong man's house and snatches his

24. Reading *liget tibi*. Apart from *liget te*, which means much the same, there are other variants: *nocet tibi*, "he can hurt you (if he comes);" *neget tibi*, "he may be withholding [favors?] from you."

goods away, unless he has tied up the strong man first.[25] By his most sacred, most glorious power, Christ bound the devil, loosing his sword to make an end of him and deliver the needy and poor, who had no other helper.[26] Who else can your helper be but the Lord, to whom you cry, *Lord, my helper and my redeemer* (Ps 18:15(19:14))? If you rely on your own strength it will let you down and you will tumble; if you rely on someone else's strength that other will want to dominate you, not support you. Him alone must we seek, who has both redeemed his servants and given them freedom, who has given his blood to ransom them, and has made his servants into his brothers and sisters.

25. See Mt 12:29.
26. See Ps 71(72):12.

Exposition 2 of Psalm 34

Second Sermon

Introduction: Christ and the Church, one body, one voice

1. Let us turn our attention to the rest of the psalm now, and beg our Lord and God to grant us a sound understanding of it, and cause it to bear good fruit in the way we live. I think you will remember the point we reached in discussing it yesterday, beloved brethren,[1] so let us pick it up from there today. We hear Christ's voice in it: the voice, that is, of Christ, Head and body. When you hear Christ mentioned, never divorce Bridegroom from bride, but recognize that great sacrament, *they will be two in one flesh* (Eph 5:31; Gn 2:24). If there are two in one flesh, why not two in one voice? It is not as though the Head endured trials here, and the body is exempt from them; nor was there any reason for the Head to suffer other than to set an example for the body. The Lord suffered of his free will, but we of necessity; he out of pity, we because it is our condition. Accordingly, his voluntary suffering is our necessary consolation, so that when we have to undergo something similar we may fix our gaze on our Head, be instructed by his example, and say to ourselves, "If he suffered so, what of us? And as he bore it, let us bear it too." However fiercely the enemy may rage, he can go only as far as killing the body; and in the Lord's case he could not even finally destroy that, for the Lord rose on the third day. And what took place in his body on the third day will take place in ours at the end of time. Our hope of resurrection is adjourned, but it is not annulled, is it?[2] So, dearest friends, let us recognize Christ's words here, and sort them out from the cries of the wicked. The words are those of the body undergoing persecution, harassment and trials in this world; but because many people suffer likewise here below, and often on account of their sins and crimes, we need to be very alert in distinguishing the reason for the suffering, rather than looking simply at the pain. A criminal may undergo torments very much like those of a martyr, but the reason is different. There were three men on crosses; one was the Savior, another was destined for salvation, the third for damnation; their torments were alike, the reasons unlike.

1. *Caritatem vestram.*
2. *Differtur, numquid aufertur?*

Verses 11-12. In what sense was Christ ignorant?

2. If, speaking in his own person, the Head says, *Unjust witnesses arose, interrogating me on matters of which I knew nothing*, we in our turn must ask him, "Lord, what was there that you did not know? Were you ignorant of anything? Did you not know even the hearts of your interrogators? Had you not foreseen their tricks? Had you not delivered yourself knowingly into their hands? Had you not come for this, to suffer at their will? Of what, then, were you ignorant?"

He knew nothing of sin, and of this sin in particular, not in the sense that he could not judge it, but in that he did not commit it. We use the same kind of expression in everyday speech. You say of someone, "He doesn't know how to keep still," because he does not keep still; or "She doesn't know how to do the right thing," because she is not given to acting rightly; or "He doesn't know how to act dishonorably," because he never does. What is uncharacteristic of a person's conduct is foreign to his or her conscience, and what is foreign to the conscience seems to be something that person knows nothing about. God can be said not to know in the same way that art does not know lapses of taste, yet it is precisely art that enables us to recognize such lapses and condemn them. When we put the question to our Head, "Lord, what was there that you did not know? How could you be interrogated on matters of which you were ignorant?" he replies to us by pointing to the truth of his own gospel. "I knew nothing of sins, and it was about sins that I was being interrogated. If you do not believe that I am ignorant of sins, look at the passage in the gospel where I say that I do not even know the sinners, to whom I am to say at the end, *I never knew you; depart from me, you who work iniquity*" (Mt 7:23). Do you think he did not know those whom he was condemning? Is not a good judge, one who knows them well, the only one who can justly condemn?[3] The Lord is the good judge, and he does know them well, yet he did not lie in saying, *I never knew you*. It implies, "You do not fit into my body; you do not keep to my rules. You are like lapses of taste in a work of art, but I am art itself, free from all fault, and it is from me that anyone learns to avoid faults."

Unjust witnesses arose, interrogating me on matters of which I knew nothing. Of what was Christ so radically ignorant as blasphemy? He was interrogated on this score by his persecutors, and because he spoke the truth he was judged to have blasphemed. Judged by whom? By those of whom the psalm goes on to say, *For good deeds they requited me with evil, and gave back to my soul only sterility.* "I brought them fecundity, but they gave me sterility in return; I brought them life, they requited me with death; I bestowed honors, they insults, I medi-

3. Variant offered by the CCL editors: "Can anyone be justly condemned, if he is not known to be bad?"

cine, they wounds. And in all these returns they made to me, there was nothing but sterility." Christ cursed a tree for its sterility when he looked for fruit on it and found none.[4] There were leaves, but no fruit, as his persecutors produced words, but not deeds. Look how prolific they were in words, though barren of deeds: "You preach against theft, but steal yourself; you say adultery is wrong, but you commit adultery."[5] Such were the people who were interrogating Christ on matters of which he knew nothing.

Verse 13. Sackcloth, fasting and prayer, as interpreted of Christ

3. *When they were troublesome to me, I clothed myself in sackcloth;*[6] *I humbled my soul with fasting, and my prayer will be directed*[7] *back into my own breast.* Yes, brothers and sisters, this is exactly what we are taught, because we belong to Christ's body, because we are members of Christ. We are advised that in any trouble we may have, we should not cast about for a retort to make to our enemies, but look to how we may propitiate God by prayer, and especially pray that we be not overcome by temptation. And, finally, we are taught to pray that even our persecutors may be brought back to spiritual health and righteousness. There is no greater thing we can do, no better way of dealing with temptation, than to withdraw from the hubbub outside and enter the secret recesses of our own minds, and there call upon God, where no one else sees either the groaning suppliant or the One who comes to our help.[8] There is nothing more profitable that we can do than to shut the door of our private room against all the annoyance that tries to invade from outside, humble ourselves by confessing our sin, and magnify and praise God who both corrects and consoles us.[9] This is most certainly the right course for us.

However, we have been talking about this as experienced by the body, that is, by ourselves. Can we discern anything of the kind in our Lord Jesus Christ? We may search the gospels thoroughly, with the utmost care, yet we do not find any mention of the Lord's having donned sackcloth when he was facing pain or trouble. We read that he fasted after his baptism, certainly, but we have never heard or read anything about sackcloth in that connection. In any case he was fasting then because the devil was tempting him, not the Jews, who were not persecuting him yet. I am not saying that the Lord fasted when they were interrogating him on matters of which he was ignorant, or when for good deeds they requited him with evil by pursuing, hounding, arresting, scourging, wounding

4. See Mt 21:19.
5. See Rom 2:21-22.
6. *Cilicio*, literally "goat's hair," because originally derived from Cilician goats.
7. Variant: "was directed."
8. See Mt 6:6.
9. Variant: "God who corrects us to our profit."

and killing him. Yet throughout all this, brothers and sisters, if we lift the veil slightly in reverent curiosity,[10] and probe the inner meaning of this part of scripture with the keen eye of our heart, we discover that our Lord did do what the psalm describes. Perhaps he uses the word "sackcloth" to represent his mortal flesh. But why sackcloth? Because it resembles sinful flesh. The apostle testifies, *God sent his Son in the likeness of sinful flesh, that he might deal with sin by condemning it within that very flesh* (Rom 8:3). In other words, God clothed his Son in sackcloth, so that, sackcloth-clad, he might condemn the goats. There was no sin in him; and I do not mean simply that there was none in the Word of God; I mean there was no sin in his holy human soul and mind, in that humanity which the Word and Wisdom of God had taken and shaped to himself. There was no sin whatever even in his body, but in the Lord there was the likeness of sinful flesh, because death comes only from sin,[11] and his body was obviously liable to death. If he had not been mortal he could not have died; if he had not died he would not have risen from the dead; and if he had not risen he would not have been for us an example and proof of eternal life.

For these reasons death is called "sin," because it comes about through sin. It is like the way we speak of "the Greek tongue," or "the Latin tongue"; we do not mean the physical organ, but what is done by that organ. The tongue is one member among others in our bodies, like the eyes, nose, ears, and so on. "The Greek tongue" means Greek words; the words are not the tongue, but the words are uttered by the tongue. So too you say of someone, "I recognized his face," referring to a part of his body; and you say, "I recognized his hand," when referring to an absent person, although it is not the hand that forms part of his body that you recognized, but the writing done by that physical hand. In a similar way we can speak of our Lord's "sin," meaning what sin brought about, because he assumed his flesh from that very stock that by sin had deserved death. To put it briefly: Mary, descended from Adam, died because of sin. Adam died because of sin, and the Lord's flesh, derived from Mary, died to abolish sins.[12] This is the sackcloth the Lord put on, and because he was concealed by sackcloth he was not recognized. *When they were troublesome to me, I clothed myself in sackcloth*, he says. In other words, while they were venting their savagery, I remained hidden. If he had not been willing to remain hidden he could not have been put to death; this is clear from that episode where, in a single moment, he released one little drop of his power, as it were, as they tried to arrest him. He asked one question

10. So there can be a devout and profitable curiosity, though in his *Confessions* Augustine associated *curiositas* with a root vice, the "lust of the eyes" (1 Jn 2:16); see *Conf.* X,35,54-55.

11. See Rom 5:12.

12. The first sentence of this brief summary gave rise to multiple variants, presumably because copyists familiar with more developed Marian doctrine found difficulty with it. Emendations include: "Mary, descended from Adam, died because of Adam's sin"; "Mary was Adam's descendant, and Adam died because of sin"; "Mary was the descendant of the first Adam, and the second Adam, born of Mary died to abolish sins."

only: "Whom do you seek?" and that was enough to hurl them backward and fell them to the ground.[13] Power like that he could not have humbled in his passion, except by keeping it hidden under sackcloth.

4. So then, *I clothed myself in sackcloth and humbled my soul with fasting.* We have understood about the sackcloth; now what are we to make of the fasting? Was it food Christ wanted, when he looked for fruit on the tree;[14] and if he had found any, would he have eaten it? And was it water Christ wanted, when he said to the Samaritan woman, *Give me a drink*, and on the cross, *I am thirsty* (Jn 4:7; 19:28)? What does Christ hunger for, what does he thirst for? Our good actions. He found none in those who crucified and hounded him, so he had to stay fasting then, for they supplied nothing but sterility to his soul. What a fast it was for him! He found barely one robber to taste on the cross. The apostles had fled and disappeared into the crowd. Even Peter, who had promised to be faithful to the point of dying with his Lord, had already denied him three times, and wept, and was now lurking among the mob, still afraid of being recognized. In the end, when they saw him dead, all of them despaired even of salvation; but after his resurrection he came and sought them out in their despair, and talked with them as they mourned and grieved, bereft of hope. This was the state of some of them who conversed with him along the road. He asked them, *What are you discussing between you?* They were talking about him. They replied, *Are you the only stranger in Jerusalem not to know what the priests and our leaders did to Jesus of Nazareth, who was so powerful in deed and word? How they crucified and killed him? And we had been hoping that he was the one to redeem Israel* (Lk 24:18-21). The Lord would have been forced to endure a grueling fast had he not been able to refresh those he meant to swallow up. But refresh them he did; he comforted them, strengthened them, and transformed them into his own body. So in this sense we can speak of our Lord fasting.

5. *My prayer will be directed back into my own breast*, the psalm continues. A mighty breast this is; may the Lord grant us to make our way into it. The breast symbolizes what is secret. It is with excellent reason, brothers and sisters, that we are instructed to pray within our own breast, where God alone sees, where God alone hears, where no human eye spies on us, where no one sees except the One who comes to our aid. This is where Susanna prayed, and though her prayer was inaudible to human beings, it was heard by God.[15] This is certainly good advice for us; but if it is to be applied to our Lord (for he too prayed), we must look for something more. We find nothing about sackcloth in the gospel, if we take it literally, nor is there any literal statement about the Lord fasting at the time of his passion. That is why we explained sackcloth and fasting in an allegor-

13. See Jn 18:4,6.
14. See Mk 11:13.
15. See Dn 13:35, 42-44.

ical way, understanding them figuratively as best we could. With his prayer it is quite otherwise, for we heard him cry even from the cross, *My God, my God, why have you forsaken me?* (Mt 27:46; Ps 21:2(22:1)). But even there, yes, even there, we were present.[16] For when did the Father, from whom he was never separated, ever forsake Christ? Again, we read that Jesus prayed alone on the mountain-side, that he spent the whole night in prayer,[17] and that he prayed as the passion drew near. So what are we to make of this line in the psalm, *my prayer will be directed back into my own breast*? I am not sure I know how to understand this of the Lord. I will tell you what now occurs to me, but perhaps something more suitable may suggest itself later, either to me or to someone better. I understand *my prayer will be directed back into my own breast* to mean that within his breast he had his Father, for God was in Christ, reconciling the world to himself.[18] Christ had within himself the Father whom he was entreating; he was never far from his Father, for he had said himself, *I am in the Father, and the Father is in me* (Jn 14:10). But prayer is proper to his humanity. As the Word, Christ does not pray, he hears prayer; and he does not beg help for himself, but together with the Father comes to the help of us all. Accordingly we can best understand *my prayer will be directed back into my own breast* as signifying, "The human nature in me is calling upon the divinity in me."

Verse 14. Being near to God, or far from him

6. *I was humbled like one mourning and grieving, yet I was as pleasing to him as to a close friend or brother.* Christ is looking to his body now; we must see ourselves in this verse. When we find joy in prayer, when our mind is at peace, contented not with the world's prosperity but in the light of truth (anyone who has experienced this light will know what I am talking about, and recognize it here), then the soul knows what this phrase means: *I was as pleasing to him as to a close friend or brother.* This is how close the soul is to God at such times, and how pleasing it is to him. *In him we move and have our being*, says scripture (Acts 17:28), as we might in a brother or sister, a near relative or a friend. But when the soul is in no state to rejoice like this, to be radiant like this, to come close to God and cling to him like this, but sees itself to be far away, then it must conduct itself in the way the psalm recommends: *I was humbled like one mourning and grieving.* When I came close to God, it says, then *I was as pleasing as to a brother*; but when I am far off, and banished to a distance, I lament, *humbled like one mourning and grieving.* What is it mourning for?

16. *Et ibi nos eramus.* The CCL editors (questionably) amend the last word to *oramus*: "even there we are praying."
17. See Mt 14:23; Lk 6:12.
18. See 2 Cor 5:19.

Because it longs for what it does not possess. Sometimes both states are experienced by the same person. We are sometimes close, sometimes far away; we approach God by the light of truth, but seem to be distant from him owing to the cloud of the flesh.

This does not mean, brothers and sisters, that we come near to God by any change of place, or distance ourselves from him by any spatial movement, for God is everywhere and is confined to no place whatever. To approach him is to become like him; to move away from him is to become unlike him. If you see two objects that are very similar, you say, "This one is very close to that," don't you? And when two dissimilar objects are shown you, even though they are in one place and can be held together in one hand, you say, "These differ widely." You are holding both, holding them together, yet you say they are different by far. They are distant not by position in different places but by their dissimilarity.

So then, if you want to come close to God, be like him. If you do not want to be like him, you will withdraw into the distance. If you are like him, be glad of it; if you are unlike him, groan over it, so that your groaning may arouse your desire, and your desire move you to groan the more. Then you will begin to draw near to him by your groaning, even though you had been heading in the opposite direction. Did not Peter draw near when he said, *You are the Christ, the Son of the living God*? But then he put himself far off by saying, *Far be it from you, Lord, this will not happen*. And what did Christ, like a close friend, say to him as he approached? *Blessed are you, Simon, son of Jonah*. But then as Peter moved away, and grew unlike the Lord, Jesus said to him, *Get behind me, Satan*. As he drew near, Jesus said, "*It is not flesh and blood that revealed this to you, but my Father, who is in heaven*; his light has flooded you, and you are shining with his radiance." But when Peter drew further away, arguing against the suffering which the Lord was to undergo for our salvation, Jesus rebuked him: *You have no taste for the things of God, but only for human things* (Mt 16:16-23). In another psalm someone vividly recorded both states: *Beside myself with fear, I said, "I have been flung far out of your sight"* (Ps 30:23(31:22)). He would not be "beside himself" as he spoke unless he were drawing near to God, because this ecstatic state is a going forth of the mind. He poured out his soul above himself[19] and approached God, but then he found himself flung back to earth, as though through a cloud and the weight of the flesh. Remembering where he had been, and taking stock of where he was now, he said, *I have been flung far out of your sight*.

May God grant it to be true for each of us that *I was as pleasing to him as to a close friend or a brother*. But when it is not so, let this be verified in us instead: *I was humbled like one mourning and grieving*.

19. See Ps 41:5(42:4).

Verse 15. Blessed are the mourners

7. *They made merry over me and made common cause.* They were merry, I was sad. But we heard just now in the gospel, *Blessed are those who mourn* (Mt 5:5). If mourners are blessed, then those who laugh are to be pitied. It was against me that they *made merry and made common cause; their scourges fell thick upon me and they knew it not,*[20] for they were interrogating me about matters of which I knew nothing, and they did not know whom they were interrogating.

Verse 16. Persecution, past and present

8. *They mocked me with derisive gestures*; that is to say, they made fun of me and insulted me. It happened to the Head, and it happens to the body. Consider the glory of the Church today, brothers and sisters, and then cast your minds back to the contempt in which it once was held. Remember how Christians were hounded out of every refuge, and how wherever they were discovered they were mocked, beaten, killed, thrown to the beasts and burnt; and remember how people made merry at their expense. What had happened to the Head happened to the body too. What had been done to the crucified Lord was done to his body as well throughout the persecution of former days. But persecution has not ceased even now. Wherever they find a Christian they make a point of insulting him or her; they taunt Christians, call them doltish, dull, lily-livered, good for nothing. But let them do what they will: Christ is in heaven. Let them do what they will: he has made his punishment glorious, and planted his cross on the brows of all. The godless are allowed to insult us, but not to use violence. And what the tongue brings forth is indicative of what the godless have in their hearts. *They hissed at me through their teeth.*[21]

Verse 17. Why help is delayed

9. *When will you have a care for me, Lord? Save my soul from their stratagems, my precious one from the lions.*[22] His help seems to us slow in coming, so it is in our name that the psalm here asks, *When will you have a care?* When shall we see your punishment fall on those who insult us? When will the judge be worn down by weariness and give that widow a hearing?[23] But in truth our Judge postpones his saving help in our case not out of weariness but out of love; of set purpose and not because he lacks the means; not because he is unable to come to

20. Variant in one manuscript: "I knew it not."
21. In the present sermon Augustine passes over the first part of this verse, but he discusses it briefly in his Exposition of Psalm 57, 20.
22. Or "my precious life"; literally "my only one," as in Ps 21:21(22:20).
23. See Lk 18:3-6.

our aid immediately, but because our numbers are to be continually augmented until the end comes. All the same, our longing impels us to ask, *When will you have a care, Lord? Save my soul from their stratagems, my precious one from the lions*: this means the Church, save it from ruthless powers.

Verse 18. Praise from the "weighty people"

10. Perhaps you would like to know what this "only one" is? Read on. *I will confess to you, Lord, in the great congregation, in a weighty people I will praise you.* Assuredly it is *in the great congregation* that *I will confess to you*, and *in a weighty people* that *I will praise you*, for while confession is made in every gathering, it is not in everyone present that God is praised. The whole assembly hears our confession, but not in the whole assembly does God's praise resound. In this whole assembly, that is, in the Church spread throughout the world, there is both chaff and wheat. The chaff blows away, but the wheat remains; that is why the psalm says, *In a weighty people I will praise you.* In these heavy, weighty folk, who are not blown away by the wind of temptation, God is praised; but on account of the chaff he is continually blasphemed. When outsiders take note of our chaff, what do they say? "Look how those Christians live! Look what Christians get up to!" And that saying of scripture comes true: *Through your fault my name is profaned among the nations* (Rom 2:24; compare Is 52:5; Ezk 36:20). Turn your jaundiced gaze on us, you scoundrel, look into the threshing-floor, you who unmistakably belong among the chaff yourself, and you will not easily see any good grain. But look harder and you will find that heavy people in whom you may praise the Lord. Do you really want to find it? Be like that yourself. If you are not, it will be difficult for you to avoid tarring everyone else with your own brush. *Measuring themselves by themselves* (2 Cor 10:12), as the apostle says, they do not understand; but *in a weighty people I will praise you.*

Verses 19-21. Christ and those who tried to trap him

11. *Do not let them insult me, those who pit themselves against me unjustly*, for they insult me over the chaff that is to be found in me, *those who hate me for no reason*, because I have done them no harm, *and wink at me*, the false hypocrites. *They spoke peaceful words to me, indeed.* Why does he say, *They wink at me*? Because they give facial signals that do not express what they have in their hearts. And who are these people who wink? *They spoke peaceful words to me, indeed, but deceitfully hatched hostile plots, and opened wide mouths against me.* At first they only winked, those lions that sought to seize and devour their prey; at first they soothed him with peaceful words, but they were full of guile and hostile intentions. What were the peaceful words they spoke? *Teacher, we*

know that you do not truckle to anyone, and truthfully teach the way of God. So is it lawful to pay tribute to Caesar, or not? (Mt 22:16-17). Yes, conciliatory words they spoke to me. But what happened? Did you not see through them; did they deceive you with their shifty, winking eyes? On the contrary, he did see through them; that was why he answered, *Why are you putting me to the test, you hypocrites?* (Mt 22:18). But later they opened wide mouths at me, shouting, *Crucify! Crucify!* (Lk 23:21). They said, *Hurrah! Hurrah! Our eyes have seen it!* This too was part of their insults: *Hurrah! Hurrah! Play the prophet for us, Christ!* (Mt 26:68). Just as their friendly behavior was insincere when they put him to the test about the tribute coin, so now was their praise intended as insult. *They said, Hurrah! Hurrah! Our eyes have seen it!*, seen your deeds, your wonderful works. This is the Christ, is it? *If he is the Christ, let him come down from the cross, and we shall believe him. He saved others, but he can't save himself* (Mt 27:42). *Our eyes have seen it.* This is the sum total of his boasting: he called himself the Son of God.[24]

But the Lord hung patiently on the cross; he had not lost his power, but he was demonstrating his wisdom. What great matter would it have been to come down from the cross, for him who was later to rise from the tomb? But then he would have seemed to yield the victory to those who mocked him; and the divine plan required that when he rose from the dead he would show himself to his own followers, not to them. This was a great mystery,[25] for his resurrection was the sign of new life, but the new life was manifested to his friends, not to his enemies.

Verse 22. God's silence

12. *You have seen, O Lord, do not keep silence.* What does that mean: *do not keep silence*? Judge them! In another text judgment is spoken of in a similar way: *I have long been silent, but shall I be silent for ever?* (Is 42:14, LXX). And with regard to judgment delayed, God says to the sinner in another psalm, *All this you did, and I was silent; you were wrong to think that I will be like you* (Ps 49(50):21). How can he be said to keep silence, when he speaks through the prophets, speaks with his own lips in the gospel, speaks through the evangelists, and speaks through us too when we speak the truth? How can this be said? Because he is silent from judgment, but not from commandments, not from teaching. But the prophet does in a way call upon him to judge, and foretells the judgment to come: *You have seen, O Lord; do not keep silence*: you will not be silent then, because you must judge. *O Lord, do not leave me.* Pending the judg-

24. See Jn 19:7.
25. *In magno sacramento.*

ment, do not leave me, for you have promised, *Lo, I am with you even to the end of the ages* (Mt 28:20).

Verses 23-24. The cause, not the pain, makes the martyr

13. *Arise, O Lord, attend speedily to my vindication.* Vindication for what? Because you have had a bad time, beset with toil and sorrows? But plenty of bad people suffer from the same things, don't they? Vindication for what, then? You expect to be declared just, because you put up with it all? No? What do you expect, then? *My vindication.* How does the psalm go on? *Attend speedily to my vindication; O my God, my Lord, champion my cause.* I am asking you to take note not of my pain, but of the reason why I am undergoing it, not of what any robber has in common with me, but of the cause in which I suffer, for *blessed are those who suffer persecution in the cause of right* (Mt 5:10).

Now this cause is something quite distinct. The suffering may be the same for both good people and bad; so it is not the pain that makes martyrs, but the cause in which they suffer. If it were the punishment that made martyrs, all the jails would be full of martyrs, all the chains there would be dragging martyrs along, and every executed felon would be in line for a martyr's crown. No, we must discern the cause. Nobody has any right to say, "Because I am suffering, I am righteous." He who was the first to suffer suffered for justice' sake, and so he added the vital qualification: *Blessed are those who suffer persecution in the cause of right.* There are plenty of people who justifiably persecute others, and many suffer it whose cause is unjust. If there could never be persecution for laudable reasons, the declaration would not have been made in another psalm, *Anyone who was secretly disparaging his neighbor, I would always pursue* (Ps 100(101):5). And anyway, brothers and sisters, does a good, just father not persecute a dissolute son? He persecutes the boy's vices, not the boy himself; he persecutes not what he has begotten but what the boy has added to that. Then consider a doctor who is called in to cure someone. He often comes armed with steel instruments, doesn't he? But they are to be used against the wound, not the patient. He cuts to heal; yet when the steel goes in the patient feels pain, and screams and struggles; if he is out of his senses with fever he may even hit out at the doctor. But the doctor does not slacken his efforts for the patient's recovery. He does what he knows to be necessary, and takes no notice if the patient curses and rails at him. And are not all those afflicted with morbid lethargy shaken, for fear they may sink down from heavy sleep into death? Some endure this treatment even from their own beloved children; no one could be called a devoted son who was unwilling to shake his sleeping father in such circumstances. Lethargic patients are aroused, the delirious are tied down; yet all of them are loved.

No one, then, has the right to say, "I am suffering persecution." Such claimants should not flaunt their sufferings but demonstrate the justice of their cause;

if they cannot demonstrate it, they may be in danger of being classed with wrongdoers. How shrewdly, how aptly the psalmist has drawn our attention to this point by praying, *Attend speedily to my vindication* (not to my pain as such); *O my God, my Lord, champion my cause.*

14. *Vindicate me, Lord, in accordance with my righteousness.* Take my cause into consideration. Not in accordance with how much it hurts me, but *in accordance with my righteousness, O Lord, my God*; on that basis vindicate me.

Verses 24-26. Swallowing the wicked

15. *Do not let my enemies jeer at me. Let them not say in their hearts, "Hurrah! Hurrah!" to our soul.* This would be as good as saying, "We have done it because he was in our power; we have killed him, made away with him." *Let them not say it* means: Show them that they have achieved nothing. *Let them not say, "We have swallowed him up."* The martyrs in similar vein say, *If the Lord had not been among us, perhaps they would have swallowed us alive* (Ps 123(124):1,3). Why do they say, *Swallowed us*? It means, They might have drawn us into their own body. What you swallow is what you absorb into your own body. The world wants to swallow you, but you must swallow the world; draw it into your own body, slaughter it and eat it. Peter was told, *Slaughter and eat* (Acts 10:13); kill in them what they are of themselves, and turn them into what you are. But if, on the contrary, they win you over to their impiety, you are swallowed by them. It is not when you are suffering persecution at their hands that you are swallowed by them, but when they persuade you to become what they are. *Let them not say, "We have swallowed him up."* Your job is to swallow the whole body of pagans. Why? Because it wants to swallow you, so you must do to it what it seeks to do to you. Perhaps this was why the golden calf was pulverized and sprinkled into water, and given to the people to drink;[26] the whole body of idolaters was to be swallowed up by Israel. *Let all of them together be shamed and struck with awe, who take pleasure in my misfortunes; let them be clothed with confusion and disgrace*, so that in their confusion we may swallow them. May *those who speak spitefully against me* be shamed and confounded.

Verses 27-28. How to praise God all day long

16. Now what have you, the Head in union with your members, to tell us? *Let them dance for joy and be glad, those who want my righteousness to prevail*, the people who have held fast to my body. *And let them say always, "May the Lord be glorified," those who want peace for his servant. Then my tongue will tell of*

26. See Ex 32:20.

your righteousness, and praise you all day long. Whose tongue can keep God's praise going all day? Even now, when our sermon has gone on a little longer than usual, you are weary; so who has the stamina to praise God all day long? I can give you a tip that will enable you to praise God throughout the day, if you want to. Whatever you have to do, do it well, and you have praised God. When you are singing a hymn, you are praising God; but what is your tongue's activity worth, unless your conscience is praising him too? Have you had enough of singing hymns? Are you off for some refreshment? All right, take care not to drink too much, and you have praised God. Or you are off to bed? Be careful that when you get up it is not to do wrong, and you have praised God. Or you are conducting business? Don't defraud anyone, and you have praised God. You are tilling your field? Don't stir up a quarrel, and you have praised God. By the probity of your actions prepare yourself to praise God all day long.

Exposition of Psalm 35

A Sermon to the People

Verse 2. Willful lack of understanding

1. A little concentration should see us through this psalm and the mysteries it holds, beloved brethren.[1] Let us run through it briskly, because in many places it is perfectly clear; and if in others the obscurity of some passages means that we have to spend more time, I hope you will bear with me for the sake of learning something useful. *The unjust person has voiced within himself the resolve to do wrong; there is no fear of God before his eyes*. It is not one person that is envisaged here, but the whole race of wrongdoers who are their own worst enemies because they fail to understand how to live good lives; and they fail to understand not because they are unable but because they refuse. It is one thing when a person tries to understand something, and cannot by reason of the weakness of the flesh, for, as scripture says somewhere, *The corruptible body weighs down the soul, and this earthly dwelling oppresses a mind that considers many things* (Wis 9:15). But it is quite a different matter when the human heart acts so destructively against itself that it does not understand what it might have understood, given a little good will. The subject-matter is not difficult, but the rebellious will poses an obstacle. This is what happens when sinners are attached to their sins and hate God's commandments. If you are a friend to your iniquity, God's word is your enemy; but if you are an enemy to your iniquity, God's word is a friend to you and an enemy to your iniquity. It follows that if you hate your iniquity, you ally yourself with God's word, and then there will be two who are bent on destroying your iniquity—you and the word of God. You can achieve nothing by your own strength, but he who has sent his word to you comes himself to your aid, and so iniquity is routed. If you hate it, God has forgiven it, and you will be free; but if you are affectionately attached to it, you will raise answering objections to every objection made against it.

Take the case of someone who is wondering how the Son can be equal to the Father. He or she has believed it and seeks now to understand it, but cannot yet do so; for this is a profound matter and demands greater capacity if it is to be comprehended. Meanwhile faith is a beginning, and keeps the soul safe until it grows stronger. The soul is nourished with milk until, sturdy and accustomed to

1. *Caritas vestra.*

more solid food, it comes to understand that *in the beginning was the Word, and the Word was with God; he was God* (Jn 1:1). Before it is capable of this it is nourished in the faith, and it does its best to understand, so that it may indeed reach such understanding as God allows it. But does anyone really have to make an effort to understand the injunction, *Do not do to another what you would not want anyone to do to you* (Tb 4:16)? It simply means that since you do not want to suffer injustice you must not deal unjustly, and since you do not want anyone to take crafty advantage of you, you must not take unfair advantage of anyone else. If you don't understand that, the fault lies in your own will. This is why the psalm says, *The unjust person has voiced within himself his resolve to do wrong*.

God is present within

2. When someone has formed this resolve to do wrong, does he announce it publicly? No, he forms it within himself. Why? Because there no human eye can see it. Yes, that is true; but doesn't God see him there, even though no human eye sees his determination to do wrong? Of course God sees him! But what has the next clause to say? *There is no fear of God before his eyes*. All the sinner has in his sights is fear of other people; he does not dare to make public declaration of his iniquity, lest he be rebuked or condemned by others. He withdraws from human observation, but where to? Into himself! He ushers himself within, where no one can see him. There within himself no one watches him as he plans his trickery, his ruses and his crimes. He would not be able to plot, even there within himself, if he considered that God is scrutinizing him; but because there is no fear of God before his eyes, he thinks he has no one to fear once he has withdrawn from human view into his own heart. But God is present there, isn't he? Assuredly, but in the sinner's outlook there is no room for the fear of God.

Verses 3-4. Dishonest searching

3. So he goes on planning his trickery, and the psalm continues—but wait a minute, perhaps he is simply unaware that God is watching him? Yes, precisely, he is unaware, and that is the point I was making earlier: he is unaware of it because he has chosen to be, and in refusing to understand he has acted against his own interests. *Because he has dealt dishonestly in his sight*. In whose sight? In the sight of God, of course, because the fear of God was not kept before the eyes of this sinner who dealt dishonestly. *In pretending to find his own iniquity, and hate it*: this suggests that he acted in such a way as to make sure he would not find it. Some people make a show of trying to find their iniquity, but they are afraid of finding it, because if they do find it, they will be challenged: "Give it up. You did this before you knew what you were doing. You committed this sin while you were still ignorant. God grants pardon; so now that you have recog-

nized it, get rid of it, so that your ignorance may easily win you pardon, and you may look straight at God and say, *Do not remember the transgressions of my youth, when I was ignorant*" (Ps 24(25):7). But no, he pretends to seek it here, seek it there, but always he is afraid of finding it. His search is a sham. When is it that a person truthfully says, "I didn't know it was a sin"? Only when he or she has perceived that it is a sin, and has given up committing it, because it was only through ignorance that he or she committed it earlier. People like that genuinely want to know iniquity for what it is, and find it, and hate it when found. But nowadays many are dishonest in the way they look for their iniquity; they go about it without sincerely wanting to find it and hate it. Consequently, because there is dishonesty in their search, there will be an attempt to defend the iniquity when it comes to light. Once it is found, its true character will be out in the open, and the sinner will not be able to deny that it is iniquity indeed. "Don't do it," you say. And what do they reply, these people who faked the search, and now that they have found the sin, do not hate it? "Oh, but everybody does it," they say. "You won't find anyone who doesn't do that. Do you imagine that God is going to send the whole lot of us to hell?" Or at any rate they protest, "If God really did not want these things to be done, would the people who do them have been left alive?" Don't you see that you were being dishonest when you pretended to look for your iniquity? If you had not been dishonest, but had acted with sincerity, you would have found it by now, and found it hateful; but as things are, you have found it and you defend it. This proves that you were acting deceitfully when you were searching.

4. *The words he utters are iniquity and guile; he has refused to understand, and so act well.* You can see from this how the psalmist attributes ignorance to a bad will. There are people who want to understand, but are unable; there are others who do not understand because they do not want to. *He has refused to understand, and so act well.*

Verse 5. Inner peace

5. *He plotted iniquity in his bedroom.* Why does it say that, *in his bedroom*? The psalm said earlier, you remember, *The unjust person has voiced within himself his resolve to do wrong*; and where that earlier verse had *within himself*, this one has *in his bedroom*. Our bedroom is our heart, for there we toss and turn if we have a bad conscience, but there, if our conscience is easy, we find rest. Any of us who love this bedroom of the heart must be sure that what we do there is good, and so it is in this bedroom of the heart that our Lord Jesus Christ commands us to pray: *Go into your private room, and shut your door.* What does he mean by *shut your door*? Do not look to God to give you the kind of good things you find outside, but those that are within. Then *your Father who sees in secret will give you your reward* (Mt 6:6). What sort of people do not close their

doors? The ones who set great store by asking external things from God, and focus all their prayers on getting this world's goods. If your door stands open, the crowd outside sees you when you pray. What does it mean to shut the door? It means to ask of God what God alone knows how to give you. What is this good thing, then, for the sake of which you shut your door, and ask him? Something that no eye has seen, no ear heard, no human heart conceived.[2] And perhaps no notion of it has found its way into your bedroom either, into your heart, I mean. Never mind; God knows what he is going to give you. When will that happen? When the Lord is revealed, when he appears as judge; for what could be plainer than the words he is to speak to those stationed at his right hand? *Come, you who are blessed by my Father, take possession of the kingdom prepared for you since the creation of the world* (Mt 25:34). Those placed at his left will hear it said, and groan in a remorse that is fruitless, because during their wicked lifetime they refused to repent fruitfully. Why will they be groaning? Because no chance of amendment is left to them. What they will hear is, *Depart into the eternal fire that was prepared for the devil and his angels* (Mt 25:41). A woeful thing to hear, that is! The just will rejoice at the good news they hear: as scripture says, *The just will be held in eternal remembrance; what they are to hear holds no terrors for them* (Ps 111(112):7). What is the bad news they need not be afraid to hear? What the others are to hear: *Depart into eternal fire.*

God can do more than we are able to ask or understand,[3] and he listens for our hidden groaning so that we may be pleasing in his sight, and not flaunt any righteousness we may imagine we have in the presence of other people. Anyone who seeks human approval for his or her good life, not with the intention of provoking those who see it to praise God, but in order to attract praise to himself, is not closing his door against the din; rather his door stands wide open to the racket outside, and God cannot hear as he wants to.

Let us make every effort, then, to clean the bedroom of our heart, and make it a place where we find peace. You know, beloved,[4] how in public places many people have a lot to put up with: in the forum, in disputes, in controversies, in the problems raised by their business; and you know too how when someone is weary of these negotiations outside he hurries back home to rest. He does his best to dispatch his public business quickly and betake himself to the peace of his own house. It is for this very reason that each of us has a home: we need it because we can rest there. So what of someone who has to put up with vexation even there, where he expects to rest? What then? It is a relief to find rest in one's own house, if nowhere else; but if a man has to endure enemies outside, and perhaps a difficult wife at home, he goes out again. When he wants a rest from

2. See Is 64:4; 1 Cor 2:9.
3. See Eph 3:20.
4. *Caritas vestra.*

the people outside he goes home, but if he cannot rest either there or outside, where is he to find any peace at all?

At least in the bedroom of your heart you will find it, so that you can take refuge there, in the depths of your own conscience. And if you have found there a spouse in whose company there is no bitterness, the very Wisdom of God,[5] unite yourself with her, be at peace there within your bedroom, and do not allow the fumes of a bad conscience to drive you out.

But the person of whom our psalm is speaking retired there to hatch his evil plots, where no one would see him. And because such wickedness was the subject of his meditation he could find no rest, even in his heart. *He plotted iniquity in his bedroom.*

Who wins the battle?

6. *He has taken his stand in every path that is not good.* What is the significance of *he has taken his stand*? It means he persevered in sinning. It has been said of a good, devout disciple that *he has not stood in the way of sinners* (Ps 1:1). The one did not stand there, but there the other has taken his stand. *But he did not hate wickedness.* This is a hint of the end, this is the harvest we must hope for: if we cannot be free from wickedness, at least let us hate it. When you have begun to hate it you are unlikely to be tricked into committing a wicked act by any stealthy temptation. It is true that sin does lurk in our mortal bodies, but what does the apostle tell us? *Do not let sin reign in your mortal body, so as to persuade you to yield to its cravings* (Rom 6:12). When shall we be free of it entirely? When *this corruptible body has put on incorruption, and this mortal body is clothed in immortality* (1 Cor 15:53-54). Before this comes to pass there remains in our bodies a tendency to sinful pleasure; but there is greater pleasure for us in the word of wisdom, in the word of God's commandment. Conquer sin and the will to sin. Hate sin and iniquity, so that you may unite yourself to God, who will hate it with you. Already you are at one with God's law in your mind, for in your mind you are the servant of God's law. If in your carnal nature you are still enslaved to the law of sin[6] because the pleasures of the flesh are still powerful in you, remember that they will be there no longer when your fight is over. To be free from the need to fight, to enjoy true and everlasting peace—this is something quite different from fighting and winning, different from fighting and being vanquished, different yet again from declining even to fight and being carried off as a prisoner. For there certainly are some people who do not put up a fight, like this one of whom the psalm says, *He did not hate wickedness*; for how

5. See Wis 8:16.
6. See Rom 7:25.

could he have been fighting against something for which he felt no hatred? Such a person is dragged away by wickedness without even resisting.

There are others who do begin to fight, but because they rashly rely on their own strength, and God wants to prove to them that it is he who wins the victory if we enlist under his leadership, they are worsted in the battle. They have apparently begun to hold fast to righteousness, but they become proud, and consequently they are knocked out. People like this fight, but are overcome. Who is it who fights and is not overcome? The one who says, *I am aware of a different law in my members that opposes the law of my mind.* Look at this fighter.[7] He does not presume on his own strength, and that is why he will be the victor. What does the next line say? *Who will deliver me from this death-ridden body, wretch that I am? Only the grace of God, through Jesus Christ our Lord* (Rom 7:23-25). He relies on the One who has commanded him to fight, and he defeats the enemy because he is helped by his Commander. But the other person we heard about *did not hate wickedness.*

Verse 6. God's good gifts, temporal and eternal

7. *Your mercy is in heaven, O Lord, and your truth reaches even to the clouds.* I don't know what this mercy of the Lord in heaven may be; but the Lord's mercy is on earth as well. You will find it written, *The earth is full of the Lord's mercy* (Ps 32(33):5). What mercy does the psalmist have in mind, then, when he says, *Your mercy is in heaven, O Lord*?

God's gifts are in part temporal and earthly, in part eternal and heavenly. Anyone who worships God in order to get these temporal and earthly goods, which are available to all, is still no better than a beast. Such a person is making use of God's mercy, to be sure, but not that specially reserved mercy[8] which is given only to the righteous, the holy, the good. What gifts are abundantly available to all? God causes his sun to rise over the good and the bad, and pours his rain on just and unjust alike.[9] Is there anyone who does not benefit from this mercy of God? First it brings us into existence, distinguishing us from the beasts by making us rational animals, capable of knowing God; then it grants us the power to enjoy this light, this air, the rain, the crops, the changing seasons, earthly comforts, bodily health, the affection of friends and the safety of our own homes. All these things are good, and they are gifts from God. Make no mistake, brothers and sisters: no one other than the one God can give them to us. There is a vast difference between people who look only to the Lord for these gifts, and those who seek them from demons, or soothsayers, or astrologers.[10] These latter

7. Variant: "Look at this law opposed to the law of his mind, look at his resistance. . . ."
8. Variant: "that mercy he can look forward to."
9. See Mt 5:45.
10. *A mathematicis*; see note on Exposition 2 of Psalm 33, 25.

are miserable on two counts: because they aspire only to earthly goods, and because they do not seek them from him who grants everything that is good. Others seek these same good things, and want to find in them their happiness, but ask God for these and nothing else. These people are better than the others, since they do seek them from God, but still they are imperiled. Did one of you ask, "Why imperiled?" Because sometimes they reflect on the way things go in human life, and they see that all these good things they long for are possessed in abundance by the godless and the unjust too. So they think they have lost the reward they should have had for worshiping God, either because what they have is what the wicked also have (although they worship God and the wicked do not), or else because it sometimes happens that the worshipers of God do not have these things, while the blasphemers do. That is why they are imperiled.

8. The psalmist understood what kind of mercy he should pray for to God. *Your mercy is in heaven, O Lord, and your truth reaches even to the clouds*. This means that the mercy you lavish on your holy ones is a heavenly, not an earthly, mercy; it is eternal, not bounded by time. But how did you proclaim it to the human race? By causing your truth to reach *even to the clouds*. Who could have had any idea of the heavenly mercy of God, unless God had announced it to human beings? How did he announce it? By sending his truth to the clouds. And what are these clouds? The preachers of God's word. This is why we hear in a scriptural passage how God was angry with a vineyard. I think you understood it, beloved brethren,[11] when you heard the reading from the prophet Isaiah. Of a certain vineyard God said, *I looked for it to produce grapes, and all it bore was thorns*. Then, in case anyone might suppose that he was speaking of some ordinary vineyard, he explained at the end of the passage, *The vineyard of the Lord of Hosts is the house of Israel, and his cherished young shoot is everyone in Judah* (Is 5:4.7). He was reproaching that vineyard which he had expected to yield grapes, but which had yielded nothing but thorns, so he continued, *I will forbid my clouds to send rain upon it* (Is 5:6). Because God was angry he issued this threat: *I will forbid my clouds to send rain upon it*; and that indeed was what happened. The apostles were sent out to preach; and in the Acts of the Apostles we read that Paul wanted to preach to the Jews, but found there no grapes, only thorns, for they began to return evil for good by persecuting him. And so, as though to fulfill the prophecy, *I will forbid my clouds to send rain upon it*, Paul told the Jews, *We were sent to you, but because you have rejected the word of God, we are turning now to the Gentiles* (Acts 13:46). In this way the prophecy came true: *I will forbid my clouds to send rain upon it*. But the truth reached the clouds, and that made it possible for the mercy of God which is in heaven, not on earth, to be proclaimed to us.

Truly, brothers and sisters, these clouds are the preachers of the word of truth. When God utters threats through his preachers, he is thundering through his

11. *Caritas vestra*.

clouds. When he works miracles through his preachers, he is sending brilliant flashes of lightning through his clouds. He terrifies us through his clouds, and through them waters the earth with rain. These preachers, through whom[12] the gospel of God is proclaimed, are God's clouds. Let us hope for mercy, then, but let it be the mercy that is in heaven.

Verse 7. God's true and humble mountains

9. *Your justice is like God's mountains, your judgments an unfathomable abyss.* Who are these mountains of God? The same people who were called clouds are God's mountains. When the sun rises it first of all clothes the mountains with light, and then its brightness penetrates the deepest valleys. So it was when our Lord Jesus Christ came: he shed his rays first on those peaks who were his apostles. He illuminated the mountains first, and from there his light spread downward to the shadowy valleys of the earth. Somewhere in a psalm it is said, *I have lifted my eyes to the mountains, from where comes help for me* (Ps 120(121):1). But you must not suppose that it is the mountains themselves that will give you help; they receive in order to give, they do not give of themselves. Even if you remain in the mountains your hope will not be firmly founded, for all your hope, all your reliance, must rest in him who illumines the mountains. All the same it is from the mountains that his help will reach you, for through these mountains, through these great preachers of the truth, the scriptures were made available to you. Nonetheless, do not attach your hope to them. Listen to the words with which the psalmist continues. He has said, *I have lifted my eyes to the mountains, from where comes help for me*; does that mean that the mountains themselves come to your aid? By no means; listen further: *my help is from the Lord, who made heaven and earth* (Ps 120(121):2). So help does come from the direction of the mountains, but it does not originate with them. With whom, then? With *the Lord, who made heaven and earth.*

There have been other mountains, so unreliable that anyone who attempted to take his bearings from them foundered at sea. Leaders of heresy arose, towering like mountains. Arius was a mountain;[13] Donatus was a mountain;[14] and now

---

12. Thus the CCL editors. The majority of codices have "These creatures of flesh through whom" (literally "these fleshes through which . . . ").
13. This heresiarch (c. 250-336) is thought to have been a Libyan who studied at Antioch under Lucian, from whom he may have imbibed the subordinationist doctrine of the person of Christ which characterized his theology. Ordained priest at Alexandria c. 312, he was revered for his asceticism but propagated his subordinationist views. In the ensuing controversy Arius was for a time supported by the Church historian, Eusebius of Nicomedia, who had also been a pupil of Lucian of Antioch. Arius was excommunicated and Eusebius withdrew his support. In 325 the Council of Nicea condemned Arius, largely under the influence of St Athanasius, who battled against the spreading Arian heresy for the rest of his life.
14. See note at Exposition of Psalm 10, 1.

Maximian seems to have become a mountain too.[15] Plenty of people have set their sights on those mountains, longing to make landfall and be delivered from the rough sea, but they have been driven onto the rocks, and all they found on land was shipwreck.

Not by mountains like this was the psalmist misled who affirmed, "*I trust in the Lord. How can you say to my soul, Migrate to the mountains like a sparrow?* (Ps 10:2(11:1)). I do not want my hope to rest in Arius, or in Donatus; *my help is from the Lord, who made heaven and earth.*" Learn from this how much you must rely on God, and how little on human agents; for anyone who rests his trust in a fellow-human is under a curse.[16] The apostle Paul was jealous for the Church, not on his own behalf, but on that of the Church's Bridegroom. So he was horrified when some tried to proclaim, *I belong to Paul; I belong to Apollos* (1 Cor 1:12). In his extreme modesty and humility he took himself as an example of someone to be put down and belittled, in order that Christ might be glorified: *Was Paul crucified for you, or were you baptized in Paul's name?* (1 Cor 1:13). He pushes them away from himself, but only to send them to Christ. He will not let the bride love him instead of the Bridegroom, for all that he is the Bridegroom's friend; for this is what the apostles were—friends of the Bridegroom. Another humble friend who was jealous on the Bridegroom's behalf was John, who was himself taken to be the Christ. He told them, *I am not the Messiah, but there is coming after me someone greater, and I am not worthy to undo the strap of his sandals* (Jn 1:20; Mk 1:7). By so deeply humbling himself he proved that he was not the Bridegroom, but the Bridegroom's friend; and so he declared, *The bride is for the Bridegroom; but the Bridegroom's friend, who stands and hears him, rejoices intensely at the Bridegroom's voice* (Jn 3:29). And even if the Bridegroom's friend is a mountain, he is still not the source of the light, but only the recipient of it. He hears the Bridegroom's voice and is transported with joy. *From his fullness we have received,* he says. From whose fullness? His, who *was the true light, which illumines every human person who comes into this world* (Jn 1:16,9). Similarly the apostle was jealous for the Church, and laid down the rule, *Everyone should regard us as servants of Christ, and dispensers of the mysteries of God* (1 Cor 4:1). This is the same advice as the psalmist gives: *I have lifted my eyes to the mountains, from where comes help for me. Everyone should regard us as servants of Christ, and dispensers of the mysteries of God.* Just in

15. By the 390s Primian, a narrow extremist, was leader of the Donatists, and Maximian, originally a deacon to Primian, led the opposition against him. Maximian was ordained bishop, but deposed by Primian in 394. Maximian and his followers then became alienated from the Donatist sect, thus creating a schism within a schism. Augustine tended to give special preference to dialogue with the Maximianists (see Letter 245,2; *Answer to Cresconius* I,4; *Revisions* 2,26,29.35). He noted also that the main Donatist faction was inconsistent in recognizing the validity of baptisms conferred by separated Maximianists.

16. See Jer 17:5.

case your hope might once more be deflected to the mountains, rather than anchoring itself in God, Paul insists, *I planted, Apollos watered, but God gave the growth. So the planter is nothing, and the one who waters is nothing; only God matters, who grants the increase* (1 Cor 3:6-7).

Already you have made your declaration, *I have lifted my eyes to the mountains, from where comes help for me*; but since *the planter is nothing, and the one who waters is nothing*, say now, *My help is from the Lord, who made heaven and earth*, and further, *Your justice is like God's mountains*, which means, "the mountains will be flooded by your justice."[17]

The depths of sin and judgment

10. *Your judgments are an unfathomable abyss*. This abyss is the depths of sin into which a person falls by despising God. Scripture says of this elsewhere, *God has delivered them to the lusts of their own hearts, so that they behave as they should not* (Rom 1:24). Let me have your attention, beloved;[18] this is a very serious matter, very serious indeed. What does it mean by saying, *God has delivered them to the lusts of their own hearts, so that they behave as they should not*? Does it imply that the reason why they commit such heinous sins is that God has handed them over like that, so that they have no option but to behave so? If that were true, one might ask, "If God does that, and causes them to behave as they should not, what responsibility have they?" This phrase, *God has delivered them to the lusts of their own hearts*, is puzzling, admittedly. It was the lust that was responsible, the lust they were unwilling to resist, and to which they were delivered by God's judgment. But to understand why they deserved to be handed over like that,[19] look at what has been said a little earlier: *Though they had known God, they did not glorify him as God, or give him thanks. Their thoughts wandered into futility and their stupid hearts were darkened* (Rom 1:21). How? By pride. *Believing themselves to be wise, they sank into folly* (Rom 1:22); that is why it goes on to say, *God delivered them to the lusts of their own hearts*. Proud and ungrateful, they were held worthy to be handed over to the lusts of their hearts, and they became an unfathomable abyss, so that not only did they sin, but they were also dishonest in refusing to know their iniquity for what it was, and detest it. This was the depth of their malice, the refusal to find out their sin and hate it. Yet look how someone sank to those depths: *God's judgments are an unfathomable abyss*. As by God's justice those who by his grace grow great are

17. Variant: "the mountains fulfill your justice."

18. *Caritas vestra*.

19. Variant: "It was the lust that was responsible, the lust they were unwilling to resist; but they were also unwilling to be delivered to it by God's judgment. But by reason of it they deserved to be handed over to other lusts."

mountains of God, so by his judgments those who sink to the basest of sins are plunged into the depths. Let the mountains be a delightful sight to you on the one hand; but on the other steer clear of that gulf, and turn instead to the truth that *my help is from the Lord*. Why will you get that help? Because you have lifted your eyes to the mountains. What does that mean? Well, I will put it in plain English.[20] In Christ's Church you find the abyss, and you also find the mountains. You find there rather few good people, because there are only a few mountains,[21] but the abyss is wide. You find there many people leading evil lives as a consequence of God's anger, because they have so behaved as to be deservedly consigned to the lusts of their hearts, and therefore they defend their sins, rather than confessing them. They say, "Why? What have I done? So-and-so did that, and someone else did that other thing." They have reached such a point that they want to put up a case for actions that the divine word condemns. This is the abyss. In another place scripture says, *A person devoid of reverence goes deep into sin and is defiant* (Prv 18:3). There is the abyss for you. Yes, Lord, *your judgments are an unfathomable abyss*.

What about you? You are not a mountain yet, but neither are you yet an abyss. Run away from the abyss, and head for the mountains. But don't stay in the mountains, for your help is from the Lord, who made heaven and earth.

Verses 7-8. God's kindness to humans and animals

11. *Men and beasts you will save, Lord, as your mercy has been multiplied, O God*. He has already said, "Your mercy is in heaven," and now, to indicate that it is on earth as well, he says, *Men and beasts you will save, Lord, as your mercy has been multiplied, O God*. Great is your mercy, and manifold is your mercy, O God, and you give it to both humans and animals. From whom does the salvation of humans proceed? From God. Does not the good estate of the beasts come from God too? He who made us made the animals as well, and he who made both saves both; but the salvation of the beasts is the safety and health that belong within time. Yet there are people who make a great point of begging from God what he has given even to animals. *Your mercy has been multiplied, O God*, in that you not only grant salvation to human beings, but give also to the beasts what you give to humans, a carnal and temporal salvation.[22]

20. Plain Latin actually. But a possible variant for *Latine* is *latius*, "I will explain more fully."
21. Augustine has now slightly shifted the meaning: mountains are no longer apostles/preachers, but more generally holy Christians.
22. Here as often, *salus* can mean "health/safety/well-being," as well as "salvation."

Becoming "sons of men"

12. Are we to gather from this that human beings do not have any special privilege with God that animals do not merit or attain? Obviously we have. Where is it, then, this special privilege? *But the sons of men will hope under the shelter of your wings.* Notice this very beautiful statement, beloved brethren.[23] *Men and beasts you will save.* The psalm has already spoken of *men and beasts*, but then it goes on to speak of *the sons of men*, as though these are a different group from "men."[24] Sometimes when scripture speaks of "sons of men" it means human beings in general, but in other cases the phrase, "sons of men," carries a particular meaning, implying that we are meant to understand some part of humanity, not the whole, especially when there is a disjunction preceding it, as there is here. The psalm deliberately says, *Men and beasts you will save, Lord, but the sons of men . . .*, as though he were setting the former aside and taking care of the "sons of men" separately. But from whom are they separated? Not from the animals only, but also from those humans who seek from God the kind of salvation which the beasts also enjoy, and ardently desire it. In that case, who are the "sons of men"? Those who hope under the shelter of God's wings. The generality of humans rejoice along with the beasts in the realization of their desires, but the "sons of men" rejoice in hope; the first group pursues the good things of the present life in company with the animals, the second hopes for future good things in company with the angels. Why is it that the former are here called "men," and the latter distinguished by the name, "sons of men"? The same distinction is found in another scriptural text: *What is a mere man that you remember him, a son of man that you visit him?* (Ps 8:5(4)). What is a mere man that you remember him? Remember him, as one who is absent is remembered. But you visit a "son of man"; to him you are present. What does "remembering" amount to? *Men and beasts you will save, Lord,* because you give that kind of salvation to the wicked too, and to people who do not long for the kingdom of heaven. God protects them; in a sense he does not desert them any more than he does his animals. He does not desert them, but he is mindful of them as though they were absent from him. But the person he visits is a "son of man," and to such is the psalm referring. *But the sons of men will hope under the shelter of your wings.*

If you want to see clearly the difference between these two types of human beings, look first at two men: Adam and Christ. Hear what the apostle has to say of them: *As in Adam all die, so in Christ shall all be made to live* (1 Cor 15:22).

23. *Caritas vestra.*
24. Insistence on inclusive language in this section would obscure the point Augustine is making. "Men" and "sons of men" must here be allowed to pass with inclusive meaning. The same play on "man" and "son of man," aided by Christ's use of the latter title for himself, is found in Augustine's Exposition of Psalm 8, 10-11.

From Adam we are born to die, in Christ we rise again to live for ever. As long as we bear the image of the earthly man, we are "men"; when we bear the image of the heavenly man (see 1 Cor 15:49), we are "sons of men," because Christ was called the Son of Man. Adam was a man, but not a son of man, and therefore those who set their hearts on material good things and a salvation restricted to this temporal life range themselves with Adam. We beg such people to be "sons of men" who may hope under the shelter of God's wings, and desire that mercy of his which is in heaven, and has been proclaimed through the clouds. But if they are not yet capable of this, let them in the meantime at least petition no one else but the one God for their temporal goods, and so do their service[25] as though under the Old Covenant, that they may progress toward the New.

13. The people of the Old Testament desired earthly blessings: the kingdom centered in Jerusalem, the subjugation of their enemies, abundant harvests, their own safety and that of their children. These things they desired, and these things they customarily received; they were guarded under the law. The good things they were accustomed to ask from God were the same good things he gives to animals, for the Son of Man had not yet come to them, to enable them to become "sons of men." Yet they already had clouds to proclaim to them the Son of Man. The prophets came and proclaimed the Messiah; some people understood and began to entertain hope of the future, and so they received the mercy that is in heaven. But there were others who longed for nothing but material things and earthly, temporal happiness. Their feet slid away under them, toward the making and worship of idols; for when God admonished them, and punished them in the very things they enjoyed, and took those things away, they suffered famine, wars, pestilence and illness, and then they would turn to idols. The good things that they ought to have so earnestly begged from God, they sought from their idols, and they abandoned their God. They observed that the good things they wanted were enjoyed in profusion by the godless and the guilty, so they thought it was no use paying homage to God, since he did not seem to give them any earthly reward. O foolish men and women! You are God's workers, and the time for receiving your wages will come later. Why do you demand your pay before you have done your work? If a worker comes to your house, do you give him his wages before he has finished his jobs? You will think him very odd if he says to you, "I'll have the money first, then I'll do the job." You are angry. Why? Because he has not trusted you, he thinks you dishonest. How, then, can God not be angry, if you do not trust in Truth itself? What he has promised you, he will give you; he does not deceive you, because he who has promised is Truth. Are you afraid he may not have it to give? He is almighty. Do not fear, either, that he may no longer be there to give it, for he is immortal. Nor need you be anxious that someone else may have moved in to take his place; he is everlasting, so do

25. Variant: "be accommodated/gratified."

not worry. If you expect your hired worker to go on relying all day on your good faith, you must believe in God all your life, because your life is only a moment of time before God. And what will you be then?[26] *But the sons of men will hope under the shelter of your wings.*

Verse 9. Thirsting for a reality beyond description

14. *They will be inebriated by the rich abundance of your house.* He is promising us something very great. He wants to name it, and he does not; is it because he is unable to, or because we cannot grasp it?[27] I make bold to assert, my brothers and sisters, that even the holy tongues and hearts through which the truth was proclaimed to us could not clearly state this thing they were announcing, nor could those holy preachers even think it. It is a great and unutterable reality; they glimpsed it partially and in enigmatic form, as the apostle says: *We see now a tantalizing reflection in a mirror, but then face to face* (1 Cor 13:12). And gazing at puzzling reflections they blurted out what they saw. What shall we be like, when we come to see face to face what they labored in their hearts to conceive, but could not bring to birth with their tongues in any way that people could comprehend? Under what pressure of necessity did the psalmist say, *They will be inebriated by the rich abundance of your house*? He searched for some expression derived from human experience which he could use to say what he meant; he saw people immersing themselves in drunkenness, taking too much wine and losing their senses; then he knew how he must express it, for we have been given a joy beyond all telling. The human mind almost vanishes, becoming in some sense divinized, and is inebriated by the rich abundance of God's house. This is why another psalm says, *How excellent is your intoxicating chalice!* (Ps 22(23):5). On this chalice were the martyrs drunk when they went forth to their passion with scarcely a glance for their own relatives. What could be more like drunken behavior than failing to recognize a weeping wife, or children, or parents? Yet the martyrs did not recognize them, or even notice that these people were there, before their eyes. How did they come to be so drunk? It is easy to see how: they drank from a cup that would intoxicate them, and the psalmist thanks God, saying, *What return shall I make to the Lord for all his bounty to me? I will take in my hands the cup of salvation, and call on the name of the Lord* (Ps 115(116):12-13).

Let us be "sons of men," my brothers and sisters, and let us hope under the shelter of his wings, and be inebriated by the rich abundance of his house. I have spoken of it as best I could, and I contemplate it as best I can, but how I see it I cannot put into words. *They will be inebriated by the rich abundance of your*

26. Variant: ". . . moment of time. Let your hope be directed to God, and you will be a 'son of man.' "
27. Variant: " . . . does not; he cannot, the mind cannot reach it."

house, and you will give them the torrent of your delights to drink. Water rushing with mighty force is called a torrent. God's mercy will flow with mighty force to water and inebriate those who in this present life fix their hope beneath the shadow of his wings. What is that delight? It is like a torrent that inebriates the thirsty. Let any who are thirsty now fix their hopes there; let the thirsty have hope, because one day, inebriated, they will have the reality. Until they have the reality, let them thirstily hope.[28] *Blessed are those who hunger and thirst for righteousness, for they shall be satisfied* (Mt 5:6).

Verse 10. Fountain and light

15. By what fountain will you be watered, then, and whence will that great torrent of his delight flow? *With you is the fount of life*, says the psalm. Who is the fount of life, if not Christ? He came to you in the flesh to bedew your thirsty throat, but he who besprinkled the one who thirsts will flood the one who hopes. *For with you is the fount of life, and in your light we will see light.* In our world a fountain is one thing, and light another; not so there. The reality that is a fountain is light also; you may call it what you will, because it is not what you call it. You cannot find a suitable name, because it is not captured by any one name. If you were to say that it is light, and only light, someone might object, "What then was the point of telling me that I am to hunger and thirst? Can anyone eat light? That other hint that was given me was obviously more apt: *Blessed are the pure of heart, for they shall see God* (Mt 5:8). I had better prepare my eyes, then." Yes, but prepare your throat too, because the reality that is light is also a fountain: a fountain because it drenches the thirsty, light because it illumines the blind. Here below we sometimes find light in one place, and a fountain somewhere else; for fountains may gush even in darkness, while you may suffer from the sun in the desert and find no fountain. Here below the two may be separated; but there you will never flag, because there will be the fountain for you, and you will never walk in darkness, for there is light.

Verse 11. Conformity with God's will

16. *Extend your mercy to those who know you, and your justice to those who are right of heart.* This deals with a subject on which I have often talked to you: those people are right of heart who in this life obey the will of God. Suppose God's will is that you should sometimes be healthy, sometimes ill. If God's will is sweet to you when you are in good health, but sour when you are sick, you are not right of heart. Why not? Because you are not prepared to align your will with the will of God, but are trying to pervert his to fit yours. His will is straight, yours

28. Word-play on *spes*, "hope," and *res*, "reality."

crooked. Your will must be straightened by alignment with his, not his bent to correspond with yours, and then you will have an upright heart. If things in this world are going well, bless God who gives you consolation; if things are going badly, bless God who corrects and tests you. Then you will be right of heart, and you will be able to say, *I will bless the Lord at all times; his praise shall be in my mouth always* (Ps 33:2(34:1)).

Verse 12. Beware of the foot of pride

17. *Let not the foot of pride come near me.* He has already told us that *the "sons of men" will hope under the shelter of your wings, and will be inebriated by the rich abundance of your house.* But anyone who has begun to experience more freely the quenching waters of that fountain must beware of growing proud. The first man, Adam, did not lack them, but the foot of pride approached him, and the hand of the sinner dislodged him, the proud hand of the devil. Scripture tells us how the seducer had said, *I will establish my throne in the north,*[29] and now, in the same vein, he persuasively suggested to humans, *Taste it, both of you, and you will be like gods* (Gn 3:5). So it was that we fell by pride, and were reduced to this mortal condition. And so too, as it was pride that wounded us, humility makes us whole. Our humble God came to heal humankind of its grievous wound of pride; he came, for the Word was made flesh, and lived among us (see Jn 1:14). He was arrested by the Jews, and insulted. When the gospel was read you heard of an occasion when they said to him, *You have a demon* (Jn 8:48); you heard what they said, and you know to whom they said it; yet the Lord did not retort, "It is you who have the demon, because you are in your sins and the devil rules in your hearts." He did not say it; if he had, he would have spoken truly, but it was not opportune to say it then, lest he appear to be exchanging curses with them, rather than preaching the truth. He let it go, as though he had not heard it. He was a physician who had come to cure a lunatic. Now a physician does not care what a deranged patient says to him, but bends his efforts to finding out how the patient may get better and be sane once more. If the madman punches him the doctor does not mind; the patient may inflict new injuries on the doctor, but the doctor concentrates on curing the patient's old fever. So too the Lord came to a sick man, a madman; and he was determined to ignore whatever he might hear or suffer. By this very attitude he was preaching humility, and it was only by being taught humility that they would be healed of their pride. The psalmist prayed to be delivered from it: *Let not the foot of pride come near me, nor the hand of sinners dislodge me*, for if the foot of pride has come near you, inevitably the hand of the sinner does dislodge you. What is the

29. Is 14:13. According to Phoenician mythology the mountain of the gods was situated in the north.

sinner's hand? The maneuvers of anyone who persuades you to evil. Have you grown proud? Then any evil persuader will quickly corrupt you. Remain steadfastly humble in God, and you will not greatly care what is said to you. That is why the prayer is made elsewhere, *Cleanse me from my secret sins, and spare your servant from the faults of others* (Ps 18:13-14(19:12-13)). What does this mean—*from my secret sins*? The same as *let not the foot of pride come near me*. And what of *spare your servant from the faults of others*? That is the same thing as asking, *Let not the hand of sinners dislodge me*. Preserve what is within you, and you will not be afraid of what happens outside.

Verse 13. Watching the tempter's head

18. But why are you afraid? Because, I think, when the psalm continues, *There they have fallen, all those who work iniquity*, it seems to be saying that they have come to the brink of that abyss mentioned earlier, *your judgments are like a profound abyss*, and that they will be plunged into that depth where the scornful sinners have fallen. *They have fallen*—but where did the fall first occur? At the approach of the foot of pride. Listen to what the foot of pride effected: *Though they had known God, they did not glorify him as God* (Rom 1:21). Thus the foot of pride came to them, and from there they plunged into the depths: *God delivered them to the lusts of their own hearts, so that they behaved as they should not* (Rom 1:24). But the psalmist who wrote, *Let not the foot of pride come near me*, was fearful of both the root and the head of sin. Why did he call it the foot? Because by growing proud humankind abandoned God and walked away; so the psalm calls its attitude a "foot." *Let not the foot of pride come near me, nor the hand of sinners dislodge me*: he means, let no sinners' activities so shift me away from you as to make me want to imitate them. But why does he direct this statement, *they have fallen, all those who work iniquity*, against pride in particular? Because those who are now iniquitous have first fallen by pride. To make the Church wary, the Lord said, *She will watch your head, and you her heel.*[30] The serpent watches for the foot of pride to approach you, and watches for you to slip, so that he may throw you down; but you must watch his head, for the beginning of all sin is pride (see Sir 10:15). *There they have fallen, all those who work iniquity; they have been driven out, unable to*

30. Gn 3:15, the "proto-evangelium." The antecedent noun ("seed") is almost certainly collective in the original Hebrew, meaning "posterity." By the time of the Greek Septuagint translation (third century B.C.) the text had been sharpened to carry a more clearly individual and Messianic sense; the antecedent noun (σπέρμα) is neuter in Greek, but the pronoun used is masculine (αὐτός). In the Vulgate, however, and in Augustine's Latin version, the pronoun is feminine. There is fluidity in patristic thought between the individual woman, Eve, to whose posterity the passage directly refers, the individual woman, Mary, seen from the second century A.D. as the new Eve, and the collective woman, Mother Church.

stand. He fell first who would not stand in the truth; then they fell through him, whom God thrust out of paradise. But the humble man who declared that he was not worthy to untie Christ's sandal[31] was not driven out; he stands and hears him and rejoices exceedingly at the Bridegroom's voice.[32] Not in his own voice does he find joy, lest the foot of pride come near him, and he be thrust out, unable to stand.

Perhaps I have worn out some of you with all this hard work, but at last we have finished the psalm, so now the labor is over and we can be pleased that the entire psalm has been explained. Somewhere in the middle I was afraid that I would overburden you, and I was minded to send you home; but I reflected that our train of thought would be cut off, and we would not be able to get back to it and deal with only half the psalm in the same way as if we ran through the whole. I therefore thought it better to put a heavy load on you than to leave the job half done and save the remainder for another day. For we owe you a sermon again tomorrow; pray for us, that we may have the strength to deliver it, and bring your thirsty throats and devoted hearts along.

31. See Jn 1:27.
32. See Jn 3:29.

Exposition 1 of Psalm 36

First Sermon[1]

Ignorance about the last day

1. To hear about the coming of the last day is terrifying for those who neglect to gain security about it by reforming their lives, and want only to go on in their sinful ways as long as possible. God has with good reason willed that the precise timing of it should be kept secret, so that our hearts may be always ready for the day we know will come, though we do not know when. This is why our Lord Jesus Christ, who was sent to be our teacher, declared that even the Son of Man did not know the day,[2] for it was not part of his teaching brief that we should be informed about the coming of that day through him. There is certainly nothing that the Father knows that is not known also to the Son, since he who is the Father's Wisdom is the Father's Knowledge; and his Son, his Word, is his Wisdom. Undoubtedly, therefore, he who had come to teach us did know the day, but he had not come to teach us anything that it was unprofitable for us to know. Like a good teacher he taught some things, and withheld others. In his role as our teacher he knew both how to teach what would be to our advantage, and how to withhold what would be a hindrance. In stating that the Son[3] is ignorant of something that he does not choose to teach us he is making use of a particular idiom: he says he does not know what he causes us not to know. We use a similar figure of speech ourselves every day. We say that today is a happy day, because it makes us happy; we call another a sad day, because it saddens us; we call a cold day a lazy day, because it makes us feel lazy. The opposite use of it is when the Lord is represented as saying, "Now I know" whatever it is. To Abraham it was said, *Now I know that you fear God* (Gn 22:12). God already knew that before putting Abraham to the test, but the test was designed to make us know what God knew already, and the story was written down to teach us what God knew before teaching it. Perhaps Abraham himself did not know beforehand the strength latent in his faith, for each of us is put to the question by our temptation, and through it we come to know ourselves. Peter, for instance, certainly did not know how much strength his faith would give him when he said to the Lord, "I

1. Preached, like the two following sermons, at Carthage.
2. See Mk 13:32.
3. Variant: "Son of Man."

will stay with you, even to death";[4] but the Lord, who knew him, gave him advance notice of his failure, and foretold his weakness to him, as though taking the pulse of his heart.

Accordingly Peter, who before being tempted relied on his own strength, came to know himself in the temptation. We may reasonably suppose that our father Abraham also learned the strength of his faith when, on being commanded to immolate his only son, he offered him without hesitation or fear to God who had given the boy. Just as before the child's birth Abraham did not know how God could give him a son, so he now believed that God had power to give him back sound and well after being sacrificed.[5] This is why God said, *Now I know*; it means, "Now I have caused you to know," as in the other examples we mentioned, where a day is called lazy because it makes us lazy, or happy because it makes us happy. So too God is said to learn something when he makes us learn it. A similar case is when scripture says, *The Lord your God tests you, in order to know if you love him* (Dt 13:3). If you think this statement means that by testing us he gains knowledge of something of which he was previously not informed, you will be imputing crass ignorance to the Lord our God, the true, infinite God; and this, as you will readily understand, is a sacrilegious opinion. What does the text mean, then, *He tests you, in order to know*? He tests you to make you know it.

Now apply the same rule of interpretation the other way round. Just as you have seen that "Now I know" means "I have caused you to know," so too when you hear it said of Christ, the Son of Man, that he does not know that day, understand that what is being said is that he causes us not to know it. But what does causing us not to know it mean? It means that he conceals it, so that something it would not profit us to be told is kept from us. This is what I was saying earlier: a good teacher knows what to pass on, and what to hold in reserve; and so we read that he did defer certain lessons. We can see why it is not a good idea to set forth everything, when those who are being taught cannot take it all in. He says elsewhere, *I have many things to tell you, but at present you are not able to bear them* (Jn 16:12); and the apostle likewise says, *Not as spiritual persons could I speak to you, but only as carnal. As if to little children in Christ I gave you milk to drink, rather than solid food. You were not capable of it then, nor are you even now* (1 Cor 3:1-2).

Where is all this leading us? This is my point: we know the last day will come, but to our own profit we know both the certainty of its coming and the uncertainty of its timing; we must therefore keep our hearts prepared by living good lives. In this way we need not fear that approaching day; we may even look forward to it. That day is to intensify the distress of unbelievers, but put an end to

4. See Lk 22:33.
5. See Heb 11:17-19.

the troubles of the faithful. Before the time arrives it is up to you to choose which of these you want to be; but once it has come, it will be too late to choose. Make your choice now, while you still have time, because what God in his mercy conceals, in his mercy he is postponing.

One is taken, another left

2. In the gospel that we have just listened to we heard about two types of people, symbolically referred to in the words with which it concludes: *One will be taken, the other left* (Mt 24:40). From this we gather that in any way of life which includes some particular profession not all are found to be persons of integrity, but neither are all reprobate. The good person will be taken, the bad left. You may see two men working in the field; their occupation is the same, but their hearts are different. Human eyes see the public face, but God knows the heart. Let the field in this example stand for anything you like; it remains that *one will be taken, the other left*. This does not mean that half will be taken and the other half left, but that there are two kinds of people. Even if one group comprises only a few, and the other the majority, still *one will be taken, the other left*, one kind taken, the other kind not. And so it will be with those in bed, and those at the mill.

You are wondering, perhaps, what these are. Their identity seems to be hidden, wrapped up in figurative expressions. The explanation that occurs to me may possibly differ from what commends itself to someone else; but when I put forward my view I am not holding him or her back from any better interpretation, nor can they forbid me to accept one rather than the other, provided each is in accord with the faith. Well then, the workers in the field seem to me to be those who preside over the churches, for the apostle says, *You are God's cultivated field, and God's building*. He even claims to be the master-builder himself: *I laid the foundation like a skilled master-builder*, and then again he says he is the farmer when he reminds them, *I planted, Apollos watered, but God gave the growth* (1 Cor 3:9,10,6).

But when the Lord spoke of the mill, he mentioned two women, not two men, and I think this suggests that the ordinary faithful are symbolized here, because prelates rule and the people are ruled. The millstone represents this world, I think, because it rolls along through cyclic time, and it crushes those who are in love with it. So then, among the people who do not withdraw from worldly activities some conduct themselves well and others badly. Some make friends for themselves from iniquitous mammon, friends who will welcome them into eternal dwellings,[6] for such people will be reminded that *I was hungry, and you fed me* (Mt 25:35). Others neglect to do so, and they are told in the same passage,

6. See Lk 16:9.

I was hungry, and you did not feed me (Mt 25:42). Since among those who are engaged in business and the affairs of this world some love to help the needy while others do not bother, the prophecy is spoken about them as about two women at the millstone: *one will be taken, the other left.*

When the Lord mentioned a bed I think he intended to signify rest. There are some people who do not want to get involved in the activities of the world, as do others who are married and have homes and households and children to look after. Nor do they have any office in the Church, as do the prelates who labor like farm workers. They keep clear of such activity as though they were not strong enough for it; they withdraw into leisure[7] and love tranquillity. They do not commit themselves to any major work, as though mindful of their own infirmity, but pray to God as if from their sickbed. And this profession too has its good practitioners and its impostors, so that of these too it can be said, *One will be taken, the other left.*

Whatever profession you turn to, be prepared to encounter impostors, because if you have not prepared yourself you will find what you hoped not to, and then you will be dismayed and lose heart. The Lord is warning you to be prepared for anything; and he is telling you this now, while it is time for him to speak, but not yet time to judge, and while it is time for you to listen, and not yet time for fruitless remorse. Repentance is not fruitless now, but it will be then. At the judgment people who have led bad lives will be all too willing to repent; but God's justice will in no way call back for them the chance they have thrown away by their own injustice; for it is just on God's part to grant mercy now, but to pass judgment then. That is why it is not being hushed up now. It is not hushed up, is it? Anyone would have a right to complain and find fault if this passage of scripture were not proclaimed and sung all over the world, if indeed it ceased to be hawked about publicly even for gain.

Verses 1-2. Why do the wicked flourish?

3. But what really troubles you, a Christian, is to see persons of evil life happy, wallowing in plentiful possessions, glowing with health, strutting proudly in their exalted rank, boasting of their secure homes, their pleasures, their obsequious hangers-on, and their powerful influence. No sadness breaks in on the lives of such persons. You observe their profligate lives, and you plainly see their affluent fortunes; and your heart tells you that there is no such thing as

7. *Otium*, a rich idea for the ancients, without pejorative connotations of idleness. *Otium cum dignitate* (dignified leisure) was an ideal for the cultured gentleman, time and freedom for philosophy, study or the arts. In Jewish and Christian contexts it is close to the idea of holiday or holy day, a time of freedom from the most pressing material demands, when God's people could remember and celebrate their dignity. In the present passage Augustine seems to be thinking of a contemplative way of life.

divine judgment, and that all things are randomly tossed about by the winds of chance. If God were really taking account of human affairs, you say, would that fellow's iniquity be allowed to flourish, while my innocence has such a hard time?

Now every illness of the soul finds its medicine in the scriptures, so any of us who are suffering from the malady that prompts us to think like this in our hearts will do well to drink a draught from this psalm. What is it? Well, let us look more carefully: what were you saying? "What was I saying?" you reply. "Why, only what you can see for yourself. Bad people flourish while the good have to struggle. How can God be looking on?" Take your medicine. Drink it. The Lord himself, about whom you are complaining, has mixed the dose for you. Just consent to take this potion; it will do you a lot of good. Let the mouth of your heart be receptive through your ear, and drink what you hear: *Do not secretly envy people of wicked intent, nor be jealous of those who commit iniquity; for they will wither swiftly like grass, and quickly fall like plants in the meadow.* What seems slow to you is swift to God; submit yourself to God and it will seem swift to you as well. The word *grass* we take to mean the same as *plants in the meadow*. They are inconsiderable things that cling to the surface of the soil and have no deep roots. They thrive through the winter, but in summer when the sun begins to grow hot they wilt. This present time is your winter. Your glory does not show yet. But like the winter trees you have the deep root of charity, and so when the cold weather passes and summer comes (judgment day, I mean) the green grass will dry up and your glory burst forth, like the foliage of the trees. *You are dead*, says the apostle: you look as dead as the trees do in winter, parched and apparently lifeless. What hope have we, then, if we are dead? We have the root within us, and where our root is fixed, there is our life, for there is our charity. *Your life is hidden with Christ in God*, the apostle continues. How can anyone with such a root ever wilt? But when will spring arrive for us? Or our summer? When shall we be arrayed in fair foliage, or laden with luscious fruit? When will that be? Listen to Paul's next line: *when Christ appears, Christ who is your life, then you too will appear with him in glory* (Col 3:3-4).

What are we to do in the meantime? *Do not secretly envy people of wicked intent, nor be jealous of those who commit iniquity; for they will wither swiftly like grass, and quickly fall like plants in the meadow.*

Verses 3-4. The wealth of the Lord's land

4. But what about you? *Hope in the Lord.* Those others hope too, but not in the Lord. Their hope is doomed to die, their hope is perishable, fragile, fleeting, transitory and vain. But you, *hope in the Lord.* "All right, I'm hoping," you say. "What else am I to do?" *Do good*, not the mischief you see them doing, those others who flourish in their malice. *Do good, and live in the land.* This last clause

is added in case you might think you could do your good deeds without living in the land; for the Lord's land is the Church, irrigated and tilled by the Father, for he is the farmer.[8] There are many people who apparently employ themselves in good works, but because they do not live in the land they do not work for the farmer. Do good, then, but not somewhere abroad; live in the land. "What wages will I get?" *You will be fed on its riches*. "What are the riches of his land?" Its riches are its Lord, its wealth is its God, the God to whom another psalm says, *You are the portion allotted to me, O Lord* (Ps 118(119):57), and of whom it is said, *The Lord is my allotted inheritance and my cup* (Ps 15(16):5). Not long ago, beloved,[9] I suggested to you in a sermon that God is our possession and we are God's possession. Now listen to our present psalm declaring that he is the wealth of this land; and see what comes next: *Delight in the Lord*. It is as though you had inquired, saying, "Show me the riches of that land where you command me to dwell," and he replies, *Delight in the Lord, and he will give you your heart's desire*.

The pleas of the flesh and of the heart

5. Notice that it expressly says, *Your heart's desire*. Distinguish this cry of your heart from the cravings of your flesh; draw the distinction as clearly as you possibly can. Another psalm says with good reason that he is *the God of my heart*, and backs this up by continuing, *God is my portion for ever* (Ps 72(73):26). Let me make this clear by some examples: suppose someone is physically blind, and asks to receive his sight. By all means let him ask, for God does this too; such benefits are also God's gifts. But even the wicked ask for these. This is a carnal request. Or suppose someone is ill, and begs for recovery, and is heard, even at the brink of death. This too is a carnal petition, and so are all similar requests. What is the petition of the heart? Just as the carnal petition envisages the healing of one's eyes, that one may see the kind of light bodily eyes are designed to see, so the petition of the heart is concerned with a different light: *blessed are the pure of heart, for they shall see God* (Mt 5:8). *Delight in the Lord, and he will give you your heart's desire*.

Verses 5-6. Darkness will give way to light

6. "Here am I desiring, asking, wanting. Will I be the one to fulfill my own desires?" No. "Who will, then?" *Reveal your way to the Lord, and hope in him,*

---

8. See Jn 15:1.

9. *Caritatis vestrae*. The passage to which he is about to refer is probably his Exposition 3 of Psalm 32, 18. It appears that the sermons on the present Psalm 36 were also preached in the Basilica of Saint Cyprian at Carthage.

and he will do it. Tell him what you are suffering, and tell him what you want. What are you suffering? *The flesh lusts against the spirit, and the spirit against the flesh* (Gal 5:17). And what do you want? *Who will deliver me from this death-ridden body, wretch that I am?* He will, if you will only reveal your way to him; that is why scripture continues, *The grace of God, through Jesus Christ our Lord* (Rom 7:24-25).

But what is this thing that the Lord will do? The psalm has urged us, *Reveal your way to the Lord, and hope in him, and he will do it*. Do what? *He will bring forth your righteousness like light*. Your righteousness is hidden at present; it is a reality, but in faith, not something that can be seen. You believe in something that prompts you to action, but you do not yet see what you believe in. When you begin to see the object of your faith, your righteousness will be led out into the light. Your faith itself was all along your righteousness, for the one who lives by faith is just.[10]

7. *He will bring forth your righteousness like light, and your judgment like high noon*. That means light at its brightest. It would have been too little merely to say, *like light*, for we already call it light when the sky pales toward dawn, and we call it light when the sun is rising; but never is the light brighter than at midday. He will not simply bring forth your righteousness like light; more than that: your judgment will be like high noon. You judge now that you should follow Christ. This is what you have decided to do, this is the choice you have made, this is your judgment. No one has shown you the things he has promised; you are still holding fast to the one who made the promise, and waiting for him to deliver. By the judgment of your faith you have chosen to follow after something you do not see. This judgment of yours is still hidden in darkness, and it is still scorned and derided by unbelievers: "What have you put your faith in? What has Christ promised you? That you will be immortal, that he will give you eternal life? But where is it? When will he give it to you? When will it ever happen?" All the same, you judge it better to follow Christ, who promises things you cannot see, than the godless critic who takes you to task for having believed in what you do not see yet. This is your judgment, and how good a judgment it is has not yet become clear, because as long as we are in this world it is still night for us. When will he bring forth your judgment like high noon? *When Christ appears, Christ who is your life, then you too will appear with him in glory* (Col 3:4). When judgment day arrives, and Christ comes to gather all nations together to be judged, what will happen then? Where will the godless hide their faithlessness, when I see my faith?

What of the present, then? Nothing but ill-treatment, troubles, temptations. And blessed is everyone with staying-power, for *whoever perseveres to the end will be saved* (Mt 24:13). Let such a person give no ground before the mockers,

---

10. See Hab 2:4; Rom 1:17.

nor choose to flourish here, which would mean ceasing to be a tree and becoming grass.

Verses 7-9. Curb your resentment if you want to see straight

8. "What ought I to do, then?" Listen to what you ought to do: *be subject to the Lord and entreat him.* Let this be your life, to obey his commandments (for this is what being subject to him implies) and to entreat him until he gives what he has promised. Let your good work endure, and let your prayer endure too. We must pray always, and never give up.[11] How do you show yourself subject to him? By doing what he commanded. You do not receive your reward yet, but that may be because you are not yet capable of it. He is already able to give it, but you are not able to receive it. Exert yourself in your tasks, labor in the vineyard, and when evening comes ask for your wages,[12] for he who brought you into the vineyard is trustworthy. *Be subject to the Lord, and entreat him.*

9. "But that is what I am doing. I am subject to the Lord, and I do entreat him. But how do you see things? That scoundrel of a neighbor—he behaves badly and yet he flourishes. I know about his thefts, his adulteries, his violence. He is haughty and proud in whatever he does, he is arrogant in his unjust dealings and he does not deign even to acknowledge me. How can I put up with all this?"

You are sick, so drink this remedial potion: *Do not be secretly envious of the person who prospers in his way.* He prospers, to be sure, but in his own way; you struggle along, but in God's way. For him there is prosperity along the way, but unhappiness when he reaches the end; for you hardship along the way, but happiness when you reach journey's end; for the way of the ungodly will perish. This is what another psalm affirms, *The Lord knows the way of the just, but the way of the ungodly will perish* (Ps 1:6). You are walking in the paths the Lord knows, and even if you find it hard going, they do not lead you astray.[13] The path of the ungodly is but a transitory happiness, and when the journey ends, the happiness is over and done with. Why? Because that road is a wide one, but it leads eventually to the depths of hell. Your path is narrow, and few walk that way, but you should think about the broad open spaces to which those few are tending.[14]

Do not be secretly envious of the person who prospers in his way. Curb your anger, and calm your indignation over the one who commits iniquity. Why are you peeved about it? How can you allow this fretful indignation to lead you into blasphemy, or near-blasphemy? *Curb your anger and calm your indignation*

11. See Lk 18:1.
12. See Mt 20:8.
13. The CCL editors of the Latin text amend to: "Walk in the paths the Lord knows; if you walk in them, they do not. . . . "
14. See Mt 7:13-14.

over the one who commits iniquity. Do you not realize where this anger is carrying you? It is on the tip of your tongue to tell God that he is unjust—that is where it is tending. "Look at him—why is he happy? And that other one, unhappy—why?" Look what those thoughts are giving birth to! Stifle their evil offspring! *Curb your anger, and calm your indignation,* come to your senses, and say rather, *My eye was troubled by anger* (Ps 6:8(7)). What eye is that, if not the eye of faith? I put my questions to the eye of your faith: Did you believe in Christ? Yes? Then why did you believe? What did he promise you? If Christ promised you happiness in this world, then go ahead and complain against him; complain when you see the unbeliever happy. But what sort of happiness did he, in fact, promise you? Nothing else but happiness when the dead rise again. And what did he promise you in this life? Only what he went through himself; yes, I tell you, he promised you a share in his own experience. Do you disdain it, you, a servant and a disciple? Do you disdain what your master and teacher went through? Do you not recall his own words: "A servant is not greater than his master, nor a disciple above his teacher"?[15] For your sake he bore painful scourging, insults, the cross and death itself. And how much of this did he deserve, he, a just man? And what did you, a sinner, not deserve? Keep a steady eye, and do not let it be deflected by wrath. *Curb your anger, and calm your indignation. Do not secretly vie with the wicked by acting viciously yourself,* as though you wanted to imitate someone who by vicious behavior contrives to flourish for a time. *Do not secretly vie with the wicked by acting viciously yourself, for those who act viciously will be destroyed.* "But I can see how happy they are!" No doubt, but you must believe him who declares that *they will be destroyed,* because his sight is better than yours, since his eye cannot be clouded by anger. *Those who act viciously will be destroyed, but all who wait for the Lord*—not for someone who might deceive them, but for Truth himself; not for someone with limited power, but for the Almighty—*all who wait for the Lord shall inherit the land.* What other land, but Jerusalem? Anyone who burns with love for her will attain to peace.[16]

Verse 10. Time passes swiftly, though to the sick it seems long

10. "But how long is the sinner to flourish? How long shall I have to wait?" What a hurry you are in! What seems to you slow in coming will soon be here. It is your illness that makes the time seem to pass slowly, when in reality it is swift. Think what the demands of the sick are like. They think nothing so long-drawn-out as the mixing of a drink for them when they are thirsty. The attendants are working fast to minimize the distress of the sick person, yet he or

15. See Jn 13:16; Mt 10:24.
16. An allusion to the popular etymology: Jerusalem = "vision of peace."

she is demanding, "When is it coming? Isn't it cooked yet? When will they give it to me?" You are just the same: the people serving you are hurrying as much as they can, but your illness makes you think their rapid work slow. Hark how soothingly our physician speaks to the patient who moans, "How long must I hold out? How long will this take?" *A little while yet*, he says, *and the sinner will not be there*. You are groaning amid sinners, to be sure, groaning over a particular sinner; but wait just a little, and no sinner will be there. Do not let my assurance that *all who wait for the Lord shall inherit the land* make you think that the waiting will be very long; no, wait just a little while, and you will receive without end what you await now. A little while yet, only a short time. Recall the years that have passed from Adam to the present day; run through the scriptures. It was scarcely more than yesterday that he fell from paradise! So many centuries have passed by and rolled on their way; where are those past ages now? The few that are still left will surely slip by in the same way. If you had been alive all through this period, from the day Adam was expelled from paradise until the present, you would certainly not think your life had been long, since it had flown past like that. So what about the life of an individual: how long is it? Add on however many years you like, eke out the time of old age, and still, what is it? Just like a morning breeze.

In any case, even if the day of judgment is far distant, the day which will bring both the unjust and the just their due deserts, assuredly your own last day cannot be far off. Prepare yourself for that. In the same state that you depart from this life you will be delivered to the life beyond. After this brief life you will not immediately be in that place to which the saints will be invited when they hear the words, *Come, you whom my Father has blessed; take possession of the kingdom prepared for you since the world was made* (Mt 25:34). You will not yet be there; everyone knows that. But it is possible for you to be in the place where someone formerly poor and covered with sores was seen at rest from afar by the proud, unproductive rich man amid his torments.[17] Established in that rest you can confidently await the day of judgment, when you will receive your body too, and be so changed as to equal an angel. How long is it, then, this waiting that makes us so impatient that we ask, "When will the day come?" Our children will be asking the same questions, and so will our grandchildren; and as succeeding generations keep on asking the same thing, the future time that still remains will speed by just as the whole of the past has done. Listen, you sick soul: *A little while yet, and the sinner will not be there*.

17. See Lk 16:23.

Sinners have their uses

11. *You will look for his place, but not find it.* He is clarifying what he has just said: the sinner *will not be there*, not because he or she will no longer exist, but because sinners will not be able to serve any further purpose. If a sinner were to cease to exist altogether, he or she could not be tormented, and then security would have been given to sinners, who could say, "I'm going to do what I like while I'm alive, because afterwards I won't exist." Can this be true; will there be no one to suffer pain, no one to undergo torments? What would have become of the text, *Off with you into the eternal fire that was prepared for the devil and his angels* (Mt 25:41)? But if they are consigned to that fire, will it not burn them up entirely, so that they no longer exist? No, that cannot be the case, because then they would not be told, *Off with you into eternal fire*; if they were ever to cease to be, the fire would not be eternal for them. Moreover the Lord did not remain silent about whether their future fate would be complete destruction, rather than pain and agony; for he said, *In that place there will be weeping and gnashing of teeth* (Mt 8:12). How will they weep and gnash their teeth if they have ceased to exist?

How, then, are we to understand the prediction that *a little while yet, and the sinner will not be there*, except in the light of the following phrase: *you will look for his place, but not find it*? What does *his place* mean? His function. Does the sinner have a function? Yes, he does. God uses sinners in the present world to test the just, as he used the devil to test Job, and used Judas to betray Christ. So the sinner does have a certain role in this life. This role is his "place," just as in a furnace there is a place for the straw. The straw is burnt so that the gold may be refined, and likewise the sinner does his worst so that the just person may be tested. But when the time of our probation is over, when there are no people left who still need probation, there will not be any left either through whom the probation need be done. Now when I said, "There will be none left who need probation," you did not think I meant that those people will have ceased to exist, did you? But because there will no longer be any need for sinners through whom the just may be tested, the psalm says, *You will look for his place, but not find it.* Look for the sinner's place now, and find it you will. God has made the sinner into a scourge, and given him high rank and a powerful position. Yes, this is what God sometimes does: he gives power to a sinner so that human activities lie under the whip, and the devout are chastised by it. To this sinner due punishment will be meted out, yet he has been used to further the progress of the devout and the downfall of the ungodly. Then *you will look for his place, but not find it.*

Verse 11. Peace and innocence

12. *But the gentle will possess the land as their inheritance.* This land is the one of which we have spoken many times: Jerusalem, the holy city, which will be freed at last from this pilgrimage and will live for all eternity with God and on God. This is why the psalm says that they *will possess the land as their inheritance.* In what will their pleasures consist? *They will be delighted by the abundance of peace.* Let an ungodly person be delighted here by abundant gold, abundant silver, a multitude of slaves, even an abundance of baths, roses,[18] wine-drinking and the most sumptuous and luxurious of banquets. Is this the sort of power you envy, this the blossom that charms you? Would not the unbeliever be the object of our mournful pity, even if he could stay in that situation always? *They will be delighted by the abundance of peace.* Peace will be your gold, peace will be your silver, peace will be your broad estates, peace your very life. Your God will be your peace. Peace will be for you whatever you long for. In this world gold cannot also be silver for you, wine cannot be bread for you, what gives you light cannot provide you with drink; but your God will be everything to you. You will feed on him and hunger will never come near you; you will drink him, never to thirst again; you will be illumined by him that you may suffer no blindness; you will be supported by him and saved from weakness. He will possess you whole and undivided, as he, your possessor, is whole and undivided himself. You will lack nothing with him, for with him you possess all that is; you will have it all, and he will have all there is of you, because you and he will be one, and he who possesses you will have this one thing, and have it wholly.

These things are *the future in store for a peaceful person* (Ps 36(37):37). We have sung that verse, though it comes a long way further on in the psalm than the verses we have been discussing. But since we have sung it, we had better conclude with it now. Do not worry: *guard your innocence*, for that is a precious thing. You are tempted to steal something and make it your own, or so I think; but look what you are stretching your hand to, and where you are stealing from. With that hand you want to gain something, and with that hand you lose something else: you gain money but you lose your innocence. Let your heart wake up, rather; you wanted to acquire money but you lose your innocence; you will do better to lose the money. *Guard your innocence and look in the right direction*, for God will so direct you that whatever he wills, you may will also. This is what being rightly directed means. If you do not want what God wants, you will be bent out of shape, and your crookedness will prevent you from being aligned with what is right. So *guard your innocence, and look in the right direction*, and

18. Abundant variants also: they include "olives," "sweet-scented plants," and (unadventurously suggested by the CCL editors of the Latin text) "various riches."

do not imagine that once this life is over, all is over for human beings too. No, for *there is a future in store for the peaceful person.*

Exposition 2 of Psalm 36

Second Sermon

Introduction: two different types of people

1. We have been ordered to speak to you about this psalm, dearest friends,[1] and we have no option but to obey, for the Lord has seen fit to delay our departure by the heavy rains. It is our bounden duty not to let our tongue remain idle in your regard, since you are always the chief preoccupation of our heart, as we also are of yours.[2]

We have already pointed out to you what God has willed to teach us in this psalm, the admonition he intended to give, what he wanted to caution us against, what we should be ready to endure and what we must hope for. This is because there are two types of people, the just and the unjust; and on this earth, in this life, the two are thoroughly mixed together. Each group has its own purposes at heart. The race of good people strives toward the heights by humility; the race of bad people is weighed down toward the depths by self-exaltation. One kind abases itself with the prospect of rising; the other hoists itself up with the prospect of falling. Consequently one race exercises forbearance while the other is the object of forbearance. The aim of the just is to win even the wicked for eternal life; the aim of the wicked is to repay good with evil and to rob those who want to bring them to eternal life—to rob them of temporal life itself, if they can. The just and the unjust find each other a strain; they are burdensome to each other. That is obvious: the irritation is mutual, but the reasons for it are different on the two sides. The good person makes a nuisance of himself to the bad one because he wants him to stop being bad, and hopes he may become good, and takes practical steps to effect this. But the bad person so hates the good that he wants him not to exist at all, rather than wanting him to be good; for the more truly good that other person is, the more of a reproach he is to the bad person's sinfulness. So the wicked one does all he can to make the good one bad; and if he cannot achieve this he tries to get rid of the good person altogether, so that his troublesome presence may no longer be there.

---

1. *Caritati vestrae*. Ordered, presumably, by his friend Aurelian, Bishop of Carthage. The autumn of 403 is a probable date. Stormy debates raged at Carthage at this time, and Augustine had been under attack from Primian, the Donatist Bishop of Carthage. At the end of this sermon he refutes some of the charges.
2. Variant suggested by the editors of the Latin text: " . . . since you always know the chief preoccupation of our heart, as we also know that of yours."

Yet even if the bad person succeeds in corrupting the good one, he will still find him just as irksome. It is not only a good person that a bad one finds it difficult to put up with: two bad people can scarcely endure each other. They may appear to have some fondness for one another, but this is only complicity in evil, not friendship. They make common cause when they conspire to injure a just person, and their concord is based not on reciprocal love but on a shared hatred of someone whom they ought to have loved.

The Lord our God enjoins on us patient endurance of people like this, and that heartfelt charity we meet in the gospel when our Lord commands us, *Love your enemies, and do good to people who hate you* (Mt 5:44). The apostle has the same thing to say: *Do not be conquered by evil; rather conquer evil with good* (Rom 12:21). Fight evil, yes, but with the weapons of goodness, for this is the real fight, the contest that issues in salvation, that the good person is pitted against evil,[3] not that there should be two who are bad.

Verses 12-13. The sinner's day is coming

2. With this in mind, let us look at the psalm. The earlier verses we have already dealt with. Now it continues, *The sinner will spy on the just person, and grind his teeth against him, but the Lord will deride him.* Who is the object of the Lord's derision? The sinner, obviously, the one who grinds his teeth against the just. Why will the Lord *deride him*? Because *the Lord knows when the sinner's day will come.* This sinful person seems pitiless when, unaware whether there will be any tomorrow for himself, he utters threats against the just; but God is looking on, and foresees the day of the sinner. What day is that? The day when God will render to each of us according to our deeds;[4] for the sinner is storing up against himself anger that will be manifest on the day of God's just judgment.[5] The Lord can see that day, and you cannot; but he who can has shown it to you.[6] You did not know when the sinner's day would come, the day when punishment is to be meted out; but God who knows has not concealed[7] it from you. It is no mean participation in knowledge, to be united with the one who knows. He has eyes that see; make sure you have the eyes of belief. What God sees, you must grasp with faith. The day of the unjust, the day God has in view, will come. What day? The day of retribution for each of us. The ungodly must be requited, whether they are first converted or not. If they are converted, the revenge is nothing else but this, that their iniquity has been destroyed. Did the Lord not laugh as he foresaw the "day" of two bad men, the traitor Judas and the perse-

3. Or "against the bad one."
4. See Mt 16:27.
5. See Rom 2:5.
6. Variant suggested by the CCL editors: " . . . but he will show you what he can see."
7. Variant suggested by the editors of the Latin text, " . . . will not conceal."

cutor Saul? He had the day of one of them in view as the occasion for punishment, but the day of the other as the time for justification. Retribution came to them both, sending one to the flames of hell, and knocking the other down with a voice from heaven. So you too, when you have to put up with a scoundrel, watch his day coming, watch it with God through the eyes of your faith; and when you find him or her savagely attacking you, say to yourself, "The offender will either be corrected and my companion, or incorrigible and with me no more."

Verses 14-16. The persecutor shoots himself in the foot

3. What do you think: does the scoundrel's wickedness harm you without harming himself? Of course not. How is it possible that the malice which springs from his ill-will and hatred, and lashes out to do you harm, should not devastate him within before making its attempt outwardly on you? Hostility rides roughshod over your body, iniquity rots his soul. Whatever he launches against you recoils on him. His persecution purifies you, but leaves him guilty. Who comes off worse, then? Suppose he has violently robbed you: who has sustained the more serious damage—the one who loses money, or the one who loses faith? Only people with inner sight know how to mourn a loss like that. Many are dazzled by the glitter of gold, but cannot perceive the radiance of faith; they have eyes to see gold, but no eyes to see faith. If they had, if they could see it, they would certainly value it more highly; and yet when someone breaks faith with them, they are loud in their protests and full of spite. "Can't you keep faith?" they demand. "Can't I ever rely on good faith?" You love it enough to demand it of others; love it enough to show it yourself.

Clearly, then, all who persecute the just are more severely damaged and more gravely wounded themselves, because in their case it is the soul itself that is laid waste. Accordingly the psalm goes on to make this point: *Sinners have drawn their swords and taken aim with the bow, to bring down the helpless and the poor, to slaughter the upright of heart. May their sword pierce their own heart.* It is easy enough for the enemy's sword[8] to reach your body, as the persecutor's sword found its way into the bodies of the martyrs, but though your body is struck, your heart remains unhurt. But as for the one who drew his sword against the body of the just person, his heart by no means remains uninjured. This psalm affirms the fact. It does not say, "May their sword pierce their bodies," but *may their sword pierce their own heart.* They wanted to inflict bodily death; may they die spiritually. The Lord reassured those whose bodies the persecutors wanted to destroy, telling them, *Do not be afraid of those who kill the body, but*

8. *Framea*; see note at Exposition of Psalm 9, Part 1, 8. In the present passage Augustine uses both *framea* and the traditional Roman word *gladius*, but seems to think the equivalence still needs explanation: "his *framea*, that is, his *gladius*, to reach. . . ."

cannot kill the soul (Mt 10:28). What sort of armed ferocity is that—to have power to kill one's opponent's body and no more, but to be fully able to kill one's own soul? They have lost their senses, they are fighting against themselves, they are crazy and cannot see what they are doing. They are like a person who tries to tear someone else's tunic by driving a sword right through his own body. You are looking only at your final target and taking no heed of where you have dragged your weapon to reach it; to rend someone else's clothes you have torn your way through your own flesh. It is quite obvious that the wrongdoers wound themselves more gravely and do themselves more harm than they think they are doing to the people they hate. So *may their sword pierce their own heart.* This is the Lord's decree, and it cannot be otherwise.

And may their bow be broken to pieces. What does that mean—*their bow be broken to pieces*? May their stratagems come to nothing. Just before this the psalm had said, *Sinners have drawn their sword and taken aim with the bow.* By the drawing of the sword it meant open attack, and by the aiming of the bow, hidden ambushes. But look what happens. The sword slays the one who drew it, and the carefully-laid ambush is futile. Why futile? Because it does no harm to the righteous person. But what if the wicked has robbed someone, for instance, and the victim has lost so much that he or she is reduced to penury? How can it be said in that case that the wrongdoer has done no harm to the righteous? Because the victim then has a song to sing, *Better are modest means to the righteous than the copious wealth of sinners.*

Verse 17. By word and example the Lord strengthens the righteous

4. But the wicked are powerful, they are very energetic and have ample resources; they can act swiftly and their commands are instantly obeyed. But will this always be the case? *The arms of sinners will be crushed.* Their "arms" are their power. What will the sinner be doing in hell? Perhaps what a certain rich man was doing, the one who up above used to feast sumptuously, but down below was tormented.[9] Yes, their *arms will be crushed, but the Lord strengthens*[10] *the righteous.* How does he strengthen them, what does he say to them? He speaks to them in the words of another psalm: *Hold out for the Lord, act manfully; let your heart be strengthened, and hold out for the Lord* (Ps 26(27):14). What does he mean by *hold out for the Lord*? You are toiling away for a time, but you will not toil for eternity; your troubles are short, but your beatitude will be eternal; you are sorrowful for a little while, but you will rejoice without end. But are you beginning to slip, amid your troubles? The example of Christ's sufferings is put before you too. Consider what he endured for you, he

9. See Lk 16:19,24. The contrast "above" and "below" may also have social connotations.
10. Variant: "will strengthen."

who had done nothing to deserve it. However much you may suffer, it will never come near those insults and scourges he bore, that ignominious cloak, or that thorny crown, and least of all will it compare with the cross, which has now been abolished as a human punishment. In days of old criminals were crucified, but no one is today. The cross has been honored, and is obsolete. Obsolete as a punishment, it is an abiding sign of glory.[11] It has passed from sites of torture to the foreheads of emperors. If Christ conferred such honor on his own sufferings, what is he keeping in reserve for his faithful followers?

With these facts, these words, this encouragement and this mighty example, *the Lord strengthens the righteous*. Let the righteous attribute whatever befalls them to the will of God, not to the power of the enemy, who can rage, but is impotent to strike if God does not permit. And if God does allow the enemy to strike, he knows how to take his own under his protection and acknowledge them as his, for *those whom the Lord loves, he corrects, and he whips every child whom he accepts* (Heb 12:6). What grounds has the wicked for congratulating himself, when my Father has made him into a whip for his own use? God picks him up as a tool, but chastises me for an inheritance. We should concentrate not on how much scope God gives to the unjust, but on how much he is keeping for the just.

Paul: persecutor, converted, sufferer, strengthened by the Lord

5. All the same, we should hope that those through whom we are being whipped may be converted, and whipped along with us. This was how God trained his faithful by first making Saul into a whip he could use, and afterwards converting Saul too. When the Lord told holy Ananias (by whom Saul was to be baptized) that he was to welcome this man Saul because he was God's chosen instrument, Ananias was fearful and horrified, because he had heard of Saul's notoriety as a persecutor. *But Lord*, he protested, *I have heard about this man, and what fierce persecution he has waged against your saints in Jerusalem. And now he has obtained authorization to search out any who call upon your name, wherever they are to be found, and drag them off and bind them and hale them before the priests*. But the Lord overruled him: *Do as I say, for I will show him how much he will have to suffer for the sake of my name* (Acts 9:13-16). "I will pay him back," the Lord promises. "I will take my revenge on him; and he who campaigned so savagely against my name will suffer for my name. Through him I am disciplining and have disciplined others, and I will use others to discipline him in his turn." That is what happened, and we know how much Saul endured, far more suffering than he had inflicted on other people, as though the Lord like a greedy creditor was demanding from him all the loan plus interest.

---

11. Variant: "of grace."

6. But consider how those words of the psalm came true in his case: *the Lord strengthens the righteous*. This same Paul, suffering intensely, declared, *We even glory in our sufferings, knowing that suffering fosters endurance, and endurance constancy, and constancy hope; but hope does not disappoint us, because the love of God has been poured out into our hearts through the Holy Spirit who has been given us* (Rom 5:3-5). That is clear enough. He says it as one now righteous and now strengthened. And as those who were pursuing him did him no harm now that he was thus strengthened, so too he had done no harm to those whom he had formerly persecuted. *The Lord strengthens the righteous*, our psalm affirms. Listen to another declaration by this righteous man, strengthened by the Lord: *Who shall part us from the love of Christ? Shall tribulation, or distress, or hunger, or nakedness, or persecution?* (Rom 8:35) How tightly must he have been glued to Christ, if he could not be dislodged by such experiences as these! *The Lord strengthens the righteous*. Again, certain prophets had come down from Jerusalem and, filled with the Holy Spirit, they prophesied to Paul that he would meet with much suffering in Jerusalem. One of them, named Agabus, went so far as to take off Paul's belt and tie himself up in it. He was giving a prophetic sign, as is customary with them, and by these significant actions demonstrating what was to come. So he said, *Just as you see me bound, so this man is to be bound in Jerusalem* (Acts 21:11). As soon as Saul (who by this time was Paul) had been warned by this utterance, the brethren began to dissuade him from running into such danger; they attempted by arguments and pleas to hold him back from going to Jerusalem. But Paul was already one of those who had been promised that *the Lord strengthens the righteous*, so he asked them, *"Are you trying to shake my resolve?* I do not reckon my life so precious." He had already declared to the children he had begotten in the gospel, *I will spend myself unstintingly for your souls* (2 Cor 12:15). So now he asserted, *I am prepared not only to be bound, but even to die for the name of our Lord Jesus Christ* (Acts 21:13).

Verse 18. The vision of God is promised to us

7. So *the Lord strengthens the righteous*. How does he do so? *The Lord knows the paths of the undefiled*. When they are suffering hardships it looks as though they are walking in bad pathways; so it seems to those who know no better, who have no idea how to assess the paths of the undefiled. But he who knows those paths knows too that he is leading his gentle followers by a very straight way. This is why another psalm says, *He will guide the meek in judgment, he will teach his ways to the gentle* (Ps 24(25):9). How do you picture those loathsome people who passed by the poor man who lay covered with sores outside the rich

man's gate?[12] Probably they held their noses and spat at him, don't you think? But the Lord knew that he was holding paradise in reserve for him. And how the passers-by must have longed to have a lifestyle like that of the rich man, who was clad in purple and fine linen, and feasted magnificently every day! Yet the Lord had his day in view, and knew what his future torments would be, torments without end. So *the Lord knows the paths of the undefiled.*

8. *And their inheritance will last for ever.* The truth of this we hold in faith; but does the Lord need faith to see it? The Lord knows those realities in a clarity of manifestation that we are not able to express, nor ever will be, even when we are equal to the angels. Even those things that we shall plainly see will never be as manifest to us as they are manifest to him who is incapable of change. Yet what does scripture say of us, even of us? *Dearly beloved, we are children of God already, but what we shall be has not yet appeared. We know that when he appears, we shall be like him, because we shall see him as he is* (1 Jn 3:2). There is reserved for us some kind of wholly delightful vision, the beauty of which can be thought of in some degree, though only through riddling reflections in a dark mirror. In no way can it be described, the ravishing beauty of that joy God keeps for those who fear him, and consummates for those who trust him.[13] For this our hearts are being made ready in all the troubles and temptations of this life. Small wonder that you are being prepared by such trials: it is for a great destiny that you are being prepared. The voice of a righteous man, strengthened by the Lord, assures you that *the sufferings of this present time are not worthy to be compared with the future glory that is to be revealed to us* (Rom 8:18). What will our future glory be? Nothing less than being equal to the angels and seeing God. How great a gift it would be to a blind person if someone healed his eyes and enabled him to see this light of day! When the blind person has been healed, he can find no adequate recompense to make to his healer; however much he may give, it will always fall far short of what the healer has given him. To give the most he possibly can, he will give gold, and plenty of it—but the other has given him his sight! To realize that what he gives is nothing in comparison, let him just look at his gift in darkness.

What shall we give, then, to the physician who heals our interior eyes, enabling them to see that eternal light which is himself? What gift shall we offer him? Let us look for something, and find it if we can, and in the anguish of our search cry out, *What return shall I make to the Lord for all his bounty to me?* And what did that seeker find? *I will take in my hands the cup of salvation, and call on the name of the Lord* (Ps 115(116):12-13). The Lord asks, *Are you able to drink the cup I am to drink?* (Mt 20:22). And to Peter likewise he said, *Do you love me? Then feed my sheep* (Jn 21:17), for it was on their behalf that he was to drink the

12. See Lk 16:20.
13. See Ps 30:20(31:19).

Lord's cup. *The Lord strengthens the righteous. The Lord knows the paths of the undefiled, and their inheritance will last for ever.*

Verse 19. A hope that does not deceive

9. *They will not be disconcerted in the bad times.* What does the psalmist mean by not being *disconcerted in the bad times*? He means that on the day of trouble, on the day they are hard pressed, the just will not be disconcerted, as any others are whose hope has let them down. Who is disconcerted? The person who says, "I have not found what I was hoping for." No wonder! You were hoping in yourself, or you pinned your hopes to some friend who is as human as you are. But a curse is on anyone who trusts in mere mortals.[14] You are disconcerted because your hope has proved illusory; hope founded on a lie is always an illusion, and every mortal is a liar.[15] If you rest your hope on your God you will not be disconcerted, because you have rested it on one who cannot be deceived.[16]

Not long since I reminded you about a righteous man who had been strengthened. When he fell upon bad times and was suffering, he was so far from being disconcerted that he said, *We even glory in our sufferings, knowing that suffering fosters endurance, and endurance constancy, and constancy hope; but hope does not disappoint us.* And why not? Because it is lodged in God. That is why Paul goes on, *Because the love of God has been poured out into our hearts through the Holy Spirit who has been given us* (Rom 5:3-5). Already the Holy Spirit has been given us; how can he deceive us after a pledge like that? *They will not be disconcerted in the bad times, and in days of famine they will eat their fill,* for even then there is a certain satisfying provision for them. The days of this present life are days of famine, in which some are hungry, but others eat their fill. What would that man have had to be pleased about, the man who said, *We glory in our sufferings*, if he had been racked with hunger within? All he saw outside him were constricting circumstances, but within there was ample freedom.

Verse 20. No place for the sinner to call home

10. But what does a bad person do when trouble looms? He or she has nothing outside, because external things have been stripped away, but no consolation in his own conscience either. He has nowhere to go outside, because things there are hard, and nowhere to go inside, because things there are bad. Inevitably the next words of the psalm come true for such a person: *sinners will perish.* How could they not perish, people who have no place to call their own? Neither things

14. See Jer 17:5.
15. See Ps 115(116):11.
16. Variant: "cannot deceive."

without nor things within hold any comfort for them. Anything which furnishes us with no comfort is alien to us, outside ourselves. All those who do not possess God give their allegiance to money, friendship, fame, or worldly power, yet no material advantage whatever can comfort them inwardly[17] as that wise man was comforted by rich inner sustenance when he belched forth from his full-fed interior, *The Lord gave, and the Lord has taken away. This has happened as the Lord willed: may the Lord's name be blessed* (Jb 1:21).

For sinners there is no place to rest in anything outside themselves, because there they endure afflictions; nor does their conscience offer them any consolation, because they are not comfortable with themselves. It is not comfortable to live with someone bad. But those who are bad live unpleasantly with themselves; inevitably such persons are tormented, and are their own tormentor. Those with a torturing conscience are their own punishment. They can flee wherever they like from an enemy, but where will they flee from themselves?

Two roving Donatists

11. It was something like this with a man who had come over to us from the Donatist sect. He had been accused and excommunicated by his own people, and he came seeking here what he had lost there. But in no way could we receive him except in the place that was due to him; for he had not abandoned that sect as someone who was in good standing with them, which would have proved that he was acting by his own choice, and not because he was forced to.[18] Because he could not have what he wanted there—empty honors, trumpery rank he came to look among us for what he had lost there, and he did not find it. So he perished. He was wounded and groaning, and refused consolation; for horrible thorns, unacknowledged, were fixed in his conscience. We tried to comfort him with the word of God, but he was not one of the prudent ants that have laid in supplies in summertime to live on during the winter. It is when things are peaceful that people should harvest the word of God for themselves, and store it in the inner recesses of their hearts, as the ant stores the results of summer's labor in the cavities of its nest.[19] There is time to do this in the summer months, but winter will overtake us—the time of trouble, I mean—and unless we can find resources within ourselves we shall inevitably starve to death. This man of whom I was speaking had not gathered the word of God for his own sustenance, and winter came upon him. He did not find among us the adulation he craved, and nothing else could console him: he derived no comfort whatever from the word of God.

17. Variant: " . . . money, friendship, fame, worldly power, slaves, and all good things cannot comfort them inwardly."

18. Variants: "proved that he was acting not because he was pleased about it, but because forced to"; or "proved that he was acting not out of love, but because forced to."

19. See Prv 6:6-8; 30:25.

He had nothing within himself, and what he sought outside himself he did not find. Firebrands of resentment and misery were smoldering inside him, and his mind was in a state of violent upheaval. All this remained hidden until one day he burst into groans clearly audible to our brothers and sisters, though he did not know he was overheard. We witnessed, and intensely deplored, such spiritual pain, such bitter anguish, such hellish torments. Need I say more? He would not tolerate the lowly station which, if only he had had the sense to see it, could have been for him the place of salvation, and his conduct was such that he even had to be expelled.

But this case should not make us despair of others, my brothers and sisters, others who may freely opt for the truth without being driven by any compulsion. I would go further: it is not only in the case of others that we must not despair; even of this man I would not give up hope as long as he is alive. We must never despair of anyone at all during his or her lifetime. It is important, beloved brethren,[20] that you should take this to heart from the episode I have described, in case anyone informs you differently. For a subdeacon of theirs, against whom no charge stood, chose the peace and unity of our Catholic Church, and leaving the Donatists came over to us. He truly came as one making his choice of the good, not as repudiated by evil persons. He was accepted among us and his conversion brought us joy. This reminds me to recommend him to your prayers, for God is powerful enough to make him better and better.

More generally we must beware of passing judgment on anyone, whether favorable or unfavorable; for as long as a person lives, tomorrow is always an unknown quantity. *The righteous will not be disconcerted in the bad times, and in days of famine they will eat their fill, for sinners will perish.*

Evanescent grandeur

12. *But as for the Lord's enemies, no sooner do they boast and exalt themselves than they will disappear, fading away like smoke.* From this simile take the point the psalmist was trying to make. Smoke bursts from the place where the fire is and wafts upward; and as it rises it billows into a great round cloud. But the bigger this cloud grows, the more tenuous it becomes; its very size means that it cannot be something durable and solid. It hangs loose and inflated, and it is carried away into the air and disperses; you can see that its very size was its undoing. The higher it rises, and the wider it spreads, and the more it extends itself over an increasing area, the weaker it is and the wispier, until it vanishes. *As for the Lord's enemies, no sooner do they boast and exalt themselves than*

20. *Caritas vestra*. In the present sentence he uses both *fratres* (vocative, second person) and *Caritas vestra* (nominative, subject of the third-person verb). It is difficult to convey this in translation; literally: "From this episode Your Charity needed to know, brethren. . . ."

they will disappear, fading away like smoke. It was of such people that scripture said, *The enemies of the truth are like Jannes and Jambres who defied Moses; they are corrupt in their minds and proved spurious by the standard of faith* (2 Tm 3:8). But what makes them enemies of the truth? Their overblown pride, as they waft off into the breeze, uplifting themselves as though they were righteous or important. What is scripture's verdict on them? Like smoke *they will not last, for their lunacy will be obvious to everyone, as was that of the opponents of Moses* (2 Tm 3:9). *As for the Lord's enemies, no sooner do they boast and exalt themselves than they will disappear, fading away like smoke.*

Verse 21. Ingratitude contrasted with generosity

13. *A sinner borrows on interest, but will not repay*. He or she receives, but will not give back. Give back what? Gratitude. What does God want of you, what does God demand of you, except what it profits you to give? What great benefits has a sinner received! Yet he makes no return. He has received his existence, and he has received his humanity, which puts him above a beast. He has received a beautiful body,[21] and within it the differentiation of corporeal senses: eyes for seeing, ears for hearing, a nose for smelling, a palate for tasting, hands for feeling things, feet for walking, and with all these the health of the whole body. But still, we have all these in common with the beast. A human being has received more: an intelligent mind with the capacity for truth, with the power to distinguish the just from the unjust, and the power to explore, to desire its Creator, to praise him and to cleave to him. All these things the sinner too has received, but he does not pay his debt by living as he should. This is why scripture says that *a sinner borrows on interest but will not repay*; he will not give anything back to him from whom he received it, he will not give thanks. Worse still, he repays good with evil—blasphemy, complaints against God, resentment. He *borrows on interest but will not repay, whereas the just person is merciful and lends*. The sinner has nothing, but the just has a great deal. Contemplate poverty on the one hand, plenty on the other. The first receives, but will not pay his debt; the second is merciful and lends, and yet is wealthy. What if the merciful person is poor? He or she is rich nonetheless. Direct those God-fearing eyes of yours at his riches. You see empty coffers, but do not see a conscience full of God. This person has no outward resources, but has charity within. And look how he keeps on giving out generously from that store of charity, yet it never runs short! Even if it happens that he has material resources, it is charity that gives from what he has; if he has nothing material to draw on, he gives kindness, or good advice, if he can; he gives some sort of help, if possible. If in the

21. *Corporis formam*. In Augustine's Platonic perspective *forma* is the principle of differentiation in created things which gives to each its identity; it also connotes the beauty of each.

end he cannot aid the other person even with advice or practical help, he at least gives the will to do so, or prays for the one in trouble, and perhaps his prayer finds a readier hearing than that of someone who hands out bread. A person whose breast is full of charity always has something to give. What we call good will is charity. God does not ask more of you than he has given you within yourself. A good will cannot be empty. If you have a coin to spare, but lack good will, you do not hand it over to a pauper. The poor themselves are generous with good will toward one another; they are not unfruitful among themselves. You will find a blind person led along by one who can see; one who had no coins to give to the needy person[22] has lent him eyes instead. How could that come about, that someone lent his own faculties to another who lacked them, unless he had within him good will, the treasure of the poor? With this treasure comes the sweetest repose, and true security. No break-in by thieves, no threat of shipwreck, can cause you to lose it. What a person has within himself, he keeps; he may escape naked, yet still he is full. *The just person is merciful and lends.*

Verse 22. Cursers become blessers

14. *For those who bless him will have the earth for their inheritance.* This refers to blessing that Just One, indeed the one and only just and justifier, who was poor among us and yet brought great wealth with which to make wealthy those whom he found poor. He it was who enriched the hearts of the poor with the Holy Spirit, and filled with the affluence of goodness souls that had emptied themselves by confessing their sins. He was able to turn a fisherman into a rich man, when by abandoning his nets the fisherman made light of what he had and began to draw up what he had not. God chose the weak things of this world to put the strong to shame;[23] and so he did not use an orator to win a fisherman, but used the fisherman to win the orator,[24] and the fisherman to win the senator, and the fisherman to win the emperor. *Those who bless him will have the earth for their inheritance*, for they will be coheirs with Christ[25] in that land of the living of which another psalm says, *You are my hope, my portion in the land of the living* (Ps 141:6(142:5)). "You yourself are my portion," the psalmist says to God, never doubting that God would secure that portion to him. *They will have the earth for their inheritance, but those who revile him will be lost.* To those who bless him the ability to bless him was his gift.[26] When he came to those who reviled him, they were turned into people who blessed instead; that was how

22. Variant: "no coins to give because needy himself."
23. See 1 Cor 1:27.
24. Perhaps the mention of "orator" before the senator and the emperor is a backward glance at Augustine's earlier profession as a teacher of rhetoric.
25. See Rom 8:17.
26. Variant: ". . . who bless him, blessing was granted."

those who reviled him were lost: they became blessers through his gift. Of their own bad will they used to curse him, but now from his good gift they bless him.

Verse 23. Following Christ

15. Consider the next verse: *a person's steps are directed by the Lord, and he will choose his way.* Our steps are guided by the Lord so that we may ourselves choose the Lord's way. If God did not direct the steps of each human being, they would go so far off course as to lead us unendingly through crooked ways, so that we would never find our way back through those twisted paths. But Christ came, and called us, and redeemed us, and poured out his blood. This is the price he paid, this the good he did; but he suffered badly. Think what he did: he is God. Think what he suffered: he is human. Who is this God-Man? If you, a human being, had not forsaken God, God would not have become human for you. Was it too small a thing to demand repayment on your part, or too small a gift on his, that he created you human, even if he had not also become human for your sake? He it is who has directed our steps, so that we choose his way. *A person's steps are directed by the Lord, and he will choose his way.*

16. Once you have set out to follow Christ's way, do not promise yourself worldly prosperity. He walked through hard things, but promised great things. Follow him. Do not think too much about the way, but more about the goal ahead of you. You will have to put up with tough conditions on your journey through time, but you will attain joys that last for ever. If you want strength to survive the hard grind, look to the recompense; a worker in a vineyard would faint if he did not keep his mind on the wages due to him. When you concentrate on your future reward, all you suffer seems trivial, and you will think it a small price to pay. You will be amazed that so much is given for such slight labor. It is undeniable, brothers and sisters, that the proper price to pay for eternal rest would be eternal labor; if you are going to get eternal happiness, you ought to face eternal suffering to merit it. But if you were condemned to eternal labor, when would you reach the eternal happiness? Never. And that is why your distress necessarily lasts only for a time, so that when it is finished you may reach infinite beatitude.

All the same, brothers and sisters, eternal happiness could demand lengthy distress as its price; I mean that if our happiness is to be without end, our wretchedness and toil and distress might be long-lasting, for even if they continued for a thousand years, is that anything when weighed against eternity? Can you weigh any finite stretch of time, however long, against infinity? Ten thousand years, ten times a hundred thousand if one can speak of it so, or a thousand thousand rather—these come to an end, and cannot be compared with eternity.

But God has willed not only that our toil shall be temporary, but also that it be brief. An entire human life lasts but a few days, even if no joyful ones are interspersed among the hard ones; and in fact joyful periods certainly occur more often and last longer than the difficult times. The hard ones are designedly briefer and fewer, so that we may hold out. So even if a person spent his or her whole life amid hard work and bitter experiences, in pain and agony, in prison, amid pestilence; if he or she were hungry and thirsty every day, every hour, throughout life, even to old age, it would still be true that human life is an affair of a few days only. Once all this toil is over the eternal kingdom will come, happiness without end will come, equality with the angels will come, Christ's inheritance will come, and Christ, our fellow-heir, will come. What did the toil amount to, if we receive so great a reward? Veteran soldiers have a hard time in the army. They get used to being wounded over the years, they enter military life in their youth and leave it as old men. What rough conditions they endure, what long marches, what biting cold, what searing heat, what short rations, what wounds, what dangers! And all for the prospect of a few quiet days in their old age, when their years are beginning to weigh heavily upon them, even if the hardships of campaigning burden them no longer. All they think about as they put up with the hardship is the few peaceful days they will enjoy in retirement, and they do not even know whether they will ever reach them.

A person's steps are directed by the Lord, and he will choose his way. So, as I began to say, if you choose Christ's way, and are a true Christian (for a Christian is one who does not reject Christ's path, but wills to walk that way through Christ's own sufferings), do not seek to travel by any route other than that by which he went. It seems a hard road, but it is a safe one. Any other may offer attractions, but is beset by brigands. *He will choose his way.*

Verse 24. Whatever you may suffer, Christ suffered before you

17. *When he falls*[27] *he will suffer no harm, for the Lord strengthens his hand.* Consider now what it means to choose Christ's way. It may happen that a Christian has to suffer some distress, some disgrace, insult, affliction, loss, or any of the other troubles that befall humankind in this life. The Christian keeps his Lord before his eyes, and the kind of trials the Lord underwent. Then *when he falls, he will suffer no harm, for the Lord strengthens his hand*, strengthens it because he suffered these things first. What are you afraid of, you poor mortal, if your steps are so surely directed by the Lord that you choose his way? What have you to fear? Pain? Christ was scourged. Insults? He had to hear them allege, *You have a demon* (Jn 8:48) when he cast demons out. A clique of bad people conspiring against you? Plots were hatched against him. Perhaps when you are accused of something you cannot prove that your conscience is clear, and you are punished

27. Variant: "When the just falls."

because the lying witnesses who testify against you are believed? But they bore false witness against Christ first, not only before his death, but even after his resurrection. Lying witnesses were put up against him[28] to secure his condemnation by the court; and the guards at the sepulcher came forward as lying witnesses too. Christ arose, accompanied by a stupendous sign; the earth trembled as it delivered up the rising Lord. Earth[29] was there, guarding the earth, but there was a harder earth that could not be moved.[30] The earth reported truthfully, but was led astray by the false earth, for the guards told the Jews what they had seen and what had happened, they accepted money, and were instructed as follows: *Say that while you were asleep his disciples came and removed him* (Mt 28:13). So there were false witnesses against the Lord even in his rising. What blindness there is in false witnesses, brothers and sisters! Their blindness is total. It often happens that lying witnesses contradict themselves, and are too blind to see how obvious it is to others that they are lying. How did these guards contradict themselves? "While we were asleep, *his disciples came and removed him*." What? Who is giving evidence? Someone who was asleep! I would not believe people who told me a story like that, even if they were to tell me their dreams! What a crazy tale: if you were awake, why did you allow it? If you were asleep, how do you know what happened?

The Donatists are in the same tradition of lying

18. Those descendants of theirs[31] are still the same. You will remember it, and we must not pass over this opportunity to remind you. The more earnestly we desire their salvation, so much the more vigilant must we be in pointing out the emptiness of their pretensions. Notice how the body of Christ is attacked by lying witnesses, for the body endures what happened in the first place to the Head. That is hardly surprising. So now, though Christ's body is extended throughout the world, it is never free from those who will taunt it, "Traitors' brood!"[32] Your charge is untrue. I can show you up as a lying witness by examining a few of your words. You fling against me the accusation, "You are a traitor." I reply, "You are a liar." But you will never and nowhere make any charge of treachery stick against me, whereas I will here and now prove you are lying from your own words. Undeniably you said that we have sharpened our swords; I read out from your Acts what your Circumcellions have done.[33] In your

---

28. See Mt 26:60.
29. The guards.
30. The priests.
31. The Donatists, object of the attacks in the next paragraphs.
32. *Progenies traditorum*, an allusion to the origins of the controversy, when some Christians allegedly "handed over" the scriptures, thus "betraying" the Church. The verb *trado* can cover both senses. See note at Exposition of Psalm 10, 1.
33. Terrorists; see note at Exposition of Psalm 10, 5.

own manifesto you claim that you let go of any property taken from you;[34] well, I can read you the passage in your own Acts where you cause an agency to be set up to demand it. Again, undeniably you claimed there that you offer nothing but the gospels; but I can quote many examples of judicial decisions which you have used to persecute people separated from you, and I can also quote your appeals to an apostate emperor, to whom you said that nothing except justice found a home with him.[35] Perhaps you regard Julian's apostasy as part of the gospel? Look how I am pinning you down as a liar. What deserves any credence, then, among the things you allege about me? Even if I could find no evidence that what you allege is untrue, it would be enough that I am showing you up as a liar in other matters. What have you to say? And all the rest of your cronies are like you. You had your reasons for promulgating your charges widely, for you wanted to have plenty of lying by association, so that you would not have to bear the shame of lying all by yourself.

The Donatists repaid in their own coin: a historical parallel

19. But our Donatist friend replies, "Let the judgment of our forefathers against Caecilian remain valid." Why should it still be valid? "Because it was the bishops who passed the judgment." Then the judgment passed on you by the Maximianists must be equally valid. In earlier days, as I think you are aware, when Maximian[36] was still a deacon under Primian, some bishops who supported Maximian came to Carthage, as we find in the Tractate which they included in the Acts; these Maximianists were in legal dispute over a house with the steward of this same Primian who professed to "let go of any property taken from him." First of all they sent the Tractate about him, complaining that he had refused to come out and meet them; this was their principal grievance. Notice how God paid them back for what they had complained of in Caecilian. It is a remarkable parallel; after the lapse of so many years God has willed to re-run before their very eyes what happened then, so that they may be left with no possibility of denying it and no route of escape. They might have said they had forgotten what happened so long ago, but God is not allowing them to forget—and if only it could bring them to salvation! God has done this in his mercy; mercy for them it will be if they consider what happened.

---

34. In the decree of the Donatist bishop Primian this claim was made. Augustine quotes it in his *Summary of the Conference with the Donatists*, Day Three, VIII, 11 (written toward the end of the year 411), and more fully in his *Answer to Cresconius* IV, 47. He refers to it again in 19 and 20 below.

35. The emperor was Julian the Apostate (361-363), whom the Donatists had approached in an effort to get their basilicas back. Augustine enlarges on this point in his *Answer to the Writings of Petilian* II, 92, 203, written in about the year 400.

36. See note at Exposition of Psalm 35, 9.

Keep before your eyes the unity of the whole world[37] at that time, brothers and sisters, from which unity they split off in their opposition to Caecilian. Keep also in view the Donatist sect today, from which the Maximianists have split off in their opposition to Primian. What the Donatists did to Caecilian at that earlier date, the Maximianists have now done to Primian. This is why the Maximianists claim to be more authentic than the Donatists, because they have given a better imitation of the actions of their forebears! They have raised up Maximian against Primian, just as the Donatists then raised up Majorinus[38] against Caecilian; and they have complained about Primian in the same terms as those others did about Caecilian. They said, you remember, that Caecilian (who was conscious of the rightness of his position) refused to come out to meet them; he knew their faction. So too the Maximianists are complaining because Primian refused to come out to meet them. Why do the Donatists admit that Primian had the measure of the Maximianist faction, but refuse to allow that Caecilian had correctly sized up the faction of the Donatists? Maximian was not yet ordained, and criminal charges were being brought against Primian; so the bishops gathered and desired him to come out to meet them. He did not come out, as the Tractate inserted in their Acts indicates. He did not emerge; I am not reproaching him for that; indeed, I commend him. If you see a gang like that, you should not go out to talk to them, but save your arguments for submission to the better judgment of your own party. There was still a large group of the Donatists left, with whom Primian hoped to clear his name; accordingly he refused to go out and meet those who had already conspired to form a breakaway group.

Well now, Primian, you see how we commend your course of action against the Maximianists. Apply the same criteria to Caecilian's case. You are unwilling to judge him as a brother? Very well, judge as an outsider. You were unwilling to go out, and what were you saying to yourself? "These people have conspired against my safety. They have been suborned against me. If I entrust myself to them, I shall be allowing my case to be prejudged. So I will not go out to them; let my case be reserved for better judges, men endowed with weightier authority." A very sensible decision. But what if Caecilian thought the same? You may be at pains to prove that another Lucilla[39] bribed those men against you, but you are unlikely to find any proof. This is something he even then knew so well that it was subsequently related in the Acts. But since you suspected some trick, and had received a report that you were in some danger, I admit that in view of your

37. That is, of the undivided Catholic Church throughout the world.
38. Soon succeeded by Donatus.
39. A rich and noble lady whom Caecilian while still a deacon had antagonized by rebuking her on some point of Church discipline. She was influential at the outbreak of the Donatist schism, and helped to secure the ordination of a rival bishop to Caecilian. She later bribed the bishops to condemn Caecilian, as Augustine explains in his Letter 43, VI, 17, so that in Carthage, "the head of Africa, altar was raised against altar." See also *Answer to Cresconius* III, 28,32–29,33.

fear your caution was justified. You acted rightly in refusing to go out and meet such people, for there were others better qualified to judge concerning you. Think now about Caecilian: you have kept Numidia for yourself, but he has kept the whole world.[40] But if you wish to maintain that the verdict of the Donatists against Caecilian was valid then, you must allow that the verdict of the Maximianists against you is valid now. Bishops condemned him; bishops condemned you. So you went on to plead your case, and the issue of it was that you landed yourself with the Maximianist schism, just as Caecilian pleaded his, and achieved the Donatist schism as the outcome.

We have, then, an amazing and incontrovertible example of history repeating itself: the Maximianists are bringing the same complaints against Primian as those others brought against Caecilian. I can hardly express to you, brothers and sisters, how moved I am, and how thankful to God, that his mercy toward them has provided an example that should illuminate their darkness, if they have the wit to see it. Now, if you will bear with me a little while, brothers and sisters, listen while I read to you the proceedings of the Maximianist council, for God has put the document into our hands.[41]

[He then read out the proceedings of the council of the Maximianists, commenting as he went along:]

20. *To our most holy brethren and colleagues throughout the whole of Africa. . .*

[Here Augustine interrupted:] This means their entire united party in Africa. But while the Catholic Church is alongside them here, in other parts of the world they are not alongside the Catholic Church.

[He continued to read:] *To our most holy brethren and colleagues throughout the whole of Africa, that is, those dwelling in Africa Proconsularis, Numidia, Mauretania, Byzacena and Tripoli; and to the priests and deacons; and to all the peoples who together with us engage in holy warfare for the truth of the gospel, the following who have attended the Council at Cebarsussa*[42] *wish eternal salvation in the Lord: Victorinus, Fortunatus, Victorianus, Miggin, Saturninus, Constantius, Candorius, Innocent, Cresconius, Florentius, Salvius, another Salvius, Donatus, Geminius, Praetextatus . . .*

40. This universality was one of the aspects distinguishing the true Church on which Augustine loved to dwell, especially in controversy with the Donatists.
41. The following is the Synodical Letter of the Maximianist Council of Cebarsussa, in Byzacena, which had met on 24 June 393. The more moderate Donatists from the Romanized cities of the coast and the Tunisian coastal plain had been appalled by the violent and unscrupulous methods of Primian, Donatist Bishop of Carthage, and their efforts to approach him peaceably had been rebuffed. This council then condemned Primian; its tone is, in the circumstances, remarkably moderate.
42. A range of variants for this place-name indicates that it has given copyists trouble.

[Augustine:] This last one is the bishop of Assuras, whom they received into their fellowship later. So Primian later accepted this man who had pronounced judgment against himself.

[He continued to read:] *Maximian, Theodore, Anastasius, Donatian, Donatus, another Donatus, Pomponius, Pancratius, Januarius, Secundinus, Pascasius, Cresconius, Rogatian, another Maximian, Benenatus, Gaianus, Victorinus, Guntasius, Quintasius, Felician . . .*

[Augustine:] This last is Felician of Musti, who is still alive—unless it is another man of the same name from somewhere else. Later in the document the signatories say where each is from.

[He continued to read:] *Salvius, Miggin, Proculus, Latinus, and the others present. It is well known to all concerning God's priests, beloved brethren, that impelled not by their own will but by divine law they both pronounce sentence against the guilty and lift any that has been passed on the innocent; this is done by them legally and rightly. For anyone who either pardons a guilty person or attempts to ruin an innocent one is exposed to no slight danger, especially as it is written, "You shall not put an innocent and just person to death, nor acquit the guilty"* (Ex 23:7, LXX). *Admonished, therefore, by this decree of the law, we were obliged under its authority to hear and discuss the case of Primian, who had been appointed to the holy people of the church at Carthage as the bishop and overseer of God's sheepfold. We did so at the instance of letters requesting the same from the elders of that same church, to the end that when everything had been investigated we might either acquit him, which would have been the most desirable outcome, or, having found him guilty, prove beyond doubt that he had been deservedly condemned. Our dearest wish was that the holy people of the church at Carthage might joyfully recognize the honor that had been conferred on it in being given a bishop holy in all respects and blameworthy in none. A priest of the Lord ought most certainly to be of such character that when the people's prayers are of no avail, the priest may deserve to obtain from God what he asks on behalf of the people; as it is written, "If the people sin, the priest will pray for them; but if the priest sins, who will pray for him?"*[43]

[Augustine:] Even the apostles wrote to ask their people to pray for them, and when the apostles themselves prayed they were accustomed to say, *Forgive us our trespasses*. The apostle John, moreover, said, *We have an advocate with the Father, Jesus Christ the righteous one, and he himself is the effectual entreaty for our sins* (1 Jn 2:1-2). But this was written about the Priest whom they do not know; the people were being prophetically taught to recognize a Priest who is of such a character that no one could pray for him. Who is this, for whom no one

43. Loosely based on 1 Sm 2:25.

prays? He who intercedes for us all.[44] In former times, in the days of the Levitical priesthood, the priest used to enter the holy place and offer victims on behalf of the people. He was not the reality, but a type of the Priest who was to come; for at that time the priests themselves were sinners like the rest of men and women, and God wanted through this prophetic type to indicate to the people that they must long for another Priest, one who would intercede for all and need no one to pray for him. This is what is meant by the text quoted, *If the people sin, the priest will pray for them; but if the priest sins, who will pray for him?* Well then, you people, choose the kind of priest for whom you are not obliged to intercede, but on whose prayer you can safely rely. He is our Lord Jesus Christ, the sole priest, the sole mediator between God and humankind, the man Christ Jesus.[45]

[He continued to read:] *The scandalous behavior of Primian and his unparalleled wickedness have therefore called down upon him the judgment of heaven, making inevitable that the author of such crimes be cut off entirely. Shortly after his ordination . . .*

[Augustine:] Now we get a list of the charges.

[He continued to read:] *Shortly after his ordination he put pressure on the priests of the aforesaid people to commit themselves by oath to join him in an ungodly conspiracy: with questionable right he demanded of them that they should immediately promise him their consent . . .*

[Augustine:] He demanded it; they refused to make the promise, but remained silent. He was quite prepared to carry through on his own the wicked deed he had planned.

[He continued to read:] . . . *should immediately promise him their consent to the condemnation of four deacons, outstanding men, of good repute for their excellent qualities, namely Maximian, Rogatian, Donatus and Salgamius.*

[Augustine:] One of these was the author of the schism. He was breaking off a fragment of what was itself only a fragment, not caring that he was cut off from the whole.

[He continued to read:] *They were dumbfounded by his unprincipled audacity, and since they might have rebutted the charges by their silence, he was fully prepared to implement single-handed the crime he had planned, so much so that he believed himself competent to pass sentence on the deacon Maximian, an innocent man, as everyone knows. He did this without due process, without counsel for the prosecution, without witnesses, in the absence of Maximian, who was ill in bed.*

[Augustine:] Look at that! What an indictment!

[He continued to read:] *For some time prior to this he had been punishing clerics with similar savagery. In contravention of the law and conciliar decrees*

44. See Rom 8:34.
45. See 1 Tm 2:5.

he was in the habit of admitting to the holy fellowship of all the priests men who had committed incest, and since the majority of the people were opposed to this practice, it was agreed in letters emanating from even the most distinguished elders that he must himself correct what he had done. But in his arrogant defiance he disdained to put matters right. The elders of the aforesaid church were deeply distressed by these events, and they dispatched letters and legates to all the clergy, begging us with tears to come to them as soon as we possibly could, in order that the matter might be duly weighed and his intentions investigated, and so the reputation of their church restored. When in accordance with the request of the aforementioned persons we came, he was seething with rage and absolutely refused to confront us.

[Augustine:] You know what is alleged against him, because by now the Donatist party has become unchaste. This was predictable: everyone, the whole mass of the people, always comes to resemble those with whom it enters into communion. It follows that if what they say is true, the whole Donatist party is unchaste by now. Of course, some of them who live in Numidia will come forward and say, "Those incestuous persons, whoever they may be, whom you have admitted into communion with you, have nothing to do with us. How could any such do us harm,[46] living far away, as we do?" So then, you would have it that what happens in Carthage does no harm to you in Numidia? How then could what happens in Africa harm the whole world? It's always the same: the arguments they use to defend themselves only incriminate them and vindicate us.

[He continued to read:] *He absolutely refused to confront us . . .*

[Augustine:] That is what they complained about in Caecilian's case.

[He continued to read:] *In every possible way he maintained a stubborn, defiant attitude and kept to his evil course, even to mustering a troop of desperados . . .*

[Augustine:] This is something else. They never accused Caecilian of doing that. Listen to what these fellows did.

[He continued to read:] . . . *who, after obtaining permission from the authorities, blocked the doors to the basilicas . . .*

[Augustine:] This was to keep the bishops out.

[He continued to read:] . . . *in order to deny us the possibility of entering and celebrating the liturgy.*[47] *Let anyone who is a lover and champion of the truth consider this, and judge whether such an action befits a bishop, or is even allow-*

46. Variant suggested by the CCL editors: "That scurrilous piece of writing has nothing to do with us. Whomsoever you have admitted to your fellowship, it could do us no harm."
47. These violent attacks were made on a preliminary meeting of the anti-Primian Donatist bishops in Carthage toward the end of 392. The meeting broke up and retired to Cebarsussa, whence the letter Augustine is quoting emerged.

able for Christians, or if the gospels endorse it. Yet it was one who had been our own brother who treated us like this, as a stranger would never have done.

[Augustine:] Do we need any more details? They give plenty, and they condemn the man. But let us read the condemnation itself.

[He continued to read:] *All of us, God's priests, in the presence of the Holy Spirit, have decreed that because the aforesaid Primian has substituted other bishops for bishops still living; has introduced unchaste persons into the communion of the saints;*[48] *has attempted to force certain priests to involve themselves in a conspiracy; has caused Fortunatus to be thrown into a sewer for bringing comfort to sick persons by baptizing them; has persistently refused communion with the priest Demetrius in order to persuade him to disinherit his son; has rebuked this same priest for giving hospitality to bishops; has sent out a gang to damage Christian homes; has caused bishops and clerics to be besieged and later stoned by his minions; has caused elders of the community to be beaten in the basilica because they objected to Claudianists*[49] *being admitted to communion; has deemed innocent clerics worthy of condemnation; has refused to present himself to us so that we can hear his case, after blocking the doors of the basilicas with his attendants and retinue to prevent us from entering; has insulted and rejected emissaries sent by us; and has seized many places, initially by force, and then by judicial authorization . . .*

[Augustine:] And this is the man who "lets go what has been taken from him"! The apostle Paul says, *Does anyone among you who has a dispute with another dare to have the case heard by the unjust, rather than by the saints?* (1 Cor 6:1). Look what a charge they have laid against Primian: that he would not negotiate about these places with the bishops, but only before a judge.

[He continued to read:] *Because he has done all these and many other unlawful things*[50] *which we have passed over in silence in order not to dishonor our pen, we have decreed that he is condemned in perpetuity by the present assembly, lest through contact with him the Church of God be defiled by any contagion or accusation. The apostle Paul urges this duty upon us when he warns, "In the name of the Lord Jesus Christ we command you, brethren, to keep clear of any brother whose conduct is irregular"* (2 Th 3:6). *And therefore, not unmindful of the Church's purity, we have judged it expedient by this Tractate to warn all our holy fellow-priests, and all clerics, and all peoples who count themselves Christians, to shun his company with the utmost care, since he has been condemned. Anyone who attempts to violate this our decree by disregarding it will be responsible for his own ruin. However, it has seemed good to us and to the Holy Spirit that a time for*

48. Or perhaps "into the communion of holy things," meaning sacramental offices.
49. A splinter-group from the main Donatist party. Claudian was one of the Donatist bishops who attended the synod in Rome in 374.
50. Variant: "seductive things."

change should be allowed to the tardy, so that if any of our fellow-priests, or any clerics, unmindful of their own salvation, shall fail to withdraw from communion with the condemned Primian within the period from the day of the condemnation, that is, from the 24 June, to the 25 December, such persons shall fall under the same sentence. Lay persons likewise shall dissociate themselves from all dealings with him by the Easter Day that follows the aforesaid day of his condemnation; if they do not, they must know that no one of them can be restored to the Church except through penance, assuming that they are aware of our decree.

Issued by the authority of us, the undersigned bishops:

Victorinus of Munatiana.[51] *Fortunatus of Dionysianum. Victorian of Carcabia. Florentius of Hadrumetum.*[52] *Miggin of Elephantaria. Innocent of Thibilis. Miggin, on behalf of my colleague Salvius of Membressa. Salvius of Ausafa. Donatus of Sabratha. Gemelius of Tanaboea.*

[Augustine:] We find among the signatories Praetextatus of Assuras and Felician of Musti.

[He continued to read:] *Praetextatus of Assuras. Maximian of Stabata. Datian of Camiceta. Donatus of Fisciana. Theodore of Uzalis. Victorian, at the behest of my colleague Agnosius. Donatus of Cebresuta. Natalicus of Thala. Pomponius of Macri.*[53] *Pancratius of Badias.*[54] *Januarius of Aquenum. Secundus of Jacondiana. Pascasius of Vicus Augusti. Creso of Conjustiacum. Rogatian. Maximian of Erumminum. Benenatus of Tugutianum. Ritanus. Gaianus of Tiguala. Victorinus of Leptis Magna.*[55] *Gustasius of Beneffa. Quintasius of Capsa.*[56] *Felician of Musti.*[57] *Victorian, from the delegation of Bishop Miggin. Miggius. Latinus of Mugiae. Proculus of Gibba. Donatus of Sabratha, on behalf of my brother and colleague Marratius.*[58] *Proculus of Gibba on behalf of my colleague Gallio. Secundian of Prisianum. Helpidius of Thysdrus. Donatus of Samurdata. Getulicus of Victoriana. Annibonius of Robauta. Annibonius at the request of my colleague Augendus of Arensi. Tertullus of Avensa. Primulian. Secundinus of Arusia. Maximus of Pittana. Crescentian of Murra. Donatus of Belma. Perseverantius of Theveste.*[59] *Faustinus of Bina. Victor of Althiburus.*

In all, fifty-three bishops.

---

51. The Primate of Byzacena.
52. A coastal town SE of Carthage.
53. In Mauretania Sitifensis.
54. In Numidia. These two, Pomponius and Pancratius, were among the few signatories who did not come from Byzacena or the Proconsular Province.
55. Leptis Magna was an important coastal town toward the east of Roman Africa, in modern Libya.
56. Capsa was far to the south of Carthage.
57. Musti was to the south of Carthage. Felician of Musti was later reconciled with the main part of the Donatist sect, see sections 20 and 22.
58. The signatory was the bishop of Sabratha who appears earlier in the list.
59. The only Numidian bishop of any standing who supported Maximian.

The historical parallel pursued, Primian and Caecilian

21. [Augustine:] Bear with me a little longer, brothers and sisters. To Primian we say, "This decree that condemned you: does it have any force, or not?" I am inclined to your point of view, Primian; indeed, I would go further and say that all those bishops made false allegations against you. Listen to my reason for saying so. You won your case before other judges, while the Maximianists were condemned. Well now, if I hold you to be innocent because, after refusing to go out and meet that faction, you were so successful in proving your innocence elsewhere that those who condemned you incurred condemnation themselves, you for your part must agree to hold Caecilian innocent, for he refused to go out and meet your predecessors, and reserved his case for the judgment of the whole world, as you reserved yours for the council of the Numidians. If the see of Bagai[60] declared you innocent, how much more right had the apostolic see to acquit him?

On the other hand, do you prefer to maintain that those who originally condemned Caecilian were in the right? In that case, they condemn you as well. No, the ruling of those who opposed Caecilian had no validity then, nor will it have in the future. But be careful not to give a verdict against yourself.

22. The Donatists make bold to say, "But we who condemned the Maximianists later were the more numerous." All right then, on that showing your judgment against Felician must stand, and so will that against Caecilian. When they[61] convoked their council at Bagai, they also condemned Felician; but now this Felician is within your fellowship, so either a guilty man has been received back, or an innocent man was condemned. If you are willing to readmit a guilty person for the sake of Donatian peace, can you not be as accommodating to all nations for the sake of the peace of Christ? If, however, it was through an error on your part that Felician was condemned, three hundred and ten conciliar members were in error. Is it not then all the more likely that seventy were in error when they condemned Caecilian? What have you to say?

Priority in time versus preponderance of numbers

When you hear the argument pressed against you, "The Maximianists were the first to issue their condemnation," you retort, "But we, who condemned the Maximianists, were the more numerous." The immediate answer is this: your predecessors had the priority when they condemned Caecilian. So if it is getting in first that counts, the Primianists must yield to the Maximianists; but if it is weight of numbers that counts, the Donatists must yield to the entire world; and I

60. See notes on Exposition 2 of Psalm 21, sections 26 and 31.
61. The bishops of the main Donatist sect.

think nothing could be more just. The Maximianists are few in number, but they had priority.

Another argument: a condemned person cannot sit as judge

Now a guilty person does not convict another person of guilt. If you agree with this principle, by what right did you[62] sign a condemnation, when you were under a condemnation yourself? (He too[63] was listed among the signatories, and they had provided no opportunity for him to plead his case. It was different with Caecilian: the right of a person to plead his case was reserved for him, as the judgment makes evident, for he was received back into communion only when he had been cleared. This man,[64] on the contrary, is found in one place as a man condemned by judges, and in another as a judge passing sentence with the rest.)

Divergences between Primian's case and Caecilian's

But let us concede that the Bagai council was competent in the matter; indeed, we concede your whole argument. The Maximianists were out of order in condemning you, but so were your predecessors in condemning Caecilian. You cleared yourself at Bagai; he cleared himself in the tribunal overseas. What are you going to say next? "We outnumber the Maximianists." Fine, boast of your numbers! We can play at that game too, and more effectively. The Maximianists condemned you in your absence, after you had refused to go out and meet them. Thus far the situations are parallel, because they condemned Caecilian in his absence too, after he had avoided their faction. But then you went on to cause decrees to be issued in the council of Bagai against your opponents in their absence, whereas Caecilian established his innocence face to face with his adversary. Then there is another significant difference: you yourself approached the Numidian judges before whom you were to clear your name, and you appointed them; the Maximianists had no say in the appointment. Caecilian won his case against Donatus before judges whom the Donatist party had sought to hear the case. Let the Maximianists reply to you, and with justice, "At first we came to you, we, the bishops from your own province, from your own diocese; we wished to be the ones to try your case. But you scorned us, and would not come out to meet us. If you were afraid of what we might decide, then even if we had chosen judges together, you still would not have appeared before them, even though you had approved them." Look at the difference between the two procedures: at that earlier time the Donatists themselves petitioned the emperor by

62. Primian, who at the time he participated in the condemnation of Felician by the council of Bagai, still lay under the condemnation issued by the Maximianist council.

63. This is an aside to the congregation.

64. Primian.

letter to appoint judges. When they lost their case they repudiated these judges, whom they had asked for before their defeat. At their request others were appointed, and again they lost their case. They then appealed to the emperor, and were defeated at his tribunal. A Maximianist whose case has gone against him in his absence keeps silence, but can a Donatist who has three times been present and three times defeated keep quiet?

The numbers game again

23. But a point of your argument against the Maximianists was preponderance of numbers. And as I said, I take your point. Three hundred and ten outnumber the hundred or so of Maximian's party who condemned Primian; but does it not weigh with you that thousands of bishops on Caecilian's side throughout the world condemned Donatus? Perhaps you will object, "But thousands of bishops throughout the world did not condemn the Donatists, did they?" Certainly they did not; but why not? Because they were not there in court, and if they were not present, they knew nothing about the case.

Why have you separated yourself from the innocent? Some baptized person comes to you from elsewhere in the world and you want to rebaptize him or her. This newcomer approaches you as you are exercising your death-dealing ministry and planning to repeat what is given once and for all, and with loud protests and distress the stranger asks you, "What do you want to do?" This Mesopotamian, or Syrian, or traveler from Pontus or somewhere even further off, asks you, "Why do you want to baptize me again?" You reply, "Because you are not baptized." This stranger, remember, has come from Galatia, or Pontus, or he is someone from Philadelphia, from the churches to which John wrote; or he comes from Colossae, or Philippi, or Thessalonica. And he says to you, "Do I have no true baptism, I who received letters from the apostle through whom you derived it? Do you presume to read a letter addressed to me, while setting your face against peace with me?"

Exposition 3 of Psalm 36

Third Sermon

Verse 25. Does it match experience?

1. The last portion of this psalm was left aside; we have not treated it or discussed it with you. Accordingly, as I see it, the Lord has called us back again to pay the debt we owe you. This was not our arrangement, but perhaps it accords with his. Let me have your attention then, brothers and sisters, so that with God's help we may at last pay off this debt which was weighing on our mind.

Who is making the declaration we have just sung? *I was young once, and now I have grown old, and never have I seen a just person destitute, or a child of righteous parents begging for bread.* Suppose we take this as an individual speaking. How long does a human life last? Is there anything remarkable in this, that a single person, living in a particular part of the world throughout his or her life (which after all is a very short period), even if such a one has journeyed from youth to old age, has never seen a just person left in the lurch, or the descendants of the just begging for bread? No, there is nothing remarkable about that. Possibly before he was born there had been some just person begging bread in that very place, or it could have been happening in some other place, where the speaker was not present. Another thing that occurs to me is this: suppose someone among you, growing old now, looks back on the course of his life and mentally revisits people he has known; it may well be that he can think of no just person begging bread, or any child of a just person begging either; yet if he looks at the sacred scriptures he finds the just man Abraham in straitened circumstances and forced by the hunger he faced in his own country to travel abroad.[1] He also finds that Isaac, Abraham's son, was obliged by similar famine to migrate elsewhere seeking food.[2] How can it be true, then, that *never have I seen a just person destitute, or a child of righteous parents begging for bread*? If the observer has found it to be true in his own life, at any rate he will find things otherwise in his reading of the scriptures, and that is a more reliable guide than one's own experience.

1. See Gn 12:10.
2. See Gn 26:1.

Spiritual paralysis

2. So what are we to do? We need the help of your devotion and insight to discern the will of God in these verses, and make out what he is trying to teach us. The danger is that some weak person with little capacity for a spiritual understanding of the scriptures may appeal to human instances and see God's good servants sometimes reduced by indigence to the necessity of begging for food. Moreover such a one is all the more likely to reflect on the apostle Paul, who says, *I have experienced hunger and thirst, endured cold and exposure* (2 Cor 11:27), and so this observer of ours may be scandalized and wonder, "Is it really true, then, what I have sung? Is that verse really true, that line I sang so devoutly as I stood in church, *never have I seen a just person destitute, or a child of righteous parents begging for bread*? The scriptures are misleading us," he may say to himself; and then all the energies he employed in good deeds may wane. I am not talking simply about the outer person. When the interior faculties are disabled the danger is all the graver, for the inner self may slacken and weary of well-doing as he says to himself, "Why should I exert myself in good works? Why break my bread to the hungry, or clothe the naked, or bring the homeless into my house,[3] putting my faith in scripture's declaration, *Never have I seen a just person destitute, or a child of righteous parents begging for bread*, when all the while I see so many people who live good lives going hungry? Of course, I could be mistaken; I could be wrongly assuming that both those who are living good lives and those who are really leading bad lives are equally good, whereas God knows otherwise; I could be counting as righteous someone who in fact is unjust. That is possible. Yes, but then what am I to make of Abraham's case? Scripture itself affirms that he was just. And what am I to make of the apostle Paul, who actually says, *Be imitators of me, as I am of Christ* (1 Cor 4:16)? Do I want to find myself subject to the same rigors that he endured, *in hunger and thirst, in cold and exposure*?"

Letting the paralytic down through the roof

3. Do you think, brothers and sisters, that we can pick up the person who thinks like this, whose inward limbs are lying slack and powerless to do good deeds; do you think we can lift him up like a paralyzed man and open the roof of this passage of scripture, and lower him to the Lord? You see that it is an obscure passage, and if obscure it is covered over as though roofed. I see on the one hand a person spiritually paralyzed, and on the other this roofed-over text; and I know that Christ is hidden under the roof. As far as my strength permits I am going to do what those people in the gospel were commended for doing, when they

3. See Is 58:7.

opened the roof and lowered the paralytic to Christ, so that Christ could say to him, *Cheer up, son, your sins are forgiven you.*[4] He healed the inner person of paralysis by forgiving his sins and bandaging up his weak faith. But there were bystanders who lacked the eyes to see that someone interiorly paralysed had been healed, and they thought the doctor who had effected the cure was blaspheming. *Who is this who forgives sins?* they demanded. *He is blaspheming. Who has power to forgive sins, except God alone?* (Lk 5:21). And because Christ was indeed God, he heard their thoughts. They were right in what they were thinking, that God alone could forgive, but wrong in not seeing that God was present. The physician therefore performed a further cure in the body of the paralytic, in order to heal the spiritual paralysis of the people who talked like that. He did something they could see, and gave something in which they had to believe.

Whoever you are, then, who are so weak and sickly that you are dissuaded from good deeds by contemplating human misfortunes, whoever you are who are enfeebled by inward paralysis, allow us to open the roof, if we can, and let you down to the Lord.

The Church's long memory

4. The Lord himself, in the Church which is his body, was young in the early days and has now advanced in age. You know this, you recognize the truth of it and understand the point, because you have your place within the body. You have believed that Christ is our Head, and we his body. But is this true of us alone, and not also of those who went before us? All the righteous since the world began have Christ as their Head. They believed that he would come, and we believe that now he has come. They too were healed by faith in him, just as we were, so that he might be the Head of the whole city of Jerusalem, in which all believers from the beginning even to the end shall be enrolled, together with the legions and armies of angels, so that there may be one city under one king, or one province under one emperor, happy in its perpetual peace and salvation, praising God without end and unendingly blissful. But the body of Christ, the Church, is like a single human being, young at first, but now at the end of time flourishing in sleek old age, for of the Church it is written, *widespreading in vigorous old age* (Ps 91:15(92:14)). Widespread the Church is, throughout all nations, and its voice is like that of a man or woman looking back to the days of youth, and reviewing all the time that has passed until this last age, for through the scriptures the Church is familiar with all those eras. It speaks exultantly and testifies, *I was young once* in the world's youth, *and now I have grown old* for I am still here in the world's last days, *and never have I seen a just person destitute, or a child of righteous parents begging for bread.*

4. See Lk 5:20.

Chewing on God's bread

5. We have recognized who this speaker is, once young and now mature; and we have reached Christ through the opened roof. But who is the just person never seen destitute, the one whose child never has to beg for bread? If you understand what this bread is, you will understand who is meant. The bread is the word of God, which is never absent from a righteous person's mouth. This righteous person was tempted in our Head, and that was his answer; for when the devil tempted the hungry, famished Christ, suggesting, *Say to these stones, "Become loaves of bread,"* Christ replied, *Not on bread alone do humans live, but on every word of God* (Mt 4:3,4). Consider then, brothers and sisters, whether there is ever a time when a just person is not doing God's will. He or she is doing it all the time by living according to his will. And God's will never leaves such a person's heart, because God's will is the same thing as God's law. What does scripture say about that? *On the law of the Lord he will reflect day and night* (Ps 1:2). You eat ordinary bread for an hour or so, and then put it aside; but you eat this bread day and night. Whenever you hear it, whenever you read it, you are eating it; and when you mull over it afterwards you are ruminating, like a clean animal, not one of the unclean.[5] A wise maxim indicates this same truth in the words of Solomon:*A desirable treasure lingers in the wise person's mouth, but the foolish gulps it down* (Prv 21:20). Someone who gulps it down, so that what he has eaten is no longer visible, has forgotten what he heard. But one who has not forgotten thinks it over, and in thinking ruminates, and in ruminating finds it delicious. That is why scripture says, *Holy meditation will keep you safe* (Prv 2:11). If holy meditation keeps you safe as you ruminate on this bread, the saying will be true: *Never have I seen a just person destitute, or a child of righteous parents begging for bread.*

Verse 26. Lending to God

6. *All day long he shows mercy and lends.*[6] (This verb means both lending on interest and receiving a loan on interest, so it will be clearer if we say *fenerat.*[7] What do we care what the grammarians say about it? It is better that you understand our colloquialisms than that our flights of eloquence leave you flum-

---

5. See Lv 11:1-8, where the distinction is drawn between clean animals (those that may be offered to God) and unclean (not acceptable). Since sheep and cattle were regarded as typical of the "clean" animals, a rough-and-ready criterion was provided: animals which have a divided hoof and chew the cud were to be regarded as clean.
6. *Feneratur.*
7. The verb exists in both a deponent form,*feneror*, and an active form,*fenero*, with no difference of meaning; but Augustine here says he intends to use*fenero* to mean "lend," as the deponent might look like a passive. He is more interested in clarity than in linguistic purity, as he goes on to say.

moxed.[8]) So the righteous person *all day long shows mercy and lends on interest*. But this is no license for usurers to make merry. We can find a special kind of lender, just as we found a special kind of bread. Wherever we open the roof we reach Christ. I do not want you to be money-lenders, and the reason why I do not want you to is that God does not want it. For if I do not want you to do something, but God does want you to, go ahead and do it; but if God does not want you to do something, then even if I did want you to, any who did it would do it to their own destruction. How do we know God does not want it in this case? Because it is written elsewhere, *He has not put his money out to usury* (Ps 14(15):5). And I think that usurers themselves know how loathsome, how hateful and abominable the practice is.

But now I myself tell you, or rather our God who forbids you to lend money on interest commands you, to be a lender. You are told, "Lend to God." Now if you lend to human borrowers, it is with expectation; and will you have no expectations if you lend to God? If you have lent to someone—handed out money as a loan, I mean—and you expect to get back from the other person more than you gave, not simply your money but something more besides, whether wheat or wine or oil or some other commodity, then in expecting to get back more than you handed out you are a usurer, and thereby you deserve blame, not praise.[9] "What am I to do, then?" you ask. "I must lend profitably." Exactly. Study the money-lender's methods. He wants to give modestly and get back with profit; you do the same. Give a little, and receive on a grand scale. Look how your interest is mounting up! Give temporal wealth and claim eternal interest, give the earth and gain heaven. "Whom shall I give it to?" did you ask? The Lord himself comes forward to ask you for a loan, he who forbade you to be a usurer. Listen to the scripture telling you how to make the Lord your debtor: *Anyone who gives alms to the poor is lending to the Lord* (Prv 19:17). The Lord needs nothing from you, but at your elbow is someone else who does need what you have. You give it to that neighbor, and he or she receives it. The poor person has no means of repaying you, yet wants to repay all the same and only lacks the

8. A pun: *quam in nostra disertitudine vos deserti eritis.*

9. The exacting of interest, at least from fellow-Israelites, was forbidden by the law in the Old Testament (see Ex 22:25; Dt 23:19-20). For Christians the prohibition was echoed by the Council of Nicea (A.D. 325) and the First Council of Carthage (A.D. 348). This teaching continued in force throughout the middle ages, though the Fourth Lateran Council (A.D. 1215) allowed the Jews to lend money at interest; this had the practical effect of making the Jews almost the only money-lenders, which may have contributed to their reputation for profiteering and the suspicion with which they were sometimes viewed. Throughout the ancient and medieval periods money was regarded as sterile, a mere means of exchange; hence the exaction of interest on a loan could reasonably be regarded as making profit out of someone else's misfortune. But with the rise of capitalism money came to be seen as productive of further wealth, for which moderate interest paid by the borrower was a fair return. The Christian Church gradually abandoned the old idea, and today the term "usury" is employed, if at all, only to denote the demanding of interest at an exorbitant rate.

wherewithal. What he does have is the kindly will to pray for you. But when a poor person prays for you it is as though he or she is saying to God, "Lord, I have borrowed money; please go surety for me." So even if you do not hold the poor person to repayment, you can certainly hold the guarantor liable. Listen to God telling you in his own scriptures, "Give, and don't worry, I will reimburse you." How do they usually talk, third-party guarantors? What do they promise? "I will repay you; I take it on myself, it is to me that you entrust it." Are we not right to think that God too says this? "I take it on myself; you are giving it to me." This is obviously the case if Christ is God, as we do not doubt, for he says, *I was hungry, and you fed me*. And when his hearers demur: *When did we see you hungry?* his reply shows that he is the warranty of the poor and the sponsor for all his members, for he is the Head and they are the limbs of his body, so that when the members are given anything, the Head receives it. *When you did that for even the least of those who are mine*, he says, *you did it for me* (Mt 25:35,37,40).

Well now, you grasping creditor, calculate what you have given, and balance it against what you will receive. Suppose you had advanced a small sum of money, and the person to whom you had given it had repaid you with a stately house, worth incomparably more than the money you had lent, how grateful you would be! You would be beside yourself with joy. Listen then to what property he promises you in return, he to whom you lent your goods: *Come, you who are blessed by my Father, take possession of . . .* Of what? Merely what you gave? By no means. All you gave was earthly wealth, which would have rotted in the earth if you had not given it away. What would you have done with it, if you had not given it? But as it is, what would have rotted on earth is kept safe for you in heaven. What we shall receive is what has been stored there for us, and what is stored is merit. Your treasure has turned into your merit. Look what you are entitled to: *take possession of the kingdom prepared for you since the creation of the world*. What about the others, the people who refused to lend; what will they be told? *Depart into the eternal fire which was prepared for the devil and his angels*. And what is the name of the kingdom we are to receive? The next line tells you, listen: *the wicked will go into eternal burning, but the righteous into eternal life* (Mt 25:34,41,46). Aim for this, buy yourselves this, lend with this in view. You contemplate Christ enthroned in heaven, but begging on earth. Now we have discovered how the righteous person must practice usury. *All day long he shows mercy and lends*.

Blessed sowing

7. *And his seed will be blessed*. Let us not take this in a material sense either. We see plenty of descendants of righteous people dying of hunger, so how can it be true that the just man's *seed will be blessed*? His "seed" is what survives him; it is what he sows here, and will reap from hereafter. This is why the apostle says,

Let us not weary of doing good, for in his time we shall reap without weariness. So while we still have the opportunity, let us do good to all (Gal 6:9-10). This is your "seed," this is what will be blessed. You commit your seed to the earth, and harvest far more than you sowed; do you fear to suffer loss when you commit it to Christ? In another text, speaking about alms, the apostle calls them "seed" more expressly: *Whoever sows sparingly will also reap sparingly, and whoever sows blessings will have blessings for a harvest* (2 Cor 9:6).

But perhaps you find sowing hard work, and commiserating with the miserable is painful. One day we shall be in better case, for there will be no one needing our alms. When we are all invested with incorruptibility no one will be hungry, so you will not need to hand out bread to anyone, no one will be thirsty and looking to you for a drink, no one naked for you to clothe, no one a traveler asking you for hospitality. In this world we are sowing our seed amid afflictions, trials, pain and groaning; but look at another psalm: *they went on their way weeping, as they scattered their seed.* But their *seed will be blessed*; listen to what follows: *when they come back they will come leaping for joy, carrying their sheaves* (Ps 125(126):6).

Verse 27. Avoid evil but also do good

8. Take note of the next verse, then, and don't be lazy: *turn away from evil, and do good.* Do not imagine that you have done enough if you have refrained from stealing anyone's clothes. By not stripping someone, you have turned away from evil, but be careful not to dry up at that point and remain barren. You must take care not to strip someone of his clothes, certainly, but you must also clothe another who is naked; this is what turning away from evil and doing good implies. "What will I get out of it?" did you say? He to whom you are lending has already told you what recompense he will make to you: he will give you eternal life, so be easy in your mind and give to him. There is something further that you need to hear: *turn away from evil and do good, and live for ever.* When you make your gift, do not suppose that no one sees you. And when you have given alms to a poor person and incurred some loss thereby, or you feel regret about what has been given away, do not suppose that God has left you in the lurch. You may say to yourself, "What have I got out of doing good deeds? I don't think God loves benevolent people." Where is the murmuring coming from, what are you all muttering about? There is always a chorus of voices with that tale to tell. Even as I speak each one of us is familiar with that story, whether on our own lips, or our neighbor's, or our friend's. May God stifle it; may he eradicate the thorns from his field, and plant productively; may he plant a tree that will bear good fruit. Why be downcast, human creature, because you have given to the poor and so lost something? Do you not see that what you have really lost is what you refused to give? Why not keep your eyes on your God? Where is your faith? Fast asleep,

is it? Wake it up in your heart. Listen to what the Lord himself told you when he exhorted you to perform good deeds of this kind: *"Get yourselves purses that do not wear out, and a treasure in heaven that never fails, where no thief can reach it* (Lk 12:33). Remind yourself of this when you are lamenting a loss. What are you sad about, you foolish mortal, so mean of spirit, so sick-hearted? Why have you lost your goods? Only because you would not lend them to me.[10] Why have you lost them? Who took them away from you? 'A thief,' you will reply. Didn't I warn you to keep them where no thief could break in?" Any of us who bemoan a loss, then, must bemoan our failure to place our goods where they could not perish.

Verse 28. Hidden and visible judgment

9. *For the Lord loves judgment and will not abandon his holy ones.* When the saints are having a hard time, do not suppose that God is not exercising judgment, or that he is judging perversely. If he commands you to judge justly, is he likely to exercise perverse judgment himself? *He loves judgment and will not abandon his holy ones.* But his way of judging is hidden, as the life of his holy ones is hidden in him. Those who now struggle on earth resemble trees which in winter have no fruit or leaves; but when he appears, like a newly-risen sun, the life that was latent in the root shows itself in the fruits. So he *loves judgment and will not abandon his holy ones.* But what if a holy person is racked with hunger? God will not abandon him, but he whips every child he acknowledges as his.[11] You make light of God's child when he is being whipped, but hold him in awe when God is treating him generously. What kind of whips are used on him? Oppressive temporal circumstances. And when will that generous reward be his? When he hears the words, *Come, you who are blessed by my Father, take possession of the kingdom prepared for you since the creation of the world* (Mt 25:34). Do not shrink from your beating, if you want to be among those worthy to be acknowledged as God's true children. So dearly does he love judgment that he does not abandon those holy ones whom he scourges for a time. And because he whips every child he acknowledges as his, he did not spare even the only-begotten Son, in whom he found no fault at all. *For the Lord loves judgment and will not abandon his holy ones.* Does that mean he will give them the things you set store by on earth—to live many years, to last into old age? You do not seem to notice that if you hope to see old age, you hope for something you will complain about when you get it.

Your soul may be ill-disposed, or weak, or limited in its outlook, and if so, do not let it say, "How can it be true that *the Lord loves judgment, and will not*

10. Variant in some codices: " . . . entrust them to me."
11. See Heb 12:6.

abandon his holy ones? Admittedly he did not abandon the three youths who sang his praises in the furnace, untouched by the fire;[12] but were the Maccabees not his saints too? Their bodies succumbed to the fire, though their faith never failed.[13] And this raises a serious question, because although they did not fall away from their faith, God forsook them." So you may think, but you must listen to the next words in the psalm: *They will be kept safe for ever*. You were hoping that they would be spared for a few more years, thinking that if God granted this he would obviously not be abandoning his holy ones. But while in a visible manner he did not abandon the three youths, in a hidden manner he did not abandon the Maccabees either. To the former he gave temporal life to shame the unbelievers; but the latter he secretly crowned that they might judge their godless persecutor. So he abandoned neither the one nor the other, he who *will not abandon his holy ones*. In fact if the three youths had not been kept safe for eternity, they would not have received anything worth mentioning. But the psalm asserts, *they will be kept safe for ever*.

10. *But the unjust will be punished, and the seed of the godless will perish*. As the sowing of the righteous will be blessed, so will the seed of the godless perish. The seed or issue of the godless must mean their wicked deeds, for we often find the son of a godless person flourishing in this world, and sometimes even turning into a righteous person and flourishing in Christ. Be careful, then, how you take this statement. Make sure you open the roof and reach Christ; do not take it in a carnal sense or you may be misled. The issue of the godless, in the sense of all the works of the godless, will perish; they will bear no fruit. They seem to achieve something for a time, but later they will look for the work they did, and not find it. We hear in another text the voice of those whose whole achievement has gone for nothing: *What good has our pride done us, what benefit has come to us from our vaunted wealth? All these things have passed away like a shadow* (Wis 5:8-9). This is how *the seed of the godless will perish*.

Verse 29. The land of the living

11. *The righteous will possess the earth*[14] *as their inheritance*. Here again take care that avarice does not creep up on you, seeming to promise you some rich estate. If here below you are commanded not to set your heart on such things, you should not hope to get them in heaven. The "earth" in this promise is the land of the living, the realm of the saints. Another psalm speaks of it: *You are my hope, my portion in the land of the living* (Ps 141:6(142:5)). If your life is the life the psalmist has in mind, consider what kind of land you are to receive. It is

---

12. See Dn 3:50.
13. See 2 Mac 7.
14. Augustine's use of *terra* fluctuates in meaning between "land" and "earth."

the land of the living. Our earth here is the land of the dying, the earth that will receive the dead whom it nourished while they were alive. Land and life are of a kind; where life is eternal, the land is eternal too. How will that earth be eternal? *They will dwell in it for ever and ever.* It will be a different earth then, that earth that is to be our home for ever; for of this present earth the Lord said, *Heaven and earth will pass away* (Mt 24:35).

Verses 30-32. The security of the just

12. *The mouth of the righteous will muse on wisdom.* Here is that bread again; look how eagerly the just person munches it, how he relishes wisdom in his mouth. *And his tongue will speak judgment. The law of his God is in his heart.* This is added to exclude the notion that he might have anything in his mouth that he does not have in his heart, and to make sure you do not count him as one of those of whom the Lord says, *This people honors me with its lips, but its heart is far from me* (Is 29:13).[15] *His tongue will speak judgment. The law of God is in his heart.* What good does that do him? The psalm goes on to tell us: *He will not be tripped as he walks.* The word of God in his heart frees him from the snare, the word of God in his heart steers him clear of the crooked path, the word of God in his heart keeps him steady in a slippery place. If God's word never leaves your heart, God is with you. What evil can befall anyone whom God is guarding? You set a guard in your vineyard and you feel safe from thieves; but the guard may fall asleep, he may lapse and let the thief in; but he who guards Israel never slumbers, never sleeps.[16] *The law of his God is in his heart, and he will not be tripped as he walks.* Let him live free from anxiety, then, even amid evildoers let him live without anxiety, even amid the godless let him live without anxiety. What harm can a godless or an unjust enemy do to the just person? He may try, as the next line suggests: *the sinner spies on the just, and seeks to kill him*, for the sinner's thoughts are along the lines foretold by the Book of Wisdom: *The very sight of him vexes us, for his life is unlike that of other people* (Wis 2:15). That is why the sinner seeks to kill the just. What of it? The Lord guards him, lives with him, and never leaves his mouth or his heart; is he likely to forsake him? What would have become of the promise we heard just now: *he will not abandon his holy ones*?

Verse 33. The persecutor's dominance is illusory

13. *The sinner spies on the just and seeks to kill him, but the Lord will not leave the just in his hands.* Then why did he leave the martyrs in the hands of the

15. Compare Mt 15:18; Mk 7:6.
16. See Ps 120(121):4.

godless? Why were the persecutors able to do what they liked to them? Some they struck down with the sword, others they crucified, others they threw to wild beasts, others they roasted in the fire. Others again were marched in chains until they dropped dead from exhaustion. It is certain that the Lord will not abandon his holy ones—but what does this mean: *the Lord will not leave the just in the hands* of the persecutor? Did he not leave even his own Son in the hands of the Jews? Why? Here again you must open the roof if you want your inner wounds bound up, wherever they are in your spirit. Make your way through to the Lord, listen to the words of scripture in another text. It foresaw that the Lord would suffer under the onslaught of the impious, and what did it say? *Earth has been given over into the hands of the ungodly* (Jb 9:24). What does that suggest—*earth has been given over into the hands of the ungodly*? It means that flesh was surrendered into the hands of persecutors. But God did not abandon his righteous servant there, because from the captive flesh he led forth the unconquered soul. God would indeed have abandoned his righteous servant in the hands of the godless if he had caused him to consent to the wishes of the godless. A just person prays against such a calamity in another psalm: *Do not let me be betrayed by my desire, Lord, and delivered to the sinner* (Ps 139:9(140:8)). It is very important that you should not be betrayed to the sinner by your own desire; if your desire is for this present life it may drive you straight into his arms and you may lose eternal life. By what desire does the just person risk being betrayed to the sinner? By that which scripture mentions elsewhere: *I have never craved the human light of day, as you know* (Jer 17:16). If someone desires and craves this human daylight, and the enemy threatens to take it away from him by killing him, then faced with the prospect of losing this life, and with no hope of any other life, the threatened prisoner gives way and yields to the enemy's demands. But the believer hears the Lord's warning, *Do not be afraid of those who kill the body, but cannot kill the soul* (Mt 10:28), and even if he or she is like earth given over into the hands of the ungodly, the spirit escapes though the earth is captive, and if the spirit escapes, the very earth will rise again. The spirit migrates to the Lord, earth to heaven. No least portion of that earth perishes, delivered though it is for a time into the hands of the ungodly. *The very hairs on your head are numbered* (Mt 10:30). The persecuted are secure, but only if God dwells within them. If the devil is cast out, God is admitted.

The Lord will not leave the just in his hands, nor will God condemn him, when the time comes for him to be judged. Some Greek codices have *and when God judges him, judgment will be given for him.* This expression, *for him*, is like the one we use when we say to someone, "Give judgment for me," meaning, "Hear my case." God will indeed hear the case of his just servant, for *we will all have to stand before Christ's judgment seat, that each of us may receive due recompense for what we have done in the body, good or bad* (2 Cor 5:10); and when the time comes for the persecuted just one to appear before that tribunal, God will not condemn him, even though he seemed for a time to be condemned by a human judge. Although the governor sentenced Cyprian,[17] an earthly judgment seat is one thing, the heavenly tribunal quite another. Cyprian received his sentence from the judge below, but his crown from One on high. *Nor will God condemn him, when the time comes for him to be judged.*

Verses 34-36. The rapid disappearance of the ungodly

14. But when will that be? Do not imagine it will happen immediately: this is the time for hard work, the time for sowing, the season when the weather is still cold. Sow your seed, then, even if the winds are howling round you and the rain pouring down. Do not be lazy; summer will come to gladden you, and then you will be happy that you sowed. "So what must I do now?" *Wait for the Lord.* "And while I am waiting, what am I to do?" *Keep to his ways.* "And if I keep them, what will I get?" *He will exalt you to possess the earth for your inheritance.* "What earth will that be?" Here again be careful not to dream about that stately home; keep in mind the inheritance the Lord promises: *Come, you whom my Father has blessed; take possession of the kingdom prepared for you since the world was made* (Mt 25:34). "But what of those who have harassed us, who have set us groaning, whose offensive behavior we have had to endure, those for whom we have prayed in vain as they raged against us—what of them?" The next line tells you: *When sinners perish, you will see.* And what a good view you will have! You will be at Christ's right hand, they at his left. But it is the eyes of faith that are needed here. People who lack the eyes of faith resent the happiness[18] of the wicked, and think that their own righteous lives are pointless, because they can see the godless flourishing. But what says the person who has the eye of faith? *I saw the godless exalting himself very high, overtopping the cedars of Lebanon.* Well, suppose he or she is exalted, lifted up very high, what follows? *But I passed further on, and look! he was not there; I searched for him, but his place was not to be seen.* Why was he not there, why was his place to be seen no longer? Because you have passed on further. If, on the contrary, you are still thinking in carnal terms, and the earthly happiness available here seems to you true happiness, you have not passed on further. Either you are on a par with the godless person or you are lower than he. Gain ground, press on; and when you have made progress and gone further, use the eyes of your faith, and consider his ultimate destiny. You will say to yourself, "Look! The one who puffed himself up like that is not here now!" It is as though you were making

17. The governor was Galerius Maximus. Cyprian died on 14 September, 258, under the Emperor Valerian.
18. Variant: "are attracted by the happiness. . . ."

your way forward past a cloud of smoke. In this same psalm we had a reference to that: *they will disappear, fading away like smoke* (v. 20). Smoke sails upward and forms a billowing sphere; the higher it rises, the more swollen this sphere becomes. But once you have passed on further, look behind you, for what is behind you is smoke, if God is ahead of you. I do not mean look back longingly, as Lot's wife did, only to remain stuck on the path;[19] look down on it, and you will not see the ungodly anywhere; you will need to search for his place. What is this place of his? It is his present station, where he wields power, enjoys wealth, and has his proper rank in human society, so that many people bend to his whims, and he gives orders and is obeyed. This place of his will not exist any longer; it will pass away, so that you[20] will be able to say, *I passed on further, and look! he was not there*. Passed on further—in what sense? I made progress, I arrived at spiritual understanding, I entered God's holy place[21] to see what would happen at the end. *And look! he was not there; I searched for him, but his place was not to be seen.*

Verses 37-38. Innocence, a straight eye, and a promised future

15. *Guard your innocence*. Hold onto it, as you used to hold tight to your purse when you were greedy for money. As you used to clutch your purse close, in case a thief might try to snatch it from you, so now guard your innocence, lest the devil try to snatch it. Let innocence be your secure inheritance, for of that both rich and poor may feel secure. *Guard your innocence*. What is the use of gaining gold, and losing your innocence? *Guard your innocence, and look in the right direction*. Have eyes that see straight, not astigmatic eyes that see evil and twisted people, eyes that squint so badly that God himself appears to you distorted and crooked, because he favors the godless and persecutes the faithful. Do you not perceive how distorted your vision is? Correct your eyesight and *look in the right direction*. What is the right direction? Do not fix your gaze on things that belong to the present world. Then what will you see? *That there is a future in store for a peaceful person*. What does that mean, *a future in store*? When you die, you will not be dead; that is what it means by *a future in store*. There will be a future for such a person even when this life is over, a future for that "seed" which will be blessed. This is why the Lord promised, *Any who believe in me, though they die, shall yet live* (Jn 11:25). *There is a future in store for a peaceful person.*

---

19. See Gn 19:26.
20. Variant: " . . . any longer; but as for you, pass by, so that you. . . ."
21. See Ps 72(73):17.

16. *But the unjust will perish entirely*. What does *entirely*[22] mean? Perhaps "for ever" or "all at once and all together." *The future hopes of the godless will come to nothing*. But for the peacemakers there will be a future, so we infer that those who are not peacemakers are godless. And the gospel confirms this, for peacemakers are blessed, because they will be called children of God.[23]

Verses 39-40. The final discrimination

17. *But the salvation of the just is from the Lord. He is their protector in time of trouble; the Lord will help them and rescue them and deliver them from sinners*. For the present let the just tolerate sinners, the wheat tolerate the tares, the grain tolerate the chaff; for the time will come for them to be separated, and the good seed will be sorted out from the refuse to be burnt up. The one will be taken into the barn, the other thrown onto the eternal bonfire; because the reason for the intermingling of the just and the unjust in the time of preparation was that the unjust might try to overthrow the just, and[24] the just thereby be tested, but that afterwards the unjust might be condemned and the just crowned.[25]

Conclusion: Donatist onslaughts

18. Thanks be to God, brothers and sisters: in the name of Christ we have paid our debt now, though charity holds us as perpetual debtors. Charity is the one thing that is always still owing, even if we pay it out every day.

We have said many things against the Donatists, and read out documents and decrees to you at length. Much of what we read to you is outside the canon of scripture; but they forced us to do it. If they reprove us for reading out such material to you, we gladly accept the reproof, provided you have been instructed in the process. On this score we may well reply to them in the apostle's words: *I have behaved foolishly, but you left me no option* (2 Cor 12:11). But above all, brothers and sisters, guard our inheritance, the inheritance of which we are rendered utterly certain by our Father's will and testament: not by any light-weight document of human origin, but by our Father's will and testament. This gives us complete assurance, because the testator is alive; he who drew up that will in favor of his heir himself proves the will. In human transactions the testator is one person and the adjudicator is another. The person named in the will establishes his or her right before the adjudicator, but not before the other one, who could have decided the matter, because he is dead. How secure is our

22. *In idipsum*.
23. See Mt 5:9.
24. Variant: ". . . might be overthrown and. . . ."
25. Augustine seems not to have quoted the final words of the psalm, but some codices supply them here.

claim, then! He who is to adjudicate is he who made the will; for even though Christ was dead for a time, he is now alive for ever.

Augustine's past life, target of Donatist attacks

19. Let them speak against us as they will, but let us love them even against their will. We know their slanders, brothers and sisters, well do we know them; but let us not be angry with them over the slanders; along with me you must bear with them patiently. They see that they have no case to make, so they turn their tongues against me and begin to slander me, alleging many things they know about, and many others of which they know nothing. What they do know are episodes in my past life; for, as the apostle says, I was once foolish and unbelieving[26] and useless for any good purpose. In my perverse error I was devoid of wisdom, demented. I do not deny it. And in not denying my own past, I am all the more praising our God, who has forgiven it.[27]

What are you hoping to gain, then, you heretic, by turning aside from the point at issue and making personal attacks instead? What am I? I ask you, what am I? Am I the Catholic Church? Am I the inheritance of Christ, diffused throughout the nations? It is enough for me to have a place within it. You disparage my past life, but what advantage do you gain from that? I take a more severe view of my misdeeds than you do; you have merely disparaged them, but I have condemned them. I wish you would take a leaf out of my book, so that at long last your error might be a past error, like mine!

These are the evil deeds of my past, which they know all about, especially those committed in this city.[28] Here I lived a bad life; I confess it. And in the measure that I rejoice in God's grace, in that same measure I—what shall I say? Deplore my past sins? Certainly I would deplore them if I were in them still. But I am not, so should I say rather that I rejoice over them? No, not that either, for I dearly wish those things had never happened. But whatever I have been is over and done with, in Christ's name. With regard to the present, their attacks deal with matters of which they know nothing. Certainly there are still faults in me that deserve their censure,[29] but they are not in a position to know about these. I have plenty of trouble in my thoughts, fighting against my sinful impulses; I have a prolonged conflict, a conflict that never seems to stop, with the temptations of the enemy who strives to overpower me. I groan to God in my weakness, and he who knows what I spawned in the past knows what my heart is bringing to birth now. But, as the apostle says, *it matters very little to me that I am judged by*

---

26. See Ti 3:3.
27. This is the logic of his greatest work, *The Confessions*, of which there are many echoes in the following lines.
28. Carthage, scene of his sins as a student; see Book III of *The Confessions*.
29. Variant: "which I must censure."

you or by any human day of reckoning, but neither do I judge myself (1 Cor 4:3). I know myself better than they do, but God knows me better than I know myself.

So do not let them scoff at you on our account; Christ forbid! For they jeer, "Who are these? Where do they come from? We know those bad fellows here, but where were they baptized?"[30] If they know us so well they must know that we traveled abroad. They know too that we came back very different from what we were when we set out. No, we were not baptized here, but the church where we were baptized[31] is known throughout the world. Plenty of our brethren know that we were baptized, and some were baptized with us. This is easy enough to check, if anyone in the congregation is anxious on this score. But what about the outsiders? Are we likely to satisfy them, or prove anything to them from the testimony of a church with which they are not in communion? How can they possibly be sure that we were baptized in Christ overseas, when they do not have any overseas Christ? The only person who does possess Christ overseas is the one who holds fast to the communion of the universal Church, abroad as well as at home. How can a Donatist, whose communion scarcely reaches across the sea, know where I was baptized? Really, brothers and sisters, I do not know what to say to them. Surmise what you like about us. If we are good, we are the wheat in Christ's Church; if we are bad, we are the chaff in Christ's Church; but either way we have not left the threshing floor. But you who were wafted away from it by the wind of temptation, what are you? No wind lifts grain from the threshing-floor. So think where you are, and from that infer what you are.

Keep to the point: what matters is the truth

20. "Who are you to make such allegations against us?" the Donatist asks. Whoever I may be, concentrate on what is said, not on who says it. "But," he replies, "the Lord says to the sinner, *What right have you to take my covenant on your lips?*" (Ps 49(50):16) Yes, perhaps the Lord does say that to a sinner, and perhaps there are some kinds of sinners to whom that rightly applies; but whomsoever the Lord means when he says it, what he is saying is that the sinner gains nothing at all by mouthing God's law. But he does not say that the hearer gains nothing, does he? Now when the Lord speaks in the Church, we have both kinds speaking, good and bad. When the good ones preach, what do they say? *Be imitators of me, as I am of Christ* (1 Cor 4:16). And what does scripture say to these good preachers? *Be an example to the faithful* (1 Tm 4:12). That is what we are laboring to be; but what we are, he alone knows, to whom we offer our groaning. But of bad preachers something different is said. *The scribes and*

30. The plurals here are not the episcopal "we"; Augustine is associating with himself his former friends and companions. One at least, Alypius, was a fellow-bishop now.

31. Milan, where Augustine was baptized by Ambrose at the Easter Vigil, 24-25 April, 387. See *The Confessions*, IX,6,14.

Pharisees have taken their place in the chair of Moses; do what they tell you, but do not imitate what they do (Mt 23:2-3). You can see that in this chair of Moses, which has been superseded now by Christ's chair, bad men sit as well as good, yet the bad do no harm to their listeners. Why then have you repudiated the chair itself, because of some bad occupants? Come back into peace; come back to the concord that can have caused you no offense. If I say good things, and do good things, imitate me; but if I do not act in accord with what I say, follow the Lord's advice: do what I say, but do not imitate what I do. But whichever is the case, do not forsake the chair of Catholic teaching.

Well now, brothers and sisters, we are about to go forth in Christ's name, and they will have plenty to say. How shall we conclude? Take care to dismiss my case summarily. Say nothing to them except this: "Keep to the point, friends. Augustine is a bishop in the Catholic Church, he has his own burden to bear and he will have to render an account to God. I have known some good of him. If he is bad, he knows it himself, but if he is good, he is not the foundation of my hope for all that. This above all I have learned in the Catholic Church, not to set my hope on any human being. It is understandable that you reproach us for the human faults among us, because you do set your hope on human beings."

Be clear about this, brothers and sisters. When they criticize us, you can be as dismissive as they are. We know what a place we have in your hearts, because we know the place you have in ours. Do not engage in battle against them to defend us. Whatever they say about us, pass over it briskly, lest you become so embroiled in defending our cause that you lose your own. This is part of their cunning. They are afraid we will discuss the real issue, and they want to prevent it; so they batter us with irrelevancies, hoping to keep us so busy exonerating ourselves that we stop trying to convict them of error.

Anyway, if you Donatists call me bad, that is nothing to the hundred-and-one bad things I could say of myself. So leave that aside, stop nagging about my case. Keep to the point, concentrate on the Church's case, consider your own position. From whatever quarter the truth addresses you, welcome it hungrily. Otherwise the bread may never come your way, because you with your malicious spirit are always fastidiously looking for something to criticize about the dish.

Exposition of Psalm 37

A Sermon to the People

Introduction: this psalm could belong to the Canaanite woman

1. The verse we have sung would have been highly suitable on the lips of the woman we heard about when the gospel was read: *I will proclaim my iniquity aloud, and take serious thought for my sin.* The Lord called her a "dog" in view of her sins, saying, *It is not good to give the children's bread to the dogs* (Mt 15:26). But she knew how to proclaim her iniquity aloud, and to take serious thought for her sin, so she did not deny what Truth had said. Rather did she confess her misery and obtain mercy,[1] seeking healing for her sin; for she had begged a cure for her daughter, and perhaps her daughter symbolized her life. Give us your attention now, as we study and expound the whole psalm, to the best of our ability. May the Lord be present to our hearts, so that we may find in it helpful things to say, and bring forth what we have found. May the finding not be too difficult, nor the utterance clumsy.

Verse 1. Wistfully remembering the Sabbath rest

2. The psalm is entitled, *A psalm for David himself, for a remembrance of the Sabbath.* If we investigate what is written about the holy prophet David, who was the ancestor of our Lord Jesus Christ according to the flesh, we do not find among the various good things that scripture reports about him that he ever "remembered the Sabbath." Why should it be so "remembered"? Since the Jews observed the Sabbath as they did, why should something that inevitably recurred every seven days need to be "remembered"? It was to be observed, but not "remembered" in that sense. No one remembers a thing unless it is absent. In this city of ours,[2] for instance, you remember Carthage, where you were some time or other; today you remember yesterday, or some day last year; or you remember some earlier year, or something you did some time ago, or where you were, or some event in which you played a part. But what does "remembering the Sabbath" mean, brothers and sisters? Does anyone call the Sabbath to mind in an act of remembrance like that? And what Sabbath is this, that is remembered with

1. A variant supported by most codices has "But she confessed his mercy and all the more obtained it."
2. Hippo, evidently.

the groaning we find in the psalm? While it was being read you heard, and as we unravel it you will hear again, how intense are the grief, the groaning, the weeping, the misery, that are there expressed.

Yet a person who is miserable in this sense is truly happy. In the gospel the Lord called mourners blessed.[3] How can anyone who is mourning be blessed? And how blessed, if he or she is miserable? But I tell you, such a person would really be miserable if he were not mourning. Here too in our psalm we must recognize this unknown mourner in the same sense; and how blessed we should be if we could be this unknown speaker! We meet here someone who is suffering, groaning, mourning, and remembering the Sabbath. The Sabbath is rest. The speaker was unquestionably in some kind of restless trouble, when with sighs he was remembering that rest.

Verses 2-3. Chastened by fire

3. He therefore describes the restless trouble in which he found himself, and commends it to God, for he is apprehensive about some calamity even worse than what he is already undergoing. There is no doubt that he is in some bad predicament; he says so plainly, and we need no interpreter, no guesswork or conjecture. His own words leave no doubt about what turmoil he is in; we do not need to look for it, but only to attend to what he is saying. Yet he is anxious about some further impending catastrophe, worse than the trouble in which he is embroiled already, so he begins by pleading, *Lord, do not rebuke me in your wrath, nor chasten me in your anger*. Certain people are destined to be chastened by God's anger in the future, and rebuked in his wrath. It may be that not all those who are rebuked will be chastened as a result, but some at least will be saved through that chastening which is to come. This will certainly happen, because otherwise it would not be called a "chastening," but it will take place as though through fire. Others there will be who are rebuked, but not chastened, for Christ will certainly rebuke those to whom he is to say, *I was hungry and you did not feed me; I was thirsty and you gave me nothing to drink* (Mt 25:42). And he will continue with the rest of the tale, chiding the wicked on his left for their inhumanity and sterile lives. To them it will be said, *Depart from me, you accursed, into the eternal fire which was prepared for the devil and his angels* (Mt 25:41).The psalmist is very much afraid of more terrible possibilities, worse than anything he bewails and groans over in this life, so he pleads, *Lord, do not rebuke me in your wrath*. Let me not be numbered among those to whom you will say, *Depart into the eternal fire which was prepared for the devil and his angels*. By pleading, *Do not chasten me in your anger,* the psalmist asks, "Purify me in this life, and make me such that I will not need that chastening fire"; this

3. See Mt 5:5.

prayer he makes with an eye to those who will be saved, but only as through fire. And why? Because here on earth they built on a foundation of wood or hay or straw. They ought to have built on gold, or silver, or precious stones,[4] and then they would have been safe from both kinds of fire: not only the eternal fire which will torture the impious for ever, but even that which will chasten those who are to be saved through it. Scripture says of the shoddy builder, *He himself will be saved indeed, though it be through fire* (1 Cor 3:15). Perhaps some people may trivialize this fire, because scripture says, *He will be saved.* Yet even though it will be for some the means of salvation, that fire will nevertheless be harder to bear than anything we can endure in this life. Think about it: how grievously the wicked have suffered, and can suffer, here. Yet for all that, they suffer no more grievously than good people do. What has any criminal, any thief, adulterer, villain or sacrilegious rascal ever suffered under the law, which a martyr has not also suffered for confessing Christ? The evils that threaten us here are far more tolerable, yet look how people will do whatever you order them in order to escape such pains! How much better advised would they be to do what God orders them, to escape far more severe penalties!

4. But why does the psalmist beg not to be rebuked in God's wrath, or chastened in his anger? Because he means to say to God, "Already the pains I am enduring are many and grievous, so let them suffice, I beg you." And he begins to enumerate them, as though making satisfaction to God and offering what he suffers, in the hope of not having to suffer anything worse: *for your arrows have found their mark in me, and you have laid upon me your heavy hand.*

Verse 4. True health is reserved for the future

5. *There is no soundness in my flesh in the presence of your anger.* Now he begins to relate what he has been suffering, yet already the trouble he mentions is a consequence of the Lord's anger, because it derives from the punishment he inflicted. What punishment was that? The penalty he imposed on Adam. Did he not truly punish Adam, did the Lord not mean what he said when he warned them, *You will certainly die* (Gn 2:17)? Do we suffer anything in this life that is not a consequence of the death we incurred through the first sin? We carry with us a mortal body (though it should not have been mortal), a mortal body seething with temptations and unease, a prey to corporal pains and manifold needs, a body changeable and of puny strength even when it is well, because it obviously is not completely well yet. Why does the psalmist say, *There is no soundness in my flesh*, if not because what passes for good health in this life is no health at all to those who have true understanding and remember the Sabbath? If you have not eaten, hunger causes you disquiet, and hunger is a kind of natural illness,

4. See 1 Cor 3:12.

because the pain imposed as a punishment has become an aspect of nature to us. What was a penalty to our first parents is for us a natural condition. This is why the apostle says, *By nature we too were children of wrath, like the rest* (Eph 2:3). *By nature children of wrath*, he says, which means bearers of the burden of punishment. But why does he say, *We were*? Because though we still are in fact, in hope we are so no longer. We have better reason to state what we are in hope, because in our hope we are entirely confident. There is no shadow of uncertainty about our hope that could make us doubtful about it. Listen to what glory is inherent in this hope: *We groan inwardly as we await our adoption as God's children, the redemption of our bodies* (Rom 8:23). What? Are you not yet redeemed, Paul? Has your ransom not been paid? Has that blood not already been poured out for you? And is it not the ransom for us all? Most certainly it is. But look at his next words: *In hope we have been saved. But if hope is seen, it is hope no longer, for when someone sees what he hopes for, why should he hope for it? But if we hope for what we do not see, we wait for it in patience* (Rom 8:24-25). Now what is he waiting for in patience? Salvation. Salvation of what? Of his very body, for he says, *The redemption of our bodies*. If Paul was waiting for the salvation of his body, the salvation he already had was not full salvation. No, you will be hungry; and thirst kills you, if not relieved. The medicine that cures hunger is food, the medicine that cures thirst is a drink, the medicine for tiredness is sleep. Withhold the medicines, and see if living creatures do not die of these ailments. If you can give up these things and not be ill, that is true health. But if your condition is such that not eating could kill you, do not boast about your health, but await with groaning the redemption of your body. Rejoice that you have been redeemed; but know that you are secure in hope, not yet in fact. Indeed, unless you groan in your hoping, you will never arrive at the reality.

Our present state is not yet one of health, then, so the psalmist laments, *There is no soundness in my flesh in the presence of your anger*. Where do they come from, the arrows that have found their mark in him? Perhaps what he calls arrows are the punishment, God's vengeance itself, plus the pains of mind and body which are unavoidable in this life. Holy Job also mentioned arrows of this sort; amid his woes he said that the arrows of the Lord had lodged in him.[5] However, we customarily take arrows as representing God's words, so surely it is impossible for anyone struck by them to suffer in this way? The arrows of God's words inflame love, not pain. Or is it that love itself cannot be free from pain? Yes, surely that is true, because if we love something and do not possess it, we inevitably feel pain. The only person who loves without experiencing any pain is the one who possesses the loved object; but, as I have said, anyone who loves but does not yet possess must of necessity groan with pain. This is why Christ's bride in the Song of Songs, speaking for the Church, cries out, *I am wounded*

5. See Jb 6:4.

with love (Sg 2:5, LXX). She says that charity has wounded her because something she loves is not yet hers, so she suffers, not yet possessing it. If she is suffering pain, she rightly says she is wounded, but this wound is sweeping her on toward true health. Anyone who has not been wounded in this fashion will find that true health is out of reach. Does that mean that the wounded person will remain in a wounded state for ever? No, certainly not. So we could understand the unerring arrows in this sense: "Your words have found their mark in my heart, and lodging there they have made me remember the Sabbath. But recalling the Sabbath without as yet having a secure hold on it makes me realize that I cannot rejoice yet. It shows me that the health I now have in my flesh is not yet true health, nor does it deserve to be called so in comparison with the health I shall enjoy in everlasting rest, when this corruptible nature has been clothed in incorruption, this mortal nature in immortality.[6] Compared with the health I shall have then, the health I have now is no better than disease."

The voice of the Head, the voice of his body: two in one flesh

6. *There is no peace in my bones in the face of my sins*. The question usually asked is, "Who is speaking here?"[7] Some take this to be Christ's voice, on account of all that is said a little later about his passion. We shall come to these statements shortly, and we too shall discover that they are indeed made about the passion of Christ. But how can one who was guilty of no sin say, *There is no peace in my bones in the face of my sins*? The need to make sense of this forces us to recognize that "Christ" here is the full Christ, the whole Christ; that is, Christ, Head and body. When Christ speaks, he sometimes does so in the person of the Head alone, the Savior who was born of the virgin Mary; but at other times he speaks in the person of his body, holy Church diffused throughout the world. We are within his body, provided that we have sincere faith in him, and unshakable hope, and burning charity. We are within his body, we are members of it, and we find ourselves speaking those words. The apostle confirms the fact. *We are members of his body*, he states (Eph 5:30), and he reiterates this in many of his letters. If we deny that these words in our psalm are the words of Christ, we should have to deny it also of that other cry, *My God, my God, why have you forsaken me?* In that earlier psalm you find, *My God, my God, why have you forsaken me? The tale of my sins leaves me far from salvation* (Ps 21:2(22:1)). The words we have in the present psalm, *in the face of my sins*, match those of the earlier one, *the tale of my sins*. Now we are quite certain that Christ was sinless

6. See 1 Cor 15:53.
7. The central question, to which Augustine's entire work on the psalms is an ever-repeated answer. The present section spells out his conviction on the subject. See Introduction, and note at Exposition 2 of Psalm 30, 3.

and free from all faults, so we might begin to think that these psalm-words are not his. Yet it would be very difficult, indeed wrong-headed, to maintain that the earlier psalm does not belong to Christ, when it describes his passion so plainly that it might almost be a reading from the gospel. We find there, *They shared out my garments among them, and cast lots for my tunic* (Ps 21:19(22:18)). And what about the fact that the Lord himself cried out on the cross, *My God, my God, why have you forsaken me?* (Mt 27:46)? What did he mean us to understand by that? Surely by reciting its first verse he was showing that the entire psalm refers to himself. But when the next line mentions *the tale of my sins* we cannot doubt that Christ is still speaking, so whose sins can these be, if not the sins of his body, the Church? The body of Christ is speaking as one with its Head. How can they speak with one voice? Because, says scripture, *they will be two in one flesh* (Gn 2:24). The apostle confirms it: *This is a great mystery, but I am referring it to Christ and the Church* (Eph 5:32). In the gospel the Lord himself replied in the same vein when they questioned him about divorce: *Have you never read what is written, that God created them male and female from the beginning? A man shall leave his father and mother, and be united to his wife, and they will be two in one flesh; so they are two no longer, but one flesh* (Mt 19:4-6). Since he himself declared that *they are two no longer, but one flesh*, is there anything strange in affirming that the one same flesh, the one same tongue, the same words, belong to the one flesh of Head and body?

Let us hear them as one single organism, but let us listen to the Head as Head, and the body as body. The persons are not separated, but in dignity they are distinct, for the Head saves and the body is saved. May the Head dispense mercy, and the body bemoan its misery. The role of the Head is to purge away sins, the body's to confess them. Wherever scripture does not indicate when the body is speaking, when the Head, we hear them speak with one single voice. We have to distinguish as we listen, but the voice is one. Why should he not speak of *my sins*, when he also claims, *I was hungry and you did not feed me; I was thirsty and you gave me nothing to drink; I was a stranger and you did not take me in; I was ill, and in prison, and you did not visit me* (Mt 25:42-43)? The Lord was certainly not in prison. Why should he not say it, though, when to their question, *When did we see you hungry, or thirsty, or in prison, and yet did not serve you?* he will reply, *As long as you did not do it for one of the least of those who are mine, you did not do it for me either* (Mt 25:44-45)? Why should he not say, *In the face of my sins*, he who cried out to Saul, *Saul, Saul, why are you persecuting me?* (Acts 9:4)? He most definitely had no one persecuting him in heaven. But just as on that occasion the Head was speaking on behalf of the body, so here too the Head speaks the words that properly belong to the body, and you hear them as the words of the Head too. Whenever you hear the voice of the body, do not separate it from the voice of the Head; and whenever you hear the voice of the Head, do not separate him from the body; for they are two no longer, but one flesh.

7. *There is no soundness in my flesh in the presence of your anger.* But perhaps, Adam, perhaps, O human race, God has been unjustly angry with you? It sounds like unjust anger on God's part, when humanity acknowledges the punishment it still suffers, even though it is already established in the body of Christ: *there is no soundness in my flesh in the presence of your anger.* Bring out into the open the justice of God's wrath, or you may look as though you are excusing yourself and accusing him. Go on with what you have to say, and show us where God's anger springs from. *There is no soundness in my flesh in the presence of your anger, nor peace in my bones.* Notice how the first part of each clause corresponds: *there is no soundness in my flesh* is repeated as *nor peace in my bones.* But notice also that the psalm does not repeat *in the presence of your anger*; instead it indicates the reason for God's anger. *There is no peace in my bones,* it says, *in the face of my sins.*

Verse 5. A weight on one's head

8. *Because my iniquities lifted up my head, they turned into a heavy burden weighing me down.* He puts the cause first, and describes the effect afterwards. In saying, *My iniquities lifted up my head,* he shows why the consequence came about, for no one is really proud except the sinner whose head is lifted high. Anyone who tosses his head in defiance of God is lifted up in this sense. Now when the passage from Ecclesiasticus was read you heard the warning, *The starting point of human pride is rebellion against God* (Sir 10:14) . When the first human refused to hear the commandment, iniquity lifted up his head against God. And because this was the sinner's condition, what did God do to him? *My iniquities turned into a heavy burden, weighing me down.* Lifting up one's head is an act of levity; anyone who does so feels there is no burden to bear. But because the sinner finds it such a light matter to lift himself up, he is given a weight to squash him down. His enterprise will rebound onto his own head, and his iniquities will descend to crown him.[8] *They turned into a heavy burden, weighing me down.*

Verse 6. The smell of sin

9. *My bruises have rotted and festered.* Obviously a bruised person is already in a bad state, but this case is worse, for the bruises themselves have rotted and festered. Why did they fester? Because they were rotten.[9] Is there anyone among

8. See Ps 7:17(16).
9. *Unde putuerunt? Quia computruerunt.*

us who does not know how this process takes place in human life? You only need a healthy sense of smell in spiritual matters to be aware how sins fester. The opposite to this reek of sin is the fragrance of which the apostle says, *We are the fragrance of Christ offered to God in every place, for those who are on the way to salvation* (2 Cor 2:15). But where does the fragrance come from? From hope. What is its source, if not the memory of the Sabbath? We bewail the bad smell in this life, but already we catch the scent of the life to come. We bewail our stinking sins, but breathe the fragrance of what awaits us. If that sweet scent were not soliciting us, we should never remember the Sabbath. But through the Spirit we can detect it, and can say to our Bridegroom, *Let us run toward the fragrance of your ointments* (Sg 1:3); so we avert our noses from our own stench and turn to him, and then we breathe a little more freely. Yet if our evil dealings were not still assailing us with their foul odor, we should not confess with sighs, *My bruises have rotted and festered.* And the cause? *In the face of my foolishness.* A little while ago he said, *In the face of my sins*; now he says, *In the face of my foolishness.*

Verse 7. Curvature of the heart

10. *I am afflicted with miseries and bowed down to the very end.* Why is the speaker bowed down? Because earlier he had been loftily proud. If you humble yourself you will be raised up, if you are proud and lofty you will be bent down, for God will certainly find a weight to bend you down with. The weight he will use is the burden of your sins. It will be tied onto your head and you will be bent over. Now what does it mean, to be bent down? It means that one cannot straighten up. That was the state of the woman whom the Lord found in the gospel: she had been bent over for eighteen years, and could not stand up straight.[10] All whose hearts are fixed on this earth are disabled in the same way. But since that woman found the Lord, and he healed her, let everyone with this infirmity hear the invitation, "Lift up your hearts!"[11] Insofar as the sinner is still bent over, he or she continues to groan, just as he too was bent down who said, *The corruptible body weighs down the soul, and this earthly dwelling oppresses a mind that considers many things* (Wis 9:15). Amid present woes let him sigh, that he may receive that other life later; let him remember the Sabbath, and by remembering deserve to attain it. The Sabbath that the Jews were accustomed to celebrate was a sign. A sign of reality—what reality? The reality the psalmist is remembering when he says, *I am afflicted with miseries and bowed down to the very end.* And what does *to the very end* signify? Even until death. *All day long I*

---

10. See Lk 13:11-13.
11. See note at Exposition of Psalm 10, 3. But the editors of Migne, PL, amend *audiat: sursum cor* to *habeat sursum cor*: "have his/her heart raised up."

was walking about in sorrow. By *all day long* he means without respite; *all day long* means throughout life. But when did the psalmist begin to take stock of his condition? Only when he began to remember the Sabbath. As long as he remembers something he does not yet possess, do you wonder that he goes about very sad? *All day long I was walking about in sorrow*.

Verse 8. Fantasies will be superseded by the vision of truth

11. *For my soul is full to the brim with deceitful fantasies, and there is no health in my flesh*. Soul and flesh—so this involves the whole human person. The soul is brimful of deceitful fantasies, and the flesh has no health in it; is there anywhere left where he can look to find joy? It is inevitable that he is very sorrowful, isn't it? *All day long I was walking about in sorrow*. Let sorrow be our lot until our soul is stripped of deceitful fantasies, and our body endued with health; for our real health is immortality. But if I try to list the deceitful fantasies that throng the soul, when would we ever find time enough? Is there anyone whose soul does not suffer them? I will remind you briefly how full our souls are with these lying fantasies. So insistent are they that we are scarcely permitted to pray. If we think about material things we have no way of doing so except through images, and often intrusive images rush in upon us, ones we are not seeking. We are tempted to pass from one to another, to flit hither and thither. Then you want to go back to your starting point and rid yourself of what you are currently thinking about, but something else occurs to you. You try to remember something you have forgotten, but it does not present itself to your mind; something else which you did not want comes instead. Where had that thing you had forgotten gone to? Why did it slip into your mind later, when you were no longer looking for it? While you were looking for it, innumerable other things occurred to you instead, things that were not required. I have sketched the situation briefly, brothers and sisters; I have sprinkled a few ideas upon you, so that if you take them in and go on thinking about them yourselves you will discover what it means to bewail the deceitful fantasies that invade our souls. These illusions came in as a penalty, and the soul lost the truth, for just as the deceitful fantasies are the soul's punishment, so is truth the soul's reward.

But when we were locked fast in those illusions, Truth came to us. He found us immersed in them, so he took our flesh, or rather took flesh from us, from the human race. He made himself visible to eyes of flesh in order to heal by faith those to whom he meant to manifest the truth, so that once those eyes were healed, truth might begin to dawn on them. He himself is the truth, and this truth he promised us when his flesh was made visible, so that there might be implanted in us the beginnings of that faith whose reward is truth. For Christ did not manifest himself to us on earth; what he manifested was his flesh. If he had manifested himself, the Jews would have seen and recognized him; but if they had recognized him they would never have crucified the Lord of glory.[12] What about his disciples, though; perhaps they did see him, when they asked him, *Show us the Father, and that is enough for us* (Jn 14:8)? No; wishing to make it evident that until then he had not been seen by them, he replied, *Have I been all this time with you, and yet you have not truly seen me? Whoever has seen me, Philip, has seen the Father* (Jn 14:9). If they had been truly seeing Christ, how could they have still wanted to see the Father? In seeing Christ they would have been seeing the Father. Evidently they had not yet truly seen Christ, these men who longed to have the Father disclosed to them. Listen now to the reason why they were not yet seeing Christ. In another place he promised this seeing as a reward: *Anyone who cherishes my commandments and keeps them, that is the one who loves me; and whoever loves me will be loved by my Father, and I will love him.* Then, as though in response to the question, "What will you give to the one you love?" he continued, *I will show myself to him* (Jn 14:21). If he has promised to manifest himself to those who love him, as their reward, it is clear that we are promised a vision of the truth that will exclude the possibility of our ever complaining again that *my soul is full to the brim with deceitful fantasies.*

Verse 9. Homesickness

12. *I have been weakened and humbled exceedingly.* The person who remembers the towering heights of the Sabbath is also the one who sees how deeply he or she is humbled, while anyone who is incapable of conceiving that sublime rest also fails to perceive where he or she is now. This is why another psalm says, *Rapt out of myself, I said, "I have been flung far out of your sight"* (Ps 30:23(31:22)). The psalmist's mind had been snatched aloft and he saw something sublime, yet he knew he was not yet fully present to what he saw. It was as though a kind of flash of divine light had reached him; he could in some degree understand it, though it came from a place he knew he had not attained. It enabled him to see his present situation, and how gravely he was weakened and cramped by human misfortunes, and this prompted his cry, *"Rapt out of myself, I said, "I have been flung far out of your sight."* What I have seen in ecstasy is such that in its light I see how far away from it I am, for I have not yet reached that place." The man who told us that he had been taken up to the third heaven, where he heard words beyond all utterance that no human may speak[13]—he had been there. But he was called back to us, to spend more time being made perfect through weakness first,[14] and so be invested with strength later. Though encouraged in his ministry by having glimpsed something of those mysteries, he added,

12. See 1 Cor 2:8.
13. See 2 Cor 12:2-4.
14. See 2 Cor 12:9.

"I heard words beyond all utterance, that no human is allowed to speak." What use is it then for you to inquire of me or of anyone else about matters no human may speak of, if even he who was allowed to hear them was not permitted to tell? Nonetheless, as we groan and confess our miseries, and recognize where we are, let us remember the Sabbath and patiently wait for what he has promised, he who has given us in himself an example of patience. Let us confess that *I have been weakened and humbled exceedingly*.

The groaning heart

13. *My heart was bellowing its groans*. Sometimes you overhear God's servants making their appeals with groaning, and you wonder why. Nothing is obvious except the groans of this servant of God—if they reach the ears of anyone nearby, that is; for there is also a hidden kind of groaning that human ears do not catch. But in the case where a person's heart has been seized by so powerful a desire that the inner anguish is expressed audibly, you seek the cause. You may say to yourself, "Perhaps he is groaning about so-and-so, or perhaps some calamity has befallen him." Who can know the reason, except the one in whose sight and into whose ears his servant is pouring out those sighs? Accordingly, says the psalmist, *my heart was bellowing its groans*. If human beings hear anyone groaning they usually take it to be the groans of the flesh; they do not overhear anyone whose groans are those of the heart. If a thief has stolen someone's property the victim may have been left bellowing, but not with the groaning of the heart. Another bewails the son he has buried, another his wife; another groans because his vineyard has been damaged by a hailstorm, or because his barrel of wine has turned sour, or because someone has made off with his beast; another because he has sustained a loss of some other kind; and another because he is afraid of an enemy. All these are bellowing their distress, but with the groans of the flesh. Quite different is God's servant, who bellows his at the remembrance of the Sabbath, that kingdom of God which flesh and blood will not possess.[15] So, says the psalmist, *my heart was bellowing its groans*.

Verse 10. Continuing desire is unceasing prayer

14. Who, then, could discern the reason for that bellowing? The psalmist continues, "*All my desire is before you, Lord*. Not before human beings, who cannot see my heart, but before you is all my desire." Let your desire too be before him, and there your Father, who sees in secret, will reward you.[16] This very desire is your prayer, and if your desire is continuous, your prayer is contin-

15. See 1 Cor 15:50.
16. See Mt 6:6.

uous too. The apostle meant what he said, *Pray without ceasing* (1 Thes 5:17). But can we be on our knees all the time, or prostrate ourselves continuously, or be holding up our hands uninterruptedly, that he bids us, *Pray without ceasing*? If we say that these things constitute prayer, I do not think we can pray without ceasing. But there is another kind of prayer that never ceases, an interior prayer that is desire. Whatever else you may be engaged upon, if you are all the while desiring that Sabbath, you never cease to pray. If you do not want to interrupt your prayer, let your desire be uninterrupted. Your continuous desire is your continuous voice. You will only fall silent if you stop loving. Who are the people who have fallen silent? Those of whom the Lord said, *With iniquity increasing mightily, the love of many will grow cold* (Mt 24:12). The chilling of charity is the silence of the heart; the blazing of charity is the heart's clamor. If your charity abides all the time, you are crying out all the time; if you are crying out all the time, you are desiring all the time; and if you are desiring, you are remembering rest.

You must also understand in whose presence that bellowing of your heart is heard. Consider what kind of desire it should be in God's sight. A desire for your enemy's death? People might think that desire justified, for we do sometimes pray misguidedly. Let us examine what people pray for, imagining that their requests are in order. They pray that someone may die, so that an inheritance may come to them. But let those who pray for the death of their enemies listen to the Lord's injunction, *Pray for your enemies*.[17] Let them not pray, then, that their enemies may die, but that their enemies be corrected; then the enemies will be dead, because when converted they will no longer exist as enemies.

All my desire is before you. "But what if my desire is before him, but my groaning does not reach him?" How can that happen, when your very desire voices itself in groans? This is why the next line says, *And my groaning is not hidden from you.* Hidden from you it is not, though it is hidden from most humans. Sometimes a humble servant of God can be seen praying, and his groaning *is not hidden from you.* And sometimes a servant of God may be seen laughing: does this mean that desire is dead in such a person's heart? No; and if desire is in him, groaning is in him too; it does not always reach human ears, but it never fails to reach the ears of God.

Verse 11. Turmoil of the heart and spiritual blindness

15. *My heart is throbbing*. Why? Because *my strength is gone*. It may happen that some catastrophe strikes suddenly. Our hearts throb, for the earth is quaking and thunder rolls round the sky, or there is a terrifying attack, or a fearful noise, or a lion is seen on the road. We are thoroughly disturbed. Robbers are lying in

---

17. See Mt 5:44; Lk 6:27.

wait, we are frightened, there is terror all around and panic strikes home. Why is this so? Because *my strength is gone*. If that strength were still with us, what would there be to fear? Whatever bad news arrived, whatever bared its teeth at us, whatever roared, whatever fell on us, whatever bristled at us, it would not frighten us. But what is the reason for the pounding heart of which the psalm speaks? *My strength has gone*. And why has it left him? Because *the very light of my eyes has forsaken me*. The light of Adam's eyes left him, for God himself was the light of Adam's eyes; and after offending God he fled into the shadow, and hid among the trees of paradise.[18] He was afraid of God's countenance, so he sought the shade of the trees. There in the wood he no longer had that light for his eyes which until now had always brought him joy. So it was for him, our first parent, and for us as his descendants. But to the second Adam, the new Adam, his members are gathered, for the new Adam has become a life-giving Spirit,[19] and from their places in his body they cry out, confessing, *The very light of my eyes has forsaken me*. But now when they make their confession, now that they are redeemed, now that they are in the body of Christ, is it still true that the light of their eyes is not with them? Yes, it is true, for they have the light only as they remember the Sabbath, as those who discern it, but only in hope. It is not yet for them the light of which it is said, *I will show myself to him* (Jn 14:21). Some portion of that light is ours, for we are children of God, and we keep hold of this in faith; but this is not the light that will be ours one day. *What we shall be has not yet appeared, but we know that when he appears, we shall be like him, because we shall see him as he is* (1 Jn 3:2). What we have now is the light of faith and the light of hope. *As long as we are in the body we are on pilgrimage and away from the Lord, for we walk by faith, not by sight. And as long as we hope for what we do not see, we wait for it in patience* (2 Cor 5:6-7; Rom 8:25). These are the tones of people on their journey, people not yet in their homeland. With good cause does anyone who prays speak in these tones; he or she speaks the truth honestly in plainly confessing, *The very light of my eyes has forsaken me*. This is the suffering of the inner person. There within, with himself, in himself and to himself he confesses it; he confesses it of no one and to no one save himself. Whatever the woes he has recounted, he has himself deserved them as his punishment.

Verse 12. The Head speaks of his sufferings, which are also ours

16. But is this all that men and women suffer? By no means. Inwardly we suffer from ourselves, and outwardly from those with whom we live. We suffer our own bad characteristics, and we are obliged to suffer those of other people.

---

18. See Gn 3:8.
19. See 1 Cor 15:45.

This is why another psalm makes the twofold petition, *Cleanse me from my secret sins, Lord, and spare your servant from the faults of others* (Ps 18:13-14(19:12-13)). In the present psalm the speaker has already made confession of his own secret sins, from which he desires to be cleansed, so let him speak now of other people's, from which he prays to be spared. *My friends . . . why need I speak of enemies? My friends and neighbors drew near and stood against me*. Make sure you understand his phrase, *stood against me*, for if they stood against me, they fell to their own ruin. *My friends and neighbors drew near and stood against me*. We must listen to the voice of the Head now, for the dawning light of our Head in his passion is beginning to show. But when the Head begins to speak, do not separate his body from him. If the Head has refused to separate himself from the voice of his body, would the body dare separate itself from the sufferings of its Head? Suffer in Christ, for Christ can almost be said to have sinned in your weakness. In this very psalm he spoke with his own lips about your sins, and seemed to claim them as his own, for he said, *In the face of my sins*, though they were not his. Just as he willed to take our sins on himself, because we are his body, so we too must will his sufferings to be ours, because he is our Head. If he suffered from friends who turned into enemies, it is unfitting that we should be spared the same. Rather let us prepare ourselves to be with him in this same experience, and not reject this chalice, so that we may find in ourselves a longing for his sublime glory, but by way of his lowliness. To certain disciples who aspired to a place close to him in his heavenly kingdom he replied, *Are you able to drink the cup I am to drink?* (Mt 20:22). Those sufferings of our Lord are our sufferings. If anyone serves God loyally, keeps faith, pays his debts, and lives justly among his fellow men and women, I should be surprised if he does not suffer, and even suffer what Christ here recounts of his own passion.

Who is near, who far?

17. *My friends and neighbors drew near and stood against me; and my neighbors stood far off*. Some neighbors drew near, other neighbors stood far off; who are these two sorts? The Jews were Christ's neighbors because they were his kinsfolk, and they approached him even as they crucified him. The apostles were his neighbors too, but they stood far off, for fear of suffering with him.

We could take it in another way: *my friends* are those who feigned friendliness with me. They did so when they said, *We know that you truthfully teach the way of God* (Mt 22:16), when they tried to tempt him to say whether or not it was right to pay tribute to Caesar, when he confounded them out of their own mouths. This was the occasion when they pretended to be his friends. But he needed no one to give evidence about what was in any human being, for he knew what was in everyone,[20] so much so that when they had mouthed their friendly words he replied, *Why are you putting me to the test, you hypocrites?* (Mt 22:18). This is why he can say, *My friends and neighbors drew near and stood against me; and my neighbors stood far off.* You understand what I mean? I have called those who approached him "neighbors," yet they stood far off; for though they drew near in body, they stood far away in their hearts. Who was so near physically as those who hoisted him onto the cross? Yet who so far away in heart as those who uttered blasphemies? Far distance of this latter kind was mentioned by Isaiah; listen to what he said about being near while really being far away: *This people honors me with its lips* (that means, they are physically near), *but its heart is far from me* (Is 29:13). The same people are said to be near, and yet far: near with their lips, far away in their hearts.

However, the fearful apostles certainly ran far away, so we can more simply and obviously refer the saying to them, understanding it to mean that some of them drew near and others stood far off, since even Peter, who had been bold enough to follow our Lord, was so far off that when questioned, and frightened, he three times denied the Lord with whom he had earlier promised to die.[21] But afterwards he came back from that far-off place to draw close again; for he heard the risen Christ ask, *Do you love me?* and he repeatedly answered, *I love you* (Jn 21:15-17). He who by denying the Lord had put himself far away was now coming near by his confession, until by his triple declaration of love he blotted out his triple denial.[22] *And my neighbors stood far off.*

Verse 13. Seeking Christ's life

18. *They who were seeking my life wrought violence.* It is already obvious who these people were who were seeking his life,[23] who did not have his life because they were not in his body. Those who were seeking his life were far away from his soul, but sought to kill it. But there is also a good way of seeking his soul, for in another text he takes issue with certain people by complaining, *There is no one to seek my soul* (Ps 141:5(142:4)). So in one place he rebukes those who do not seek his soul, and in another he rebukes those who do. Who is it who seeks his soul in a good sense? Anyone who imitates his sufferings. And who are they who seek his soul, or his life, in a bad sense? Those who were treating him violently and crucifying him.

19. It continues, *Those who looked for evil deeds in me made empty accusations.* What does that mean—*those who looked for evil deeds in me*? They

20. See Jn 2:25.
21. See Mt 26:69-74; 35.
22. Variant: "his triple declaration of fear."
23. *Qui quaerebant animam eius.* The word *anima*, which occurs eleven times in this paragraph, can mean "life" or "soul;" Augustine is playing on the ambiguity.

looked for many grounds of accusation, but found none. Perhaps this is a way of saying, "They looked for crimes," because they did indeed hunt for charges to bring against him, but could not find any.[24] They were looking for evil actions in a good man, for crimes in one who was innocent. How could they find any in him who had no sin? But since they were looking in vain for sins in the sinless one, no resort was left to them but to fabricate what they could not find. Accordingly *those who looked for evil deeds in me made empty accusations*, not charges of substance. And *they devised*[25] *treachery all day long*; that is, they unceasingly devised lying allegations. You know what a plethora of false evidence was brought against the Lord before his passion, and you know how much was falsely alleged even after he had risen from the dead. The soldiers who guarded his tomb were like those of whom Isaiah had prophesied: *I will assign the wicked to his sepulcher* (Is 53:9), for they were indeed wicked in refusing to tell the truth, accepting a bribe, and disseminating falsehood. Listen to what empty accusations they made: *While we were asleep, his disciples came and removed him* (Mt 28:13). That is certainly an empty accusation, for if they were asleep, how did they know what had happened?

Verses 14-15. The Lord's silence under attack

20. *But I was like a deaf man who heard nothing*, says the psalm, because when Christ made no reply to what he heard, it looked as though he did not hear. *I was like a deaf man who heard nothing, and like a dumb man who does not open his mouth.* Then it repeats the same thought: *I became like someone who does not hear, and has no refutation to offer.* He appeared to have nothing to say to them, no grounds for rebuking them. Yet had he not earlier censured them on many points? He had criticized them extensively: *Woe to you, scribes and Pharisees, hypocrites* (Mt 23:13), he said, and many similar things. Yet when the time came for his passion he said nothing of the kind, not because he had nothing that he could say but because he was giving them a chance to fulfill all that had been foretold, so that all the prophecies might be verified in him, of whom it had been said, *Like a sheep voiceless before its shearer, he did not open his mouth* (Is 53:7). It was therefore necessary for him to be silent in his passion, but he will not be silent at the judgment. He had come then to be judged, he who later will come to judge; and because he submitted to judgment in such profound humility he will come as judge in mighty power.

24. See Mt 26:60; Jn 8:46.
25. Variant: "will devise."

Verse 16. Trust God when you have no human advocate

21.*You will hear me, O Lord my God, because in you, Lord, I have trusted.* It is as though Christ were being asked, "Why did you not open your mouth? Why did you not beg them, Stop? Why did you not rebuke them as you hung on the cross?" The psalm replies for him, *Because in you, Lord, I have trusted, for you will hear me, O Lord my God.* In this saying he has advised you what to do, if you find yourself in trouble. You seek to defend yourself, and perhaps no one undertakes your defense. You are extremely worried, and think you have lost your case because you have no counsel for defense and no evidence on your side. Guard your innocence within yourself, where no one seeks to undermine your case. Perhaps false evidence has swayed the verdict against you, but this is so only in the human court; will it have any weight with God, before whom your case is to be heard? When God is judge, there will be no other witness than your own conscience. Between the just judge and your own conscience you will have nothing to fear except the state of your case itself. If your case is not a bad one, you need be terrified of no plaintiff, and you need neither rebut a lying witness nor call a truthful one. Simply arm yourself with a good conscience, so that you may say, *You will hear me, O Lord my God, because in you, Lord, I have trusted.*

Verse 17. Gloating enemies

22. *I said, Let my enemies never gloat over me, for when my feet slipped, they had much to say against me.* The Lord turns once more to the weakness of his body, the Head looks to the needs of his feet. He is not so high in heaven as to abandon what belongs to him on earth; he takes good care of it and keeps us in sight. In the conditions of this life it sometimes happens that our feet slip, and we slide into some sin. Then the wicked tongues of our enemies get busy, and from their reaction we understand what their objective has been all along, even though they did not admit it. They comment harshly, with no hint of gentleness,[26] delighted to have found what they ought to have deplored. *I said, Let my enemies never gloat over me*; yes, I prayed so, yet perhaps for my correction you have made them speak unrestrainedly against me *when my feet slip*. They were triumphant, and had plenty of scurrilous things to say when I lost my footing. They should have been merciful to me in my weakness, and not gloated, as the apostle enjoins, *My brothers and sisters, if someone is involved in some wrongdoing, you who are spiritual must instruct such a person in a spirit of gentleness.* And he includes the reason why: *taking heed to yourself, lest you be tempted as well* (Gal 6:1). But very different were these people of whom the psalm complains, *When my feet slipped, they had much to say against me.* They were more like the

26. Variant: "harshly against the gentle."

ones of whom it is said elsewhere, *Those who harass me will make merry if I am shaken* (Ps 12:5 (13:4)).

Verse 18. Scourging

23. *I am ready for scourging.* This is a wonderful verse! It is as though the Lord were saying, "I was born for this—to endure scourging," for he could not have been born[27] except as a descendant of Adam, to whom the scourging was due. Yet in this life sinners are sometimes subjected to no whipping at all, or very little, because their orientation is beyond possibility of change. Those for whom eternal life is being prepared fare otherwise; it is necessary for them to be whipped, for scripture warns us with good reason, *My child, do not faint under the Lord's chastisement, nor lose heart when you are rebuked by him, for those whom the Lord loves, he corrects, and he whips every child whom he accepts* (Heb 12:5-6; compare Prv 3:11-12). Let not my enemies gloat, then, let them not talk triumphantly. Even if my Father whips me *I am ready for scourging,* because an inheritance is being prepared for me. Every son or daughter must be whipped. So universal is this rule that even he who was without sin[28] was not exempt. *I am ready for scourging.*

Verses 18-19. The proper motive for grief

24. *My pain is always before me.* What pain is meant? The pain of the lash, perhaps. But truly, brothers and sisters, most truly I tell you, people feel pain under the whipping they undergo, but no pain over the reasons for it. Christ was not like that. Listen, beloved: if someone sustains a loss, he or she is more inclined to say, "I didn't deserve that," than to consider the reason for it; he feels the pain of losing money, but not the pain of losing righteousness. If you have sinned, mourn the loss of your interior treasure; perhaps your house has been stripped, but your heart may be emptier still. But if your heart is full of its true wealth, which is your God, why do you not say, *The Lord gave, and the Lord has taken away. This has happened as the Lord willed: may the Lord's name be blessed* (Jb 1:21)? What about the speaker in the psalm, what pain caused him grief? The pain of the scourging? No, certainly not. *My pain is always before me,* he says; and then as though we had asked him, "What pain?" he continues, *I will proclaim my iniquity aloud, and take serious thought for my sin.* This is the source of his pain. Not the pain of the scourge: his is the pain of the wound, not of the wound's remedy; for the whip is a medicine against sins.

27. Variant: "could not have suffered."
28. See 1 Pt 2:22.

Listen now, brothers and sisters. We are Christians, yet it often happens that when someone's child dies, the parent mourns over him, whereas if the child sins, the parent does not mourn. He ought to have wept and felt pain when he saw his child sinning; he ought to have exercised control then; he ought to have taught the child the right way to live, and imposed discipline on him. Or, if he did so, and the child would not listen, that would have been the occasion for grieving over him; for then it would have been worse for the child to go on living in licentious fashion like one dead, than to have brought the licentiousness to an end by dying; for when the child behaved disgracefully in your house, he was not merely dead, but even decomposing. These are the things that should give us pain, not the chastisement we merit for them. The chastening is to be borne, but the sins are to be grieved over.

But we must mourn over them in the way you have heard the psalmist mourn: *I will proclaim my iniquity aloud, and take serious thought for my sin*. After you have confessed your sin, do not be so carefree that you are always ready to confess and commit it again. Proclaim your iniquity in such a way that you take serious thought for your sin. What does that imply? Take serious thought for your wound. If you were to say, "I will take serious thought about my wound," what else would you mean but "I will see to it that my wound gets healed"? This is what it means to take serious thought for your offense: always to use your best endeavors, always to direct your intention, to act always with the utmost care to heal your sin. Well now, you may bewail your sin every day, but perhaps while your tears flow your hands hang idle. Let almsgiving atone for your sin, let the poor rejoice over your gift so that you too may rejoice over the gift of God. The pauper is in need, and you too are in need, he of what you can give, and you of what God can give. If you spurn the needy person who looks to you, will not God spurn you when in your need you look to him? Fill up the needy person's void, so that God may fill the void within you. This is what *I will take serious thought for my sin* means: I will do whatever needs to be done to blot out my sin and heal it. *And I will take serious thought for my sin.*

Verse 20. My enemies are alive and well

25. *But my enemies live on*, they fare well, they enjoy happiness in this world where I toil and bellow the groans of my heart. What is their life like, the life of those enemies who, as he has told us, have made empty accusations? Listen to the description of them in another psalm: *Their sons are like well-set saplings*; yet he has said of these people earlier, *Their mouths have spoken empty words*. Nevertheless *their daughters are gathered round them like the pillars of the temple, their store rooms are full to overflowing, their oxen are sturdy and their ewes fruitful, increasing at every lambing-time. Never is their hedge broken down, nor is there rioting in their streets* (Ps 143(144):8,12-15). My enemies

live on; this is their lifestyle; they flaunt it, they love it, and they get it by their evil deeds, for what does the next line say? *People who have these things are called blessed* (Ps 143(144):15). But what about you, who take serious thought for your sin? What about you, who proclaim your iniquity aloud? That psalm concludes, *Blessed is the people whose God is the Lord.*

Yet *my enemies live on; and those who hate me without reason have been strengthened against me and increased.* Why does he say, *Who hate me without reason*? They hate one who wills good to them. If they rendered evil for evil, they would not be good; if they failed to return good for benefits they had received, they would be ungrateful; but those who hate without reason are the people who render evil for good. The Jews were like that: Christ came to them, offering good things, but they repaid this good with evil. Beware of this bane, brothers and sisters, for it can creep in quickly. Just because we have said, "The Jews were like that," none of you must think that you are beyond its reach. Perhaps your fellow-Christian rebukes you with kindly intention; you hate him for it, and you are like that too. See how quickly it can happen, and how easily. Shun this great danger, this nimble sin.

Verse 21. The accursed upon the tree

26. *Those who return evil for good malign me because I pursued justice.* That was why they returned evil for good. But what does it mean by saying, *I pursued justice*? It means, "I would not let it go." In case you might think that "pursue" always had a pejorative sense, the psalmist said *persecutus*, that is, "I followed it perfectly": *I pursued justice.* Now listen to our Head lamenting[29] in his passion: *They cast me out, me, the beloved one, like a dead man of ill omen.* Was it too little for you that he was dead, that you must abhor him like a thing of ill omen? This was because he had been crucified. Death by crucifixion was an abomination among them, because they had not understood the prophetic word, *Accursed is anyone who is hanged on a tree* (Dt 21:23; compare Gal 3:13). He did not himself bring death, but found it propagated here from the curse inflicted on our first parent; and taking this death of ours upon himself, he hung what had been derived from sin upon a tree. The prophet's intention in saying, *Accursed is anyone who is hanged on a tree*, was to exclude the opinion of some heretics[30] and others who think that our Lord Jesus Christ had only phantom flesh, and did not really die on the cross. The prophecy showed that God's Son died a real death, the death to which mortal flesh was liable, lest if he were regarded as exempt from the curse, you might think he did not truly die. But his death was no sham; it had been passed down through the descendants of the man who was

29. Variant: "clearly visible."
30. Notably the Manicheans.

originally condemned when God said, *You shall certainly die* (Gn 2:17). To Christ indeed it descended as true death, so that to us it might descend as true life; upon him came the curse of death so that on us might come the blessing of life. So they cast me out, me, the beloved, like a dead man of ill omen.

Verse 22. The person of the sinner is transfigured into Christ

27. *Do not abandon me, O Lord my God, do not leave me alone*. Let us make this prayer in him, let us make it through him, for he intercedes for us;[31] let us say, *Do not abandon me, O Lord my God*. Yet elsewhere he had prayed, *My God, my God, why have you forsaken me?* (Ps 21:2(22:1); Mt 27:46), and here he prays, *O my God, do not leave me alone*. If God does not abandon the body, is it conceivable that he abandoned its Head? Whose voice is this, then, if not that of the first human being? Christ proves that his flesh is true flesh inherited from Adam when he cries, *My God, my God, why have you forsaken me?* But God had not forsaken him. If he does not forsake you when you believe in him, did the Father and the Son and the Holy Spirit, one holy God, abandon Christ? No, but Christ had taken the identity of the first human being to himself.[32] We know this from the apostle's words, *Our old humanity has been nailed to the cross with him* (Rom 6:6). We should never have been rid of our old nature, had he not been crucified in weakness.[33] He came for no other purpose than that we should be renewed in him, for it is by longing for him and imitating his passion that we are made new. It was the voice of weakness, our voice, that cried out, *Why have you forsaken me?* And the next words were, *the tale of my sins*, as though Christ were saying, "Those words were the words of a sinner, but I have transformed them into my own." *Do not leave me alone*.

Verse 23. The denarius of eternal life

28. *Make haste to help me, Lord of my salvation*. This is the salvation the prophets sought to discover, as the apostle Peter says.[34] They did not receive what they sought, but they inquired about it and foretold it, and now we have come along and found what they sought. Yet we have not received it either, and others will be born after us who will also find yet not receive, and they too will

---

31. See Rom 8:34.
32. *Personam in se transfiguraverat primi hominis*, a packed phrase and difficult to render in English, but the key to Augustine's understanding of the psalms. *Persona* (like πρόσωπον in the Greek Fathers) is best understood here from its theatrical background, rather than in the light of the philosophical and psychological usages associated with it later. The *persona* was originally a mask through which an actor spoke, and hence the "character" or role assumed.
33. See 2 Cor 13:4; but some codices have "had he not crucified us," and others "unless the old nature had been crucified."
34. See 1 Pt 1:10-12.

pass away, so that at the day's end we may all receive together, along with the patriarchs and prophets and apostles, the denarius of salvation.[35] You know how the hired workers had been brought into the vineyard at different hours, yet all received the same wages.[36] So too the prophets and apostles and martyrs, and we ourselves, and those who come after us even to the end of the world, will receive at that last hour everlasting salvation. Contemplating God's glory and seeing him face to face we shall be enabled to praise him for ever, without wearying, without any of the pain of iniquity, without any of the perversion of sin. We shall praise God, no longer sighing for him but united with him for whom we have sighed even to the end, albeit joyful in our hope. For we shall be in that city where God is our good, God is our light, God is our bread, God is our life. Whatever is good for us, whatever we miss as we trudge along our pilgrim way, we shall find in him. In him will be that quiet that we remember now, though the memory cannot but cause us pain; for we remember that Sabbath, and about its memory so much has been said, and we must still say so many things, and never cease to speak of it, though with our heart, not our lips; because our lips fall silent only that we may cry the more from our heart.

---

35. Like Saint Paul, Augustine believed that Christ's resurrection had inaugurated the final age of the world; but he did not think it would necessarily be short, as is evident from the present paragraph.
36. See Mt 20:8-10.

Exposition of Psalm 38

A Sermon preached at Carthage, at the shrine of Saint Cyprian,[1] *on a Wednesday*[2]

Verse 1. Learning to leap

1. The psalm which we have just sung, and are now undertaking to expound, is entitled, *To the end, Idithun's song for David himself.* We are to expect the words of someone called Idithun, then, and we must listen to what he has to tell us. If anyone among us is able to be an Idithun, that person will find and hear himself or herself in what is sung. Who the original Idithun was in that far-off generation they only can determine who lived at that time,[3] but we shall be in a better position to understand the truth he tells us if we look first at the interpretation of his name. As far as we have been able to discover by studying these names, which have been translated for us from Hebrew into Latin by students of sacred scripture, Idithun means "one who leaps across." So who is this leaping speaker, and across whom did he leap? Notice that the name means not simply "one who leaps," but "one who leaps across." Does he sing while leaping across, or leap across by singing? Whichever it is, we sang a few minutes ago the song of someone leaping across; and God, to whom we sang it, must judge whether we too are people who leap across. If anyone here did leap across while singing it, let such a one rejoice to be what he has sung about; but if anyone who sang it is still stuck fast in the earth, that person must aspire to be a leaper in accord with the psalm. This psalmist whose name is Leaping Across has jumped over people who cling to the soil, people bowed down to the earth with their minds attached to what is lowest and their trust in things that pass away. Whom could he have leapt across, otherwise? He could only leap over those who stand still.

2. You know that certain psalms are called "Songs of Ascents."[4] In Greek this is quite plain, for they are called ἀναβαθμῶν. This means songs about steps, but steps up, not down. The distinction cannot be made in Latin; we just have to say "steps" without being specific, and leave it vague whether people on them are

1. *Ad mensam sancti Cypriani.*
2. Possibly in September 416.
3. Thus the CCL editors of the Latin text, amending an original "is for you to determine."
4. The group of psalms 119-133 (120-134) was traditionally referred to as "Gradual Psalms" or "Songs of Ascents," probably because they were used by pilgrims "going up" to Jerusalem for festivals.

going up or down. But since no speech, no utterance, goes unheard[5] the earlier language clarifies the one that came later, and what is ambiguous in one is made clear by another. So just as in one type of psalm the singer was going up, in this one the singer is leaping across. But the leaping across is also an ascent, though not on foot or by using scaling-ladders or wings. Yet if you refer it to our inner life, feet and scaling-ladders and wings are available. If we had no feet in this inward sense, why does a person of spiritual discernment pray, *Let not the foot of pride come near me* (Ps 35:12(36:11))? If there were no spiritual ladders, what was it that Jacob saw, with angels going up and down on it?[6] And if we could not use spiritual wings, what does a psalmist mean by the question, *Who will give me wings like a dove's? Then I will fly away and find rest* (Ps 54:7(55:6))? When we are dealing with material matters, feet are one thing, scaling-ladders another, and wings something else again; but within ourselves feet and ladders and wings are all the loving impulses of a good will. By means of these we walk and climb and fly. When any of you hear about this man who is leaping across, and you aspire to imitate him, you must not think to leap across ditches in a bodily sense by leaping lightly into the air, or to fly over some highish obstacle by jumping. But I am talking now in bodily terms because there is a sense in which a spiritual person does leap even across ditches. Another psalm declares, *Burnt up by fire and dug out, they will perish at your frowning rebuke* (Ps 79:17(80:16)). But what are these things that are *burnt up by fire and dug out*, these things that will perish at the Lord's *frowning rebuke*? Sins, obviously. Anything that has been set alight by disordered greed is burnt up by fire, and whatever is dictated by supine fear is like a ditch dug out. All sins spring from one or other of these two, greed or fear. Spiritual persons must therefore leap across all the things that could trap them on earth. Let all of us erect our ladders and spread our wings, and see whether we recognize ourselves here.

But we should more truly say that by the grace of the Lord many people do recognize themselves in these words: people who, detached from this world and all the delights it offers, choose to live rightly, even as they live here amid spiritual joys. Where will they find such joys, while still walking the earth? Surely from the divine oracles, from the word of God, from some parable in holy scripture which they have studied and pondered, from the sweetness of finding after the labor of the search. There are indeed good and holy pleasures in these books, pleasures that are not to be found in gold and silver, feasting and luxury, hunting and fishing, games and jesting, frivolous theatrical entertainments, or the high offices which people try to seize, though they crumble to nothing. It is not the case that true enjoyment is to be derived from all these, and none from the sacred books; quite the contrary. A soul that has leapt over these baser things and found

5. See Ps 18:4(19:3-4).
6. See Gn 28:12.

itself delighted by the holy scriptures is compelled to say, *The unrighteous have told me titillating tales, but they cannot compare with your law, O Lord,*[7] and it says this confidently, knowing it to be true. Let our Idithun come forward and leap across people who still look to the base things for their pleasure; let him or her take delight in the higher things and find joy in the word of the Lord, in the delightful law of the Most High.

But is there more to say? Must we make yet another leap, from here to somewhere else again? If we desire to leap across, is there still a further place to which we must leap? We need to listen to what our psalmist has to say, for it seems to me that he is still leaping across the place where he was accustomed to dwell in the divine oracles, where he learned the lessons we are about to hear.

Verse 2. No one avoids all faults in speaking; the hearers must take it in good part

3. *I said, I will keep guard over my conduct, so that I do not offend with my tongue*. One can well believe that in the course of reading, discussion, preaching, administering reproof, encouraging people, or while engaged in work, or beset by human problems, living as a man among fellow men and women, the psalmist had said some things he regretted and admitted that some expressions had fallen from his lips that he wished to recall, but could not. This is likely to have been the case even though he was already leaping across people who did not delight in the same things as he did, for it is difficult for anyone not to slip up and sin with the tongue. As scripture says, *If anyone has not sinned with his tongue, he is a perfect man.*[8] The moist saliva that surrounds the tongue makes it slippery. The psalmist was aware how difficult it is for a person who is obliged to speak to say nothing in his discourse that he will afterwards regret having said, so he felt disgusted about these sins and sought to avoid them. This very Leaper-Across felt how hard it was, so no one who is not yet leaping across ought to pass judgment on me. Let any such critic make the leap across and experience for himself or herself what I mean; then such a person will be both a witness to the truth and a child of truth.

In the light of this experience Idithun had made up his mind not to talk, in order to avoid saying anything he might wish unsaid. His opening words indicate his resolution: *I said, I will keep guard over my conduct, so that I do not offend with my tongue*. Well said, Idithun: keep guard over your conduct, and do not offend with your tongue; weigh what you are going to say, scrutinize it, refer

---

7. Ps 118(119):85. Augustine had heard this verse from the symbolic figure of Continence, who encouraged him as he stood on the brink of decision; see his *Confessions* VIII,11,27.
8. Jas 3:2. The last word in Augustine's Latin version is *vir*, denoting a male person. So too the Greek behind it, ἀνήρ.

it to the truth within you, and then bring it forth to the hearer outside. No doubt you often try to do this[9] amid the turmoil of business and when minds are preoccupied, but the soul itself is weakened and weighed down by the corruptible body,[10] and although it wishes both to hear and to speak—to hear within and to speak outside—it is sometimes troubled by the effort that speaking demands and fails through insufficient attention and inadvertence, and says something that should not be said. A surer remedy against these failures is silence; for a sinner will stand up, someone notorious for some particular sin, someone proud and malicious, and will hear the Leaper speaking. He will take careful note of the words, and set traps. It is hardly possible that anyone with this intention will be unable to find anything that has not been fittingly said, and as he listens he does not make allowances, but cavils out of ill-will. Confronted with people like this Idithun had chosen to say nothing as he leapt over them, so he sang of his intention: *I said, "I will keep guard over my conduct, so that I do not offend with my tongue*. As long as I am liable to be ensnared by those who misrepresent me, or as long as they snatch at me, even though I am not ensnared, *I will keep guard over my conduct, so that I do not offend with my tongue*. Although I have leapt beyond earthly pleasures, although fleeting desires for temporal gain do not hold me fast, although I now despise those lower things and climb to what is better, I find it enough to enjoy in God's presence the understanding I have from these better things. Why need I speak and lay myself open to their traps, why give the accusers their opportunity? So I resolved, *I will keep guard over my conduct, so that I do not offend with my tongue. I have set a guard over my mouth*." What is the purpose of that? To defend yourself against the devout, the zealous, the faithful, the holy? Of course not. They listen with a mind to approve and commend, and if among the many things they find to commend there may be some they cannot approve, they are more inclined to forgive than to prepare malicious accusations. Against whom, then, do you seek to protect yourself in keeping guard over your conduct and in setting a guard over your mouth, so that you do not offend with your tongue? He explains: "It was *when the sinner took his stand against me*. He did not take his stand at my side, but *against me*. What shall I ever find to say that will satisfy him? I am speaking to a carnally-minded person about the things of the spirit, to one who sees and hears only on the outside, but is deaf and blind within. A materialist has no perception for what concerns the Spirit of God. If he were not a materialist, would he misrepresent me so? Happy the person who speaks a word into the ear of a listener,[11] not into the ear of a sinner who has taken his stand against him."

---

9. Variants: "Who tries to . . . ?"; "The person who observes this rule. . . ."
10. See Wis 9:15.
11. See Sir 25:12.

Many people of this kind stood round grinding their teeth when Christ was led like a sheep to the slaughter, when like a lamb voiceless before its shearer he did not open his mouth.[12] What can you say to the inflated, the turbulent, the vexatious, the litigious, the chatterboxes? What can you say that is holy and edifying, what can you say to them concerning religious truth that leaps beyond them,[13] when the Lord himself said even to willing hearers, people who longed to learn, who hungered for the food of truth and received it avidly, *I have many things to tell you, but at present you are not able to bear them* (Jn 16:12)? The apostle likewise said, *Not as spiritual persons could I speak to you, but only as carnal*, yet they were not to be despaired of, for all that, but nourished; for he went on to say, *As if to little children in Christ I gave you milk to drink, rather than solid food. You were not capable of it then.* Tell it to us now. *Nor are you capable even now* (1 Cor 3:1-2). Do not be in a hurry, then, to hear what you cannot yet take in, but grow up so that you may become capable of it. This is how we address a little child, who needs to be nourished with holy milk at the breast of Mother Church, and so eventually made capable of sharing the Lord's table. But what am I to say even in childish mode to a sinner who has taken his stand against me, thinking or pretending that he is suited to what is beyond him, who, when I say things to him that he cannot take in, will attribute it not to incapacity on his own part but to failure on mine? It is with this sinner in view, the one who has taken his stand against me, that *I have set a guard over my mouth*, declares Idithun.

Verse 3. Woe betide a preacher who falls silent

4. And what followed that decision? *I have become deaf, and have been humbled, and have fallen silent even from good words.* This leaping speaker has encountered a difficulty in the place to which he has now leapt, and he is looking for some way to leap out of it, to escape this difficulty. "I was so afraid of committing sin that I imposed silence on myself. I had resolved, *I will keep guard over my conduct, so that I do not sin with my tongue*; but in my fear of speaking *I have become deaf, and have been humbled, and have fallen silent even from good words.* Through my excessive fear of saying something bad, I have been left with nothing good to say. *I have become deaf, and have been humbled, and have fallen silent even from good words.* How did I say anything worthwhile before, except because I had heard it? *You will give me delight and gladness to hear*" (Ps 50:10(51:8)). And the Bridegroom's friend stands and

12. See Is 53:7.
13. Variants: "What is a holy and pious person, one who from his religious faith leaps beyond them . . . ?" and "What can you say to the holy and the pious, to anyone who from his religious faith leaps beyond them . . . ?"

hears him, and is transported with joy at that voice not his own, but the Bridegroom's.[14] In order to say anything true, he must first hear what he has to say. Anyone who lies, on the contrary, speaks from his own store.[15] The psalmist has suffered a sad and irksome fate, and by confessing it here he is warning us to avoid it, not imitate it. As I have said, in his exaggerated fear of saying something that might not be good, he decided to say nothing, not even good things; and because he resolved to keep quiet, he began to lose his hearing. If you are a leaper, you stand and wait to hear from God what you are to say to your fellow men and women. You leap between our rich God and the needy people who look to you, so that you may hear in one quarter and speak in the other. But if you choose not to speak on the one side, you will not deserve to hear on the other: you are scorning the poor, so you will be scorned yourself by God, who is rich. Have you forgotten that you are a servant, whom the Master has appointed over his household to give your fellow-servants their rations?[16] Why do you seek to receive anything, if you are unwilling to dole it out? Give what you have, that you may deserve what you have not.[17] "Accordingly," says Idithun, "when I had placed a kind of guard over my mouth, and imposed silence on myself because I saw how dangerous speech was, something happened to me that I had not bargained for: *I became deaf, and was humbled.* I did not humble myself; rather *I was humbled. I became deaf, and was humbled, and fell silent even from good words*. I have stopped saying even good things, so afraid am I that I may say something amiss, and my teaching be censured. *I have fallen silent even from good words, and my pain has come back.* In silence I had found a respite from one kind of pain, that which my slanderers and critics had inflicted on me; the pain I endured from them had ceased. But when I began to keep silence from good words, my pain was renewed. My policy of keeping quiet about what I ought to have said began to cause me more intense pain than having said the wrong things would have done. *My pain has come back.*"

Verses 4-5. Longing for the goal

5. *Fire will blaze up during my meditation.*[18] My heart began to be troubled. Often I saw people behaving foolishly; it sickened me, but I did not rebuke them, and zeal for your house devoured me as I remained silent.[19] I thought of my Lord saying, *You wicked, lazy servant, you should have handed my money over to the*

14. See Jn 3:29.
15. See Jn 8:44.
16. See Mt 24:45.
17. These remarks clearly come from Augustine's own heart and experience. The double duty of hearing and speaking was an essential ingredient in his idea of a bishop's office.
18. Some codices supply the first half of this verse, which Augustine omits.
19. See Ps 68:10(69:9).

bankers, so that I could have recovered it with interest on my return. And may God shield his stewards from the fate mentioned in the next verse: *Let him be cast into outer darkness* (Mt 25:26-27,30) bound hand and foot. Remember that he was not one to squander and bring financial ruin, but a servant indolent in paying out what was due. What are people to expect who have used up the Lord's property in self-indulgence, if those who have simply held it back through laziness are condemned so severely? *Fire will blaze up during my meditation*. The psalmist finds himself caught in this vacillation between speaking and keeping silence, between those who are poised to censure him and those who long to receive instruction, between those who have plenty and those in need. To the affluent he has become an object of abuse, to the proud the butt of their scorn,[20] yet he is conscious of the blessed ones who are hungering and thirsting after righteousness.[21] Whichever way he turns he is hard pressed, in trouble either way, in danger of casting his pearls before swine[22] and equally endangered if he does not dispense their rations to his fellow-servants. In such a ferment he sought a better place, somewhere better than this stewardship where one works so hard and is in such peril. He sighed for some kind of end, where he would not have to suffer all this, and the end he longed for was that final reckoning when the Lord will say to his good steward, *Enter into the joy of your Lord* (Mt 25:21). *I spoke with my tongue*, says the psalmist. "Amid the ferment, the dangers, the difficulties (for though the law of the Lord is a delight to us, it still permits the charity of many to grow cold[23] as scandals abound), amid this ferment, I say, *I spoke with my tongue*." To whom? "Not to any hearer whom I want to instruct, but to that unfailing hearer by whom I want to be instructed. *I spoke with my tongue* to him, to whom I must listen within if I am to hear anything good, anything true." And what did you say? "*Make known to me my end, O Lord*. I have leapt across certain things, and arrived at certain others, and the things I have reached are better than those from which I leapt away, but there is still something over which I must leap; for we shall not always remain here to endure temptations, obstacles, and accusing listeners. *Make known to me my end*, show me the goal still far away, not the race immediately in front of me."

6. The "end" he mentions is that goal the apostle kept in view as he sped along his way, though he confessed his own imperfection and knew the distance between his present life and that other place to which he was running. *Not that I have gained it already, or am already perfect, brethren; I do not judge myself to have taken hold of it yet*, he says. On hearing that you might say, "If the apostle has not taken hold of it, can I?" But look at what he is doing, and pay attention to

20. See Ps 122(123):4.
21. See Mt 5:6.
22. See Mt 7:6.
23. See Mt 24:12.

what he says. So what are you saying,[24] apostle? Do you really mean that you have not laid hold on it yet, that you are not yet perfect? What are you saying? To what kind of activity are you exhorting me? What model do you propose to me, for me to imitate and follow? *One thing only I do*, he says. *Forgetting what lies behind and straining to what lies ahead, I bend my whole effort to follow after the prize of God's heavenly call in Christ Jesus* (Phil 3:12-14). *I bend my whole effort*, not claiming to have arrived, not claiming to have laid hold of the prize. Let us not slip back again into the place from which we have already leapt across, but neither let us remain in the place we have reached. Let us run ahead, keeping our eyes on the finishing-post, for we are still on the way. Do not be complacent about the things you have left behind; rather be concerned for those you have not yet gained. *Forgetting what lies behind and straining to what lies ahead*, says Paul, *I bend my whole effort to follow after the prize of God's heavenly call in Christ Jesus*. For Christ is the end. The "one thing" Paul mentions is the one thing the apostles longed for: *Lord, show us the Father, and that is enough for us* (Jn 14:8). It is the "one thing," the one request made in another psalm: *One thing have I begged of the Lord, and that will I seek after. Forgetting what lies behind and straining to what lies ahead, one thing have I begged of the Lord, and that will I seek after, to live in the Lord's house all the days of my life*. For what purpose? *That I may contemplate the Lord's delight* (Ps 26(27):4). There I shall rejoice in my ally, no longer fearing him or her as an adversary; there he will be a friend who joins me in contemplation, not an enemy to accuse me.

This was Idithun's desire. He wanted that end to be revealed to him while he was still here, that he might know what was still lacking to him; he wanted not so much to rejoice in the things he had attained as to long for those he had not reached yet. Though he had leapt beyond some things, he prayed not to halt on the way, but to be carried on by desire to the things of heaven, until after leaping over some things he might at last leap over all. Droplets of divine dew were falling on him from the scriptures, arousing his thirst to run like a hart to the fountain of life, and in that light to see light, and to be sheltered in the recess of God's face, far from human disturbance.[25] There he would be able to say, "At last! I want nothing else. Here I love everyone and fear no one."

This is a good desire, a holy desire. If any of you have it already, rejoice with us, and pray that we may persevere in our desire, and never slacken in it by reason of the scandals around us. For our part we make the same prayer for you; for it is not as though we were fit to pray for you, and you unworthy to pray for us, The apostle habitually commended himself to his hearers, to whom he was preaching the word of God. So you too, brothers and sisters, pray for us, that we

24. This is the variant suggested by the CCL editors, here and in the following line. The codices have "What are you doing?"
25. See Pss 41:2(42:1); 35:10(36:9); 30:21(31:20).

may clearly see what should be seen, and aptly say what is to be said. However, I know that this desire exists in only a few people, and only those who have tasted the realities of which I speak understand me perfectly. Nonetheless we speak to all of you, to those who have such a longing and to those who do not have it yet: to those who have it, that they may sigh together with us for the things we speak of, and to those who do not yet long for them, that they may shake off their sluggishness, leap beyond base things, and come to experience the sweetness of the divine law, rather than linger amid the pleasures of the wicked. For many people tell many titillating tales, and there are plenty of people singing the praises of plenty of attractions, and wicked people offering wicked suggestions. And it is true that those wicked things do afford pleasure, but none to compare with your law, O Lord.[26] Let those who are convinced that we too are testifying about these realities come and testify along with us, for though this is a process that goes on inside ourselves, and cannot be expressed in words, anyone who engages in it must believe that it goes on in others too. None of us must think ourselves to be the sole recipients of this gift from God. Let Idithun say on their behalf, *Make known to me my end, O Lord.*

Time, the dimension of contingent being

7. *And make known to me the number of my days, the number that is.*[27] Now I am looking for a number of days "that is." I can speak about, and understand, a number that is not really a number, just as I can speak of years where there are not really any years, for ordinarily where there are "years," a number is implied, yet a psalm says to God, *You are the selfsame, and your years will not fail* (Ps 101:28(102:27)).

But here the prayer is not simply, "Make me know the number of my days," but "Make me know the number of them that *is*." What does that mean? That numbered day in which you are now—does it not exist? Well, I have to say that if I look hard, it does not exist. If I am sticking fast on the road, I have the illusion that it does exist, but when I leap across, it does not exist. If I shake myself free of earthly things to contemplate the things of heaven, if I compare transient things with those that abide, I see what has true being, and what has more the appearance of being than true existence. Am I to say that these present days of mine have true being? I repeat, am I to say that these days really exist? Shall I be so rash as to use the great word "being" of this flux of things that slide toward extinction? For myself, in my weakness I am so nearly non-existent that God has eluded my memory, God who said, *I AM WHO AM* (Ex 3:14).

26. See Ps 118(119):85.

27. *Et numerum dierum meorum qui est.* The phrase is awkward. The translation here offered assumes that this is the correct reading, though two codices ease it by amending *qui* (relative) to *quid* (interrogative): "the number of my days, what it is."

Is there some "number of days" that truly exists, then? Indeed there is, it exists without end. But in these present days I can only say that something "is" if I am able to hold onto something of the day on which you ask me whether it exists, or if you can hold onto something of that day in order to ask me. But do you hold onto it? If you have held onto yesterday, you hold onto today as well. "But," you will reply, "I am not holding onto yesterday, because it no longer exists; I hold onto this day where I am now, the day that is present to me." Really? Has not the part of it which has passed since first light already escaped from you? Did not "today" begin from its first hour? Give me its first hour; give me its second hour too, for by now that may have flown away as well. "At least I will give you its third hour," you say, "if that is where we are now. Certainly these days do exist, and there is a third day,[28] and if you accept that, you must grant me that the third hour also exists." But no, I will not concede to you even that, if you have in any degree leapt across these things with me. Give me just this third hour where you are now. If some portion of it has already slipped by, and some other portion still remains, you cannot give me either what has passed (because it no longer exists) or what remains (because it does not exist yet). What are you going to give me, then, of this present hour? How much of it will you give me—enough for me to speak the word, "is"? When you say the word "is" you utter one syllable, and that only takes a moment. But this syllable has three letters,[29] and even in that tiny moment you will not reach the second letter of the word until the first has ended, nor will the third make itself heard until the second has died away. What can you give me, then, of this one syllable? And do you think you can hold onto a day, if you cannot hold onto a syllable? As the moments fly past all things are snatched away. The torrent of things flows on, but from tnis torrent he drank for us on his way, he who has now lifted up his head.[30] These days of ours do not have being; they depart almost before they arrive, and when they do arrive they cannot stand still. They join onto each other,[31] they follow one another and cannot hold themselves together. Nothing of the past can be called back, and the future that we await will pass away; as long as it has not come, we do not possess it, and when it has come we cannot keep hold of it.

I want to know *the number of my days, the number that is*, not this number that is not, or rather this number that both is and is not. It is this last aspect that disturbs me more and is to me more difficult and dangerous, for we cannot say

28. Allusion to the resurrection?
29. Two in English of course, three in Latin: *est*.
30. See Ps 109(110):7. The quotation points the contrast between the elusive quality of our time, characteristic of creaturely existence which is close to non-being, and the eternity of God, whose Word has neither beginning nor ending. Yet the incarnate Word "drank from the torrent" of our transient human existence. See also Exposition of Psalm 76,8, and note there.
31. Variant: "press upon each other."

something "is" if it does not stand still, but neither can we say it has no being at all, if it comes and goes. What I am seeking is the simple "is." I seek the true "is"; I am looking for the genuine "is," the "is" that we shall find in that Jerusalem which is the bride of my Lord, where there will be no death, no deficiency, where the day passes not, but abides, the day that is preceded by no yesterday and hustled on by no tomorrow. *Make known to me the number of my days,* this number, *the number that is.*

What I have and what I lack

8. *That I may know what I lack,* for this is what is wanting to me as I struggle along here, and as long as I lack it I do not claim to be perfect. As long as I have not received it, I confess, *Not that I have already gained it, or am already perfect; but I bend my whole effort to follow after the prize of God's heavenly call* (Phil 3:12,14). I shall receive it as my prize at the end of my race. The end of our running will be a stillness, and in this stillness a homeland where there will be no journeying, no unrest, no temptation. So then, *make known to me the number of my days, the number that is, that I may know what I lack.* I am not there yet, so let me not become proud about the place I have attained, but let me be found in Christ, not having any righteousness of my own.[32] With my eyes on him WHO IS, and comparing with him these present things which have no being in that sense, I shall see that what I lack is greater than what I have, and so I shall be more humbled about what is missing than elated about what is at hand. People who while living here think they possess anything deserve by their pride not to receive what they lack, for they think what they have is something great; but any who think themselves something, whereas they are nothing, deceive themselves.[33] The illusion does not make them great, for while inflation and swelling look like greatness, they are no bearers of health.

Verse 6. The passage from the old to the new

9. Our leaping psalmist is carrying on a secret business in his heart which only someone who is engaged in the same will know. He has obtained what he asked: his end has been made known to him, and so has the number of his days—not the number of days that passes, but that which "is." He has a true estimate of the things he has leapt over and has compared it with a higher knowledge. Now you might ask him, "Why did you want to know the number of your days, the number that is? What have you to say about these present days?" With regard to this other

32. See Phil 3:9.
33. See Gal 6:3.

number,[34] the days of this present life, he replies, "*How old you have made my days!* They are growing old, and I want new ones, days that never grow old, so that I may say, *The old things have passed away, and lo, everything is made new!*" (2 Cor 5:17), even now in hope, and hereafter in reality. Though already made new by faith and hope, how much old business we still have to deal with! We have not so put on Christ as to wear nothing any longer of Adam. Look at Adam growing old, and Christ being made new in us: *Though our outer self is decaying,* says scripture, *our inner self is being renewed daily* (2 Cor 4:16). As we regard our sin, our mortality, our fleeting seasons, our groaning and toil and sweat, the stages of our life that succeed one another and will not stand still, but slip by imperceptibly from infancy to old age as we regard all these, let us see in them the old self, the old day, the old song, the Old Covenant. But when we turn to our inner being, to all that is destined to be renewed in us and replace the things subject to change, let us find there the new self, the new day, the new song, the New Covenant, and let us love this newness so dearly that the oldness we meet there does not frighten us. As we run our race we are passing from the old things to the new. This transition is effected as the old things decay and the inner are made new, until our outer decaying self pays its debt to nature and meets its death, though it too will be renewed at the resurrection. Then all things which for the present are new only in hope will be made new in very truth. You further the process now as you strip yourself of the old and run toward the new.

Our psalmist was running toward these new things and straining toward what lay ahead when he said, *Make known to me my end, O Lord, and the number of my days, the number that is, that I may know what I lack.* He is still dragging Adam along, but look how he is hastening toward Christ. *How old you have made my days!* he says. These old days derive from Adam, and you have rendered them old; every day they grow older, so much so that eventually they will be consumed altogether. *And my substance is as nothing in your sight.* In your sight, Lord, it is as nothing, nothing in the presence of you who see this. When I see it too, it is in your sight that I see it. I do not see the truth in the presence of fellow-mortals, for what can I say, what words can I use to demonstrate that what I am is nothing when compared with HIM WHO IS? But within myself it can be said,[35] within myself it can be experienced in some measure. *In your sight,* Lord, where your eyes see me, not where human eyes see . . . . What do I see there, where your eyes are? That *my substance is as nothing.*

34. Variant: "having regard to that high knowledge."
35. Variant: "learned."

Emptiness all round

10. *Nonetheless all things are empty, for everyone who lives.* Why does he say, *Nonetheless*? Well, what has he been saying? "By now I have leapt across mortal things, I have learned to despise what is lowest, I have trampled earthly things underfoot and have soared to the enjoyment of the law of the Lord. I have been afloat in the number of days the Lord gives,[36] and I have longed for that end which knows no ending. I have desired to know the number of my days, the number that truly is, for the present numbered days have no true being. This is what I am like; I have leapt beyond so much and now I pant with longing for the realities that are still and lasting. *Nonetheless*, in my present state, as long as I am here, as long as I am in this world, as long as I carry mortal flesh, as long as human life on earth is all temptation,[37] as long as I gasp, beset by scandals, as long as I who stand must be wary lest I fall,[38] as long as both my bad points and my good deeds are opaque to me, *all things are empty, for everyone who lives.* Everyone, I say, both the person who sticks fast and the one who leaps along. Even Idithun still belongs in this universal state of emptiness; for all things are empty, and vanity of vanities, and what wealth does anyone get from all the work he toils at under the sun?[39] Is Idithun still under the sun? He has some stake in this world under the sun, and some stake in the world beyond it. Here under the sun he has the business of waking and sleeping, eating and drinking, feeling thirst and hunger, thriving and being tired, growing from a child into a youth, and then into an old man, being unsure what to hope and what to fear. All these even Idithun experiences under the sun, even though he is one who leaps beyond. Where does he get the impetus for his leaping? From his desire: *Make known to me my end, O Lord.* The desire is something beyond this sunny world; it does not arise from the world under the sun. All the things we can see are under the sun, but whatever is invisible is not under the sun. Faith is not visible, hope is not visible, charity is not visible, kindliness is not visible, neither is that chaste fear that abides for ever.[40] In all these Idithun finds sweetness and consolation; he lives beyond this sun, because he is a citizen of heaven.[41] The things that still preoccupy him under the sun wring groans from him; he scorns them and suffers

36. *Fluctuavi in dispensatione numerorum dierum dominicorum.* If this is the correct reading, the reference is presumably to the contemplation of eternal realities that he has mentioned, and this would suit the immediate context here. But the phrase is difficult and has given rise to a number of variants. Some codices omit *dierum*, others substitute *nummorum* ("coins," "money"). This last may be right; he would then be harking back to the dilemma he faced in 5, where the words *fluctuo* and *dispensatio* also occur, together with the idea of investing money. We could then translate "I have wavered in my stewardship of the Lord's money, but. . . . "

37. See Jb 7:1.

38. See 1 Cor 10:12.

39. See Eccl 1:2-3.

40. See Ps 18:10(19:9).

41. See Phil 3:20.

pain, longing ardently for the things he truly desires. Of these latter he has already spoken, and now he must speak of things here below. You have heard what he yearns for; listen now to what he spurns. *Nonetheless all things are empty, for everyone who lives.*

Verse 7. For whom are you amassing your wealth?

11. *Although each human being walks as an image.* What image is meant? Surely the image of him who said, *Let us make humans in our own image and likeness* (Gn 1:26)? *Although each human being walks as an image*: he puts in the word *although* because this image is something great, yet after the "although" comes a "nonetheless," to show that what you heard after "although" refers to what is beyond the sun, and what follows "nonetheless" refers to what is under the sun. The one belongs to truth, the other to emptiness. So *although each human being walks as an image, nonetheless his perturbation is vain.* Listen to what makes him fret, and see if it is not empty; listen so that you may leap over it and dwell in heaven, where there is no such emptiness. What is the emptiness here? *He heaps up treasure, but does not know for whom he will be gathering it.* A crazy vanity this is! *Blessed is the one whose hope is the Lord, who has had no regard for empty things and lying foolishness* (Ps 39:5(40:4)). No doubt, you miser, I seem to you to be mad when I say things like this; such statements are old wives' tales as far as you are concerned. Clearly you are a person of considerable shrewdness and acumen; every day you think up ways of making money from business, or from agriculture, perhaps even by oratory or by practicing at law, or from warfare; you might even dabble in moneylending. Like the intelligent man you are you let slip no opportunity to pile money upon money, and to stow it away secretly[42] with ever greater care. You plunder the next man and take precautions against anyone who may rob you; you fear the possibility of yourself suffering what you do to others, and you do not learn better ways from what you do suffer. But I am wrong: of course you do not suffer, do you? You are a prudent man, well able not only to acquire wealth but also to hang onto it. You have safe places to put it, and safe hands to entrust it to, so that nothing you have amassed may be lost. Well now, I want to put a question to your heart, and subject your shrewdness to scrutiny. You have gathered these riches, and preserved them so ably that you can lose nothing of what you have preserved; tell me, then: for whom are you keeping your wealth? I am not tackling you about any other evil aspect of your vain greed, I will not make a point of this or magnify its importance. I am putting this one question; this is all I want to discuss, since our

42. *Castigetur* usually means "punish, chastise" but occasionally "confine" (as a punishment). It evidently surprised copyists, who offered variants: *congregetur* or *collocetur* ("gather together") or even *cartigetur* ("record in a charter").

reading of this psalm gives me a good opportunity. Quite clearly you are picking up all the wealth you can; I am not telling you to watch out while you are picking it up in case you are picked up yourself; I am not saying, Take care that when you plan to be a predator you do not become the prey. No, I will emphasize it even more plainly, in case you are blinded by your greed and have not heard or understood—I am not, I tell you, saying, Take care that when you plan to prey on smaller fry you do not become the prey of someone more powerful. After all, you do not consider yourself to be in the sea, do you, where you might watch small fish being swallowed by larger ones? No, that is not what I am saying. I am not even concerned with the difficulties and dangers inherent in acquiring money, or the hardships endured by those who collect it and are exposed to perils on every side as they do so, almost coming face to face with death. All these aspects I am passing over. Granted, then, that you make money and no one challenges you, and you save it and no one robs you, now shake out the creases from your heart, and from that great prudence of yours which leads you to deride me and think me a simpleton for saying these things, tell me this: you are laying up treasure, but for whom? I see what you intend to say (did you think it would not have occurred to me?). You will say, "I am keeping it for my children." This sounds like family loyalty, but it is an excuse for injustice. "I am keeping it for my children," you say. Really? You are keeping it for your children, are you? Did not Idithun know about this? Certainly he did, but he reckoned that such a practice belonged to the old days, and so he despised it, because he was hurrying toward the new days.

There is a safer place to store it

12. All right then, now I will include your children in this question I am discussing with you. You who will pass away are storing up wealth for children who will pass away; or rather you who are already fading away are storing it up for those who are already fading away. I should not have said, "You will pass away," as though you were stable at present. You are not; for even today, from the point when we began speaking until the present moment, you know we have grown older. You cannot see your hair growing, yet even now as you stand here, or while you are busy with some work, or talking, your hair is growing. It does not grow suddenly, so as to send you scurrying for a barber. Our lifetime is flying past, for those who understand, and for those who take no notice, and for those intent on evil designs. You are passing away, and keeping your wealth for a son who is also passing away. I ask you, first, do you know that this son for whom you are saving will in fact ever possess it? Or, if he is not born yet, do you know that he will be born? You are keeping it for your children, yet you know neither that they will exist nor that they will possess it. Moreover you are not storing your treasure where it ought to be stored, for your Lord did not advise his servant

to squander the allowance he made to him. You are the servant of a great householder, and as such you are entrusted with money. What you love, what you have, he has given you, and it is not his wish that you waste what he gave you, he who intends even to give you himself. But even what he gave you temporarily he does not want you to waste, believe me. Perhaps there is a lot of it; it is overflowing and your needs cannot keep up with it; it must certainly be deemed superfluous. "But I do not want you to waste even that," your Lord says. "What am I to do?" Move it. The place where you have stored it is unsafe. You want to act in the best interests of your avarice; very well, see whether what I advise does not consort well even with your avarice. You want to keep what you have, not lose it, so I will show you where to store it. Do not pile up treasure on earth, without knowing for whom you are collecting it, or how the person who will possess it later, the future holder, may run through it. Perhaps the person who possesses it then will be possessed by someone else, and will be unable to hold onto what he inherits from you. Or perhaps even while you are saving it for him you may lose it, before he even comes into the money. Let me give you a piece of advice in your anxiety: *Lay up for yourselves treasure in heaven* (Mt 6:20). If you wanted to keep your valuables safe here on earth you would look for a storage-place; perhaps you would not entrust them to your own home because of your servants, so you would commit them to the banking quarter,[43] for accidents are unlikely to happen there and a thief cannot easily break in, so everything is kept safe. Why do you plan to do this? Because you have no better place to keep them? What if I show you a better place? I will tell you of one: do not entrust your wealth to someone unsuitable. There is someone eminently suitable, leave it with him. He has vast storerooms from which no riches can be lost, and he himself is very great, and richer than all the wealthy in the world. So perhaps you will reply, "How could I dare to entrust my goods to such a personage?" But suppose he himself asks you to? Recognize him: he is not simply a householder, he is also your Lord. "I do not want you to waste the money I allowed you, my servant," he says. "Be careful where you put it. Why are you putting it where you may lose it, and where you cannot yourself remain permanently in any case? There is another place, to which I am going to transfer you. Let your wealth travel there ahead of you. Do not fear to lose it, for I was the giver, and I will be its guardian." This is what your Lord says to you; question your faith, and see if you are willing to trust him. You will object, "What I can't see is as good as lost. I want to see it here." But if you are determined to see it here, you will neither see it here nor have anything at all there. You have some treasures hidden in the earth perhaps—I don't know what they are. When you go out, you do not carry them with you. You have come here to listen to this sermon, to acquire interior riches. Think about your exterior riches: have you brought them with you? No? Well

43. Variant: "to a neighboring banker."

then, you cannot actually see them now, can you? You believe that you have them at home, because you remember where you put them; but are you sure you have not lost them? How many people have returned to their homes and failed to find what they left there! Ah, some covetous people felt a clutch at their hearts when I said that![44] Because I said that it has often happened that people have gone home and not found what they left there, some of you may perhaps say in your hearts, "Stop it, bishop! Say something of good omen, and pray for us. Don't bring it on, please don't let it happen! I trust in God to let me find what I left there safe and sound." So you trust in God, but do not believe him? "I trust in Christ, that what I left at home will be safe, and no one will break in or steal it." So you want to play safe by trusting in Christ in order to lose nothing from your house. You will be much safer if you believe Christ, and put your money where he advised you to put it. Do you trust your servant, yet feel suspicious of your Lord? Are you secure about your house, and uneasy about heaven? "But how can I put money into heaven?" you will ask. I have given you good advice; put your money where I tell you. I do not want you to know how it gets to heaven. Put it into the hands of the poor, give it to the needy. What does it matter to you how it gets there? Will I not deliver what I receive? Have you forgotten the promise, *When you did it for even the least of those who are mine, you did it for me* (Mt 25:40)? Suppose some friend of yours had certain tanks or cisterns or other containers made to store liquid—wine or oil, perhaps—and you were looking for somewhere to store your produce, and your friend said to you, "I will store it for you." But suppose he had connected to his cisterns pipes and conduits that were out of sight, so that what was poured in as you watched drained away unseen; and he said to you, "Pour what you have in here," but you saw that the place where you had meant to store your produce was not what you thought, and you were afraid to pour it in. He would know the secret workings of his own plant, so he would say to you, "Don't worry, just pour it in. It flows from here to that other place over there. You can't see how it gets there, but trust me, I built it." Now he who made all things has built mansions for us all, and he wants our possessions to go there ahead of us, lest we lose them on earth. But if you have hoarded them on earth, tell me for whom you will be gathering them. You have children? Very well, then, increase their number by one, and give Christ something. *He heaps up treasure, but does not know for whom he will be gathering it. His perturbation is vain.*

Verse 8. Still waiting

13. *And now*, says Idithun, as he looks down at vanity and looks up at truth, standing midway between the two, with something below him and something

44. Evidently a frisson in the congregation evoked the next few remarks.

else above him (for below him is what he has leapt away from, and above is what he is straining toward). "*And now*," he says, "that I have leapt beyond some things, and trampled many things underfoot, now that I am no longer held captive by temporal things, I am still not perfect, for I have not yet received what I want." *In hope we have been saved. But if hope is seen, it is hope no longer, for when someone sees what he hopes for, why should he hope for it? But if we hope for what we do not see, we wait for it in patience* (Rom 8:24-25). So he asks, "*And now, what am I waiting for? Surely for the Lord.* For him I am waiting, for him who gave all these things by which I now set little store. He will give me himself, he who is above all things, he through whom all things were made and by whom I was made among all these things. He, the Lord, is my hope." You see our Idithun, brothers and sisters, you see how he waits for God. Let none of us claim to be perfect here: we should be deceiving ourselves, making a mistake, misleading ourselves, for none of us can reach perfection here. And what advantage would we gain by losing humility? *And now, what am I waiting for? Surely for the Lord.* When he has come we shall not have to wait for him any more, and then the perfection we seek will be ours. But for the present, Idithun is still waiting, however much he has already leapt over. *And all I have is continually before you.* I am making some progress, and already tending toward him; already I am beginning to attain true being, in some measure; but *all I have is continually before you.* What you have on earth is before the eyes of men and women. You have gold, silver, slaves, estates, trees, cattle, servants; all these can be seen by other men and women. Yet all you truly have is in God's sight all the time. *All I have is continually before you.*

Verse 9. Perfection through knowing one's imperfection

14. *Pluck me free from all my iniquities.* I have leapt across many things, yes, many indeed, yet *if we say that we have no sin, we deceive ourselves, and the truth is not in us* (1 Jn 1:8). I have leapt beyond many things, but still I beat my breast and say, *Forgive us our debts, as we forgive those who are in debt to us.* For you I wait, you who are my end, for *Christ is the end of the law, bringing justification to everyone who believes* (Rom 10:4). Free me from all my sins: not only from those of the past, lest I roll back again into the ones I have leapt across, but from absolutely all of them, for which I now beat my breast and say, *Forgive us our debts. Pluck me free from all my iniquities,* as I make my own the wisdom of the apostle's words. *Let those of us who are perfect be wise about this,* he says (Phil 3:15). He had just confessed that he was not yet perfect, yet he immediately added, *Let those of us who are perfect be wise about this.* How can he speak of *those of us who are perfect*? What do you mean, Paul? You said a moment ago, *Not that I have gained it already, or am already perfect.* "Read the whole verse

in order," he replies. *One thing only I do: forgetting what lies behind and straining to what lies ahead, I bend my whole effort to follow after the prize of God's heavenly call in Christ Jesus* (Phil 3:12-14). He is not yet perfect, because he is following after the prize of God's heavenly call, and he has not yet caught up with it; he has not yet arrived. But if he is not perfect, and has not reached his goal, which of us is perfect? Yet he goes on to say, *Let those of us who are perfect be wise about this.* If you are not perfect yourself, apostle, do you suppose we are? Remember, he has just said that he is! He did not say, "As many of you as are perfect, be wise about this"; what he said was, *Let those of us who are perfect be wise about this*, and he gave this exhortation just after saying, *Not that I have gained it already, or am already perfect.*

We learn, then, that in this life you can be perfect in no other way than by knowing you cannot be perfect. Your perfection will consist in having leapt over certain things in order to hasten on toward certain others, but in having leapt over them in such a way that there still remains something further, to which after all your efforts you must still leap. Faith like this is safe, for those who think they have already reached the goal are exalting themselves and are heading for a fall.

On show before mortals and angels

15. Since I am wise on this score, since I acknowledge that I am both imperfect and perfect (imperfect because I have not yet attained what I want, but perfect because I know this thing that I lack), since then I am wise enough to spurn human pleasures and refuse to find my joy in things that perish, since I am ridiculed by the miser who prides himself on his shrewdness and mocks me for being a simpleton—since this is how I live, he says, *you have made me an object of reproach to the unwise.* Your will is that I live among those who are set on vanity, and that I preach the truth to them. Inevitably we shall be taunted by them, for we have become a spectacle to this world, to both angels and mortals.[45] The angels praise us and mortals insult us; or rather angels both praise and revile, while mortals too both praise and revile. We have weapons in both right hand and left with which to fight, through glory and ignominy, through bad repute and good, as seducers and trustworthy people.[46] These varied fortunes are ours among angels as among mortals, for among the angelic hosts there are angels who are pleased when we live our lives well, and traitor-angels whom we offend by our good lives, just as among mortals there are holy people who applaud our life, and wicked people who deride our goodness. All these reactions are our weapons, some for the right hand, others for the left; both kinds are useful, and I employ both: right-handed and left-handed, the commendations and the insults,

45. See 1 Cor 4:9.
46. See 2 Cor 6:7-8.

those which do us honor and those which defame us. With both sorts I do battle with the devil and with both I strike home at him, in favorable times if I do not let success go to my head, and in adversity if I do not flinch.

Verses 10-11. Struck dumb

16. *You have made me an object of reproach to the unwise. I grew deaf and did not open my mouth.* But it was only to the unwise that *I did not open my mouth*, for to whom could I speak about what goes on within me? Rather will I *listen to what the Lord God speaks within me, for he will speak peace to his people*, whereas *there is no peace for wicked people*, says the Lord (Ps 84:9(85:8); Is 48:22). *I grew deaf and did not open my mouth, because it is you who made me.* Do you mean that was why you did not open your mouth—because it was God who made you? That is a strange thing to say. Did not God make a mouth for you so that you could speak? Does he who planted ears in us not hear? Does he who fashioned the eye not see?[47] God gave you a mouth to speak with, yet you say, *I grew deaf and did not open my mouth, because it is you who made me*?

But perhaps the phrase, *Because it is you who made me*, should be taken with the following verse, so that we read, *Because it is you who made me, take your scourges away from me*. Because you are my Maker, do not kill me; beat me only enough to help me succeed, not succumb;[48] buffet me only to bring me up, not to break me down.[49] *Because it is you who made me, take your scourges away from me*.

Verse 12. Salutary correction

17. *I fainted under your strong hand as you accused me*; that is, when you rebuked me, I tottered. What does it mean to be accused by you, Lord? The psalm goes on to explain: *You have chastised human beings for their sin, and brushed my soul away like a spider*. This Idithun understands a great deal; are any of us prepared to understand, and leap across with him? He confesses that he has fainted under God's censure, and asks that the divine rod be removed from him, since it is God who made him. It is for the Maker to remake his work, for the Creator to recreate. But are we to suppose, brothers and sisters, that Idithun's fainting, the tottering that made him long to be recreated and formed anew, was pointless? *You have chastised human beings for their sin*, he says. All my

47. See Ps 93(94):9.
48. *Ut proficiam, non ut deficiam.*
49. This phrase could also mean "Hammer me only to stretch me out further, not to pound me to pieces."

fainting, all my weakness, all my need to cry from the depths—all of this is because of my iniquity, and in this situation you did not condemn me, but chastised me. *You have chastised human beings for their sin.* This truth is stated even more clearly in another psalm: *It is good for me that you have humbled me, so that I may learn your righteous judgments* (Ps 118(119):71). I was humbled, yet I recognize that it did me good: it is both punishment and grace. What must he be holding in reserve for us when the punishment is over, if his very punishment is grace? God it is of whom a psalm says, *I was humbled, and he saved me* (Ps 114(116):6), and *it is good for me that you have humbled me, so that I may learn your righteous judgments.* For *you have chastised human beings for their sin.* There is another text which could be spoken to God only by one who leaps over, because only by such a leaper could its truth be seen: *You who shape our pain as your precept* (Ps 93(94):20). Yes, he says to God, *you shape our pain as your precept*, you fashion pain into a precept laid on me. You give form to my pain; you do not leave it shapeless but mold it to your purpose, and this carefully formed pain inflicted on me will be for me a commandment from you, so that you may set me free. You form pain, scripture says, you shape our pain, you mold our pain, you do not send any unreal pain to us. As an earthenware pot is so called because it is a potter's work, so do you like a potter mold our pain into shape. This is why it can be said, *You have chastised human beings for their sin.* I see myself full of bad things, I see myself undergoing punishment, and in you I see no injustice at all. So if I am undergoing punishment, and in you there is no injustice, what other explanation is there but that you chastise men and women in their sin?

Experienced weakness leads to humility

18. How have you chastised them? Tell us about the chastisement itself, Idithun. How were you disciplined? *You brushed my soul away like a spider.* This was the chastisement. What is more fragile than a spider—the creature itself, I mean, though I could also ask, what is more fragile than a spider's web? But look how frail the spider itself is: if you lay a finger on it even lightly, it disintegrates; nothing else at all is so easily crushed. You have treated my soul like that by chastising me for my iniquity, says the psalmist. When such weakness is the effect of God's correction, there is a kind of strength that is really a vice. (I can see that some of you are flying ahead and have grasped the point already, but you swift ones must not leave the slower ones behind; they need to follow the course of the sermon with the rest.) As I was saying, try to understand why this is. If it is the correction administered by a just God that has reduced a person to such weakness, there is a certain kind of strength that is simply vicious. Human beings displeased God by a show of that kind of strength, and therefore needed to be corrected by weakness; they displeased him by their pride, and therefore

needed to be disciplined by humility. All proud people claim to be strong. This is why the many who are coming from the east and the west have been victorious, the many who are to sit down with Abraham and Isaac and Jacob in the kingdom of heaven. Why have they been victorious? Because they refused to be strong. What do I mean by that: they refused to be strong? They were afraid to rely on their own strength, and they did not set up any righteousness of their own, but chose to be subject to God's righteousness.[50] When you hear the Lord's words, *Many will come from east and west and will sit down with Abraham and Isaac and Jacob in the kingdom of heaven; but the children of the kingdom* (the Jews who knew nothing of God's righteousness and wanted to establish their own) *will be thrown into the outer darkness* (Mt 8:11-12)—when you hear him say that, remember the faith of the centurion, a Gentile, who was so weak in himself, so lacking in any strength, that he confessed, *I am not worthy to have you coming under my roof* (Mt 8:8). He was unworthy to receive Christ in his house, but he had already welcomed him into his heart. Indeed, the Son of Man who teaches us humility had already found in the centurion's breast a place to lay his head.[51] When the centurion spoke like this, the Lord looked round at those who were following him and said, *Truly I tell you, I have not found faith to match this in Israel* (Mt 8:10). He found[52] this man weak, and the Israelites strong, so he drew the contrast between the two: *It is not the healthy who need the physician, but the sick* (Mt 9:12). For this reason, then, because they were humble, the Lord declared that *many will come from east and west and will sit down with Abraham and Isaac and Jacob in the kingdom of heaven; but the children of the kingdom will be thrown into the outer darkness*. Face the fact that you are mortal, that you carry about decaying flesh. You shall fall as any lordly ruler falls, you shall die as mortals die, and fall as the devil fell.[53] What good does the medicine of mortality do you? The devil is proud of being an angel without mortal flesh; but you[54] have been given mortal flesh, and it has done you no good because you are not humbled by this glaring weakness; therefore you shall fall as any lordly ruler falls. The first grace that God in his kindness confers on us is to bring us to confess our weakness, to confess that whatever good we can do, whatever strength we have, is ours only in him, so that anyone minded to boast may boast in the Lord.[55] *When I am weak, then I am strong*, says Paul (2 Cor 12:10). *You have chastised human beings for their sin, and brushed my soul away like a spider.*

50. See Rom 10:3.
51. See Mt 8:20.
52. Variant: "I found."
53. See Ps 81(82):7.
54. Here the "you" which has been plural, initially addressing the Jews, becomes singular.
55. See 1 Cor 1:31.

Only death is certain

19. *Yet all human anxiety in this life is pointless.* The psalmist returns now to the truth of which he reminded us earlier. However much progress a person has made here, *all human anxiety in this life is pointless*, for we live in uncertainty. Which of us can be secure even about the good in ourselves? We fret in vain. Each of us must cast our anxiety upon the Lord, cast on him whatever worries us, believing that he will sustain and protect us.[56] What is certain on this earth? Only death. Consider all the vicissitudes of this life, both good and bad, all that befalls us in our righteousness or in our iniquity. What among all these is certain? Only death. You have made some progress, have you? You know what you are today, but you do not know what you will be tomorrow. A sinner, are you? You know what you are today, but not what you will be tomorrow. You hope to get money, but whether it will come your way is uncertain. You hope to find a wife, but it is uncertain whether you will find one, or what she will be like if you do. You hope to have children, but you cannot be certain that any will be born. If they are born, it is not certain that they will survive. If they do live, you cannot know whether they will grow up well or prove to be weaklings. Whichever way you turn, everything is uncertain, except for one sole certainty: death. If you are poor, there is no certainty that you will ever be rich; if you are uneducated, you cannot be certain of being taught; if you are in poor health, it is uncertain whether you can recover your strength. You have been born, and so you can at least be certain that you will die, but even in this certainty of death uncertainty lurks, because you do not know the day of your death. We live beset with uncertainties, holding one thing only as certain, that we shall die, but without even the certainty of when that will be. The only thing we ultimately fear is the one thing that we cannot possibly avoid. *All human anxiety in this life is pointless.*

Verse 13. Weeping for the distant prospect

20. Although he is already leaping over these things, already to some extent living in things above and spurning those below, the psalmist still finds himself amid these earthly realities, and so he prays, "*Hear my prayer.* What have I to rejoice over, and what to groan about? I rejoice over the stages passed, but groan over what still remains. *Hear my prayer and my entreaty; let your ears listen for my weeping.* Just because I have leapt over so many things, and mounted above so many, am I not to weep? Have I not reason to weep all the more bitterly? In piling up knowledge we only pile up grief.[57] The more I long for what is still distant, the more I groan until it comes, and the more I weep. Am I not right to

56. See Ps 54:23(55:22).
57. See Eccl 1:18.

weep? Should I not weep the more as scandals become more widespread, as iniquity increases, as the charity of many grows colder?[58] *Who will give water to my head, and to my eyes a fount of tears?* (Jer 9:1). *Hear my prayer and my entreaty; let your ears listen for my weeping. Do not be silent toward me.* Do not let me become permanently deaf. *Do not be silent toward me*, but allow me to hear you." God speaks in secret, and he speaks to many in their hearts. Very loud is his voice in a very quiet heart, where with mighty power he cries, *I am your salvation.* That is how another psalm prays: *Say to my soul, I am your salvation* (Ps 34(35):3). Now he prays, "Let that voice never fall silent for me," that voice with which God says to the soul, *I am your salvation.* "I beg you," says he, "*Do not be silent toward me.*"

No security of tenure

21. *Because I am no more than a lodger in your house.* Whose lodger? I was the devil's lodger once, and a bad landlord I had then. But now I am with you, and am I a lodger still? What does "lodger" mean?[59] A lodger I am with respect to this place from which I shall be moving on, but not in that other place where I shall live for ever. The place where I shall abide for eternity should be called my home; but this place which I shall leave is the place of my sojourning. Yet even while I am a sojourner here, I am my God's lodger, as I shall be at home with him when I have gained my final dwelling. What is this home to which we shall move when the time comes for us to leave this present lodging? The apostle mentions it. You can recognize it when he says, *We have a building from God, a home not made by hands, an everlasting home in heaven* (2 Cor 5:1). If this home will be eternal in heaven, we shall not be lodgers or tenants any longer when we reach it. How could you be a lodger in your eternal home? But as for your earthly lodging, when the Master of the house says to you, "Move on," you must be prepared to go; and you do not know when he will say it. But your longing for your eternal home will itself prepare you. You must not be indignant with him for choosing any moment he likes to say, "Move on." It is not as though he had given you any guarantee, or had bound himself by any agreement, and not as though you had paid advance rent to cover any definite period. When the owner of the house decides, you will be out. For the time being you stay only by his favor. *Because I am no more than a lodger in your house, and a pilgrim.* There beyond is my homeland, there is my house; but here I am no more than a tenant in your property, a traveler lodging with you. Many travelers are the guests of the devil; but those who have believed and stayed faithful, though travelers still because they

58. See Mt 24:12.

59. *Inquilinus*, one who lodges in the house of another. Sometimes it means a serf, or sometimes a non-Roman in Roman territory.

have not yet reached their own land and their home, are travelers who lodge with God. *As long as we are in the body we are on pilgrimage and away from the Lord; but we make it our business to please him, whether we stay here or are on our way* (2 Cor 5:6,9). I am only a traveler and a lodger, *like all my forebears*. If I am like all my forebears, have I any right to say that I shall not be departing, when they have all moved on? Are the conditions of my sojourning likely to be different from theirs?

Verse 14. The goal of true being

22. What petition remains for me to make, then, since I shall undoubtedly move on from here? *Forgive me, so that I may find some cool refreshment before I go away*. But, Idithun, look carefully at those knots you need to have untied if you are to find cool refreshment before you go. What are they? You presumably suffer from some fever that makes you long for coolness, so that you cry out, "Let me find cool refreshment," and "Forgive me." What has God to forgive, unless it is some minute fault[60] that prompts you to pray, *Forgive us our debts*? Yet he begs, *Forgive me, before I go away to be no more*. Set me free entirely from my sins before I go, for I do not want to go with my sins on me. Forgive me, that I may have peace in my conscience, that my conscience may shed its burden of feverish anxiety, for I must take serious thought for my sin.[61] *Forgive me, so that I may find some cool refreshment*, and above all forgive me *before I go away to be no more*; for if you do not forgive me and allow me this cool refreshment, I shall go and not be. *Before I go away* to a place where I shall not be, *forgive me that I may find some cool refreshment*.

This raises the question: in what sense will he not be? Was he not going to his rest? God forbid that Idithun should have failed to find that rest! Obviously Idithun was going away, but going away to his rest. But think instead of some malefactor, not Idithun: someone who does not leap over earthly things, someone who lays up treasure here and watches over it jealously, someone unjust, proud, boastful, haughty, disdainful of the pauper lying at the gate. Will such a person "not be"? Of course he or she will still exist. Then what does the psalm mean by saying, *Before I go away to be no more*? If that rich man in the gospel did not exist anymore, who was burning? Who was longing for a drop of water to be trickled onto his tongue from Lazarus' finger? Who was it who kept saying, *Father Abraham, send Lazarus* (Lk 16:24)? If he could speak he undoubtedly existed; this man who was on fire existed, the man who will rise again at the end, to be condemned to eternal flames along with the devil. What

60. *Scrupulum* (or *scripulum*), the 24th part of an ounce, applied metaphorically to a source of worry or unease.
61. See Ps 37:19(38:18).

does *to be no more* mean, then? I think Idithun had in mind the difference between being and non-being. He was looking forward with all the longing of his heart, with all the power of his mind, to that end which he had desired should be shown him when he prayed, *Make known to me my end, O Lord*. He was looking to the number of his days, the number that truly *is*; he considered that all the things that exist here below have no being at all when compared with that eternal being; and he habitually declared that he himself did not truly exist either. The things of heaven abide, but the things of earth are changeable, subject to death and fragile. As for that eternal pain, it is full of decay, and the only reason it does not end is that it is doomed to be coming to an end unendingly.[62] Idithun gazed toward that blessed country, his blessed land, his blessed home, where the saints share eternal life and unchangeable truth; and he feared to go away from it and be exiled to a place where there is no true being. He longed to be, there where being is being at its supreme perfection. Comparing the two, and finding himself standing between them, he was still fearful, so he said, "*Forgive me, so that I may find some cool refreshment before I go away to be no more*, for if you have not forgiven my sins, I will go away from you for ever. And from whom would I then be going away for ever? From him who said, *I AM WHO AM*, from him who said, *Thus shall you say to the children of Israel, HE WHO IS has sent me to you*" (Ex 3:14). Anyone who takes the road away from him who truly *is* necessarily goes toward non-being.

23. Well, brothers and sisters, if I have burdened and wearied you, put up with it, for this sermon has been hard work for me too. But in fact you have only yourselves to blame if you feel overworked, because if I felt you were getting bored with what was being said, I would stop immediately.

62. *Ad hoc non finitur, ut sine fine finiatur.*

Exposition of Psalm 39

A Sermon to the People

Persecution, overt and insidious

1. Our Lord Jesus Christ made many prophecies about the future. Some of them we know to have been fulfilled; others we hope to see fulfilled later. But all of them most certainly will be fulfilled, because Truth has said so; and as he speaks with total fidelity, so he seeks people who will believe him with like fidelity. When these prophecies come true, believers will be glad, but unbelievers will be thoroughly dismayed. Nonetheless these things will come to pass whether human beings want it or not, and whether they believe or not; as the apostle says, *If we deny him, he will deny us; if we do not believe, he still remains faithful, for he cannot deny himself* (2 Tm 2:12-13). But above all, brothers and sisters, remember the brief piece of advice we all heard just now in the gospel, and hold onto it: *Whoever perseveres to the end will be saved.*[1] In former days our ancestors were arrested and haled before councils, and pleaded their case before enemies whom they loved. To the enemies who judged them they offered as much reproof as they could, and love to the limit of their strength. Righteous blood was splashed about, and from that blood, like seed sown throughout the world, sprang the crop of the Church.[2]

But the period that followed has been one of scandals, and pretense, and temptations, provoked by those who say, *Look, here is Christ!* or *There he is!* (Mt 24:23). Our enemy was a lion in earlier days when he used to rampage openly, but now he is a snake, lying hidden in ambush. But another psalm says to Christ, *On both lion and snake you will trample* (Ps 90(91):13), and because we are his body and his members, he will trample[3] on the snake and save us from harm today, just as of old he trampled on the lion with the feet of our forebears, the lion that roared openly against them and dragged the martyrs off to their deaths. The apostle warned us about the wiles of this snake: *I have prepared you for presentation to your one husband, Christ, as a chaste virgin; but I am afraid*

1. Mt 24:13. This gospel, which had been read before Augustine began to preach, deals with the persecutions the faithful are to expect in the last days, and is the background to many of his reflections in this sermon.
2. The simile recalls Tertullian's famous remark that "the blood of martyrs is the seed of Christians." Augustine echoes Tertullian again toward the end of the present sermon; see section 26 and note there.
3. So the CCL editors; variants have "he tramples" and "let him trample."

that, just as the serpent seduced Eve by his cunning, so too your minds may be led astray, and fall away from that chastity which you have in Christ (2 Cor 11:2-3). The snake is that ancient seducer who tries to violate the virginity not of the flesh, but of the heart. As a human seducer exults in his wickedness when he violates the body, so the devil is triumphant when he corrupts the mind. As our ancestors needed patient fortitude when pitted against the lion, so do we need vigilance against the snake. Persecution of the Church never ceases, whether it is from the lion or from the snake; and the devil is more to be feared in the guise of deceiver than when he rants and roars. In former days he forced Christians to deny Christ; nowadays he teaches them to deny Christ. Then he used force, now doctrine. Then he attacked them violently, but now insidiously. Then he raged in full view, but now he weaves and slithers and is difficult to see. It is plain how he applied force to Christians in those earlier days to make them deny Christ. They were dragged off and ordered to apostatize, and when they confessed Christ instead they earned their crowns. But today the persecutor persuades by teaching, and he misleads because anyone so deceived does not think that he or she is forsaking Christ. What do the heretics says nowadays to a Catholic Christian? "Come along and be a Christian." They say this to elicit the question, "But am I not a Christian already?" There is a world of difference between saying, "Come and be a Christian," and saying, "Come and deny Christ." This latter is an obvious invitation to wickedness; the lion's growl is audible from afar, and a Christian gives him a wide berth. But the slippery snake approaches unseen with silent, gliding motion, drawing his length along softly[4] as he creeps in, craftily whispering; and he does not say, "Deny Christ." Who would listen to him if he did, now that we have seen the martyrs crowned? What he does say is, "Be a Christian." The hearer is struck by this remarkable saying.[5] If the poison has not yet penetrated, he or she replies, "I am a Christian, that's obvious." But if he is swayed and captivated[6] by the serpent's tooth, he replies, "Why do you say to me, Be a Christian? How can you say that? Am I not a Christian already?" The snake answers, "No." "I'm not?" "No." "Well, make me a Christian then, if I'm not one." "Come along, then. But when the bishop begins to question you about what you are, do not say, I am a Christian, or I am a believer; but say you are not. If you follow this advice, you may become one."

The truth is that if this bishop discovers that the profession he hears is that of a believing Christian, he will not dare to baptize him over again;[7] but if he hears the candidate say he is not, he gives him what he apparently did not have until

4. Variant: "with gentle touch."
5. Variant; "wretched saying."
6. Variants: "scorched"; "worn down."
7. A law enacted under the Emperor Theodosius (A.D. 379-395) had forbidden the repetition of baptism; see *Cod. Theod.*, xvi. Donatist methods of recruitment seem to be Augustine's target in the present polemic.

now, trusting to be held faultless himself since he is only acting in accordance with the candidate's own statement. But I want to take you up on this point, you heretic. Why do you think yourself immune to criticism? Why should I listen to such excuses, that you do not deny the validity of such a candidate's baptism, because the denial is his only? If the person who denies it is at fault, what of the one who teaches him to deny it? Are you really exonerated, you, a Christian, who achieve by your false teaching what the pagan achieved by threats? What are you trying to do, anyway? Do you rob him of what he has, by persuading him to deny that he has it? You do not take it away from him, but cause him to keep it in such a way that it becomes for him a title to punishment. What he has, he has: that baptism is imprinted on him like a brand, and as it was a proud badge for the soldier, so it convicts the deserter. What are you doing? You are trying to superimpose Christ on Christ. If you were single-hearted, you would not duplicate Christ. What is more, I put this to you: have you forgotten that Christ is called a stone? *The stone rejected by the builders has become the headstone of the corner* (Ps 117(118):22; see Mt 21:42; 1 Pt 2:4). If then Christ is a stone, and you are attempting to superimpose Christ on Christ, you must have forgotten what you heard in the gospel, that no stone will be left standing upon another.[8] So strong, by contrast, is the bonding of charity, that although many living stones come together in the building of God's temple, one stone is formed out of the many. You, on the other hand, have torn yourself away. You lure people away from the building and invite them to ruin. These crafty tricks of yours are ever multiplying and never cease. We see them, we endure them, and we do our best to circumvent them by disputation, by persuasion, by attempts to reach agreement, and by a show of force, and yet by loving you throughout it all.[9]

Yet in spite of all our efforts these people continue in their pernicious practice, and our heart grieves over our dead brethren. But while we mourn those outside our unity we fear for those inside it; so what are we to do amid the manifold pressures and incessant temptations that surround us in this life? When iniquity is so rampant, charity seems to grow weary; as scripture says, *With iniquity increasing mightily, the love of many grows cold* (Mt 24:12). What indeed are we to do, except follow the advice of the next verse, with God's help? *Whoever perseveres to the end will be saved* (Mt 24:13).

Verses 2-3. Waiting for the Lord

2. Let us make the words of this psalm our own: *I waited and waited for the Lord*. The psalmist says, "*I waited and waited*, not for some human promise-maker who is liable to deceive or be deceived, nor for some human

8. See Mt 24:2.
9. Variant: "by loving you all."

comforter who may be overwhelmed by his or her own sorrow before cheering me. By all means let my brother or sister comfort me by sharing my sadness; let us groan together, weep together, pray together and wait together, but for whom? For the Lord," who never withdraws what he has promised, but only defers it. He will deliver it, he will most assuredly deliver it, for he has delivered many things already, though we would have no right to doubt God's faithfulness even if he had not yet delivered anything. We should think along these lines: "He has promised us everything. He has not given us anything yet, but he is a reliable promiser and faithful in keeping his promise." Your job is to be an assiduous creditor. Even if you are small or weak, exact the promised mercy. Haven't you noticed how the young lambs butt their mothers' udders with their heads to get the milk they need?

I waited and waited for the Lord, says the psalmist. And what did the Lord do? Did he turn away from you, or despise you for waiting, or did he perhaps fail to see you? Certainly not. What, then? *He looked after me, and listened to my plea*. He looked after you and listened, so your waiting was not in vain, was it? His eyes were on you and his ears attentive to you, for *the eyes of the Lord are upon the righteous, and his ears are open to their prayers* (Ps 33:16(34:15)). But what about when you were behaving badly, when you were blaspheming him? Did he not see then? Or hear then? If not, what would have become of the next line in that other psalm, *The Lord frowns on evildoers*? And to what purpose? *To blot out their memory from the earth* (Ps 33:17(34:16)). So when you were bad he was looking at you, but not looking after you.[10] Accordingly this person who was waiting for the Lord in our psalm would have thought it insufficient to say, "He looked at me." Rather he says, *The Lord looked after me*; that is, he heeded me in order to comfort me, he looked to my interests. What did he heed? *He listened to my plea.*

Verse 4. Out of the mud

3. And what did he give you? What did he do for you? *He led me out of a pit of misery and from slimy mud; he set my feet upon a rock and guided my steps. And he put a new song into my mouth, a hymn to our God.* He has granted you great benefits, yet he still owes you more. But anyone who is in possession of so much already paid must be confident about the balance, all the more so since he was bound to be confident in any case even before he had received anything. By these tokens our Lord has convinced us that he is both faithful in his promises and generous in his giving. What has he done in this instance? *He led me out of a pit of misery*. What is this pit of misery? The murky depth of iniquity to which carnal lusts consign us; that is why he calls it *slimy mud*. From where did he lead

10. *Adtendebat te, sed non adtendebat tibi.*

you out? From a deep place. So that explains your cry in another psalm, *Out of the depths I have cried to you, Lord* (Ps 129(130):1). We must notice this, though: people who are already crying out from a deep place cannot be entirely sunk in it, for their cry is already beginning to lift them. Others, however, are more deeply immersed in the mire, because they do not even realize that they are in the depths. These are the proud, scornful folk, not the devout who pray, not the tearful ones who cry out, but those of whom scripture says elsewhere, *A person devoid of reverence goes deep into sin and is defiant* (Prv 18:3). In such a case it would not matter so much that he or she is a sinner; far worse is his determination not to confess his sins but to defend them; and this sinks him deeper. But the one who has cried out from the depths has already lifted his head from the deepest place in order to utter the cry. In this psalm such a person has been heard, and led out of the pit of misery and the slimy mud. Already he has faith that he did not have before; he has hope where formerly there was none; and he who was going astray with the devil now walks with Christ. This is unmistakable, for he says, *He set my feet upon a rock and guided my steps*. But the rock is Christ.[11]

Let us be on this rock, and may our steps be guided, for we still need to keep on walking if we are to arrive anywhere. The apostle Paul was already on the rock, and knew that his steps were guided, yet what did he have to say? *Not that I have gained it already, or am already perfect, brethren; I do not judge myself to have taken hold of it yet* (Phil 3:12-13). What has been granted to you, then, if you have not taken hold yet? For what are you giving thanks when you say, *I received mercy* (1 Tm 1:13)? He is thankful because his steps were guided and he is now walking upon a rock. This is how he puts it: *one thing only I do: forgetting what lies behind* . . . and what does lie behind? The pit of misery. What does "lying behind" evoke? Slimy mud, carnal lusts, the darkness of iniquity. *Forgetting what lies behind, I strain to what lies ahead*. He would not say he was straining ahead if he had already reached the goal; for the mind stretches out in desire for the thing it longs for, not in delight over what has been attained. *Straining to what lies ahead*, he says, *I bend my whole effort to follow after the prize of God's heavenly call in Christ Jesus* (Phil 3:13-14). He kept on running, for he was intent on winning the prize. In another text he speaks from a point very close to the winning-post: *I have run the whole course* (2 Tm 4:7). When he said, *I bend my whole effort to follow after the prize of God's heavenly call*, he was already well onto the right path, because his steps had been guided on the rock, so he had matter for thanksgiving and also something still to ask for; he gave thanks for what had been given and pleaded for what was still owing. What had been given already that moved him to gratitude? The forgiveness of his sins, the illumination of faith, the strength of hope, the fire of charity. But in what

11. See 1 Cor 10:4.

respect could he still hold the Lord his debtor? *All that remains for me now is the crown of righteousness*, he says. Something is still owing to me. What is it? *The crown of righteousness, which the Lord, the just judge, will award me on that day* (2 Tm 4:8). At first God is a kindly father, drawing us out of the pit of misery so that he can forgive our sins and disengage us from the slimy mud; then he is a just judge who awards what he has promised to us as we walk well, though it is only by his prior gift that we do walk well. The just judge will make due award, then, but to whom? *Whoever perseveres to the end will be saved* (Mt 24:13).

A hymn of praise, but for our benefit, not God's

4. *He put a new song into my mouth.* What new song? *A hymn to our God.* Possibly you were accustomed to sing hymns to other gods, old hymns; it was the old person who sang them, not the new person. Let the new person come to birth and sing a new song; let the renewed person love what has made him or her new. What is more ancient than God, who exists before all things, with no end and no beginning? Yet when you come back to him he is new for you. When you went away from him you grew old and complained, *I have grown old amid all my enemies* (Ps 6:8(7)). We sing a hymn to our God, and the hymn itself gives us freedom,[12] for *I will call upon the Lord in praise, and I shall be saved from my enemies* (Ps 17:4(18:3)). A hymn is a song of praise. Make sure when you call on God that you do so in praise, and not in an attempt to coerce him. If you invoke God, begging him to suppress your enemy, or if you invoke God as your ally when you are minded to make merry over someone else's misfortune, you are making him collude with your malice. And if you do that, you are not calling upon him with praise, but trying to manipulate him. You think God is a replica of yourself. But another text of scripture puts you right about that: *All this you did, and I was silent; you were wrong to think that I will be like you* (Ps 49(50):21). Be sure to invoke the Lord with praise; do not suppose that he is like you. And if you avoid that, you may become like him. Your business is to *be perfect, like your Father in heaven, who causes his sun to rise over the good and the wicked, and sends rain upon just and unjust alike* (Mt 5:48,45). Accordingly you must praise the Lord in such a way that you wish no harm to your enemies. "But how much good ought I to will them?" you ask. As much as you want for yourself. It is not as though they will become good by stealing some of what belongs to you, or that you will receive less because something good is given to them. Your enemy is only your enemy because he or she is bad; but if your enemy becomes good, he or she will be your friend and companion. Indeed, that erstwhile enemy will be your brother or sister, so that you will want to share with him or her every good thing you loved.

---

12. Variant: "Let us sing . . . and let the hymn itself give. . . ."

Invoke the Lord with praise, and sing a hymn to your God. *By a sacrifice of praise I shall be honored*, he tells us (Ps 49(50):23). How can that be? Is there more glory for God, because you glorify him? Do we add something to God's glory when we say to him, "Glory be to you, my God"? Do we render him more holy when we say, "I bless you, O my God"? No. When he blesses us, it is a different matter; he does make us holier and happier. When he glorifies us, he does indeed make us more glorious and increase our honor; but when we glorify him, the gain is ours, not his. After all, how do we glorify him? By declaring him glorious, not by making him so. This is why, after telling us that *by a sacrifice of praise I shall be honored*, he continues with another statement to help you understand that you are not conferring some benefit on God by offering him this sacrifice of praise: *And along that road I will show him my salvation* (Ps 49(50):23). So you see, when you praise God, it is not God who profits thereby, but you. Are you praising God? Then you are walking on the right road. Are you trying to coerce God? Then you have lost your way.

Christ's voice in the song of his members

5. *He put a new song into my mouth, a hymn to our God.* Someone may perhaps ask who the speaker is in this psalm. Briefly, it is Christ. But as you know, brothers and sisters—and it can never be said too often—Christ sometimes speaks in his own person, as our Head. He is the Savior of the body and its Head, the Son of God who was born of a virgin, suffered for us, rose for our justification and sits at God's right hand to intercede for us.[13] He will bring due retribution at the judgment, good things for the good and bad things for the wicked. He is our Head because he graciously willed to become the Head of the body by taking flesh from us in order that he might in that flesh die for us; but he also raised it from death for us, that we might learn to hope where before we could only despair, and find our feet on the rock, and walk in Christ. Accordingly he sometimes speaks as our Head, and at other times as from ourselves, his members, just as he spoke in the name of his members and not from himself when he said, *I was hungry and you fed me* (Mt 5:35). Again, when he said, *Saul, Saul, why are you persecuting me?* (Acts 9:4) it was the Head crying out in the person of his members, yet he did not say, "Why are you persecuting my members?" but, *Why are you persecuting me?* If he suffers in us, we shall also be crowned in him. This is the charity of Christ. Can anything else compare with it? He put a hymn about this matter into our mouths, and sings it with the voice of his members.

13. See Rom 4:25; 8:34.

Leaders and followers

6. *The righteous will see and be afraid, and will hope in the Lord.* The righteous, it says, will see. Who are these righteous people? Believers, clearly, because it is the one who lives by faith who is just.[14] Moreover this is the way things are ordered in the Church: some forge ahead and others follow; but those in front provide an example for those who follow, and the followers imitate those in front. But does this mean that the leaders who furnish an example have no one to follow? If they follow nobody, they will go astray. They do indeed have someone to follow—Christ himself. These better people in the Church may have none of their fellows left to imitate, because they have made such progress that they have outstripped them all; but Christ is left to them, and they must follow him to the end. You can see this order of things[15] sketched by the apostle Paul when he says, *Be imitators of me, as I am of Christ* (1 Cor 4:16). Any whose feet have already been guided onto the rock must be an example to other believers; as Paul says elsewhere, *Be an example to the faithful* (1 Tm 4:12). The faithful themselves are the righteous, who should keep their eyes on those who are ahead of them in goodness, and follow by imitating their lives.

How are they to follow? *The righteous will see, and be afraid.* As they watch they will learn to fear evil paths, for they will see that people better than themselves have chosen paths that are good. The righteous are like wayfarers who see others walking with assurance down a certain road, while they themselves are doubtful about the right way and hesitating which road to take. They say to themselves, "Those others must have good reason for going that way, and they are making for the same place as we are. Why would they take that road so confidently, if they did not know that the one we are on is dangerous?" Similarly *the righteous will see and be afraid.* They see on the one hand a narrow path, and on the other a wide road; few take the former, but many the latter.[16] But if you are a righteous person, counting is not important; you will do better to weigh. Use reliable scales, not deceptive ones, since you have been called righteous. *The righteous will see and be afraid*: this was said about you. Do not count the crowds of people who throng the wide roads, filling the circus tomorrow, shouting their glee on the city's birthday while degrading[17] the city by their disgraceful behavior. Take no notice of them. They are very numerous, beyond counting, whereas few are to be seen on the narrow path. Use a reliable balance, I tell you, and weigh the matter: look how much straw you can send sailing up against only a few grains!

So much for the righteous believers who follow; what of those who go ahead? Let them not be proud or self-important, and let them not mislead those who

14. See Hb 2:4; Rom 1:17.
15. Variant: "Charity has arranged this order of things."
16. See Mt 7:13-14.
17. Variant: "disturbing."

follow. How might they do that? By promising salvation through themselves. Recall the duty of the followers: *the righteous will see and be afraid, and will hope in the Lord*, not in those who walk ahead. They must indeed watch those in front, and follow and imitate them, but they must also remember from whom those in front received the strength to go ahead like that, and in him they must hope. Let them imitate their betters, yes, but put their trust only in him by whose gift those leaders are what they are. *The righteous will see and be afraid, and will hope in the Lord.* It reminds us of another psalm where we read, *I have lifted my eyes to the mountains*, and there we understand the mountains to represent certain illustrious people, great spiritual men in the Church, people who are great because of their massive worth, not because swollen with pride. Through them the whole of scripture was mediated to us; they are the prophets, the evangelists, the good teachers. In their direction, therefore, *I have lifted my eyes to the mountains, from where comes help for me*. But in case you should think this means human help, the psalm immediately specifies: *My help is from the Lord, who made heaven and earth* (Ps 120(121):1-2). *The righteous will see and be afraid, and will hope in the Lord.*

Verse 5. Steer clear of the broad road

7. Well now, those who want to hope in the Lord, those who see and are afraid, must beware of walking in bad ways, broad ways. Let them prefer the narrow path, where the steps of some people have already been guided onto the rock; and let them listen now to how they must conduct themselves. *Blessed is the one whose hope is the Lord, who has had no regard for empty things and lying foolishness.* These are the ways you were tempted to take. Look at the crowds on the broad road; it is a sure path to the amphitheatre and a sure path to death. The broad road is lethal; its spaciousness is pleasant for a time, but its end is narrow constraint for eternity. Yet the crowds bawl and the crowds hurry along and the crowds make merry and the crowds all run in the same direction. Do not imitate them, do not turn aside; these are empty things and lying foolishness. Let the Lord your God be your hope; do not hope to get anything else from the Lord your God, but let the Lord your God himself be your hope. Many people hope to get money from God, many hope to get from him honors that are transitory and perishable, or they want some other thing from God, something other than God himself. But you, you must simply ask for your God. Hold all those other things cheap and make your way to him; forget all the rest and remember him; leave them all behind and stretch out toward him. He has brought back to the right way any of us who have erred, he leads the right-minded along,[18] and he himself leads them to the very end. Let him be your hope, then, for he leads us,

18. Variant: "he leads the one he has brought back."

and leads us all the way. Where does earthly avarice lead, what is its end? You were trying to get your hands on country estates, you were greedy for land, you ousted your neighbors. Then, having bought them out, you gazed covetously on the property of a new set of neighbors, and eventually your avarice stretched so far that you reached the coast! But when you had arrived at the coast you coveted the islands. So having secured ownership of the earth, perhaps you now intend to seize heaven? Abandon all these infatuations; he who made heaven and earth is far more beautiful.

Fanatical addiction

8. *Blessed is the one whose hope is the Lord, who has had no regard for empty things and lying foolishness.* Why are these insane pursuits called "lying"? Because insanity does tell lies, while soundness of mind is truthful. When you think these things good, you are deceived, you are not of sound mind, you have become delirious through high fever and are enamored of something unreal.[19] You sing the praises of some charioteer, you shout to him, you go crazy about him. This is empty, and lying foolishness. "No it's not," shouts the fan. "There's nothing better, nothing is so much fun." What am I to do for someone in the grip of a fever like this? If you have any pity in you, pray for people in this plight. It often happens that a doctor feels desperate as he turns to the people in the house, who stand around tearfully, hanging on his every word as they wait for his report on the patient who is dangerously ill. The doctor stands there undecided, for he cannot give any encouraging promise, but fears to tell them the bad news lest he arouse alarm. So he resorts to a discreet pronouncement: "The good God can do all things. Pray for him." So which of these insane folk can I hope to control? Which of them will listen to me? Who among them will not call us spoilsports? Because we do not share their frenzy they think we are missing their intense and manifold pleasures, in which they themselves are losing their minds, and they fail to see that these things are deceptive. When shall I have the chance to give the patient an egg, even against his will,[20] or offer him a restorative drink;[21] how can I heal him, when shall I find a way? I beg him to eat lest he collapse from

19. The vehemence of Augustine's polemic against "shows" in the following paragraphs is explained by his early experience of their power to seduce the mind and create addictions. As a student at Carthage he had been enamored of the spurious emotions aroused by theatrical performances, and later had trembled at the near-disaster that had befallen his friend Alypius through contamination with the blood-lust of the crowds at gladiatorial fights (see his *Confessions*, III,2,2; VI,7,11-VI,8,13). He called it *curiositas* and came to see it as an aspect of the "lust of the eyes" condemned in 1 Jn 2:16, a craving for superficial and titillating knowledge that was a perversion of the mind's thirst for truth.

20. The many variants to which the projected treatment has given rise include: "How can I give him wine, even against his will?" and "When can I give him an egg, if he does not want it?"

21. Variants: "a drink of restorative juice/medicine"; "lest he harm himself with a restorative drink"; "persuade him to accept a restorative drink."

malnutrition and never regain his health,[22] but he clenches his fists and tries to attack the physician. Even if he does land a punch, he must still be loved, and if he inflicts some injury he must not be abandoned; he will recover one day and then he will be grateful.

How many people recognize themselves in this description, and look at each other, and talk about each other in God's Church? In the bosom of Holy Church they apply themselves now to good pursuits connected with the word of God and with the duties and responsibilities of charity. They habitually seek the company of Christ's flock instead of staying away from the church; they see this and they speak to each other about one another. "Who is that circus-fan now? Look at the once fanatical admirer of that gladiator, that actor!" The speaker means someone else, and that other speaks similarly of him. These exchanges undoubtedly take place, and we are certainly happy about such people. And if we are happy about them, let us not despair of others like them. Let us pray for them, dearest friends, for after being numbered among the impious they come to swell the number of the saints. *They have had no regard for empty things and lying foolishness.*

"So-and-so has won! He drove such-and-such a horse!" shouts the fanatic. Does he think to be godlike in his forecasts? By affecting divinity he loses the source of divinity; he is often liberal with his tips and he is often wrong. Why? Because this is lying foolishness. But why are the forecasts sometimes correct? To lead crazy people astray, people who by falling in love with a semblance of the truth will stumble into the trap of falsehood. Let them be left behind, abandoned, amputated from the body. If they were once our members, let them be cut off as dead; as scripture enjoins, *Put to death your members that belong to the earth* (Col 3:5). Let our God be our hope. He who made all things is better than all things; he who made beautiful things is more beautiful than all of them; he who made all that is strong is himself stronger; he who made all greatness is greater than any. Whatever you have loved, he will be that for you. Learn to love the Creator in the creature, the Maker in what is made. Do not let something he has made so captivate you that you lose him by whom you were made yourself. *Blessed is the one whose hope is the Lord, who has had no regard for empty things and lying foolishness.*

Verse 6. There are better shows in God's Church

9. If anyone has been struck by that verse, and wants to correct his or her life, if the righteousness that comes from faith has filled such a person with fear, and he has begun to want to walk in the narrow path, he will perhaps say to us, "I shall never keep up this walking, if I have no shows to watch." What are we going to do about that, brothers and sisters? Are we going to leave him starved of shows?

---

22. Variant: "I beg him to eat, lest he collapse from malnutrition; I beg him to regain his health."

He will die, he will never hold out, he will not follow us. What shall we do, then? Let us give him other wonderful things to watch, in place of the shows he has given up. And what kind of entertainments are we going to offer to a Christian man or woman, whom we want to wean away from those other shows? I give thanks to the Lord our God, for in this next verse of the psalm he has indicated what shows we must provide and put on for show-addicts who want shows[23]. Our convert has turned away from the circus, from the theater, from the fights in the stadium, so let him inquire what there is to look at among us; yes, by all means let him inquire, for we do not want to leave him with no spectacle to enjoy. What shall we give him instead? Listen to the next verse: *You have wrought many wondrous deeds, O Lord my God.* He used to watch prodigies performed by human beings, let him now watch God's wondrous deeds. Many are the wondrous feats of the Lord, so let him look at them. Why did they ever become worthless in his eyes? He applauds the charioteer who controls four horses which run their course without slipping or stumbling; but has the Lord not performed feats just as wonderful in the spiritual sphere? Let him control licentiousness, let him control cowardice, control injustice, control rashness;[24] let him, I mean, control the passions which, when they fall into excess, produce those vices. Let him harness them and subject them to himself, and hold the reins, and not be whirled away; let him steer where he chooses, and not be dragged off in a direction where he does not want to go. He was used to applauding a charioteer, and as a charioteer he will be applauded; he used to shout for a charioteer to be invested with the victor's insignia, but he himself will be clothed with immortality. These rewards, and these wonderful events, God provides. He shouts to us from heaven, "I am watching you. Fight bravely, I will help you; win, and I will crown you." *You have wrought many wondrous deeds, O Lord my God; deep are your thoughts and no one is like you.*

Now consider an actor.[25] After much practice a man has learned to walk a tightrope, and as he hangs balancing there he has you hanging in suspense. But look at one who achieves feats even more worth watching. Your acrobat has learned to walk on a rope, but he has never made anyone walk on the sea, has he? Forget your theatrical shows and watch our Peter, who is not a tightrope-walker but a sea-walker, if I may so express it. But that is not all: walk yourself, not on those same waters where Peter walked, because his walking was a sign, but on other waters, for this world is a sea. It has its undrinkable saltiness, its waves of tribulation and its storms of temptation; it is inhabited by men and women like

23. The repetitiveness seems deliberate and a trifle mocking: *Quae spectatoribus spectare volentibus spectacula* . . . .

24. The vices opposed to the traditional four cardinal virtues: temperance, fortitude, justice, and prudence. The list was derived from Plato and Aristotle, and taken over by Ambrose and Augustine, and Christian tradition more generally.

25. *Histrio*, evidently here of the acrobatic variety.

fishes, rejoicing in their misdeeds as they devour one another. Walk on it, tread it beneath your feet. You want to watch spectacles? Very well, be a spectacle yourself. And in case you weaken, keep your eye on someone who went before you and said, *We have been set up as a spectacle to this world, and to angels and to mortals* (1 Cor 4:9). Tread the sea underfoot, or you may sink into it. But you will not be able to walk there, you will not be able to tread on it, unless he who first trod the sea himself has commanded you. Peter said to him, *If it is you, tell me to come to you over the water* (Mt 14:28). And because it was indeed the Lord who walked there, he heard Peter as he asked, granted him what he longed for, called him as he walked, and pulled him out as he sank. The Lord worked these marvels; gaze at them, let faith be your avid eye. And then perform similar wonders yourself, for even if the winds batter you, and the waves roar against you, and human weakness throws you into some doubt about your salvation, you have a recourse: you can cry out, "Lord, I'm sinking!" He who told you to walk will not let you drown. Since you already have your feet on a rock you need have no fear even in the sea; if you were not on the rock you would certainly sink, but the rock on which we are to walk is not covered by the sea.

10. Witness God's wonders. *I announced the news and spoke the message, and they were multiplied, in numbers beyond reckoning*. There is a definite number, and there are also others beyond reckoning. The number is definite because it pertains to Jerusalem, the heavenly city; for the Lord knows who belong to him:[26] God-fearing Christians, faithful Christians, Christians who keep the commandments, walk in God's ways, refrain from sin and, if they have fallen, confess it. These are the people who are included in the number. But are these all? No, there are others outside this number. Even if there are but a few of them in comparison with the far greater crowds outside, still look how our churches are bursting with them, how the walls are bulging with them, how they tread on each other and nearly suffocate each other, so closely are they packed. But then, let there be but a public show on offer, and many of these make for the amphitheater. These are "beyond reckoning," outside the number. But we are saying this in the hope that they may become part of the number; they will not hear it from us, because they are not present, but when you go home make sure they hear it from you. *I announced the news and spoke the message*, says the psalm. This is Christ speaking. He announced it in his own person as our Head, and he announced it through his members. He sent heralds out to announce it, he sent his apostles: *Their sound went forth throughout the world, their words to the ends of the earth* (Ps 18:5(19:4)). How very many believers there are, all piled up together, how great the crowds that gather! Many of these are truly converted, but many make only a pretense of conversion. Those truly converted are fewer than the shams, for these last are *multiplied, in numbers beyond reckoning*.

26. See 2 Tm 2:19.

Verse 7. The course of love

11. *I announced the news and spoke the message, and they were multiplied, in numbers beyond reckoning. Sacrifice and offering you did not desire.* These are the miracles of God, these the thoughts of God which have no rival. Let the person addicted to shows be led away from that gratification of the eyes,[27] and in our company seek better and more profitable sights, which will give him joy when he discovers them. And the joy will be such that he need not fear that his favorite may be defeated. He is enamored of a charioteer, but if that man is beaten, the supporter must bear the ignominy. If the charioteer wins, it is only he himself who is invested with the insignia. Does the poor man who cheered him on win any honors? No, only the champion. If the favorite loses, though, the fan is jeered at on his behalf. Why should you feel the sting of failure for his sake, when you have no share in the decoration he wins? With our shows it is quite different. Speaking of the pagan stadium and the shows put on there, the apostle Paul said, *All run, to be sure, but only one receives the prize* (1 Cor 9:24); the rest depart as losers. They have run their race with perseverance, yet when one receives the guerdon, all the rest who have tried just as hard are left with nothing. Not so among us. Let all who run the race persevere in their running, for all of them are rewarded. The one who is first at the winning-post waits, to be crowned with the latecomer. The reason for this is that the contestants are animated not by greed but by charity. All the runners love one another, and the course itself is love.

Sacrifice, old and new

12. *Sacrifice and offering you did not desire*, says the psalm to God. The ancients celebrated rites which prefigured the future reality; for our sacrifice, which the faithful know about, was being foreshadowed by symbols. Many knew this, but far more did not. The prophets and the holy patriarchs understood what they were celebrating; but the rest, the sinful multitude, were so carnal that they could only be used as a sign of what would come later. Then the truth came, and the first kind of sacrifice was abolished. The holocausts of rams, goats, calves and other victims were done away with, for God did not want them. Why did he not want them? Or rather, why had he wanted them earlier? Because all those rites were like the assurances of someone who is making a promise; and when what has been promised is delivered, the words of promise are no longer spoken. The speaker is making a promise until he delivers, and once he has delivered he uses different words. No longer does he say, "I will give . . . " what-

27. A curiositate; see note at section 8 above. A variant has "be drawn to gratify his eyes" [in the Church].

ever he said he would give; now he says, "I have given. . . ." He has changed the verb. Why did one word seem suitable to him at first, and why did he then change it? Because it was a word referring to its own time, and for that time it served his purpose. While he was still making his promise that word was spoken; but when what had been promised was given, words expressive of promise were superseded, and words expressive of fulfillment used instead. So those earlier sacrifices were like the words of a promise, and now they have been discarded. What is it that has now been given as a fulfillment? The body which you know, though not all of you know it.[28] And may you who do know about it not know it to your own condemnation. Notice the time when this statement was made, for it is Christ our Lord who made it, speaking at one time in his members, at another in his own person. *Sacrifice and offering you did not desire*, he says. What does that imply? That we are left in our days with no sacrifice? Far from it. *But you have perfected a body for me*. The reason why you did not want those old sacrifices now was that you meant to establish this perfect sacrifice; but before you had established this perfect one you did want the old. The perfect accomplishment of what had been promised rendered the words of promise obsolete. If words of promise were still appropriate now, it would mean that the promises had not yet been fulfilled. The reality was for a long time promised by certain signs, but now these sign-promises have been done away with, because the truth that was promised has been given to us. We are in this body, we are sharers in this body, and we know what we receive. You who do not yet know will know, and I pray that when you have learned about it, you may not receive it to your own condemnation, for any who eat and drink unworthily bring judgment on themselves.[29] The body has been made perfect for us; let us be made perfect in the body.[30]

Verse 8. The mark of Cain

13. *Sacrifice and offering you did not desire, but you have perfected a body for me. For holocaust and sin-offering you did not ask; then I said, Lo, I am coming*. Does this need any explanation? *Sacrifice and offering you did not desire, but you have perfected a body for me. For holocaust and sin-offering you did not ask*, the very things he did require in earlier days. *Then I said, Lo, I am coming*. It is time for what was long promised to come, and so the signs through which it was promised are taken away. Indeed, brothers and sisters, look how the old sacrifices have been superseded, and the new brought to fulfillment. Let the Jewish people show me a priest now, if they can! What has become of their sacri-

---

28. He means the catechumens, from whom explicit teaching on the Eucharist was withheld.
29. See 1 Cor 11:29.
30. Christ's mortal body, his eucharistic body and his ecclesial body are brought together here in one perspective.

fices? They have undeniably perished, done away with in this era. Should we have found fault with you in earlier days for offering them? No, but we do find fault with you now, and if you attempted to offer them now it would be unseasonable, inopportune and unfitting. You are still making promises, but I have received what was promised.

But something has remained to them that they can celebrate, so that they are not left entirely without a sign. Cain, the elder brother who killed the younger, was given a mark so that no one should kill him, as Genesis records: *God put a mark on Cain, so that no one should kill him* (Gn 4:15), and the Jewish nation likewise has survived. All the peoples who came under Roman rule reached common consent in adopting Roman law;[31] they shared the general superstitions, but later began to separate themselves from them through the grace of our Lord Jesus Christ. But the Jewish people remained unaltered with its sign, the sign of circumcision and the sign of unleavened bread; Cain was not killed. No, he was not killed, for he still had the mark on him. But he was cursed and banished from the earth that had opened its mouth to receive a brother's blood shed by his hand. He shed that blood, but he did not receive it; he shed it and another land received it, while Cain was cursed and banished from the earth that opened its mouth to receive the spilt blood. The earth where the blood has been received is the Church, and from here Cain was cursed. This blood "cries out to me from the earth," for it was of this same earth that the Lord said, *The voice of your brother's blood pleads to me from the earth* (Gn 4:10). It clamors to me from the earth, the Lord says. It cries out to the Lord, but the one who shed it is too deaf to hear, because he does not drink it. So now those people are like Cain with his mark. The sacrifices that used to be offered were done away with, and what has remained to them like Cain's mark has achieved its purpose, but they do not know it. They kill a lamb and eat unleavened bread, but *Christ has been immolated as our passover* (1 Cor 5:7). This is the slain lamb that I recognize: Christ has been immolated. What about the unleavened bread? *Accordingly*, says Paul, *let us keep the festival not with the leaven of malice and ill-will* (he is indicating the old mixture; the flour is stale and musty), *but with the unleavened bread of sincerity and truth* (1 Cor 5:8). They have remained in shadow and cannot see the glorious sun; we are already in daylight, for we hold fast to the body of Christ, we hold fast to the blood of Christ. If we have new life, let us sing a new song, a hymn to our God. *For holocaust and sin-offering you did not ask; then I said, Lo, I am coming.*

31. Variant suggested by the CCL editors: "the Jewish nation has survived among all the peoples who came under Roman rule. Those peoples reached. . . ."

Verse 9. Christ's obedience

14. *At the foremost place in the book it is written of me that I should do your will; O my God, this I have wanted, your law in the midst of my heart.* See how he now turns to his members, and how he himself did the will of his Father. But what book does he mean, where this is written of him at its foremost place? Perhaps it is written at the opening of this very Book of Psalms. What need is there for a more extensive search? Why should we investigate other books? Look where it is written on the opening page of this Book of Psalms, *Blessed is the person who has not gone astray in the council of the ungodly, and has not stood in the way of sinners, and has not sat in the seat of pestilence, but in the law of the Lord was his will.* This is the same thing as in our psalm here: *O my God, this I have wanted, and your law is in the midst of my heart*; and this again means the same thing as *on his law will he reflect day and night* (Ps 1:1-2).

Verse 10. The mouth speaks the heart's thoughts. The repentant thief

15. *I have freely proclaimed your righteousness in the great Church.* Christ is addressing his members, and exhorting them to do what he did. He proclaimed, so let us proclaim; he suffered, let us suffer with him; he has been glorified, and in him we shall be glorified too. *I have proclaimed your righteousness in the great Church.* How great? Spread throughout the world. How great? Throughout all nations. Why throughout all nations? Because it is the progeny of Abraham, in whom all nations are to be blessed.[32] Why throughout all nations? Because its sound has gone forth through all the earth,[33] *in the great Church.*

See, Lord, I will not keep my lips sealed, you know it. My lips speak, and I will not restrain them. My lips speak to the ears of men and women, but you know my heart. *Lord, I will not keep my lips sealed, you know it.* A human being hears one thing, but God perceives something else. This is emphasized because our proclamation must not be with our lips only, so that it could be said of us, *Do what they tell you, but do not imitate what they do* (Mt 23:3). Nor must it be said of us, as it was said of that people who praised God with their mouths but not their hearts, *This people honors me with its lips, but its heart is far from me* (Is 29:13). Sing with your lips, but draw near to him with your heart, for *the faith that issues in righteousness is in the heart, and the confession that leads to salvation is made with the lips* (Rom 10:10). This was true of the thief who hung on the cross with the Lord, and from the cross acknowledged the Lord. Others failed to recognize the Lord even as he performed miracles, but this man recognized him as he hung upon the cross. The thief was nailed securely in all his limbs: his hands were

32. See Gn 12:3.
33. See Ps 18:5(19:4).

immobilized by nails, his feet transfixed, and his whole body fastened to the wood. That body had no use of its other members, but his heart had the use of his tongue. With his heart he believed, and with his lips he made confession. *Lord, remember me when you come into your kingdom*, he said (Lk 23:42). He hoped for salvation as a distant prospect, and would have been content to receive it after a long delay; his hope stretched toward a far-off future, but the day was not delayed. He prayed, *Remember me when you come into your kingdom*, but Christ replied, *Truly I tell you, today you will be with me in paradise* (Lk 23:43). *Today*, he says, *you will be with me in paradise*. In paradise grow trees of happiness. Today you are with me on the tree of the cross, and today you will be with me on the tree of salvation.

Neither fear nor falsehood

16. *See, Lord, I will not keep my lips sealed, you know it*. This is said to warn us that we must not out of fear restrain our lips from proclaiming what we have believed. There are Christians who live among ill-disposed pagans, among people who are sophisticated[34] in an unwholesome way, squalid, unfaithful people without good sense, mockers. These Christians nonetheless have faith in their hearts, but once they begin to find themselves hounded for being Christians they are afraid to confess with their lips the faith they have in their hearts, and they restrain their lips from giving expression to what they know, what they have within. The Lord rebukes them: *If anyone is embarrassed about me in the presence of men and women, I will be embarrassed about that person in my Father's presence* (Mk 8:38); that is to say, "I will not recognize anyone who has been ashamed of confessing me before other people; I will not confess that person before my Father." The lips must proclaim what is in the heart: this is an injunction against fear. But the heart must have in it what the lips say: this is an injunction against insincerity. Sometimes you are afraid, and dare not say what you know to be true, what you believe; but at other times you are tempted to be insincere, and say something that is not in your heart. Your lips and your heart must be in agreement. If you seek peace from God, be reconciled with yourself; let there be no harmful conflict between your mouth and your heart. *See, Lord, I will not keep my lips sealed, you know it*. How does he know it? What does the Lord know? He knows what is within the heart, where human eyes do not see. This is why the psalmist says elsewhere, *I believed . . .*, so he has a heart, he has something God can see. But he must not restrain his lips, and he does not; for what does he say next? *Therefore I spoke* (Ps 115(116):10). And because he has uttered what he believed, he looks for some return he can make to the Lord for all the Lord has bestowed on him, so he adds, *I will take in my hands the cup of*

34. Variant: "live among pagans, and like to mix with people who are sophisticated."

salvation, and call on the name of the Lord (Ps 115(116):13). When the Lord asked, *Are you able to drink the cup I am to drink?* (Mt 20:22) he did not shrink away. He confessed with his lips what he had in his heart, and so he encountered suffering. But because he had gone like that to face his passion, what could the enemy do to harm him? Nothing at all, because *precious in the sight of the Lord is the death of his righteous ones* (Ps 115(116):15). Those deaths in which the pagans gave vent to their savagery are today our source of refreshment.[35] We celebrate the birthdays of the martyrs,[36] we keep the example of the martyrs before us, we contemplate their faith, remember how they were discovered and dragged off, and how they stood before their judges. In the Catholic Church, scorning all pretense, bonded closely to one another, they confessed Christ. They were his members, and they longed to follow where their Head had gone before. And who were the people possessed by such longing?[37] People brave under torture, faithful in their confession, truthful in speech. They were shooting God's arrows into the faces of their interrogators, and wounding them, and provoking them to anger, though many they wounded even to salvation.

We keep all these examples before us, and feast our eyes on them, and hope to imitate them. These are the shows that Christianity puts on. God himself watches from on high, encourages us to participate, and gives us his help; he sets the prizes for the contests and awards them at the end. Make sure you are not fearful. Do not keep your lips sealed. *Lord, you know* that what the lips utter is also in the heart.

Verse 11. Speaking the truth under threat

17. *I have not hidden my justice in my heart*. What does *my justice* mean? My faith, because the one who lives by faith is just.[38] Take an example. Suppose someone is being interrogated by a persecutor under threat of punishment; they were sometimes allowed to do this. "What are you—pagan or Christian?" "Christian." This is the Christian's justice; he or she has believed, and lives from that faith. This Christian has not hidden his justice in his heart. He did not say to himself, "I believe in Christ, certainly I do, but I am not going to tell this savage persecutor who is threatening me what I believe. My God knows within me, in my heart, that I believe, and he knows that I am not giving him up." So you say you have this faith in your heart, but what is on your lips? "I am no Christian." Then your lips are bearing witness in opposition to your heart.

35. Variant: "today help us to become perfect."
36. That is, the anniversaries of their deaths, their birthdays into heaven. One codex has "the birthday of a martyr."
37. This sentence is omitted by some codices.
38. See Hb 2:4; Rom 1:17.

Christ is truth and salvation

18. *I have declared your truth and your salvation.* This means, "I have proclaimed your Christ." When we say, *I have declared your truth and your salvation,* how can we say that "truth" means Christ? Because he said, *I am the Truth* (Jn 14:6). And why can we say that God's salvation is Christ? Because when Simeon recognized the child in his mother's arms in the temple, he said, *My eyes have seen your salvation* (Lk 2:30). An old man recognized an infant, for in this child he had become a child himself, being made new by faith. He spoke so because he had received an assurance: the Lord had told him that he would not leave this life before he had seen God's salvation. It is good that this salvation of God should be manifested to human beings, but let them cry out to him, *Show us, Lord, your mercy, and grant us your salvation* (Ps 84:8(85:7)). But it must be God's salvation for all nations, because after praying, *May God have mercy on us and bless us, may he make his face shine upon us, that we may know your way upon earth,* the psalmist added, *your salvation among all nations* (Ps 66:2-3(67:1-2)). So we find him praying first, *That we may know your way upon earth,* but then making it more precise by saying, *Your salvation among all nations.* You might have asked him, "What is this way that you long to see? Usually men and women come to a way; are you suggesting that this way will come to them?" Indeed our Way has come to men and women; he found them going astray and called the wanderers back to himself. "Walk in me," he said, "and you will not miss the path, for *I am the Way, and the Truth, and the Life*" (Jn 14:6). Do not say, then, "Where is God's way? To what country must I travel? What mountain shall I climb? What plains must I seek?" Are you looking for the way of God? God's way is God's salvation, and this way is everywhere, because his salvation is among all peoples. *I have declared your truth and your salvation.*

Mercy now, justice later

19. *I have not concealed your mercy and your justice from the great congregation.* Let us be part of it, let us be numbered within that body, and let us not conceal either the Lord's mercy or the Lord's justice. Do you want to hear what the Lord's mercy is like? Give up your sins, and he will forgive your sins. And do you want to hear about his justice? Hold fast to righteousness, and your righteousness will be crowned. At present his mercy is preached to you, but later his justice will be manifested, for God is not merciful in such a way as to be unjust, nor just in such a way as to leave no room for mercy. Is it a small thing, the mercy shown to you? No, for he will not impute to you all those sins of your earlier days. You lived sinfully until today, but you are still alive, so live rightly today,

and then you will not conceal his mercy.[39] So if this is mercy, what is his justice? All nations will be gathered before him, and he will sort them out as a shepherd separates sheep from goats. He will place the sheep at his right hand, the goats at his left. What will he say to the sheep? *Come, you who are blessed by my Father, take possession of the kingdom prepared for you.* And to the goats? *Depart from me into the eternal fire* (Mt 25:34,41). That will be no place for repentance. If you have spurned God's mercy you will feel his justice; but if you have not spurned his mercy, his justice will be your joy.

Verses 12-13. The near mercy

20. *But you, Lord, do not take your mercies far away from me.* Christ has turned his eyes toward his wounded members, and he prays, "Because I have not concealed your mercy and your justice from the great congregation, from the Church united throughout the world, look upon my wounded members, look upon delinquents and sinners, and do not withdraw your mercies." *Your mercy and your justice have always upheld me.* I would not dare to turn back to you if I were not confident of your forgiveness; I would not go on persevering, were I not confident of your promise. *Your mercy and your justice have always upheld me.* I see you to be good, and I see you to be just; I love you because you are good, and fear you because you are just. Love and fear jointly are my guides, for *your mercy and your justice have always upheld me.* Why do they uphold me, and why is it that I must never take my eyes off them? *Because evils have encompassed me, evils beyond counting.* Who, indeed, can count sins? Which of us can make a reckoning of other people's sins and our own? What a great pile of them was pressing down on the psalmist who groaned, *Cleanse me from my secret sins, Lord, and spare your servant from the faults of others* (Ps 18:13-14(19:12-13))! Perhaps our own were slight, but other people's were piled upon us; so now I am afraid on my own account and afraid for my good brother or sister; and I have to put up with a brother or sister who is bad. What would become of us, weighed down by this heap of sins, if God's mercy were to cease? *But you, Lord, do not go far away*, be near to me. To whom is God near? To those who have bruised their hearts.[40] He is far from the proud, but near to the humble, for though the Lord is most high, he has regard for the lowly.[41] Yet the proud must not flatter themselves that they are hidden, for the Lord recognizes the proud from afar. He certainly did recognize from afar the boastful Pharisee, but he came from very near to help the tax-collector who confessed his sins.[42]

---

39. Variant: "No, for he did not cut you off in your earlier days . . . so I have not concealed his mercy."
40. See Ps 33:19(34:18).
41. See Ps 137(138):6.
42. See Lk 18:10-14.

The first flaunted his merits and covered his wounds; the other had no merits to flaunt but exposed his wounds. He had come to the doctor; he knew he was ill, he knew he needed healing. He did not presume to raise his eyes to heaven, but beat his breast; he hoped that what he was prepared to admit, God would remit.[43] He punished himself so that God might set him free.

This same attitude is found in our psalm. Let us listen devoutly to its humble pleas, and love God devotedly; let us make these prayers our own with heart and tongue and our whole inner being. Let none of us think ourselves just. Each one who speaks is alive—alive, yes, and let us hope that he or she may have true life! But we still live here, and that means we still live with death; and though the spirit is very life through being justified, the body is dead because of sin.[44] And the corruptible body weighs down the soul; its earthly dwelling oppresses a mind that muses on many things.[45] Your job, then, is to cry out, to groan, to make confession, not to exalt yourself, nor to boast, nor to preen yourself on your merits; for even if you do have anything to be pleased about, what have you that you did not receive?[46] *Evils have encompassed me, evils beyond counting.*

The cure for spiritual blindness

21. *My iniquities have seized me, and I cannot manage to see.* There is something there to be seen, so what is oppressing us and blocking our vision? Iniquity. If some disease attacked your eye you could not see this natural light; nor could you if smoke or dust or something else invaded your eye. If you could not lift your sore eye toward the light, do you suppose you will be able to lift your sore heart to God? Must it not be healed first, to enable you to see? Are you not proved proud if you say, "Let me see first, so that I may believe"? Who is it who speaks like that? Who will ever see, if he or she demands, "Let me see first, so that I may believe"? I will show you the Light, or rather the Light wishes to manifest itself. And to whom? It cannot manifest itself to a blind person, who is incapable of seeing it. Why? Because his eyes are clogged by so many sins. So what does the psalmist say? *My iniquities have seized me, and I cannot manage to see.* Let these iniquities be cleared out of the way, and all his sins forgiven; let the pressure on his eye be relieved and the injured organ healed; let the stinging commandment of the Lord be applied like eye-salve. Begin by doing what you are commanded to do: heal your heart, cleanse your heart, love your enemy.[47] Which of us loves our enemy? But this is what the doctor prescribes. It stings us, but it is salutary. "What shall I do for you?" he asks. "You have been subjected to

43. *Se agnoscebat, ut ille ignosceret.*
44. See Rom 8:10.
45. See Wis 9:15.
46. See 1 Cor 4:7.
47. See Mt 5:44; Lk 6:27,35.

this unpleasant treatment so that you may recover." And he has something further to say. "Once you are healed, this will not seem painful to you. When you are well you will find it intensely pleasurable to love your enemy. Try hard to get better. Be brave in troubles, in all kinds of constraints, in temptations. Hold on; this is the doctor's hand at work, not some ruffian's." "Yes," replies the believer, "I have taken the commandments seriously, and held onto my faith, and I will heal my heart first, as you order me. Then, with a heart cleansed and healed, what shall I see?" *Blessed are the pure of heart, for they shall see God* (Mt 5:8). "This is what I cannot see yet," says the psalmist, for *my iniquities have seized me, and I cannot manage to see*.

Small sins are very numerous

22. *They have become more numerous than the hairs of my head.* He compares his vast number of sins to the hairs on his head. Who could count those? Far less, then, can we count our sins, which are still more numerous. They seem trifling, but there are very many of them. You have guarded against great sins: no longer do you commit adultery or murder, you do not steal other people's goods, you do not blaspheme, you do not give false testimony. All these are mountainous sins. You have guarded against the great sins, but what about the small ones? Unconcerned about them, are you? You have got rid of the mountain, but take care you are not buried by sand. *They have become more numerous than the hairs of my head.*

Verses 13-14. Hearty incomprehension

23. *My heart forsook me*. If your heart has deserted itself, small wonder if it is deserted by your God. What does the psalm mean by saying, *My heart forsook me*? It means, "My heart is incapable of knowing itself." *My heart forsook me* means, "In my heart I want to see the Lord, but I cannot, for the multitude of my sins. But that is not all: my heart does not comprehend itself either." None of us comprehend our own hearts, so let none of us presume on ourselves. Did Peter comprehend his own heart—really comprehend it with his heart, I mean—when he said to the Lord, "I will stay with you even to death"?[48] In his heart there was false presumption, and the real fear that was also in his heart was covered over and out of sight. Consequently his heart was in no fit state to understand his heart. His heart was ailing and hidden, but to the physician it was plain to see. What the Lord foretold of it came true. The Lord knew something about him that Peter did not know himself: that his heart had forsaken him, and his heart was hidden from his heart. *My heart forsook me*. What are we to do, then? What plea

48. See Mt 26:35; Lk 22:33.

can we make? What are we to say? *May it please you to deliver me, Lord.* This is like saying, *If you will, you can cleanse me* (Mt 8:2). *May it please you to deliver me, Lord; look on me and help me.* This is the cry of his members repenting, his members caught in sorrow, his members screaming under the surgeon's knife, yet still hoping. *Lord, look on me and help me.*

Verse 15. Seeking Christ's soul/life

24. *Let them be confounded and filled with awe, all of them together, who seek my soul to take it away.*[49] In another text he speaks reproachfully: *I looked to right and to left, but there was no one to seek my soul* (Ps 141:5(142:4)); and there he means, "No one to imitate me." There Christ speaks in his passion: "I looked toward the right—not at the impious Jews, but to my true right-hand men, my apostles—*but there was no one to seek my soul.* So far was anyone from seeking it, that the man who had spoken so presumptuously was denying my soul."

But a person can be "sought" in two different ways, either as someone whose company you wish to enjoy, or as someone you are hounding; and therefore in the present text it is not the apostles he has in view but others, people who are seeking his life, people he hopes to see confounded and filled with awe. He makes sure that you do not understand this search in the same sense as when he complains that there is no one to seek his soul; he adds, to make this clear, *To take it away* (that is, they are seeking my life, seeking to kill me), and *let them be confounded and filled with awe.* Indeed there were many seeking his life, and they were confounded and filled with awe. They sought his life and, as seemed good to them, took his life away; but he had the power to lay down his life, and the power to take it up again.[50] They were pleased when he laid it down, but confounded when he took it up again. *Let them be confounded and filled with awe, all of them together, who seek my soul to take it away.*

The place for followers is behind the Lord

25. *Let them be thrust back and filled with awe, who make malicious plans against me.* He says, *Let them be thrust back,* but we must not take this in any spiteful sense. He wills good to them, and the voice that prays is that of him who begged from the cross, *Father, forgive them, for they do not know what they are doing* (Lk 23:34). Why then does he say they should be thrust back? Because these people who at first were proud, and deserved to be thrust back, were

49. In this, as in his Exposition of Psalm 37, section 18, Augustine plays on the double meaning of *anima*: "soul" or "life."
50. See Jn 10:18.

humbled in the process and so deserved to get up again. When people are in front they want to rush ahead of the Lord, they want to go one better than the Lord; but if they are behind him they are acknowledging that he is ahead, he is their leader, and they his followers. He leads and they follow along behind. This is why the Lord was so severe with Peter, who tried to give him bad advice. The Lord was destined to suffer for our salvation, and was foretelling future events connected with his passion, and Peter intervened: "*Far be it from you, Lord*, show yourself some kindness, *this will not happen*" (Mt 16:22). He wanted to run ahead of the Lord, and to give advice to his teacher. But the Lord decided to put him in his place as a follower, not as one going ahead, so he replied, *Get behind me, Satan* (Mt 16:23). "You are a Satan," he implies, "because you want to get in front of him whom you should follow;[51] but once you have been pushed back, and begun to follow, you will no longer be a Satan. What will you be then? A rock, and *upon this rock I will build my Church*" (Mt 16:18).[52]

Verses 16-17. Open malevolence and false flattery

26. *Let them be thrust back and filled with awe, who make malicious plans against me*. Some people curse you from the bottom of their hearts even while they are speaking to you approvingly; and such people are malevolent. This is what I mean: you may say to someone, "Become a Christian," and he or she replies, "Be a Christian yourself." Now what he has wished on you is something good in itself, but it is not the words that will be imputed to him, but the intention with which they were spoken. When the man born blind received his sight, the Jews browbeat him and bullied him with their insults, and when he said to them, *You don't want to be his disciples too, surely?* they cursed him for it. Notice carefully what the evangelist says: *They cursed him and said, "You be his disciple yourself"* (Jn 9:27-28). They were cursing the man, but the Lord blessed him; he brought about the very thing they had flung at the man as a curse, but what they truly meant was imputed to them, and the Lord punished them for their cursing. *Let them be thrust back and filled with awe, who make malicious plans against me*.

There are other people again who are not good, but intend good to us, after their fashion; and of these we should be wary. We thought just now of the kind who curse us, and though they wish us something that will be to our advantage,

51. The Hebrew word *Satan* that lies behind the Greek text originally meant "adversary" in general, anyone who gets in the way, but came to be specialized as a name for the superhuman adversary, the devil. In the episode to which Augustine is referring here the implication is that by trying to dissuade Jesus from his vocation to suffering, Peter is resuming the same attempt made by the devil in the story of Jesus' temptations; see Mt 4:1-11; Lk 4:2-13.

52. Augustine reflected similarly on going ahead and following, with reference to Peter, in his Exposition 1 of Psalm 34, section 8, but here he has taken the idea a little further.

do so with hostile intention. But many of the second kind say something to our harm, but mean it in a spirit of approval. What I mean is this: if someone says to you, "Get away, be a Christian yourself," he is wishing you something that will be good for you, though he means it maliciously; but if someone says to you, "You're the best of the lot,"[53] with reference to some bad aspects of your life, he is proclaiming your shabby points and praising them; after all, scripture tells us that the sinner does receive praise for the longings of his soul, and whoever does evil is blessed.[54] In the one case a foul-mouthed enemy wished you something that was for your good; in the other a well-wisher hoped for something that would harm you. Both are your enemies, shun them both, beware of both. One rages, the other flatters, but both are bad. One is furious with you, the other praises you craftily, one insults you and the other commends you; but the former is your enemy in his invective, and the latter your enemy in his deceit. Keep away from both, and pray against both.

The psalmist who prayed, *Let them be thrust back and filled with awe, who make malicious plans against me*, gave thought also to another class of people, cunning in their malevolence and insincere in their smooth speech. *May they speedily be shamed, those who say to me, "Splendid! Well done!"* Their praise is spurious. "So-and-so is a great man," they say, "and a good man. He is cultured and learned, but why, Oh why, must he be a Christian?"[55] They praise those aspects of your life that you would not wish to be admired, and deprecate the very thing that brings you joy. But perhaps you say to them, "Why praise me as a good person, or a just person, my friend? If you think I am, praise Christ, for he has made me so." The other then replies, "No, don't say that, you are not doing yourself justice. You have made yourself what you are." *May they be shamed, those who say to me, "Splendid! Well done!"* And how does the psalmist continue? *Let all who seek you dance with delight, O Lord.* They are not seeking me; it is you whom they are seeking. Not to me are they saying, "Splendid! Well done!" They see that I am glorious in you,[56] if I have any shred of glory; for if anyone has a mind to boast, let it be in the Lord.[57] *Let all who seek you dance with delight, O Lord, and say, "May the Lord's greatness always be told,"* for even

53. Variants include: "Your [achievements] are so great that no one will have a better name"; and "No one will so greatly excel others in achievements."
54. See Part 2 of Ps 9:3(10:3).
55. Augustine's reflections here are very similar to Tertullian's (*Apol.* 3): "They [the pagans] will say, 'Gaius Seius is a good man, but for the fact that he is a Christian,' or 'I am amazed that a wise man like Lucius should have become a Christian all of a sudden.' No one thinks it necessary to consider whether perhaps Gaius is good or Lucius wise precisely because of being a Christian, or a Christian because he is wise or good. They praise what they recognize, but what they are ignorant about they denounce."
56. A crop of variants includes: "they seem to glorify me in him and in you"; "they seem to glorify me in you;" "in that they see that I am glorified in you."
57. See 1 Cor 1:31.

though someone has changed from a sinner into a righteous person, give the glory to him who justifies the impious.[58] So if we think of the person as a sinner, let the praise be to him who calls the sinner to forgiveness; and if we think of the person as already walking in the path of righteousness, let the praise be to him who calls the righteous to their crown. *May the Lord's greatness always be told* by those *who set their love on your salvation.*

Verse 18. God's care for his poor

27. *But I*, I, against whom they planned maliciously, *but I*, whose life they were seeking to take it from me. . . . Turn now to persons of a different stamp. *But I*, to whom they were saying, "Splendid! Well done!" *I am needy and poor.* There is nothing of my own in me that deserves praise. May he tear off my sackcloth and clothe me in his own robe,[59] for it is not I who live now, but Christ lives in me.[60] If Christ lives in you, and all the good you have belongs to Christ, and all the good you ever will have belongs to Christ, what are you of yourself? *I am needy and poor.* I am not rich, because I am not proud. That Pharisee who said, *O Lord, I thank you that I am not like other people*, he was a rich man. But the tax-collector who said, *Lord, be merciful to me, a sinner* (Lk 18:11,13), was a poor man. The one was belching from satiety, the other wailing with hunger. *I am needy and poor.* So what are you going to do, you needy, poor thing? Beg at God's gate; knock[61] and it will be opened to you. *I am needy and poor, but the Lord will care for me.* Then *cast your care upon the Lord, and hope in him, and he will bring it to pass* (Ps 54:23(55:22)). What kind of care can you take of yourself? What provision can you make for yourself? Let him who made you take care of you. Since he cared for you before you even existed, how can he fail to care for you now that you are what he willed you to be? You are a believer now, you are already walking the path of righteousness. Is it likely that he will not care for you, he who makes his sun rise over good and bad people, and sends his rain on just and unjust alike?[62] Now that you are righteous by living through faith, will he neglect you, abandon you, send you away? Of course not. In your present life he cherishes you, and helps you, and provides all you need here, and cuts away all that could harm you. By giving you all these things he comforts you so that you can hold out, and by taking them away he corrects you so that you may not perish. The Lord has you in his care, so don't worry. He who made you is carrying you;[63] do not fall out of your Maker's hand. If you do fall out of it, you

58. See Rom 4:5.
59. See Ps 29:12(30:11); Lk 15:22.
60. See Gal 2:20.
61. Variant: ". . . to do, you needy, poor thing, you beggar? At God's gate knock. . . . "
62. See Mt 5:45.
63. Variants: "May he who made you carry you"; "He who made you will protect you."

will break. But a will set on good ensures that you stay in your Maker's hand. This is what you must say: "My God wanted me. He will carry me and hold onto me." Cast yourself upon him; do not think this is a rash thing to do, as though you might risk falling headlong. Not at all. He has said, *I fill heaven and earth* (Jer 23:24). In no place whatever is he absent from you. Be sure you are not absent from him, or absent from yourself. *The Lord has care of me.*

The prayer of one single poor man, Christ and his members

28. *You are my helper and protector; O my God, do not delay.* He is calling on God and imploring him, for he is afraid of his own weakness: *do not delay.* What does it mean, *do not delay*? Remember what was read just now in the gospel about the time of tribulation. *If those days were not curtailed, no mortal could be saved* (Mt 24:22). All the members of Christ, the body of Christ diffused throughout the world, are like a single person asking God's help, one single beggar, one poor suppliant; and this is because Christ himself is that poor man, since he who was rich became poor, as the apostle tells us: *Though he was rich he became poor, so that by his poverty you might be enriched* (2 Cor 8:9). He enriches those who are the true poor, and impoverishes the falsely rich. This poor man cries out to God, *From the ends of the earth I have called to you, as my soul grew faint* (Ps 60:3(61:2)).

The days of tribulation will come, days of trouble upon trouble, as scripture forecasts, and the nearer those days approach, the more will tribulations increase. None of us can afford to promise ourselves anything the gospel does not promise. I beg you, brothers and sisters, to study our scriptures. Have they deceived us on any point, have they made any prediction that misled us, in that things turned out differently? No, indeed; and it is necessary that until the very end everything must take place as they have prophesied. And our scriptures promise us nothing in this world except tribulations, afflictions, painful straits, mounting sorrows and abundant trials. Let us concentrate on preparing for all these, lest we be taken unawares and fall away. You heard the gospel warning, *Woe betide those who are pregnant in those days, or suckling their babies* (Mt 24:19). The pregnant referred to here symbolize people who are swollen with expectant hope, and the nursing mothers suckling babies stand for those who have obtained what they earlier desired; for a pregnant woman grows large with her hoped-for child, but does not see the child yet, but a lactating mother holds in her arms the child she was expecting. Let me give you a parallel to this. Suppose someone says to himself, "My neighbor's house is very fine. If only it were mine, if only I could annex it, and make that estate and this one into a single property!" You see, even greed loves unity! What the speaker loves is a good thing, but he does not understand where love for it is appropriate. Here he is, looking longingly at his neighbor's estate. But that neighbor is rich, he needs nothing, he is a person of rank, even of power. You would be better advised to take care you do not fall foul of his power, than to hope you may get your hands on any part of his estate. In this case, then, the one who was hoping conceives nothing; his soul does not become pregnant. But suppose his nearest neighbor is a poor man, who is either in difficult circumstances and may wish to sell, or can be bullied and forced to sell. Then he casts his eyes on his neighbor's property and hopes for that estate; his soul becomes pregnant and he expects to be able to gain possession of his poor neighbor's house and lands. When this poor man is in dire straits he approaches his rich neighbor, whom he is perhaps accustomed to treating obsequiously, deferring to his wishes, rising at the other's approach and greeting him with a bow. "I beg you," says the poor man, "give me what I need. I am in a tight spot, under pressure from a creditor." But the rich man replies, "I have no spare cash just now." If the poor man sold his property, he would get it.[64]

We recognize this situation. There have been people like this among us; please God there may not be any again. We were alive yesterday, and we are still alive today, aren't we? So we have an opportunity for conversion, for the separation has not been made yet, with some at Christ's right hand and others at his left.[65] Nor are we yet in hell, with that rich man who was thirsty and longing for a drop of water.[66] While we still have life, let us listen and correct ourselves. Let us not covet other people's things, or swell up as though pregnant, or try to get hold of them and when we have them kiss them like new-born babies. *Woe betide those who are pregnant in those days, or suckling their babies.*

We must change our heart, lift up our heart, and not allow our heart to make its home here, for this is a bad place to live. Let us be content with what is still necessary for us in our fleshly condition, and get rid of what is not necessary. Let each day's troubles be enough,[67] but let us live here with our hearts uplifted.[68] *If you have risen with Christ, have a taste for what is above, where Christ is seated at the right hand of God. Seek the things that are above, not the things on earth; for you are dead, and your life is hidden with Christ in God* (Col 3:1-3). What has been promised to you is not visible yet; it is prepared already, but you cannot see it. If you want to become pregnant, this is what you must conceive; let this be your hope. Your birthing will be safe and certain, you will not miscarry. But it will not be a temporal birth, for what you will have brought to birth you will embrace for all eternity. Isaiah speaks in the same terms: *We have conceived, and given birth to the spirit of salvation* (Is 26:13). It is postponed and not given to us now, but it will be given. How much has been given, though, brothers and sisters! If you try to count up all these gifts by checking through the scriptures,

64. Variant: "he has to sell, willy-nilly."
65. See Mt 25:33.
66. See Lk 16:22-24.
67. See Mt 6:34.
68. *Sursum corde habitemus*; see note at Exposition of Psalm 10, section 3.

you find them beyond reckoning. In the scriptures the Church is mentioned, and look, here it is. The scriptures foretell that idols will not last, and clearly they do not exist now. It was prophesied there that the Jews would lose their kingdom, and so they have. It was written that there would be heretics, and so there are. The scriptures speak of the day of judgment, of the rewarding of the good and the punishment of the wicked; if we have found God to be trustworthy in all the other instances, will he fail and deceive us on this last point? *The Lord will care for me. You are my helper and protector; O my God, do not delay*. The gospel tells us, *If those days were not curtailed, no mortal could be saved, but for the sake of the elect they will be cut short* (Mt 24:22). Days of tribulation there will be, but they will not be as long as expected. They will pass quickly, but the peace and rest that will come to us will never pass away. However long the bad time, it must be endured for the sake of the good without limits.

Exposition of Psalm 40

A Sermon to the People

Christ, leader of martyrs

1. The martyrs' solemn festival has dawned, so let us see if this psalm has anything to tell us about the passion of Christ and the glory of it. He is the commander-in-chief of martyrs, who before ordering his troops into battle engaged in battle first, not sparing himself. He first won the victory, so that he could afterwards encourage them by his own example, and aid them with his majestic power, and crown them as he had promised. But I must remind you before we begin, as I so often do (and I do not mind how often I have to repeat this, because it is useful for you to remember it), that sometimes our Lord Jesus Christ speaks in his own person, as our Head, but also often in the person of his body. We are his body as well as his Church. When he speaks in this latter way the words seem to come from a single voice, so that we understand Head and body to form an indivisible unity; these two cannot be separated from each other, for this is a marriage like the one of which it was written, *They will be two in one flesh* (Gn 2:24; Eph 5:31). So if we acknowledge two in one flesh, let us equally acknowledge two in one voice.

Let us begin this sermon from a verse we sang in response to the reader, even though it occurs in the middle of the psalm: *My enemies reviled me, asking, When will he die, and his name disappear?*[1] The speaker here is our Lord Jesus Christ, but we must consider whether his members are not concerned too. The same question was bandied about when our Lord was walking on earth in the flesh, for when the Jews noticed that the crowd was attracted by his authority, his divine presence and the majesty attested by his miracles, they said to each other, just as the Lord had predicted in one of his parables that they would, *This is the heir. Come on, let's kill him, and the inheritance will be for us* (Mt 21:38). Caiaphas, the high priest, had an answer for them when they said, *You see that a great crowd is following him, the whole world has gone after him. If we leave him alone like this, everyone will believe in him, and then the Romans will come, and sweep away our land and our nationhood.* Caiaphas told them, *It is expedient that one should die for all, rather than the whole nation perish* (Jn 12:19;

1. Verse 6, perhaps used as the antiphon which the congregation interjected during the reading or singing of the psalm.

11:48.50). But the evangelist explained for our benefit the words of this man who did not know what he was saying: *He did not say this as of himself. In virtue of his office as high priest he prophesied that it was necessary for Jesus to die for his people and the nation* (Jn 11:51). Nonetheless when the Jews saw the people going after Jesus they said, *When will he die, and his name disappear?* What they meant was, "When we have killed him his name will be known on earth no longer, and when he is dead he will not lead anyone astray. The very fact of his being killed will convince people that they were following a mere human being, in whom they could not hope to find salvation. So they will abandon his name and memory, and it will exist no more."

He died, but his name did not disappear; far from it. Rather was his name sown like seed. He died, but like a grain of wheat,[2] and as soon as the grain was dead the harvest sprang up. No sooner had our Lord Jesus Christ been glorified than people came to believe in him far more strongly and in much greater numbers; and then his members began to hear the same mutterings that their Head had heard. Our Lord Jesus Christ is enthroned in heaven, but in us his members he is still struggling on earth; and his enemies persisted in saying, *When will he die, and his name disappear?* for the devil stirred up persecutions against the Church to destroy the name of Christ. Do you suppose, brothers and sisters, that when the pagans broke out in fury against the Christians, they were not saying the same thing to themselves, not planning to wipe out Christ's name? The martyrs were killed so that Christ might suffer anew, not in himself, but in his body. The holy blood was shed because it was powerful for the growth of the Church, and the death of the martyrs was added to Christ's sowing. *Precious in the sight of the Lord is the death of his righteous ones* (Ps 115(116):15). The Christians multiplied and multiplied again, and the expectations of their enemies who asked, *When will he die and his name disappear?* were not fulfilled.

But the same thing is still being said today. The pagans sit down and count the years,[3] they listen to soothsayers in their company who say, "The time will come when there won't be any Christians, and then the idols will be worshiped as they used to be in earlier days." Still they are asking, *When will he die, and his name disappear?* You have been proved wrong twice; at least have some sense this

2. See Jn 12:24-25.
3. In *The City of God* XVIII, 53, 2, Augustine wrote as follows: "When the pagans observed that even by so many fierce persecutions the Christian religion was not destroyed, but even grew amazingly, they thought up some Greek verses, which purported to have been spoken by some divine oracle in response to a suppliant. These allege that Peter contrived by spells that Christ's name should be venerated for three hundred and sixty-five years, and predicted that once this number was completed, it would vanish at once." The Maurists add that if we count from Peter's Pentecost sermon the three hundred and sixty-five years would have been up in A.D. 399, at which time not only did the veneration of Christ's name not cease, but it even grew, for such temples of the gods which still survived were dismantled and their idols smashed, as Augustine notes in *The City of God* XVIII, 54.

third time. Christ died, and his name will not disappear. The martyrs died, and the Church grew all the more; the name of Christ is spreading throughout all nations. Christ foretold his own death and resurrection; he foretold the deaths of his martyrs and their crowning; he also foretold the future fortunes of his Church. If he spoke truly in the first two instances, did he lie in the third?

Verse 2. Christ the poor man

What you believe in opposition to him is futile; you would be better advised to believe in him, and so *understand about the needy and poor man*, because *though he was rich he became poor so that by his poverty you might be enriched*, as scripture tells us (2 Cor 8:9). But because he became poor people think slightingly of him today, and say, "He was only a man, after all. What else? He died, he was crucified. You are worshiping a mere man, pinning your hopes to a mortal man, adoring a dead man!" But you are quite wrong. Try to understand about this needy, poor man, so that you may become rich through his poverty. What does that mean—*understand about this needy, this poor man*? It means that you must accept Christ himself as this needy, poor person, like the speaker in another psalm who cries out, *I am needy and poor, but the Lord cares for me* (Ps 39:18(40:17)). What does understanding about this needy, poor man imply? Understanding that *he emptied himself and took on the form of a slave, bearing the human likeness, sharing the human lot* (Phil 2:7). He was rich in the bosom of the Father, and poor among us; rich in heaven, and poor on earth; rich as God, poor as man. Does this disconcert you, that you see a human being, that you look on flesh, that you witness a death, that you find the cross an object of ridicule? Does this disconcert you? Try to understand about the needy, poor man. What does that mean? Understand that where weakness is displayed before your eyes, there godhead lies hidden. He is rich, because that is what he is, but poor, because that was what you were. His poverty is our wealth, just as his weakness is our strength, his foolishness our wisdom,[4] and his mortality our immortality. Pay close attention to what this poor man is, and do not measure him by the poverty of others. He who was made poor came to fill the poor; so open wide your faith and embrace this poor man, lest you remain a poor person yourself.

Christ, divine and human, rich and poor

2. *Blessed is everyone who understands about the needy and poor man; the Lord will deliver him on the evil day*. The evil day is coming, whether you like it or not. The day of judgment will arrive, and it will be an evil day for you if you have not understood about the needy, poor man. What you are reluctant to

4. See 1 Cor 1:25,30.

believe now will be plainly revealed at the end. But when it is revealed you will not escape, because you do not believe now while it is hidden. You are being invited to believe what you do not see, so that when you do see it you may not be shamed. Try to understand, then, about the needy, poor person that is, about Christ. Understand the riches hidden in him whom you see as a poor man, for *in him are hidden all the treasures of wisdom and knowledge* (Col 2:3). Inasmuch as he is God, he will deliver you on the evil day; but inasmuch as he is man, and he raised up and transformed what was human in himself, he has raised it up to heaven.[5] Though he willed to form one person with humanity, he who is God could neither be diminished nor increase; nor could he die or rise again. He died in human weakness; God does not die. It should not surprise you that the Word of God does not die, if you reflect that in the case of a martyr the soul does not die. Did we not hear the Lord saying just now, *Do not be afraid of those who kill the body, but cannot kill the soul* (Mt 10:28)? If when the martyrs died their souls did not die, would it have been possible for the Word to die when Christ died? The Word of God is unquestionably far greater than the soul of any human being, because the human soul was made by God; and if it was made by God it was made by the Word, for through him all things were made.[6] Obviously, then, if even the soul made by the Word does not die, neither does the Word himself. But just as we correctly say that a man has died, even though his soul does not die,[7] so too we say that Christ died, even though his godhead does not die. How could he truly die, then? Because he was the needy, poor man. Do not be so fixated on his death that you turn away from contemplating his divinity. *Blessed is everyone who understands about the needy and poor man.* Keep in mind all the poor, needy, hungry and thirsty people, travelers far from home, the ill-clad, the sick, the prisoners. Try to understand about a poor person of this sort, because if you do, you will understand about him who said, *I was hungry, I was thirsty, naked, a stranger, sick and in prison* (Mt 25:35-36). Then on that fateful day the Lord will pluck you out of danger.

Verse 3. Eternal life and temporal help are both God's gift

3. Now consider the blessing promised you. *May the Lord keep him safe.* The prophet is praying that it may be well with anyone who understands about the needy, poor man. This prayer is also a promise; so let those who act accordingly be confident in their hope. *May the Lord keep him safe and give him life.* What does that suggest—keep him safe and give him life? What kind of life is in ques-

5. Slightly obscure; we should perhaps read "will raise it up to heaven," unless he means it in the proleptic Pauline sense, as in Eph 2:6.
6. See Jn 1:3.
7. Variant: "even though only his flesh dies."

tion here? The life to come, when the person who was dead is brought to life. A dead person could hardly be expected to understand about the needy, poor man, surely? The making-alive here promised to us is that of which the apostle speaks: *The body indeed is a dead thing by reason of sin, but the spirit is life through righteousness. If he who raised Christ from the dead lives in you, he who raised Christ from the dead will bring life to your mortal bodies too, through his Spirit who dwells in you* (Rom 8:10-11). This is the gift of life promised to anyone who understands about the needy, poor person.

But the apostle also says to Timothy, *We have the promise of life both in the present and in the future* (1 Tm 4:8). Those who do understand about the needy, poor man might be tempted to think that though they will indeed be welcomed into heaven, they are neglected on earth. They might restrict their hopes to their eternal future, assuming that, as far as the present life is concerned, God has no care for his holy, faithful servants. To guard against this error the psalmist, after speaking of what we must hope for above all—*May the Lord keep him safe and give him life*—turns his gaze toward this present life and adds, *And render him blessed on earth.* Lift your eyes with Christian faith to these promises. God does not abandon you on earth, but he still promises you more in heaven. There are plenty of bad Christians who pore over astrological almanacs, inquiring into and observing auspicious seasons and days. When they begin to hear themselves reproved for this by us, or by good Christians, better Christians, who demand why they meddle with these things, they reply, "These precautions are necessary for the present time. We are Christians, of course, but that is for eternal life. We have put our faith in Christ so that he may give us eternal life, but the life in which we are engaged now does not concern him." Not to put too fine a point on it, their argument could be briefly stated like this: "Let God be worshiped with a view to eternal life, and the devil be worshiped for this present life." Christ replies to this, *You cannot serve two masters* (Mt 6:24). You are paying homage to one with an eye to what you hope for in heaven, and to the other to get what you hope for on earth. How much better off you would be worshiping one only, him who made heaven and earth! Will he who cared enough to bring this earth into existence neglect his own image on earth? So then, when anyone understands about the needy, poor person, *may the Lord keep him safe and give him life.* But that is not all. Although this gift of life is to last for ever, may the Lord also *render him blessed on earth.*

The devil revises his tactics

4. *And not deliver him into the hands of his enemy.* This enemy is the devil. When we hear these words, none of us must refer them to any human enemy we may have. Perhaps you were thinking of a neighbor, of someone with whom you had a dispute in court, someone who tried to steal your goods, or one who is

attempting to coerce you into selling your house? No, do not think along these lines; but refer the verse to the enemy of whom the Lord says, *An enemy has done this* (Mt 13:28). This enemy is the one who suggests to us that he should be worshiped to guarantee temporal prosperity. This enemy has no power to destroy the Christian name, for he has seen himself worsted by Christ's renown and the praise accorded to him. The devil saw too that his slaughter of Christ's martyrs had resulted only in their winning their crowns and himself being led captive in Christ's triumphal procession.[8] So he began to think he would never persuade people that Christ is nothing. Since it was so difficult to deceive them by slandering Christ, he now attempts to hoodwink them by praising Christ. What was his line of attack in earlier days? "Whom are you worshiping? A dead Jew, a crucified man, a human being of no importance who couldn't even keep death at bay!" But when he saw that the human race is making rapid progress in Christ's name, that temples are being dismantled in the name of the Crucified, idols smashed and sacrificial fires stamped out, that people are astonished and awed at seeing these things happening as the prophets foretold, and that they are now shutting their hearts against his slanderous attacks on Christ—when he saw all this he assumed a new disguise, as one who praises Christ. He began to deter people from faith by different tactics. "Christianity is a magnificent rule of life, a powerful, divine law that defies description. But who can keep it?"

In the name of our Savior you must trample on both lion and snake.[9] The lion used to rampage and savage his victims; now the snake cunningly insinuates himself by compliments. Let any who have been wavering come to faith, and not say, "But who can keep such a law?" If they rely on their own strength they will not keep it. But relying on God's grace let them believe, relying on God let them come; let them come[10] to be helped, not to be judged. All believers live in Christ's name, and all in their different walks of life fulfill Christ's commandments, whether as married people, or as celibates and virgins; they live the best and fullest lives the Lord's gift enables them to live, and they do not rely on their own powers to do so, but know that they may boast only in him.[11] For what have you that you did not receive? And if you received it, why boast as though you did not?[12] So do not say to me, "Who is able to keep such a law?" He keeps it in me, he who was rich but came to the poor, indeed came as a poor man to the poor, but as fullness to those who were empty. Anyone who bears all this in mind understands about the needy, poor person, and does not disdain Christ's poverty but

8. *Et se triumphatum.* When a Roman general was accorded a triumph, notables among the defeated enemy were sometimes displayed at the end of the procession.
9. See Ps 90(91):13. A variant suggested by the CCL editors is: ". . . who can keep it? It is kept in the name of our Savior, who tramples on. . . ."
10. Variant: "they come."
11. See 1 Cor 1:31.
12. See 1 Cor 4:7.

rather understands Christ's riches. Such a person is blessed on earth, and is not delivered into the hands of that enemy who tries to persuade us that we should worship God with an eye to heavenly benefits, but the devil for our earthly needs. *May the Lord not deliver him into the hands of his enemy.*

Verse 4. The uncomfortable bed

5. *May the Lord bring him relief.* But where? In heaven perhaps, only in eternal life perhaps, so that it behooves us to pay cult to the devil because of our earthly penury, because of our needs in this life? God forbid! You have the promise of life in both present and future.[13] He who came to earth, and came to you, is he through whom heaven and earth were made. In any case, take note of what the psalm says: *May the Lord bring him relief on his bed of pain*. The bed of pain is the infirmity of our flesh. Do not protest, "I cannot control my flesh; I cannot carry and restrain it"; for you are given help to enable you to do so. May the Lord bring you relief on your bed of pain. The bed was supporting you, not you the bed, for you were inwardly paralyzed; but he is at hand, he who says to you, *Pick up your sleeping-mat, and go home* (Mk 2:11). *May the Lord bring him relief on his bed of pain.*

But then the psalmist turns to the Lord as though to ask, "If God does bring relief, why do we suffer so much in this life? Why do we meet such formidable obstacles, such arduous labor, so much distress from both our flesh and the world?" He turns to God, but at the same time makes clear to us God's program for our healing, as he says, *You have disarranged all his bedding in his illness.* What can that mean *you have disarranged all his bedding in his illness*? Bedding[14] suggests something to do with the earth. Every weakly soul looks for something earthly to rest on in this life, because it is too great an effort to keep the mind stretched toward God uninterruptedly. It looks for something on earth on which it can rest, where it can take time off from its efforts and lie down. This could be an attraction for innocent people just as much. We need not speak of the desires of bad people, the theatrical shows that are the relaxation of many, or the crowds who find their recreation in the circus, in the amphitheatre, in gaming and dicing, or in the food-shops that pander to greed. We have no wish to speak of the great numbers who look to adulterous affairs, or to violent theft, or to guile and fraud for the same purpose, though indeed people do find relaxation in all these things. Relaxation, did I say? They find pleasure in it all. But let us leave all these aside, and speak only of innocent people. A good man finds rest in his own home, in his household, his wife and his children, in his modest way of life, in his

13. See 1 Tm 4:8.

14. *Stratum*, from the verb *sterno*, to spread, strew, spread blankets, etc., on the ground for lying on; hence the link Augustine makes with "earth."

smallholding, in the young plants he has set with his own hands, in some building that has been put up through his initiative. Innocent people find their relaxation in things like these. Yet because God wants us to be in love only with eternal life he mingles bitter elements even with these innocent pleasures, so that even in them we experience distress. He overturns all our bedding in our illness. So the psalm says to him, *You have disarranged all his bedding in his illness.* The patient must not complain if he encounters various troubles in his innocent pastimes. We are being taught to love better things by the pain we endure in those that are inferior; the wayfarer traveling toward his homeland must not fall in love with a stable instead of home. *You have disarranged all his bedding in his illness.*

Verse 5. Confession of sin—Christ's words?

6. But why should this be? Because God whips every child he acknowledges as his.[15] Still, why does it have to be so? Because on a human being who had sinned the sentence was passed, *In the sweat of your face you shall eat your bread* (Gn 3:19). We humans must realize that the corrective pains we feel when all our bedding is disarranged are the penalty we suffer for our sins; and therefore we must turn to God and say, as the psalm goes on to say, *I said, Lord, have mercy on me; heal my soul, for I have sinned against you.* O Lord, train me by these troubles. You see fit to whip every child you intend to acknowledge as yours, you who did not spare even your only Son. He was scourged, though sinless, but I must say, *Have mercy on me; heal my soul, for I have sinned against you.* If he in whom there was no disease submitted to the surgeon's knife, if he who is himself our healing did not refuse the searing remedy, should we be rebellious against the doctor who cauterizes and cuts, the doctor who trains us through all our troubles and heals us of our sin? No, indeed. Let us entrust ourselves to the doctor's hand, for he makes no mistakes, never lances sound flesh instead of morbid tissue; he knows what he is examining; he knows our vices because he made our nature. He is well able to distinguish between what he himself created and what our evil desires have introduced. He knows that to healthy people he gave a command, so that they might not fall sick; he knows that he said to them in paradise, "Eat this; but do not eat that." But those healthy people did not listen to the command from the doctor that would have saved them from falling; so let them at least hear it now, while they are ill, and so rise up again. *I said, Lord, have mercy on me; heal my soul, for I have sinned against you.* I do not blame my deeds, my sins, on luck. I do not say, "Fate brought this upon me." I do not say, "It was Venus that made me an adulterer, and Mars that

15. See Heb 12:6.

made me a robber, and Saturn who made me grasping." Rather *I said, Lord, have mercy on me; heal my soul, for I have sinned against you.*

But surely Christ cannot say this? Could our sinless Head make these words his own? Could they be the words of him who paid back where he had stolen nothing?[16] Could he speak so, who alone of all was free among the dead?[17] Free among the dead he was, because he had no sin, and *whoever commits sin is the slave of sin* (Jn 8:34). Could he, then, make these words of the psalm his own? No, not as from himself; but as from his members he could, for the voice of his members is his voice, just as the voice of our Head is our voice. We were in him when he said, *My soul is sorrowful to the point of death* (Mt 26:38). He was not afraid of dying, for he had come to die; nor was the one who had power to lay down his life and power to take it up again[18] refusing to die. But the members were speaking through their Head, and the Head was speaking on behalf of his members. This is why we can find our own voice in his in the psalm-verse, *Heal my soul, for I have sinned against you.* We were in him when he cried out, *My God, my God, why have you forsaken me?* for in the psalm which opens with those words the next phrase speaks of *the tale of my sins* (Ps 21:2(22:1); see Mt 27:46). What sins could there be in him? None whatever, but our old nature was crucified together with him, that our sinful body might be destroyed, and that we might be slaves to sin no more.[19] Let us say to him, then, and also say in him, *I said, Lord, have mercy on me; heal my soul, for I have sinned against you.*

Verse 6. Already expounded

7. *My enemies reviled me, asking, When will he die, and his name disappear?* We have discussed this verse already, because it was the starting-point of this sermon. We want to move on to the rest, and there is no need to repeat here what must be fresh in your ears and your hearts, since we spoke of it so recently.

Verse 7. Spies within who spread slander abroad

8. *And they kept coming in to see.* What Christ suffered, the Church suffers; what the Head suffered, the members suffer too. Is a servant greater than his master, or a disciple than his teacher? *If they have persecuted me, they will persecute you as well*, the Lord said, and *if they have called the master of the household Beelzebub, how much more his servants?* (Jn 15:20; Mt 10:24-25). So then, *they kept coming in to see.* Judas was close to our Head; he was accustomed to

16. See Ps 68:5(69:4).
17. See Ps 87:6(88:5).
18. See Jn 10:18.
19. See Rom 6:6.

come in and see: to spy on him, I mean, not looking for something in which he might believe, but hoping to find grounds for betrayal. So there was one who kept coming in to see in the case of our Head, and this serves as a precedent for us. How does it work out for us, who are his members, now that he has been taken up to heaven? The apostle Paul speaks of *false brethren who infiltrated in order to spy upon our freedom* (Gal 2:4). These too were accustomed to come in and see. Such people are hypocrites, wicked dissemblers who join us with feigned charity, taking careful note of every movement and every word on the part of the saints, ever seeking the means to entrap them. What does the psalm go on to say of these spies? *Their heart has said empty things*. They make a show of love when they speak, but what they say is empty; it is untrue and has no substance. And what is the psalm's verdict on the way they amass pretexts for their accusations? *They have collected iniquity for themselves*. As our enemies prepare their false charges they think highly of themselves, because they seem to have damaging evidence. *They have collected iniquity for themselves*. Notice, though, that it says, *for themselves*, not "against me." As Judas heaped it up to his own detriment, not Christ's, so do these bogus members of the Church heap it up against themselves, not us. Elsewhere it is said of them, *Iniquity lied to itself* (Ps 26(27):12). *They have collected iniquity for themselves*, and having come in to see, *they would go outside and talk*. The same one who came in to see used to go outside and talk. If only he were inside, and spoke the truth! Then he would not go outside, where he tells lies. He is a traitor and a persecutor, and after going outside, he talks. If you belong among Christ's members, come inside and hold fast to the Head. If you are the wheat, put up with the tares; if you are true grain, endure the chaff; if you are a good fish, make allowances for the bad fish in the net with you.[20] Why did you fly away before the time for winnowing? Why did you uproot the crop along with yourself before harvest-time? Why have you torn the nets before they reached the shore? *They would go outside and talk*.

What counts is the intention behind the words

9. *With common purpose all my enemies kept whispering against me*. With common purpose[21] they all opposed me; how much better it would have been if they had united in a common purpose with me! What does it mean, *with one accord against me*? With a single agreed plan, in one conspiracy. Christ says to them, therefore, "You agree against me. Agree with me instead. Why must it be against me? Why not with me?" If you were always united in a common mind, you would not splinter into schisms, for the apostle says, *I beg you, brothers and sisters, to be united in what you say, and not to allow schisms to form among you*

20. See Mt 13:24-30, 47-48.
21. *In idipsum*.

(1 Cor 1:10). *With common purpose all my enemies kept whispering against me; they plotted to do me harm.* To harm themselves, rather, because *they collected iniquity for themselves*; but they meant it against me, and it is by their intention that they make themselves liable to punishment. That they were unable to achieve anything does not mean that they did not want to. The devil desired to get rid of Christ entirely, and Judas wanted Christ killed. Christ was killed and he rose again; we were given life, but to the devil and to Judas due punishment was meted out, not the salvation that was awarded to us. To make it clear that all of us are assessed on our intention as deserving either reward or punishment, let me remind you that in certain cases we find people wishing someone good, wishing him or her the kind of benefit we would want for ourselves, and yet we call it cursing. An instance of this was the argument between the once-blind man, now enjoying light in both body and heart, and the Jews. He was showing them up, these Jews who had bodily sight but were blind in their hearts, and now, in his healed condition, he said to them, *You don't want to be his disciples too, surely?* But, as the gospel puts it, *they cursed him and said, "You be his disciple yourself."*[22] May such an outcome be the fate of us all, yet they wished it on him as a malediction. We call it a "malediction" from the misguided malevolence of those who speak so, not from anything bad in the words as such. The evangelist who described it like this had regard to the spirit in which they spoke, not the words they uttered. *They plotted to do me harm.* But what harm could they do to Christ, and what harm to the martyrs? God turns all things to good.

Verse 9. Eve is created from Adam's sleep

10. *They directed a wicked word against me.* What kind of wicked word? Think what it was in the case of our Head: *Let's kill him, and the inheritance will be for us* (Mt 21:38). What fools you are! Why do you think you are going to get the inheritance? Because you killed him? Well, you did kill him, but the inheritance will not fall to you. *Will he not go further, and rise again, he who has fallen asleep?* You exult over your success in killing him, but he has only fallen asleep, for in another psalm that is what he says, *"I fell asleep.* They raged, they were bent on killing me, but I fell asleep; for if I had not been willing, I would not even have slept. *I fell asleep, for I have the power to lay down my life, and I have the power to take it up again. I rested, and fell asleep, and I arose*" (Ps 3:6(5); Jn 10:18). Let the Jews rage, then, and let earth be delivered into impious hands,[23] let flesh be surrendered to the hands of persecutors; let them fasten it to the cross and pierce it through with nails, and dig into it with a lance; but *will he not go*

---

22. Jn 9:27-28. Augustine meditated similarly on how an apparent good wish can be a curse, and *vice versa*, in his Exposition of Psalm 39, 26.
23. See Jb 9:24.

further and rise again, he who has fallen asleep? Why did he sleep? Because Adam was a type of the one who was to come,[24] and when Adam slept, Eve was formed from his side.[25] Adam prefigured Christ, and Eve prefigured the Church, which is why she was called the mother of the living.[26] When was Eve fashioned? While Adam slept. And when did the Church's sacraments flow forth from Christ's side?[27] While he slept on the cross. *Will he not go further and rise again, he who has fallen asleep?*

Verse 10. How could Jesus have trusted Judas?

11. But whose fault was it that Christ slept? It was the fault of the man who had come in to see, and collected iniquity for himself. *"Even the one who was my friend, the one whom I trusted and who ate my bread, has lifted his foot against me.* He raised his foot over me, meaning to trample on me." Who is this man who was his friend? Judas. But does the phrase, *whom I trusted*, really mean that Christ trusted Judas? Surely he had known what Judas was from the outset? He must have known, because he had said to all his disciples, *Have I not chosen all twelve of you? Yet one of you is a devil* (Jn 6:71). How then was it possible for Christ to trust Judas? It was possible, because Christ is present in his members. There were plenty of believers who must have trusted in Judas, and the Lord made their attitude his own.[28] Many people who had come to believe in Christ were accustomed to see Judas walking about among the twelve disciples, and some of them would have trusted him, because he seemed like the others. But Christ was present in these trustful members of his, just as he is in his members who hunger and thirst; and as he can say, *I was hungry*, so too he can say, *I trusted*. It follows that if we ask him, "Lord, when did you trust him?" just as we can also ask him, "Lord, when were you hungry?" he can reply to us, "Whenever one of the least of those who are mine trusted him, I trusted him," as he also replies, *What you did for even the least of those who are mine, you did for me* (Mt 25:40).

"And who was this, in whom I trusted? *The one who was my friend, the one whom I trusted and who ate my bread.*" Did Christ use these prophetic words to point to Judas at any moment in the passion? Yes; he designated Judas as the betrayer by handing him a morsel of bread,[29] so it was clearly Judas who was meant by the words, *who ate my bread*. Then again when Judas came to hand him

24. See Rom 5:14.
25. See Gn 2:21.
26. See Gn 3:20.
27. See Jn 19:34.
28. *Hoc in se transfiguravit Dominus.*
29. See Jn 13:26.

over he gave Jesus a kiss,[30] proving that the rest of the verse also referred to him: *the one who was my friend.*

Verse 11. The green wood did not burn

12. *But you, Lord, have mercy on me.* He speaks here in the guise of a servant,[31] in the form of a needy, poor person; remember how the psalm declared, *Blessed is everyone who understands about the needy and poor man.* Now he prays, *Have mercy on me, and raise me up; then I will requite them.* Notice when this prayer was made, and how it has been answered. The Jews killed Christ in order not to forfeit their national place.[32] But after killing him they lost it: they were uprooted from their territory and dispersed. When Christ was raised from the dead he requited them with tribulation, but the recompense was dealt out as a warning, not a final condemnation. The Jews were rooted out from that city where the populace, like a ravening, roaring lion, had shouted, *Crucify, crucify!* (Ps 21:14(22:13); Lk 23:21; Jn 19:6); it belongs to Christians now, and no Jew lives there. In the place from which the thorns of the synagogue were uprooted Christ's Church was planted. And truly the fire burned among the Jews as it does among thorns;[33] but the Lord was like green wood. He made this comparison himself, when certain women were lamenting over him because he was about to die. *Do not weep over me, but weep over yourselves and your children,* he told them, alluding to the retribution mentioned in our psalm: *raise me up, and I will requite them*; for *if they do this to the green wood, what will be the fate of the dry?* (Lk 23:28,31). How could green wood ever be consumed by burning thorns? The Jews went up like a fire amid thorns; fire devours thorns, but does not easily catch any green wood it touches, for the sap in the wood resists the flame, causing it to gutter feebly, though it is vigorous enough to make the thorns blaze.

Raise me up; then I will requite them. You certainly must not think, brothers and sisters, that the Lord's prayer, *Raise me up,* implies that the Son is less powerful than the Father, and was unable to raise himself. Not at all. What he raised up was what was prone to die; flesh died, and flesh was raised up. God, the Father of Christ, had the power to raise up Christ—to raise the flesh of his Son, that is; but this does not mean that Christ himself, who is the Word of God and equal to the Father, had no power to raise his own flesh. To exclude such a misapprehension he promised in the gospel, *Destroy this temple, and in three days I will raise it up again*; and to make sure we should be in no doubt about

30. See Mt 26:49; Mk 15:45; Lk 22:47.
31. See Phil 2:7.
32. See Jn 11:48.
33. See Ps 117(118):12.

what he meant, the evangelist added, *He spoke of the temple of his body* (Jn 2:19,21). *Raise me up; then I will requite them.*

Verse 12. The killers' glee was premature

13. *This is how I know that you wanted me: my enemy will not rejoice over me.* The Jews thought they had succeeded in their purpose of harming Christ when they saw him crucified, and so they rejoiced. In Christ hanging on the cross they contemplated the fruit of their savage efforts, and they wagged their heads, saying, *If he is the Son of God, let him come down from the cross.*[34] He had the power to do so, but he did not choose to come down; his intention was not to display his power,[35] but to teach us patience. If in response to their gibes he had come down from the cross he would have appeared to yield the victory to his mockers; people would have thought that he was defeated and could not bear their taunts. All the more firmly did he stay on the cross while they insulted him, fixed immobile as their heads wagged about. Those heads were wagging because the Jews were not holding fast to the true Head. And certainly he did give us a lesson in patience. He refused to do what the Jews were trying to provoke him to do, but he did something mightier, for it is a far more powerful act to rise from a grave than to come down from a cross.

My enemy will not rejoice over me. At that time they did rejoice; but Christ rose again, Christ was glorified, and now the Jews see the human race being converted in his name. Let them mock now, let them do their head-wagging now! They will do better to keep their heads still, or shake them only in wonder and admiration. Nowadays they ask, "Can this man be the one of whom Moses and the prophets spoke? Of him who was to come the prophets said, *He was led like a sheep to the slaughter, and like a sheep voiceless before its shearer, he did not open his mouth; by his wounds we were healed* (Is 53:7,5). We watch this crucified man drawing the whole human race after him, and it seems that our fathers achieved nothing by their resolve, *Let us kill him, lest the whole world go after him.*[36] Perhaps it would not have gone after him if he had not been killed." *This is how I know that you wanted me: my enemy will not rejoice over me.*

Verses 13-14. The Christian case against the pagans is proved from the Jewish scriptures

14. *But you have upheld me because of my innocence.* His was innocence indeed: sinless integrity, the repayment of debts he did not owe, a scourging he

34. See Mt 27:39,40.
35. Variant: "this was no proof that he lacked power."
36. See Jn 12:19.

did not deserve. *"You have upheld me because of my innocence, and strengthened me for ever.* You have strengthened me for ever, though you weakened me for a time; you have strengthened me in your sight, though you weakened me in the sight of men and women." What shall we say, then? All praise to him, all glory be to him. *Blessed be the Lord, the God of Israel.* He is truly the God of Israel, that is, our God, the God of Jacob, the God of the younger son, the God of the junior people. Let no one say, "This line refers to the Jews; I am not Israel." It would be truer to say that the Jews are not Israel. The elder son represents the senior people that was rejected; the younger son stands for the junior people God chose to love. The prophecy that *the elder shall serve the younger* (Gn 25:23) has been fulfilled now. Consider, brothers and sisters: the Jews serve us now; they are like slaves[37] carrying our satchels; they carry books for us, the students. Look how the Jews are like slaves to us, and deservedly. Cain, the elder brother who killed the younger, was given a mark to ensure that he would not be killed;[38] this means that the Jewish people was to remain in existence.[39] The prophets and the law are cherished among them, and in the law and the prophets Christ was made known. When we deal with the pagans, we demonstrate to them that what is happening in Christ's Church is what was prophesied about the name of Christ, about Christ as Head and members; and if they suspect that we have forged these prophecies, and written them up after the event though they purport to refer to something future, we bring forward the books of the Jews. This is all the more convincing inasmuch as the Jews are our enemies, so our opponent is convinced by our enemy's documents.

God has disposed all things, and ordered all things for our salvation. He foretold it before we existed, he has fulfilled it in our time, and what he has not fulfilled yet, he will. We hold fast to him as one who keeps his promises, and therefore we can believe him to be our debtor still; for as he has already given what had not been given when it was prophesied, so will he give what has not been given yet. Any who want to find out where these things are written should read Moses and the prophets. If any noisy protester among our enemies says, "You have concocted those prophecies to suit your own case," let the Jewish books be produced, for the elder will serve the younger. Let them read there the predictions we now see fulfilled, and let us all say, *Blessed be the Lord, the God of Israel, from of old and unto all ages.* And all the people will say, *So be it, so be it.*

37. The *capsarius* was the slave who followed a boy to school, carrying his books. There may be an echo of Gal 3:24; but the analogy has a special point in the present passage in view of the following argument about the books of Hebrew scripture which serve the Christian purpose.
38. See Gn 4:15.
39. In the Exposition of Psalm 39, 13, the "mark of Cain" was the continuing observance of the Passover lamb and unleavened bread; here it is the permanence of the Hebrew scriptures.

Exposition of Psalm 41

A Sermon to the People

Introduction: longing on both sides

1. Our soul has been longing for some time past to rejoice with you in God's word, and to salute you in him who is our help and our salvation.[1] So listen now to what God gives you through us, and together with us be glad about his words, and about his truth and charity; for we have undertaken to talk to you about this psalm in response to your own longing.[2] The psalm begins in fact with holy longing, for the singer says, *As a deer longs for springs of water, so does my soul long for you, O God.* Who is it saying that? If we will, it is we ourselves. Why bother to inquire any further who it is, when it is within your power to be yourself the answer to the question? Remember, though, that the speaker is not a lone individual, but a single body: the Church, which is the body of Christ. A longing like this is not found in everyone who comes into church, yet those who have tasted the sweetness of the Lord,[3] and recognize that savor in this song, should not think they are alone in this experience. They must believe that similar seeds have been sown widely in the Lord's field all over the world, and that it is a single, united Christian voice which sings, *As a deer longs for springs of water, so does my soul long for you, O God.* We could well hear the voice of our catechumens here too, for they are hurrying toward the holy, grace-giving bath.[4] This is why we customarily sing the psalm to arouse in them a longing for the fountain of forgiveness for their sins, like the longing of a deer for the springs of water.[5] Fair enough, and may this interpretation keep its place in the Church; it is both true and sanctioned by usage. All the same, brothers and sisters, I cannot believe that a longing of such intensity is satisfied in believers even at baptism. If the candidates know where their pilgrimage is tending, and what that land is to

1. A pun in the Latin links verb with noun: *in illo vos salutare, qui est nostrum adiutorium et salutare*: "to wish you good health in him who is our help and our health."
2. Variant: "our desire."
3. See Ps 33:9(34:8).
4. *Lavacrum.*
5. The catechumens were instructed during Lent and baptized at Easter. The psalm was sung as they processed to the baptistery, where they received the sacrament by immersion. Ambrose has left an account of baptismal practice in two works: *On the Sacraments* and *On the Mysteries.*

which they must cross over, their longing will be kindled to even greater intensity.

Verse 1. Understanding offered to the "children of Korah"

2. The psalm is entitled, *Unto the end, understanding for the children of Korah.* We have come upon these children of Korah in the titles of other psalms;[6] and we remember having discussed the name and its meaning before. Nonetheless we ought to mention the title now. The fact of having expounded it earlier should not deter us, for you were not all present in the various places where we discussed it previously. Now Korah may have been an historical person, as indeed he was, and may well have had children who were called "the sons of Korah." But we must peer into the holy secret implicit here, and persuade this name, pregnant with mystery, to bring forth what it holds. It is a great and holy mystery that Christians should be designated "children of Korah." Why can they be called that? Because they are children of the Bridegroom, children of Christ; that is what Christians are called: the Bridegroom's children.[7] But why does Korah stand for Christ? Because the name Korah means Calvary; but that is a more obscure point. I was inquiring why Korah stood for Christ, but I am far more interested in inquiring why Christ is seen to be connected with Calvary. You already know, don't you? Of course you do. Christ was crucified at a place called Calvary. So "the children of the Bridegroom," the children of his passion, the children redeemed by his blood, the children of his cross who wear upon their brows the sign of that gibbet his enemies set up on Calvary—these are called "children of Korah." For them this psalm is sung, to bring them understanding.

Let us bestir ourselves to understand, then. If it is sung for us, we should try to understand it. What are we going to understand? Into what kind of comprehension will the singing of this psalm lead us? I will tell you, boldly I will tell you: since the world was first created men and women have seen the invisible realities of God, understood through things that are made.[8] Well then, brothers and sisters, catch my eagerness, share my longing. Let us love, all of us together; let us burn together with this thirst; let us run together to the fountain of understanding. Let us long for it as a hart yearns for a spring. I do not mean that spring which the baptismal candidates long for, that their sins may be forgiven; let us who are baptized long rather for the well-spring of which scripture says, *With*

6. The collection "of the sons of Korah" was one of the groups incorporated into the final form of the Psalter. It includes Pss 43-48, 83, 84, 86, 87 (44-49, 84, 85, 87, 88). In his Exposition of Psalm 83, 2, and Exposition of Psalm 84, 2, Augustine discusses the meaning of the name Korah, interpreted as "bald," and associates this with Calvary, "the place of a skull." In the present context he seems to assume that this link is known to his hearers: he did not comment on the psalms in numerical order. See also the Expositions of Psalm 43, 1; Ps 44, 1; Ps 46, 2.

7. See Mt 9:15; Lk 5:34.

8. See Rom 1:20.

you is the fountain of life; for God is both a spring and light, as that other psalm goes on to say: *In your light we will see light* (Ps 35:10(36:9)). If he is both fountain and light he obviously is understanding, for while he fully satisfies the soul athirst to know, everyone who understands is illumined by a light that is not corporeal or carnal or external, but is an inward radiance. There is an interior light, brothers and sisters, which people without understanding do not know. The apostle has some exhortation to offer to believers who long for the fountain of life and already experience it in some degree: *Walk no more now as the pagans walk*, he says. *Their minds are empty; they are darkened in their understanding and estranged from the life of God by the ignorance that is in them, owing to the blindness of their hearts* (Eph 4:17-18). If they are darkened in their understanding—darkened, that is, precisely because they do not understand—it follows that they who do understand are illuminated. Run to the springs, long for the fountains of water. With God is the fountain of life, a fountain that can never dry up; and in his light is a radiance never dimmed. Long for this light; long for the well-spring, and for a light such as your eyes have never known. Your inner eye is being prepared to see that light, and your inner thirst is burning ever more fiercely for that fountain. Run to the fountain, long for the fountain; but do not run to it in any random fashion, do not run like any animal you may chance to think of: run only like a deer. Why like a deer? Because there must be no tardiness about your running. Run energetically, long untiringly for the fountain. I say this because the deer stands for fleetness of foot.

Verse 2. Deer kill snakes, and then feel thirstier

3. Perhaps this is not the only characteristic of deer that scripture wished us to consider. There may be something else. Listen now to another peculiarity of theirs. A hart kills snakes, and after font them he burns with a more intense thirst than before; so after dealing with the snakes he runs to the well-springs even more urgently. These snakes represent your vices; put the snakes of your iniquity to death, and you will long all the more keenly for the font of truth. Perhaps a miserly spirit is hissing dark suggestions in you, hissing something opposed to God's word and forbidden by his commandments? You know what you are told: "Give that thing up, and stay clear of sin." But if you would rather commit the sin than turn your back on some temporal gain, you are choosing to be bitten by the snake instead of killing it. If you prefer your vice, your lust, your greed, your snake, when am I going to find in you the kind of longing that will send you running to the well-spring? How are you going to yearn for the font of wisdom, if you are still floundering in the venom of ill-will? Kill off whatever in you is opposed to the truth; but when you judge yourself to be free of crooked desires, do not sit down as though that were all, and you had nothing else to long for. There is something for which you must arouse yourself and go, if you have

already done your best to rid yourself of anything in you that could hold you back. I know that if you are a good deer you are going to say to me, "God knows that I'm not a money-grubber now, that I no longer covet other people's property, that I'm not on fire with adulterous lust, not tormented by hatred or envy of anyone," and so forth. You are going to tell me, "I no longer have these sins"; and so you look for something you can enjoy, don't you? Long for what will truly give you delight, long for the fountains of water. God has everything that will refresh you. He is able to fill anyone who comes to him, anyone who comes parched from slaughtering snakes, like a fleet-footed deer.

Kindly arrangements among deer

4. There is another point to notice about deer. People have seen them doing what I am about to describe; it would not have been recorded about them in writing unless previously observed. It is said, then, that when deer are walking in single file, or want to swim to a different place to find fresh grazing, they rest their heavy heads on each other. One goes in front, another rests its head on him, and others on them, and so on until the whole line is supported. When the hart who has been bearing the weight in the foremost position is exhausted, he moves to the rear, and another takes his place to carry what the first one was carrying, while this previous leader rests himself by supporting his head on another, as all the others have been doing. They go on like this, carrying the heavy weight for each other; so they make good progress, and do not let each other down. Was it not deer like these that the apostle had in mind? *Bear one another's burdens*, he says, *and so you will fulfill the law of Christ* (Gal 6:2).

Verse 3. The longing is intensified by waiting

5. Once a deer of this kind is established in faith, but does not yet see the object of that faith and yearns to understand what he or she loves, this deer has to endure other people who are not deer at all, people whose understanding is darkened, who are sunk in their inner murk and blinded by vicious desires. Nor is this all, for they jeer at the believer who cannot yet point to the reality in which he or she believes: *Where is your God?*. Let us listen to how our hart handled these attacks, so that we may meet them in the same way if we can. To begin with he expressed his thirst: *as a deer longs for springs of water, so does my soul long for you, O God*. Did I hear someone ask, "Perhaps the deer is longing for springs of water because he needs a wash?" We can't tell whether it was for drinking or for washing, but listen to the next line; and don't ask questions: *my soul has been athirst for the living God*. The line, *as a deer longs for springs of water, so does my soul long for you, O God*, means the same as *my soul has been athirst for the living God*. What was this soul thirsting for? *When shall I reach him and appear*

before the face of God? "This is what I am thirsting for, to reach him and to appear before him. I am thirsty on my pilgrimage, parched in my running, but I will be totally satisfied when I arrive. But *when shall I reach him?"* What is soon to God seems late to our longing. *When shall I reach him and appear before the face of God?* A like longing evoked the cry in another psalm: *One thing have I begged of the Lord, and that will I seek after: to live in the Lord's house all the days of my life.* To what purpose? *That I may contemplate the Lord with delight* (Ps 26(27):4). *When shall I reach him and appear before the face of the Lord?*[9]

Verse 4. A diet of tears

6. Meanwhile I mull over these things as I run my course, as I am still on the way, not yet arriving, not yet appearing there. And all the while *my tears have been bread to me day and night, as every day I hear the taunt, Where is your God?* Notice that he says, *My tears have been bread,* bread, not bitterness. "My very tears were delicious to me. I was thirsting for that spring, and because I could not yet drink from it, I ate my tears the more hungrily." He did not say, "My tears have been my drink." If he had, we might have thought he had thirsted for his tears as he thirsted for the well-springs; but no: "My thirst, my burning thirst, remains unquenched, and it drags me toward the springs of water; but as I wait, my tears have become bread to me." And in eating his tears he would certainly find his thirst for the springs all the keener. "My tears became bread for me, by day and by night." It is in the daytime that people eat food, which is represented by the term "bread"; at night they sleep. Yet the psalmist eats his bread of tears by day and by night. You could take this to mean "all the time"; or you could understand "day" as prosperity in this world, and "night" as worldly misfortune. "In both prosperity and adversity, as this world sees them, I pour out my tears," he says. "Never do I take the keen edge off my desire. Even if things are going well by worldly standards they are bad for me, until I appear before the face of God. Why try to force me into enjoying the daylight, if some worldly prosperity smiles on me? Is prosperity not a deceiver? Is it not labile, unsteady, mortal? Is it not ephemeral, fleeting, transient? Does it not harbor more of deceitfulness than delight? Why then should my tears not be bread for me, even in prosperity?" It is true, indeed, that even if the happiness of this world bathes us in its light, as long as we are in the body we are still on our journey and absent from the Lord,[10] and *every day I hear the taunt, Where is your God?* If a pagan says this to me, I cannot retort, "What about you? Where is *your* God?" because

9. Perhaps because of contamination from the quotation immediately preceding, the last word here is *Domini*, not *Dei* as in his citation of the same verse above. One of the characteristic features in the psalms of the Korah collection is the use of "God" rather than the divine name usually rendered in English by "the Lord." But a few codices amend to *Dei* here.

10. See 2 Cor 5:6.

the pagan can point to his god. He indicates some stone with his finger and says, "Look, there's my god! *Where is yours?*" If I laugh at the stone, and the pagan who pointed it out is embarrassed, he looks away from the stone toward the sky; then perhaps he points to the sun and says again, "Look, there's my god! *Where is yours?*" He has found something he can demonstrate to my bodily eyes. For me it is different, not because I have nothing to demonstrate, but because he lacks the kind of eyes to which I could demonstrate it. He was able to point the sun out to my bodily eyes as his god, but how can I point out to any eyes he has the sun's Creator?

Where is your God? The search through creatures and in oneself

But as I listened daily to the taunt, *Where is your God?* and was nourished by my daily diet of tears, as I pondered day and night on this question hurled at me, *Where is your God?* even I came to wonder if was possible for me not merely to believe in my God, but even to see something of him. I see the things my God has made, but my God himself, who made them, I do not see. Yet like a deer I long for the springs of water, and the fountain of life is with him; and since this psalm was written to bring understanding to the children of Korah, and the invisible realities of God are seen and understood through things that are made,[11] what shall I do to find my God? I will consider the earth, for the earth was made. Great is the beauty of earth's many faces, but it was an artist who made it. Great wonders there are in seeds and in the generation of living things, but all of them come from their Creator. I point to the immensity of the sea all around us; I am astonished and filled with wonder, and I look for the artificer. I look up to the sky and the loveliness of the stars; I marvel at the sun's radiance with its power to awaken the day, and the moon that relieves the darkness of night. These things are marvelous, we must praise them, even be astounded at them, for they are not earthly things; they belong to the heavens. But not yet is my thirst slaked, for though I admire them and sing their praises, it is for him who made them that I thirst. So I return to myself, and examine who I am, I who can ask such questions. I find that I have a body and a soul: the one I must rule and by the other be ruled: the body serves and the soul commands. I observe that my soul is a better thing than my body, and that the investigator of these mysteries is not my body but my soul; and yet I recognize that when I surveyed all these things, I surveyed them through my body. I was praising the earth, but I knew it only through my eyes; I praised the sea, but my eyes had revealed it to me; I praised the sky, the stars, the sun and the moon, but only through my eyes had I come to know them. The eyes are bodily organs, the windows of the mind; it is the inner self that looks out through them, and if the mind is preoccupied with some other thought, the eyes

11. See Rom 1:20.

are open to no purpose. My God, who made these things I see with my eyes, is not to be sought with my eyes.

My mind even has the power to see objects through itself alone. It may be aware of something like colors and light not actually present to my eyes, music or other sounds not available to my ears, sweet scents not perceived by my nose, a savor not in contact with my palate or tongue, a feeling of hardness or softness, of cold or heat, of roughness or smoothness, which my body might have perceived, but does not. Or again it may be aware of something that I see within myself. See within? How is that? Something, I mean, that is neither a color, nor a sound, nor a scent, nor a taste, nor heat, nor cold, nor hardness nor softness. When we think about justice, and appreciate the beauty of it within ourselves, in our thought, what sound do our ears catch? Does any steamy scent rise to our nostrils? What enters the mouth? What pleasant surface meets the exploring hand? Yet justice is within us; it is beautiful, it moves us to praise, we see it; and even if our bodily eyes are in darkness, the mind enjoys its light. What was it that Tobit saw, when in his blindness he was giving advice to a son who could see?[12] The mind which governs the body, guides it and dwells in it, is aware of something that reaches it not through the body's eyes, or ears, or nose, or palate, or sense of touch, but through itself; and unquestionably what the mind knows through itself is better than what it comes to know through its servant. But still there is more: the mind sees itself through itself; it sees itself so as to know itself. In no way does it seek the help of the bodily eyes to see itself; on the contrary, it withdraws from all its bodily faculties, finding them a hindrance and a noisy one, and betakes itself to itself that it may see itself in itself and know itself in its own presence.

But is the mind's God something similar, something like the mind itself? To be sure, God can be seen only with the mind, but he cannot be seen as the mind itself can be seen. This mind is seeking a reality that is God, a reality of which the mockers cannot say, *Where is your God?* It is seeking the unchangeable truth, the substance that cannot fail. But the mind itself is not like that: it fails and makes progress, it knows and then knows not, it remembers and forgets, it wants something at one moment and then wants it no more. No such mutability is found in God. If I say, "God is subject to change," they will have the right to jeer at me, those who say, *Where is your God?*

Verse 5. The soul is poured out above itself

8. I sought my God in visible, material creatures, and I did not find him. I sought the substance of him in myself, as though he were something like what I am, and did not find him there either; so I have become aware that my God is

12. See Tb 4:1-23.

some reality above the soul. *I reflected on these things, and poured out my soul above myself* that I might touch him,[13] for how could my soul ever attain what it seeks, the reality above the soul, unless it poured itself out above itself? If it remained within itself it would see nothing other than itself; and in seeing only itself it would certainly not be seeing its God. Let the onlookers who deride me go on saying, *Where is your God?* Yes, let them say it, and as long as I do not see him, as long as I am made to wait, I will eat my tears day and night. Let them go on saying, *Where is your God?* I look for my God in every bodily creature, whether on earth or in the sky, but I do not find him. I look for his substance in my own soul, but do not find him there. Yet still I have pondered on this search for my God and, longing to gaze on the invisible realities of God by understanding them through created things, *I poured out my soul above myself*; and now there is nothing left for me to touch, except my God. For there, above my soul, is the home of my God; there he dwells, from there he looks down upon me, from there he created me, from there he governs me and takes thought for me, from there he arouses me, calls me, guides me and leads me on, and from there he will lead me to journey's end.

In the admirable tabernacle he catches the sound of another festival

9. For he who has his most lofty home in a secret place has also a tent on earth. His tent[14] is the Church, the Church which is still a pilgrim; yet he is to be sought there, because in this tent we find the way that leads to his home. When I resolved to pour out my soul above myself to reach my God, why did I do it? *Because I will walk into the place of the tent.* If I seek my God away from that camp-site I will go astray. *I will walk into the place of the wonderful tent, even to the home of God.* I will walk into the place where this tent is pitched, this wonderful tabernacle, and so reach God's home. And already I find many wonderful things in the tent, great things that move me to admiration and amazement. The faithful are God's tent on earth; and in them I admire the obedience of their bodily parts, for sin does not reign in them to exact obedience to its desires, nor do they put their members at sin's disposal as implements of iniquity, but rather subject them to the living God in good works.[15] So I marvel at bodily members enlisted for action under the soul that serves God. Moreover I watch the soul obeying God, organizing its activities, restraining its wayward desires, banishing ignorance, stretching out to endure all that is harsh and testing, and exercising justice and kindness toward other people.

13. One manuscript specifies, "touch him with my mind's understanding."
14. *Tabernaculum.* See Augustine's observations on homes and tents in his Exposition of Psalm 26, 6.
15. See Rom 6:12-13.

These virtues I do indeed admire in the soul, yet still I am walking in the wonderful tent. Then I go further still and pass beyond it; and though the tent is admirable, I am dumbfounded when I arrive at God's house. In another psalm the speaker tells us that he had put a hard, puzzling question to himself: why on this earth good fortune usually comes the way of the wicked, while misfortune dogs the good. Then he speaks of the house of God: *I tried to solve the problem, but it is too hard for me until I enter God's holy place, and understand what the end must be* (Ps 72(73):16-17); for there, in God's holy place, in God's house, is the spring of understanding. There that psalmist understood what the end must be, and solved his problem about the happiness of villains and the travail of the just. What was his solution? He saw that while the life of the wicked is prolonged here, they are being reserved for punishment without end, but while the good struggle along they are being trained until they are ready at last to gain their inheritance. This is what the psalmist understood in God's holy place: he understood the final outcome. He climbed up to the tent, then arrived at God's house. Yet it was while he marveled at the members of that company in the tent that he was led to God's house. He was drawn toward a kind of sweetness, an inward, secret pleasure that cannot be described, as though some musical instrument were sounding delightfully from God's house. As he still walked about in the tent he could hear this inner music; he was drawn to its sweet tones, following its melodies and distancing himself from the din of flesh and blood, until he found his way even to the house of God. He tells us about the road he took and the manner in which he was led, as though we had asked him, "You admire the tent on earth, but how did you reach the secret precincts of God's house?" *By the voice of exultation and praise*, he says, *the sounds of one celebrating a festival.*[16] When people celebrate in this world with their various forms of indulgence, they usually set up musical instruments outside their houses, or assemble singers there, or provide some kind of music which enhances the pleasure of the guests and entices them to immoderate behavior. If we are passing by and happen to hear it, we say, "What's going on?" And they tell us that it's some kind of party. "It's a birthday party," they say, or "There's a wedding reception." They tell us this so that the songs may not seem out of place, and the lavish expenditure[17] may seem to be justified by the festive occasion. In God's home there is an everlasting party. What is celebrated there is not some occasion that passes; the choirs of angels keep eternal festival, for the eternally present face of God is joy never diminished. This is a feast day that does not open at dawn, or close at sundown. From that eternal, unfading festival melodious and delightful sound reaches the ears of the heart, but only if the world's din does not drown it. The sweet strains of that celebration are wafted into the ears of one who walks in the

16. Variant: "of a banquet."
17. Variant: "the joy."

tent and ponders the wonderful works of God in the redemption of believers, and they drag the deer toward the springs of water.

Verse 6. Subsequent sadness

10. Nonetheless, brothers and sisters, as long as we are in the body we are still on pilgrimage and away from the Lord.[18] Our corruptible body weighs down the soul, and this earthly dwelling oppresses a mind that considers many things.[19] At times we may in some measure scatter the clouds as our yearning draws us on, and even come within earshot of that melody, so that by pressing forward we may conceive something of the house of God. Yet under the weight of our weakness we fall back into familiar things, and slide down again into our ordinary way of life. As we have found there a cause for joy, so here there is no shortage of things to groan about. The deer made tears his food by day and by night; he was possessed by yearning for the well-springs, those springs of God's spiritual delight, and he poured out his soul above himself in his longing to touch what was above his soul. He walked into the admirable tent, and even to the house of God; he was drawn onward by the charm of a spiritual, intelligible music until he despised all external things and was rapt by love for what is within. But for all that, he is still a human being, still groaning, still carrying frail flesh, still imperiled amid the stumbling-blocks of this world. So he looked again at himself as he returned from that place, and as he found himself amid his woes he compared them with the glories he had gone in to see, the wonder he had seen and left behind as he came out. *O my soul, why are you sorrowful, and why do you disquiet me?* he asked. "Remember how we were gladdened by an inner sweetness, remember how we found it possible to perceive with the sharp point of our mind something that does not change, even though we could but brush against it for a swift moment. Why, then, do you still disquiet me? Why are you still sorrowful? You do not doubt your God. It is not as though you had no retort to make to those who ask, *Where is your God?* Already in my deepest being I have known something beyond change, so how can you still disquiet me? *Hope in God.*"

His soul seems to reply silently to him, "Why do I disquiet you? Why else, than because I am not there, in that place of delight to which I was carried away, but so briefly? Am I yet drinking from that fountain, free from fear? Am I yet beyond all danger of falling? Am I secure, as though all sinful desires were subdued and overcome? Is my adversary, the devil, not still on the watch? Does he not set cunning traps for me every day? Can you seriously ask me not to

18. See 2 Cor 5:6.
19. See Wis 9:15.

disquiet you, while my place is still in this world, while I am a pilgrim still, and far from God's house?"

But he has an answer for the soul that disquiets him, and gives him such plausible reasons for its unease by pointing to the evils that abound in this world. "*Hope in God*," he says. "Dwell in hope for this in-between time." If hope is seen, it is hope no longer; but if we hope for what we do not see, we wait for it in patience.[20]

Verse 7. Hope and salvation

11. *Hope in God*. Why? *Because I will confess to him*. And what will you confess to him? "That he is *the salvation of my countenance, my God*. There can be no salvation for me derived from myself, so this is what I will say, this I will confess: he is *the salvation of my countenance, my God*." The speaker knows that caution is necessary in spite of the things he has in some measure understood, so he is on his guard lest the enemy approach by stealth, and he does not yet make bold to say, "I am saved in every respect." We do indeed possess the first-fruits of the Spirit, yet we groan within ourselves, waiting for our full adoption in the redemption of our bodies.[21] When that salvation has been brought to perfection in us we shall live in God's house for ever, praising without end the God to whom another psalm cries out, *Blessed are they who dwell in your house; they will praise you for ever and ever* (Ps 83:5(84:4)). This is not our situation yet, for the salvation promised us is not yet fully accomplished, but I confess to my God in hope, and say to him, "You are *the salvation of my countenance, my God*." We are saved in hope; but if hope is seen, it is hope no longer.[22] Persevere until you get there, persevere until salvation comes to you. Listen to God himself speaking to you inwardly: *Hold out for the Lord, act manfully; let your heart be strengthened, and hold out for the Lord* (Ps 26(27):14), for *whoever perseveres to the end will be saved* (Mt 10:22; 24:13). In view of all this, *O my soul, why are you sorrowful, and why do you disquiet me? Hope in God, because I will confess to him*. This is my confession: You are *the salvation of my countenance, my God*.

Turn away from yourself

12. *My soul was troubled as it turned to me*. It would not be, would it, if it turned to God? It is troubled when it turns to myself. When turned toward the unchangeable it received new strength, but when turned to what is prone to change it was disturbed. I know that my God's righteousness abides, but whether

20. See Rom 8:24-25.
21. See Rom 8:23.
22. See Rom 8:24.

my own will abide, I know not, for the apostle's warning terrifies me: *Anyone who thinks he stands must take care not to fall* (1 Cor 10:12). Since there is in me no stability, neither is there any hope for me in myself. *My soul was troubled as it turned to me*. Would you like to free your soul from its anxiety? Then do not let it linger in yourself. Say rather, *To you, Lord, have I lifted up my soul* (Ps 24(25):1). Listen, I will make the point clearer. Put no trust in yourself, but only in your God. If you trust in yourself, your soul will be turned toward yourself and gravely troubled, because it cannot yet find any grounds for security in you. So then, if my soul turned toward myself and found itself disturbed, what is left to me but humility, the humble refusal of the soul to place any reliance on itself? What course is open to it, except to make itself very small indeed, and to humble itself so that it may be raised up? Let it attribute nothing to itself, and then what is profitable may be granted to it by God.

My soul was troubled when it focused on itself, and what aroused that turbulence was pride. *Therefore I remembered you,*[23] *O Lord, from the territory of the Jordan and the little hill of Hermon*. From where did I remember you? From an insignificant mountain and from the Jordan region. Perhaps that means from baptism, where our sins were forgiven. I think this may be right, because no one runs toward the forgiveness of sins except those who are displeased with themselves; no one runs toward the forgiveness of sins except those who acknowledge that they are sinners; and none can confess their sinfulness without humbling themselves before God. This is why *I remembered you from the territory of the Jordan, and from a little hill*, not from a high mountain. From this paltry hill I want you to bring about great things, because *anyone who exalts himself will be humbled, but the one who humbles himself will be exalted* (Lk 14:11; 18:14). An additional point is that if you investigate the interpretation of the names, you find that Jordan means "their descent." Descend then, so that you may be lifted up; do not lift yourself up, or you may be suppressed. *And from the little hill of Hermon*. The name Hermon is said to mean "putting under a ban." Put yourself under a ban in your displeasure with yourself; for if you are self-satisfied you will be displeasing to God. God grants us all good things because he is good, not because we are worthy, because he is merciful and not because we have deserved them in any way. Therefore *I remembered God from the territory of the Jordan and from Hermon*. Because he remembers God in humility, he will be found worthy to be exalted and to enjoy God to the full, for those who make the Lord their boast are not exalted on their own account.

23. Variant: "I will remember you."

Verse 8. The human heart is a great deep

13. *Deep calls to deep at the sound of your cataracts.* I may be able to get through this whole psalm if you help me by your concentration, for I can see how eager you are. I am not too worried about any fatigue you may feel as you listen, for you can see how I am sweating in the effort that speaking costs me. And as you watch me laboring, you will certainly help me, for you know I am laboring not for my own benefit, but yours. Go on listening, then; I can see you want to.

Deep calls to deep at the sound of your cataracts. The one who remembered God from the Jordan region and from Hermon now says this to God. He says it wonderingly: *Deep calls to deep at the sound of your cataracts.* What is this deep that is invoking another deep, and what is the depth invoked? The latter must be the depth of understanding,[24] for a depth is an unsearchable place, a profundity beyond comprehension. The word "depth" is usually applied to some vast ocean, because there we find such depth, such profundity, that we can never fathom it.

Now in another place it was said, *Your judgments are an unfathomable abyss* (Ps 35:7(36:6)), and by this metaphor scripture meant to teach us that God's judgments are deeper than our minds can comprehend. What then is the deep that is calling out here, and what the deep that is invoked? If "deep" signifies profundity, surely the human heart is a deep abyss? Could anything be more profound? Human beings can speak, they can be observed as they use their limbs, and heard in their speech; but can we ever get to the bottom of a person's thoughts, or see into anyone's heart? Who can grasp what another person is intent upon there within the heart, what are the possibilities, the activity, the purposes of the heart, its will and its refusals? The profundity of a human being is surely referred to in a saying we find elsewhere: *A mortal will draw near to the heart's depths, and God will be exalted* (Ps 63:7-8(64:6)).

But if a human being is a deep abyss, how does a deep call upon a deep? Can it mean one human invoking another? Can a human being do that, in the way we invoke God? No, certainly not. But we do use the word "invoke" to mean "invite" or "call something to oneself." For instance, it might be said of someone that he invites death;[25] this means that he lives in such a way as to call death down upon himself, for no one will actually pray for it, or explicitly invite it; but by living in a wicked fashion people implicitly call it down upon themselves. So in this sense deep does call to deep when one human being calls to another. This is how wisdom is imparted, and faith is learned, when one deep invokes another. Holy preachers of God's word call to a deep abyss. But are they not a deep abyss themselves? They certainly are, as you know. The apostle says, *It matters very little to me that I am judged by you or by any human day of reckoning.* What a

24. Mentioned in the title of the psalm.
25. See Wis 1:16.

deep abyss he is! But he goes further: *Neither do I judge myself* (1 Cor 4:3). Do you find it difficult to believe that there could be such profundity in any human being that it is hidden from the person himself? Think, then, what a depth of human weakness lay hidden in Peter. He did not know what was going on within him when he kept promising so rashly that he would die with the Lord or for the Lord.[26] What a deep abyss he was! Yet even that depth lay open and naked to God's eyes, for Christ told him in advance what Peter himself did not know.

Any human being, even a holy, good-living person, even one who has made great progress, is a deep place, and such a person calls upon another depth when he preaches to another some part of the faith, some part of the truth, with a view to eternal life. But the deep that preaches is profitable to the deep he calls to if he calls in the sound of God's cataracts. *Deep calls to deep*, one person wins over another, but not with his own voice only: he calls in *the sound of your cataracts*.

The depth of God's judgments

14. Now consider an alternative interpretation. *Deep calls to deep at the sound of your cataracts.* I already began to tremble when my soul turned to myself and was troubled, but I am thoroughly terrified by your judgments, for *your judgments are an unfathomable abyss* (Ps 35:7(36:6)), and *deep calls to deep*. As we struggle in this mortal flesh, this travailing, sinful flesh, full of troubles and handicaps and liable to immoderate desires, we are already subject to the penalty imposed by your judgment, for of old you said to a sinner, *You shall certainly die* and *In the sweat of your face you shall eat your bread* (Gn 2:17; 3:19). But this is only the first abyss of your judgment. If people live sinfully here, *deep calls to deep*, because they pass from punishment to punishment, from darkness to darkness, from depth to depth, from torment to torment, from burning lust to the flames of hell. Perhaps it was of this that the psalmist was afraid when he said, *My soul was troubled as it turned to me; therefore I remembered you, Lord, from the territory of the Jordan and from Hermon.* I must be humble, for I am exceedingly frightened by the prospect of your judgments. I was in sheer terror at the thought, and as it turned to me *my soul was troubled.* What judgments of yours struck fear in me? Were they some trivial judgments on your part? No, your present judgments are already great, and severe, and grievous; but if only they were all! *Deep calls to deep at the sound of your cataracts.* You threaten us, you tell us that after our present travail a further condemnation awaits us: *at the sound of your cataracts deep calls to deep.* Where shall I go, then, from your face, whither flee from your spirit,[27] if even after our present pains more severe pains are to be feared?

---

26. See Jn 13:37.
27. See Ps 138(139):7.

Waves and breakers

15. *All your breakers and waves have coursed over me.* The waves wash over me in the sufferings I undergo now, but your threats are judgments poised above me.[28] All my present hardships are your waves, but all your menaces hang over me, ready to break on my head. In the waves this abyss that I am calls out, but behind your impending threats is that other abyss to which this one calls. Already I flounder amid your waves, but your threats are far more serious and they hang over me, for a threat is something not yet pressing down, but poised overhead. Yet you set me free, and therefore I have said to my soul, *Hope in God, because I will confess to him, the salvation of my countenance, my God.* The more my woes are multiplied, the gentler will be your mercy.

Verse 9. Gather the word while you can

16. With this in mind the psalmist continues, *The Lord has assured*[29] *us of his mercy in daylight, but he will demonstrate*[30] *it at night.* When tribulation strikes, no one has time to listen. Take note while things are going well for you, listen while you are prospering, learn while you are tranquil. Collect the teachings of wisdom and the word of God like food, for when we are in trouble we need to feel the benefit of what we heard in our carefree days. So it is that in your times of prosperity God assures you of his mercy, telling you that if you serve him faithfully he delivers you from trouble; but only at night does he demonstrate to you that mercy of which he assured you in the daytime. When the trouble is visited upon you, he does not leave you bereft; he proves to you that his daytime assurance was true. This is why scripture says, *Very lovely is the Lord's mercy in time of trouble, like a rainy cloud in drought* (Sir 35:26). *The Lord has assured us of his mercy in daylight, but he will demonstrate it at night.* He can only prove to you that he comes to your help when tribulation overwhelms you, because then he who made his promise to you in daylight has the chance to deliver you.

We are urged to imitate the ant, for the same reason.[31] Worldly prosperity is symbolized by daylight, and worldly adversity by the darkness of night; but another image is provided by the changing seasons. Summer represents prosperity, and winter adversity. What does the ant do? Throughout the summer she collects what will be useful in winter. So you must do likewise: in summertime, when your enterprises are going well and you are tranquil, listen to the word of the Lord. How is it possible that in this stormy world you could make your entire crossing of the sea without running into trouble? How is that possible? Does

28. *Suspensiones.*
29. Variant: "will assure."
30. Variant: "has demonstrated."
31. See Prv 6:6.

anyone? If anyone did, that person's tranquil course would be all the more suspect. *The Lord has assured us of his mercy in daylight, but he will demonstrate it at night.*

Verses 9-10. The inner prayer: "Why have you forgotten me?"

17. What must you do, then, while you are on your pilgrimage? How must you conduct yourself? *My prayer to the God of my life is within me.* This is what I do, I, a thirsty deer, longing for the springs of water, remembering the sweetness of the sound that has led me through the tent, even to God's house. As long as my corruptible body weighs heavily on my soul[32] *my prayer to the God of my life is within me.* To offer supplication to God I have no need to seek exotic gifts from overseas; for God to hear me I have no need to sail afar and bring back incense and aromatic spices, or to bring calf or ram from the flock, for *my prayer to the God of my life is within me.* Here within me I have the victim I must offer, here within the incense I must burn, here within me is the sacrifice with which I may propitiate my God: *a sacrifice to God is a troubled spirit* (Ps 50:19(51:17)). Listen to what this inner sacrifice is like, this offering from a troubled spirit: *"I will say to God, You are my protector; why have you forgotten me?* I am struggling here as though you were no longer mindful of me. But you are training me, and I know that you are only delaying what you promised, not disavowing it.[33] All the same, *why have you forgotten me?* Just as our head cried out in our voice, *My God, my God, why have you forsaken me?* (Ps 21:2(22:1); Mt 27:46), so too *I will say to God, You are my protector; why have you forgotten me?*"

Verses 10-11. Even my bones are broken

18. *Why have you thrust me back?* Why have you thrust me away from that sublime source of understanding and unchangeable truth? I am already panting for it, so why have I been thrown down to my old life by the burdensome weight of my sinfulness? This same plea is made in another psalm: *Beside myself with fear* or after some kind of ecstasy, where he had seen some glorious vision, *Beside myself with fear, I said, I have been flung far out of your sight* (Ps 30:23(31:22)). That suppliant compared his present lot with the wonders he had attained in his uplifted state, and he saw himself now flung far away from God's gaze, as the psalmist does here: *Why have you thrust me back? Why must I walk in deep sadness, while my enemy harasses me and breaks my bones*, my enemy the devil, the tempter? As scandals increase all around, the charity of many

32. See Wis 9:15.

33. *Differs mihi, non mihi aufers, quod promisisti.*

grows cold.[34] When we see even the powerful people in the Church so often giving way under pressure, does not Christ's body cry out, "The enemy is breaking my bones"? Bones are our strong framework, yet even these strong supports sometimes yield to temptation. When any member of Christ's body thinks of this, does he or she not cry out with the voice of Christ's body, "*Why have you thrust me back? Why must I walk in deep sadness, while my enemy harasses me and breaks my bones?* It is not just my flesh that is under attack, but my bones too." You watch them crumble under temptation, even those bones in which you thought there would be some strength, and so the weak members lose heart when they see the strong succumb. How dangerous this is, my brothers and sisters!

Verses 11-12. Where is your God?

19. *Those who trouble me have insulted me.* And here it comes again, the same mocking question: *They insulted me, as every day they taunt me: Where is your God?* Most of all do they say this when the Church is beset by temptations: *Where is your God?* What a lot of insults the martyrs heard, as they suffered valiantly for Christ's name: "Where is your God? Let him deliver you, if he can." People saw them enduring torments outwardly, but did not see them inwardly crowned. *Those who trouble me have insulted me, as every day they taunt me: Where is your God?* When I have this to contend with, and as my troubled soul turns to me, what else am I to say to it, except, *O my soul, why are you sorrowful, and why do you disquiet me?* But my soul seems to reply, "And how could I not disquiet you, trapped as I am amid such great evils? I am longing for the good, I am thirsting, laboring; and you think I could refrain from disquieting you?" But *hope in God, because I will still confess to him.* My soul makes the same confession; it reiterates its hope yet more strongly: "You are *the salvation of my countenance, my God.*"

34. See Mt 24:12.

Exposition of Psalm 42

A Sermon to the People

The song of Christ's body

1. This psalm is a short one, so as you listen it will satisfy your minds without putting too much strain on your fasting stomachs. Let us hope that our soul may find nourishment in it, that soul which the psalmist speaks of as sad. I think it is probably sad because of some fasting on the part of the psalmist, or I should say because of his hunger, because fasting is a voluntary state, whereas hunger is something we cannot help. The Church is hungry, Christ's body is hungry. This person who is spread worldwide, whose head is on high and whose limbs are here below—this whole person is hungry. We should hear his voice, her voice, in all the psalms, jubilating or groaning, rejoicing in hope or sighing with love in fulfillment; we should hear it as something already well known to us, a voice most familiar because it is our own. There is no need to make heavy weather over indicating to you who the speaker is. Only let each of us be within Christ's body, and we shall be the speaker here.

A common lot for all, but different desires

2. Now you know that all those Christians who are making progress are like good seed. These are the people who groan with longing for the heavenly city, who know they are on pilgrimage, who hold steadily to their road, and who by their desire for that abiding country have cast their hope ahead like an anchor.[1] Christians of this stamp are the good seed, Christ's wheat which moans amid the weeds until the time arrives for harvest at the end of the world. Truth himself has explained this to us, Truth who is never deceived.[2] The good seed mourns amid weeds, amid bad people I mean, cheats and seducers, violent and angry folk and those poisoned by intrigue; it looks round and sees itself growing with them in the same field all over the world, watered by the same rain, blown on by the same wind, finding the same nutriment with them and going through the same hardships. It knows that it shares with them all this bounty of God in one common provision, and that all of it is granted to wicked and to good people without distinction by him who makes his sun rise over good and bad alike, and sends his

1. See Heb 6:19.
2. See Mt 13:24-30.

rain on just and unjust.[3] The good seed, the holy seed, the seed of Abraham, is aware of how much it has in common with those from whom it will one day be separated; it is aware of being born in the same way as they are, of inheriting the same human condition, of carrying a mortal body exactly as they do, of enjoying the one daylight, the springs and fruits and abundance of this world, and of enduring its adversities in hunger or plenty, in peace or war, in health and disease. The holy people knows how much it has in common with the wicked, yet knows too that it does not make common cause with them; and so it bursts out, *Judge me, O God, and distinguish my cause from that of an unholy people*. It says, "Judge me, O God; I am not afraid of your judgment, because I have experience of your mercy. In this in-between time while I am on pilgrimage you do not yet assign me any distinguished place, because I have to live with the weeds until the season for harvest. You do not yet distinguish the rain that falls on me, you do not yet distinguish my daylight; but please distinguish my cause." Let a distinction be drawn between one who believes in you, and one who does not. In weakness they are equal, but in conscience far apart; there is parity of travail, disparity of desire. The desire of the ungodly will be extinguished; but what of the desire of the just? We should certainly be apprehensive about that, if the one who makes the promise were not totally reliable. The goal of our desire is the one who has promised; he will give us himself because he has already given us himself. He will give his immortal self when we are immortal, as he has already given himself to us as mortal in our mortality. *Judge me, O God, and distinguish my cause from that of an unholy people; deliver me from the wicked and deceitful*. The wicked and deceitful are the same as the *unholy people*. The psalm mentions them to indicate that it means people of a certain type, for there will be two people working together, and one will be taken, the other left.[4]

Verse 2. The cause of your sorrow

3. It takes patience to endure until the harvest a kind of undistinguished distinction, if we can put it that way. I mean that since the two sorts of growth are still together, they are still undistinguished; but since the weeds are weeds and the grain is grain, in that sense they are distinguished already. We need fortitude as we wait, and we must beg it from him who ordered us to show fortitude, for if he does not make us into brave people we shall not be so. Let us entreat him to grant us fortitude, then, since he has said, *Whoever perseveres to the end will be saved* (Mt 10:22; 24:13). The psalmist saw the danger that if his soul arrogated fortitude to itself, it might be enfeebled thereby, so he immediately added, *Since you are my fortitude, O my God, why have you thrust me back? Why must I walk*

3. See Mt 5:45.
4. See Mt 24:40.

in deep sadness, while my enemy harasses me? He is looking for the cause of his sorrow. *Why must I walk in deep sadness, while my enemy harasses me?* he asks. I am walking in sorrow, and the enemy attacks me with daily temptations, throwing into my path either attractive things which I should not love, or bogeys that it would be wrong to fear. The soul battles against both, and though not captured it is endangered and huddled up in sadness, so it says to God, *Why?* Let it ask him, and let it hear the reason why, for here in this psalm we have someone looking for the cause of the same sadness we know, and demanding of God, *Why have you thrust me back, and why must I walk in deep sadness?*

He may find the answer in Isaiah; possibly the reading we have just heard may help him in his quest: *From me, who gave life to all, a breath of life will go forth. For a little while I afflicted him on account of his sin, and struck him, and turned my face away from him; and so he went away disconsolate and walked in his own ways* (Is 57:16-17). So did you need to ask, *Why have you thrust me back, and why must I walk in deep sadness?* You have heard the reason why: *on account of sin*. The cause of your sadness is sin; try to let righteousness be the cause of your joy. You had the will to sin but did not want the unpleasant consequences. So not content with being unrighteous yourself, you wanted God, from whose punishment you shrank, to be unrighteous too. A better counsel is offered you in another psalm: *It is good for me that you have humbled me, so that I may learn your righteous judgments* (Ps 118(119):71). I learned my iniquities in my arrogance; now let me learn your righteous judgments in my humiliation. *Why must I walk in deep sadness, while my enemy harasses me?* Complaining about your enemy, are you? Yes, he certainly does harass you, but it was you who gave him a foothold.[5] You have a recourse now, though. Accept sound advice, open the door to your King and shut out the tyrant.

Verse 3. Light and truth; the mountain and the tent

4. Now notice what the psalmist says, what prayer he makes to God, so that this may indeed happen. And offer the very prayer that you hear, make the same prayer yourself even as you hear it, because this must be the petition of us all: *Send forth your light and your truth. They have led me, bringing me all the way to your holy mountain and into your tents*. "Your light" and "your truth": we have two names here, but one single reality, for what else is God's light, if not God's truth? And what is God's truth, if not God's light? But both of these are the one Christ, who says, *I am the light of the world. Whoever believes in me will not walk in darkness. I am the Way, the Truth and the Life* (Jn 8:12; 14:6). He is light and he is truth. May he come, then, and deliver us, distinguishing our cause from

5. See Eph 4:27.

that of an unholy people even now; may he deliver us from the wicked and deceitful. May he separate wheat from weeds, for he will send in his angels at harvest-time to collect from his kingdom all the things that make people stumble, and throw them into a blazing fire, but his wheat they will gather into the barn.[6] He will send forth his light and his truth, for these have already led us, already brought us to his holy mountain and into his tents. We have the advance payment, and we hope for the final award. His holy mountain is his holy Church. This is the mountain that grew out of a tiny stone to smash earthly kingdoms, as Daniel saw in his vision; so great did it grow that it filled the whole surface of the earth.[7] It is on this mountain that a psalmist knew his prayer had been heard when he told us, *With my voice I cried to the Lord, and he heard me from his holy mountain* (Ps 3:5(4)). Those who pray elsewhere than on this mountain should not hope to be heard in such a way as to be brought to eternal life. It is true that many people are heard when they pray with other objects in view, but they have no cause to congratulate themselves on that, for the demons too were heard when they begged to be sent into the pigs.[8] Let us long to be heard so that the issue is eternal life, in accord with the longing expressed here: *Send forth your light and your truth.* This Light seeks the eye of our hearts, for he says, *Blessed are the pure of heart, for they shall see God* (Mt 5:8). We are on his mountain at present—in his Church, that is—and in his tent. A tent is something nomads lodge in, but a house is where people live together at home.[9] A tent is for travelers and for soldiers. So when you hear mention of a tent, understand that there is a war on, and watch out for the enemy. But what will our home be like? *Blessed are they who dwell in your house; they will praise you for ever and ever* (Ps 83:5(84:4)).

Verse 4. God is praised with both lyre and psaltery

5. We have already been brought to the tent and assigned our place on his holy mountain, so what further hope do we cherish? *I will go in to God's altar.* There is an invisible altar on high, to which no unrighteous person has access. The only person who approaches that altar is one who has no qualms about approaching this altar here below; there will he find his life, Christ, who at this altar distinguishes his cause.[10] *I will go in to God's altar.* From his holy mountain, from his

6. See Mt 13:41-42.
7. See Dn 2:31-45.
8. See Mk 5:11-13.
9. See note at Exposition of Psalm 26, 6.
10. *Illic inveniet vitam suam, qui in isto discernit causam suam.* Since God was the subject of *discernit* in earlier paragraphs, and Christ has been referred to as the Life, this seems the best interpretation; but it would be grammatically possible to take the believer as the subject of both verbs, and translate, "The person who at this altar distinguishes his cause will find his life at that other altar." In either case the background is probably 1 Cor 11:28-29, but the allusion would be clearer if this latter interpretation is the right one.

tent, from his holy Church, I will make my entrance to God's altar on high. What kind of sacrifice is offered there? The one who enters is taken up into the holocaust. *I will go in to God's altar.* What does he mean by this approach to God's altar? He goes on to develop the idea: *to God who makes my youth joyful.* "Youth" symbolizes newness. It is as though he said, "To God who gives joy to my new condition." He who saddened my old state now gladdens my newness. At present I step sorrowfully in my old state, but then I shall stand joyfully in my newness.

I will confess to you on the lyre, O God, my God. What is the difference between confessing to him on the lyre,[11] and confessing to him on the psaltery?[12] We cannot praise him all the time on the lyre, nor always on the psaltery. These two musical instruments work quite differently, and the distinction between them is worth considering and committing to memory.[13] Each of them is carried in the hands and plucked manually, which suggests that they represent our bodily activities. Each of them is good, provided that the player is skilled at the psaltery and equally skilled on the lyre. But here is the difference: the psaltery has its vaulted part[14] at the top: that wooden, concave, sounding-chamber, its drumlike piece, I mean, on which the strings are stretched and which gives them their resonance. The lyre has its hollow sounding-chamber at the bottom. Accordingly our activities can be distinguished into those which are played on the psaltery and those played on the lyre; but both are pleasing to God and melodious in his ears. When we do something in harmony with God's commandments, obeying his orders and careful to comply with his precepts, and when we feel no pain in the doing,[15] that is the music of the psaltery. The angels do this all the time, and they never feel pain. But sometimes we do suffer from the troubles and temptations and obstacles on earth. Our pain is then only in our lower part, because it is due to our mortal condition and the debt of tribulation we contract from our primitive origins. Moreover the things that give us pain are not above us. In these cases we are playing the lyre. The sweet sounds proceed from the lower part; we suffer as we sing our psalms; or rather, we sing and play the lyre. The apostle used to say that he preached the gospel, and preached it the world over, in response to God's command, because he had received this gospel not from human sources nor through human agency but through Jesus Christ;[16] and when he spoke in those terms, the strings were resonating from above. At other

11. *In cithara.*
12. *In psalterio.*
13. He draws it out in several places in his Expositions: see Exposition 2 of Psalm 32, 5; Exposition 2 of Psalm 70, 11; Exposition of Psalm 80, 5.
14. *Testitudinem*; see note at Exposition 2 of Psalm 32, 5.
15. *Ubi facimus et non patimur.* This could also be understood as "when we are active and not passive," and the following remark about the angels translated in the same sense. But the emphasis on suffering in the next few lines suggests otherwise.
16. See Gal 1:12.

times he would say, *We even glory in our sufferings, knowing that suffering fosters endurance, and endurance constancy, and constancy hope* (Rom 5:3-4); and then it was the lyre sounding from below, but still very melodiously, for all patient endurance is melody to God's ears. But if you give way under tribulations like that, you have broken your lyre.

Why, then, does the psalmist now say, *I will confess to you on the lyre*? Perhaps because he had asked earlier, *Why must I walk in deep sadness, while my enemy harasses me?* He was experiencing some pain from lowly troubles, yet even in these circumstances he wanted to please God. He was strong amid his afflictions and very keen to give God thanks; and since he could not be free from trouble he paid to God his debt of patient endurance. *I will confess to you on the lyre, O God, my God.*

Verse 5. The higher part of the mind converses with its soul

6. The psalmist turns again to his sad soul, hoping to coax some notes from that sounding-chamber underneath. *Why are you sorrowful, O my soul; why do you disquiet me?* he asks. "I find myself amid troubles, sickness and grief. O my soul, why do you disquiet me?" Who is speaking here, and to whom? He is speaking to his soul; we all know that. It is obvious that the words are addressed to his soul. *Why are you sorrowful, O my soul; why do you disquiet me?* But what I am asking is this: exactly who is the speaker? It can't be the flesh talking to the soul, can it? Apart from the soul, the flesh has no power to speak. It would be more fitting for the soul to address the flesh than for the flesh to address the soul. Yet he did not say, "Why are you sorrowful, O my flesh?" What he said was, *Why are you sorrowful, O my soul?*

We might suppose that if he had indeed been addressing his flesh, he might have said not, *Why are you sorrowful?* but rather, "Why are you in pain?" The pain of the soul is called sorrow; the body's distress may be called pain, but not sorrow. It is true, of course, that the soul is often saddened by bodily pain, but even then there is a difference between what is in pain and what is sorrowful, for the flesh is feeling pain, but the soul is sad; and our psalm says quite plainly, *Why are you sorrowful O my soul?* So it cannot be the soul addressing the flesh, because the psalm did not say, "Why are you sorrowful, my flesh?" Nor can it be the flesh addressing the soul, because it is absurd to suppose that the lower part could speak to the higher.

We are therefore given to understand that we have something within us where the image of God is to be found: our mind or reason. It is this mind that was just now calling upon God's light and God's truth. It is with our mind that we apprehend what is just and what unjust, and with it we distinguish the true from the false. This mind is called our understanding, and it is a faculty not granted to the beasts. Anyone who neglects his understanding, or subordinates it to other things, or throws it away as though he had none, is admonished in another psalm: *Do not be like a horse or a mule, devoid of understanding* (Ps 31(32):9). So it is our understanding that is addressing our soul here. The soul is drooping in its troubles, wearied amid anxieties, cringing under temptations and sick with its toil. But the mind, which apprehends truth from on high, cheers its soul, saying, *Why are you sorrowful, O my soul; why do you disquiet me?*

You cannot be wholly free from sin

7. A conversation of this kind was surely taking place in the conflict where the apostle typified others, and perhaps even ourselves. *I take great delight in God's law as far as my inner self is concerned,* he says, *but I am aware of a different law in my members* (Rom 7:22-23), that is, certain carnal impulses. In his wrestling, nearly desperate, he invokes the grace of God: *Who will deliver me from this death-ridden body, wretch that I am? Only the grace of God, through Jesus Christ our Lord* (Rom 7:24-25). Even the Lord himself deigned to prefigure all who engage in a fight like this, for he said, *My soul is sorrowful to the point of death* (Mt 26:38; Mk 14:34). He knew what was coming. But could he have been afraid of suffering, he who had said, *I have the power to lay down my life, and I have the power to take it up again. No one takes it away from me, but I lay it down of my own accord and take it up again* (Jn 10:18)? No, but he who said, *My soul is sorrowful to the point of death,* was representing his members in advance. Often enough our minds firmly believe, and hold it as certain in faith, that we shall make our way to Abraham's embrace; yet though we believe it, the soul is troubled by the imminence of death owing to its familiarity with the present world. But then it bends its ear to the inner voice of God, and hears within itself the song of reason. In our silence something sounds softly to us from above, reaching not our ears but our minds. Any who hear that music are so disenchanted with material noise that the whole of human life seems to them a confused uproar, which stops them hearing another sound that is delightful, a sound like no other and beyond description. Indeed, whenever someone in a very stressful situation feels battered, he or she addresses the soul: *Why are you sorrowful, O my soul, and why do you disquiet me?*

This is all the more so because our life can never pass muster as truly pure, since he who judges us will deliver a perfectly clear, unclouded judgment. A person's life may win general approval in human society, so that other people can find in it no just grounds for reproach. But God's eyes judge the matter, and from him proceeds a standard of measurement supremely fair and incapable of error. In any human being God finds things he must indeed reproach, reprehensible things unseen by anyone else, things which even the person who stands under judgment was unaware of. Perhaps this was what the soul feared when it felt so troubled; but the mind spoke to it, as though to offer encouragement:

"Why be afraid about your sins, when you know you have not the strength to avoid them all? *Hope in the Lord, for I will confess to him."* This encouragement effects some healing at once, and the rest of its sins are purged by faithful confession. You have good cause to fear if you claim to be just, and do not make your own the plea in another psalm, *Do not sit in judgment on your servant* (Ps 142(143):2). Why this prayer, *Do not sit in judgment on your servant*? Because I need your mercy. If you hand down judgment without mercy, what will become of me? *If you make an inventory of our law-breaking, O Lord, Lord, who will stand?* (Ps 129(130):3). *Do not sit in judgment on your servant, for no living person will be found righteous in your sight.* So then, if no living person is found righteous in his sight, woe betide anyone who lives here, however righteously he or she may live, if God undertakes to judge. In the words of another prophet God frequently reprimands the arrogant and proud: *Why do you want to dispute your case at law with me? You have all abandoned me, says the Lord* (Jer 2:29). Do not dispute with him at law; concentrate on being righteous. But then, however righteous you have managed to be, confess that you are a sinner, and always hope for mercy. Freed from anxiety by this humble confession,[17] speak to the soul that troubles you and raises its hubbub against you: *"Why are you sorrowful, O my soul, and why do you disquiet me?* You wanted to trust in yourself, did you? *Hope in the Lord*, not in yourself. What are you in yourself? What are you by your own efforts? Let him be your healing, who was willingly wounded for you." *Hope in the Lord, because I will confess to him.* And what will you confess? That he is *the salvation of my countenance, my God.* You are my face-saving God, and you will heal me. I speak as a sick person to you; I acknowledge you to be my physician; I do not boast of my health. What do I mean by saying that I acknowledge the physician, and do not boast of my health? I mean exactly what another psalm means: *I said it myself: Lord, have mercy on me; heal my soul, for I have sinned against you* (Ps 40:5(41:4)).

Fasting, almsgiving and prayer

8. This is a safe saying,[18] brothers and sisters; but be vigilant also about good works. Pluck your psaltery by obeying the commandments, and pluck your lyre by accepting suffering. You heard Isaiah's advice: *Break your bread for the hungry* (Is 58:7), so do not delude yourself that fasting is all that is required. Fasting punishes you, but brings no refreshment to anyone else. Your restriction will be fruitful if it brings amplitude to another. So you have deprived yourself, have you? But to whom do you mean to give what you denied to yourself? How do you intend to dispose of what you went without? How many poor people

17. Variant: "persist in this humble confession."
18. Variant: "This is your voice."

might grow fat on that luncheon we missed! Fast in such a fashion that while another person is fed you may feel the contentment of having lunched on your prayers, which are now more likely to win a hearing, for in the same prophecy the Lord says, *While you are yet speaking, lo, I am here, if you willingly break your bread for the poor* (Is 65:24; 58:9,10,7). This kind of gift is often made grudgingly and in a sulky spirit by those who want to be rid of beggars rather than to refresh hungry bellies, but *God loves a cheerful giver* (2 Cor 9:7). If you give your bread grudgingly, you have lost both the food and the merit. Do it with a good will, so that he who sees within you may say, *Lo, I am here*, even before you have finished speaking. How swiftly are the prayers of those who do good works accepted! This is what human righteousness consists of in this life: fasting, almsgiving and prayer.[19] Do you want your prayer to fly to God? Then make two wings for it, fasting and almsdeeds.

May the Light of God and the Truth of God find us so employed, and therefore free from anxiety, when he comes to deliver us from death, he who has already come to undergo death for us. Amen.

19. The three classic "good works" already in Jewish piety. See, for example, Tobit 12:8.

Exposition of Psalm 43

A Sermon to the People

Verse 1. Why God's favor seems to be withdrawn

1. This is a psalm for the children of Korah, as the title prefixed to it declares. But Korah is interpreted "baldness,"[1] or "Calvary," and we find in the gospel that our Lord Jesus Christ was crucified at a place called Calvary. Clearly, then, this psalm is sung for the children of his passion. What is more, we have the very plain and firm testimony of the apostle Paul, who plucked a verse from this psalm to slip into one of his letters as an exhortation of endurance and a message of comfort, at a time when the Church was undergoing persecution by the pagans. The verse he quoted in his letter belongs here: *for your sake we are done to death all day long, reckoned as sheep for the slaughter.*[2] That means that we should be prepared to hear the voice of martyrs in this psalm. Notice one special point: the worthiness of the martyrs' cause is manifested by the words, *for your sake*. Similarly the Lord added the phrase, *in the cause of right*, when he said, *Blessed are those who suffer persecution in the cause of right* (Mt 5:10); he did not want anybody and everybody who was persecuted to seek honor simply from the fact of suffering penalties, if their cause was not a good one. In the same vein he encouraged his disciples by saying, "Blessed will you be when people do or say this or that to you," but he added, "on my account." And the same point is made by the verse in our psalm: *for your sake we are done to death all day long*.

2. God's plan is very deep indeed, a plan of profound wisdom which we must ponder. He led our ancestors, the patriarchs and the whole people of Israel, out of Egypt with a mighty hand; he drowned their pursuing enemies in the sea; he conducted them through the territories of peoples who opposed them, trounced their foes and installed them in the promised land. He won resounding victories with a mere handful of his own people in the face of vast enemy forces. Yet after this he chose to turn away from his people, or so it seemed, with the result that his holy ones were mown down in widespread slaughter, while God lifted no hand to resist, or defend them, or prevent it. He had apparently turned a deaf ear to their groaning, as though he had forgotten them, as though he were not the same God who in his incontestable strength had delivered them from Egypt with a

1. *Calvitium*; see note at Exposition of Psalm 41, 2.
2. Verse 22; see Rom 8:36.

mighty hand and outstretched arm, who had settled them in their own realm after expelling its previous inhabitants, and had struck amazement into all who saw it by granting to such small numbers victory over powerful forces, time and again.

Now this puzzling fact is what the present psalm sets out to sing about, in a tone of lament and confession. These things did not happen without purpose, and we are meant to discover what that purpose was. The events are plain to see, but the reason for them is something that we must search deeply to find. This is why the psalm is entitled not simply, "for the children of Korah," but *for understanding for the children of Korah.* A like purpose is suggested in that other psalm which begins, *My God, my God, look upon me, why have you forsaken me?* When our Lord said that from the cross, he included us in what he was saying, for we are his body and he is our Head. He was speaking from the cross not with his own voice but with ours, for God never forsook him, nor did he ever leave the Father; it was for our sake that he said, *My God, my God, why have you forsaken me?* This is clear from the line that follows: *The tale of my sins leaves me far from salvation*; this demonstrates that it was not in his own person that he spoke, because no sin could be found in him. *I will cry to you all day, and you will not listen to me*, he lamented in that psalm, *and in the night* there was no hearing for him either. But he added, *You will not collude with my foolishness* (Ps 21:2-3(22:1-2)). So if God's refusal to hear was no collusion with foolishness, it must have been to promote understanding. What can it mean, to say, "You will refuse me a hearing, so that I may understand"? It means, "You will not hear me when I ask for temporal things, so that I may understand that eternal goods are what I must desire from you."

God does not forsake you, even when it looks like that. He takes away what you misguidedly longed for, and teaches you what you must long for to your true profit. If God always looked so favorably on our petitions concerning present prosperity that we had an abundance of everything, and suffered no lack at all in this time of our mortality, and never felt the pinch or had to go without things, we would think that these benefits alone are what God grants to his servants, and we would desire nothing greater from him. This is why God infuses bitter troubles into what is sweet but harmful to us in this life, to teach us to seek other things that are sweet and salutary. This is what the title, *For understanding for the children of Korah*, suggests. So now let us listen to the psalm, and try to see the point more clearly.

Verses 2-3. Contrast: then and now

3. *We have heard with our own ears, O God, for our fathers have told us the story, of the mighty deeds you wrought in their days, in the days of old.* They are perplexed about the reason for God's apparent decision to abandon them and

subject them to painful trials, and they recall[3] the past events of which they have heard from their forebears. The implication is, "These troubles we are undergoing now are nothing like what our ancestors related to us." It is the same contrast as that pointed to by the other psalm: *Our fathers hoped in you; they hoped in you and you delivered them. But I am a worm and no man, scorned by all and an outcast from the people* (Ps 21:5.7(22:4.6)). "They trusted you, and you delivered them. Have I not trusted you? Yet have you not forsaken me? Was I mistaken in believing in you, and was it to no purpose that my name was written in your book, and your name inscribed on me?" So too in our present psalm: "This is what our ancestors described to us, how *your hand scattered the Gentiles and planted our people, how you reduced those races to weakness and drove them out.* You cleared other nations out of their land in order to bring in our people, and plant them there, and establish their sovereignty by your loving kindness. This is what our forebears told us."

Verse 4. Strength comes from God's presence

4. But perhaps that earlier generation achieved such feats because they were strong, because they were warriors, because they were invincible, because they were highly trained, because they were warlike? "By no means," says the psalm. "That is not the tradition our ancestors passed on to us, nor what scripture relates." What does it say, then? Only what the next verse tells us: *For it was not by their own sword that they took possession of the land, nor did their own arm save them, but your right hand, and your arm, and your illuminating face*. By *your right hand* it means "your power," and by *your arm*, "your Son." But what does it mean by *your illuminating face*? That you stood by them and manifested yourself by such signs that they were aware of your presence. When God helps us by some wonderful intervention, do we see his face with our own eyes? No, of course not; but by his miraculous effects he makes people aware that he is present. Yet all who have been astounded by an event of this sort will say, "I saw God present there," won't they? So when the psalm speaks of *your right hand, and your arm, and your illuminating face, because you were well pleased with them*, it means, "You so dealt with them that you might take pleasure in them, and that whoever observed your work in them might acknowledge, Truly God is with these people, God is driving them on."

3. The verb here, as in "are perplexed" above, is singular in all the manuscripts, but amended to plural by the CCL editors.

Verse 5. God yesterday, tomorrow and today

5. What are we to make of that? Was it a different God then? Different from now? Absolutely not. Look at the next line: *You are my same king, my same God.* You are yourself, the same, unchanged. I see the times changing, but the Creator of time does not change. *You are my same king, my same God.* As always you lead me, as always you rule me, as always you come to my help. *You who ordain salvation for Jacob.* What does *you ordain* mean? Even if in your own substance, O God, in that nature whereby you are what you are, you remained hidden; even if you were not present to our fathers in your own essence, in such a way that they could see you face to face, still through some created being you ordain salvation for Jacob. Face-to-face vision is reserved for those who have been set free by the resurrection. Even though the New Testament fathers saw your mysteries unveiled, even though they announced the revelation of your secrets, they still avowed that they saw only in a glass darkly, and that a vision in face-to-face clarity was reserved for the future,[4] when the apostle's promise will come true: *You are dead, and your life is hidden with Christ in God, but when Christ appears, Christ who is your life, then you too will appear with him in glory* (Col 3:3-4). Direct face-to-face vision is kept for us until that day, of which John also speaks: *Dearly beloved, we are children of God already, but what we shall be has not yet appeared. We know that when he appears, we shall be like him, because we shall see him as he is* (1 Jn 3:2). Therefore although our fathers did not see you face to face, as you truly are, even though that vision is reserved for the resurrection, and even though it was angels that appeared to them, nonetheless it is you who *ordain salvation for Jacob.* Not only in your own nature are you present. Even when you choose to be present through some creature of your own making, you ordain this for the salvation of your servants, and it is you yourself who are at work. What is done by those whom you thus ordain for your own purposes is done for the sake of your servants' salvation. So then, asks the psalmist, "Since you yourself are my king and my God, and since you ordain salvation for Jacob, why do we now endure such distress?"

Verses 6-7. Hope for the future too

6-7. But perhaps what they told us was valid only for the past, and nothing of the kind is to be hoped for in the future? On the contrary, it certainly is to be hoped for. *By your power we will toss our enemies like straw.* Our ancestors described for us the deeds you wrought in their days, in the days of old, because it was your hand that scattered the Gentiles, you who uprooted alien peoples and planted our race instead. Those things are long past; but what of the future? *By*

4. See 1 Cor 13:12.

your power we will toss our enemies like straw. The time will come for all the enemies of Christianity to be tossed in the air like straw; may they be blown about like dust in the wind and swept off the earth. Well then, if the victories of the past have been recounted for us so graphically, and such great feats announced for the future, why are we struggling in our present circumstances? Why else, if not to promote *understanding for the children of Korah*?

By your power we will toss our enemies like straw, and in your name we will scorn those who rise against us. This is a promise for the future. *For I will put no trust in my bow*, just as our fathers put none in their swords. *And my sword will not save me.*

Verse 8. Future salvation is as sure as though already past

8. *You have saved us from those who afflict us.* This statement seems by its form to refer to the past, but it is made about the future; the verb is in the past tense to indicate that salvation is as certain as though accomplished already. Give a moment's thought to this. Why do many prophets speak as though future happenings, not seen as yet, were already past? For instance, the passion of our Lord was still in the future when it was foretold, yet a psalm said, *They dug holes in my hands and my feet, and numbered all my bones*; it did not say, "They will dig," or "they will number." It continued, *They looked on and watched me*, not "They will look on and watch me." *They shared out my clothing among them* (Ps 21:17-19(22:16-18)), it said, not "They will share out." All these actions were described as though they were past, yet in fact they were still future, because to God future events are as certain as though they had already taken place. For us, things that have happened are certain, but future events are uncertain. We know something has happened, and it is impossible for something that has happened not to have happened. Now take the case of a prophet: to him or her a future event is as certain[5] as a past event is to you and me; and just as you cannot conceive that a past event, something you remember occurring, cannot not have happened, so to the prophet it is inconceivable that what he knows will happen should not happen. This is why events that are still future are confidently spoken of as though past. This, then, is a statement of our hope: *You have saved us from those who afflict us, and put those who hate us to shame.*

5. One manuscript by inserting a *non* changes the sense slightly: "Can you find a prophet to whom a future event is not as certain . . ."

Verse 9. Definitely a future prospect

9. *Our boast shall be in God all day long*. Notice, though, how the psalmist does introduce some verbs in the future tense, to help you understand that what has been couched in the past tense is a prophecy of the future. *Our boast shall be in God all day long, and in your name we will sing praise for ever*. Why does it say here, *Our boast shall be* and *we will praise*? Because you have rescued us from all who afflict us, because you will give us an eternal kingdom, and because that promise will be fulfilled in us: *Blessed are they who dwell in your house, O Lord, they will praise you for ever and ever* (Ps 83:5(84:4)).

Verses 10-11. Present failure

10. Since then the future outcome is certain for us, and equally certain the past events we heard about from our ancestors, what of the present? *But now you have pushed us away and shamed us*. You have shamed us not in our consciences, but in the eyes of other people. That did happen; for there was a time when Christians everywhere were under attack and hounded, and everywhere taunted with the cry, "Look at him, he's a Christian!" as though that were an insult and a reproach. Where then is our God, our king, who ordains salvation for Jacob? Where is he who wrought all those mighty deeds our fathers recounted to us? Where is he who will do all those things he has revealed to us through his Spirit? Surely he cannot have changed? No; but these things happen to further the *understanding of the children of Korah*. We need to understand something of why he has willed us to suffer all these things in the intervening period. All what things? *But now you have pushed us away and shamed us, and you no longer go forth with our armies, O God*. We march out against our enemies, but you do not march with us; we come within sight of them, and they are stronger, and we find ourselves no match for them. Where is that ancient valor of yours? Where is your right hand, where is your might? Where the dried-up sea, where the pursuing Egyptians overwhelmed by the waves?[6] Where is Amalek offering battle, but defeated by the sign of the cross?[7] *You no longer go forth with our armies, O God*.

11. Instead *you have forced us back in the face of our enemies*, so that it seems they are in front, we behind, they the victors and ourselves the vanquished. *And those who hate us plundered as they wished*. Seizing what? Ourselves.

6. See Ex 14:21-28.
7. See Ex 17:8-13.

Verses 12-13. Disaster

12. *You have handed us over like sheep for butchering, and scattered us among the nations.* We have been devoured by the nations, he means. They suffered in such a way that they seemed to be absorbed into the body of the Gentiles. So the Church mourns its own members that have been devoured by the pagans.[8]

13. *You have sold your people for nothing.* We have seen the ones you paid out, but have not seen anything that you received in return. *And there was no great crowd at their celebrations.* No, for when Christians were fleeing from the idolatrous enemies who persecuted them, was that a time for gatherings and songs of joy to God? Were hymns being sung then by God's churches, the hymns that are our favorites in peacetime, and sound in God's ears with the sweetness of fraternal harmony? No, *there was no great crowd at their celebrations.*

Verses 14-15. The example of the cross

14. *You have made us an object of scorn to our neighbors, a butt for their hissing and derision to all around us. You have set us up as an example among the nations.* What does that mean—*an example*? People who curse others sometimes point to some third person whom they hate as a standard of comparison: "May you die like that, may you be punished like him or her." Plenty of curses were uttered in those terms, weren't they? "May you be crucified like him!" Even today there is no lack of enemies against whom we have to stand up for Christ, including the Jews themselves, who say to us, "May you die in the same way as he did!" for they would not have condemned him to such a death if they had not held that manner of dying in the utmost abhorrence, or if they had understood the mystery concealed in it. If a blind person's eyes are anointed, he does not see the salve in the doctor's hand. For the cross was set up for the persecutors too. Later on it became the instrument of their healing, and they came to believe in him whom they had themselves killed. *You have set us up as an example among the nations, a thing at which the peoples wag their heads.* This head-wagging was an insulting gesture, as in another psalm: *they mouthed at me and wagged their heads* (Ps 21:8(22:7)). They did that to the Lord; they did it also to all his saints whom they managed to persecute, and arrest, and mock, and deliver to judgment, and torment and kill.

8. The reverse of the process mentioned in his Exposition of Psalm 3, 7 where the command "Rise, Peter, slaughter and eat" (Acts 10:13) is interpreted as the Church assimilating the (unclean) pagans into its own body.

Verses 16-17. Disinterested love: further understanding

15. *My shame confronts me all day long and my blushing face covers me with confusion, as I hear them berating me and talking me down*, as I hear their insulting words and the charge they fling against me: that I worship you, that I confess you. They turn that name into a crime to charge me with, the name through which all charges against me will be blotted out. *As I hear them berating me and talking me down*: talking against me, he means. *I am ashamed before the enemy, the persecutor.*

Now what understanding can we glean from this? The events spoken of as past will not happen again among us. The future happenings we hope for, but they are not in evidence yet. In the past you led your people out of Egypt in your great glory; they were rescued from their pursuers, conducted through Gentile territory and established in their own kingdom after the expulsion of its previous tenants. What about the future? Your people are to be led out of the Egypt of this world when their leader, Christ, appears in his glory; the saints are to be placed at his right hand, and the wicked at his left condemned to be the devil's companions in everlasting punishment; the kingdom is to be awarded to the good by Christ, for them to enjoy with the saints for ever. These events are still in the future, and the earlier series is past. What comes in between? Troubles. Why? So that every soul that worships God may be shown up, and how truly it worships him be brought into the open; so that the test may be applied: does it freely and disinterestedly worship him from whom it freely received salvation?[9] Suppose God were to say to you, "What did you give me, to induce me to create you? Even if, once created, you have deserved me, you could not have deserved me before I made you." What are we to say to him who in the beginning made us absolutely gratis, simply because he is good, and not because we deserved anything? And then what can we say about our re-creation, our second birth? That eternal salvation was sent to us by the Lord in response to our merits? Certainly not: if our merits had weighed at all in the matter, he would have come to condemn us. He came not to assess our deserts but to forgive sins. You did not exist, and you were created: what did you give to God? You were evil, and you were set free: what did you give to God? With good reason is grace called grace, for it is given gratis. So what is required of you is that you worship him gratuitously, not because he bestows temporal things but because he grants you the good things of eternity.

16. However, you must take care not to go adrift in your thoughts even about these eternal goods, for if you think about eternal things in a carnal way you will no longer be worshiping God gratis. How is that? Well, if you worship God because he gives you a farm, will you refuse to worship him because he takes your farm away? But perhaps you will counter this by saying, "Yes, I do worship

9. *Utrum gratis colat eum a quo salutem gratis accepit.*

him because he is going to give me a house,[10] but it is not a temporal dwelling I'm thinking of." All the same, your attitude is still a mercenary one. You do not worship God out of pure love, but because you are seeking a reward from him. You want to inherit in the next world the things you are bound to leave behind here; your idea is to transmute your carnal pleasure, not to cut it out. We do not think highly of the kind of fasting undertaken by someone who is simply saving himself up for a sumptuous banquet, do we? Sometimes when people are invited to a great feast they fast beforehand because they want to arrive at it hungry; is that sort of fasting to be deemed a sign of self-control, or of self-indulgence? Do not hope that God will give you in heaven the things he commands you to set little store by on earth. The Jews used to think along those lines, which was why a certain question preoccupied them. They do indeed hope for resurrection, but they hope to be raised up to enjoy the same bodily pleasures they love here. Inevitably then they faltered when a question was put to them by the Sadducees, who do not believe in resurrection. The question concerned a woman who married seven brothers in succession: whose wife would she be at the resurrection? The Jews were nonplussed, and could not answer. But when the question was put to the Lord, he replied, *You are going wrong because you know neither the scriptures nor the power of God. In the resurrection they will not marry or take wives, for they will not be faced with death* (Mt 22:29-30; Lk 20:35-36). He means that no replenishment of numbers will be needed where there will be no diminishment,[11] and that we are promised a resurrection in which there will be no mere revisiting of the pleasures we know here, but the possession of eternal joy in God himself. What will there be? *They will be equal to God's angels* (Lk 20:36), he says. You don't suppose, surely, that the angels find their enjoyment in daily banquets, and in the wine on which you get drunk? Or do you imagine that the angels have wives? Among angels there is none of this. What is the source of their joy, then? The Lord tells us: *Do you not know that their angels perpetually see the face of my Father?* (Mt 18:10). If the angels rejoice in contemplating the Father's face, you must prepare yourself for the same joy—unless you can find something better than seeing the face of God? Woe betide any such infatuation on your part, if you so much as surmise that there could be anything more beautiful than he, from whom derives all beauty, anything that could so captivate you that you are not worthy to think of him. The Lord was among us in the flesh, and appeared as a human being among humans. What did he look like? I have already told you: like a human being among humans. What was special about his appearance? He was flesh, visible to fleshly creatures. What was so special about the appearance of one of whom it had been said, *We saw him, and there was no fair form or comeliness in him* (Is 53:2)? But who was this, who had

10. *Villam.*
11. *Non ibi quaeritur successor, ubi non erit decessor.*

neither fair form nor comeliness? None other than he of whom it had also been said, *Fairer are you than any human being* (Ps 44:3(45:2)). As man, he had neither fair form nor comeliness, but he was beautiful from his status above all human beings. Showing this deformed form of his flesh[12] to the eyes of those who gazed at him, he said, *Anyone who cherishes my commandments and keeps them, that is the one who loves me; and whoever loves me will be loved by my Father, and I will love him, and will show myself to him* (Jn 14:21). He was promising to show himself to them – himself, whom they were already looking at. How was that? It was as though he said, "You see the form of a servant, but the form of God is concealed. With the one I am wooing you, but the other I am keeping for you; with the one I am nourishing you now while you are still children, but with the other I feed you in your maturity."

This provision is made so that our faith, by which we are purified, may be made ready for the contemplation of what is invisible. The same was done to promote *understanding in the children of Korah*. All those disasters befell them so that as God's holy ones were stripped of their possessions, and even of temporal life itself, they might learn not to worship the eternal God for the sake of temporal advantages, but in pure love for him to endure all the trials which they had to undergo for a time.

Verses 18-20. The hard way

17. Now at last the children of Korah have understood. And what do they say? *All these things came upon us, and we did not forget you*. Then they expand the phrase, *we did not forget you*, by continuing, *We did not transgress your covenant, nor did our heart turn back, and you have caused our paths to diverge from your way*. Yes, this really does show understanding, that our heart has not turned back, that we have not forgotten you, and that we have not transgressed against your covenant even amid great distress and under persecution from the Gentiles. *You have caused our paths to diverge from your way*. Our paths led us among the pleasures of the world; our paths meandered among temporal prosperity and wealth; you moved those paths of ours far from your way, and showed us how narrow and confined is the path that leads to life. *And you have made our paths diverge from your way*. What does it mean—*you have made our paths diverge from your way*?[13] He is saying to us, "You are caught amid troubles and you suffer grievously; you have lost much of what you valued in this world. But I

---

12. *Formam illam deformem carnis ostendens*: an oxymoron which the CCL editors soften by amending to *forman illam de forma carnis ostendens*: "showing this form from the form of his flesh."
13. What, indeed? The thought would have been easier if Augustine's Latin version had carried on the negative from the three preceding clauses, to read "and our feet have not strayed from your way."

have not abandoned you on this way which, as I am proving to you, is narrow. You were looking for broad paths, but what do I tell you? This is the road that will lead you to eternal life; if you take the one you are tempted to walk on, you are heading for death. *How broad and spacious is the road that leads to perdition, and how many there are who walk along it! But how narrow and confined is the way that leads to life, and how few they are who walk in it!*" (Mt 7:13-14). Who are these "few"? Those who endure distress, those who bear up under trials, those who amid all these troubles do not give way, those who do not rejoice for a mere hour or two at hearing the word, but then when things become difficult dry up as though under scorching sun, but have the root of charity in them, as we heard in the gospel that was read just now.[14] Have that root of charity in you, brothers and sisters, have the root of charity, I tell you, so that when the sun rises it will not scorch you, but foster your growth. *All these things came upon us, and we did not forget you; we did not transgress against your covenant, nor did our heart turn back.* But because we bear ourselves like this amid tribulations, already walking along your narrow way, we can say that *you have caused our paths to diverge from your way.*

18. *Because you have humbled us in a place of weakness*, you will exalt us in a place of strength. *And the shadow of death has covered us.* Our present mortality is the shadow of death, but real death is damnation with the devil.

Verses 21-22. God knows our hearts, though we may not

19-20. *If we have forgotten the name of our God*: but they have not; this is a mark of the understanding granted to Korah's children. *And if we have stretched out our hands to any other god, will God not inquire about these things? For he knows the secrets of the heart.* He knows, and he inquires? If he knows the secrets of the heart, why does he bother to inquire about them there?[15] *Will God not inquire about these things?* He knows them in himself, but he inquires about them for our instruction. Sometimes God inquires and seems to be finding out about some matter because he is making it known to you. He is telling you about his work, not making some new discovery on his own behalf. We often use a similar figure of speech: we say, "What a happy day!" when conditions are favorable, but it isn't the day itself that is rejoicing, is it? Yet we speak as though the day were joyful because it makes us joyful. Or again we say, "The sky looks gloomy." There is no such emotion in the clouds, but if people see the sky with a certain aspect they are saddened, and so they call the sky gloomy because it induces gloom in them. In the same way God is said to learn something when he

14. See Mt 13:3-23; Mk 4:3-20; Lk 8:5-15.

15. Or "If he knows the secrets of the heart, what is that question, *Will God not enquire about these things?* doing in the verse?"

causes us to learn it. God says to Abraham, *Now I know that you fear God* (Gn 22:12). Had he been unaware of it until then? No, but Abraham had not known himself, because only in this trial did he come to know himself. Often enough a person thinks himself able to do something that in fact he cannot do; and then by God's dispensation a testing experience comes his way. Through this testing the person comes to know himself, and then God is said to have found out the true facts, which he caused the person concerned to discover. Peter scarcely knew himself, did he, when he said to the physician, "I will stay with you even to death"?[16] But the doctor had felt Peter's pulse and knew what was going on inside the sick man, though the patient was ignorant of it. Along came the crisis that put him to the test; the doctor proved that his diagnosis had been right, and the patient lost his presumption. This is how God both knows and enquires. If he knows, how can he enquire? Because of you, so that you may find yourself, and give thanks to him who made you.[17] *Will God not enquire about these things?*

21. *For he knows the secrets of the heart.* What is the meaning of this? What secrets are meant? *For your sake we are done to death all day long, reckoned as sheep for the slaughter.* You may see someone put to death, but the true reason he or she is put to death you do not know. God knows it, but it is a hidden matter. When I said that, did someone object, "We do know. He is imprisoned for the name of Christ, for confessing the name of Christ"? But the heretics confess Christ's name too, don't they? Yet it is not really for him that they die.[18] That is not all: even in the Church itself—yes, in the Catholic Church, I mean—don't you think there have been some in the past, and may still be some, who have suffered for the sake of winning renown? If there were no such people, the apostle would hardly have said, *If I deliver my body to be burnt, yet have no love, it profits me nothing* (1 Cor 13:3). He must have known that there would be some who would do even that for boastful motives, not out of love. This is why we must recognize that the real motive is obscure; God alone sees it, we cannot. He alone who knows the secrets of our hearts is competent to judge. *For your sake we are done to death all day long, reckoned as sheep for the slaughter.* As I have pointed out already, the apostle Paul used this text to encourage martyrs not to faint under the sufferings they face for Christ's name.

16. See Mt 26:35.
17. The ideas in this paragraph are very similar to those in Exposition 1 of Psalm 36, 1.
18. Augustine's view on "good works" performed outside Catholic unity was very stern; here he seems logically but harshly not to recognize true martyrdom when those put to death are heretics. But there is some doubt about the correct reading, some manuscripts inserting a *non*: "Why do the heretics not confess. . . ."

Verse 23. Arise, Lord!

22. *Arise, why do you sleep, O Lord?* To whom is that cry addressed, and who utters it? Should we not rather think that the person who could say, *Arise, why do you sleep, O Lord?* was asleep and snoring[19] himself? But the psalmist replies, "I know what I am saying. I know that he who guards Israel does not fall asleep";[20] yet the martyrs shout, *"Arise, why do you sleep, O Lord?* O Lord Jesus, you were slain, you fell asleep in your passion, and for us you are already risen, for we know it, we know you have risen. Why did you arise? The pagans who are persecuting us think you dead; they do not believe that you rose again. Arise for them too. Why do you sleep—not for us, but for them? If they believed that you are already risen, would they have been able to persecute those who believe in you? But why do they persecute us? 'Stamp them out, kill them, whoever they are, any who have believed in some fellow who met a shameful death,' they say. For them you are still asleep; arise, so that they may understand that you are risen, and may cease their uproar."

And so while the martyrs are dying, and praying like this, they fall asleep themselves, and by their falling asleep they arouse Christ who was truly dead; for Christ can be said to have risen among the pagans in the sense that they have come to believe that he is risen. Little by little, as they have believed and have been converted to Christ, they have so greatly swelled our numbers that the persecutors have taken fright and stopped persecuting us. How has it happened? Because Christ, who was formerly asleep for the pagans when they did not believe, has now risen among them. *Arise, and do not reject us for ever.*

Verses 24-25. Ultimate humiliation

23-24. *Why do you turn your face away* as though you were not present, as though you had forgotten us? *Why do you forget our need and our distress? For our soul was crushed down in the dust.* Where is it crushed down, humiliated? In the dust, he says, which implies, "The dust is persecuting us. These people are persecuting us of whom you said elsewhere, *The ungodly are not like the righteous, but like dust which the wind sweeps away from the face of the earth* (Ps 1:4). Our soul was crushed down in the dust; our belly stuck to the ground." It seems to me that the psalmist describes here the pain of ultimate humiliation by using the image of someone who has fallen flat on his face, so that his belly is stuck to the earth. If a person is so far humiliated that he is brought to his knees, there is still further down to go; but if he is brought so low that his belly is sticking to the ground, no further humiliation is possible for him, for if anyone

19. *Halare.* Variants include *balare* "to bleat, talk foolishly"; *balare et ululare* "bleat and wail."
20. See Ps 120(121):4.

tries to push him down further, it will not be humiliation[21] but burial. So perhaps what the psalm is saying here is, "We have been utterly humiliated in the dust, crushed so low that no further humiliation remains for us. Since our humiliation has reached its nadir, may your mercy reach us now."

Another interpretation: those who fail

25. Another thought, brothers and sisters: could we not think that in these words the Church is mourning those whom the persecutors persuaded to deny their God? Then it would be those who held firm under persecution who say, *Our soul was crushed down in the dust*, that is, "At the hands of that dust, at the hands of godless persecutors, *our soul was crushed down in the dust*, so as to evoke from us a prayer to you, a cry for your help to deliver us from our ordeal. But *our belly stuck to the ground*." They mean that "our belly" consented to the impious persuasion of that dust; for that is what the expression "stuck to" implies. When you love God, when you burn with charity toward him, you rightly say to him, *My soul has clung to you* and *It is good for me to cling tightly to God* (Ps 62:9(63:8); 72(73):28). To cling to God is to do his will. It makes sense, then, to say of the belly that it clung to the earth, when we mean those people who could not hold out under persecution, but yielded to the will of the wicked; for this is how they "stuck to the earth."

But why are they called "the belly"? Because they are carnal. It suggests that the Church's mouth is to be found in the saints, in spiritual people, and the Church's belly in the carnal. This is why the Church's mouth is plainly visible, but its belly is covered up, as befits something weaker and more vulnerable. Scripture supports this interpretation in the passage where someone says he was given a book to eat, *and the book was sweet in my mouth, but bitter in my stomach* (Rv 10:10). What can that mean? Surely that the highest precepts, which spiritual persons accept, are unacceptable to the carnal, and that commands which delight the spiritual only give the carnal indigestion. What is in that book, brothers and sisters? *Go and sell all you possess, and give the money to the poor* (Mt 19:21). How sweet is that command in the Church's mouth! All the spiritual have obeyed it. But if you tell any sensual person to do that, he or she is more likely to walk sadly away, as the rich man in the gospel walked away from the Lord, than to fulfill the injunction. Why does a carnal person walk away? Because that book, so sweet to the mouth, is bitter in the belly. You have given any amount of gold and silver, have you? But now the question arises about some particular item: unless you give it up, you may commit some sin, or perhaps cheat the Church, or be tricked into some blasphemy. You are in a tight spot, caught between losing money and losing righ-

21. The root of the word "humility" is *humus*, "earth, ground, soil."

teousness. You are advised, "Let go of the money, and keep hold of righteousness." But righteousness does not taste pleasant in your mouth, for you are still weak, still among those members the Church assigns to its stomach. You are grieved, and you choose to drop some element from your righteousness rather than even a coin from your money. By so doing you wound yourself more seriously, keeping a full purse but being left with an empty heart. Perhaps it was of people like these that the psalm said, *Our belly stuck to the ground.*

Verse 26. Unmerited help

26. *Arise, Lord, help us.* Truly, truly, dearest friends, he did arise and he has helped, for when he arose—rose from the dead, I mean—and when he made himself known to the pagans, and the persecutions ceased, even those who had stuck to the earth were scraped off it, and did penance, and were restored to the body of Christ. Weak they were, imperfect they were; but they were restored, so that the scripture might be fulfilled in them: *Your eyes beheld my imperfection, and in your book all shall be written* (Ps 138(139):16).

Arise, Lord, help us, and redeem us for the sake of your name. That means, "gratis." Not for any deserving on my part, but because of your name; because it is worthy of you to do this and not because I am worthy to receive your help. Even the fact that we did not forget you, that our heart did not turn back, that we did not stretch out our hands to any other god—even this would have been beyond our power had you not been helping us. How could we have found the strength for it had you not been speaking to us within, encouraging us, and never deserting us? Whether we are enduring amid troubles or rejoicing amid prosperity, redeem us, not for any merit of ours, but for your own name's sake.

Exposition of Psalm 44

A Sermon preached in the Restored Basilica on Wednesday, 2 September[1]

Verse 1. Childish mockery of a bald man

1. We have joyfully sung this psalm with you, and now I beg you to study it carefully with us. It is a song about a sacred marriage, about a bridegroom and his bride, a king and his people, the Savior and those who are to be saved. Anyone who has arrived at this wedding properly dressed in wedding clothes (not to attract attention to himself or herself, but in honor of the Bridegroom) will not be content just to listen eagerly. That is what people ordinarily do when all they are looking for is entertainment, and they have no intention of letting what they see or hear affect their behavior. But a properly disposed guest also takes to heart a word that will not lie there idle, but will germinate, burst into flower, grow, reach perfection, and yield fruit for harvesting. As the title of the psalm indicates, we must be the children of Korah. No doubt the original children of Korah were historical persons; but every title found in the divine scriptures offers a hint to alert minds, demanding not merely a hearer, but a perceptive one. We can investigate the meaning of the Hebrew word, and find out what "Korah" means and, as is the case with all the words in scripture, an interpretation is at hand. "The children of Korah" means "the children of the bald man." You must not think that funny. We do not want to be like those tittering boys with their childish minds, whom we read about in the Book of the Kingdoms.[2] They mocked the prophet Elisha by shouting after him, *Off you go, baldy, off you go, baldy!* Those silly, prattling children jeered at him to their own destruction, for wild beasts came out of the woods and devoured them. This is what scripture says, and we have reminded you where it was written.[3] Let those who remember it recognize the reference, and those who do not remember look it up, and those who have not read it at all take our word for it. Since that episode was a symbol of future realities, it should not upset us. Those boys represented stupid people, people with ignorant minds, and the apostle does not want us to be like that. *Do not be childish in your outlook*, he says. But then he qualifies it, because he remembers that the Lord invited us to imitate children when he placed a little

1. Possibly in A.D. 403.
2. That is, 2 Kings 2:23-24, in our system.
3. See note at Exposition of Psalm 41, 2.

child before him and warned us, *Only someone who becomes like this child will enter the kingdom of heaven* (Mt 18:3). So after bidding us grow out of childish attitudes, the apostle is careful to remind us in what sense we must be childlike: *Do not be childish in your outlook*, he says. *Be babes in your innocence of evil, but mature in mind* (1 Cor 14:20). Anyone who delights to be childlike is not delighted by the immaturity of children, but by their innocence; for it was immaturity that incited the boys to jeer at God's holy man for his baldness, and shout after him, *Baldy! Baldy!* So it came about that they were devoured by wild animals, and represented people who with the same childish attitude mocked at a certain man who could be called "bald" because he was crucified at a place named Calvary. Such people behaved as though they had been seized by wild beasts, because they were in fact possessed by demons, by the devil and his angels, for he is at work in God's rebellious subjects.[4] Childish onlookers they were who stood before the sacred tree wagging their heads and saying, *Let him come down from the cross, if he is the Son of God* (Mt 27:42).

We are Christ's children, because we are the children of the Bridegroom,[5] and this psalm is written for us, as its title proclaims: *For the children of Korah, for those things which will be changed.*[6]

The world has changed, and so have we

2. There is no need, is there, for me to explain what is meant by *for those things which will be changed*? What should I say about it? Anyone who has been changed will recognize from personal experience what it means. Let all who hear this phrase, *for those things which will be changed*, reflect on what they once were, and what they are now. And let them consider first of all how the world has altered. Not long ago it worshiped idols, now it worships God; until recently it paid cult to the things he made, but now to him who made it. Notice when this was said, "for those things which will be changed." The pagans who are still left are terrified by the changed state of affairs; unwilling to be changed themselves, they see our churches brought into commission again and their temples abandoned, celebration in the one and desolation in the other. They are astonished at the change, but let them read the prophecies that announced it; let them bend an ear to him who promised it, and believe him now that he has made his promise good.

But that is not all, brothers and sisters. Each one of us is being changed from an old self into a new self, from an unbeliever into a believer, from a thief into a

4. See Eph 2:2.
5. See Mt 9:15; Lk 5:34.
6. One codex has "Unto the end, for the children. . . ." The CCL editors amend the second clause to "for those [people] who will be changed."

generous giver, from an adulterer into a chaste person, from a spiteful trouble-maker into a kindly neighbor. So let the psalm be sung for us, *for those things which will be changed*; and now let him be delineated through whom the changes are brought about.[7]

The Word weds the Church; the Bridegroom's beauty

3. The full title is, *For those things which will be changed, for the children of Korah, for understanding. A song for the beloved one.* This beloved one was seen by his persecutors, but not for their understanding, for if they had known him, they would never have crucified the Lord of glory.[8] It was for the purpose of understanding that he himself was seeking a different kind of eyes when he said, *Whoever sees me sees the Father* (Jn 14:9). Let the psalm now sing of him, and let us rejoice at his marriage, and so be among those of whom the marriage is made, who are invited to the wedding: these invited guests are themselves the bride, for the Church is the bride, and Christ the Bridegroom. It is customary for appropriate songs to be sung by students[9] to both spouses. These songs are called epithalamia, and are devoted to honoring bridegroom and bride. Perhaps you are wondering whether there is any bridal chamber[10] at this wedding to which we have been invited? Yes, there is; why else would another psalm say, *He has pitched his tent in the sun, and he is like a bridegroom coming forth from his tent* (Ps 18:6(19:5))? The nuptial union is effected between the Word and human flesh, and the place where the union is consummated is the Virgin's womb. It is flesh, very flesh, that is united to the Word; as scripture says, *They are two no longer, but one flesh* (Mt 19:6; see Eph 5:31). The Church was drawn from the human race, so that flesh united to the Word might be the Head of the Church, and all the rest of us believers might be the limbs that belong to that Head.

Do you want to see who he is, who has come to his wedding? *In the beginning was the Word, and the Word was with God; he was God* (Jn 1:1). Let the bride be happy, then, for she has been loved by God. And when was she loved? While she was still ugly, for, as the apostle says, *All have sinned, and are in need of the glory of God*, and again, *Christ died for the impious* (Rom 3:23; 5:6). She was loved in her ugliness, that she might not remain ugly. It was not because she was ugly that she was loved; her ugliness was not itself the object of his love. If he

7. *Per quem commutata sunt*, "through whom these [things] have been changed"; but the CCL editors amend to *per quem commutati sunt*, "through whom they [Christians] have been changed."

8. See 1 Cor 2:8.

9. *Ab scholasticis*. The CCL editors supply a doubtful suggestion from one codex that the word should be *scoliasticis*, derived from a Greek word for a festive song sung between servings of drinks at a banquet.

10. *Thalamus*.

had loved that, he would have preserved it, but in fact he rid her of her ugliness and formed beauty in her.

To what kind of bride did he come, and what did he make of her? Let him come himself in the words of the prophets, let him come now. Let the Bridegroom come forth and show himself to us, and let us love him. But if we find any trace of ugliness in him, let us love him not. What a strange thing! He found plenty of ugly features in us, yet he loved us; but if we find anything ugly in him, we must not love him. It is true that he put on our flesh in such a way that it could be said of him, *We saw him, and there was no fair form or comeliness in him* (Is 53:2), but if you take account of the mercy that caused him to be reduced to such a state, he is beautiful even in his deformity. The prophet was speaking from the standpoint of the Jews when he said, *We saw him, and there was no fair form or comeliness in him*. Why is that so? Because his lowly state was no use to them *for understanding*. For all who do understand, the truth that *the Word was made flesh* (Jn 1:14) is supremely beautiful. A friend of the Bridegroom prayed, *Far be it from me to boast, save in the cross of our Lord Jesus Christ* (Gal 6:14). It would be a mean-spirited thing merely not to be ashamed of it; you must boast of it. Why did Christ have neither fair form nor comeliness? Because Christ crucified was a scandal to the Jews, and foolishness to Gentiles. But in what sense was he fair of form on the cross? Because God's foolishness is wiser than human wisdom, and God's weakness more powerful than human strength.[11] Let us therefore, who believe, run to meet a Bridegroom who is beautiful wherever he is. Beautiful as God, as the Word who is with God, he is beautiful in the Virgin's womb, where he did not lose his godhead but assumed our humanity. Beautiful he is as a baby, as the Word unable to speak,[12] because while he was still without speech, still a baby in arms and nourished at his mother's breast, the heavens spoke for him, a star guided the magi, and he was adored in the manger as food for the humble. He was beautiful in heaven, then, and beautiful on earth: beautiful in the womb, and beautiful in his parents' arms. He was beautiful in his miracles but just as beautiful under the scourges, beautiful as he invited us to life, but beautiful too in not shrinking from death, beautiful in laying down his life and beautiful in taking it up again, beautiful on the cross, beautiful in the tomb, and beautiful in heaven.

Listen to this song to further your understanding, and do not allow the weakness of his flesh to blind you to the splendor of his beauty. The supreme and most real beauty is justice: if you can catch him out in any injustice, you will not find him beautiful in that regard; but if he is found to be just at every point, then he is lovely in all respects. Let him come to us, so that we may gaze on him with the

11. See 1 Cor 1:23.25.
12. *Infans Verbum*.

eyes of our spirit, as he has been delineated for us by the prophet who sang his praises, and began, *My heart overflows with a good word.*

Verse 2. The Father speaks

4. *My heart overflows with a good word.* Who is speaking here—the Father, or the prophet? Some have understood these words to be spoken by the Father, who by saying, *My heart overflows with a good word*, gives us an inkling of a birth beyond the power of human telling. But notice that he says, *Cor meum*; this is to save you from any mistaken idea that God needed to undertake something in order to beget a Son. A human being does have to undertake something, namely sexual union, in order to procreate children; without this human parents cannot bring children to birth. But you must not suppose that God needed any such union in order to beget his Son; and to exclude that mistake he says, *My heart overflows with a good word.* Think, every one of you: this very day your heart generates a plan, but your heart does not need to seek a wife in order to do so. Through this plan that has been born from your heart you perhaps build something. Before your construction stands there built, it stands already in your plan; what you are going to construct is already present in your intelligence, through which you are going to make it. So you can take satisfaction in an edifice that does not yet exist, not because you can see it as a building but because you have brought it to birth as a plan, though no one else can approve your plan unless you have told others about it, or they see the finished job.

If, then, all things were made through the Word, and the Word is from God, contemplate the fabric that was made through the Word, and proceed from the completed building to admire the master-plan. What must the Word be like, if through him were made the sky and the earth, and all the sky's array, all the earth's fecundity, the vast expanse of the sea, the wide air, the shining stars and the radiance of sun and moon? All these things are visible; but pass beyond even these, and consider the angels, the authorities, thrones, sovereignties and powers;[13] all these were made through him. And how comes it that all these things were created good? Because the *good Word* was uttered, through whom they came to be. So the Word is good, and this Word was addressed by someone as *Good Teacher*, yet the Word himself deprecated this address: *Why do you ask me about what is good? No one is good, except the one God* (Mt 19:17; Mk 10:18). How are we to interpret this? Someone addressed him as *Good Teacher*, and he asked, *Why do you ask me about what is good?* He even added, *No one is good, except the one God.* How then can he himself be good? Because he himself is God, and moreover is one God together with the Father; for when he said, *No one is good, except the one God*, he did not separate himself from the Father, but

13. See Col 1:16.

asserted their unity. *My heart overflows with a good Word*: this can be understood, then, as God the Father's statement about his good Word, our God, our benefactor, that good Word through whom alone whatever we have of goodness is possible.

5. The next line is, *I tell my works to the king*. Is this still the Father speaking? If it is, let us see how we can also interpret this consistently with the true Catholic faith. *I tell my works to the king*. If it means that the Father tells his Son, our King, about his works, what can it mean? What works can the Father tell his Son about, when all the Father's works are performed through the Son?

Perhaps the verb, *I tell*, refers to the eternal generation of the Son? Can that be it? I am afraid that this explanation may at some points be difficult for those of slower intelligence to grasp; but I will offer it all the same, and let anyone follow who can. It is better so, because if I don't explain at all, even those capable of following will not have the chance. Here we are, then: in another psalm we read, *Only once has God spoken* (Ps 61:12(62:11)). He spoke many times through the prophets, and many times through the apostles; today he speaks through his saints; yet the psalm says, *Only once has God spoken*. How can he be said to have spoken once only, unless we take it to mean his utterance of his Word? In the preceding line we understood *my heart overflows with a good Word* to mean the begetting of the Son, and this next line seems to me to be a repetition of the same truth: *my heart overflows with a good Word* is reiterated in the verb, *I tell*. After all, what does *I tell* mean? "I bring forth a word." And from where does God bring forth a Word, if not from his heart, from his innermost being? Any word you speak yourself you bring forth from your heart; there is no other source for the word that sounds audibly and then fades away. Are you surprised that the same should be true for God? But there is this difference: God's speaking is eternal. You say something now, because you were silent a moment ago. Or perhaps you do not yet speak your word, you hold it back. When you do begin to bring it out you are breaking your silence and giving birth to a word that did not previously exist. Not in this manner did God generate his Word, for God's speaking has no beginning and no end; yet he speaks one Word only. He could speak another only if what he had spoken could pass away; but as he by whom the Word is spoken abides eternally, so too does the Word he speaks abide. This Word is spoken once, and never ceases to be spoken; nor had the speaking of it any beginning; nor is it spoken twice, for what is spoken once never passes away. Accordingly *my heart overflows with a good Word* signifies the same as *I tell my works to the King*.

But still, why does it say, *I tell my works*? Because in this uttered Word are all the works of God. Whatever God was to create was already present in the Word. Nothing could have existed in the created order that was not present in the Word, just as nothing can be in your own handiwork that was not present in your plan. The gospel makes this plain by saying, *What was made was alive in his life* (Jn

1:3-4). Created beings existed, but only in the Word; they were there in the Word, though they had as yet no existence in themselves. But the Word was, and this Word was God; this Word was with God and was the Son of God, and was one God with the Father. *I tell my works to the King*. Let anyone who understands about this Word listen to the Speaker, and contemplate both the Father and his everlasting Word, in whom are present all things that will come to be in the future, as are present still all those that have passed away. These are the works of God: works in his Word, in his only-begotten Son, in the Word of God.

6. Now, how does the psalm continue? *My tongue is the pen of a scribe writing swiftly*. What possible resemblance can there be, brothers and sisters, between God's tongue and a scribe's pen? Well, what resemblance is there between a rock and Christ? Or a lamb and our Savior? Or a lion and the strength of the only-begotten Son?[14] Yet these comparisons were made, and it is only because they were that we are in some measure educated through visible things toward apprehension of the invisible. So too with this humble metaphor of the pen: we should neither equate it with the excellent reality it points to, nor reject it as unworthy. But I wonder why God willed to call his tongue the pen of a swiftly-writing scribe? After all, however rapidly a scribe might be able to write, it would not bear comparison with the speed of which another psalm speaks: *Very swiftly runs his word* (Ps 147:15). However, insofar as the human mind may presume to understand, I think that this comparison, *my tongue is the pen of a scribe*, may also be taken as spoken by the Father. Ordinarily what is spoken with the tongue makes a sound and then fades away, whereas what is written endures; but when God speaks his Word, it does not make a transient sound and then fade, but is spoken and abides, and therefore God has chosen to compare it with the abiding written word rather than with sounds. By adding, *A scribe writing swiftly*, he has prodded our minds toward further understanding; and they must not be lazy, content to think of those who copy ancient texts, or very nimble secretaries. If we concentrate on these, our minds will proceed no further. Think swiftly of the word, *swiftly*; turn that word, *swiftly*, over in your mind. What does it suggest—*swiftly*? God's speed is so great that nothing could be swifter. When people write they form letter after letter, syllable after syllable, word after word; and there is no passing on to the next until the one before has been properly written. But with God there are not many words, nor is anything left out, but all things are comprised in one Word; so nothing could be swifter.

Verse 3. The Bridegroom brings grace

7. But look—this eternal Word so uttered, the coeternal Word of the eternal Father, will come as Bridegroom. *Fair are you beyond all humankind*. Why does it

14. See 1 Cor 10:4; Jn 1:29; Rv 5:5.

not say, "Beyond the angels"? What did it imply by *beyond humankind*? Surely, that he too is human. But to ensure that you do not put the man Christ on a par with any other human, it says that he is *fair beyond all humankind.* He is human indeed, but beyond all humans; he is among humans, but beyond them; he takes his human birth from humankind, but he is beyond all humankind. *Grace bedews your lips.* Elsewhere we read, *The law was given through Moses, grace and truth came through Jesus Christ* (Jn 1:17). *Grace bedews your lips.* Truly such help was necessary for me, because *I take great delight in God's law as far as my inner self is concerned, but I am aware of a different law in my members that opposes the law of my mind, and imprisons me under the law of sin inherent in my members. Who will deliver me from this death-ridden body, wretch that I am? Only the grace of God, through Jesus Christ our Lord* (Rom 7:22-25). This is why our psalm says, *Grace bedews your lips.* He came to us with the word of grace on his lips, with the kiss of grace. What could be sweeter than grace like this? And with what is it concerned? *Blessed are those whose iniquities are forgiven, and whose sins are covered* (Ps 31(32):1). If he had come as a strict judge, without this grace bedewing his lips, who would have had any hope of salvation? Would anyone have been unafraid of what was owing to a sinner? But he came bringing grace, and so far from demanding what was owed to God, he paid a debt he did not owe. Did one who was sinless owe a debt to death? But you, what was owing to you? Punishment. He canceled your debts, and paid off debts that were none of his. This is mighty grace. Grace—why "grace"? Because it is given gratis. It is up to you to give thanks, then, but not to repay him, for that you cannot do. Looking for some means of making recompense to God, a psalmist asked, *What return shall I make to the Lord for all his bounty to me?* Then he seemed to find something: *I will take in my hands the cup of salvation, and call on the name of the Lord* (Ps 115(116):12-13). So you think to make sufficient repayment to him, because you take in your hands the cup of salvation, and call on the name of the Lord? But who gave you this cup of salvation?

The psalmist confined himself to thanksgiving, since he fell far short of making due recompense. Find something that you can give to God that you did not receive from him, and then you will be in a position to make proper repayment. But be careful, because when you look for something to render to him that you did not first receive from him, you may find it, certainly, but all you will find is your sin. That certainly you did not receive from him, but neither is it fit for you to offer. That is what the Jews gave him—evil for good. They received rain from him, but yielded him no fruit, only painful thorns. Whatever good there is in you that you want to give to God, you will discover that you received it from no one else but God. This is the grace of God, bedewing Christ's lips. He made you, and made you gratis, for he could not give anything to you before you were there to receive it. Then when you had gone to ruin, he sought you; he found you and called you back again. He did not hold your past sins against you, and he promised you good things for the future. Truly, O Christ, *grace bedews your lips.*

8. *Therefore God has blessed you for ever*, says the psalm. It would be straining the text to understand this phrase also—*therefore God has blessed you for ever*—as spoken by God the Father. It seems better to assume that the prophet is speaking here in his own person. Sudden changes of speaker, even entirely unexpected changes, are commonly found in the sacred scriptures; anyone who looks carefully will find that the pages of holy writ are full of them. For instance, another psalm prays, *O Lord, rescue my soul from wicked lips and the guileful tongue*; but immediately it continues, *What is to be given to you, what shall be added to you, that you may withstand the deceitful tongue?* Obviously there are two different speakers here, one making a petition, the other responding with help. One speaker says, *Sharp arrows of the mighty one, with all-devouring coals*, the same one who asked, *What is to be given to you, what shall be added to you?* But in the next line the petitioner resumes, *Alas, how long-drawn-out is my wayfaring!* (Ps 119(120):2-5). Such frequent switches within a few lines alert us to use our intelligence. The place where the speaker changes is not noted; there is no indication, "Man says this; God says that"; but the words themselves make clear to us which belong to the human speaker, and which to God.

It was a man who said, *My heart overflows with a good word; I tell my works to the king*. A man said this, the man who wrote the psalm, but he said it in God's name. But now he begins to speak in his own person: *Therefore God has blessed you for ever*. God had said, *Grace bedews your lips*, to the one whom he had made fair beyond all humankind, for this Son whom he had begotten before all ages, this eternal Son whom he, the eternal Father, had brought forth, God had also made to be a man. On this account the prophet was filled with a joy that he could scarcely express. He had spoken earlier as from God, but now, contemplating what God the Father would reveal about his Son to humankind, the prophet says as from himself, *Therefore God has blessed you for ever*. Why blessed? Because of grace. With what is grace concerned? With the kingdom of heaven. The Old Testament had promised a land; but the reward promised to those subject to the old law was different from that promised to us under grace. The land slipped away from them, and that land was all the kingdom that they were destined for, those people subject to the law; but the kingdom of heaven that belongs to the children of grace does not slip away. That is why our psalm says here, *God has blessed you*, not for a time only, but *for ever.*

An alternative interpretation: the psalmist has spoken throughout

9. However, some people have preferred to consider all the words we have so far considered as spoken by the prophet himself. Thus the line, *My heart over-*

flows with a good word, would be the prophet's way of announcing his hymn (for when anyone sings a hymn to God, his or her heart is blurting out a good word, just as when anyone blasphemes God, that person's heart is belching out a bad word). On this showing the next line, *I tell my works to the king*, would signify that the highest duty of every human being is to praise God. It is proper to God to delight you by his beauty, and your business to praise him with thanksgiving. If your works are not praise offered to God, you are beginning to be in love with yourself, and to join the company of those people of whom the apostle predicts, *They will be lovers of themselves* (2 Tm 3:2). Find no pleasure in yourself, and let him be your delight who made you; because what you find displeasing in yourself is what you have yourself brought about in you. Let your work be praise offered to God; let your heart overflow with this good word. Tell your works to the King, because the King has created you for this purpose, and himself given you what you are to offer him. Give back to him his own gifts; do not try to snatch a share of your inheritance and go off abroad, there to squander it on harlots and feed pigs. Remember that story in the gospel. But of us too the glad cry has gone up, *He was dead, but has come back to life; he had perished, but is found* (Lk 15:24,32).

10. *My tongue is the pen of a scribe writing swiftly*. There have been interpreters who similarly understood this in the sense that the prophet indicated what he was going to write, and therefore compared his tongue with a scribe's pen. He would have mentioned in particular a scribe writing at speed to suggest that he would write about things which would come to pass swiftly. So we should understand "writing swiftly" to mean "writing about swift matters," or events which were not to be long delayed. In fact God did not delay long before sending Christ. How quickly time seems to have rolled by, once it is past! Recall the generations that preceded you, and you will find that Adam seems to have been made only yesterday. In the same way we read about all the things that have happened since that beginning, and they seem to have been accomplished very swiftly. The day of judgment will arrive swiftly too, so you must forestall it by even greater promptitude. It will come quickly, so you must be even quicker about changing your life. The face of the judge will be upon us, but look to the prophet's advice: *Let us hasten before his face confessing* (Ps 94(95):2). *Grace bedews your lips, therefore God has blessed you for ever.*

Verse 4. The sword of division

11. *Gird your sword upon your thigh, mighty warrior.*[15] What sword is this? Surely your word. With that sword he laid low his enemies, and with that sword

15. This and the following paragraph are quoted by Eugippius (A.D. c.455-535), in his compilation of extracts from Augustine, much used in the middle ages; he thus provides an independent witness to the text. The discrepancies are minor.

he severed son from father, daughter from mother, daughter-in-law from mother-in-law; for in the gospel we read, *I have come to bring not peace, but a sword*, and again, *There will be five in one household ranged in opposition, two against three, and three pitted against two: a son against his father, a daughter against her mother, and a daughter-in-law against her mother-in-law* (Mt 10:34; Lk 12:52-53). What sword sliced them apart, if not the sword Christ brought? Truly, brothers and sisters, even now we see the same thing happening daily. Some young man decides to serve God, and thereby offends his father; they are at loggerheads, one promising an earthly estate, the other in love with a heavenly inheritance, one promising one thing and the other setting his heart on something quite different. The father should not think himself slighted, for no one except God is being preferred to him, yet he goes to law against this son who wants to serve God. Nonetheless the spiritual sword that divides them is more powerful than the bonds of flesh that unite them. The same division is effected between a daughter and her mother, and far more so between a daughter-in-law and her mother-in-law,[16] for sometimes in one household where there is a daughter-in-law and her mother-in-law, one may be heretical and the other Catholic. But where this sword is powerfully at work, we need not fear any repetition of baptism.[17] If a daughter can be set in opposition against her mother, how much more a daughter-in-law against her mother-in-law?

12. This division has taken place also on a larger scale, affecting the whole human race: a son has been severed from his father, because we were once children of the devil. To people who were still unbelievers it was said, *You are children of your father, the devil* (Jn 8:44); and where did all our unbelief come from, if it was not handed down to us from him? He was not our father by creating us, but we made ourselves his children by imitating him. But now we see the child set against the father, divided from him. The sword has come into play, the sons and daughters have found another father and another mother. The devil, who presented himself as our model, made us into children doomed to death, but the two parents we have found bring us forth to eternal life.[18] So a son has been divided against his father.

There is also an instance of the division between a daughter and her mother, because those of the Jewish race who became believers were divided from the synagogue. Again, a daughter-in-law was set against her mother-in-law,

16. Possibly he is thinking of Monica's tact in handling difficulties between herself and her mother-in-law, as described in his *Confessions* IX,9,20. The division was all the more likely to be felt in this relationship, where only one party might be Christian, though he goes on to consider the situation where both are Christian, but one Catholic and the other heretic (or schismatic).
17. Presumably because the elder relative, if Donatist, might try to insist on it, but a Catholic daughter-in-law would accept the inevitability of division, and refuse.
18. Evidently God and holy mother Church. But Eugippius has *terrenam* (earthly) instead of *aeternam* (eternal), presumably understanding it of biological parents who are Christians.

because the Christian people of Gentile origin could be called a daughter-in-law, since its Bridegroom, Christ, was a son of the synagogue. Yes, he was; for where did his human birth in the flesh come from? From the synagogue. He left his father and mother to cleave to his wife, that they might be two in one flesh. This is not some fancy of mine, but a truth attested by the apostle, who says, *This is a great mystery, but I am referring it to Christ and the Church* (Eph 5:32). In a certain sense he did leave his Father: not that he was ever separated from him, but in that he took human flesh. How was that a leaving of his Father? Inasmuch as *being in the form of God he deemed it no robbery to be God's equal, yet he emptied himself and took on the form of a slave* (Phil 2:6-7). And how did he leave his mother? By leaving the Jewish race, as represented by the synagogue, which clung to the old rites. This was symbolically suggested by the episode where he asked, *Who is my mother, who are my brothers?* (Mt 12:48; Mk 3:33). He was teaching inside[19] but they were standing outside. Think about it: aren't the Jews standing outside like that even now, while Christ is teaching in the Church? Now, who is the mother-in-law? The Bridegroom's mother. And the mother of our Bridegroom, our Lord Jesus Christ, is the synagogue. Obviously her daughter-in-law is the Church, which has come from the Gentiles and will have no truck with circumcision of the flesh, so she is set against her mother-in-law. *Gird on your sword.* We have indicated its power.

The sacredness of the thigh

13. *Gird on your sword*—your word, that is; and gird it *upon your thigh, mighty warrior*. Buckle your sword to your thigh. What significance is there in the thigh? It represents the flesh. That is why a prophecy said, *The scepter shall not be taken from Judah, nor a leader from his thighs* (Gn 49:10). And remember Abraham: he had been promised that in his seed all nations would be blessed,[20] and the time came for him to send his servant to find and bring home a wife for his son. It was from this son that would descend the holy seed in whom all nations would be blessed. Abraham, holding fast in faith to the great name that would come through the apparent lowliness of his own seed, that is, the Son of God who would be born from the human race as Abraham's descendant, ordered the servant he was dispatching to swear to him by using a special gesture. *Place your hand under my thigh,* he said, *and so swear* (Gn 24:2-3). It was like saying, "Place your hand on the altar," or "on the gospel," or "on the prophet," or on anything sacred. "Put your hand under my thigh," he said, because he had faith, and so far from fearing any suggestion of indecency, he understood the truth. This is why the psalm says, *Gird your sword upon your thigh, mighty warrior.*

19. Variant: "was leading them within."
20. See Gn 1:3.

You are a mighty warrior even in respect of your thigh, for God's weakness is stronger than any human power.[21] *Mighty warrior.*

Verse 5. Gentleness and power

14. *In your beauty and dignity.* Receive your endowment of justice, because in your justice you are always beautiful and dignified. *Ride forth victoriously and seize your kingdom.* Do we not see this fulfilled already? It has undeniably taken place. Look round at the whole world: he has ridden forth victoriously and seized his kingdom, for all nations are his subjects. What was it like, to see all this in spirit? Just what it is for us to experience it now. When these things were spoken, Christ was not yet reigning, he had not yet ridden forth victoriously. These things were preached, but now they have been manifested in reality, and they are within our grasp. We know God to be a faithful keeper of his promises in very many matters; in only a few does he still owe us a fulfillment. *Ride forth victoriously and seize your kingdom.*

15. *By your faithfulness, gentleness and justice.* He kept his promise about truth and faithfulness when faithfulness sprang up from the earth, and justice looked down from heaven.[22] Christ was revealed to an expectant human race, so that in Abraham's offspring all nations might be blessed. The gospel was preached, and truth was faithfully imparted. What about gentleness? The martyrs suffered, and thereby God's victorious cause was greatly advanced, and his reign extended throughout all nations. The martyrs neither flinched nor resisted; they spoke up frankly, concealing nothing; they were ready for any fate and refused none. This was mighty gentleness! It was the body of Christ that achieved this, because it had learned the lesson from its Head. He had been the foremost to be led like a sheep to the slaughter, like a lamb that does not open its mouth in the presence of the shearer.[23] So gentle was he that hanging on the cross he prayed, *Father, forgive them, for they do not know what they are doing* (Lk 23:34). But what of his justice? He will come to judge, and to requite each of us in accordance with our deeds.[24] He spoke the truth, he endured injustice,[25] but he will settle matters equitably. *Your right hand will conduct you wonderfully.* We are conducted by his right hand, but he himself by his own. He is God, we are human. By his right hand he was conducted: by his power, that is; for whatever power the Father has, Christ has also, as he also possesses the same immortality as the Father, the same divinity as the Father, the same eternity as the Father, and

21. See 1 Cor 1:25.
22. See Ps 84:12(85:11).
23. See Is 53:7.
24. See Rom 2:6.
25. Variant: "he displayed meekness."

the strength of the Father. His right hand will conduct him wonderfully as he does good, shares human suffering, and foils the malice of his human enemies by his goodness. He is still being conducted to places where he does not yet reign, and it is his right hand that conducts him, for what takes him there is the gift he has given to his saints. *Your right hand will conduct you wonderfully.*

Verse 6. Christ's piercing shafts

16. *Your arrows are sharp and very powerful.*[26] These are his piercing words that arouse love. In the Song of Songs the bride moans, *I am wounded by love*,[27] by which she means that she is in love, she is afire with love, and she is yearning for her bridegroom, who has pierced her with the arrows of his word. *Your arrows are sharp and very powerful*, penetrating and effective. *Peoples will fall under your assault.* Who are these who have fallen? Those who were struck, and so brought low. But though we see peoples subject to Christ, we do not see them falling, so the psalm goes on to explain where this falling occurs: *in the heart.* There they exalted themselves against Christ, and there they fall before Christ. Saul was accustomed to blaspheme Christ, and stood proudly erect; but now he prays to Christ, for he was struck down and fell prostrate. Christ's enemy was slain so that Christ's disciple might be raised to life. From heaven the arrow was aimed, and Saul was struck in his heart. It was in Saul that it found its mark, for he was not Paul yet, but still Saul, still upright, not yet fallen flat. But the arrow struck him and he fell low in his heart. This falling down in his heart was not a consequence of his falling on his face; it happened when he asked, *What do you want me to do, Lord?* (Acts 9:6). So recently you were putting Christians in chains, Saul, and dragging them off to punishment; and now you are saying to Christ, *What do you want me to do?* What a sharp arrow that must have been, what a potent arrow, which felled the wounded Saul to turn him into Paul! As he fell, so too did the peoples; look at the Gentiles and see how they have been brought into subjection to Christ. This is why the psalm says, *Peoples will fall under your assault, in the hearts of the king's enemies your arrows will find their mark.* Your enemies, it means, for the psalmist calls you a king, and knows that is what you truly are. *Peoples will fall under your assault, in the hearts of the king's enemies your arrows will find their mark.* They were your enemies, they were wounded by your arrows, and they fell before you. So from enemies they were transformed into friends; your enemies died, and your friends live. This is the same transformation that the title of our psalm proclaimed: *for those things*

26. *Potentissimae*, agreeing with "arrows;" but a variant supported by the CCL editors has *potentissime*, agreeing with "Christ" (understood). The following lines support the former alternative.
27. See Sg 2:5; 5:8.

that will be changed. We study to understand individual words and particular verses of the psalm, but we study in such a way that none of us may doubt that the whole refers to Christ. *Peoples will fall under your assault, in the hearts of the king's enemies your arrows will find their mark.*

Verse 7. The straight ruler

17. *Your throne, O God, stands for ever and ever*, because God has blessed you for ever by the grace that bedews your lips. The throne that stood in the Jewish kingdom stood for a time only, as befitted those who were under the law, but not those under grace. Then he came to deliver those who were under the law, and establish them under the regime of grace. *Your throne, O God, stands for ever and ever.* Why? If the throne that belonged to that former kingdom was a temporary one only, how is it that this throne will stand for ever and ever? Because it is God's. *Your throne, O God, stands for ever and ever.* O eternal Godhead![28] God could not possibly have a temporary throne. *Your throne, O God, stands for ever and ever, your royal scepter is a scepter of righteous rule.* It is a scepter of righteous rule because it guides us aright. People were bent, distorted, they wanted regal power for themselves, they were in love with themselves, they cherished their own evil ways. They did not submit their wills to God, but sought to bend the will of God to their own lusts. A sinner or an unjust person often gets angry with God for dropping no rain on him, but he does not want God to get angry with him for dropping so low himself.[29] Nearly every day people sit down to find fault with God: "He ought to have done this . . . that other arrangement was not a good idea." You see what you ought to do, evidently, but you think he doesn't? You are twisted out of shape, but he is perfectly straight. How can you make a twisted thing sit well with a straight one? They cannot be aligned. You may attempt to lay a warped beam along a level floor, but it does not meet or fit properly, it will not lie flush with the pavement. The floor is perfectly level all over, but the beam is warped and will not fit a flat surface. In the same way, God's will is level and yours is bent. You think his will is not straight because you cannot fit in with it; but you must straighten yourself to fit his will, not attempt to bend his to suit you. You can't, anyway. Your effort is futile, because his will is always perfectly straight. Do you want to be united with him? Then allow yourself to be corrected. Then it will be his rod or scepter that rules you, his scepter of righteous rule. That is why we speak of a sovereign as a "ruler"; and anyone who does not correct his subjects is a defective ruler. Our ruler is sovereign over those who have been made straight. As he is a priest

28. *O aeternitatis divinitas!* But a variant has *divitias*: "Oh the riches of eternity!"

29. A slightly forced pun this time, not as good as some of Augustine's others: "*. . . Deo quia non pluit; et non vult sibi Deum irasci, quia fluit.*"

because he sanctifies us,[30] so too he is our king or ruler because he rules us.[31] But what does scripture say in another text? *With a holy person you will be holy, and with the innocent man you will be innocent. With the chosen you will be chosen, and with the perverse you will deal perversely* (Ps 17:26-27(18:25-26)). This does not mean that God is perverse, but that those who are perverse themselves think him so. If you take delight in what is good, you find God good; if the good does not please you, you think God depraved. If God seems tortuous to you, it is your own tortuousness that is the trouble, for his rectitude abides unchangeably. Listen to the testimony of another psalm: *How good God is to Israel, to those of straightforward hearts!* (Ps 72(73):1).

Verse 8. Attend to your sins before God does

18. *Your royal scepter is the scepter of righteous rule. You have loved justice and hated iniquity.* Here you see what the scepter of righteous rule is: *you have loved justice and hated iniquity.* Draw near to this scepter and let Christ be your king, allow this scepter to rule you, because otherwise it may break you; it is an iron rod, and inflexible. What did another psalm have to say about it? *You will rule them with an iron rod, and you will dash them to pieces like a potter's vessel* (Ps 2:9). Some it rules, others it breaks; it rules the spiritual, but breaks the carnal. Come near to this scepter, then. What are you afraid of about it? The whole of the scepter is summed up in this: *you have loved justice and hated iniquity.* What are you afraid of? Perhaps you were an iniquitous person, and you hear that your king hates iniquity, so you are afraid. But he is what you make him to be. What does he hate? Iniquity. He doesn't hate you, does he? But there is iniquity in you? All right. God hates it, so you must hate it as well, so that both of you are in accord, hating the same thing. You will become God's friend if you hate what he hates. So too will you be his friend if you love what he loves. Let the iniquity that is in you become loathsome to you, and let what he has created delight you. You are a human being, and you are sinful. There, look, I have called you by two names: "human being," and "sinful." One of these names indicates your nature, the other your guilt; one was made for you by God, the other you made yourself. Love what God made, and hate what you made, because he hates it too. Now look how you are beginning to find yourself united to him, since you hate what he hates! He will punish sin, because his royal scepter is a scepter of righteous rule. Would you wish him not to punish sin? That is impossible. Sin demands to be punished; if it did not, it would not be sin. Forestall him, then; if you don't want him to punish your sin, punish it yourself. It is to this very

30. *Sacerdos a sanctificando nos.*
31. Variant: " . . . a priest for the purpose of sanctifying us . . . a king/ruler to rule us."

end that he continues to spare you, putting it off, holding his hand, bending his bow, threatening you. Would he make such a display of shouting that he is going to strike you, if striking you was what he really wanted? No, and that is why he delays in dealing with your sins; but you must not delay. Turn your attention to punishing your sins, because it is not possible for them to go unpunished in the long run. They must needs be punished, either by yourself or by him. Admit them, so that he may remit them.[32] A penitential psalm exemplifies this attitude: *Turn your face away from my sins* (Ps 50:11(51:9)). Did it say, "from me"? No, it didn't, and in another place a psalm expressly begs God, *Do not turn your face away from me* (Ps 26(27):9). Accordingly we must understand the first one to mean, "I don't want you to see my sins," because for God to see something means to take it into account. When a judge is said to take something into account, it means that he turns his attention to it, and therefore must punish it, because he is a judge. And God is a judge too. *Turn your face away from my sins.* But you, for your part, should not turn your face away, if you want God to turn his face away from them. In that same psalm this very offer is made to God: *I know my wrongdoing, and my sin confronts me all the time* (Ps 50:5(51:3)). He wants it to be before his own eyes, but not before God's. *Your royal scepter is a scepter of righteous rule.* No one should be complacent about God's mercy, for his scepter is a scepter of righteous rule. Are we saying that God is not merciful? Far from it; what could be more merciful than God, who so generously spares sinners, God who takes no notice of any past sins in any of those who turn back to him? Love him for his mercy, but in such fashion that you want him to be true to himself; for his mercy cannot diminish his justice, nor his justice his mercy. In the meantime, as long as he delays, be sure that you do not delay, because his royal scepter is a scepter of righteous rule.

God's anointing of God

19. *You have loved justice and hated iniquity, for, O God, your God has anointed you.* That is why he anointed you, so that you might love justice and hate iniquity. Notice how this is phrased: *for, O God, your God has anointed you.*[33] It means, "Oh you who are God, your God has anointed you." God is anointed by God. In Latin it looks as though the word "God" is just repeated in the nominative case, but in Greek the distinction is perfectly clear: one name belongs to the person addressed, and the second to the person who addresses him, saying, *O God, he has anointed you.* So the phrase, "O you who are God, your God has anointed you," is like saying, "This is why your God has anointed

32. *Tu agnosce, ut ille ignoscat.*
33. *Propterea unxit te, Deus, Deus tuus.*

you, O God." You have to accept this and understand the verse in this way, because it is quite clear in the Greek.[34]

Who, then, is the God who was anointed by God? Let the Jews tell us that. After all, these scriptures are theirs as well as ours. God was anointed by God, and when you hear the word, "anointed," understand that it means Christ, for "Christ" is derived from "chrism," and the name "Christ" means "Anointed one."[35] Nowhere else were kings and priests anointed; it was done only in that kingdom where Christ's coming was prophesied, where he was anointed, and from where the name Christ was to come. Nowhere else at all do we find this, in any other nation or kingdom. So God was anointed by God, and with what kind of oil? Spiritual, obviously. Visible oil is a sign; invisible oil is a sacramental mystery,[36] for the spiritual oil is within. God was anointed for us, and sent to us. He was God, but he became man so that he could be anointed; yet he was man in such wise that he was God, and he was God in such a way that he did not disdain to be man. He is true man and true God, and there is no falsehood in him, for he is in every respect true, in every respect the very Truth. God became man, and it can be said that "God was anointed," because God became man, became Christ the Anointed One.

Jacob's anointed stone and Jacob's ladder

20. We have a prefiguration of this in the episode where Jacob had put a stone under his head and gone to sleep.[37] The patriarch Jacob used the stone as a pillow for his head, and while he was asleep he saw the heavens opened, and a ladder extending from heaven to earth, with angels passing up and down on it. When he awoke he poured oil on the stone and went away. In that stone he recognized Christ; that was why he anointed it. Notice what a long time ago preaching about Christ began. Now what is the significance of that act of anointing a stone, particularly among the patriarchs, who worshiped the one God? It was a symbol only, and Jacob left it at that. It was not as though he anointed the stone and came back to it regularly, and offered sacrifice there; the mystery was given symbolic expression and that was all; there was no initiation of sacrilegious cult.

Now consider the stone, and remember another text: *the stone rejected by the builders has become the headstone of the corner* (Ps 117(118):22). The stone was placed at Jacob's head because Christ is the head of a man.[38] Think about

---

34. In the Septuagint, as in the quotation of the verse by Heb 1:9, it runs as follows: *Διὰ τοῦτο ἔχρισέν σε· ὁ Θεός· ὁ Θεός σου*. Since in Greek, as equally in Latin, the first noun could be either nominative or vocative, only the punctuation as inserted here makes Augustine's point.
35. See note at Exposition 2 of Psalm 26, 2.
36. A variant supported by two codices makes the thought slightly clearer: "Visible oil functions as a sign of invisible oil, for it is a sacrament. . . ."
37. See Gn 28:11-22.
38. See 1 Cor 11:3.

this carefully, for there is a great mystery here. The stone is Christ; he is *the living stone, rejected by men, but chosen by God* (1 Pt 2:4), and the place for a stone is at a man's head, because Christ is the head of a man. The stone was anointed because Christ's name is derived from chrism. By Christ's revelation ladders were shown to Jacob, stretching from earth to heaven, or from heaven to earth, with angels ascending and descending on them. We shall understand the significance of this more clearly if we recall the statement made by the Lord himself in the gospel. Now you are aware that Jacob is the same person as Israel. His name was changed to Israel when he was wrestling with the angel, and winning; he received a blessing from the opponent he was beginning to overcome.[39] Similarly Israel—the people of Israel, I mean—overcame Christ in the sense that they crucified him, yet in the persons of those Israelites who came to believe in Christ, Israel was blessed by the one it had defeated. However, many of them did not believe, and the crippling of Jacob symbolizes this. A blessing, and a lameness. A blessing, certainly, in those who believed, and we know that very many from their race did come to believe later. But a crippling in those who did not believe. And because those who did not were many, and those who did were comparatively few, the adversary touched the broad part of Jacob's thigh to strike him lame. What is "the broad part of the thigh"? The majority of his race.

Now for the ladders. In the gospel, when the Lord saw Nathanael, he said, *Look, there is a true Israelite, in whom there is no guile* (Jn 1:47). Something like that had been said about Jacob: *Jacob was a man without guile, who lived at home* (Gn 25:27); and the Lord remembered that description when he caught sight of Nathanael, a man free from guile who came from that same people. So he said, *Look, there is a true Israelite, in whom there is no guile*. He called Nathanael a guileless Israelite because he had Jacob in mind. But Nathanael replied, *How did you come to know me?* to which the Lord answered, *When you were under the fig tree, I saw you*. That means, "Even when you were among a people subject to the law, which spread its material shade over them as a protection, I saw you." And what is implied by "I saw you?" It means, "Even there, I took pity on you." Nathanael remembered that he really had been under a fig tree, and he was amazed, because he thought no one had seen him there, so he confessed, *You are the Son of God, you are the King of Israel*. Who said that? None other than the man who had just been told that he was a true Israelite, and that there was no deceit in him. The Lord continued, *Have you believed because I said, "I saw you under the fig tree?" You will see greater things than that*. He is talking to Jacob, to Israel, to the man who had put a stone under his head. *You will see greater things that that*. What greater things can he have in mind? The stone is already at Jacob's head. *To all of you I say, you will see heaven opened, and God's angels ascending and descending over the Son of Man* (Jn 1:47-51). May

39. See Gn 32:24-31.

this be true now, in the Church; may it be true that God's angels ascend and descend on those ladders. The angels of God are charged with announcing the truth. Let them mount high and see that *in the beginning was the Word, and the Word was with God; he was God.* Then let them come down and see that *the Word was made flesh, and dwelt among us* (Jn 1:1,14). Let them ascend, and lift up the great, but let them descend to nourish the little ones. Look how Paul ascended: *If I seem to be out of my mind, it is because I am talking to God*; but then watch him coming down again: *but if I am talking sense, it is for you* (2 Cor 5:13). Then, see, up he goes again: *We speak wisdom among the perfect*, and down: *I gave you milk to drink, rather than solid food* (1 Cor 2:6; 3:2). And this is what happens all the time in the Church: God's angels ascend and descend upon the Son of Man, because the Son of Man is enthroned on high, and to him we ascend in our hearts; in this respect he is our Head. But the Son of Man is here below, inasmuch as his body is on earth. His members are here, the Head is in heaven; we ascend to the Head, and descend to his members. Christ is there, and Christ is here. If he were present above only, and not here, how could the voice from heaven have demanded, *Saul, Saul, why are you persecuting me?* (Acts 9:4). Who was giving him any trouble in heaven? No one, neither the Jews, nor Saul, nor the diabolical tempter; no one was causing him trouble in heaven, but he complained, just as when our foot is trodden on, our tongue yells, because of the organic unity of the human body.

21. *You have loved justice and hated iniquity, for, O God, your God has anointed you.* We have already spoken about this anointed God, that is, about Christ. There was no clearer way in which Christ's name could have been expressed, than by calling him "Anointed God." As he is *fair beyond all humankind*, so too he is anointed *with the oil of joy, more abundantly than all who share with him.* Who share with him? The children of men, because he is the Son of Man, who became a sharer in their mortality in order to make them sharers in his immortality.

Verse 9. The scent of Christ

22. *From your garments drift the perfumes of myrrh, spices and cassia.* Your clothing diffuses sweet scents. His garments are his saints, his elect, the whole Church which he makes fit for himself, free from spot or wrinkle;[40] for he washed away its every spot in his blood, and smoothed out every wrinkle as he stretched it on the cross. From him proceeds the sweet scent evoked by the various plants named in the psalm. Listen to Paul, the smallest of men,[41] who was

40. See Eph 5:27.
41. His name resembles the Latin *paulus*, "small," and he called himself "the least of the apostles," 1 Cor 15:9.

like that fringe of the Lord's garment which a woman with a hemorrhage touched, and was healed;[42] listen to him: *We are the fragrance of Christ offered to God in every place, both for those who are on the way to salvation, and for those who are perishing* (2 Cor 2:15). You will notice that he did not say, "We are a sweet scent for those on the way to salvation, but a foul stench for those who are perishing." What he said was, *We are a sweet fragrance, both for those who are on the way to salvation, and for those who are perishing*. We may well believe that a person can be saved by a good scent; there is nothing improbable about that. But how could anyone be destroyed by a good scent? This is something profound, a great truth is here; even if we find it impossible to grasp, it is true nonetheless. Paul himself indicates that it is difficult, for he immediately adds, *Who is equal to this?* How can anyone understand why people should die from a sweet perfume? But I will make a suggestion, brothers and sisters. Paul was preaching the gospel. Many loved him for doing so, but many others were jealous of him. Those who loved him were in process of being saved by the delicate perfume, but this same perfume was provoking the jealous to their own destruction. So for those who were on their way to perdition it was not a bad smell; it was a good scent, and that made them all the more jealous of Paul, because it was obvious that God's good grace had its way with him. No one is jealous of a miserable person. Paul was glorious in his preaching of God's word, and was living under the guidance of the scepter of righteous rule. All those who loved Christ in him, and were running after Christ's beautiful perfume, loved Paul. The bride, who says in the Song of Songs, *Let us run toward the fragrance of your ointments* (Sg 1:3), loved her Bridegroom's friend; but the others were all the more tormented by jealousy as they saw Paul glorious in his preaching of the gospel and blameless in his life, so they were slain by the sweet scent.

Verse 10. The apostles' daughters

23. *From your garments drift the perfumes of myrrh, spices and cassia; kings' daughters from ivory palaces have found favor with you*. Whichever ivory palaces, whichever great houses or regal mansions you care to name, there have been kings' daughters from there who have been pleasing to Christ. Would you like me to suggest to you a spiritual interpretation of these ivory palaces? The great houses, the mighty tabernacles of God are the hearts of the saints, and the kings who live there are royal because they rule their flesh, subordinate their crowding human affections to their will, chastise their bodies and bring them into submission. This is how you should understand the palaces, and from there come the kings' daughters in whom Christ finds his joy, because when these kings preach and spread the gospel, many souls are born to them, and all these

42. See Mk 5:28; Mt 9:20; Lk 8:44.

souls are "the daughters of kings." The churches are the apostles' daughters, kings' daughters. Christ is the *King of kings* (Rv 19:16), and under him the apostles too are kings, for to them it was said, *You will sit upon twelve thrones, judging the twelve tribes of Israel* (Mt 19:28). They preached the word of truth, and through it they begot churches, not for themselves but for him. In the law it was laid down that *if a man dies, his brother shall marry the dead man's wife, and raise up offspring for his brother* (Dt 25:5). The brother is to *marry the dead man's wife, and raise up offspring*, not for himself, but *for his brother*. Now Christ himself used the expression, *Tell my brothers* (Mt 28:10);[43] and in a psalm he said, *I will tell of your name to my brothers* (Ps 21:23(22:22)). Christ died, he rose again, he ascended, and he withdrew his bodily presence, so his brothers took his wife for the purpose of begetting children through the preaching of the gospel—not by their own power, but through the gospel—so that their Brother's name might be perpetuated. That is why Paul said, *In Christ Jesus through the gospel I have begotten you* (1 Cor 4:15). Accordingly, as they were raising up offspring for their Brother, they did not call the children they begot "Paulines" or "Petrines," but "Christians." The same wide-awake caution is to be found in these verses too. Examine them, and see if this is not the case, for after speaking of *ivory palaces*, and evoking royal, spacious, beautiful, comfortable dwellings, such as are the hearts of the saints, the psalmist added, *kings' daughters from ivory palaces have found favor with you, and come to do you honor*. They are the daughters of kings, certainly, for they are the daughters of your apostles, but they come *to do you honor*, because the apostles have raised up offspring for their Brother. Paul had raised some up for his Brother, and when he saw some of them running after his own name he exclaimed, *Was Paul crucified for you?* (1 Cor 1:13). What does the law enjoin? That the newborn should be named after the dead man.[44] Let the child be born to the dead man, and bear the dead man's name. Paul observes this prescription and recalls his converts to their senses when they try to adopt his name: *Was Paul crucified for you?* And what about the time when you begot them, Paul; did you put your own name on them? No, for he continues, *Or were you baptized in Paul's name?* (1 Cor 1:13). *Kings' daughters have found favor with you, and come to do you honor*. Hold onto that phrase, *to do you honor*, keep it in mind always, for this is what it means to wear the wedding garment: that you seek his honor, his glory.

The daughters of kings can also be taken to represent the cities which have believed in Christ, and were founded by kings; and the phrase, *from ivory palaces* can be understood to mean that they were founded by the rich, the proud, the arrogant. *Kings' daughters have found favor with you, and come to do you honor*, because they are no longer seeking to promote the reputation of their city

43. Compare Jn 20:17.
44. See Dt 25:6.

fathers, but are concerned to honor you. Let anyone point out to me in Rome any temple of Romulus that is held in anything like the same veneration as the memorial of Peter, which I can point out! And who is being honored in Peter, if not the one who died for us? For we are Christians, not Petrines. Even though fathered by the dead man's brother, we are named after the dead man. We came to birth through Peter, but we are born to Christ. As Rome, so too Carthage, and many another noble city: all of them are daughters of kings, but they have found favor with their true King and come to do him honor. And from all of them is formed one single queen.

The queen's apparel

24. What a nuptial hymn this is! As songs full of joy are resounding, the bride herself enters. Until now it was the bridegroom's coming that preoccupied us, and he was being described throughout; all eyes were on him. But now it is time for the bride's entry. *The queen has taken her place at your right hand.* If she were on your left, she would not be a queen. There are indeed some persons at your left, but to them will be said, *Depart from me into the eternal fire* (Mt 25:41). Your queen will stand to your right, and to her will the invitation be spoken, *Come, you who are blessed by my Father, take possession of the kingdom prepared for you since the creation of the world* (Mt 25:34). *The queen has taken her place at your right hand in a golden gown, decked with variety.* What is this queenly apparel? It is precious, and of varied colors; this represents the mysteries of our teaching, and the variety of languages in which they are expressed. The African tongue is one, the Syriac another, the Greek another, the Hebrew another . . . and many others there are. These languages make up the variety with which the queen's gown is adorned. Just as all the different colors in a dress harmonize to form a unity, so do all these tongues express the one faith. Let there be plenty of variety in the garment, but no tear made.

So we have interpreted the variety as the diversity of languages, and the gown itself as unity; but now what does the gold represent amid this variety? It symbolizes wisdom. However great the variety of languages, it is one and the same gold that is preached. The gold itself does not vary, but there is variety in the way the gold is spoken about. All tongues preach the same wisdom, the same doctrine and discipline. There is variety in the languages, but gold in their meaning.

Verse 11. The admonition to the bride

25. The prophet now addresses the queen, and delighted he is to sing to her. He addresses each one of us too, provided we know where we belong, and try to be members of that body, and persevere in faith and hope, united with one

another as limbs of Christ. He addresses us, *Hearken, my daughter, and see*. He speaks as one of the fathers to a daughter, even though the speaker is a prophet or an apostle (for after all, we speak of "our fathers the prophets," and "our fathers the apostles," and if we call them our fathers, they have the right to call us their children). The daughters of these kings are being addressed, therefore, but the admonition is delivered by a single fatherly voice, and to one single daughter: *Hearken, my daughter, and see*. Listen first, and afterwards see. The gospel was brought to us, and realities we do not yet see have been preached to us; we have believed on the strength of what we have heard, and by believing we shall come to see. The bridegroom mentions this in another psalm: *A people I never knew has come to serve me, and as soon as they heard me they obeyed me* (Ps 17:45(18:43-44)). Why does he say, *As soon as they heard me*? Because that people has not yet seen. The Jews saw him, and crucified him; the Gentiles did not see him, but believed. Let the queen make her entry from amid the Gentiles, let her come in a golden gown, bedecked with variety; let her come from the Gentiles adorned with all the foreign tongues but with a single undivided wisdom, and let the admonition be spoken to her, *Hearken, my daughter, and see*. Unless you hear first, you will not see. Hear, so that you may cleanse your heart by faith, as the apostle said in the Acts of the Apostles: God was *cleansing their hearts by faith*.[45] This is why we must hear what we are to believe before we see it: our hearts need to be cleansed first by believing, so that we may be able to see with them. Listen, so that you may believe; cleanse your heart by faith. "And when I have cleansed my heart, what am I going to see?" *Blessed are the pure of heart, for they shall see God* (Mt 5:8).

Hearken, my daughter, and see, and bend your ear. Merely to hear would not be enough; we must hear with humility, so *bend your ear. And forget your own people and your father's house*. In another nation, in another father's house, you were born. The nation was Babylon,[46] and its king the devil. From whatever quarter the Gentiles have come flocking in, they have come from their father, the devil; but they have repudiated him.[47] *Forget your own people and your father's house*. The devil begot you as an ugly child when he made you a sinner; but God who justifies the ungodly gives you new birth as a beautiful creature. *Forget your own people and your father's house*.

45. Acts 15:9. It was Peter who said this, though usually by the title, "the apostle," Augustine means Paul.
46. Babylon is for Augustine the type of the earthly city; he will develop the theme later in *The City of God*. See also his *Confessions* II,3,8, and note at Exposition 2 of Psalm 26, 18.
47. Possibly an allusion to the renunciations preceding baptism.

Verse 12. Her beauty is the king's gift

26. *For the king has desired your beauty.* What beauty is this, if not what he himself created in her? He has desired beauty, but whose? The beauty of a sinner, a wicked, ungodly woman, as she was in the house of her father the devil, and among her own people? No, no; but the beauty of the bride described in the Song of Songs: *Who is this who comes up washed white?* (Sg 6:9.5). She was not white before, but now she has been washed pure white: as the Lord promises through a prophet, "Even if your sins are brilliant red, I will wash you white as snow."[48] *He has desired your beauty.* But who is this king? *He is your God.* See now how right it is for you to abandon that other father, and that other nation that was yours, and come to this King who is your God. He is your God and your King, your King and your Bridegroom. The King you are marrying is God; he provides you with your portion, by him you are adorned, by him redeemed, by him healed. Whatever you have in you that can please him, you have as his gift.

Verse 13. The homage of the Gentiles and of the rich

27. *And Tyrian maidens will pay homage to him with their gifts.* It is to your King, your God, that these *Tyrian maidens will pay homage with their gifts.* The maidens from Tyre represent maidens from all Gentile races: the part stands for the whole. Tyre was a neighbor to the land where prophecy flourished, so Tyre symbolized the Gentiles who were to believe in Christ. From there came the Canaanite woman who was at first called a dog; you remember where she came from, because the gospel says, *He withdrew to the region of Tyre and Sidon, and a Canaanite woman who lived in those parts came out and kept shouting* (Mt 15:22). And the rest of the story you know. She had been a "dog" earlier, in her father's house and among her own people, but by crying out and coming to the King she became beautiful through her faith in him. So she deserved to hear, *Woman, your faith is great* (Mt 15:28). *The king has desired your beauty. And Tyrian maidens will pay homage to him with their gifts.* Even so does the King will to be approached and to see his treasury filled; and he himself has provided the gifts with which they are to be filled, filled by you.[49] Let them come, says the psalm, let them come to pay him homage with their gifts. What kind of gifts are acceptable? *Do not lay up treasures for yourselves on earth, where moth and rust will destroy, and thieves may break in and steal them; lay up for yourselves treasures in heaven, where neither thief nor moth can touch them. For where your treasure is, your heart will be too* (Mt 6:19-21). *Come with your gifts, give*

48. See Is 1:18.
49. Variant: "and they are filled for you/us."

alms, and everything will be clean for you (Lk 11:41). Come with your gifts to him who says, *I want mercy rather than sacrifice* (Hos 6:6; Mt 9:13; 12:7). In days of old there was a temple that foreshadowed what was to come, and people used to bring bulls, rams, goats, and various other animals for sacrifice. By their blood-shedding one thing was done, but something else signified. But now blood has been shed for us, the blood prefigured by all those sacrifices; the King himself has come, and he demands gifts. What gifts? Alms. For he will sit in judgment, and will himself award gifts to certain people. *Come, you who are blessed by my Father*, he will say, *take possession of the kingdom prepared for you since the creation of the world.* And why? Because *I was hungry, and you fed me; I was thirsty, and you gave me a drink; naked, and you clothed me; a stranger, and you made me welcome; sick and in prison, and you visited me.* These are the gifts that the Tyrian maidens bring as homage to the King, for when they ask him, *When did we see you so?* he who is both enthroned on high and present here below can say, thinking of those who go up the ladder and those who come down, *When you did that for even the least of those who are mine, you did it for me* (Mt 25:34-38).

28. *Tyrian maidens will pay homage to him with their gifts.* The psalmist now intends to state more clearly who the daughters of Tyre are, and how they are to do homage to the king. *All the rich among the people will seek favor with you.* So these daughters of Tyre who come with their gifts are the rich citizens for whom the Bridegroom's friend has this advice: *Instruct the rich of this world not to be high-minded, nor to put their trust in unreliable wealth, but in the living God, who gives us everything to enjoy in abundance. Let them be rich in good works, give readily, and share what they have.* Let them do honor to the King with their gifts, but not think that they are losing what they give. They should have no anxiety about putting it where they will find it again for ever. *Let them use their wealth to lay a good foundation for the future, and so attain true life* (1 Tm 6:17-19). As they do honor to the King with their gifts they *will seek favor with you*, for they all come to the Church and give alms there. They should not do it elsewhere, outside; the Church is the right place to do it, because a favorable reception from this bride and queen will be to their advantage when they give alms. This is why we read that people who sold their goods used to come with the proceeds to seek the queen's acceptance, and what they brought they would lay at the feet of the apostles.[50] Love grew very strong in the Church. The queen with her gracious countenance is the Church, but the daughters of Tyre who pay homage—the wealthy who bring gifts, that is—they are the Church too. *All the rich among the people will seek favor with you.* Both those who seek acceptance,

50. See Acts 4:34-35.

and the queen whose acceptance is entreated, are all the one bride, all one queen, for mother and children together all belong to Christ, belong to the Head.[51]

Verses 14-15. Inner beauty

29. Good works and almsgiving can trap us in human pride, however, so the Lord warns, *Be careful not to do your good works in the sight of other people, to attract their attention* (Mt 6:1). Yet he also tells us in what sense these things must be done publicly, in order to win the bride's favor: *Let your deeds shine before men and women in such a way that they see the good you do, and bless your Father who is in heaven* (Mt 5:16). Do not seek recognition for yourselves by the good works you carry out in public, but seek the honor of God. Someone objects, perhaps, "But who knows whether it is God's glory I am seeking, or my own? If I give something to a poor person, I can be seen doing it, but who sees what my intention is?" The one who sees can take care of that; he who will reward you sees your intention. He who sees you within loves you within; he loves you within, and you must love him within, for he fashions your inner beauty. Do not seek your reward in being seen by onlookers, and praised for what you do; consider the next words of the psalm: *All the glory of the king's daughter is within.* Not only does she wear an outer garment of gold, decked with variety; he who has fallen in love with her knows her to be inwardly lovely as well. What is the inner face of beauty? Beauty of conscience. There Christ regards us, there Christ loves us, there Christ punishes, there Christ bestows the crown. Let your almsgiving be done in secret, then, for *all the glory of the king's daughter is within. With her golden fringes she is girdled with varied embroidery.* Her beauty is within, but in her fringes is a variety of tongues, setting forth the splendor of her teaching. But what would be the use of them, if there were no beauty within?

30. *Virgins will be conducted after her to the king.*Yes, this surely has happened. The Church has believed, and the Church has spread throughout all nations. Look how virgins now long to be pleasing to the King! What motivates them? That the Church has led the way. *Virgins will be conducted after her to the king, her nearest and dearest will be led to you.* Those who are conducted are no strangers, but her nearest and dearest, those who belong to her. Notice that the psalm first said, "To the king," then turned toward him and said, "To you." *Her nearest and dearest will be led to you.*

51. The paradox Augustine plays with in this paragraph, that the Church is the people, yet more than the people, is taken up again in sections 31 and 33 below.

Verse 16. The joyful entry of the virgins

31. *They shall be conducted with joy and gladness, they shall be ushered into the temple of the king*. The temple of the king is the Church itself, and yet the Church enters his temple. Of what is the temple built? Of the people who enter the temple. Who are its living stones?[52] God's faithful. These are the ones who *will be ushered into the temple of the king*. There are virgins outside the King's temple, heretical nuns; virgins they are indeed, but what advantage is that to them if they are not brought into the King's temple? The King's temple stands firm in unity; it is not a tumbledown place, or torn apart, or divided against itself. The mortar binding its stones together is the charity of those who live there. *They shall be ushered into the temple of the king*.

Verse 17. Sons to take the place of fathers for the Church

32. *To take the place of your fathers, sons have been born to you*. Nothing could be more obvious. Look carefully at this temple of the king, because the psalmist speaks on its behalf, with its worldwide unity in mind. Those who have chosen to remain virgins cannot be pleasing to the Bridegroom unless they are brought into his temple. *To take the place of your fathers, sons have been born to you*. The apostles begot you; they were sent out, they preached, they are the Church's fathers. But was it possible for them to remain with us in bodily form for ever? It is true that one of them said, *I long to die and to be with Christ, for that is much the best; but it is necessary for you that I remain in the flesh* (Phil 1:23-24). Yes, he said that, but how long was he able to stay? Even until our day? Even into the future? No; but was the Church abandoned when the apostles departed? Far from it. *To take the place of your fathers, sons have been born to you*. What does that mean? The apostles were sent to be your fathers, but in their place sons have been born to you, because bishops have been appointed. Where did they spring from, the bishops who are found throughout the world today? The Church calls them "fathers," although the Church itself brought them forth, and appointed them to the sees of the fathers. Do not imagine yourself forsaken then, O Church, because you do not see Peter, do not see Paul, do not see any of those from whom you were born. A new fatherhood has grown up for you from your own offspring. *To take the place of your fathers, sons have been born to you; and you will appoint them princes all over the world*. Look how widely the King's temple has been extended, and let any virgins who are not being ushered into it learn from this that they have no place at the wedding. *To take the place of your fathers, sons have been born to you; and you will appoint them princes all over the world*. This is the Catholic Church: her sons have been set up as princes

52. See 1 Pt 2:5.

worldwide, her sons have been appointed in her fathers' stead. Let those who are cut off from us recognize the truth, let them come back into unity, let them be led into the temple of the King. God has built his Church in every place, laying the firm foundations of the prophets and apostles.[53] The Church has given birth to sons, and appointed them in place of our fathers as princes over the whole earth.

Verse 18. The city of God

33. *They will be mindful of your name in generation after generation. Therefore the peoples will confess to you.* What is the use of confessing, if it is done outside the temple? What is the point of praying, if prayer is not offered on the mountain? *With my voice I have cried to the Lord,* says another psalm, *and he heard me from his holy mountain* (Ps 3:5(4)). And what mountain is that? The mountain of which scripture says, *A city founded upon a mountain cannot be hidden* (Mt 5:14). What mountain? The mountain Daniel saw growing from a small stone, and smashing all earthly kingdoms, and filling all the surface of the earth.[54]

Let anyone who hopes to receive, worship there; let anyone who wants to be heard, ask there; let anyone who wants to be forgiven, confess there. *Therefore the peoples will confess to you for ever, and for unending ages,* for though in eternal life there will no longer be any groaning sinners, the everlasting confession of sheer happiness will never cease in the praises sung to God in that heavenly, imperishable city. To this same city will the peoples confess in praise for ever, this city to which another psalm sings, *Glorious things are spoken of you, city of God* (Ps 86(87):4). To her who is Christ's bride, who is a queen, a king's daughter and a King's wife, will they sing, for her princes are mindful of her name in generation after generation, which means as long as this age shall last, this age which rolls on through succeeding generations. So long shall they continue to care lovingly for her, until she is set free from this passing world to reign with God for ever. Therefore will the peoples confess to her through all eternity, for there will the hearts of all be transparent and manifest as they shine with charity made perfect. Thus she will know herself entirely in utter fullness, she who is in many of her parts hidden now even from herself. This is why we are warned by the apostle to pass no judgment prematurely, before the Lord comes to light up all that is hidden in darkness, and lay bare the thoughts of all hearts; then each one will receive due commendation from God.[55] That holy city will in some sort confess to herself, for the peoples who form her will confess for ever to

---

53. See Eph 2:20.
54. See Dn 3:35.
55. See 1 Cor 4:5.

the city. No part of her may remain hidden from herself, for nothing in any one of her citizens will be hidden from sight.

Exposition of Psalm 45

A Sermon to the People

Verse 1. Christ's cross unlocks mysteries

1. What we are going to talk about to you, dearest friends,[1] is something very well known to you, so there is no need to delay long over it: it will be sufficient to remind you briefly of what you already know. I mean that we must understand the "children of Korah" to be ourselves. As you are aware, "Korah" means "baldness." You know too that because our Lord was crucified at the place called Calvary,[2] he drew many people to himself, like that grain of wheat which would have remained one lonely grain if it had not been put to death.[3] Accordingly those who have been drawn to him are "children of Korah." This is the mysterious implication of the title. No doubt there were some children of Korah at the time when these verses were originally sung, but the important thing is that the spirit should give us life; we must not stick at the letter which veils the true meaning.[4] So let us recognize ourselves here, and see whether the following lines in the main text of the psalm fit our situation. We shall find ourselves in them as long as we remain inseparably united to the members of that body whose Head is in heaven. After his passion he ascended there in order to take with him those who were grounded in their lowly state on earth; he willed to take them, richly productive now, bearing fruit through their patient endurance.[5]

But the full title is *Unto the end, a psalm for the children of Korah, about the hidden things*. It is concerned with what is hidden; but, as you know, he who was crucified on Calvary rent the veil asunder so that the secret places of the temple were exposed to view.[6] Our Lord's cross was like a key for opening what was locked away, so let us be confident that he will be with us now, that these hidden things may be unveiled. When we see the words, *Unto the end*, we should always understand them as a reference to Christ, because *Christ is the end of the law, bringing justification to everyone who believes* (Rom 10:4). He is called its "end" not in the sense that he abolishes it, but because he brings it to perfection.

1. *Caritati vestrae.*
2. "The bald place": see his comments in the Exposition of Psalm 83, 2; Exposition of Psalm 84, 2; and note at Exposition of Psalm 41, 2.
3. See Jn 12:24-25.32.
4. See 2 Cor 3:6.
5. See Lk 8:15.
6. See Mt 27:51.

We speak of food we have been eating as "finished," but also of a garment that was being woven as "finished"; in the first case the food is all gone, in the second a tunic has reached completion. So with Christ: when we reach him, we shall have nowhere further to go, and so he is called the "end" of our journey. It would be wrong to think that when we have reached him we shall have to go on striving to attain to the Father. Philip made that mistake when he said to Christ, *Lord, show us the Father, and that is enough for us*. His words, *that is enough for us*, imply a further search for perfect satisfaction and fullness. But Christ replied, *Have I been all this time with you, and yet you have not known me? Whoever has seen me, Philip, has seen the Father* (Jn 14:8-9). In him we possess the Father, because he is in the Father, and the Father in him. He and the Father are one.[7]

Verse 2. Insecure refuges, and the worst tribulations

2. What advice has the singer for us in this psalm where, as long as we share the singer's attitude, we shall recognize our own voice in his? *Our God is a refuge and strength*. Some refuges are anything but strong, so that anyone who flees to them is weakened rather than securely established. Suppose, for example, you take refuge with some person of importance in this world, hoping to find in him a powerful friend. That looks like a safe haven for you. But so very uncertain are worldly fortunes, and so increasingly frequent the ruin of powerful people, that in taking refuge under such a person's protection you will simply find your own reasons for apprehension all the greater. In your previous situation it was only about your own affairs that you needed to worry, but now that you have taken refuge with him you need to be anxious on his account as well. There have been many who sought that kind of security only to find that when their ostensible protectors fell, they themselves were under investigation. No one would have been interested in questioning such small fry, if they had not taken refuge with powerful people like that.

But our refuge is quite different; our refuge is "strength." When we flee to it we shall be secure and unshakable.

3. *Our helper in the terrible tribulations that have come upon us*. There are many kinds of tribulation, and in all of them we must seek refuge in God, whether the trouble concerns our income, our bodily health, some danger threatening those we love, or something we need to support our life. Whatever it is, there should be no refuge for a Christian other than our Savior. He is God, and when we flee to him, we are strong. No Christian will be strong in himself or herself; but God, who has become our refuge, will supply the strength. However, dearly beloved, I must tell you that among all the tribulations that beset the human soul, there is none worse than a guilty conscience. If there is no wound

7. See Jn 10:30.

there, and that inner part of ourselves called conscience is in a healthy state, then wherever else we have troubles to endure we can flee to that inner place and there find God. But if there is no peace within us because of our abundant sins, which cause God to be absent from that place, what are we to do? Where shall we flee, when troubles begin to strike? We may flee from the country into the city, or from the public domain into our own home, and from our home into our private room, but tribulation comes hard on our heels. Once in our private room we have nowhere left to run to except our inner bedchamber. But what if that is filled with uproar, and the fumes of iniquity, and the fire of our sins? We cannot find security there. On the contrary, we are driven out, and once driven out from there we are banished from ourselves. The person we had thought to find refuge with has turned out to be our enemy, and where can we go to escape our very self? Wherever we run, we drag this self after us, and wherever we drag a self in this state, we make it our tormentor. These are the terrible tribulations that overwhelm a person, and none are more grievous; other troubles can never be as harsh as these, because they are not as intimate.

Consider this, dearly beloved. When trees are cut down and passed as satisfactory for building purposes, it sometimes happens that some areas on the outer surface are flawed or rotten. But the builder inspects the innermost heart of the tree, and if he has checked that the trees are sound at the core, he promises that they will last in the building. He will not be particularly concerned about lesions on the surface, provided he can certify the inner part as sound. Well now, nothing is more interior to a person than his conscience. So if the conscience is not found to be healthy, what is the point of external health, when the core, the conscience, is rotten?

These kind of tribulations are extremely fierce and terrible, as the psalm says; yet even in these the Lord has become our helper by forgiving our sins. For the consciences of sinners there is no cure at all, except forgiveness. Think of the plight of someone who has admitted his debt to the tax system. He sees his money running out, and knows he cannot pay. He laments that his troubles are very severe, knowing that the bailiffs may arrive at any time. He has no shred of hope, unless that his debt may be written off, and this anxiety concerns only worldly goods.[8] How much worse then is the plight of one who, because of his or her numerous sins, is a debtor who owes condign punishment? How is such a person ever going to pay the debt owed by a bad conscience? If he pays up, he himself will be done for! To pay the debt, he must undergo the penalty. There is no way out for us, except to find safety in God's forgiveness. But once we have received it, we must not get ourselves into debt again.

8. Variant: "unless earthly rulers let him off."

The remedy

4. We could take the "children of Korah" to be the crowds Peter addressed in the Acts of the Apostles. They were startled by the miracles that attended the coming of the Holy Spirit, for those on whom he had fallen were speaking in the languages of them all. Peter proclaimed Christ to them as the one who had demonstrated such mighty power by sending his Holy Spirit. They could see for themselves how the man they had crucified with their own hands, regarding him as worthy of nothing but contempt when they killed him, was now most high and ennobled in God's presence, as was evident from his having filled uneducated people with the Holy Spirit, and loosened the tongues of the dumb.[9] They were pierced to the heart, and asked, *What shall we do?* It was certainly severe tribulation that had come upon them, for they had not themselves discovered their sins; rather had their sins been found for them by the admonition of the apostles. So the tribulations found them, not they the tribulations. When a person reflects on his own action without being admonished by anyone else, and entreats God, what does he say? *I have found anguish and sorrow, and I called on the name of the Lord* (Ps 114(116):3-4). So there is a difference between the tribulation you find for yourself, and the tribulation that finds you. But whichever kind you are in—the kind that finds you out, or the kind you find for yourself—you should beg him who is our helper in tribulations to drive it away. That is what the psalmist did, for he testifies, *I called on the name of the Lord*, and those who admitted that the tribulations they suffered had come upon them unsought equally acknowledged, *Our God is a refuge and strength, our helper in the terrible tribulations that have come upon us*. He has become their helper, then, but why? Because *they were pierced to the heart, and asked, "What shall we do?"* A very desperate plea. "He whom we killed has proved to be so great, and now what is to become of us?" Peter gave them their answer: *Repent, and let every one of you be baptized in the name of the Lord Jesus Christ, that your sins may be forgiven* (Acts 2:37-38). He spoke with good reason, for they could imagine no sin greater than this. What greater sin can a sick person commit than to murder the physician? Can the patient do anything worse than killing his doctor? But if that can be forgiven, is anything unforgivable? From God, whom the psalmist called *a refuge and strength*, they received complete assurance. *Let every one of you be baptized in the name of the Lord Jesus Christ*: accept baptism in the name of him whom you killed, *and your sins will be forgiven*. You have recognized your physician, though belatedly. Now that you have received his assurance, drink the blood you shed.

9. See Wis 10:21.

Verse 3. Christ stills the storm

5. What have they to say, now that they have been given such firm reassurance? *Therefore we shall not be afraid when the world rocks*. Such a short time before, they were anxious, but now they know they are safe, and after overwhelming troubles they find themselves established in great tranquillity. Christ had been asleep for them, and that was why they were apprehensive, but when Christ woke up, he commanded the winds, and they died down, as we have just heard in the gospel.[10] Christ dwells in the heart of each one of us through our faith. This episode shows us that if we forget our faith, our heart is like a boat battered and tossed about in this stormy world, because Christ seems to be asleep. But when he awakes, there is calm. This interpretation is beyond dispute, because the Lord himself demanded, *Where is your faith?* (Lk 8:25). When Christ awoke he awakened their faith, so that what had been done for the boat might happen also in their hearts. *Our helper in the terrible tribulations that have come upon us*, he acted there to bring about a great calm.

The mountains move

6. Consider what a calm it is: *therefore we shall not be afraid when the world rocks, and the mountains are shifted out to sea*. No, we shall not be afraid. Let us look for these mountains that have been moved; if we find them, we shall obviously be secure there. Now the Lord said to his disciples, *If you have faith even the size of a mustard-seed, you will say to this mountain, "Up with you, be thrown into the sea," and it will happen* (Mt 17:19). Possibly by *this mountain* he meant himself, for he was called a mountain in a prophecy: *In the last days the mountain of the Lord shall be established above all other mountains* (Is 2:2; Mi 4:1). It towers above the peaks of all other mountains, its place is upon all mountain-tops, because those other mountains are there to proclaim this supreme mountain. The sea represents this world, in comparison with which the Jewish people were like an island of dry land, for they were not drenched by the salty waters of idolatry, but were like a dry patch surrounded by the salty sea of the Gentiles. The time was to come when this dry land, the Jewish race, would be shaken, and then the mountains would be shifted out to sea, especially that mountain which had been atop them all. He abandoned the Jews and found his place among the Gentiles, like a mountain moving from dry land into the sea. By whom was he moved? By the apostles, to whom he had promised, *If you have faith even the size of a mustard-seed, you will say to this mountain, "Up with you, be thrown into the sea," and it will happen*. He means, "If you preach with absolute faith, this mountain, which represents me, will be preached among the

10. See Mt 8:24-26; Mk 4:37-40; Lk 8:23-25.

Gentiles. I shall be glorified, I shall be acknowledged among the Gentiles, and in me the prophecy will be verified, *A people I never knew has come to serve me"* (Ps 17:45(18:44)).

But what about the other mountains? They were shifted too; when did it happen? Let scripture enlighten us. When the apostle was preaching to the Jews, they scorned the word, and Paul said to them, *We were sent to you, but because you have rejected the word of God, we are turning now to the Gentiles* (Acts 13:46). So the mountains moved over into the sea. The Gentiles truly believed the mountains, so that the mountains found a home out in the open sea. Very different were the Jews, of whom it was said, *This people honors me with its lips, but its heart is far from me* (Is 29:13; Mt 15:8). And this faith among the Gentiles fulfilled the Lord's promise through a prophet concerning the new covenant: *I will put my laws into their hearts* (Jer 31:33; Heb 8:10). These laws, these commandments that were stamped upon the faith and believing hearts of all nations by the apostles, were figuratively called mountains transplanted into the middle of the sea. For our part, we shall have no fear when it happens. Who among us will be fearless? Those who are pierced to the heart, and so spared from being numbered with the repudiated Jews, who are like branches broken off.[11] Some of the Jews believed, and threw in their lot with the apostles who preached to them.[12] But those whom the mountains abandoned have cause to be afraid. We have not left the mountains, and when they were transplanted out into the sea, we followed.

Verse 4. The apostles raise a storm

7. What follows the removal of the mountains into the open sea? Pay attention, and see the truth of it. When these predictions were made, they were obscure, because the events had not yet taken place; but is there anyone around today who is unaware that they have? The page of divine scripture is open for you to read, and the wide world is open for you to see. Only the literate can read the books, but even the illiterate can read the book of the world. So what happened when the mountains were shifted out to sea? *Its waters roared and heaved.* When the gospel was preached people said, *What is this? He seems to be peddling foreign deities* (Acts 17:18). That was the Athenians' attitude. But remember the Ephesians: what a hullabaloo they raised, what a din they made in support of their Diana in the theater when, intent on killing the apostles, they shouted, *Great is Ephesian Diana!* (Acts 19:28). Amid these pounding and roaring waters the apostles were not afraid, for they had taken refuge in God. Paul even wanted to go into the theater, but he was restrained by the disciples,

11. See Rom 11:17-20.
12. Thus the CCL editors. Many codices have "They believed, and the apostles approached."

because they wanted to keep him alive. All the same, *its waters roared and heaved, and mountains were shaken by the force*. The force of what or of whom? The force of the sea? The power of God, more likely, the God who has been called *a refuge and strength, our helper in the terrible tribulations that have come upon us*. By this power mountains were shaken, and this time, I think, the mountains represent the authorities of this world; for there are mountains of God and mountains of the world. The head of this world's mountains is the devil, but the mountains of God have Christ for their head. So now one lot of mountains was shaken by the other, and as the worldly mountains were rocked by the resounding waves, they raised their voices[13] against Christians. Secular mountains trembled, a great earthquake ensued and the waters raged. But against whom? Against a city founded on a rock. When the gospel is preached the waters heave and mountains quake, but what about you, city of God? Listen to what comes next.

Verse 5. The river of the Holy Spirit

8. *The vehement impulses of a river give joy to God's city*. Mountains quiver, the sea rages, but God stays faithful to his city by means of this impetuous river. What is it, and what are its impulses? They are the inundation of the Spirit, of which the Lord said, *Let anyone who is thirsty come to me and drink. If anyone believes in me, rivers of living water shall flow from within that person* (Jn 7:37-38). And, sure enough, these rivers gushed from within Paul, Peter, John and the rest of the apostles, and from the other faithful messengers of the gospel. Since all these rivulets derived from the one great river, there are many *vehement impulses to give joy to God's city*. To make it quite clear that this promise referred to the Holy Spirit, the evangelist continued in the same passage, *He said this of the Spirit which those who believed in him were to receive; for the Spirit had not yet been given, because Jesus was not yet glorified* (Jn 7:39). When Jesus had been glorified after his resurrection and ascension, the Holy Spirit came on the day of Pentecost and filled the believers. They spoke in tongues, and began to preach the good news to the Gentiles. At this the city of God was overjoyed, though the sea was heaving with its noisy waves, and the mountains were quaking and asking themselves what they should do, and how they could get rid of this new teaching, and how they might uproot the Christian race from the earth. But against whom was all this agitation directed? Against the irresistible impulses of the river which were giving joy to God's city. The psalmist goes on to make clear what river he meant, and that he was indeed referring to the Holy Spirit when he said, *The vehement impulses of a river give joy to God's city*, for he continues, *The Most High has sanctified his own tent*. If the word "sanctified"

13. Variant: "passed laws."

is used, it is obvious that we should understand these powerful impulses to be those of the Holy Spirit, by whom every godly soul that believes in Christ is sanctified, to make it a citizen of the city of God.

Verse 6. Divine indwelling

9. *God is in the center of it, and it shall not be upset.* Let the sea rage and the mountains quake, still *God is in the center of it, and it shall not be upset.* Why *in the center of it*? The image suggests that God stands in one spot, and those who believe in him are ranged around him. Does this mean that God is confined in a place, in such a way that, while the things around him have ample room, he who is encircled is cramped for space? Heaven forbid! You must not think of God like that. He whose throne is in the souls of the devout is not hemmed in by any place. God's throne is in human hearts in such wise that if a man or woman falls away from God, God remains unchanged in himself; it is not as if he falls too, deprived of any place to call his own. It is the other way round: he lifts you up, so that you may be in him; he does not lean on you in such fashion that if you withdraw your support, he falls. If he withdraws his support, you will fall; but if you withdraw yours, he will not fall.

What does the psalm mean, then, when it says, *God is in the center of it*? It suggests that God is completely fair to everyone, and has no favorites. Just as some object that is placed in the center of a circle is equidistant from all parts of the circumference, so God is said to be central because he cares for everyone equally. *God is in the center of it, and it shall not be upset.* Why will it contrive not to be upset? Because God is at its center. *God will help it with his gracious countenance.* He is our helper in the terrible tribulations that seek us out remorselessly. *God will help it with his gracious countenance.* What is signified by *his gracious countenance*? The manifestation of his power. How does God manifest himself, and how can we see his countenance? I have reminded you already:[14] you have learned that God is present; we have all learned it, by what he does. Whenever we receive some help from him in such a way that we cannot doubt that it was granted by the Lord, the gracious countenance of the Lord is with us. *God will help it with his gracious countenance.*

Verse 7. The rain of salvation

10. *The nations were disturbed.* How disturbed, and why? By their plans to overthrow the city of God, the city at whose center God dwells? Or to destroy the sanctified tent, which God helps with his gracious countenance? No. The disturbance among the Gentiles is now a salutary one, for what comes next? *And king-*

14. Perhaps he means in his Exposition of Psalm 43, 4.

doms were bent low. Bent low, they were, he says; no longer are they proudly erect to wreak havoc, but bent low to worship. When were kingdoms bent low? When the prophecy found in another psalm was fulfilled: *all the kings of the earth will worship him, and all nations will serve him* (Ps 71(72):11). What induced kingdoms to bow low? The next line tells us: *the voice of the Most High was heard, and the earth trembled*. Fanatical devotees of idols croaked like frogs from the marshes, all the more frantically for coming from that foul and filthy mud. But what is the croaking of frogs compared with thunder from the clouds? It was from the clouds that *the voice of the Most High was heard, and the earth trembled*, because God thundered from his own clouds. What are they? His apostles, his preachers, through whom he thundered his commandments and flashed the lightning of his miracles. The clouds are the same people as the mountains: they are mountains by their height and stability, and clouds by their rain and the fertility they bring; for these clouds have irrigated the earth, and it was of them that the psalm said, *The voice of the Most High was heard, and the earth trembled*. They were mentioned also when the Lord threatened a barren vineyard, from which the mountains had been removed and relocated in the sea: *I will forbid my clouds to send rain upon it* (Is 5:6). This prophecy was fulfilled in the events we have already recalled, when the mountains were shifted out into the sea, and when the apostle said, *We were sent to you, but because you have rejected the word of God, we are turning now to the Gentiles* (Acts 13:46). Yes, the threat was carried out that *I will forbid my clouds to send rain upon it*. In the end the Jewish people was left like a dry fleece on the threshing-floor. You know the story of how this miraculous event took place.[15] At first the threshing-floor was dry, and the fleece alone was wet, but no rain could be seen upon it. Similarly the mystery of the new covenant could not be seen in the Jewish race. There it was a fleece, here a veil,[16] for the mystery was present in the fleece, but veiled. Now, however, in the open threshing-floor, among all nations, Christ's gospel is plain to see. The rain is obvious, and the grace of Christ is laid bare, with no veil covering it.[17] The fleece had to be wrung out to get rid of the rain, and so did the Jews squeeze Christ out from themselves. Now the Lord has sent ample rain upon the threshing-floor from his clouds, while the fleece has remained dry. From these clouds *the voice of the Most High was heard*, so that kingdoms might be bent low and brought to worship.

15. See Jgs 6:37-40.
16. A pun: *Illic vellus, hic velum*.
17. He is combining two unrelated scriptural passages: Jgs 6:37-40 on the sign given to Gideon, and Paul's allegory about the veiled face in 2 Cor 3:13-18.

Verse 8. God undertakes to support us

11. *The Lord of hosts is with us, our supporter is the God of Jacob.* Not on any human whatsoever, not on any potentate, not even on any angel, not on any creature earthly or heavenly do we rely. But *the Lord of hosts is with us, our supporter*[18] *is the God of Jacob.* He sent angels to us, and after the angels came himself; he came to receive service from the angels and to make us mortals the angels' equals. This was tremendous grace. If God is for us, who stands against us?[19] *The Lord of hosts is with us.* Who is this Lord of hosts? If God is for us, I repeat, who can stand against us? *If he did not spare even his own Son, but delivered him up for us all, how can he fail to give us everything else along with that gift?* (Rom 8:32). Let us be secure, then, and in tranquillity of heart nourish a good conscience on the bread of the Lord. *The Lord of hosts is with us, our supporter is the God of Jacob.* However abysmal your weakness, see who lifts you up.[20] Suppose someone is ill, and a doctor is called in. The doctor undertakes responsibility for the sick person.[21] Who has taken him on? The doctor. So there is great hope for recovery, because a great doctor has taken him on.[22] But in our case, who is the doctor? Any doctor other than ours is a mere human, who will be ill himself some time or other—but not ours. *Our supporter is the God of Jacob.* Make yourself a tiny infant, such as parents pick up.[23] Those who are not picked up and acknowledged are exposed, but those who are taken into their parents' arms are nourished and reared. But do you imagine that God has taken you into his arms in the same way as your mother took you up when you were a baby? Not so, because he has taken you up forever. It is your own voice that testifies in another psalm, *My father and mother have abandoned me, but the Lord has taken me up* (Ps 26(27):10). *Our supporter is the God of Jacob.*

Verse 9. The stone that grew into a mountain

12. *Come and see the deeds of the Lord.* Now what has the Lord done, after undertaking to support us? Cast your eyes over the whole wide world; come and see. For if you do not come, you do not see; if you do not see, neither do you believe; if you do not believe, you are still standing far off. But if you believe,

---

18. *Susceptor noster.* The verb *suscipio* is rich in meaning: support, lift up, accept, undertake responsibility for something or someone, and (of a parent) take a child into one's arms in a gesture of acknowledgment, as opposed to disowning and exposing it. All these meanings are in the background in the following lines. See also Exposition of Psalm 3, 3, and Exposition of Psalm 83, 9, and notes there.
19. See Rom 8:31.
20. *Quis te suscipiat.*
21. *Susceptum suum dicit medicus aegrotum.*
22. *Suscepit.*
23. *Quales a parentibus suscipiuntur.*

you come near, and if you believe, you see. How can we approach this mountain? On foot? By ship? With wings? On horseback? No, none of these. As far as distance is concerned you need not be preoccupied or worried, for the mountain itself comes to you. At first only a tiny stone, it grew up into a mighty mountain, so great that it filled the whole surface of the earth. Why bestir yourself to travel through foreign lands trying to reach it, when it fills all lands? It has come already—wake up! As it grows larger it knocks on the doors of those still asleep: surely their slumbers are not so profound that they are insensible even to the arrival of a mountain! Let them rather hear the call, *Arise, sleeper, rise from the dead: Christ will enlighten you* (Eph 5:14), for the Jews were unable to see the stone. It was a small stone then, so they despised it for its diminutive appearance, and in their contempt they tripped over it, and in tripping they dashed themselves against it. Now all that remains to them is to be crushed entirely, for it was prophesied of this stone, *Anyone who trips over this stone will be dashed against it, and anyone on whom it falls will be crushed* (Lk 20:18). It is one thing to be dashed, quite another to be crushed; being dashed against it is less than being crushed. When the stone comes in glory from above, the only people it will crush are those who dashed themselves against it when it lay humbly on earth. At this present time, before our Lord comes again, he has been lying humbly before the Jews, but they have stumbled against him and bruised themselves. One day in the future he will come to judge, glorious and noble, great and powerful; he will come not as a weak man to be judged, but as the strong one to judge and to crush those who stumbled and dashed themselves against him, for to those who do not believe, he is a stone to stumble over, a rock to trip them.[24]

Dearest friends, we may find it unremarkable that the Jews did not recognize someone who lay like a very small stone before their feet, attracting only their disdain. Much more amazing is it that some refuse today to recognize so lofty a mountain. The Jews tripped over the little stone because they failed to see it, but today's heretics trip over a mountain; for that stone has grown mightily by now, and we can say to them, "Look how Daniel's prophecy has come true: *That stone*, the one that was once so small, *grew into a lofty mountain, and filled the whole earth* (Dn 2:35). Why do you persist in stumbling over it, instead of climbing it? Can anyone be so blind as to trip over a mountain? Anyone would think that he had come on purpose to trip you up, instead of coming so that you could climb." *Come, let us go up to the mountain of the Lord* (Is 2:3; Mi 4:2): this is the invitation addressed to us through Isaiah. *Come, let us go up*. What does he mean by *Let us go up*? *Come* means "believe," and *let us go up* means "let us make progress." But the heretics will neither come, nor ascend, nor believe, nor press forward. They simply yap at the mountain. They have been bruised so many times by tripping over it and dashing themselves against it, yet they will

24. See 1 Pt 2:8.

not go up the mountain, but persist in stumbling against it. Let us extend the invitation to them: *Come and see the deeds of the Lord, the prodigies he has performed on earth.* They are called *prodigies* because they are portentous; they are the miraculous signs that were given when the world first believed. What did they lead to, and what did they portend?

Verse 10. Banishment of war, and of weapons

13. *Banishing war even to the ends of the earth.* We do not see this promise fully realized, for wars still rage. They are fought between nations for dominance; and they are fought also between sects, between Jews, pagans, Christians and heretics. Wars are waged, and with increasing frequency, as some fight for the truth, and others for falsehoods. The prophecy that God is *banishing wars even to the ends of the earth* has not been completely fulfilled yet, but perhaps it will be.

But is there a sense in which it is fulfilled already? I think it is in some people. It is realized in the wheat, but not yet in the chaff. In what sense is God *banishing wars even to the ends of the earth*? Does the psalm perhaps mean wars waged against God? But who goes to war against God? Impiety does. And what can impiety achieve against God? Nothing. What does an earthenware vessel achieve against a rock, even if hurled with great force? Nothing: the harder its impact against the rock, the more damage it incurs itself. Wars of this kind used to be waged often and fiercely. Impiety tried conclusions with God, and the earthenware vessels were smashed. Human contenders relied on their own resources, they thought themselves strong enough to prevail. Job called this effrontery their "shield" when he said of an impious man, *He charged against God with his gross arrogance for a shield* (Jb 15:26). What does he imply by saying that the assailant's gross arrogance served him as a shield? That he was recklessly presuming on his ability to defend himself.

Was this the attitude of the others we heard about, those who kept saying, *Our God is a refuge and strength, our helper in the terrible tribulations that have come upon us*? Or of those who professed in another psalm, *I will put no trust in my bow, and my sword will not save me* (Ps 43:7(44:6))? When anyone realizes that we are nothing in ourselves, and cannot look to ourselves for any help at all, that person's weapons have all been broken, and the wars that raged within him or her are quelled. Wars like these were abolished by that voice of the Most High that thundered from his holy clouds, the voice that caused the earth to tremble and kingdoms to bow low. Wars of this kind he has banished even to the ends of the earth. *He will shatter the bow and smash the weaponry, and the shields he will burn with fire.* Bows, weaponry, shields, and fire. The bow represents an ambush, the weaponry open attack, the shield vain self-reliance. And the fire that burns them all up is the fire of which the Lord spoke: *I have come to set fire to the earth* (Lk 12:49). Another psalm says of it, *No one can hide from his heat* (Ps 18:7(19:6)). Once this fire gains a hold, nothing of the armory of impiety will remain in us; all its pieces will inevitably be shattered, smashed and burnt up. You must stay unarmed, without any succor from yourself; and the weaker, the more undefended, you are, the more does he take up your cause,[25] he of whom it was said, Our supporter[26] is the God of Jacob. You thought you could win by yourself, so you are gravely shaken in yourself. Throw away the weapons you relied on, and listen to the Lord telling you, *My grace is sufficient for you*. You too must say, *When I am weak, then I am strong*. This is Paul's declaration. He had lost all the weapons which appeared to be his strength when he admitted, *Of nothing but my weaknesses will I boast* (2 Cor 12:9-10). It was as though he were saying, "No longer am I charging against God with my own gross arrogance for a shield. *I was originally a persecutor and a blasphemer, and harmed people, but I received mercy so that Christ Jesus might give proof in me of his long forbearance toward those who will believe in him unto eternal life*" (1 Tm 1:13,16). *Banishing wars even to the ends of the earth*. If God takes up our cause, will he abandon us in our unarmed condition? By no means. He equips us, but with weapons of a different order, the evangelical weapons of truth, self-control, salvation, hope, faith and charity. We shall wield these weapons, but they will not come from ourselves. The arms we did have as from ourselves will have been burnt, provided that we are enkindled by that fire of the Holy Spirit of which the psalm declares, *The shields he will burn with fire*. You aspired to be powerful in yourself, but God has made you weak in order to make you strong with his strength, for your own was nothing but weakness.

Verse 11. Be still and see

14. What comes next? *Be still*.[27] To what purpose? *And see that I am God*. "See that you are not God, but I am. I created you, and I recreate you; I formed you, and I form you anew; I made you, and I remake you. If you had no power to make yourself, how do you propose to re-make yourself?" But the contentious uproar in the human mind is oblivious, so to this uproar the command is given, "*Be still*: clear your minds of their disputatious noise. Do not argue with God, as though to take up arms against him; if you try that, those weapons which are not

25. *Te suscipit*.
26. *Susceptor*.
27. *Vacate*. An important concept. At the material level it signifies that a thing, place, building, etc., is vacant, unoccupied, idle or uncultivated. Of persons, it can suggest idleness, but more significantly "being free for" some higher activity, a purposeful disengagement for something more worthwhile, a fruitful leisure. In the present context the notion of "empty-handed," "unarmed," is obviously still part of the meaning, but tradition has rightly fastened on this verse as implying an invitation to contemplation: "Let go" or "be still" and "know that I am God." This sense is already implicit in Augustine's remarks immediately following.

yet burnt will be in action again. But if they have been truly burnt, *be still*, because you no longer have anything to fight with. If you are still and empty within yourselves, you who formerly presumed on yourselves may entreat me for all you need. *Be still*, and you will see *that I am God*."

Christ's triumph among both Gentiles and Jews

15. *I will be exalted among the Gentiles, and exalted on earth*. A little while ago I pointed out that the word "earth" signified the Jewish people, and "sea" the Gentiles. The mountains were shifted out into deep sea, the nations were disturbed and kingdoms bent low, the Most High sent forth his voice and the earth quaked. *The Lord of hosts is with us, our supporter is the God of Jacob*. Miracles were worked among the nations, the Gentiles' faith grew to full stature, and now the arms of human presumption are going up in flames. There is leisure and tranquillity of heart that permit us to recognize God as the author of all his gifts. But now that he is so glorified, will he abandon the Jewish people? Of that race the apostle said, *This I must say to you, to save you from conceit about your wisdom, that blindness has fallen upon part of Israel, until the full tally of the Gentiles comes in* (Rom 11:25). Until, that is, the mountains have passed over to us, and the clouds have sent rain here, and the Lord has humbled our kingdoms by his thunder—*until the full tally of the Gentiles comes in*. And then what? *So that all Israel may be saved* (Rom 11:26). This is why the psalm in its last verse preserves the same order: *I will be exalted among the Gentiles*, it says, *and exalted on earth*. In the sea, and then on the land. Thus may all of us together sing the refrain, *The Lord of hosts is with us, our supporter is the God of Jacob*.

Exposition of Psalm 46

A Sermon to the People

One truth, varied expressions

1. Through the holy books that make up his scriptures, the Lord our God has poured out for us the faith in which we live, and on which we live; and he has done so in a great variety of different modes. He constantly varies the words he uses, and these words are laden with mystery;[1] but he commends to us one same faith through them all. The same thing is expressed in many different ways so that the mode of expression may always seem fresh and never bore us, but the underlying truth be held firmly and maintain our hearts in unity. Keep this fact in mind as we come to consider the psalm we have just heard sung, and to which we have sung our response, because although we shall be telling you what you already know, with the Lord's help and his kindly gift it is possible that we may bring you some special sweetness, as you ruminate on things you have heard already here or there, but now think about once more as we remind you. When God laid down regulations about animals that chew the cud being classed as clean,[2] he meant to teach us by this reference to rumination that each of us should consign what we hear to our hearts, and not be slow to mull over it afterwards. When we listen, we are like the clean animal eating, and when later we call to mind what we heard, and turn it over in our thoughts to extract the utmost savor from it, we are like the animal ruminating. This is why the same truths are spoken in different ways, giving us the opportunity to find delicious new flavors in what we already know, and enticing us to listen to them again with delight; for when the idiom is diversified, the ancient truth seems ever new as it is presented differently.

Verse 1. The children of Korah

2. The title of the psalm is *Unto the end, for the children of Korah. A psalm for David himself.* Quite a few other psalms have this title which refers to the children of Korah.[3] They point to a sweet mystery, hinting at a holy meaning hidden under a sign.[4] All the more reason for us to open our minds to understand it, and

1. *Sacramenta verborum*: for Augustine, words were essentially signs, and hence "sacramental."
2. See Lv 11:2-7; Dt 14:4-8.
3. See note at Exposition of Psalm 41, 2.
4. *Insinuant magnum sacramentum.*

to recognize in the title nothing other than ourselves, who are listening and reading, and may use the title like a mirror presented to us so that we can look into it and discover who we are.

Now who are the children of Korah? Korah certainly was someone's proper name; undoubtedly there was a real person who bore it.[5] But when these scriptures are read, we find the divine word speaking to people who cannot readily be understood to be the descendants of that individual named Korah; and so our minds come back to the mystery, wondering what the name "Korah" signifies. It is a Hebrew word, one which is in ordinary use and can be translated into Greek and Latin. And this has been done; many Hebrew names have been interpreted for us, and when we investigate the meaning of this one we find that "Korah" is equivalent to "bald;"[6] Ah, that alerted you, didn't it? It was obscure enough when the "children of Korah" were mentioned, but is it not more obscure still when they are called "children of the bald man"? Who are these children of the bald man? Could they perhaps be the children of the Bridegroom? Yes, that's it, because the Bridegroom was crucified at a place called "Calvary." Recall the passage in the gospel about the Lord's crucifixion, and you will find that Calvary is the place. What is more, the people who mock his cross are devoured by demons, as though by wild beasts, and that is what another scriptural passage foreshadowed. God's prophet Elisha was climbing a hill when teasing boys shouted after him, *Up you go, baldy! Up you go, baldy!* (2 Kgs 2:23). Elisha summoned bears to come out and catch them, so the boys were devoured; but his action was not so much cruel as mysteriously prophetic. If those boys had not been eaten up, would they still be alive today? Of course not. Were they not born mortal, and could they not just as easily have been carried off by a fever? But if they had been, the mysterious warning that was to terrify later generations would not have been displayed in them. In the light of this, no one should presume to mock at the Lord's cross. The Jews were demon-possessed, and they were similarly devoured, for when they crucified Christ at the "bald place," and lifted him high on the cross, they were as good as saying with their childish, uncomprehending minds, *Up you go, baldy!* What else does *Crucify! Crucify!* mean,[7] but *Up you go*? The state of childhood is put before us both as an example of humility we must imitate, and as a foolish attitude we must avoid. The Lord proposed childlikeness to us as humility to be practiced when he called children to him, and then, when people tried to hold them back, said, *Let them come to me; the kingdom of heaven belongs to such as these* (Mt 19:14).[8] But a childish cast of mind was held up by the apostle as something silly to be shunned: *Do not be childish in your outlook, brethren.* Yet even he puts it before them as a good

5. See Nm 16:1.
6. *Calvum.*
7. See Lk 23:21.
8. See Mt 18:2-4.

example, under another aspect: *Be babes in your innocence of evil, so as to be mature in mind* (1 Cor 14:20).

Now our psalm is sung *for the children of Korah*, and therefore is sung for Christians. So let us listen to it as children of the Bridegroom, that Bridegroom whom childish lunatics crucified at a place called Calvary. They deserved to be savaged by beasts, but we to be crowned by angels, for we acknowledge the Lord in his degradation and are not ashamed of it. We are not embarrassed to belong to one who in a mystical sense is called "the bald man" because of his association with Calvary, for by that very cross on which he was the butt of insults he has not left our brows bald and shamefully exposed; instead he has signed them with his cross.

Well now, it is time for you to see for yourselves that the verses which follow are addressed to us; so let us see what they say.

Verse 2. The joy of the Gentiles

3. *All nations, clap your hands.* Does "all nations" mean Israel only? No indeed. Blindness fell upon part of Israel, so that stupid children shouted, *Baldy! Baldy!* But the Lord was crucified on that bald place, Calvary, in order to redeem the Gentiles by his outpoured blood, and thus the apostle's prophecy was fulfilled: *Blindness fell upon part of Israel, until the full tally of the Gentiles should come in* (Rom 11:25). Let those empty-headed, doltish, crazy folk fling their insults; let them shout, *Baldy! Baldy!* if they want to. But you, all you nations redeemed by the blood he shed on Calvary, *all nations, clap your hands*, because God's grace has come to you. *Clap your hands*: what does *clap* suggest? Rejoice. Yes, but why with *your hands*? Because you must express your joy in good actions. You must not make merry with your voices and leave your hands idle. If you are happy, *clap your hands*. Let him who has graciously granted you such joy see the hands of the Gentiles at work. And what do I mean by "the hands of the Gentiles"? I mean the deeds of those who work in a way that pleases him. *All nations, clap your hands, raise a shout of joy to God with exultant voices*. So you must use both voice and hands. It is not a good thing to employ your voice alone, because then your hands are lazy, but neither is it good to use only your hands, because then your tongue is dumb. Hands and tongue should be in harmony: the tongue confessing, the hands at work. *Raise a shout of joy to God with exultant voices.*

Verse 3. King of the Jews, and of all the earth

4. *For the Lord is most high, and terrible*. He is most high because, though in his descent he seemed ridiculous, by ascending to heaven he has shown himself terrible, *a great king over all the earth*. Not only over the Jews, then, though he is indeed their king; for the apostles believed, and they were of the Jewish race, and many thousands of their fellow-Jews sold their property and laid the proceeds at

the apostles' feet.[9] So in them was verified the prophecy written as a title over the cross: *King of the Jews* (Mt 27:37; Mk 15:26; Lk 23:38; Jn 19:19). King of the Jews, certainly, but that is too little to say of him. *All nations, clap your hands, for God is king over all the earth.*[10] It would not be enough to assign him one lone nation as his subjects; he paid so heavy a price from his pierced side because he meant to buy the whole world. He is *a great king over all the earth.*

Verse 4. Worldwide sovereignty?

5. *He has subjected peoples to us, put nations under our feet.* What nations, and to whom were they subjected? Who are the speakers here? The Jews, perhaps? Well, yes, if we take it to be the apostles and saints, for God did indeed so subject peoples and nations to them that they who earned death at the hands of their fellow-Jews are today honored among the Gentiles. Just so was their Lord killed by his compatriots, but honored now among the Gentiles, crucified by his own race but worshiped now among foreigners, those foreigners he made his own at such a price.[11] This was his purpose in buying us: to ensure that we should not be aliens to him. Do you think, then, that it is the apostles' words we are hearing in this verse, *he has subjected peoples to us, put nations under our feet*? I don't know. It would be strange if the apostles were to speak so proudly, rejoicing that Gentiles had been subdued under their feet, in the sense that Christians are subordinate to the apostles. Much more likely is it that they rejoice to be themselves subjected along with us under the feet of the one who died for us. There were some Christians once who were running after Paul and trying to get under his feet, wanting to belong to Paul, but he rebuked them: *Was Paul crucified for you?* (1 Cor 1:13).

What are we to understand here, then? How are we to take it? *He has subjected peoples to us, put nations under our feet.* Here is a suggestion: those who form part of Christ's inheritance are found among all nations, but equally those who do not belong to Christ's inheritance are found among all nations. Yet you see Christ's Church so highly respected in his name that all those who do not yet believe lie under the feet of Christians. What crowds of people, not yet Christians themselves, come running to the Church and begging the Church to help them! They want temporal assistance from us, even if they are still unwilling to reign eternally with us. Since everyone wants help from the Church, including those who are not yet its members, can it not be truly said that *he has subjected peoples to us, put nations under our feet*?

9. See Acts 4:34-35.
10. See verse 8 below.
11. Variants specify "at the price of his blood."

Verse 5. Jacob and Esau

6. *He has chosen his inheritance for us, the beauty of Jacob that he loved.* It is a certain beauty of Jacob, his own inheritance, that he has chosen to be ours. Esau and Jacob were twin brothers. They wrestled with each other in their mother's womb, causing her grave internal upheaval. Even while the two of them were in the womb, the younger was chosen and given ascendancy over the elder, for even as early as that the promise was made, *There are two peoples in your womb, and the elder shall serve the younger* (Gn 25:23). The elder is found among all nations today, and so is the younger. The younger is represented by good Christians, the elect, the devout, the believers; and the elder by the proud, the arrogant, sinners, the obstinate, and those who defend their sins instead of confessing them. These latter are like the Jews, who took no account of God's righteousness and tried to set up their own instead.[12] But the promise was made, *the elder shall serve the younger* and, sure enough, it is undeniable that the godless are subject to the godly, the proud to the humble. Esau was born first, and Jacob second, but the later-born was preferred to the first-born, because the elder bartered away his birthright through gluttony. Scripture tells us the story: Esau hungered for the lentil stew, and his brother bargained with him: "If you want me to give you some, give me your birthright."[13] Esau valued the food he carnally desired above the privilege he had spiritually deserved by his seniority at birth, so he gave up the rights of the first-born in order to eat lentil stew. Now we find that lentils are typically the food of the Egyptians, because they grow plentifully in Egypt. That is why Alexandrian lentils have a high reputation, and are imported into our own country—as though we could not grow them here. This suggests that it was by coveting Egyptian food that Esau lost the rights of the first-born, and in this respect he was like the Jewish people, of whom it was said, *In their hearts they turned back to Egypt* (Acts 7:39), for they too in a sense have hungered for lentils and thereby lost their birthright. *He has chosen his inheritance for us, the beauty of Jacob that he loved.*[14]

---

12. See Rom 10:3.
13. See Gn 25:30-34.
14. Augustine's treatment of the Jacob-Esau story in this paragraph has reversed the meaning attached to it by Old Testament compilers and Jewish tradition. For them, Esau represented the other nations, typically Edom, of whom he was thought to be the progenitor; and Jacob stood for Israel, the chosen one, God's inheritance. For Augustine, Esau is the Jews, and Jacob the Gentiles chosen in the Jews' stead. Another part of the background here is the traditional view of Egypt as the home *par excellence* of idolatry, partly because of the highly developed system of worship in ancient Egypt, and partly because of Egypt's special role in the early history of the chosen people. Thus the desire to "return to Egypt" of which they are accused symbolizes a denial of the covenant and the special relationship with God to which it committed them.

Verse 6. Joy at Christ's ascension

7. *God went up amid shouts of joy*. Our Lord Christ, he who is indeed our God, *went up amid shouts of joy, the Lord at the sound of a trumpet*. When it says, *Went up*, where was he going? We know very well. He went to a place where the Jews did not follow him,[15] even with their eyes, for they had mocked him when he was raised up on the cross, but could not see him as he was lifted up to heaven. *God went up amid shouts of joy*. What does it mean, to shout with joy? It means to give voice to a wondering happiness that cannot be adequately expressed in words. It was with wonder and happiness like this that the disciples were filled as they watched the Master they had mourned as dead now going up to heaven; no words could do justice to such joy, so all they could do was shout wordlessly about a happiness beyond telling. And there was a trumpet-call there too: the voice of the angels, which can rightly be compared to a trumpet, for scripture says, *Raise your voice like a trumpet* (Is 58:1). The angels proclaimed the Lord's ascension, but they also had an eye to the disciples who, as the Lord ascended, lingered there amazed and marveling, saying nothing but shouting with joy in their hearts. Then the clear voices of the angels rang out like trumpets: *Why stand here, men of Galilee? This is Jesus* (Acts 1:11). As though they did not know it was Jesus! Had they not seen him in their company so short a time before? Had they not heard him talking to them? And more: besides seeing him visibly present, they had even handled his limbs.[16] Were they likely to be in any doubt that this was Jesus? But the angels were talking to men almost out of their minds with wonder and shouting with joy, so they said, "This is Jesus," as if to say, "If you believe in him, this is the one at whose crucifixion you tottered, at whose murder and burial you thought you had lost your hope. This is the same Jesus. He is ascending before your eyes, but *he will come again, even as you have seen him go to heaven* (Acts 1:11). His body is taken from your sight, but God is not distanced from your hearts. Watch him ascend; believe in him while he is away; hope for his return; but all the time be aware that he is present with you through his hidden mercy. He who has ascended into heaven to remove himself from your sight has made you this promise: *Lo, I am with you even to the end of the ages*" (Mt 28:20). With good reason did the apostle encourage us by saying, *The Lord is very near, have no anxiety* (Phil 4:5-6). Christ is enthroned above the heavens, and the heavens are a long way away, yet he who is seated there is near to us. *The Lord has gone up at the sound of a trumpet*. If you have understood, you children of Korah, you can see yourself in this, and you too can rejoice, seeing that this is your story as well.

15. See Jn 8:21.
16. See Lk 24:39.

Verse 7. Christ is God from eternity

8. *Sing psalms to him as our God, sing him psalms.* Those who were estranged from God jeered at Christ in his manhood, but you *sing psalms to him as our God*, for he is not only man; he is God. He is man from the seed of David,[17] but as God he is David's Lord. He took flesh from the Jews, *to whom belong the patriarchs, and from whom Christ was born according to the flesh*, as the apostle reminds us (Rom 9:5). So Christ is truly sprung from the Jews, but only according to the flesh; for who is this Christ, who took fleshly nature from the Jews? *He is sovereign over all, God, blessed for ever* (Rom 9:5). He was God before being made flesh, God in the flesh, God with flesh. Not only was he God before he took flesh: he was God before the earth, from which flesh was made, and not only God before the earth whence flesh was made, but God before the sky which was made earlier, and God before the first day was created, and God before all the angels came to be. Christ is God, because *in the beginning was the Word, and the Word was with God; he was God. Everything was made through him; no part of created being was made without him* (Jn 1:1-3). He through whom all things were made exists before all things. *Sing psalms to him as our God*, then, *sing him psalms.*[18]

Verse 8. The universal God

9. *For God is king over all the earth.* Does this mean that he is God of all the earth only now, and not formerly? Is he not God of heaven and earth, since there is no doubt that all things were made through him? Has anyone the right to say, "He is not my God"? No, but not all humankind recognized him as their God, so it could in a way be said that he was only God where he was acknowledged. God was made known only in Judah,[19] and not yet was the command given to the children of Korah, *all nations, clap your hands*. Yet the God who was made known in Judah was the God who is king of the whole earth; and now he is acknowledged by all peoples, because Isaiah's prophecy has been fulfilled: *Your God, who has delivered you, will be called the God of the whole earth* (Is 54:5). *For God is king over all the earth; sing psalms to him with understanding.*[20] He is teaching us, warning us that we must sing psalms with our minds tuned to understanding, not just making a sound to please the ear, but seeking light for our hearts. *Sing psalms with understanding*, we are told. You were called from Gentile races to be Christians, and those Gentile pagans used to worship gods made by human hands, and sing psalms to them, but not with understanding. If

17. See Rom 1:3.
18. Augustine omits the last words of this verse.
19. See Ps 75(76):1.
20. *Intellegenter*. A variant is *sapienter*, "wisely," "with discernment."

they had been singing with understanding, they would not have worshiped stones. When a human person endowed with reason sang to a stone devoid of reason, was that singing with understanding? It is different for us, brothers and sisters: we do not see with our eyes what we are worshiping, yet we have been put right in the matter of worship.[21] Not seeing God with our eyes, we have a far higher notion of him. If we did see him, we would perhaps make light of him. The Jews saw Christ, and made light of him, whereas the Gentiles who had not seen him worshiped him. To them was the exhortation addressed, *Sing psalms with understanding*; and, as another text admonishes us, *Do not be like a horse or a mule, devoid of understanding* (Ps 31(32):9).

Verse 9. The Lord's enthronement in the souls of the just

10. *The Lord will reign over all nations.*[22] He who was at that time reigning over one nation only *will reign over all nations*, the psalm promised. When these words were spoken, God was reigning only over the one nation, so this was a prophecy, and the reality had not yet been manifested. May God be thanked, that we today see the fulfillment of what was prophesied long ago. Before the time was ripe, God wrote a bond for us, and now that the time has come, he has paid. The words, *God will reign over all nations*, were prophetic.

God sits upon his holy throne. What is this holy throne? The heavens perhaps? That would be a good way to understand it. Christ has ascended, as we know, in the same body in which he was crucified, and is enthroned at the Father's right hand; we await his coming from there to judge the living and the dead.[23] *He sits upon his holy throne*. So the heavens are his holy throne? Yes, but do you want to be his throne too? Do not think such a thing beyond you; if you prepare a place for him in your heart, he comes and is pleased to set his throne there. We know for certain that Christ is the power of God, and the wisdom of God;[24] and what does scripture say of Wisdom? The soul of a righteous person is the throne of Wisdom.[25] So then, if the soul of a righteous person is Wisdom's throne, make sure your soul is righteous, and it will be a regal chair for Wisdom. I would go further, brothers and sisters: surely God is enthroned in all those who lead good lives, perform good works, and treat others with reverent charity, and surely God rules them? The soul obeys God who is seated within it, and the soul in turn commands its bodily members. Your soul sends orders to the appropriate member of your body, telling the foot to move, or the hand, eye, or ear to perform

21. *Tamen correcti adoramus*. A variant has *corde recti*, "we worship as people who are right of heart."
22. A variant adds "for ever."
23. See 2 Tm 4:1.
24. See 1 Cor 1:24.
25. See Wis 7:27-28.

its function. The soul treats these members as its servants, but the soul itself is the servant of its Lord who is enthroned within it. It cannot rule its subordinates well, unless it consents to obey its own superior. *God sits upon his holy throne*.

Verse 10. Abraham's progeny

11. *The princes of the peoples have rallied to the God of Abraham*. The God of Abraham and the God of Isaac and the God of Jacob: this is the truth as God himself declared it;[26] and the Jews made it a matter for boasting: *We are Abraham's descendants* (Jn 8:33). They took pride in their father's name and wore his flesh, but they did not hold fast to his faith. They were his close relatives by carnal descent, but degenerate in their conduct. Notice what the Lord said to these arrogant people: *If you are Abraham's children, act as Abraham did* (Jn 8:39). John the Baptist spoke in a similar way to certain Jews who came to him quivering with fear and anxious to straighten themselves out by repentance. *Brood of vipers*, he called them. They were wicked, abandoned characters, they were sinners, they were impious, but they came to John for baptism, and what did he have to say to them? *You brood of vipers!* They called themselves descendants of Abraham, and he called them a brood of vipers. How was that? Abraham was not a viper, was he? But by their evil lives they had become children of the demons they were imitating, and so John challenged them: *You brood of vipers, who has taught you to flee from the wrath that is coming? Bring forth the fruit that befits repentance, and do not say to yourselves, We have Abraham for our father*. Then, as though realizing that they might still make their pedigree a matter for pride, he went on, "*For God is able to raise up children to Abraham even from these stones* (Mt 3:7-9). Abraham will not be left childless if God damns you, for he is quite capable of damning those he hates and still giving to Abraham the offspring he promised." But from where will he raise the children he must restore to Abraham, if he condemns the Hebrews who sprang from Abraham's flesh? *From these stones*. John pointed to the stones there in the desert. But who were "stones," if not the Gentiles, who were accustomed to worship stones? But did that make them stony themselves? Truly it did; they could be called stones for adoring stones, as a psalm had foretold: *May those who fashion them become like them, and all who put their trust in them* (Ps 113B(115):8). And yet it was from those same stones that God restored posterity to Abraham, for now all of us, who used to be stone-worshipers, have turned to God and become Abraham's children, not by claiming carnal descent from him but by imitating his faith. This is how *the princes of the peoples have rallied to the God of Abraham*. Observe that the psalm says, *The princes of the peoples*;

26. See Ex 3:6.

not the princes of one people only, but those of all peoples *have rallied to the God of Abraham.*

The centurion

12. One of these princes was the centurion you heard about just now when the gospel was read. This centurion was a man who enjoyed reputation and a powerful position among his fellows; he was a prince from the princes of the peoples. He sent his friends along when Christ was coming his way—or, more accurately, he sent his friends to intercept Christ who would otherwise have passed by—and asked that Christ would heal his servant, who was dangerously ill. But when the Lord indicated his willingness to come, the centurion sent him this message: *I am unworthy to have you entering my house; but just say the word, and my servant will be healed. For I am myself a man under authority, and I have soldiers under me*. Notice how he suggested a chain of command.[27] First he mentioned that he was subject to someone else, and then that others were subordinate to him. "I am under authority, and I am in authority; I am under someone, and I have others under me. *I say to this one, Go, and he goes, to another, Come, and he comes; and to a servant, Do this, and he does it*." This is a way of saying, "If I, who am under the power of others, give orders to those who are under me, can't you, who are under no one's power, give orders to your creation, when all things were made through you, and without you nothing was made? *Just say the word*, then, *and my servant will be healed*, for to receive you into my house is an honor I do not deserve." He trembled at the thought of bringing Christ within his four walls, yet Christ was already in his heart. The centurion's heart was already Christ's throne, for he who was seeking out the humble had already taken his seat there. On hearing these words, Christ *marveled, and he turned to his followers and said, I tell you truly, I have not found such great faith in Israel* (Lk 7:6-9). Another evangelist who tells the same story adds something else that the Lord said: *In truth I tell you, many will come from east and west and will sit down with Abraham and Isaac and Jacob in the kingdom of heaven* (Mt 8:11). Now this centurion was not from the race of Israel. Among the Israelites proud people thrust God away from them, but among the princes of the Gentiles there was this humble man who invited God to come to him. Jesus' admiration of his faith was a rebuke to the faithlessness of the Jews. They considered themselves healthy, but they were dangerously sick when they killed the physician they could not recognize. Christ denounced and reprobated their pride, and how did he make this clear? *In truth I tell you,* he said, *many will come from east and west*, people who are no kin of Israel. Those crowds will come, to whom the psalm says, *All nations, clap your hands*. And

27. Or "kept his rank."

they *will sit down with Abraham in the kingdom of heaven.* Abraham did not engender them from his body, yet they will come and sit down with him in the kingdom of heaven, and they will be his children. By what right? Not by being born from his flesh, but by following his example of faith. *But the children of the kingdom*—the Jews, that is—*will be thrown into the outer darkness, where there will be weeping and gnashing of teeth* (Mt 8:12). Those who were born of Abraham's flesh will be condemned to the darkness outside, while those who have imitated Abraham's faith will dine with him in the kingdom of heaven. Here too, certainly, *the princes of the peoples have rallied to the God of Abraham.*

The high and mighty

13. And what is to become of those who belonged by right to the God of Abraham? The psalm goes on to say, *The mighty gods of the earth were highly exalted.* The people of God, that vine of God's cultivating of which he said through a prophet, *Give judgment between me and my vineyard* (Is 5:3), these are the "gods" who are to go into the outer darkness, forbidden to sit down with Abraham and Isaac and Jacob. They do not join the throng that resorts to the God of Abraham. Why not? Because they are *the mighty gods of the earth.* Being mighty gods of the earth, they put their reliance on the earth, and what earth was that? On themselves, for every man and woman is but earth, as a man was once reminded: *Earth you are, and back to earth you shall go* (Gn 3:19). Every human being must rely on God, and hope for help from God, not self. The earth does not send itself rain or sunlight; and just as the earth awaits rain and sunlight from the sky, human beings must await mercy and truth from God. But the Jews, *mighty gods of the earth, were highly exalted*; that is, exceedingly proud. They did not think they needed a doctor, and therefore they remained in their diseased state, and that disease brought them to death. The natural branches were lopped off, so that the humble wild olive might be grafted in,[28] *because the mighty gods of the earth were highly exalted.* Let us, then, hold firmly to humility, charity and piety, my brothers and sisters, for while they have been rejected we have been called; so let us learn a lesson even from their example, and beware of being proud.[29]

28. See Rom 11:17.
29. The last lines of Augustine's Exposition of Psalm 45 give another view of the New Testament's teaching on the destiny of the Jews.

Exposition of Psalm 47

A Sermon to the People

Verse 1. The second day of creation: the Church

1. The title of this psalm is *A song of praise for the children of Korah, on the second day of the week.* Now on the second day of the week of creation, the day after the one we call Sunday or the Lord's day, the firmament was made.[1] As I will go on to explain, we are children of the firmament, so try to take in what the Lord graciously gives us to understand about it. This day is called the second feria, and the firmament was called "sky," for that was the name the Lord assigned to it. On the first day he had created light, and separated it from darkness; he had called the light "day," and the darkness "night." But as the full text of this psalm will show, when God spoke so at the beginning of his creative work, he foreshadowed something that was to be fulfilled in us, and the ages have run their course toward this fulfillment that was inherent in creation from the first. It was with excellent reason that the Lord said of Moses, *He wrote about me.*[2] Everything that was written, even about God's first creation, can be interpreted as a sign of things to come. So you can say that God created light when Christ rose from the dead, for then light was truly divided from darkness, when immortality was marked off from mortality.[3] What was his next task? To provide the Head with a body, the Church.

Moreover, there is a psalm assigned to the first day of the week, in which Christ's resurrection is unambiguously proclaimed: *Away with your gates, you princes!*[4] *But you, everlasting gates, lift yourselves up, and the King of glory will enter* (Ps 23(24):7.9), for it is abundantly clear that Christ is the king of glory. Scripture says of his killers, *If they had known him, they would never have cruci-*

---

1. See Gn 1:6-8.
2. Jn 5:46. Moses was regarded as the author of the Pentateuch.
3. Augustine's insights throughout this paragraph are deeply attuned to the whole movement of salvation history as presented in the scriptures. Even within the Old Testament the story of creation is not told for its own sake, but to form a backdrop to the exodus and the creation of a chosen people: creation is like Act I of salvation. This is all the more true in the perspective of the New Testament. Creation is a prelude to the new creation in Christ; and the light of God's first day points toward the dawn of Easter, and the ultimate day of that city that needs no sun or moon, being lit by the glory of God and the Lamb (see Rv 21:23).
4. Here and in his Exposition of Psalm 23 Augustine read *principes vestri*, which makes little sense. Variants include *principis vestri* ("lift up the gates of your prince") and from the CCL editors, *principes vestras.*

fied the Lord of glory (1 Cor 2:8). Obviously, then, we must understand the work of the second day to be the Church of Christ, but the Church of Christ as it exists in the saints, the Church of Christ in those whose names are written in heaven, the Church of Christ in those who do not give way under the temptations of this world. These are the people who are worthy to be named "the firmament." The Church of Christ is to be found in those who stand firm, of whom the apostle says, *We who have firm footing must bear with the weaknesses of the infirm* (Rom 15:1), and hence the Church is called the firmament.

This is the subject of our psalm. Let us listen, and recognize the Church here, and unite ourselves with its fellowship, and be proud of it, and accept our kingdom. It is also called a firmament in the apostolic letters; listen, and remember what is said: *God's house is the Church of the living God, the pillar and firmament of truth* (1 Tm 3:15). The psalm sings about this firmament to the children of Korah who, as you know, are the children of the Bridegroom who was crucified at a place called Calvary, for Korah translates as "baldness."[5] Now for the rest of this psalm which is entitled, *On the second day of the week*.

Verse 2. The city and the mountain

2. *Great is the Lord, and exceedingly worthy of praise*. Yes, the Lord is great, and *exceedingly worthy of praise*, but do unbelievers praise the Lord? And what about those who do believe, but lead bad lives—do they praise the Lord? Do they not rather cause the name of God to be profaned among the pagans?[6] Do they praise the Lord? No; or, at any rate, if they do, is the praise they offer acceptable, when scripture warns us, *Praise is not seemly in a sinner's mouth* (Sir 15:9)? You have told us, psalmist, that *great is the Lord, and exceedingly to be praised*, but where is this observed? *In the city of our God, on his holy mountain*. This mountain is mentioned elsewhere, when another psalm asks, *Who will climb the mountain of the Lord? One with clean hands and a pure heart* (Ps 23(24):3-4). For such people the Lord is indeed *great, and exceedingly worthy of praise*, but *in the city of our God, on his holy mountain*. This is the city set on a mountain that cannot be hidden, the lantern that is not concealed under a meal-tub but known to all and universally renowned.[7] Not everyone is a citizen of it, but only those for whom the Lord is *great and exceedingly worthy of praise*.

Let us see what this city is, because if we are unsure, we may think on hearing the words, *in the city of our God, on his holy mountain*, that we need to go in search of this mountain in order to find a hearing there. After all, another psalm was quite right to say, *With my voice I have cried to the Lord, and he heard me*

5. *Calvitium*.
6. See Rom 2:24.
7. See Mt 5:14-15.

from his holy mountain (Ps 3:5(4)). So it was that mountain that helped you, and won you a hearing; for if you had not climbed it, you might well have cried out from your prone position below, but you could not have made yourself heard. What is this mountain, brothers and sisters? We ought to seek it with the utmost zeal, explore it very diligently indeed, and spare no effort to move in and climb it. But what if it is in some other country; what are we to do then? Shall we leave home and journey into a foreign land to reach the mountain? It would be truer to say that if we are not there on the mountain we are even now exiles in a foreign land, for that city is our own homeland, if we are members of the King who is the Head of the city. Where is the mountain, then? If it is located in some particular spot, we shall have a lot of trouble getting there, as I have said. But why make busy preparations? I would have you as prompt to climb the mountain as the mountain itself was eager to come to you while you were still asleep; for there was a cornerstone that seemed of little importance, and the Jews fell over it.[8] It was hewn out of the mountain-side without hands; that is to say, it came from the Jewish realm without human hands, for it came by no human agency to Mary, from whom Christ was born. But if the stone that tripped up the Jews had remained there, you would not have been in a position to climb it. But what happened? What does Daniel's prophecy say? That little stone grew, and became a lofty mountain. How big did it grow? Big enough to cover the whole surface of the earth.[9] And this meant that by growing and filling the entire world it came even to us. Why should we go looking for the mountain, as though it were far away? It is here with us, and our business is to climb it, so that among us the Lord may be *great, and exceedingly worthy of praise*.

Verse 3. The "companions of the north" join with Zion

3. Still, there could have been some risk of your not recognizing the mountain in this psalm, and thinking that you needed to look for it in some other part of the world. The next verse excludes misunderstanding, for after saying, *In the city of our God, on his holy mountain*, the psalmist adds, *He increases the gladness of all the earth, the mountains of Zion*. But Zion is only one mountain, so why does it say, *Mountains*? Perhaps because Zion embraces peoples coming from different quarters to meet each other and be joined to the cornerstone, and these two walls are like two mountains, one from the circumcised, the other from the uncircumcised, one from the Jews, the other from the Gentiles. They are no longer adverse even though diverse in origin; and once fitted into the corner they are diverse no longer. *He himself is our peace, since he united the two*, says scripture (Eph 2:14). Christ is the cornerstone *rejected by the builders*, which

8. See Rom 9:32.
9. See Dn 2:34-35.

has *become the headstone of the corner* (Ps 117(118):22). Christ is the mountain who joined two mountains in himself. There is one house, and two houses; two in that they came from different quarters, but one because of the cornerstone in which they are joined. This same truth is reiterated; listen: *the mountains of Zion and the companions*[10] *of the north, the city of the great king*. You were accustomed to think of Zion as a single place, where Jerusalem was founded, and you thought to meet there one people only, that of the circumcision; for the remnant of Israel was gathered up by Christ, although that people had been for the most part winnowed away like straw. That was prophesied: *A remnant shall be saved* (Rom 9:27).[11] But consider the Gentiles, watch the wild olive being grafted into the succulent olive.[12] That means the Gentiles, who here are called *companions of the north*. These companions of the north are built into the city of the great king. Ordinarily the north would be in the opposite direction to Zion, which lies toward the south. Who is "the north" then? Surely the one who said, *I will set my throne in the north, I shall be like the Most High* (Is 14:13-14). The devil had held sway over the godless, and made idol-worshiping Gentiles his possession, for it was truly to demons that they were paying homage. Thus it had come about that the entire human race, wherever any part of it was to be found throughout the world, had by close association with the devil become "the north." But Christ binds the strong one, takes away his weapons,[13] and commandeers them for his own purposes. The peoples set free from unbelief and demonic superstition, now believers in Christ, have been aligned with the city. They have come to meet the wall that juts out from the circumcised, and have joined it at the corner; accordingly those who were once companions of the north have become part of the city of the great king. This is why in another passage it is said, *From the north come golden clouds, and in them is great glory and praise for the Almighty* (Jb 37:22, LXX); for it redounds to a doctor's credit when a desperately sick person recovers. From the north come not black clouds, not murky or dark clouds, but clouds tinged with gold. How can that be? Surely because of the illuminating grace they receive through Christ.

Look at the result. *The companions of the north* are built into *the city of the great king*. Companions[14] they certainly were, since they stuck fast to the devil, for those who stick by anyone are rightly said to be "at his side." Our own ordinary speech has the same idiom. We say, "He is a good man, but has bad fellows alongside him," meaning that he may himself be outstanding for honorable behavior, but his associates are of dishonorable intent. The companions of the north are those who stand by the devil and make common cause with him. From

10. *Latera*, literally "sides," hence "those at someone's side," associates, connections.
11. See Is 10:22.
12. See Rom 11:17.
13. See Mk 3:27; Mt 12:29.
14. *Latera*.

their ranks came a certain son who had died, but came to life again, had been lost, but was found, as we heard just now in the gospel.[15] He had set out for a distant country and traveled even as far as the north; and there, as you heard, he had thrown in his lot with one of the important people of the country. So he became a "companion of the north" by entering the employment of that powerful person; but because the city of the great king draws its members even from the associates of the north, he came to himself and said, "I will arise, and go to my father." And his father ran out to meet him, exulting that "my son was dead, and has come back to life; he was lost, but is found." The fatted calf represents the cornerstone. The elder son was at first reluctant to come and share the feast, but at his father's plea he did come in, and those two sons who feasted together on the calf were like the two walls that form the city of the great king.

Verse 4. Sheer grace

4. Let the psalm proceed now. *God will be acknowledged in her houses.* Because of the mountains, because of the two walls and the two sons, it can now speak of "houses." *God will be acknowledged in her houses.* But to emphasize that this is the effect of grace, it adds, *When he upholds*[16] *her*, for what would that city have been, if God had not upheld her? She would collapse immediately if she had no such foundation, wouldn't she? No one can lay any foundation other than that which is laid already, Christ Jesus.[17] That city is truly great, and the Lord is acknowledged in her, only when he upholds her. It is like the case where a doctor takes on[18] a patient because he needs healing, not because he is attractive as he is. Attractive he certainly is not, and the doctor hates the disease. We might say that in one sense the doctor does not love the sick person, but in another he does. If he simply loved him as sick, he would hope that the patient would remain permanently sick; but on the other hand, if he did not love him at all, he would not come near him. So he does love the sick person, but in such a way as to want him well.

In a similar way the Lord has upheld this city, and made himself known in her; he has been acknowledged within the city, but only by his own grace, because nothing that is possessed by this city that makes her boast in the Lord does she possess of herself. Scripture confirms it: *What have you that you did not receive? And if you did receive it, why boast as though you had not?* (1 Cor 4:7). *God will be acknowledged in her houses when he upholds her.*

15. See Lk 15:11-32.
16. *Suscipiet*; see note at Exposition of Psalm 45, 11.
17. See 1 Cor 3:11.
18. *Suscipit.*

Verses 5-7. The King and the kings

5. *Look, the kings of the earth have gathered.* Look at those companions of the north now! Look how they are flocking, and listen to them saying, *Come, let us go up to the mountain of the Lord, for he has made his way known to us, that we may walk in it* (Is 2:3; Mi 4:2). *Look, the kings of the earth have assembled and gathered as one.* One? Who would this one be? The cornerstone, undoubtedly. *They are filled with wonder at what they see.* After seeing and wondering at Christ's miracles and his glory, how do they react? *They are troubled and thrown off balance, and panic has seized them.* Why else would panic seize them, if not because they are conscious of their transgressions? Let the kings come running to the King, let the kings acknowledge the King. Another passage celebrates their submission: *I have been established by him as king over his holy mountain, preaching the Lord's decree. The Lord said to me, "You are my Son, today have I begotten you. Ask of me, and I will give you the nations as your heritage, and the ends of the earth for your possession. You will rule them with an iron rod, and you will dash them to pieces like a potter's vessel"* (Ps 2:6-9). The news had gone forth that he had been set up as King in Zion, and that the whole earth, to its furthest bounds, had been made over to him as his domain. Earthly kings have to take care they do not lose their kingdoms, as the wretched Herod feared to, and killed little boys in place of one little boy.[19] So afraid was he of losing his kingdom that he could not recognize the King. If only he could have gone with the magi to worship the King! If he had, he would not in his malevolent obsession with sovereignty have harmed the harmless, and by destroying them been himself destroyed.[20] Herod destroyed innocent children; but Christ crowned these little ones who died in his cause. Earthly kings were understandably afraid when the edict went forth, "I have been established by him as King, and he who established me will give me an inheritance that stretches to the ends of the earth." But why do you look askance, you kings? Look indeed, but do not look askance.[21] Very different from yourselves is he who said, *Mine is not a kingship of this world* (Jn 18:36). Do not be so frightened that your earthly kingdoms may be confiscated. A different kingdom will be given you, a kingdom in heaven, where he is King. This is why that other psalm continues, *And now, kings, understand.* You were ready to be jealous, but understand. The psalm is speaking of another King, whose kingship does not derive from this world. *The kings of the earth have gathered as one; they are troubled and panic has seized them,* so they needed to be admonished, *Now, you kings, understand; be instructed, all you who judge the earth. Serve the Lord in reverence, and rejoice*

19. See Mt 2:3-8,16-18.
20. A double pun: *Innocentes perderet, et nocens periret.*
21. *Videte, non invidete.*

before him with awe (Ps 2:10-11). And how did they respond? They endured *pangs like those of a woman in travail.* What can these *pangs of a woman in travail* be, except the pangs of a penitent? The same conception of pain and travail is mentioned in Isaiah: *Through fear of you we have conceived, and given birth to the spirit of salvation* (Is 26:18). From their fear of Christ the kings conceived, and when the time for parturition came they brought forth salvation by believing in the One whom they feared. They endured *pangs like those of a woman in travail.* When you hear of anyone on the point of giving birth, wait for the child. Our old self is in travail, but the new self is coming to birth, amid *pangs like those of a woman in travail.*

Verse 8. The destruction of the proud ships

6. *With a violent wind you will smash the ships of Tarshish.* This is easy to understand: "You will overturn the pride of the Gentiles." But how does the idea of the Gentiles' pride emerge from the story? What gives it away is the allusion to the *ships of Tarshish.* Scholars have done research on this, seeking to discover what city is meant by "Tarshish." Some have thought that Cilicia was "Tarshish," because its principal city is Tarsus. The apostle Paul hailed from there; he was born at Tarsus in Cilicia.[22] Other scholars have decided that Carthage is meant, either because it was once called Tarshish or because in some language it still is. In Isaiah we read, *Wail, you ships of Carthage* (Is 23:1, LXX). Ezekiel mentions a city[23] that is interpreted as Tarsus by some and as Carthage by others, and this divergence among commentators suggests that the city named Carthage was called Tarshish. It is well known that in the early days of Carthage's hegemony ships were very plentiful, so much so that they surpassed those of other peoples in trading and sea-voyages. This was said to have been due to Dido. When she fled from her brother she had taken over some merchant ships from her native region,[24] with the consent of local dignitaries. She came ashore in Africa, and founded Carthage. That was why, from its very foundation, Carthage never lacked ships. So proud did the city become of its reputation that its ships can well stand for Gentile pride, which relies on things as uncertain as the winds. But we should no longer put our trust in setting our sails, or in the favorable tide of worldly prosperity; our foundation must be in Zion. There we must find our stability, and not be tossed about by every gust of teaching.[25] Those whose sails are swollen with the uncertain fortunes of this life are liable to be capsized, and all the pride of the Gentiles must be subjected to Christ, who

22. See Acts 21:39.
23. See Ez 38:13, LXX.
24. According to legend, she was the daughter of the King of Tyre.
25. See Eph 4:14.

smashes the ships of Tarshish with a violent wind. Not those of any other city, but the ships of Tarshish. But why *with a violent wind*? It means with enormous fear, for all such pride has so trembled at the prospect of his future coming as judge that it has believed in him in his humility, and so has no need to be terrified of his majesty.

Verse 9. The Church contemplates prophecies fulfilled

7. *As we have heard, so too we have seen.* O blessed Church, at one time you heard, and at another time you saw. The Church heard the promises, and now sees the promises fulfilled; it heard in prophecy what it now sees made manifest in the gospel. Everything that is now being realized was prophesied beforehand. Lift up your eyes, let your gaze sweep round the world, look at the inheritance that stretches to the ends of the earth; see how the promise is being made good that *all the kings of the earth will worship him, and all nations will serve him* (Ps 71(72):11). See too how a psalmist's prayer is answered: *Be lifted up above the heavens, O God, and may your glory spread all over the earth* (Ps 107:6(108:5)). Contemplate him whose hands and feet were fixed with nails, whose bones were counted as they hung from the tree, whose clothes were diced for—contemplate him reigning, whom they saw hanging, contemplate him seated in heaven, whom they despised as he walked the earth. See too how in this the promise is fulfilled that *all the ends of the earth will be reminded and will turn to the Lord, and all the families of the nations will worship in his presence* (Ps 21:28(22:27)). And as you look on all these things, exclaim with joy, *As we have heard, so have we seen.* It is with good reason that when the Church is called from the Gentiles it receives the invitation, *Hearken, my daughter, and see; forget your own people and your father's house* (Ps 44:11(45:10)). Your father belonged to the north, but you for your part must come to Mount Zion. Hearken and see; do not think to see and then hearken, but hearken and see. Hearken first, and see later. At first you hearken to what you cannot see, and afterwards you will see what you heard about. The Lord declares, *A people I never knew has come to serve me, and as soon as they heard me they obeyed me* (Ps 17:45(18:44)). If it was as soon as they heard, that implies that they did not yet see.

But then what becomes of the prophecy, *Those who heard no tidings of him will see, and those who have never heard of him will understand* (Is 52:15)? There is no contradiction: it means that those to whom the prophets had not been sent were the very people who first heard and understood the prophets; though at first they did not hear, later they heard and marveled. The others, to whom the prophets had been sent, were left with the books in their hands but no understanding of the truth in their minds; they had the tablets of the testimony, but had lost hold of their inheritance.

But we, on the contrary, *as we have heard, so have we seen, in the city of the Lord of hosts, in the city of our God.* There we have heard, and there also we have seen. Anyone who is outside the city neither hears nor sees, but no one inside can be deaf or blind. *As we have heard, so too we have seen.* And where do you hear, where do you see? *In the city of the Lord of hosts, in the city of our God. God has founded it to last for ever.* Let not the heretics insult it as they shred away into sects, nor let those who claim, *Look, here is Christ!* or, *There he is!* (Mk 13:21) make themselves out to be important. Those who say, *Look, here is Christ! There he is!* are promoters of schisms. But God has promised us unity; the kings have gathered as one; they have not been scattered into schisms.

But can it be that this city, which has hold of all the world, will one day be destroyed? Absolutely not. *God has founded it to last for ever.* And if God has founded it to last for ever, why be afraid that its foundation will collapse?

Verse 10. A mixed crowd in the Church

8. *We have received your mercy, O God, in the midst of your people.*[26] Who have received it, and where? Is it not "your people" that has received your mercy, and, if so, how can we say that *we have received your mercy* and immediately add, *in the midst of your people*, as though those who have received it, and those in whose midst it was received, were two different groups?

This is a great mystery,[27] yet one familiar to you. When the truth you already know has been chiseled out from these verses, it will seem not so much awkward as comforting. All those who have received his sacraments are today considered to be God's people, but not all are included under his mercy. All who have received Christ's baptism are called Christians, but not all of them live in a way that befits the sacrament. There are some of whom the apostle says, *They have the appearance of religion, but deny its real virtue* (2 Tm 3:5). Yet because of their outward show of piety they are classed as members of God's people, just as chaff has its place with the grain on the threshing-floor as long as the threshing is in progress. But will the chaff have any place in the barn? Now amid this unworthy people is a good people which has received God's mercy. It lives in a way worthy of divine mercy, for it listens to the apostle's exhortation, and holds onto what it hears, and acts on it: *We order you, we beg you, not to receive God's grace to no purpose* (2 Cor 6:1). A person who does not allow the grace received to be ineffective is one who receives both the sacrament and the mercy of God. What harm does such a person incur by living amid a disobedient people until the time for winnowing, when the good will be sifted out from the wicked? What

26. Some codices have "in the midst of your temple." The Greek would entail a difference of only one letter. But the rest of the paragraph makes it evident that Augustine read "people."
27. *Magnum sacramentum.*

harm, to stay amid such people meanwhile? He or she must belong to those who deserve to be called the firmament[28] and continue to be open to God's mercy; he or she must be a lily amid thorns. Do you question whether thorns can belong to God's people? Listen, I will tell you. There is a comparison made in scripture: *Like a lily in the midst of thorns, so is my dearest one amid the daughters* (Sg 2:2). Now, did it say, "In the midst of foreign women"? No, it said, *Amid the daughters*. There are bad daughters, then, and amid them is the beloved, like *a lily in the midst of thorns*. In a similar sense people who receive the sacraments but do not live good lives can be said both to belong to God and not to belong to him; they are his and yet they are strangers. His, because of his sacrament, but strangers because of their vices. That is what the foreign daughters suggest: they are daughters inasmuch as they have the outward form of devoted love, but foreign because they have lost their virtue.[29] So let our Christian placed in these circumstances be like a lily, and receive the mercy of God, and hold onto the root that will produce a good flower, and not be ungrateful for the gentle rain that falls from heaven. The thorns may be ungrateful, but let them grow all the same under the showers, though they are growing for the fire, not the storage barn. *We have received your mercy, O God, in the midst of your people*. Amid a people who are closed to it, we have received your mercy, for though he came to his own, his own did not receive him. Nonetheless, in the midst were some who did receive him, and he empowered these to become children of God.[30]

How many will be saved?

9. Now any thinking person may wonder, "How can that be true? This people that receives God's mercy in the midst of God's people—what sort of numbers are we talking about? Very small indeed! In fact there are hardly any of them. And is God going to be content with those few, and damn the vast majority?" Those who talk in this vein are promising themselves something that they have not heard God promising. "Can you really believe it?" they persist. "Is God going to let us be lost if we live bad lives, and enjoy the pleasures this world has to offer, and pander to our lusts? After all, how many are there who appear to be keeping God's commandments? One or two, perhaps, a few at most. Is God going to save them alone, and damn all the rest? Not a bit of it," they say. "When he comes and sees what a huge crowd he has on his left, he will take pity on them and forgive them."

But remember that this was precisely what the serpent promised to our first parents. God had threatened them with death if they tasted the forbidden fruit,

---

28. See the first paragraph of this sermon.
29. Or "lost the essence of it," *propter amissionem virtutis*.
30. See Jn 1:11-12.

but the serpent assured them, "Not a bit of it, you will not die" (see Gn 3:4). They believed the serpent, and found out that God's threat was truthful, and the devil's promise false. Now, brothers and sisters, think of the Church as the realization of what was symbolized by the mystery of paradise. The serpent never tires of insinuating now what he insinuated then. But the fall of the first humans should be for us a proof of the need for caution, not an example of how to sin. Adam fell so that we may rise. Let us reply to such suggestions as Job did. He had a wife who played the role of Eve, but he who had been vanquished in paradise vanquished his tempter on the dunghill.[31] So let us refuse to listen to wheedling voices, and not assume that the elect are few. They are numerous, but they do not show up amid the crowd. To be sure, we cannot deny that there are very many bad people, so many that the good can scarcely be seen among them, just as the grains of wheat are almost invisible on the threshing-floor. Anyone who glances at the threshing-floor will think there is nothing there but straw. An inexperienced onlooker regards it as a waste of time to send in oxen, and have workers sweating away in the heat threshing the straw. But hidden within it is a mass of grain that will be winnowed out. Then the bulky yield of grain, which was hidden by the bulk of the straw, will be evident. Do you want to find the good people? Be one yourself, and you will find them.

Verse 11. God is praised not in a sect, but worldwide

10. Notice now how the psalm counters the desperate attitude we have been discussing. By saying, *We have received your mercy, O God, in the midst of your people*, the psalm indicated that there is also a people of God that is not open to his mercy, but that in the heart of it there are some who do receive the mercy of God. Now, to counter the idea that may have occurred to some of us, that these latter are so few as to be almost negligible, what consolation does it offer in the next lines? *As does your name, O God, so too your praise extends to the ends of the earth*. How are we to understand this? *Great is the Lord, and exceedingly worthy of praise, in the city of our God, on his holy mountain*. He can be praised only in his saints, for people who live sinful lives do not praise him. Even if they preach him with their tongues, they blaspheme him by their lives. Since he can be praised only in his saints, the heretics have no business to say to themselves, "His praise has been safeguarded among us, because we are a small group, separate from the crowd. We live righteously, and we praise God not only in words but by our conduct".[32] They have their refutation in this psalm. How can you say that God is praised in a sect? The psalm confesses to him, *"As does your name, O God, so too your praise extends to the ends of the earth*. As you have become

31. See Jb 2:9-10.
32. A thrust at the Elitism of the Donatists.

known throughout all lands, so too are you praised throughout all lands; throughout all lands there is no lack of people who praise you." But only they praise him who live good lives. *As does your name, O God, so too does your praise extend* not just to some schismatic group, but *to the ends of the earth. Your right hand is filled with justice.* This last statement means "Those who stand at your right hand are very numerous." The big crowd will not be only those at his left; there will be a full complement, a great heap at his right hand too. *Your right hand is filled with justice.*

Verse 12. The discerning winnower

11. *Let Mount Zion rejoice, and the daughters of Judea*[33] *dance for joy, on account of your judgments, O Lord.* O Mount Zion, O daughters of Judea, you are struggling amid tares now, amid straw, amid thorns; but dance for joy over God's judgments. God makes no mistakes when he judges. Let your life stand out in contrast, though by birth you blend in with them,[34] for the plea that went up from your lips and your heart has not gone unheard: *Do not destroy my soul with the ungodly, nor my life with those who shed blood* (Ps 25(26):9). God is a highly skilled winnower. He will bring his winnowing-shovel with him,[35] and will not let a single grain of wheat fall into the heap of chaff for burning, or a single wisp of straw get into the barn to be stored. Dance for joy, daughters of Judea, over the judgments of a God who makes no mistakes, and do not arrogate to yourselves the right to make judgments in advance. It is your job to garner, his to sift what has been garnered.

Let Mount Zion rejoice, and the daughters of Judea dance for joy, on account of your judgments, O Lord. You must not think that "daughters of Judea" means only the Jews. The name "Judah" means "confession." All the children of confession are children of Judea. The statement that *salvation comes from the Jews* means that Christ sprang from the Jews, neither more nor less. But the apostle tells us, *A Jew is not one who is so outwardly, nor is circumcision an external mark in the flesh. A Jew is one who is such inwardly, by circumcision of the heart, not literally but in spirit; and he receives commendation not from human beings, but from God* (Rom 2:28-29). Be a Jew of that kind yourself, and make circumcision of the heart your boast, even if you are not circumcised in your flesh. *Let the daughters of Judea dance for joy on account of your judgments, O Lord.*

33. Variant: "Judah," here and in the next few lines.
34. *Discretae vivite, etsi concretae natae estis.*
35. See Mt 3:12; Lk 3:17.

Verses 13-14. The strength of charity

12. *Encircle Zion and embrace it.* This is what should be said to the wrong-doers, among whom is living that people of God which has received his mercy. In the midst of you is a right-living people, so *encircle Zion*. But how? *Embrace it.* Do not hem it in with constrictions, but embrace it with charity. Imitate those Christians of holy life in your midst, so that you too may be incorporated into Christ, whose members they are. *Encircle Zion and embrace it. Make your proclamation from its towers.* From its high ramparts proclaim its praise.

13. *Set your hearts on its virtue.* Beware of having the appearance of religion while denying its real virtue;[36] rather *set your hearts on its virtue*. What is the characteristic virtue of that city? Anyone who seeks to know its virtue must understand the power of charity. This is the virtue that no one can defeat. No stormy waves of this world, no rivers of temptation, can quench the fire of charity.[37] Scripture says of it, *Love is as strong as death* (Sg 8:6). When death comes it cannot be resisted, whatever the contrivances, whatever the medicines, you use to oppose it; for no one born mortal can escape the violent onslaught of death. Just so, neither can the world withstand the violence of charity. Death is taken as the term of comparison because it is the direct opposite of charity, for as death is unstoppably violent in snatching us away, so is charity equally violent in saving us. Through charity many people have died to the world, because they wanted to live to God. By this charity the martyrs were set on fire. They were not pretending, nor were they puffed up with vanity, nor were they like those of whom scripture says, *If I deliver my body to be burnt, yet have no love, it profits me nothing* (1 Cor 13:3). Since they were truly impelled to suffer by love of Christ and love of truth, what impact could the attacks of ferocious men have on them? The weeping eyes of their families and friends worked upon them more violently than the hatred of their persecutors. How many were clutched by their children, who did not want them to die! How many saw their wives begging on their knees not to be left widowed! How many parents implored their children not to die! We know this well, and have read about it in the Passion of the blessed Perpetua.[38] So many pleas were made, so many bitter tears shed, but when did they ever quench the fire of charity? This is the virtue of Zion, for whom else-

---

36. See 2 Tm 3:5.
37. See Sg 8:7.
38. Saints Perpetua and Felicitas were celebrated African martyrs. Perpetua, a noble woman, said to have been 22 years of age, was killed along with the slave-girl Felicitas in the persecution of Septimius Severus, on 7 March 203, in the arena at Carthage. A vivid contemporary account relates various visions, and conversations between Perpetua and her relatives and companions. It describes in detail her father's attempts to dissuade her, both before and after she was condemned to face the wild beasts. On one occasion he brought with him Perpetua's infant son to reinforce his arguments, but she stood firm. The Basilica of Saints Perpetua and Felicitas was one of the most important in Carthage.

where the prayer is made, *May peace reign in your virtue, and abundance in your towers* (Ps 121(122):7). Our psalm continues, *Make this proclamation from its towers: Set your hearts on its virtue, and distribute its houses.*

14. What are we to make of this *Set your hearts on its virtue, and distribute its houses*? It means, "Distinguish one house from another, do not confuse them." There is one house that has the semblance of religion, but not the substance of it, and another house that has both the appearance and the reality of religion. Distinguish them, do not confuse them. You will distinguish them when you set your hearts on its virtue, which is to say when you have become spiritual through charity. Then you will pass no rash judgment; then you will see that the wicked are no hindrance to the good as long as we are together in the threshing-floor. *Distribute its houses.*

Another interpretation is possible. The apostles were instructed to treat separately the two houses, the one that came from the circumcision and the other from the Gentiles. After Saul had been called, and had turned into the apostle Paul, and joined the fellowship of his co-apostles, he agreed with them that they should go to the Jews, and he to the Gentiles.[39] By this division of labor in their apostolate they distributed the houses in the city of the great King, and by bringing both together at the corner they kept distinct spheres in their evangelization, but bound them together in charity. Certainly this explanation seems preferable, for the next words suggest the instructions given to preachers: *Distribute its houses, so that you may tell the story in a new generation.* This mediation of their gospel was to reach us who would be born later. The apostles did not labor exclusively for those with whom they lived while on earth, nor did the Lord's concern extend only to the apostles, to whom he graciously showed himself alive after his resurrection. He cared about us too, for when he said, *Lo, I am with you throughout all days, even to the end of the ages* (Mt 28:20), he was addressing them directly, but meaning it for us as well. Were they going to be there to the end of the ages? No, obviously not. The Lord also said, *Not for these only do I pray, but for those also who through their word shall believe in me* (Jn 17:20). He had us in mind, because he died for us. It was necessary, therefore, that the apostles should be sent to *tell the story to a new generation.*

Verse 15. This is our God

15. And what will you tell? That *this is God, our God.* The earth was visible, but the Creator of the earth was not. Christ's flesh could be touched, but God in the flesh was not so readily recognized. They from whom his flesh was taken (for the Virgin Mary was from Abraham's stock) held onto his flesh; but they stayed at the level of the flesh and did not perceive his godhead. O you, apostles, O you,

39. See Gal 2:9.

great city, preach from your towers and tell them, *This is our God.* Yes, even as he is, despised, and lying before the feet of those who stumble over him, that he may humble the hearts of those who confess him yes, even like that, *this is our God.* Undoubtedly he was seen, as it had been prophesied: *At last he was seen on earth, and consorted with human beings* (Bar 3:38). *This is our God.* He is truly a man, yet who may recognize him? For *this is our God.* Does this perhaps mean God only for a time, like the false gods? Well, although these cannot truly be gods, I suppose they can be called such, at least temporarily; for what does a prophet say to them, or recommend should be said? *You shall say to them. . . .* What? *The gods that did not make sky or earth must perish from the earth, and from the sight of all who are under the sky* (Jer 10:11). Our God is not like that; our God is above all the gods. And who would they be? *The gods of the heathen are demons, but the Lord made the sky* (Ps 95(96):5). He then is our God, *this is our God.* And for how long? *for ever and for ages unending; he it is who will guide us for ever.* If he is our God, he is our King as well. He protects us, because he is our God, and saves us from death; he rules us, because he is our King, and saves us from falling. But in ruling us he does not crush us; it is those whom he does not rule that he breaks. *You will rule them with an iron rod*, says another psalm, *and you will dash them to pieces like a potter's vessel* (Ps 2:9). But these are the people who do not accept his sovereignty, so he does not spare them, but smashes them like a potter's jar. For our part, let us choose to be ruled and liberated by him, for *this is our God for ever and for ages unending; he it is who will guide us for ever.*

Exposition 1 of Psalm 48

First Sermon

Introduction: Trying to bend God to our perverse desires

1. All the words that God speaks to us are salutary for those who understand them rightly, but perilous for those who attempt to twist them to suit the perversity of their own hearts, instead of reshaping their hearts to the rectitude of God's word. This deplorable form of human perversity is all too common. The duty of human beings is to live in accord with God's will, yet they want God's will to conform to theirs. Unwilling to be corrected, they attempt to distort God, judging what they want rather than what he wants to be the right thing. All too often we hear people grumbling against God, complaining that the wicked prosper in this life, while the good have a hard time. They speak as though God were out of line, and did not know his job, or averted his gaze entirely from human affairs, or were so reluctant to have his peace disturbed that he took no notice—as though God could only see and correct such anomalies by going to a lot of trouble. People who want to worship God in order to ensure that things go well with them murmur with discontent when they see others, who do not worship him, going from strength to strength and enjoying earthly happiness, whereas they themselves, who worship God, have to struggle amid the pressures, poverty, pain and other difficulties that beset our mortal life.

Against this attitude, and against this blasphemous grumbling, God's word is ever singing a different song to lure us away from the serpent's bite; for such perversity is the foul discharge from a heart infected by the serpent's venom and belching its stinking blasphemies against God. What is worse still, it pushes away God's caring hand, but the serpent's bite it does not ward off. I repeat: the human heart thrusts the hard edge of God's word away from it, but welcomes the persuasive, deceitful flattery of the serpent. The divine word has a different song to sing, and addresses us now in this psalm. I would be urging you to give it your attention, holy brethren,[1] were it not that God himself makes us all attentive, and not us alone, but the whole world. Listen, then, to its opening words.

1. *Sanctitatem vestram.*

Verse 2. Two ways of listening, two ways of dwelling

2. *Hear these things, all you nations.* Evidently it is not just you who are present whom the psalm is addressing. How could our feeble voice shout so loudly as to make itself heard among all nations? But our Lord Jesus Christ has shouted through his apostles; he has shouted in as many tongues as he has sent,[2] with the result that we find this psalm, formerly recited by one nation alone in the synagogue of the Jews, now being recited all over the world and in all the churches.[3] The prophecy implied in its opening words has therefore been fulfilled: *hear these things, all you nations.*

I want to remind of you of something, in case the length of this psalm frightens you off, and you are unable to give your minds to it fully because of the bodily weariness you anticipate. It is this: if possible we will finish it today, but if we can't, some verses can be left over for us to deal with tomorrow. Either way, be attentive all the time, for if the Lord grants it, you will hear as much as will uplift you but not weigh you down.

Well, then, *hear these things, all you nations*, and that includes you. *Take them in with your ears, all you who dwell in the world.* This seems to be a repetition, as though the first injunction, *Hear*, had not been strong enough. The psalmist is saying, "Listen to what I say, take it in with your ears, do not let it go in one ear and out of the other." What does this command, *take them in with your ears*, call to mind? It reminds us of our Lord's warning, *Let anyone who has ears for hearing, listen!* (Mt 11:15). Since all those about him obviously had ears, what ears was he trying to reach when he said, *Let anyone who has ears for hearing, listen*? The ears of their hearts, evidently, and at these same ears the psalm is beating. *Take them in with your ears, all who dwell in the world.*

Possibly there is another distinction implicit here. There is no need to restrict ourselves, nor anything wrong in spelling out the full meaning. There may be a difference between *all you nations* and *all you who dwell in the world.* The psalmist perhaps wanted us to grasp an extra nuance when he said, *You who dwell*, and meant us to understand *nations* as all wicked people, and *dwellers in the world* as all the righteous. A person who "dwells" is one who is not held captive, for anyone who is a prisoner is "dwelt in" rather than dwelling.[4] A man who has possessions is considered to be master of his property, but he alone is truly master of it who is not ensnared in the meshes of greed; for anyone who is entangled in greed is not a possessor but possessed. We have another similar indication about "dwelling" in God's scripture, in the passage that says, *I would rather be degraded in the Lord's house than dwell in the tents of sinners* (Ps

2. Variant: "to those to whom he has sent them."

3. There is an implied contrast between "synagogue" and "church"; see Augustine's remarks in his Exposition of Psalm 77, 3.

4. *Habitatur, non habitat.*

83:11(84:10)). Does that mean that you do not dwell in the Lord's house, if you are in a degraded position there? In a sense you do; but it confines the word "dwell" to those who rule, and possess, and exercise sovereignty, and govern. Those who have a lowly, despised status are not said to "dwell," but to be subject. The psalmist affirmed, though, that he would rather occupy such a subordinate place in God's house than have dominion in the tents of sinners.

It may be, then, that there is some difference in meaning between *all nations* and *all you who dwell in the world*, as there also is between *hear* and *take them in with your ears*. This latter also looks like a mere repetition, but in fact a difference is suggested, because not only sinners and godless folk, but righteous people too, were to hear the words of the psalm. All will listen, all of them indiscriminately, but when the time for reckoning has come, those who heard to no purpose will be separated from those who have taken it in with their ears. So let the sinners listen: *hear these things, all you nations*; but let the righteous hear them too, the people who do not hear in vain, and rule the earth rather than being ruled by it: *take them in with your ears, all you who dwell in the world.*

Verse 3. Rich and poor listeners

3. The psalmist continues, *All you earthlings and sons of men*. By the term *earthlings* he has indicated sinners, and by *sons of men* the faithful and just. So you see, he is maintaining the distinction, for who are the *earthlings*? The earth-born. And who are they? Those who hope for an earthly inheritance. But who are the *sons of men*? Those who belong to the Son of Man. We pointed out this distinction to you on another occasion, holy brethren,[5] and we discovered that Adam was a man, but not a son of man, whereas Christ was Son of Man, and was God. All those who belong to Adam are *earthlings*, and all who belong to Christ are *sons of men*. Nonetheless, let them all listen; I am not withholding my words from anyone. If someone is an earthling, let him or her hear it because of the judgment to come; but if anyone is a son of man, let him or her listen because of the kingdom.

Rich and poor together. This is a reiteration of the same idea. The word *rich* applies to the earthlings, and *poor* to the sons of men. Take the rich to be the proud, the poor to be the humble. Someone may have plenty of money and resources, and yet not be haughty about it, and then he or she is poor. Another may have nothing, yet be covetous and puffed up, and then God classes him or her with the rich and reprobate. God questions both rich and poor in their hearts,

5. *Sanctitati vestrae*. Augustine elaborated a distinction between "men" and "sons of men" in his Exposition of Psalm 8, 10-11, and Exposition of Psalm 35, 12. Here, as in both the other contexts, it is not possible to insist on gender-inclusive language without obscuring his point about the Son of Man.

not in their treasure-chests[6] or their houses. They are truly poor who take to heart the advice given by the apostle to Timothy: *Instruct the rich of this world not to be high-minded* (1 Tm 6:17). How did Paul turn these rich people into poor people? He took away from them their reason for wanting to be rich. No one wants to be rich except to give himself airs among his fellows, and to seem more important than they are. But when Paul ordered the rich *not to be high-minded* he put them on the same level as the have-nots. A beggar may be more arrogant over his handful of coins than a rich person who hearkens to the apostle's warning, *Instruct the rich of this world not to be high-minded.* And how are they to avoid becoming high-minded? By acting in the way he goes on to describe: *nor to put their trust in unreliable wealth, but in the living God, who gives us everything to enjoy in abundance.* Notice that he did not say, "Who gives them," but *who gives us.* Did Paul not have riches himself? Certainly he did. What were his riches? Those of which scripture testifies elsewhere, *To a faithful person there is a whole world of riches* (Prv 17:6, LXX). Listen to Paul's profession: *We are like people who have nothing, yet possess all things* (2 Cor 6:10). Anyone who aspires to be rich must beware of clutching at a mere part; then he or she will possess the whole. Let such a person remain immovably attached to him who created the whole. *Rich and poor together.* Another psalm foretells, *The poor shall eat and be satisfied* (Ps 21:27(22:26)). How did it characterize the poor? They are the ones who will *eat and be satisfied.* What do they eat? The faithful know the answer.[7] How will they be satisfied? By imitating the Lord's passion, and not allowing the price he paid for them to go for nothing. *The poor shall eat and be satisfied, and those who seek the Lord will praise him.* What about the rich, though? They too eat, but how? *All the rich of the world have eaten, and worshiped* (Ps 21:30(22:29)). The psalm does not say, "They ate, and were satisfied," but *they ate and worshiped*; they do indeed worship God, but are not prepared to show human kindness to their brothers and sisters. They eat, and worship, whereas the poor eat and are satisfied; yet all eat. The eater is under an obligation to provide the same food in return; let him or her not be forbidden to eat by the Giver,[8] but be warned to fear him as Creditor.[9]

---

6. *In arca.* Variants: *in area,* "on the threshing-floor"; *in horreo,* "in the barn."
7. Another of Augustine's fairly infrequent allusions to the Discipline of the Secret; see note at Exposition 2 of Psalm 32, 2.
8. Or perhaps "by the steward," the preacher.
9. As in his Sermon 329 Augustine teaches that those who at the Lord's table are fed with the fruit of his self-sacrificing charity must in their turn show the same charity, even to the point of martyrdom. The martyrs have done this. "It is written, *You are a guest at a magnificent table. Take careful note of all that is set before you, for you in your turn must serve a like banquet*. . . . No host feeds his guests with himself, yet this is what Christ our Lord does . . . he is our food and drink. The martyrs were well aware of the nature of the food and drink they were given, and prepared to do the same. . . ." He goes on to compare it with the cup of suffering Christ drank.

Let both sinners and just people listen to these things, both the nations and those who dwell in the world, the *earthlings* and the *sons of men, rich and poor together*; let them all listen without distinction, without separation. Harvest-time will sort them out, the winnower's hand will be powerful enough.[10] But for the present let rich and poor listen together, and let kids and lambs graze together, until the coming of him who will pick out some to stand at his right hand, and leave others at his left. Let them listen to him teaching all together, as one, lest they be forced to listen in a separate group to their judge condemning them.

Verses 4-5. Practicing what we preach

4. Now what are they about to hear? *My mouth will speak wisdom, and the meditation of my heart, understanding*. The statement is perhaps repeated because you might think that when he said, *My mouth*, someone was speaking to you with wisdom only on his lips; for many people have it on their lips, but not in their hearts. Scripture says of them, *This people honors me with its lips, but its heart is far from me* (Is 29:13). So what about the psalmist who is speaking to you here? After declaring, *My mouth will speak wisdom*, he wanted to make sure you would understand that what he pours out from his mouth wells up from his heart, so he added, *And the meditation of my heart, understanding*.

5. *I will bend my ear to a parable, and on the psaltery I will set forth what I have to say*. Whose heart is this, that meditates and utters its understanding in such a way that it is no superficial word on the lips, but takes possession of his innermost being? Who is this man who first listens, and then speaks accordingly? Many people there are who say what they do not hear. Who are they? They are the people who do not practice what they preach, like the Pharisees who, as the Lord said, were sitting in the chair of Moses. He wanted to speak to you from Moses' chair, and to speak through them, though they did not act in accordance with their teaching. And the Lord wanted to reassure you about this. "Do not be afraid," he said, *do what they tell you, but do not imitate what they do, for they talk, but do not act accordingly*" (Mt 23:3). They do not listen to what they say. The people who act, and speak in accordance with their actions, listen to what they are saying, and their admonition is fruitful because they are listening to it themselves. But anyone who speaks but does not listen may profit someone else but is useless to himself. Now this psalmist who is addressing you wanted to be both listener and speaker, so before declaring, *On the psaltery I will set forth what I have to say* (by which he means speaking in a physical way, for the soul plays on the body like a musician on the psaltery), he said, *I will bend my ear to a parable*. "Before I speak to you in a bodily way," he says, "before the

10. See Mt 3:12.

psaltery sounds its notes, I will first of all *bend my ear to a parable*; that is, I will listen first to what I have to tell you." But why *to a parable*? Because, says the apostle, *What we see now is a tantalizing reflection in a mirror. As long as we are in the body we are on pilgrimage and away from the Lord* (1 Cor 13:12; 2 Cor 5:6). Not yet do we enjoy face-to-face vision, where there will be no more parables, no more enigmatic sayings or puzzling comparisons. Whatever we understand now, we perceive only through enigmas. An enigma is an obscure parable that we understand only with difficulty. However carefully we cultivate our hearts, and withdraw into ourselves to understand what is within, as long as we see only through our corruptible flesh we see only in part. But when at the resurrection of the dead we have been endowed with incorruptibility, when the Son of Man appears to judge the living and the dead, then this Son of Man, who once was judged, will be manifest as judge. He will distinguish the bad from the good, and place the bad at his left, the good at his right. Both good and bad will see him then; but to the bad he will say, "*Depart from me into eternal fire*," and to the good, "*Come, you whom my Father has blessed, take possession of the kingdom." Thus the wicked will go into eternal burning, but the righteous into eternal life* (Mt 25:41.34:46). There the just will enjoy the face-to-face vision of which the others were not worthy.

Pay careful heed to what I am saying. When the Son of Man was on earth, and due to be judged, both bad people and good people saw him. The apostles who followed him saw him, and so did the Jews who crucified him. So it will be when he comes to judge. Both good and bad will see him: the good, so as to receive their reward for following him, and the wicked, so as to receive their punishment for crucifying him. Will it be only those who crucified him who will be damned? Yes, I dare to say it: only those. "So we're all right," say today's sinners. You are all right only if God does not question the soul. What do I mean by that? You must understand, beloved, for at God's judgment-seat they must not be able to say that they never understood. The Jews crucified Christ because they could see him; but you, because you do not see Christ, resist his word. If you resist his word, would you not crucify his flesh if you could see him? The Jews sneered at him hanging on a tree; you sneer at him seated in heaven. Even as both types of people saw him when he was on earth, so will both types see him when he comes again. The Son of Man will come to judge because the Son of Man came to be judged. The Father did not take flesh, and the Father did not suffer; therefore he judges through the Son of Man. The Lord himself told us this in the gospel: *the Father judges no one, but has entrusted all judgment to the Son*; and he continued a little later, *and he has given him authority to pass judgment, because he is the Son of Man* (Jn 5:22.27). As Son of God he is the Word eternally with the Father; and since he is always with the Father he always exercises judgment with the Father; but as Son of Man he both underwent judgment, and will judge. As at that earlier time, when he was judged, he was seen both by those who believed and by those who crucified him, so too when he approaches as our judge he will be seen both by those whom he will condemn and by those whom he will crown. But the impious will not enjoy that vision of his godhead which he promised to his lovers when he said, *Whoever loves me will be loved by my Father; and anyone who cherishes my commandments and keeps them, that is the one who loves me; and I will love him, and will show myself to him* (Jn 14:21). This self-disclosure is something intimate that he keeps for his chosen ones; he does not grant it to the godless. What is that vision like? Well, ask yourself, what is Christ like? He is equal to the Father. What is Christ like? *In the beginning was the Word, and the Word was with God; he was God* (Jn 1:1). We sigh for that vision now, and we groan for it through all the stretch of our pilgrimage. In the end we shall be brought home to that vision, but we see it now only through an enigmatic parable. But if we do see it at all, albeit through a parable, let us bend our ear to the parable, and with the psaltery set forth what we have to say. Let us listen to what we are saying, and practice what we preach.

Verse 6. The serpent at our heels

6. So what did he say? *Why should I be afraid on the evil day? The iniquity of my heel will encompass me*. This is a rather strange way to begin. *Why should I be afraid on the evil day?* he asks, but then adds, *The iniquity of my heel will encompass me*. Surely he ought to be all the more afraid if the iniquity of his heel is likely to encompass him? It is as good as saying, "There is no reason to be afraid of some peril you cannot possibly avoid." If a person fears death, for instance, what is he or she going to do to avoid dying? How is anyone descended from Adam going to escape paying the debt Adam incurred? Tell me that. But let such a person reflect that though he was born from Adam, he has followed Christ, and that though he is liable for Adam's debt, he is also due to win what Christ has promised. So anyone who fears death has no way of evading it; but anyone who fears damnation, fears to hear the sentence which the godless will hear, *Depart from me into eternal fire* (Mt 25:41), certainly does have a way to evade it. Has he any reason to be afraid, then? Why should he be? Because the iniquity of his heel will encompass him? But if he avoids the iniquity of his heel, and walks in the ways of God, he will never arrive at the evil day, for the evil day is the last day, but for him it will not be evil. We must be aware that the last day will indeed be evil for some people, but good for others. It will scarcely be an evil day, will it, for those to whom the Lord will say, *Come, you whom my Father has blessed, take possession of the kingdom* (Mt 25:34)? But evil it certainly will be for those who are bidden, *Depart into eternal fire*. Even if the iniquity of his heel does surround him, why need anyone be afraid on the evil day?

During this present life people must make prudent provision, kick the iniquity away from their heels, and walk in the way of which the Lord spoke: *I am the way, and the truth, and the life* (Jn 14:6). Then they have no reason to be afraid on the evil day, for he who has become our Way gives them security. *Why should I be afraid on the evil day? The iniquity of my heel will encompass me.* All the more reason, then, to avoid the iniquity that lurks at our heels. It is the heel that causes a person to slip. Let me have your attention, beloved.[11] What did God say to the serpent? *She will watch for your head, and you her heel.*[12] The devil is watching your heel, waiting for you to slip, so that he can throw you down. He watches your heel, but you must watch his head. What is his head? The first emergence of an evil suggestion. When he begins to suggest evil acts to you, get rid of him before pleasure surges up and consent follows. Then you will avoid his head, and he will not catch your heel. But why was this warning addressed to Eve? Because a person is tripped up through the flesh, and for each one of us our flesh is an interior Eve. It is clear that Eve represents the flesh from scripture's teaching: *By loving his wife, a man loves himself.* But what does *himself* imply? It goes on to tell us: *For no one ever hated his own flesh* (Eph 5:28-29). As the serpent tripped Adam up through Eve, so too the devil hopes to trip us up through our flesh, and therefore Eve was commanded to keep an eye on the devil's head, since he is watching her heel.

Even if the iniquity of our heels encompasses us, then, why should we be afraid on the evil day? If we have turned to Christ we have it in our power not to commit iniquity; then there will be nothing to encompass us and we shall not mourn, but rejoice, on the last day.

Verses 7-8. Reliance on Christ, our brother

7. But who are the people who truly will be entangled by the iniquity around their heels? *Those who trust in their own strength and boast of their abundant wealth.* I shall be careful to avoid such traps, then, and make sure that the iniquity of my heel does not encompass me. How can we avoid them? Let us not trust in our own strength, nor boast of our abundant wealth, but boast only of him who has promised us that the humble will be exalted, and has threatened the arrogant with damnation. Then the iniquity of our heels will not encompass us, as it may entangle *those who trust in their own strength and boast of their abundant wealth.*

8. Some people rely on their friends, others on their own strength, others on riches. These things are the presumptuous reliance of a human race that does not rely on God. But with strength in view, with riches in view, with friends in view, the psalmist demands, "*If your brother does not save you, will any human being save you?* Are you expecting some man or woman to redeem you from the wrath

11. *Caritas vestra.*
12. Gn 3:15. On the feminine pronoun, *ipsa*, see note at Exposition of Psalm 35, 18.

that is coming? If your brother does not redeem you, will any mere human redeem you?"

Now, who is this brother? If no man or woman is going to save us unless he does, who is he? None other than he who after his resurrection says, *Go and tell my brothers* (Jn 20:17). He has willed to be our brother, and when we say, "Our Father," to God, the reality of it is manifest in us; for anyone who says "Our Father" to God is saying "Brother" to Christ. Now whoever has God for Father and Christ for Brother need have no fear on the evil day. Such a person will not be encompassed by any iniquity that dogs our heels, because he or she does not rely on strength, or boast of plentiful riches, or brag about powerful friends. Let us put our reliance on him who died for us so that we may not suffer eternal death, on him who was humbled for our sake so that we may be exalted, on him who sought us in our unbelief so that we may seek him now that we are believers. If he, then, does not redeem us, will any mere human redeem us? Will some other man redeem us, if the Son of Man does not? If Christ does not redeem us, will Adam? *If your brother does not save you, will any human being save you?*

Verses 8-9. Making a good investment

9. *He will offer to God neither propitiation nor the cost of redeeming his soul.* A person who will not *offer propitiation to God*, that is, one who will not attempt to placate God for his sins, is the one who trusts in his own strength and boasts of his abundant wealth. Nor does a person who relies on his own strength, friends or riches offer to God *the cost of redeeming his soul*. But who are the ones who do pay the price of redeeming their souls? The people to whom the Lord says, *Make yourselves friends from sinful mammon, so that they may welcome you into the tents of eternity* (Lk 16:9). Yes, those who assiduously give alms are the ones who meet the cost of redeeming their souls. Through Timothy the apostle advises them not to be proud, and not to boast about their plentiful wealth. Moreover, he did not want their assets to grow stale by being kept to themselves, but urged the rich to make something out of them, and so realize the price of redeeming their souls. *Instruct the rich of this world not to be high-minded*, he tells Timothy, *nor to put their trust in unreliable wealth, but in the living God, who gives us everything to enjoy in abundance*. Then he seems to anticipate an objection from them: "In that case, what are we to do with our money?" *Let them be rich in good works, give readily, and share what they have*, he recommends. Then they will not lose it. How do we know they won't? Because he continues, *Let them use their wealth to lay a good foundation for the future, and so attain true life* (1 Tm 6:17-19). That is how they will hand over the price of their souls' redemption. Our Lord enjoins the same thing: *Get yourselves purses that do not wear out, and a treasure in heaven that never fails, where no thief can reach it,*

or moth destroy it (Lk 12:33). God does not want you to lose your wealth; he simply advises you to change the place where you keep it. I want to make this very clear to you, beloved.[13] Suppose a friend came into your house, and found that you had stored your grain in a damp place. Perhaps he had more experience of how grain goes bad than you had, and he gave you some advice. "You will lose what you laboriously garnered, brother. You have put it in a damp place, and it will go bad within a few days." You ask him, "What shall I do, then, brother?" "Take it higher up," he replies. So you would be willing to listen to your friend if he suggested carrying your grain up from the cellar to the loft, but you do not hear Christ advising you to lift your valuables from earth to heaven! What you will recover there is not what you are safeguarding, though. He is telling you to safeguard the earth and win heaven, to safeguard perishable things in order to gain those that last for ever. You must lend your money to Christ; make sure he receives these trifling things on earth, that he may pay you back most handsomely in heaven.

But those who are entrapped by the iniquity of their heels, who rely on their own strength and boast of their abundant wealth, who presumptuously count on human friends who have no power to help them in any way—none of these *offer to God propitiation or the cost of redeeming their souls.*

Verses 9-10. Reversal of fortunes after this life

10. What has the psalm to say about this type of person? *He labored*[14] *for eternity, but will live only until the end.* His labor will be endless, but his life will have an end. Why does it say, *He will live only until the end*? People like this reckon that life consists in daily pleasures. And so lacking in firm faith are many of our poor and needy folk, who do not keep their eye on what God promises them for their present labors, that when they see the rich at their daily banquets, glittering and gleaming amid their gold and silver, they say—what do they say? "These are the only people worth talking about,[15] they really live!" This is a common saying, but I wish it would drop out of use now. I am warning you, yet it is still current. At any rate I hope it may be said henceforth by fewer people than it would have been if I had not warned you about it. Not that I am so presumptuous as to think that it will altogether cease to be said because of my admonition, but at least let it be said less commonly; though I am afraid some people will go on talking like that until the end of time. It would not matter so much if the poor onlooker just said that the rich person is the one who lives; he goes further, insists on it, thunders it. Do you really think that rich person is the only one who

13. *Caritas vestra.*
14. The reading of the best codices, but the CCL editors amend to "will labor."
15. Most codices have *soli sunt isti*; but one witness has *felices sunt isti*, "they are the lucky ones."

lives?[16] Let him live; his life will come to an end. Because he does not hand over the price of his soul's redemption, his life will end but his labor will be endless. *He labored for eternity, but will live only until the end.* In what sense will he *live only until the end*? In the same sense as did a certain man who dressed in purple and fine linen, and was accustomed to feast sumptuously every day, and in his pride and swollen self-esteem despised a man who lay covered with ulcers at the gate, with dogs licking his sores, longing for any crumbs that might fall from the rich man's table.[17] What good did his wealth do him? The two of them changed places: one was taken up from his place at the gate into Abraham's embrace, the other was swept away from his lavish banquets into the fire. The one found rest, the other burned; one was satisfied, the other athirst; one had labored until the end came, but was now living for ever, the other had lived until the end came, but was now to labor for ever. What use was it for the rich man, stuck there below in torments, to beg that a drop of water might be trickled onto his tongue from Lazarus' finger, pleading, *I am in agony in this flame*? It was not granted to him. His longing for a drop of water from a finger was like the other's former longing for a few crumbs from the rich man's table; but the poor man's labor came to an end, as the rich man's life came to an end. The latter would then labor for ever, the former live for ever. We who may have to labor and struggle here do not have our life here; but afterwards we shall not be in this state, for Christ will be our life for all eternity, whereas those who want to have their life here will labor for ever, and have life here only until the end comes.

Verse 11. Death and eternal life

11. *For when he sees the wise dying, he will not see untimely extinction.* The person who labors for ever, and will live only until the end, *will not see untimely extinction, when he sees the wise dying.* What does this mean? It means that he will not understand what death is when he sees the wise dying. He says to himself, "That fellow was a wise man, one who lived in accord with wisdom, and devoutly worshiped God. But it didn't save him from death, did it? So I will make the most of all good things as long as I am alive, since people who take a different view are powerless. They must be, otherwise they would not die." The speaker sees a wise man die, but does not see what death is. *When he sees the wise dying, he will not see untimely extinction.* The Jews saw Christ hanging on the cross, and mocked him: "If this man were God's Son, he would come down from the cross," but they failed to see what extinction truly is. If only they could

16. The text is printed thus in CCL: *Adiungit et dicit, tonat: Putas eum solum vivere.* This makes the last clause what the poor man thunders; but the sense is not good. By altering the punctuation it is possible to understand the "Do you think" clause as spoken by Augustine, as the translation here offered assumes.

17. See Lk 16:19-31.

see what it is, if only they could see! He was dying within time that he might rise to life that lasts for ever, but they were living within time in such a way as to incur eternal death. But because they saw him dying, they did not see untimely extinction; that is, they did not understand the nature of real extinction. What do they say in the Book of Wisdom? "*Let us condemn him to the most shameful of deaths, for his claims will be taken care of. If he truly is the Son of God, he will deliver him from the hands of his adversaries* (Wis 2:20,18). God will not permit his Son to die if this really is his Son." But when they saw him on the cross, saw themselves insulting him and saw him refusing to descend from the cross, they said, "He was only a man, after all." Thus they spoke. Undoubtedly he who had the power to rise again from the grave also had the power to come down from the cross, but he taught us to bear with those who insult us, taught us to be patient when we come up against vilification from others, to drink the bitter chalice now and receive eternal health later. Drink this bitter cup, for you are ill; drink it, so that you who are diseased to the core may get well. Do not shrink from it, for the doctor drank from it first so that you would not be afraid: the Lord, I mean, was the first to drink the bitter cup of suffering. He who had no sin drank it, he who had nothing in him that needed healing. Drink it then, until the bitterness of this world passes away, and there comes another world where there is no obstacle to stumble over, no anger, no decay, no fever, no dishonesty, no quarrels, no old age, no death, no argument. Labor here, for you will reach the end; labor, lest by refusing to labor you reach only the end of your life and never reach the end of your labors. *For when he sees the wise dying, he will not see untimely extinction.*

Prudent use of riches

12. *The imprudent person and the unwise will perish together.* What sort of person is imprudent? One who makes no provision for his future. And who is the unwise? One who does not understand the trouble he is in now. But you, you must understand your present woes, and prudently ensure that you will find yourself in a good state later. By understanding your present unfavorable situation you will prove you are no fool, and by making provision for your future you will show that you are not imprudent. But who does make provision for the future? That servant did, the one whom his master entrusted with money to administer. But later the master said to him, *You cannot handle my business any longer. Render an account of your dealings.* The steward asked himself, *What am I to do? I am not strong enough to dig, but ashamed to beg* (Lk 16:2.3). But even with his master's property he made himself friends, who would be ready to take him in when he was sacked from his post. He cheated his master, certainly, in his efforts to win friends who would stand by him; but you must not be afraid of cheating, because you are only doing what the Lord himself exhorts you to do. *Make yourselves friends from sinful mammon*, he says (Lk 16:9). Perhaps the

money you made was made sinfully; or perhaps its sinfulness consists simply in the fact that you have it and someone else doesn't, you have plenty and someone else is in need. If so, use this sinful mammon to make friends for yourself; use your riches (or what sinners call riches), and you will be making a prudent provision. You are doing yourself a good turn, not robbing yourself. True, you seem to be the loser in the short term. But will you be losing money if you put it in your safe? Think how your children behave, my brothers and sisters. No sooner do they come by a few coins that they may use to buy themselves something than they put them in their money-box, and they do not open it until later. Does that mean that because they cannot see what they are saving up, they have lost it? Of course not. It is the same for you, don't worry. Children put money into their money-boxes and have no anxiety about it; and are you fearful about putting yours into the hand of Christ? Be prudent, and make provision for your future in heaven. Be prudent, and imitate the ant, as scripture bids us,[18] lay in your stores in summer, so that in winter you may not go hungry. "Winter" means the last day, the day of tribulation; "winter" means the day of stumbling and bitterness. Gather now what will be useful to you in the future. If you don't, you will perish as an imprudent fool with others like you.

13. But when that rich man died, he was given a grandiose funeral. Look at the public's volte-face! They forget what a bad life he lived, and focus on the pomp accorded to him when he dies. How fortunate is the person mourned by so many! Yet the poor man lived in such a fashion as to make few mourn his demise, though they ought to have lamented his wretched life. But for the wealthy man there is an elaborate funeral, he is laid in a rich tomb, dressed in costly apparel, and buried with ointments and scented spices. Then look at the monument they raise over him—all encrusted with marble! Is there any life inside that monument? No, within it he lies stone dead. In judging such observances to be good, people have lost their way and strayed from God. They have not sought the truth but have been beguiled by false values, and how far this is the case is demonstrated by the next line of the psalm. This man who did not pay the price of his soul's redemption, who did not understand death when he saw the wise dying, has been so imprudent and unwise that he perished with the like-minded. How will they perish who *will leave their wealth to strangers? The imprudent person and the unwise will perish together.*

Who are the strangers?

14. Pay close attention now, brothers and sisters. *They will leave their wealth to strangers.* The psalm seems to have reckoned accursed those whose goods will be owned by strangers after their deaths. Conversely, those are blessed who

18. See Prv 6:6-8; 30:25.

leave their children as heirs to their estates, those whose own kindred succeed them. "He had children, so he isn't dead," people say. But what about those children? They preserve what their parents left them; or rather, they do more than preserve it: they augment it. And for whom are they in their turn saving it up? For their children, and those again for their children, and the third generation again for theirs. But what does Christ get? And what accrues to the rich man's soul? He leaves the whole lot to his children. The rich would be better advised to include among their children on earth that extra brother whom they have in heaven, for they ought to be giving it all to him, or at least giving him a share.

One of you may object, however. "But look, if scripture declared accursed those who perish and leave their wealth to strangers, it follows that a man who leaves it to his own relatives is blessed." I dispute this interpretation, because I am bending my mind to the parable, and I see that scripture made good sense when it spoke as it did. For I see plenty of wicked people dying, and being succeeded by their children, and I cannot think scripture can have meant that such people are exempt from a wretched fate, since it censures their lifestyle. So, brothers and sisters, how do you think I understand it? I think it means that all of them are in fact leaving their wealth to strangers. But how can their children be strangers? Like this: the children of wicked people can be called strangers because we find in scripture an instance of an outsider who became a neighbor through being helpful. If someone of your own close kin does not come to your help, he or she is as good as a stranger. Now, where do we find this instance of someone from outside the pale becoming a neighbor by being helpful? In the gospel. A man was lying wounded after being attacked by robbers. But just before telling the story, the Lord had replied to a questioner, *You shall love your neighbor as yourself.* And he had objected, *But who is my neighbor?* Then the Lord told the story. *A man was going down from Jerusalem to Jericho when he fell in with robbers, who wounded him and left him half dead.* His compatriots passed by, for this was a Jew, traveling down from Jerusalem to Jericho. A priest came that way, and passed by; a Levite came, and he too passed by; then a Samaritan came along—just some unknown Samaritan, an outsider. He approached the wounded man and took note of his wretched condition, and mercifully tended his injuries. He *lifted him onto his own mount, and took him to an inn, and entrusted him to the innkeeper's care*. All this is narrated in a mysterious style and seems to call for further explanation; but the Lord says distinctly what I just now proposed to you, brothers and sisters. *"Which of them was a neighbor to the wounded man?" The other replied, "I suppose the one who dealt mercifully with him." Jesus answered, "Go and do the same yourself"* (Lk 10:27.29.30.34-37). The person to whom you show mercy is your neighbor. So if the Samaritan, a foreigner, became the wounded man's neighbor by treating him kindly and helping him, it follows that those who cannot come to your help when you are in trouble have become strangers to you.

Now let us see how this applies to rich people who have lived bad lives, and borne themselves proudly, and then died and left their wealth to their children—to their children, I say, not to strangers. Then the children follow their parents' example. As the parents were proud, so are the children; as they were grasping, so are the children; as they were miserly, so are their children. Yet for all that, the children are strangers to their parents. To prove the point, think of that other man who was burning in hellfire: did the heirs to his fortune come to help him? But perhaps he had no direct heirs, and strangers had come into the property? No, we find in the gospel proof that he did have close relatives, for he says, *I have five brothers* (Lk 16:28). But his brothers could not come[19] to help him even when he was roasting in the fire. What would that rich man say to you? "I have five brothers,[20] but I neglected to make a friend of that one brother of mine who used to lie at my gate. My other brothers, the ones who now own my wealth, cannot help me; they have become strangers to me." So you see, all those who lead bad lives leave their wealth to strangers.

Verse 12. The dead are not helped by feasts at their tombs

15. But surely these strangers do provide something for the dead whom they recognize as their relatives? Yes indeed, just listen to what they provide, and how the dead are mocked. *The imprudent person and the unwise will perish together, and will leave their wealth to strangers.* Why did the psalm call them *strangers*? Because they cannot be of any service to those who left them the money. Yet they make a show of being serviceable: *their tombs are their homes for ever.* Because the tombs are built up so grandly, they are like houses. You may often hear some rich person saying, "I have a marble home, and I shall have to leave it behind. I have not yet begun to think about my permanent home, where I shall be for good." When he does take thought for making a marble monument or carved memorial for himself, he thinks of it as though it were an eternal home. Anyone would think that rich man in the gospel remained resident in his tomb! If he had stayed there, he would not have been burning in hell. What we need to keep in mind is where the spirit of an ill-living person remains, not where his or her mortal body is laid. Yet the psalm says, *Their tombs are their homes for ever, their tents last from generation to generation*. By *tents* it means their temporal dwellings, by *homes* those in which they will stay for ever, namely, their tombs. They leave to their relatives the tents they stayed in while they lived, and they move into their tombs as into eternal homes. What does it profit them that *their tents last from generation to generation*? You can think of these generations as their children, then their grandchildren, then their

19. Variant: "did not come."
20. Variants: "Who are my brothers?" or "What of my brothers?"

great-grandchildren; but what do all these do for their ancestors? How do those tents help them? Listen, the psalm answers: *These will invoke their names in their own lands*. What does that mean? They will carry bread and wine to the tombs, and there call upon the names of the dead.[21] Just think how fervently the name of that rich man in the gospel must have been invoked after his death! People would have been getting drunk at his grave-cults, yet not a drop found its way below to his burning tongue. The celebrants are providing a treat for their own bellies, not for the spirits of their ancestors. Nothing reaches the spirits of the dead except what they did for themselves while they were alive; if they did no good in their lifetime, nothing will avail them when they are dead. So what do their descendants effect? Nothing but *invoking their names in their own lands*.

Verses 13-14. Loss of insight, and hypocrisy

16. *Human beings failed to understand how they were honored; they were no better than the foolish beasts, and became like them*. Notice how scornful the psalm is about people who did not understand what to do with their riches during their lifetime, but deluded themselves that they would be happy in the future if they provided for themselves a marble-encrusted tomb (as though they could live in it for eternity), and made sure that the relatives to whom they would leave their fortunes would invoke their names on their home ground. How wrong they were. They should have prepared an eternal home for themselves by good works; they should have secured immortal life for themselves, sent the cost on ahead so that they could follow their good deeds, taken care of their needy neighbors and given alms to their companions along the road, instead of despising the Christ who lay in his sores at their gates, Christ who declared, *When you did that for even the least of those who are mine, you did it for me* (Mt 25:40). But the psalm says that when human beings were honored, they failed to understand, so what does being honored imply? Human beings are made in the image of God,[22] and are of higher dignity than the beasts, for God did not make men and women in the same way as he made any animal. God made beasts to be subject to human beings; and surely this does not mean to our strength only, and not to our understanding? Yet humans have *failed to understand*; and they who have been made in the image of God *are no better than foolish beasts, and have become like them*.

21. The Roman festival, *Parentalia*, was celebrated from 13 to 21 February with offerings to the shades of the ancestors, and similar grave-cults were popular in Roman Africa. They took on Christian coloring when the custom spread of ritually sharing in food and wine at the tombs of the martyrs; but the association with pagan rites, and the occasion they gave for drunken excess, drew episcopal condemnation on these customs. Ambrose tried to stamp them out in Italy, as Augustine relates in his *Confessions* VI,2,2; and he himself discouraged them in Africa.

22. See Gn 1:26.

The same comparison is made elsewhere: *Do not be like a horse or a mule, devoid of understanding* (Ps 31(32):9).

17. *This path that they tread is an occasion of stumbling for them.* Let it be their downfall, not yours. When would it be so for you? If you believed that people of that sort are blessed. But if you understand that they are not blessed, then the way they walk will be an occasion of stumbling for them, but not for Christ, not for his body, not for his members. *But later they will bless with their mouths.* What can that mean—*later they will bless with their mouths*? When they have so far deteriorated that they seek only temporal good things, they become hypocrites, and when they bless God they do so with their lips only, not their hearts. When they are reminded of the glory of eternal life, or they are told that they ought to despise riches in Christ's name, Christians who have so deteriorated grimace in their hearts[23] and scornfully dismiss what they hear. If they do not dare to do so openly, for fear of being shamed or of being rebuked by others, at any rate they do so in their hearts; and so while blessing stays on their lips, in their hearts there is cursing. *But later they will bless with their mouths.*

It would take us too long to finish the psalm, beloved, so let what you have heard today be enough to be going on with. Tomorrow you will hear whatever the Lord grants.

23. *Torquent os in corde suo.*

Exposition 2 of Psalm 48

Second Sermon

Verse 14, continued. Yesterday's conclusion recalled

1. You will remember, dearly beloved,[1] that yesterday we had to cut short the discussion of the psalm we had begun. But we had reached the verse where the Spirit of God describes people who have no concern except for worldly, earthly, present-day affairs, and give no thought to what comes after this life. In their estimation there is no happiness other than riches and rank in this world, and transitory strength;[2] they make no provision for what is to come after their death, except for making sure that they get a grandiose funeral, and are buried in wonderfully elaborate tombs, and have their names invoked on their home ground by members of their households. But they make no arrangements for themselves as to where the spirit will be after this life ends, and they are foolish enough to ignore Christ's warning, *You fool: your life will be taken from you this very night; and then who will own what you have prepared?* (Lk 12:20). They do not notice that after lavish daily banquets, after the purple and the fine linen, the rich man in the gospel was condemned to hell and its torments; nor do they remember how the poor man found repose in Abraham's embrace after his toil and ulcers and hunger. They care nothing for these things, and focus only on what is present, neglecting to make any provision for their fate after death, apart from ensuring that their names, which are rejected by heaven, shall be lauded on earth.

People of this stamp are described by the Holy Spirit, who says of them, *This path that they tread is an occasion of stumbling for them, but later they will praise with their mouths*. This reminds us of what the Lord Jesus Christ said about certain people who approach the faith, cleansed by the word of God and exorcisms performed in his name,[3] desirous of receiving God's grace and being baptized, but afterwards slide back into sins worse than those they committed previously. *Their later doings are even worse than what they did earlier*, he says—no, that was the apostle Peter, wasn't it; but the Lord says something almost the same: *The last state of that person will be worse than the first* (2 Pt

1. *Caritas vestra.*
2. *Virtutem.* Variants include *vitam*, "life"; *felicitatem*, "happiness"; *virtutem et felicitatem*, "strength and happiness."
3. The pre-baptismal rites.

2:20; Lk 11:26). Why is this worse? Because earlier he was at least openly a pagan, but afterwards his paganism is cloaked by the Christian name, and his wickedness hidden under a veil of piety. So he will be worse because disguised, and hence the psalm says, *Later they will bless with their mouths*. In other words, you hear the name of God and the name of Christ on their lips, but do not find them in their hearts. It was said of these folk, *This people honors me with its lips, but its heart is far from me* (Is 29:13). This is the point we reached in the psalm yesterday.

Verse 15. Shepherded by death

2. The verses we must discuss and deal with today begin like this: *They are consigned like sheep to the underworld, where death will be their shepherd.* Whose shepherd? Those whose path is an occasion of stumbling to them. And who are they? The people whose entire concern is present affairs, who give no thought to the future, and who think this life is the only life, whereas in reality it is more justly called death. They fully deserve to be like sheep in hell, with death for their shepherd. But what is meant by that—having death for their shepherd? Is death something real, is it some kind of power? We can say with certainty that death is either the separation of soul from body, which is what people fear especially, or the separation of the soul from God, which people do not fear, although this is true death. In fact it often happens that by shunning the death which severs soul from body, people fall prey to that other death by which the soul is severed from God. This is death, then; but in what sense is *death their shepherd*? If Christ is life, the devil is death. In many places scripture tells us that Christ is life. The devil is death not precisely because he is identified with death, but because it comes about through him. This was the case with the death into which Adam fell, the death which at the devil's persuasion was given to humankind to drink. But the devil also had a hand in the other kind of death, the death that separated soul from body, because he who first of all fell through pride envied the human creature who was still standing, and so by tempting him into invisible death he knocked over the man who had been still on his feet, thus making him liable to pay the debt of visible death as well.[4] Those who make themselves the devil's allies have death for their shepherd; but we whose thoughts are on future immortality, and with good reason wear the sign of Christ on our foreheads, have no shepherd except Life itself. Death is the shepherd of unbelievers, Life the shepherd of believers. If the sheep who are shepherded by death have their home in

4. *Ut etiam mortem visibilem penderet*. This reading assumes that Adam is the subject of the verb. Variants assume that the devil is the subject: *morte visibili perderet*, "might destroy him [Adam] by visible death;" *morte invisibili perderet*, "through [the aforesaid] invisible death he might destroy him."

hell, we conclude that the sheep whose shepherd is Life are to be found in heaven. What? Are we in heaven already? Yes, we are in heaven through our faith. If we are not, what becomes of the invitation, "Lift up your heart"?[5] If we are not in heaven, what right had Paul to say, *We have citizens' rights in heaven* (Phil 3:20)? In the body we walk about on earth, but in our hearts we dwell in heaven. Or at least, we dwell there provided we send on ahead something to hold us there, for each one of us dwells in the place we think about, the place where we store our treasures. If one amasses treasures on earth, one's heart never leaves the earth, but if one builds up treasure in heaven, one's heart never comes down from heaven. The Lord tells us this quite plainly: *Where your treasure is, your heart will be too* (Mt 6:21).

Night and daybreak, winter and summer, trees and grass

3. Now these folk who have death for their shepherd apparently flourish for a time, while the just seem to have a hard time of it. Why is this? Because it is still night. What do I mean by night? That the merits of the just cannot be seen, whereas the good fortune of the impious is a byword. As long as winter lasts, grass seems to be in better shape than a tree, for grass stays green through the winter, while the tree seems to have dried up. But when the sun grows hotter in summertime, the tree which looked so dry all winter bursts into leaf and produces fruit, while the grass grows parched. Now you can see the tree's glory, but the grass is dry and brown. In just this way do the righteous struggle on now, before summer comes. Their life is in the root; it does not show in the branches yet. But our root is charity. And what does the apostle tell us? That we must be rooted up above, so that life may be our shepherd. We must keep our dwelling-place fixed in heaven, and walk about on this earth as though we were already dead. Let us be dead here below, since we live on high, and beware of so living here below as to be dead on high. Our life, our hearts, must never abandon heaven, and so the apostle tells us, *You are dead*; but do not be afraid, because *your life is hidden with Christ in God*. That is where our root is fixed. But one day our glory will appear, like that of a tree burgeoning in leaves and fruit, so he continues, *When Christ appears, Christ who is your life, then you too will appear with him in glory* (Col 3:3-4). Then it will be morning; it is not morning yet. Let the proud and rich folk of this world go on swelling with self-importance, let the impious jeer at the good and unbelievers at the faithful. Let them go on saying, "What good has faith in Christ done you? What more do you have through having Christ?" And the faithful, if truly faithful they are, must answer, "It is still night, so you can't see what we have hold of."

---

5. *Sursum cor*; see note at Exposition of Psalm 10, 3.

Let your hands not grow weary of good works. In another place scripture says, *On my day of trouble I searched for God; with hands outstretched before him I sought him in the night, and I was not disappointed* (Ps 76:3(77:2)). When day breaks our labor will be revealed, and our fruit will show in the morning. Those who struggle with difficulties now will be powerful then, and those who now boast and brag will be subservient later; for what does the psalm promise next? *They are consigned like sheep to the underworld, where death shall be their shepherd. And in the morning the righteous will have dominion over them.*

4. Since we have already said, *In the morning the righteous will have dominion over them*, I think this verse is quite comprehensible. Endure the night, and long for the morning. Do not suppose that because the night has life in it yet, the morning has no life. Is a sleeping person alive, and someone else who has risen not alive? Surely the one asleep is more like a dead person? Now, who are the sleepers? They are the ones Paul shakes in the hope of waking them up, the people to whom he says, *Arise, sleeper, rise from the dead: Christ will enlighten you* (Eph 5:14). Those who are enlightened by Christ must already be awake, but the fruit of their night vigil is not yet plainly seen. It will appear in the morning, which is to say when the uncertainties of this life have passed away. Our present life is a night; doesn't it seem like darkness to you? Someone lives a bad life, yet he or she lives on, flourishes, strikes fear into others, and is widely honored. Someone else leads a good life, but is criticized, reviled and slandered, but he or she toils on. It seems like darkness. But hidden in the root are vigor, fertility and rich promise. There is as yet no sign of life in the branches, but the root has not dried out, though it may appear to be withering. Come the summer, and the tree is clothed with glory and proves its fertility by its fruits.

And then what will be the fate of the people we are bidden not to envy? What does another psalm say of them? *They will wither swiftly like grass, and quickly fall like plants in the meadow* (Ps 36(37):2). They will fall when they see at Christ's right hand the saints who are struggling now, the saints who are the butt of their mockery. The wicked will rue it inwardly then, and repent of their taunts, but their repentance will be too late, and sterile. They refused to repent fruitfully in the present life, so they will repent unfruitfully hereafter. And what will their lament be, in that sterile repentance? *These are the people we once held in derision, as a byword and a butt for our mockery!* The words I am quoting come from the Book of Wisdom; those of you who are familiar with it will recognize them. They are the words that will be spoken in the future by the wicked when they see the judge, with all the faithful already grouped at his right, and all the saints exercising judgment with him. Here are the words scripture assigns to them: *these are the people we once held in derision, as a byword and a butt for our mockery! Fools that we were, we thought their life madness* (Wis 5:3-4). Yes, this rings true. When someone begins to live for God, to despise the world, to refrain from seeking revenge when injured, to give up the desire to be rich here below; when such a person resolves not to seek earthly happiness, to set no store by anything but fix his or her mind on God alone, and persevere in the way of Christ, other people say, "He's mad." It would be bad enough if this were said only by pagans. But since so many people are spiritually asleep and refuse to awaken, the faithful hear even from their nearest and dearest, even from their fellow-Christians, the question, "What's the matter with you?" My brothers and sisters, if someone says to a person who is following Christ, "What's the matter with you?" can we understand what is implied? We find it horrifying that the Jews said to our Lord Jesus Christ, *You have a demon* (Jn 8:48), and when we hear that gospel passage read, we beat our breasts. The Jews said a shameful thing to Christ, *You have a demon*; but what about you, O Christian, when you see that the devil has been driven out of someone's heart and Christ dwells there instead? Do you dare to ask, "What's the matter with you?" Do you suspect that that person has a demon? When our Lord was speaking to the Jews in a way they could not comprehend it was said of him—yes, even of him—that he was mad. *He is possessed, he has a demon*, they said; but a few of them were beginning to wake from sleep, and they objected, *These are not the words of a man who has a demon* (Jn 10:20,21). And so it is today, brothers and sisters, as long as his words are heard by all nations and all who dwell in the world, by earthlings and sons of men, by rich and poor, which is to say by those who belong to Adam and those who belong to Christ. Some say, *He has a demon*, and others demur: *These are not the words of a man who has a demon*; for some of them cling to the way of the world and hear only for a time, while others hear his words to good purpose and do as the psalm advises: *Take them in with your ears, all you who dwell in the world.* But when they do so, the good effect is not seen yet.[6] As for those who behave sinfully, and deliberately choose the way of the world, *death is their shepherd*, whereas for all who choose the way of God, Life is shepherd. Life in Person will come to judge, and he will damn along with their shepherd those to whom he will say, *Depart from me into the eternal fire which was prepared for the devil and his angels* (Mt 25:41). But those who were insulted, who were derided for their faith, will hear from their Shepherd, who is very Life, *Come, you who are blessed by my Father, take possession of the kingdom prepared for you since the creation of the world* (Mt 25:34). Then will be fulfilled the promise that *the righteous will have dominion* over the wicked, not now, but *in the morning*. Let no one say, "Why am I a Christian? I have no one to boss about. If only I could boss the wicked!"[7] Don't be in too much of a hurry; you will lord it

---

6. *Incertus est fructus*; but some codices have, perhaps rightly, *certus est fructus*, "the good effect [literally, fruit] is certain."

7. *Impero nemini, imperem iniquis*. But there is a crop of variants. Some codices omit *impero nemini*; some have *improperium iniquis* as the second clause: "I am a reproach to the wicked."

over them, but only when morning breaks. *Their support will wear out in hell, the support that is their glory.*[8] They have some glory now, but in hell it will wear out. What is *their support*? The money that bolsters them, the friends, their own strength. But when a person dies, all his plans will perish with him, on that very day.[9] The more glory he appeared to have among his fellows while he lived, the more he will find rottenness and corruption to torment him in hell after his death.

Verse 16. "As if . . ."

5. *But God will indeed save my soul.* You can detect here the voice of someone who has hopes for the future: *God will indeed save my soul.* This could be the prayer of someone who is still hoping to be freed from constriction or pain. Suppose a person is in prison. He says, "God will save me." Or someone is in chains, and says, "God will save me." Or again, someone is in danger at sea, tossed by waves and raging gales: what does he say? "God will save me." They all hope for deliverance so that they may continue their present life. This is not what the psalmist envisages. Listen to the next line: *God will indeed save my soul from the grasp of hell, when he takes up my cause.* The psalmist has in mind the salvation which Christ has already demonstrated in himself. He descended into hell, and ascended into heaven. What we have seen in the Head, we find also in the body. What we believe to have been accomplished in the Head was reported to us by those who witnessed it; we have seen it through them, because we all form one body. Does that mean that those who saw were better people, and we to whom they testified are inferior? That is not what Life himself said, our shepherd. He rebukes one of his disciples who doubts and wants to feel the scars, the one who after touching the scars exclaims, *My Lord and my God!* (Jn 20:28). The Lord looked at the doubting disciple, and saw through him the whole world that would come to believe. *Because you have seen, you have believed,* he said; *blessed are those who do not see, yet believe* (Jn 20:29).

God will indeed save my soul from the grasp of hell when he takes up my cause, but what of the time before that? Hard work, afflictions, troubles, temptations—you may not hope for anything different. Where is the joy? In our hope for the future, for the apostle says, *We always have cause for joy.* Amid such severe troubles, we are always rejoicing, yet sad too: always rejoicing, because Paul's precise words were, *as if sorrowful, we always have cause for joy* (2 Cor 6:10). Our sadness has an "as if" prefixed to it, but there is no "as if" quality about our joy, because it springs from certain hope. Why is an "as if" attached to

8. *Et auxilium eorum veterascet in inferno a gloria eorum*, obscure. The variants suggest (1) that *gloria* be understood as nominative, in apposition to *auxilium*, "their support, their glory, will . . ."; or (2) "they were driven out from their glory."

9. See Ps 145(146):4.

our sadness? Because it will fade away like a dream, and *the righteous will have dominion in the morning*. You know, beloved,[10] how when someone relates a dream, he puts in the phrase, "as if." "It was as if I were sitting there; it was as if I were speaking, as if I were dining, as if I were on horseback, as if I was having an argument. . . ." All of it is described in terms of "as if," because when the dreamer wakes, he does not find things as they were in the dream. A beggar might say, "It was as if I had found a treasure;" if there were no "as if" about it he would be a beggar no longer, but there was an "as if," so beggar he remains. Now for people who open their eyes to worldly delights but shut their hearts, the "as if" dream passes, and reality takes its place. Their "as if" dream is the happiness this world offers, but the reality for them is punishment. For us, it is the other way round: our sadness carries an "as if" label, but there is no "as if" qualification about our joy. The apostle did not say, "As if rejoicing, but always sad," or "As if rejoicing, and as if sad." What he said was, *As if sorrowful, we always have cause for joy*. He continued, *Apparently poor* (and here he said "apparently,"[11] which is equivalent to "as if"[12]), *we enrich many*. Yet when the apostle made that claim he possessed nothing; he had given away all his property and had no wealth at all. And how did he go on? *Seeming like people who have nothing* (this state of seeming to have nothing was the apostle's experience of the "as if"), *we possess all things* (2 Cor 6:10). No "as if" to that last statement, you see. He was "as if" poor, but he truly did bring riches to many; there was no "as if" about that. He was "as if" without any possessions, yet he truly possessed all things; no "as if" applied there. How did he truly possess all things? By clinging to the Creator of all things. *God will indeed save my soul from the grasp of hell, when he takes up my cause*.

Verse 17. Do not lose your nerve

6. What about those whose ambition is to flourish here? You will see a bad person doing well, and perhaps you will feel your feet slipping away under you, and in your thoughts you will say, "O God, I know what that man has done, what crimes he has committed. But look, he is prosperous, he intimidates people, he throws his weight about, he is arrogant, nothing gives him a headache, and his house never suffers any damage." You will be frightened then, because you have become a believer, and perhaps your heart says to you, "It's very hard on me. I think I made a mistake in believing. God does not take any notice of human affairs." But God arouses us, and what has he to say? *Do not be alarmed: a person may have become rich*. Why did you begin to lose your nerve, when some

10. *Caritas vestra*.
11. *Sicut*.
12. *Quasi*.

fellow grew rich? You began to be afraid that you had made a wrong decision when you became a believer, that all your struggle for faith was wasted, and that the hope in which you turned to God was futile. Perhaps you could by fraud have made the same fortune as the other man, and been rich, and not needed to work; but you heeded God's threats and held back from fraud, and turned your back on the fortune. Yet you see how the other fellow did commit fraud, and made his pile, and nothing bad has happened to him. So you lose your nerve about being good. But the Spirit of God says to you, *Do not be alarmed: a person may have become rich. . . .* Do you really want to have eyes only for present things, and no more? He who rose from the dead gave us promises about the future, but he did not promise us peace on this earth or rest in this life. Every one of us seeks rest, and what we seek is good, but not in our own country do we seek it. There is no peace in this life. What we seek on earth has been promised us in heaven; what we seek in this world has been promised us for the next.

Verses 17-18. Dying in style

7. *Do not be alarmed: a person may have become rich, and the splendor of his household may have increased.* Why does it tell us not to be alarmed? Because *when he dies he will take nothing with him.* You see a rich man living, yes; but now imagine him dying. You observe what he possesses here; but now consider what he can take with him. What does he take with him? He has plenty of gold, plenty of silver, plenty of land and slaves. Then he dies, and all these things are left behind—for whom, he does not know. Even if he bequeaths them to persons of his own choosing, he cannot ensure that they will remain with persons of his own choosing. Many people have acquired goods that were not left to them, and many others have lost what they did inherit.

All these things are left behind, then, and he takes with him . . . what? Someone may say, perhaps, "Well, he does take with him the clothes they wrap him in, and the money they lavish on an expensive marble tomb and on setting up a memorial to him. Those at any rate he does take." But I tell you, no, not even those; for they are expended on a non-sentient thing. If you dress someone up while he is asleep, without waking him, the things you put on him will be with him in bed. The adornments may be attached to the sleeper's body, but perhaps in his dreams he sees himself in rags. Now, what he feels is more significant than what he does not feel. When he wakes up, even what he dreamed will not be his; nonetheless, what he saw in his dreams while he slept was more to him than what he was unaware of. Well now, brothers and sisters, suppose people say to themselves, "Let sufficient money be set aside for my death; after all, why should I leave my heirs rich? They will get plenty from me anyway, so let me keep some of my own money to spend on my corpse." But what, I ask you, will a dead body get out of it? What will decaying flesh possess? What will insentient flesh call its own? If the rich man in the gospel, the one whose tongue was parched, had anything, then a dead person will indeed possess something of his estate. But is that what we read in the gospel, brothers and sisters? Do we read that the rich man made his entrance into hellfire dressed all in silk and apparelled in fine linen? Did he in hell look much the same as he had at his well-stocked table? I do not think so. When he was thirsty and longed for a drop of water, none of those things was available to him. So a person cannot hold onto any of it; nor does the dead man take with him what the burial takes. Only the erstwhile container of the person lies there, the house in which he used to dwell. We call the body a house, and its inhabitant is the spirit. When the spirit is being tormented in hell, what advantage accrues to it if the body is lying amid cinnamon sticks and aromatic herbs, wrapped in precious linen? You might as well decorate the walls of a house whose owner has been sent into exile. He is languishing in a foreign land, subject to penury and hunger, scarcely finding any poky little place to sleep in, and you say, "What a lucky fellow, to have his house decorated like this!" Anyone who heard you would conclude that you were either joking or crazy. But it is the same when you embellish the body while the soul is in torment. If you give the spirit some help, you will have given the dead person something worthwhile; but what will you give, when that rich man begged for even a single drop of water, and did not get it? The fact is, he had disdained to send any goods on ahead of him. Why did he disdain to do so? Because *the path they tread is an occasion of stumbling for them*. He thought there was no life except the present life, and had no concern except that he should be wrapped in exquisite clothes when he was buried. His soul was snatched away from him, as the Lord warned: *You fool: your life will be taken from you this very night; and then who will own what you have prepared?* (Lk 12:20). So in him the prediction our psalm makes is verified: *do not be alarmed: a person may have become rich, and the splendor of his household may have increased, but when he dies he will take nothing with him, nor will his glory*[13] *follow him below.*

Verse 19. Teeth on edge

8. *During his lifetime his soul will be blessed.* You must be alert here, dearly beloved:[14] *during his lifetime his soul will be blessed.* As long as he lived, he did well for himself; so say all, but they are wrong. The so-called blessings derive only from the lips of the one who draws attention to them; they are not blessings in fact. For what are you saying? That he ate and drank, that he did whatever he liked, that he enjoyed sumptuous banquets, and therefore did well for himself? Not at all, I tell you; he did himself harm. It is not I who tell you this, but Christ:

---

13. Variant: "the glory of his house."
14. *Caritas vestra.*

he did himself harm. Remember the rich man who feasted splendidly every day. He thought he was doing well for himself, but when he began to roast in hell, what he thought had been good was shown up as bad, for what he had eaten on earth he was now digesting in hell. I assure you, brothers and sisters, what he had been accustomed to feast on was iniquity. While he was eating luxurious food with his bodily mouth, he was eating iniquity with the mouth of his heart. What he had been accustomed to eat on earth with his corporeal mouth, he was now digesting with agony in hell. What is more, though his eating had lasted only for a time, the process of digesting the evil was to be eternal.

Can iniquity be eaten, then? Someone among you is saying, perhaps, "What is he talking about? Is iniquity edible?" Yes, but it is not I who say so; listen to scripture: *As sour grapes hurt the teeth, and smoke the eyes, so does iniquity hurt those who commit it* (Prv 10:26, LXX), for anyone who has eaten iniquity—freely chosen to eat it, that is—is in no state to eat righteousness. Righteousness is bread. What is our bread? *I am the living bread which has come down from heaven* (Jn 6:41). This is the bread for our hearts. If someone eats sour grapes with his bodily mouth his jaws become so rigid and paralyzed that he is less able to eat bread: he can only commend what he sees, for he is unable to eat it. So too anyone who has committed iniquity, and fed on sin in his heart, becomes less and less equal to eating this bread; he praises God's word, but does not act on it. Why not? Because when he attempts to act on it, he finds it hard work, just as our teeth find it hard work when we begin to eat bread after eating sour grapes. So what can people do, when their teeth have been set on edge? Refrain from sour grapes for a while, until their jaws work normally again, and then they can attack the bread. It is the same with us: we praise righteousness; but if we want to eat it, let us abstain from our sins. Then there arises in our hearts not only the pleasurable appetite to praise righteousness, but also the ability to eat it easily. If a Christian says, "God knows that I have the appetite for it, but I can't practice it," he or she has teeth set on edge by the prolonged eating of iniquity. So it looks as though righteousness is edible too, doesn't it? If it were not, the Lord would hardly have said, *Blessed are those who hunger and thirst for righteousness* (Mt 5:6). We must conclude, then, that because the rich man's soul *will be blessed in his lifetime*, this is true for his lifetime only, for in death he will suffer agony.

Mercenary praise

9. *He will praise you when you confer benefits on him.* Pay close attention to this, and let it nourish you. Let it be firmly rooted in your hearts. Eat, and observe people of this type, but do not be like them. Steer clear of such professions of gratitude. *He will praise you when you confer benefits on him.* How many Chris-

tians there are, brothers and sisters, who thank God only when some windfall comes their way! That is what the psalm means by saying, *He will praise you when you confer benefits on him*. He will praise you, declaring, "Truly you are my God. God has delivered me from prison, and I will praise him for it." He makes some gain, and he confesses; he comes into an inheritance, and he confesses; he suffers a loss, and he blasphemes. What kind of a son are you, if your father offends you when he corrects you? Would he be correcting you, if you had not offended him? Or, if you had offended him so seriously that he had come to hate you, would he bother to correct you? You should rather give thanks to God when he corrects you, so that you may receive your inheritance from him; for when you are corrected, you learn. He corrects you a great deal, because there is a great inheritance awaiting you. If you weigh the corrections you undergo against what you are to inherit, you will find that the correction is nothing. This is the point the apostle Paul makes: *The slight momentary thing that distresses us now is working in us toward an eternal glory in heaven that far outweighs it*. How long will it take? *We keep our eyes not on things that are seen, but on those which are not seen, not on temporal things, but on those that are eternal; for things which are seen are temporal, but things unseen are eternal*. And again, *I consider that the sufferings of this present time are not worthy to be compared with the future glory that is to be revealed in us* (2 Cor 4:17-18; Rom 8:18). What is it, after all, that you have to put up with? Yes, you have to put up with it all the time; I admit that. But suppose you have to endure what Job endured, and that all your life long, from the day of your birth and through all the stages of life, even to old age and death? Yes, suppose someone suffers even from infancy what Job suffered for a few days? Even then, remember that what you suffer will come to an end, but what you are to receive will have no end. I would not have you reckoning the pain equal to the prize. Equate time with eternity, if you can.

10. *He will praise you when you confer benefits on him*. Do not be that sort of person, brothers and sisters. Surely you understand that this is why we say these things to you, this is why we sing, this is why we explain the psalm, this is why we sweat over preaching: that you should not behave so. Your own dealings test you. Sometimes in your dealings you hear a truth, and you curse. It is the Church you are cursing. Why? Because you are Christians. "If that's how it is," you say, "I'm taking myself off to the Donatist sect. Or I would rather be a pagan." Why this reaction? Because you bit into the bread, and hurt your teeth. When you were only looking at the bread, you spoke highly of it, but now that you have begun to eat it, your teeth hurt. What I mean is that while you were listening to God's word, you joined in the common praise of it; but when you are bidden, "Act on it," you curse. Do not take that line. Better to admit, "The bread is good, but I am not up to eating it." But this is not your attitude. You commend the bread while you are only looking at it, but as soon as you begin to sink your teeth into it

you say, "This is horrid bread. What must its maker be like?" And so you praise God only as long as he confers benefits on you, and you are lying when you proclaim, *I will bless the Lord at all times; his praise shall be in my mouth always* (Ps 33:2(34:1)). The song on your lips demands a like song from your heart, and you have sung in church, *I will bless the Lord at all times*. But how is this true *at all times*? If there is gain coming your way at all times, you bless him all the time; but if things go wrong for you, you bless him no more, but curse. If you do not bless God at all times, if his praise is not always in your mouth,[15] you will be like the person described in the psalm: *he will praise you when you confer benefits on him.*

Verses 20-21. Wicked and righteous lines of descent

11. *He will make his way into the generations of his fathers*; that is to say, he will imitate the conduct of his ancestors, for the wicked who are alive today have brothers and sisters, and also forebears. The wicked of former ages are the fathers and mothers of today's wicked people, and today's wicked folk are in their turn the ancestors of tomorrow's wicked. In the same way the righteous people of earlier days are the fathers and mothers of today's righteous people, who are themselves the progenitors of the righteous of the future. The Holy Spirit wanted to demonstrate that just dealing is not wrong even when it provokes resentment in others, for the just had their own ancestor at the very beginning, right back at the origin of our race. Adam begot two sons. In one there was iniquity, in the other righteousness: iniquity in Cain, righteousness in Abel. Iniquity appeared to triumph over righteousness, for Cain, the unjust, slew the just Abel in the night. Had morning dawned yet? No, but *in the morning the righteous will have dominion* over the unjust. Morning will break, and then everyone will see where Abel is, and where Cain. The same is true of all those who follow Cain's example, and all who follow Abel's, even to the end of time. *He will make his way into the generations of his fathers, and will not see the light forever.* While he was here on earth, he lived in darkness, gloating over false goods and not valuing those that are real, and he will depart from this world into the black infernal regions; those dark torments will summon him from his dark slumbers on earth, and *he will not see the light forever*. But why not? The answer comes in a verse found in the middle of the psalm, and repeated here at the end: *Human beings failed to understand how they were honored; they were no better than the foolish beasts, and became like them.*

15. The translation here follows the emendation suggested by the CCL editors, which twice inserts *quia non*. Unamended, the text does not make good sense: "Are you sure you bless him at all times, sure that his praise is always in your mouth? You will be like. . . ."

Not so you, brothers and sisters. You must regard yourselves as human creatures made in the image and likeness of God. The image of God is within you, not in your body; it is not in those ears you can see, nor in the eyes, the nose, the faculty of taste, the hands, the feet. Yet God's image was truly created in you where the understanding resides, where the mind is, where the reason with its power to seek out the truth, where your faith is, your hope, your charity—there God has his image; and there you understand and see that material things pass away, as another psalm affirms: *although each human being walks as an image, nonetheless his perturbation is vain. He heaps up treasure, but does not know for whom he will be gathering it* (Ps 38:7(39:5-6)). Don't worry, because however wonderful these things may be, for you they are transient, if you are honored human beings endowed with understanding. But if you do not understand this, then, honored human beings though you are, you are no better than foolish beasts, and become like them.

Exposition of Psalm 49

A Sermon to the People

Verse 1. Christ calls

1. It is up to each one of us, brothers and sisters, to assess how effective God's word is in correcting our life. How far does it incite us to hope for the rewards he promises, and to fear the punishments he threatens? Each one of us must confront our own conscience honestly without any self-flattery, for we stand in great danger. As you see, our Lord God himself flatters no one. Even though he consoles us by promising us good things and thereby strengthening our hope, nonetheless he will not spare any of us who live bad lives and scorn his word. While there is still time we must question ourselves to determine where we are; then we must either persevere in a good course, or turn away from an evil one.[1] As the psalm affirms, it is no mere human, nor even any angel, but *the God of gods, the Lord* who *has spoken*. And to what purpose did he speak? *He has summoned all the earth from the sun's rising-place to its setting*. The one who has summoned all the earth from the sun's rising-place to its setting is our Lord and Savior, Jesus Christ. The Word was made flesh in order to live among us. Our Lord Jesus Christ is therefore the God of gods, because through him all things were made, and nothing was made apart from him. If the Word of God is God, he is most certainly God of gods; and if we ask whether he is indeed God, the gospel answers, *In the beginning was the Word, and the Word was with God; he was God* (Jn 1:1). And if, as it goes on to say, all things were made through him, it follows that the gods, if any were made, must have been made through him. But the one God himself was not made, and he alone is truly God. He alone, Father and Son and Holy Spirit, is the one God.

The truly deified and the false gods

2. Now who are these gods, of whom he, the true God, is God, and where are they? Another psalm tells us: *God has taken his stand in the synagogue of the gods, to make a distinction among them* (Ps 81(82):1). We still do not know

1. One codex inserts here the following lines, and then omits all the rest of Augustine's remarks on verses 1-2. "Between the just judge and your own conscience you have nothing to fear except your case itself, for he who at present is the witness of your life will be the judge of your case. If your case is not a bad one, you need fear neither opponent nor false witness."

whether perhaps some gods are assembled in heaven, so that there, in that assembly, in their "synagogue," I mean, God has taken his stand to make a distinction among them, for you must observe whom that same psalm is addressing when it says, *This is my sentence: you are gods, sons of the Most High, all of you; yet you shall die as mortals die, and fall as any lordly ruler falls* (Ps 81(82):6-7). It is quite obvious that God called human beings "gods" in the sense that they were deified by his grace, not because they were born of his own substance. It is proper to God to justify us because his is just of himself and not by derivation from anyone else; and similarly he alone deifies who is God of himself, not by participation in any other. Moreover he who justifies is the same as he who deifies, because by justifying us he made us sons and daughters of God: *he gave them power to become children of God* (Jn 1:12). If we have been made children of God, we have been made into gods; but we are such by the grace of him who adopts us, not because we are of the same nature as the one who begets. Our Lord and Savior Jesus Christ is the unique Son of God; he is God, one God with the Father, the Word who was in the beginning, the Word who was with God, the Word who is God. Others, who become gods, become so by his grace. They are not born of God's very being in such a way that they are what he is; it is through a gracious gift that they come to him and become with Christ his coheirs. So intense is the Heir's charity that he wanted to have fellow-heirs. What avaricious human being would want to have coheirs? Even if one such were found who was willing to have coheirs, and he divided the inheritance with them, he would have less himself than if he had kept the whole. But the inheritance we look to, as coheirs with Christ, is not diminished by the crowd of people who are to inherit, nor does it dwindle because they have become so numerous; there is as much when the heirs are many as when they are few, and as much for each individually as for all. *See what love the Father has bestowed on us*, says an apostle, *that we should be called God's children, and rightly, for so we are*. And further, *Dearly beloved, we are children of God already, but what we shall be has not yet appeared*. So only in hope, not yet in reality, are we what we are. *But*, he continues, *we know that when he appears, we shall be like him, because we shall see him as he is* (1 Jn 3:1-2). The only-begotten Son is like him by being born of him; we become like him by seeing him. We are not like God in the same way as the Son is, for he is of one nature with the Father from whom he is born. We are like God, but not equal to him; the only Son is like him because equal to him.

We have heard, then, who have been made gods through being justified, for they are called children of God. Now, what about the "gods" who are not gods at all, to whom he who is God of gods is a source of terror? Another psalm declares, *He is more to be feared than all the gods*; and in case you might wonder, "What gods are these?" the psalm explains: *The gods of the heathen are demons* (Ps 95(96):4-5). God instills fear into the demons, into the gods of the heathen, but he is lovable to those whom he has himself deified, his own sons and daughters. I find instances of both groups confessing God's majesty, however: the demons confessed Christ, and the faithful too confessed Christ. *You are the Christ, the Son of the living God*, said Peter (Mt 16:16). *We know who you are: you are the Son of God*, said the demons.[2] I hear comparable confessions, but I do not find comparable love; indeed, I find in one case a love that chooses,[3] and in the other only dread. His sons and daughters are those to whom he is lovable, but those who find him terrible are not his children. Those who find him lovable he makes gods, but those who fear him as terrible are convicted by him of being no gods at all. The former become gods, the latter are only believed to be; truth makes gods of the one group, and error imagines the other lot to be gods.

Christ's universal lordship

3. *The God of gods, the Lord, has spoken.* He has spoken in many ways. He spoke through angels, he spoke through prophets, he spoke with his own lips, he spoke through his apostles, he speaks through his faithful servants, he speaks through our humble ministry when we say anything that is true. Consider how though his ways of speaking are so varied, though he uses many tools and plays on so many instruments, he himself is sending forth his sound through them all: touching, restraining, inspiring. Yes, consider what he has done: *he has spoken, he has summoned all the earth.* What "earth" does that mean? Africa? So it would seem, from the claims of those who say, "Our Donatist party is the Church of Christ." No, he did not call Africa exclusively, but neither did he exclude Africa; for he who *summoned all the earth from the sun's rising-place to its setting*, leaving no region outside his summons, has indeed found Africa among those he has called. Let Africa rejoice, then, at being within that unity, and not grow proud in isolation. We have good reason to say that the voice of the God of gods has reached Africa, but not been confined to Africa, for *he has spoken; he has summoned all the earth from the sun's rising-place to its setting*. There is no hiding-place for the trickery of the heretics, no place where they can take refuge under the shadow of falsehood, for no one can hide from that sun's heat.[4] He who summoned the earth has summoned the whole earth; he who called the earth has called as much of it as he himself fashioned. What do pseudo-Christs and false prophets think to gain by attacking me? What is the point of their efforts to ensnare me with their sophistical words: *Look, here is Christ!* or *There he is!* (Mt 24:23)? I will not listen to people who try to show me only parts: the God of gods shows me the whole. He who *summoned all the earth from the sun's rising-place*

2. See Mk 1:24; Lk 4:41.
3. *Dilectionem*, see note at Exposition 2 of Psalm 31, 5.
4. See Ps 18:7(19:6).

to its setting has redeemed the whole, but has condemned the parts that make spurious claims.

Verse 2. "Beginning from Jerusalem"

4. When we hear that the earth has been summoned from the sun's rising-place to its setting, we may wonder whence his call went out. The psalm informs us: *His beauty shines forth from Zion*, and here we see clearly that the psalm accords with the words of the gospel, *throughout all nations, beginning from Jerusalem.* Notice the close correspondence between *throughout all nations* and *he has summoned all the earth from the sun's rising-place to its setting*, and between *beginning from Jerusalem* and *his beauty shines forth from Zion.* So the psalm's assertion that *he has summoned the earth from the sun's rising-place to its setting* is in harmony with the Lord's words, *It was necessary for Christ to suffer, and to rise from the dead on the third day, and for repentance and forgiveness of sins to be preached in his name throughout all nations* (Lk 24:46-47), because all nations are to be found within this sweep from the sun's rising-place to its setting. Furthermore the psalm's indication that *his beauty shines forth from Zion*, that the beauty of his gospel proceeded from there, that he who is fairer than any mortal[5] began to be proclaimed from that city, is in accord with the Lord's instruction, *beginning from Jerusalem.*

The new is in harmony with the old, and the old with the new. The two seraphs sing to each other, *Holy, holy, holy, is the Lord, the God of hosts* (Is 6:3). The two Testaments are in agreement, the two Testaments speak with one single voice. Let this voice of the two harmonious Testaments win a hearing, not the voice of the disinherited[6] with their bogus claims. So this was indeed what he did, the God of gods: *he summoned the whole earth from the sun's rising-place to its setting*, and from Zion his beauty proceeded; for that was where the disciples were gathered when on the fiftieth day after his resurrection they received the Holy Spirit sent from heaven. Thence the gospel set forth, from there proceeded their preaching, from that city the whole world was filled, and all this came about through the grace of faith.

5. It was through faith that it happened, for when the Lord first came, he came in hidden guise, for he had come to suffer. Strong in himself, he appeared in the weakness of our flesh. It was necessary that he should be seen, but not recognized; that he should be despised, so that he might be killed. His glorious beauty inhered in his divinity, but was concealed by his flesh, for if his enemies had

5. See Ps 44:3(45:2).

6. This mention of the disinherited implies that by "testaments" Augustine had in mind the meaning "will" in addition to "covenant." See the play on the double meaning in Heb 9:15-20.

recognized him they would never have crucified the Lord of glory,[7] And so among the Jews, among his enemies, he walked about incognito, working wonders and bearing injuries, until he was hanged upon the cross. As the Jews watched him hanging there they despised him all the more, and wagged their heads in the presence of the cross, jeering, *If he is the Son of God, let him come down from the cross*.[8] There the God of gods lay hidden, and his cry was uttered more out of compassion for us than from his own majesty, for where could those words have come from, if he had not taken our voice to himself: *My God, my God, why have you forsaken me?* (Mk 15:34; Mt 27:46)? When did the Father ever forsake his Son, or the Son his Father? Are the Father and the Son not one God? Is it not profoundly true that *I and the Father are one* (Jn 10:30)? How, then, could he cry, *My God, my God, why have you forsaken me?* Only because through his weak flesh the voice of a sinner made itself heard. If he took on himself the likeness of sinful flesh,[9] why should he not also take to himself the likeness of a sinful voice? To this end the God of gods was hidden while he walked about among human beings, when he hungered and thirsted, when he was tired and sat down, when bodily weariness overcame him and he slept, when he was arrested, when he was scourged, when he was haled before the judge, and when he replied to the insolent governor, *You would have no power over me, had it not been given you from above* (Jn 19:11). He was still the hidden God of gods when he was led out to the sacrifice, when like a sheep before its shearer he did not open his mouth,[10] when he was crucified and buried: through it all he was ever the hidden God of gods. And what about afterwards, when he had risen? The disciples were astonished and did not believe at first, until they had touched and handled him. But what had arisen was flesh, because it was flesh that had died; the godhead which could not die stili lay concealed in the flesh of the Risen One. His human shape could be seen, his limbs grasped, his scars felt, but could anyone see the Word through whom all things were made? Could anyone hold onto that? Or handle that? And yet *the Word was made flesh, and dwelt among us* (Jn 1:14). Thomas, who held onto him as man, apprehended him as God, as best he could; for after feeling the scars, Thomas exclaimed, *My Lord and my God!* (Jn 20:28). Yet what the Lord displayed to them was the same human form, the same flesh, that they had seen on the cross and that had been laid in the grave. This he did for them through the space of forty days. He did not show himself to the impious Jews, but only to those who had believed in him before his crucifixion, so that when he rose again he might render strong those who had gone reeling off when he was crucified.

---

7. See 1 Cor 2:8.
8. See Mt 27:40.
9. See Rom 8:3.
10. See Is 53:7.

Finally, on the fortieth day, he entrusted his Church to them, entrusted the world he had summoned from the sun's rising-place to its setting, to ensure that any people who were minded to perish in schism would have no excuse. He ascended into heaven, telling them, *You will be witnesses to me in Jerusalem* (that was where his beauty was to shine out from) *and through Judea and Samaria, and throughout the whole world* (Acts 1:8). When he had said this, a cloud took him away from them. They went on gazing after him whom they had known; but it was in his lowly condition that they had known him and they did not know him yet in his radiant glory. As he departed from them into heaven they were admonished by the voice of an angel, asking, *Why stand here gazing up to heaven, men of Galilee? This Jesus, who has been taken up from you to heaven, will come again, even as you have seen him go* (Acts 1:11). So he ascended, but they went home full of joy and remained in the city as he had ordered them until they were filled with the Holy Spirit.

But what was it that had been said to Thomas as he fingered the Lord's scars? *Because you have seen, you have believed; blessed are those who do not see, yet believe* (Jn 20:29). That was a prediction about ourselves. The earth which has been summoned from the sun's rising-place to its setting does not see, but believes. The God of gods was hidden not only from those among whom he walked about, and from those who crucified him, and from them before whose eyes he rose again, but from us too, who did not see him walking this earth but believe that he is enthroned in heaven. Even if we were to see him, would not what we saw be the same as what the Jews saw and crucified? We have something better in not seeing Christ, yet believing him to be God, than they had who saw him and thought him nothing more than a man; for in the end through thinking wrongly about him they compassed his death, whereas we by believing rightly are brought to life.

Verse 3. Hidden and silent now, Christ will be manifest later as judge

6. What are we to infer from this, brothers and sisters? That the God of gods, who was hidden then, and is hidden now, will be hidden always? Certainly not. Listen to the next line: *Our God will come openly.* He who came once in a hidden way will come again openly. He came in hidden guise to be judged, but he will come openly to exercise judgment; he came concealed so that he might stand before a judge, but he will come again openly to pass judgment even on the judges. *Our God will come openly; he will not keep silence.* Does this mean that he is silent now? If so, where do we get these things from, the things we are speaking about? Where do his commandments come from? And his warnings? And the terrifying trumpet? No, he is not silent; yet in another way he is. He does not keep silent from warning us, but he is silent from avenging his own; he does not keep silent from giving commandments, but he is silent from judgment. He

bears with sinners who daily commit evil deeds, caring nothing for God's presence, whether in their own consciences or in heaven or on earth;[11] but none of these things escapes him, and he cautions all without exception. Even when he chastises some people in their lifetime it is a caution only, not yet a condemnation. So he keeps silent from passing judgment: he is hidden away in heaven and there he still intercedes for us;[12] he is patient with sinners and does not unleash his wrath but awaits our repentance. Yet in another place he says, *I have long been silent, but shall I be silent for ever?* (Is 42:14, LXX).[13] And when he breaks his silence, then *God will come openly*. What God is this? *Our God*. Our God is very God, for there is no God other than our God. The gods of the heathens are demons (see Ps 95(96):5), but the God of Christians is the true God. He will come, he will come in person, but this time he will come openly, no longer to be mocked, not now to be struck and scourged, not now to be beaten about the head with a reed, not now to be crucified, killed and buried, for it was the hidden God who willed to suffer all this. *Our God will come openly; he will not keep silence*.

The fire of judgment

7. The following lines indicate that he will come to judge: *Fire will go before him.*[14] Are we afraid? Let us amend our lives, and then we shall not be. Straw is afraid of fire, but what harm can it do to gold? You have it in your power now to decide what you are going to do about it, but if you fail to correct yourself you will be tested by the fire that is coming whether you like it or not. But you know, brothers and sisters, I think it would be very inadvisable to lead a bad life, even if we had the power to prevent judgment day ever coming. Imagine a situation where there is no threat of fire on judgment day, and the only menace hanging over sinners is that they will be separated from God and never see his face. Whatever the plethora of enjoyment in which they might find themselves, however secure they might be in an eternity where their sins would always go unpunished, they would still inevitably mourn their lot, being shut out from the vision of their Creator and exiled from that loveliness of his countenance which defies all description. But how can I speak of a loss like that? To whom can I speak of it? Only to his lovers, who know what the pain of it would be, not to those who

---

11. A variant supplied by one codex has " . . . caring nothing in their consciences; for nothing escapes him, nothing in heaven or on earth, but he. . . ."
12. See Rom 8:34.
13. The codex last mentioned inserts here, "Let us listen, brethren, when he does not keep silent from words, lest we find no opportunity to listen when he does not keep silent from judgment."
14. The received text has here *Ignis ante eum praeibit*, which is quoted from Ps 96(97):3 rather than from the present psalm, though the thought is very similar. Probably Augustine was quoting from memory at this point. The codex which has been providing variants over the last couple of pages has here the corresponding verse from Ps 49(50), *Ignis in conspectu eius ardebit*. When Augustine repeats it a few lines further on he does so in this form.

scorn him. Any of you who have begun to experience the delights of wisdom and truth, in however small a degree, will know what I am talking about, and how grievous would be the punishment of simply being banished from the face of God. As for others, who have not yet tasted that sweetness, and do not yet long for the vision of God's face, they must at least fear the fire; if the rewards do not entice them, let the prospect of torments terrify them. If what God promises seems trifling to you, tremble before what he threatens. You are told that the sweetness of his presence will be granted to you, yet you do not change your life, you are not stirred to any action, you do not sigh for it, do not desire it. You hug your sins and your carnal pleasures; and all the while you are piling up straw around yourself, ready for the fire that is coming. *Fire will blaze out before him.*[15] This fire will not be like the one you have in your hearth at home. Yet even with that one, if somebody threatens to force your hand into it, you will do whatever he wants. Suppose he says to you, "Sign your father's death-warrant, sign the death-warrants of your children. If you refuse, I will thrust your hand into the fire." You will comply to save your hand from being burnt. Yet all that threatens you is the brief burning of a single member. It will not go on hurting for ever. So when your enemy threatens you with so slight an injury, you commit the evil act; but when God threatens you with everlasting evil, you will not do good! The enemy's threats ought not to coerce you into doing wrong, nor should they deter you from doing what is right. But by God's threats, by his threats of eternal fire, you are forbidden to do wrong and invited to do right. Why are you so dilatory? Because you do not believe.

Let each one of us shake out his or her own heart, and discover what faith is holding onto there. If we believe that judgment is coming, brothers and sisters, let us lead good lives. This present age is the season for mercy, but that future day will be the time for judgment. No one must plead, "Let me have my earlier years back again." Such a suppliant will be repenting then, but to no avail; we must repent now, while repentance is fruitful. A bucket of manure must be be applied to the roots of the tree now—the manure of a grieving heart and tears, I mean—lest God come and uproot the tree;[16] for once uprooted, there is no place for it except the fire. At the present time branches can still be grafted in again even if they have been broken off;[17] but then every tree that does not bear sound fruit will be cut down and thrown into the fire.[18] *Fire will blaze out before him.*

---

15. The aforementioned codex inserts here, "Let us amend ourselves, then, beloved brethren, and by fearing this fire allow ourselves to be corrected, so that we may be delivered from it on that day when we know we shall be shown up, through Christ our Lord. Here Saint Augustine's treatise ends happily."
16. See Lk 13:8.
17. See Rm 11:19-23.
18. See Mt 3:10.

8. *And a mighty storm will rage round him.* It will have to be a mighty storm indeed, since it will have to blow through such an enormous threshing-floor. This storm will effect the winnowing that will separate every trace of impurity from the saints, all pretense from the faithful, and every dismissive or proud person from the devout who tremble at God's word.[19] At present there is a mingling of all these, stretching from the sun's rising-place to its setting. Let us inquire how he who is coming will sort them out, how he will make use of that storm which *will rage round him*, that mighty storm. There can be no doubt that the storm will bring about a separation, the same kind of separation which the fishermen did not expect, those men whose nets burst before they reached the shore.[20] In that process a distinction will be drawn between bad and good. There are some people who in this present life follow Christ, carrying no load of worldly cares on their shoulders,[21] people who to good purpose have heard the Lord's invitation, *If you want to be perfect, go and sell all you possess and give the money to the poor: you will have treasure in heaven. Then come, follow me.* They are the kind to whom he says, *You will sit upon twelve thrones, judging the twelve tribes of Israel* (Mt 19:21.28). It seems, then, that some will be exercising judgment in association with the Lord, while others are to be subject to judgment, even though they are placed at his right hand; for we have very clear evidence that certain people will be exercising judgment with the Lord in the text I have just quoted: *You will sit upon twelve thrones, judging the twelve tribes of Israel.*

Will there be enough thrones?

9. But someone may object, "The twelve apostles will sit down there together, but only the twelve. Where will the apostle Paul sit? Surely he won't be excluded?" Heaven forbid that we should say so, or even silently think such a thing. What about his taking Judas' place? No, that won't do; the divine scripture has made it plain who was ordained to fill the place of Judas. Matthias is expressly named in the Acts of the Apostles, to eliminate all doubt.[22] Through him the number twelve was restored, even though Judas had fallen. Now since this group of twelve has occupied the twelve seats, does that mean that the apostle Paul will not be judging? Or that he will have to stand when he judges? No, it cannot be like that; the Lord who makes just awards will not arrange

19. Compare Is 66:2, which verse is almost a description of the "poor" who are beloved of God.
20. See Lk 5:6.
21. *Expeditis humeris*, an evocative expression. A Roman soldier was said to be *expeditus* when unencumbered with baggage and other items carried on the march, and with his weapons ready for action.
22. See Acts 1:23-26.

matters so, and the man who labored more strenuously than all the others[23] will not be left to stand while judging. But admittedly this one apostle Paul does force us to think more carefully about it, and inquire why the number twelve was mentioned in connection with the seats. Elsewhere in scripture we find other numbers that represent great crowds. Five virgins are invited in, while five are shut out.[24] You can look where you choose for what these virgins represent: they may stand for the chastity and integrity of heart which must characterize the whole Church, which is a virgin in this sense; for to the whole Church the apostle says, *I have betrothed you to your one husband, Christ, as a chaste virgin* (2 Cor 11:2). Or you can understand them to represent those women who have dedicated even the integrity of their flesh to God. But surely among so many thousands there are more than five of these? Yes, of course; but the number five represents self-restraint in the use of all the senses of the body. Many people are corrupted through their eyes, many through the ears, many through illicit scents, many through tasting forbidden things, and many through adulterous embraces. Others restrain themselves from all these five doorways of corruption, and restrain themselves in such a manner that the approval they receive is from their own consciences alone; they look for no accolade from others. These people are the five wise virgins, who carry their oil with them. What does that mean, to carry our oil with us? It means that all we have to boast about is the witness of our own conscience.[25] Then again, remember the man who while enduring torments in the underworld said, *I have five brothers* (Lk 16:28). These represent the Jewish people subject to the law, for Moses, their legislator, wrote five books.

Moreover, after his resurrection the Lord orders the disciples to cast the net to starboard, and a hundred and fifty-three fish are hauled up, yet large as they were, the apostle tells us, the nets did not split.[26] Notice that he had commanded them to cast the nets before his passion, but on that earlier occasion he had not indicated right or left. If he had said right, it would have suggested that they were to catch good people only; if left, that they were to catch only the bad. But by saying neither right nor left he indicated that both good and bad are to be taken, mixed up together. And caught they were, as the gospel's reliable account testifies, and in such numbers that the nets burst. This catch symbolized the present age, and the torn nets symbolized the rents and tears made by heretics and schismatics. But the Lord's action after his resurrection signified what will happen for us after our own resurrection, in that multitude in the heavenly kingdom where no bad person will be found. Accordingly the nets cast out toward the right prefigured those who will be on the Lord's right hand, after the ones destined for his left hand have been removed.

---

23. See 1 Cor 15:10.
24. See Mt 25:10-12.
25. See 2 Cor 1:12.
26. See Jn 21:6-11.

But are we to think that only a hundred and fifty-three just people will be at his right? No, scripture suggests thousands of thousands.[27] And read the Apocalypse: it would seem from what is said there that there will be twelve times twelve thousand from the Jewish people alone.[28] Then think of the huge number of martyrs. To go no further afield, our own Massa Candida numbered more than a hundred and fifty-three martyrs.[29] Finally, remember those seven thousand of whom the Lord speaks when he responds to Elijah: *I have seven thousand men left to me who have not bent their knees to Baal* (1 Kgs 19:8; Rom 11:4). These far outnumber the catch of fishes. So the hundred and fifty-three fish do not correspond to the exact number of the saints; rather does scripture for its own reasons suggest by this high number the whole multitude of the saints and the righteous, so that by a hundred and fifty-three we may understand all those who have part in the resurrection to eternal life.

But there is something else. The law comprises ten precepts, but the Spirit of grace, through which alone the law is fulfilled, is said to be sevenfold.[30] We need to examine these numbers, and find out what 10 + 7 means. Ten for the commandments, and seven for the Holy Spirit's grace, through which the commandments are observed: this suggests that all who have part in the resurrection, who belong at the Lord's right hand, who form part of the kingdom of heaven and share in eternal life, all these hold onto the 10 + 7; that is, they fulfill the law through the grace of the Spirit, not as though by their own striving or their own merits. But now, if you take the numbers from one to seventeen, and progressively add each to the previous total, you get a hundred and fifty-three.[31] And so you will find that the immense number of the saints is related to this number of a few fish. Just as by five virgins an innumerable number of virgins is represented, and by the five brothers of the man tormented in hell the thousands of Jews are signified, and by the hundred and fifty-three fish the thousands of thousands of saints, so too when twelve thrones are mentioned we should not think of twelve individuals, but of the enormous number of those who have been made perfect.

10. But I know what you are going to ask me next. "You have given a plausible account of how in the five virgins many others are comprised, and why

---

27. See Dn 7:10.
28. See Rv 7:4.
29. The martyrs of Utica, north of Carthage, were known as *Massa Candida*, or "White Lump." This may originally have been the name of the place where they suffered, but a legend grew up that in the time of the Emperor Valerian (c. 258) they were thrown alive into quicklime, which reduced their bodies to white powder. Augustine's Sermon 306 was preached on the anniversary of their death.
30. See Is 11:2-3.
31. He spells it out for them, as follows:
1+2=3+3=6+4=10+5=15+6=21+7=28+8=36+9=45+10=55+11=66+12=78+13=91+14=105 +15=120+16=136+17=153.

many Jews are to be understood as included in the five brothers, and why a great crowd of perfect people are to be understood by the hundred and fifty-three. Very well, now show us why and how the twelve thrones symbolize not twelve individuals, but a multitude. What do those twelve thrones mean, if they signify all those from all parts of the world who have become so perfect that to them it could be said, *You will sit upon twelve thrones, judging the twelve tribes of Israel*? Why can all these, coming from every quarter, have some connection with the number twelve?"

Because that very thing we are saying about them—that they come from every side—means that we are speaking about the whole world. But this world consists of four parts, which we name east, west, south and north. From all these regions people are called in the Trinity, and made perfect by faith in the Trinity and obedience to the commandments. If you multiply three by four you get twelve, and so you see why the saints, who will sit on the twelve thrones to judge the twelve tribes of Israel, belong to the whole world. Moreover, by the twelve tribes of Israel, Israel as a whole is meant, since it consisted of twelve tribes. It is clear, then, that as those who are to exercise judgment will come from the whole world, so too will those who are to be judged.

When the apostle Paul was reprimanding the faithful laity for not bringing their disputes to the Church for adjudication, but dragging off those against whom they had a case to the public tribunal, he demanded, *Do you not realize that we shall judge angels?* (1 Cor 6:3). He said this with reference to himself, so you see how he claimed the prerogative of a judge, and not for himself alone, but for all who have the right to exercise the judicial office in the Church.

Verse 4. "Heaven" is Christ's partner as he sorts out the earth

11. It is quite evident, then, that many will be invited to sit with the Lord in judgment, and that others too will be called, not as equals, but to be judged according to their merits. This will occur when the Lord comes with all his angels, and when all nations assemble before him. Those who have become so perfect that they are privileged to sit on the twelve thrones, judging the twelve tribes of Israel, will be counted among his angels. This is not the only instance of humans being called angels, for the apostle said, with reference to himself, *You welcomed me like an angel of God* (Gal 4:14); and of John the Baptist it was said, *Look, I am sending my angel ahead of you, to prepare your way before you* (Mk 1:2; Mt 11:10; Lk 7:27). We may infer, therefore, that when he comes with his angels, he will have his saints with him as well. Isaiah makes the point plainly: *The Lord will come in judgment, with the elders of his people* (Is 3:14). The elders of his people, these who have been called angels, are the many thousands of the perfect who have come from every corner of the world, and they are also called "heaven." The rest are called "earth," but they are a fruitful earth. What is

this fruitful earth? It is those who are destined to be placed at the Lord's right hand, those to whom he will say, *I was hungry, and you fed me* (Mt 25:35). Fruitful earth they are indeed, and the apostle delighted in them because they had sent him what he needed. *Not that I seek your gift,* he tells them; *all I seek is the fruit accruing to you.* And he thanks God for them, *because at last I see you putting forth new shoots of care for me* (Phil 4:17,10). That image, *putting forth new shoots,*[32] is appropriate to trees which have become brown and dried up.

Well then, brothers and sisters, when the Lord comes to judge, what will he do? Let us listen to the psalm: *He will call heaven above.* "Heaven" means all the saints, all those perfect ones who will sit in judgment; he will call them up to sit with him and judge the twelve tribes of Israel. This must be what it means, because how otherwise could he call heaven above, when heaven is always above? But the psalm here calls "heaven" the people who elsewhere are called "the heavens," when another psalm says of them, *The heavens proclaim God's glory.* And of them it testifies that *Their sound went forth throughout the world, their words to the ends of the earth* (Ps 18:2,5(19:1.4)). Observe how the Lord makes a distinction when he comes to judge: *He will call heaven above, and the earth below, to separate out his people.* From whom would his people be distinguished? From the wicked, obviously. After this there is no further mention of the wicked; they have already been judged and condemned to punishment. Concentrate now on the good people, and see how they are distinguished.

He will call heaven above, and the earth below, to separate out his people. He summons the earth as well, you see, but not to confuse all its inhabitants together: rather to sort them out. At the beginning he did call them all indiscriminately; that was when *the God of gods, the Lord, spoke, and summoned all the earth from the sun's rising-place to its setting.* At that stage he had not yet made any distinction among them; his servants were sent to invite everyone to the wedding, and they gathered in good and bad together.[33] But it will be different when the God of gods *comes openly, and no longer keeps silence*; then he will *call heaven above* to join him in giving judgment, for what "heaven" is, these "heavens" are. (It is the same when we speak of "the earth": we mean what the various lands are; and we know that what the Church is, the various churches are.) *He will call heaven above, and the earth below, to separate out his people.* Now in association with "heaven" he sorts out the earth; that is to say, "heaven" sorts out the earth with him. How does he sort out the earth? In such a way that he places some at his right hand, and others at his left. To this "earth" that he has singled out, what does he say? *Come, you who are blessed by my Father, take possession of the kingdom prepared for you since the creation of the world. For I was hungry, and you fed me,* and so on. They will reply, *When did we see you*

32. *Repullulastis.*
33. See Mt 22:10.

hungry? And he will answer them, *When you did it for even the least of those who are mine, you did it for me* (Mt 25:34-35.37.40). Heaven points out to the earth those most insignificant ones who are its own, and shows them exalted from their humble station, for *when you did it for even the least of those who are mine, you did it for me*. Thus the Lord *will call heaven above, and the earth below, to separate out his people*.

Verse 5. Mercy is better than sacrifices

12. *Gather his just ones to him*. The divine voice, a prophetic voice, speaks here; the speaker sees the future as though it were present, and charges the angels who are to gather the peoples, for he will send out his angels on that day, and all nations will be assembled before him.[34] *Gather his just ones to him*. And who are the just? Those who live by faith[35] and perform works of mercy, for works of mercy are works of justice. The gospel affirms this: *Be careful not to do your righteous works in the sight of other people, to attract their attention*, it says; and then, as if to forestall the query, "What righteousness does it mean?" it continues, *Therefore when you give alms . . .* (Mt 6:1.2). In this way it makes plain to us that almsgiving is a righteous, just activity. The psalm therefore commands, "Gather his just ones, gather those who have treated the helpless with compassion and have understood about the needy and poor; gather them, and may the Lord keep them safe and give them life."[36] *Gather his just ones to him, who regard his covenant above sacrifices*: that is to say, those who think more highly of what he has promised than of their works,[37] for these works are sacrifices, as we know from the Lord's words, *I want mercy rather than sacrifice* (Hos 6:6; Mt 9:13). *Who regard his covenant above sacrifices*.

Verse 6. Infallible discernment

13. *The heavens will proclaim his justice*. The heavens certainly have announced this justice of God to us, for the evangelists have foretold it. From them we have heard that there will be some at his right hand, to whom the Master of the house will say, *Come, you whom my Father has blessed, take possession of. . . .* Of what? *The kingdom*. And what price have they paid for it? *I was hungry and you fed me* (Mt 25:34,35). What action could be so insignificant, so earthy, as to break your bread for a hungry person? Yet that is the price of the

34. See Mt 25:32.
35. See Heb 2:4.
36. See Ps 40:2-3(41:1-2).
37. *Qui cogitant de promissis eius super illa quae operantur*. He could mean "think about his promises over and above their works," or even "during their works."

kingdom of heaven. *Break your bread for the hungry, and take the person with no shelter into your home. If you see anyone naked, clothe him* (Is 58:7). But suppose you have no opportunity to break your bread for them, or have no house into which you can invite them, or no garment to clothe them with? Give only a cup of cold water, or put two tiny coins into the treasury.[38] A widow purchased with two mites, and Peter purchased by leaving his nets, as much as Zacchaeus purchased by giving away half his fortune.[39] What it costs is what you have.

The heavens will proclaim his justice, because God is the judge. Truly he is a judge, not confusing things but discriminating, for the Lord knows who belongs to him.[40] Even if grains of wheat are hidden under chaff, they are known to the farmer. No one should be anxious about being a grain amid the chaff, for the eyes of the winnower make no mistake. Do not fear that the mighty storm that will rage around him may muddle you up with the straw. That storm will certainly be a violent one, but it will not take a single grain away from the place where it belongs, to sweep it into the chaff, for the judge is not some countryman with his three-pronged fork but the triune God. *The heavens will proclaim his justice, because God is the judge*. Let the heavens go forth, let the heavens proclaim it, let their sound echo throughout the earth, and their words to the furthest parts of the world;[41] and let the body declare, *From the ends of the earth I have called to you, as my soul grew faint* (Ps 60:3(61:2)). At present it groans in its confused state, but once the discernment has been made it will rejoice. Let it go on crying, then, *Do not destroy my soul with the ungodly, nor my life with those who shed blood* (Ps 25(26):9). He does not destroy it, because the judge is God. Let it insistently cry, then, *Judge me, O Lord, and distinguish my cause from that of an unholy people* (Ps 42(43):1); yes, let it keep making this plea, and God will act; his just ones will be gathered to him. He has summoned the whole earth in order to distinguish his own people.

Verse 7. He is God, and your God

14. *Listen, my people, and I will speak to you*. Take note, for he who will come, and will be silent no longer, is not silent even now, if you are willing to listen. *Listen, my people, and I will speak to you*. If you do not listen, I will not speak to you. *Listen, and I will speak to you*, for if you are not listening, then even if I speak, it will not be to you. So when do I speak to you? When you listen. And when do you listen? Only when you are my people. *Listen*, then, *my people*; you do not listen if you are some alien people. *Listen, my people, and I will speak to*

38. See Mk 9:40; 12:42-43.
39. See Lk 19:8.
40. See 2 Tm 2:19.
41. See Ps 18:5(19:4).

you; Israel, I will testify to you. Listen, Israel; listen, my people. Israel is the name that signifies God's choice of you: *you will no longer be called Jacob; your name shall be Israel* (Gn 32:28). Listen then as Israel, as the one who sees God, if not yet in clear vision, at least already in faith; for the name Israel means "one who sees God."[42] Let anyone who has ears for hearing hear, and anyone who has eyes for seeing see. *Listen, Israel, and I will testify to you.* The former phrase, *my people*, corresponds to the subsequent *Israel*; and the former declaration, *I will speak to you*, matches the subsequent *I will testify to you.* What will the Lord our God say to his people? What testimony will he give to Israel? Let us hear him. *I am God, I am your God.* I am God, and I am also your God. How should we understand *I am God*? In the sense of his revelation to Moses: *I AM WHO I AM* (Ex 3:14). And the other utterance, *I am your God*? In the sense that "I am the God of Abraham, and the God of Isaac, and the God of Jacob.[43] I am God, and I am your God; and even if I were not your God, I would be God still. I am God in my own goodness; but if I am not your God, it is because of the evil in you." The expression *your God* is spoken to someone whom God takes into a more intimate relationship with himself, as his slave or part of his personal property. *I am God, I am your God.* What more do you desire? Are you looking to get some profit from God, are you wanting God to give you something, so that what he has given you may be your very own? But look, he who might give you something like that is God himself, and he is yours! What is more valuable than he is?[44] You were seeking his gifts, when all the time you possess the Giver.

Verse 8. Genuine sacrifice

15. Let us inquire what he demands from humankind. He is our God, our emperor, our king, so what taxes does he impose on us, since he has willed to be our sovereign and to make us his domain? We must find out what revenue he requires. No poor subject must quail at the thought of what God may demand, because when God exacts any payment he first gives what he sets as the contribution we must make to him. All that is required of you is to be loyal. God exacts nothing that he has not given, and he gives to each of us what he demands. So what does he demand? Listen as he tells us: *"I will find no fault with you about your sacrifices.* I will not say to you, Why have you not slaughtered your sleek bull for me? Why did you not select the best buck from your flock? Why is that ram roaming about among your ewes, instead of being laid on my altar? I will not say to you, Inspect your fields, your farmyard and your buildings, to find what you can offer to me. *I will find no fault with you about your sacrifices.*" What do

42. See note at Exposition 1 of Psalm 21, 4.
43. See Ex 3:6.
44. Variant: "sweeter than you are?"

you want, then? Do you not accept my sacrifices? Surely you do, for you say, *Your holocausts are before me always*. Holocausts of a special kind, these are, the kind of which another psalm says, *If you had wanted a sacrifice I would certainly have offered it; but you take no pleasure in holocausts*. But then the psalmist turns to God, and to another thought: *A sacrifice to God is a troubled spirit. God will not scorn a contrite and humbled heart*. What are these holocausts that he does not scorn? What are the holocausts that are continually offered in his sight? The psalm continues, *In your good will, O Lord, deal kindly with Zion, and let the walls of Jerusalem be rebuilt. Then you will accept a sacrifice of righteousness, oblations and holocausts* (Ps 50:18-21(51:16-19)). This shows that God will accept certain holocausts. Now what is a holocaust? A sacrifice entirely consumed by fire. This is what the word means: *καῦσις* means "burning," and *ὅλον* means "the whole." So a holocaust is a sacrifice completely burnt up. But there is another kind of fire: the fire of intense, ardent charity. May our minds be inflamed with charity, and may charity take possession of all our members for its own purposes, not allowing them to fight in the service of our wayward desires. Anyone who wants to offer a holocaust to God must be wholly on fire with divine love. These are the kinds of holocausts which are *before me always*.

Verse 9. The old sacrifices are superseded

16. Perhaps, though, the Israel whom he addresses does not understand which of its holocausts God keeps ever in view; perhaps it is still thinking about oxen and sheep and goats? Let it stop thinking of these, for the Lord continues, *"I will not accept calves from your homestead*. I have specified my holocausts; but in your mind, in your planning, you were still running to your herds of animals, still selecting from them some fat beast for me. But I tell you, *I will not accept calves from your homestead*." He is foretelling the New Covenant, under which all those old sacrifices have ceased. They had a part to play in prefiguring a special sacrifice that was to come, by the blood of which we would be cleansed, but now *I will not accept calves from your homestead, nor he-goats from your herds*.

Verse 10. All animals, wild and tame, are God's

17. *For all the animals in the forest are mine*. Why should I ask you for what I created? Is what I gave you as your possession more yours than mine, when I made it? *All the animals in the forest are mine*. But perhaps Israel might object, "The wild animals, the ones I do not confine in my farmyard or tether at my manger, those belong to God, certainly. But this ox is mine, and this goat, and this sheep." No, says God. *"The cattle on the mountains and the oxen* are mine as

well. All those you do not own are mine, and these that you do own are mine too. If you are my servant,[45] all your personal property belongs to me. If the property a slave has gained for himself belongs to his master, it cannot be the case that property the Master has created for the servant does not belong to its Creator.[46] The forest animals that you have not caught are mine, and so are your cattle that graze upon the mountains, and the oxen that feed at your manger. They are all mine, because I created them."

Verse 11. God's knowledge of creatures

18. *I know all the birds in the sky*. How does he know them? He weighs them and numbers them.[47] Which of us knows all the birds in the sky? But even if God were to endow someone with knowledge of all the birds under heaven, still God would not himself know them in the same way as he granted a human being to know them. God's knowledge is one thing, human knowledge another, just as God's manner of possessing is one thing, and a human being's way of possessing quite different. You do not own anything in the same way that God owns it. What you possess is not entirely in your power: as long as your ox is alive it is not in your power to decide that he will not die, or will not graze. But in God there is supreme power, and there is supreme and secret knowledge. We must attribute this to God, and praise God for it. Let us not have the effrontery to ask, "How does God know?" I hope you are not expecting me to explain to you how God knows, brothers and sisters. But I will say this much: he does not know as any human being knows, nor as any angel knows; but how he knows I do not dare to state, for it is beyond my power to know it.

One thing I do know, and it is this: even before any of the birds in the sky came into existence, God knew what he had determined to create. What kind of knowing is that? You, human creature, only began to see the birds after you had been formed yourself, after you had received the faculty of sight. But those birds were born from the water at the command of God, when he said, *Let the waters bring forth birds* (Gn 1:20). Where did God get his knowledge of those creatures he ordered the waters to produce? Obviously he knew what he had created, but he also knew it before he had created it. So profound is God's knowledge that created things were in some indescribable manner present to him before they had been created; and do you think he is waiting to receive anything from you, when

45. Or "slave."

46. The contrast in this sentence seems to be not between domesticated and wild animals, but between material goods or money a servant might gain, and animals which are more obviously God's creation.

47. Probably an echo of Wis 11:21, "You have disposed all things according to measure and number and weight." Augustine saw this text as a hint of the trinitarian structure of created being, imparted to it by the creative Trinity.

he possessed it even before he had created it? *"I know all the birds in the sky*; you cannot give them to me. Whatever you decide to offer me in sacrifice, I know them all. I did not come to know them because I had made them, but knew them so as to make them.

"*And the loveliness of the field is with me*. The beauty of the field, the exuberant life of all the things that grow in the earth, all of it is with me," says God. In what sense is it with him? Was it with him even before those things came to be? All things that would come to be in the future were with him, and all things that have been in the past are with him; but the future things are with him in such wise that they do not push the past things out of his sight.[48] All things are established with him through a mode of knowing proper to God's ineffable wisdom in the Word, and all of them are created for the Word.[49]

Or should we infer that the loveliness of the field is with him because he is himself present in every place? He said, *I fill heaven and earth* (Jer 23:24); and can anything not be with him to whom the psalmist says, *If I mount to heaven, you are there; if I sink down to hell, even there you are present* (Ps 138(139):8)? Everything is with him, the whole of creation is with him, but not with him in such a way that he is contaminated by anything he has made, or suffers any need for his creatures. You may have a pillar beside you as you stand there, and when you feel tired you lean against it. You need that thing you have with you; but God does not need the field that is with him. With him is the field, with him the loveliness of the earth, with him the fair heavens, and with him all the birds, because he is present everywhere. And why are they all present to him? Because before ever they came to be, before they were created, all of them were known to him.

Verses 12-13. God is not hungry

19. Who can explain the words spoken to God in another psalm, *You have no need of any good things from me* (Ps 15(16):2)? Who can make that plain? God has told us that he does not stand in need of anything from us: *If I am hungry, I will not tell you*. He will not hunger, or thirst, or labor, or fall asleep, he who guards Israel.[50] "But," he says, "I am accommodating my words to your carnal nature. Because you are hungry when you have not eaten, you may think that God too suffers hunger and needs to eat. But even if he is hungry, he does not tell you; all that exists is spread out before him, and he takes whatever he needs from

48. Behind this assertion lies Augustine's pondering on the mystery of time, as a dimension of created, contingent being. We think we have it, but we deceive ourselves, because the past has slipped away, and the future is flying toward us and past us, to be lost likewise. But God is eternal and suffers no such loss.

49. Reading *in ipsum Verbum omnia*, as the CCL editors suggest. The received text *et ipsum Verbum omnia* does not yield clear sense.

50. See Ps 120(121):4.

wherever he chooses." These assertions are made to convince our puny minds, of course. They are not an admission by God that he is hungry.

In another sense, though, the God of gods did graciously will to be hungry for our sake. He came to be hungry himself and fill us with rich food, he came to endure thirst and give us drink, he came to be clothed in our mortal nature and clothe us in immortality, he came poor to make us rich. Yet he did not lose his wealth by taking our poverty upon himself, for in him are hidden all the treasures of wisdom and knowledge.[51] "*If I am hungry I will not tell you; for the round world is mine, and all its fullness*. Do not work to supply my needs; without any work I have everything I want."

20. Why are your thoughts still running on your flocks? *Am I to eat the flesh of bulls, or drink the blood of he-goats?* You have heard what he does not want from us, though he does mean to exact some payment. If you were worrying about that kind of tribute, banish the thought from your minds; do not even think of making that sort of offering to God. If you have a bull in peak condition, slaughter him for the poor; let them eat bulls' flesh, even if they don't want to drink goats' blood. If you do this, he will reckon it in your favor, he who said, *If I am hungry, I will not tell you*; because he will say to you in the future, *I was hungry, and you fed me* (Mt 25:35). *Am I to eat the flesh of bulls, or drink the blood of he-goats?*

Verse 14. The sacrifice of praise

21. Ask him, then, "O Lord our God, what payment do you exact from your people, your Israel?" And he answers, *Offer to God a sacrifice of praise*. Let us too respond to him, *The vows I must perform for you, and the praises I will render you, O God, are within me* (Ps 55(56):12). I had been fearful that you might demand something beyond my means, something I used to have on my farm, until a thief made off with it. But what do you demand of me? *Offer to God a sacrifice of praise*. I only need to return to myself to find the victim I must immolate. Let me return to myself, and find within myself this offering of praise; let my soul[52] be your altar. *Offer to God a sacrifice of praise*. We need have no anxiety: we do not need to travel to Arabia to find frankincense; we need not ransack some miserly merchant's bundle. All God demands of us is a sacrifice of praise. Zacchaeus had this sacrifice of praise in his fortune, the widow had it in her little purse, and some poor man who took in a stranger had it in his jar. Someone else had nothing, either in a fortune or in a little purse or in a jar, but had the whole price in his own soul. Salvation came to Zacchaeus' house, and the widow put in more than all the wealthy, and the one who gave a thirsty trav-

51. See Col 2:3.
52. Literally "conscience."

eler a drink of cold water will not lose his reward; but there is peace on earth to all people of good will.[53] *Offer to God a sacrifice of praise*, a sacrifice that costs us nothing, given to us gratis! I did not buy what I must offer; you gave it to me, for I could never have found it for myself. *Offer to God a sacrifice of praise*. The offering of this sacrifice of praise consists in giving thanks to him from whom you have every good thing you have, to him by whose mercy whatever evil you have from yourself is forgiven you. *Offer to God a sacrifice of praise, and address your prayers to the Most High*. The Lord delights in this sweet fragrance. *Address your prayers to the Most High*.

Verse 15. Longing for heaven is painful

22. *Call upon me on your day of trouble. I will rescue you, and you will glorify me*. You should not rely on your own strength, for all your resources are deceptive. *Call upon me on the day of trouble; I will deliver you, and you will glorify me*. "That is why I allowed the day of trouble to catch up with you. If you were not in trouble, perhaps you would not invoke me, but when you are in distress you call on me, and when you call on me, I will rescue you, and when I rescue you, you will give glory to me, and never afterwards stray away from me." There was someone who had grown slack about his prayer and let his fervor cool, and he cried, *I found anguish and sorrow, and I called on the name of the Lord* (Ps 114(116):3-4). He found tribulation to be something useful. He had become gravely infected by the corruption of his sins, and had lost his understanding; but then he found trouble that worked like cauterization and surgery. *I found anguish and sorrow*, he says, *and I called on the name of the Lord*.

It is undeniable, brothers and sisters, that there are tribulations well known to us all. These are the troubles that abound in the human race: one person suffers financial loss and bewails it; another is bereaved and left to mourn; another is exiled from his homeland, and grieves, longing to return and feeling sojourn in a foreign land to be unbearable; another person's vineyard is destroyed by hail, and he surveys his labors, seeing it all destroyed and all his toil gone for nothing. When can any mortal be free from sorrow? Someone may suffer from a friend who has turned into an enemy; what greater grief than that can there be in human experience? Everyone bewails these things, and feels the pain. These are our tribulations, and in all of them people invoke the Lord, and they are right to do so. Let them call upon God, for he is powerful enough to teach us how to bear them, or to heal them when they have been borne. He knows how not to let us be tried beyond our strength.[54] Let us call upon God even in this kind of trouble. All the same, these are the troubles that come to find us, as another psalm puts it: *Our*

53. See Lk 2:14.
54. See 1 Cor 10:13.

helper in the tribulations that have come upon us (Ps 45:2(46:1)). There is another kind which we ought to look for. The troubles we have spoken of come to find us, and let them come; but there is a kind of tribulation we must seek, and find. What is that?

It cannot be our happiness in this world, can it, our ample supplies of temporal things? They are hardly troubles; rather are they the things that console us in our troubles. Yes, but what troubles? The troubles of our pilgrimage. This very fact that we are not yet at home with God, that we are tossed about amid temptations and vexations, that we cannot be free from fear—all this is tribulation. This is not the security promised to us. Any of us who have not discovered this tribulation that dogs our pilgrimage are not under pressure to return to our homeland. This really is a tribulation, my brothers and sisters. We do good works, to be sure, when we hand out bread to a hungry person, give shelter to a traveler, and so on; but even these actions are part of the trouble we suffer, for we are confronted by miserable people to whom we show mercy, and the misery of the miserable arouses compassion in us. How much better off you would be if you were in a country where you found no hungry person to feed, no wayfarer to be taken into your house, no ill-clad person to clothe, no sick person in need of a visit from you, no quarrelsome person to be reconciled with an opponent! In that country all things are perfect, all are true, all are holy, all are eternal. Our bread there will be justice, our drink wisdom, our vesture immortality, our house an eternal home in heaven, our stable strength immortality. Will any sickness sneak in there? Will any weariness lure us toward sleep? There will be no death, no quarreling; there will be only peace, rest, joy, justice. No enemy will intrude, no friend let us down. What rest that will be!

If we think about where we are now, and reflect carefully on it, and then remember where we shall be, according to the promise of him who is incapable of deceit, we discover from his very promise how grave is our trouble in our present condition. But no one finds this trouble except by seeking it. You are in good health? Ask yourself if you are wretched. It is easy enough for a sick person to recognize that he or she is wretched; but when you are in good health, ask yourself whether you are miserable because you are not yet with God. *I found anguish and sorrow, and I called on the name of the Lord.*

So *offer to God a sacrifice of praise*. Praise him who promises, praise him who calls us, praise him who encourages us, praise him who is our helper; and be sensitive to the tribulation of your present circumstances. Call upon him, and you will be delivered, you will glorify him, and you will abide for ever.

Verse 16. Preachers, beware!

23. Consider what follows now, brothers and sisters. God had said to this person, whoever he or she may have been, *Offer to God a sacrifice of praise*,

thereby imposing a kind of tax. So on hearing this he began to reflect in his own mind, and to say, "I will get up each morning and go to church, and I will sing one hymn in the morning and another in the evening, and a third or fourth at home. In this way I will offer a daily sacrifice of praise as a victim to God." Now you are certainly doing well if you do that; but take care not to be over confident because you are doing it, because while your tongue is blessing God, your life may be cursing him. The Lord, the God of gods who has spoken, summoning the whole earth from the sun's rising-place to its setting, warns you, "O my people, even though you are still growing amid the tares, *offer a sacrifice of praise* to your God, and *address your prayers to him*; but make sure you do not live discordantly even while singing sweetly." Why does he say this? *To the sinner the Lord says, What right have you to expound my just judgments, and take my covenant on your lips?* You can see how sorely afraid I am as I say this, brothers and sisters. We take God's covenant on our lips, and we instruct you, preaching the just deeds of God. And what does God demand of the sinner? *What right have you?* Does this mean that he bans sinful preachers? If that were the case, what would we make of the admonition, *Do what they tell you, but do not imitate what they do*; or that other text, *Whether in sincerity or through opportunism, let Christ be preached* (Mt 23:3; Phil 1:18)? No, these things were said so that the hearers should have no anxiety about whom they hear the message from, not to encourage complacency on the part of preachers who speak well but live badly. So you are all right, brothers and sisters: if you hear good words, you are hearing God, no matter through whom you hear them. But God did not intend to let the speakers off unrebuked; they are not permitted to be smug simply because of what they say, or to fall asleep in their deplorable way of life, or to say to themselves, "God isn't going to damn us. He has willed to use our mouths to communicate such a lot of good stuff to his people." Don't be so sure: whoever you are, you speaker, listen to what you are saying. If you want to be listened to, first listen to yourself. Make your own the words spoken in another psalm: *I will listen to what the Lord God speaks within me, for he will speak peace to his people* (Ps 84:9(85:8)). What am I worth, then, if I do not hear what he speaks within me, yet expect others to hear what he speaks through me? I will listen first, indeed I will listen, and most of all I will listen to what the Lord God speaks within me, for he will speak peace to his people. I will listen, and I will chastise my body and reduce it to subjection, lest after preaching to others I be disqualified myself.[55] *What right have you to expound my just judgments?* Why do you take to yourself what does you no good? God warns the preacher to listen. He must not leave off his preaching, but he must take on obedience. But you, what right have you *to take my covenant on your lips?*

55. See 1 Cor 9:27.

Verses 17-18. Contempt for God's words; complicity in sin

24. *But you hate instruction*, you hate discipline. When I spare you, you sing and praise me; when I chastise you, you grumble, as though I were your God only when I spare you, and not when I chastise you. Yet I rebuke and chastise those whom I love.[56] *You hate instruction, and have thrown my words behind you*. What is said through you, you throw behind you. *You have thrown my words behind you*, where you cannot see them, but where they will be a load on your back. *You have thrown my words behind you.*

25. *Whenever you saw a thief, you would collude with him, and you threw in your lot with adulterers*. This is pointed out so that the accused cannot say, "I have not committed theft or adultery." No? But what if you approved someone else's action? Did you not concur simply by approving? Did you not throw in your lot with the perpetrator by commending him? My brothers and sisters, this is what it means to comply with a thief, or to throw in your lot with an adulterer, because even if you do not commit the sin yourself, you commend what is done and support the deed. The sinner is praised for the longings of his soul, and whoever does evil is blessed.[57] You don't do wrong, but you praise those who do. Is that a trivial wrong? *You threw in your lot with adulterers.*

Verse 19. More collusion with evildoing

26. *Your mouth overflowed with malice, and your tongue embraced guile*. The Lord is speaking, brothers and sisters, about the malice and guile of people who flatter others from whom they hear stories of wrongdoing. They know that what they are hearing about is wrong, but they are reluctant to offend their informants, so not only do they not rebuke them, but by keeping silence they connive. It is bad enough that they refrain from saying, "What you have done is bad"; they even say, "You did well." They know that it was bad, but their mouths overflow with malice, and their tongues embrace guile. Guile is a kind of cheating with words, saying one thing outwardly while thinking something different. Notice that God does not say, "Your tongue was guilty of guile," or "acted guilefully"; he wished to show that there was a kind of pleasure in the evil deed, so he said that it *embraced guile*. And even then, it would not be so bad if you simply did it, and took pleasure in the doing; but you praise the other person in outward show while deriding him inside yourself. This other person unguardedly flaunts his vicious actions, not knowing whether they are vicious, and you—you bring him crashing down. You know that what he did was wrong, but you do not say, "Watch out! Look where you're going!" If you saw him walking carelessly in

56. See Rv 3:19.
57. See Ps 9:24(10:3).

the dark in a place where you knew there was a pit, and you kept quiet, what kind of person would you be? Would you not be reckoned his enemy, a threat to his life? And yet if he fell into the pit it would not be his soul that died, but only his body. But when he is about to hurl himself down into his vices, and he brags about his misdeeds in your hearing, you know those things are bad, yet you commend them, and within yourself you deride him. Please God that person whom you mock, whom you would not correct, may sooner or later be converted to God, and say, "To hell with those who say to me, Splendid! Well done!"[58] *Your tongue embraced guile.*

Verse 20. Further charges: slandering a brother and scandalizing the weak

27. *You sat down to slander your brother.* This expression, *you sat down*, matches what he said earlier, *your tongue embraced.* What a person does standing up, or just passing by, is done without pleasure, but if someone sits down to it, he or she is seeking ample time for the deed. *You sat down to slander your brother*; you applied yourself thoroughly to the business of slandering him, you did it sitting down. You wanted to be fully engaged in it, you were embracing your malevolent deed, you were kissing your guile.

You sat down to slander your brother, and put a stumbling-block in the way of your mother's son. Who is your mother's son? The same person as your brother, surely? So the psalmist simply intended to repeat what he had already said, *your brother*? Perhaps so. Or did he mean to drop us a hint of some distinction? Yes, I think there is a distinction between the two. When a brother is said to be slandering his brother, you can imagine a situation where one who seems to be strong, a teacher, a scholar of some importance, slanders a brother who perhaps also teaches competently and conducts himself well. But there is another brother too, and in his path the first brother places a stumbling-block by slandering the second. When slanderous accusations are made against good people by those who are considered to be of some importance and well educated, weak persons who are not yet capable of judging for themselves are made to fall. This weak brother is here referred to as *your mother's son*, but not yet your father's, because he still needs milk and clings to his mother's breasts. He is still being carried in the bosom of Mother Church, for he is not yet able to manage the solid food of his Father's table. He draws his nourishment from his mother's breast, and is too inexperienced to judge, being still unspiritual and carnal. *The spiritual person judges everything; but the unspiritual person has no perception for the things that belong to God's Spirit, for to him they are foolishness* (1 Cor 2:15,14). To people like this the apostle says, *Not as spiritual persons could I speak to you, but only as carnal. As if to little children in Christ I gave you milk to*

58. See Ps 39:15-16(40:14-15).

drink, rather than solid food. You were not capable of it then, nor are you even now (1 Cor 3:1-2). "I was a mother to you," he tells them elsewhere: *I became very small among you, like a nurse fostering her children* (1 Thes 2:7)—her own children, he implies, not like a nurse feeding someone else's children. Some mothers after childbirth hand their babies over to nurses; those who have borne the children do not foster their own little ones but delegate the duty to others; and then the nurses who do foster them are fostering not their own babies but other people's. Not so Paul: he had both given birth to his children and was fostering them himself. He did not entrust to any nurse the little ones he had brought to birth; as he tells them, *I am in travail with you over again, until Christ be formed in you* (Gal 4:19). He fostered them, and nourished them with milk. But there were certain people with a reputation for learning and spirituality who slandered Paul: *"His letters are weighty and powerful, to be sure," they say; "but his bodily presence is weak, and his speech contemptible"* (2 Cor 10:10).This is what his slanderers had said, according to Paul's testimony in his letter. They sat down and slandered their brother, and in so doing they placed a stumbling-block in the way of a weaker son of their mother, one still at the breast. By their actions they forced this same mother to give birth all over again. *You put a stumbling-block in the way of your mother's son.*

Verse 21. You should be like God; do not try to make him like you

28. *All this you did, and I was silent.* One day the Lord our God will come, and will not keep silence, but for now, *all this you did, and I was silent.* What is implied by *I was silent*? "I have refrained from avenging myself, I have stayed the hand of my severity, I have prolonged my patient dealing with you, I have waited and waited for you to repent. *All this you did, and I was silent.* But while I delay, precisely to give you time to repent, *you with your hard and impenitent heart are storing up against yourself anger that will be manifest on the day of God's just judgment*, as the apostle warned you (Rom 2:5). *You were wrong to think that I will be like you.* It is not enough for you to find your wicked deeds pleasant; you think they please me too. Because you cannot bear to envisage God as avenger, you want to make him your accomplice, and have him as a sharer in the profits of your crime, like a corrupt judge. *You were wrong to think that I will be like you,* but neither have you any wish to be like me. The gospel tells you, *Be perfect, like your Father in heaven, who causes his sun to rise over the good and the wicked alike* (Mt 5:48.45). But you do not want to imitate God, who gives good things even to bad people; you want to sit down and slander even the good. *You were wrong to think that I will be like you. I will rebuke you.*" That will be when God comes openly, when our God comes, and no longer keeps silence. And, he asks, "What shall I do by way of rebuking you? What shall I do

to you? You do not see yourself now, but I will make you see yourself. If you could see yourself, you would be unpleasant to yourself, but pleasing to me. But because in your refusal to see yourself you think yourself pleasant, you will later be displeasing both to me and to yourself: to me when you are judged, and to yourself when you are burning. What shall I do to you? *I will bring you face to face with yourself.* Why do you try to hide yourself from yourself? You are behind your own back, and you do not see yourself, but I will make you. What you have thrust behind your back I will put before your face, and you will see your ugliness. But not in order to correct it: only so that you may be ashamed."

This is what God says, brothers and sisters, so are we to conclude that there is no hope for the person admonished? Not necessarily. Remember that city of which it was prophesied, "Just three more days, and Nineveh will be destroyed."[59] Within three days the city was moved to conversion: it prayed, it lamented, and it deserved mercy instead of the threatened punishment. Let all whom the description fits hearken, then, while there is still time for them to hearken to the Lord in his silence; for he will come again and keep silence no longer, and he will rebuke them; and at that time there will be no chance of correction. *I will bring you face to face with yourself,* he says. But you must do that for yourself now, whoever you are to whom this psalm applies: you must do now for yourself what God threatens to do for you. Bring yourself out from behind your back, where you are unwilling to look at yourself and where your deeds are concealed, and place yourself in front of you. Take your seat in the tribunal of your own mind, and be judge of yourself. Let fear rack you, and let confession burst out of you; say to your God, *I know my iniquity, and my sin confronts me all the time* (Ps 50:5(51:3)). Let what was behind you be in front of you, lest on some future day you are placed in your own sight by God, your judge, and there is no refuge where you can flee from yourself.

Verse 22. The lion

29. *Understand these things, you who forget God.* Look, here he is, crying out to us; he does not stay silent, he spares no effort. You had forgotten the Lord, and you were accustomed to pay no attention to the evil character of your life. Understand now that you have forgotten the Lord. *Otherwise he may seize you like a lion, and there will be no one to rescue you.* What does *like a lion* mean? Like someone strong and powerful, someone irresistible; this is what the psalm has in mind when using the image of a lion. The same simile can be used either to praise or to revile. The devil has been called a lion: *your enemy the devil prowls about like a roaring lion, looking for someone to devour* (1 Pt 5:8). Is it fair that the devil can be called a lion on account of his savage ferocity, but Christ cannot be

59. See Jn 3:4-10.

called a lion for his enormous strength? What would become of the claim, *the lion from the tribe of Judah has conquered* (Rv 5:5)?

Try to give your minds to the short passage that remains, beloved. I beg you to shake off your fatigue; he will help you who has kept you going until now. A little earlier the Lord said, *Offer to God a sacrifice of praise, and address your prayers to the Most High*, and by this command he was imposing a tax on us, as it were. You have heard about this already. But later in the psalm we found, *To the sinner the Lord says, What right have you to expound my just judgments, and take my covenant on your lips?* God seemed to be saying to the sinner, "Praising does you no good. I exact a sacrifice of praise from people who live good lives, and they benefit from offering it; but if you give praise to me, you will gain nothing thereby. How dare you praise me? *Praise is not seemly in a sinner's mouth*" (Sir 15:9). He brings the psalm to an end by addressing both groups. Rebuking the evildoers who forget God, he says, *Understand these things, you who forget God. Otherwise he may seize you like a lion, and there will be no one to rescue you.*

Verse 23. Who offers the sacrifice of praise?

30. *By a sacrifice of praise I shall be honored.* How will a sacrifice of praise honor him? It is certain that the offering of a sacrifice of praise brings no benefit to bad people, because while they presume to take his covenant on their lips, they commit villainous deeds which are not pleasing in his sight. "All the same," says the Lord, "to them also I say, *By a sacrifice of praise I shall be honored.* You had been thinking that praising me did not profit you; but offer praise, and you will find that it does, for if you live a bad life but profess good words, you are not yet truly praising. However, if you have begun to live righteously, and you attribute your good life to your own merits, you still are not yet offering praise. I would not have you be like the robber who vilified the Lord on the cross, but neither would I have you like the man who vaunted his merits in the temple and concealed his wounds.[60] If you are an evildoer and you persist in your iniquity, I do not say to you, Praising me will not help you, but, You are not praising me at all, because I do not reckon what you offer me to be praise. But then again, if you have the semblance of righteous living (semblance only, because none are righteous except the humble and devout), and you enter the temple puffed up by your righteous conduct, despising others whom you compare with yourself, and boastfully putting yourself on a pedestal on account of your own merits, you are not praising me then either. A person of sinful life does not praise me, but neither does any man or woman who claims to live righteously without help from me. But what of that Pharisee? He surely was not claiming that his good life was his

60. See Lk 23:39; 18:10-14.

own doing? After all, he said, *O God, I thank you that I am not like other people*. Yes, he gave thanks to God for the fact that he had good in himself. So even if there is some good in you, and even if you already understand that the good in you does not originate in you but has been given you by God, still, if you exalt yourself above someone else who lacks it, by that very attitude you prove yourself guilty of envy, and you are not yet a praiser of me."

Your first job, then, is to allow yourself to be corrected, to give up your wicked ways and begin to live rightly. Recognize that you are corrected only by the gift of God, for *a person's steps will be directed by the Lord* (Ps 36(37):23). And when you have understood this, look kindly on other people, so that they may become like you; after all, you were once like them. Be as kind to them as you possibly can, and do not despair of them, for God's bountiful gifts are not limited to you.

The man or woman who by sinful living offends the Lord does not praise him; the one who has begun to live a good life but does not recognize this as a gift from God, but thinks it comes from his own resources, does not praise God; and the one who does know that his own good way of life is a gift from God, but wants God to be bountiful only to him, does not praise God either. What about the man who said, *O God, I thank you that I am not like other people: robbers, cheats, adulterers; or like that tax-collector there*: could he not have prayed, "Give to that tax-collector what you have given to me, and supply in me what you have not yet given"? But no, he was full-fed, and belching. He did not say, *I am needy and poor* (Ps 69:6(70:5)); he did not say what the tax-collector was saying, *Lord, be merciful to me, a sinner* (Lk 18:13). For this reason it was the tax-collector who went home justified, not the Pharisee.

Listen, then, you who live good lives, and you listen too, who live bad lives. "*By a sacrifice of praise I shall be honored*. There is no one who offers this sacrifice of praise to me, and yet is bad. I am not saying, No bad person may offer it to me; what I say is that no one who is bad does offer it. Everyone who does offer it is good, because whoever offers it is also living a good life, praising me not only with the tongue, but with tongue and life in harmony."

Discovering Christ as God's salvation

31. *By a sacrifice of praise I shall be honored, and that is the way where I will show him the salvation of God*. In this sacrifice of praise there is a *way where I will show him the salvation of God*. But what is God's salvation? Christ Jesus. And how is Christ shown to us in this sacrifice of praise? In that Christ comes to us bringing grace. This is what the apostle says, *I live my own life no longer; it is Christ who lives in me. The life I still live in the flesh I live by faith in the Son of God, who loved me, and delivered himself up for me* (Gal 2:20). Sinners must

realize that there would be no need of a physician if they were healthy;[61] it was for the wicked that Christ died.[62] So when they acknowledge their wicked ways, and begin by imitating the tax-collector, who prayed, *Lord, be merciful to me, a sinner*, they display their wounds and beg the physician to help them. And because so far from praising themselves they blame themselves, so that anyone minded to boast may boast not of self but only of the Lord,[63] they acknowledge the reason for Christ's coming. He came to save sinners, as Paul testifies: *Christ Jesus came into this world to save sinners, among whom I am foremost* (1 Tm 1:15). Accordingly those Jews who boasted of their own achievements were so severely rebuked by the same apostle as to be declared by him strangers to the economy of grace, since they held that wages were owed to them for their merits and good works.[64] Everyone who knows that he or she belongs within the scope of grace, which is Christ and is bestowed by Christ, knows that he or she needs grace. It is called grace because it is given gratis; and if given gratis it is not earned by any preceding merits of yours. If your merits had come first, the reward given to you would come not as grace, but as payment owed to you.[65] If you claim that your merits had priority, you are seeking praise for yourself, not for God. And that means you are not acknowledging Christ, who came to bring the grace of God. Turn and look at your so-called meritorious deeds, and see that they were bad, so that what was owing to you was not a reward, but punishment. And then, having seen what you deserved, confess what is given to you through grace, and you will glorify God with a sacrifice of praise. For there is the way where you will know Christ to be God's salvation.

61. See Mk 2:17; Mt 9:12; Lk 5:31.
62. See Rom 5:6.
63. See 1 Cor 1:31.
64. See Gal 5:4.
65. See Rom 4:4.

Exposition of Psalm 50

A Sermon[1]

Introduction: pray for the absentees

1. There is a great crowd here today, and we must neither cheat it of what it expects, nor try its patience beyond the limit. We beg you to be silent and still, so that our voice may last out with sufficient power, even after the exertions of yesterday.[2] I take it, beloved,[3] that you have assembled today in greater numbers than usual in order to pray for those who are kept away by their perverted and unworthy mania. We are not speaking of pagans, or of Jews, but of Christians; and not even of our catechumens, but of many baptized persons. How close you are to them through that saving water, yet how unlike them in your hearts! How many of our brothers and sisters are in our minds today, as we sorrowfully watch them running off after empty things and lying foolishness,[4] careless of their primary vocation! It is ironic that if while they are there in the circus something happens to frighten them, they will immediately sign themselves with the cross. Bearing the cross on their foreheads they stand in a place they would never go near if they bore the cross in their hearts. Let us implore our merciful God to grant them understanding to condemn such amusements, and a change of mind to shun them. And may that mercy forgive them.

It is fitting, therefore, that the psalm sung today should deal with repentance. Let us speak with those who are absent, yes, with them too, for what you remember to tell them will be as good as my speaking directly to them. But you must remain healthy yourselves if you are not to neglect the wounded and sick, and are to heal them more easily. Correct them with your reproofs, comfort them by talking to them, give them an example by your own good lives; and then God

---

1. Preached at Carthage, as appears from section 11 below, perhaps in the summer of 411.
2. Some weakness of the chest was an habitual trial for Augustine. In his *Confessions* he relates that it was a factor in his decision to abandon his career as a teacher of oratory, though his conversion occurred at almost the same time and his life would in any case have taken a new direction: "In that same summer [386] my lungs had begun to fail under the severe strain of teaching, making it difficult for me to draw breath and giving proof of their unhealthy condition by pains in my chest. My tone was husky and I could not manage any sustained effort . . ." (IX,2,4). The length and frequency of his sermons after becoming a bishop must have taxed his voice severely.
3. *Caritatem vestram.*
4. See Ps 39:5(40:4).

who has been with you will be with them as well. It is not as though the bridge[5] of God's mercy was demolished after you had crossed over it and left those dangers behind. The path you took, they will take; the crossing you made, they will make too. But it is a very bad thing, an extremely dangerous, harmful and even fatal thing, for them to sin with their eyes open. It is one thing when a person who does not know what to avoid goes running after these empty pleasures, but quite another when someone disregards the voice of Christ in order to do so. Yet even of these we must not despair, as our psalm demonstrates.

Verses 1-2. David's adultery

2. Its title is *A psalm for David himself, when the prophet Nathan came to him after he had gone in to Bathsheba.* This woman Bathsheba was another man's wife. We say this with grief and trepidation, yet since God wanted the matter to be written about, he does not mean us to hush it up. What I am going to say, therefore, is not what I want to say, but what I am forced to. I say it not to encourage you to imitation, but to teach you caution. David, who was both king and prophet, was captivated by the beauty of this woman, who was the wife of another man, and he committed adultery with her—David, from whose seed our Lord was to be born according to the flesh.[6] The event is not recorded in this psalm, but is alluded to in its title. In the Book of the Kingdoms[7] it is recounted in full. Both are parts of canonical scripture, both are to be accepted by Christians with unhesitating faith. They tell what was done; it was committed to writing. David arranged for the woman's husband to be killed in battle, thus making his adultery worse by murder. Afterwards the prophet Nathan was sent to him by the Lord, to rebuke him for the grave sin he had committed.

3. We have read about what we must shun; now let us listen to what we must imitate if we have slipped into sin, for there are many who are very willing to fall with David, but unwilling to rise again with him. The story is not put before you as an example of falling, but as an example of rising again if you have fallen. Consider it carefully, so that you do not fall. The lapse of the great should not give glee to lesser folk; rather should the fall of the great cause lesser folk to tremble. This is why the story is presented to us, why it was written in the first place and why it is often read and sung in church. Let all who have not fallen listen, to ensure they do not fall; and let all who have fallen listen, so that they may learn to get up again. The sin of this man, great as he was, is not passed over

5. Variant: "fountain."
6. See Rom 1:3.
7. That is, 2 Samuel 11-12, according to our usage.

in silence, but proclaimed in church. Those who are living bad lives[8] listen to find themselves a patron saint for their sinning; they look at it eagerly for something to justify the sin they have decided to commit, not for a reason to avoid one they have not committed. "If David did that," they say to themselves, "why shouldn't I?"

A soul that commits the same sin as David, making that its excuse, is all the more guilty, for it is doing something worse than what David did. I will make this point more clearly, if I can. Listen: David had no one before him as a precedent in the way you have. He fell because his lust tripped him up, not because he looked to any holy man's patronage. But if you take him as your holy exemplar in your sin, you do not imitate his holiness, but only his downfall. You are loving in David what David hated in himself.[9] You are preparing yourself to sin, you are making your arrangements to sin. You read God's book in order to sin, you listen to God's scriptures for the purpose of doing something that displeases God. This is not what David did: he was reprimanded by a prophet, he did not fall over a prophet into sin.

Other people listen to the story in a way conducive to their salvation. From this fall of a strong man they take the measure of their own weakness, and because they desire to avoid actions that God condemns they restrain their eyes from wanton roving. They do not fix their gaze on the beauty of anyone's body, nor do they lull themselves into security by any wrongheaded naiveté, telling themselves, "I looked at her with the best intentions, I just looked at her kindly. It was only out of charity that I went on looking at her for so long." They keep David's fall in mind, and see that this great man fell so that lesser men may keep their eyes away from whatever could make them fall too. They withhold their eyes from wanton glances, they do not readily join or mingle with the wives of other men, they do not raise careless eyes to other people's balconies or sun-traps. It was from a distance that David espied the woman to whose charms he fell prey. The woman was far off, but his lust was very near. What he could see was some way off, but the cause of his fall was within him.

We must be very careful about this weakness of our flesh, and remember the apostle's words, *Do not let sin reign in your mortal body* (Rom 6:12). He did not say, "Do not allow it to be there," but *Let it not reign*. Sin is in you when you feel the pleasure, but it reigns only if you consent. Carnal pleasure must be bridled, not given its head, especially when it is proceeding toward unlawful and inappropriate objects. It must be subdued by a command, not put into a commanding position. You can listen to this without a care only if you have nothing in you that

8. Accepting the emendation *audiunt male viventes* instead of the reading of most codices, and of Caesarius of Arles in his Sermon 155, *audiunt male audientes*, "those who hear in the wrong way."
9. Variant: "You should love in David what David did not hate in himself."

could unsettle you. But you reply, "I am powerfully in control." So you are more powerful than David, are you?

4. In giving us this example scripture is warning us that no one should exalt himself or herself when things are going well. Plenty of people fear adversity, but are not afraid of prosperity. Yet prosperity is more dangerous to the soul than adversity is to the body. Success first corrupts us, so that when calamity strikes it may find us fragile enough to break. We must keep a very sharp look-out when we are happy, my brothers and sisters. This is why God's word strips us of our carelessness in happy circumstances by warning, *Serve the Lord in reverence, and rejoice before him with awe* (Ps 2:11): rejoice because we must give him thanks, but with awe lest we fall. David did not commit that sin while he was being persecuted by Saul. While the holy David was enduring Saul's enmity, while he was hounded hither and thither by Saul's pursuit, while he was fleeing from one hiding-place to another in his effort not to fall into Saul's hands, he did not desire any woman who was not his, nor did he murder any man with whose wife he had committed adultery. The more wretched he perceived himself to be in his weakness and distress, the more intent he was on God. Tribulation is a useful thing, just as the surgeon's knife may be more useful than the devil's blandishments. But once David had defeated his enemies and gained security, the pressure was off him and his pride grew to excess. His example is therefore valid for us in this sense too, that we must beware of complacency. *I found anguish and sorrow*, says another psalm, *and I called on the name of the Lord* (Ps 114(116):3-4).

The prospect of pardon

5. But there is no denying it; it did happen, and I have said all this so that those who have not done likewise may vigilantly guard their chastity, and as they contemplate a great man's fall, know that they as lesser people must be afraid. But if any who hear this have fallen already, and study the words of this psalm with some evil thing on their consciences, they must indeed be aware of the gravity of their wounds, but not despair of our noble physician. Sin allied to despair is certain death. No one must say, "If I have already done something wicked I am already worthy of damnation. God does not forgive such evils, so why should I not pile sins upon sins? Let me enjoy this world's pleasures, in licentiousness and forbidden lusts. There is no longer any hope of rehabilitation for me, so let me at least grab hold of what I can see, if I can't have what I believe in."

But as this psalm warns the unfallen to be wary, so too it will not leave the fallen to despair.[10] Whoever you are who have sinned, and are holding back from

10. Variant: "so it uplifts those who have fallen."

repenting of your sin because you despair of salvation, listen to David groaning. It is not the prophet Nathan who has been sent to you; David himself has been sent. Listen to him crying out, and cry out with him; listen to him groaning, and groan too; listen to him weeping, and add your tears to his; listen to him corrected, and share his joy. If sin could not be denied access to you, let the hope of forgiveness not be debarred. The prophet Nathan was sent to that man; and notice how humble the king was. He did not brush his mentor's words aside, nor did he demand, "How dare you speak to me like this? I am the king!" King in his majesty though he was, he listened to the prophet; now let Christ's lowly people listen to Christ.[11]

Verse 3. Mercy for witting and unwitting transgressions

6. Listen, then, and say with David, *Have mercy on me, God, according to your great mercy*. A person who is driven to beg for great mercy is confessing great misery. Those who have sinned unwittingly may beg for only slight mercy; but David says, *Have mercy on me according to your great mercy*. Treat a grave wound with your mighty medicine. Grave indeed is my condition, but I take refuge with the Almighty. I would despair of so fatal a wound if I could not find such powerful medicine. *Have mercy on me, God, according to your great mercy, and in your manifold pity blot out my iniquity*. His words, *blot out my iniquity*, echo the preceding *have mercy on me, God*; and the phrase, *in your manifold pity*, means the same as *according to your great mercy*. Because your mercy is great, many are your acts of mercy, and from your great mercy springs your manifold pity. You look upon those who scorn you, to correct them; upon the ignorant, to teach them; upon those who confess, to forgive them. Did David sin through ignorance? There was another man who had done some bad deeds, many bad deeds, who could say, *I received mercy, because I acted in ignorance* (1 Tm 1:13). But David could not say, *I acted in ignorance*. He knew very well how wrong it was to lay hands on another man's wife, and how wrong it was to kill her husband, who knew nothing and was not even angry with him. So those who do wrong in ignorance obtain the mercy of the Lord; and those who do wrong knowingly obtain not just any kind of mercy, but his great mercy.

Verse 4. Mercy does not nullify justice

7. *Wash me more and more from my guilt*. Why does he say, *Wash me more and more*? Because the stain goes deep. Wash more and more the sins of one who sinned knowingly, you who have washed the sins of the ignorant clean away. Not even in this deeply stained condition must we despair of your mercy.

11. *Plebs eius humilis*; a variant has *plebeius humilis*, "a lowly commoner/common people."

And cleanse me of my offense. What inducement do you propose to offer? He is a physician, so present him with a fee; he is God, so present a sacrifice. What will you pay for your cleansing? Consider whom you are calling upon: you are invoking the Just One, and if he is just, he hates sins; if he is just, he punishes sins. You cannot rob the Lord God of his justice. Implore his mercy, but watch out for his justice. In his mercy he forgives the sinner; in his justice he punishes the sin. What then? If you seek his mercy, will your sin go unpunished? Let David reply, let the fallen reply, and let them reply with David so that they may deserve the same mercy that he received. Let them say, "No, Lord, my sin will not go unpunished. I know the justice of the One whose mercy I seek, and my sin will not go unpunished. But I do ask you not to punish me, because I am punishing my sin myself. So I beg you to remit what I admit."[12]

Verse 5. Nathan's parable; the adulteress and Christ

8. *For I admit my wrongdoing, and my offense confronts me all the time*. "I have not thrust my deed behind my back; I do not look askance at others while forgetting myself; I do not presume to extract a speck of straw from my brother's eye while there is a timber in my own;[13] my sin is in front of me, not behind my back. It was behind me until the prophet was sent to me, and put to me the parable of the poor man's sheep." What the prophet Nathan said to David was this: *There was a certain rich man who had a large flock of sheep. His neighbor was a poor man who had only one little ewe lamb; she rested in his arms and was fed from his own dish. Then a guest arrived at the rich man's house. The rich man took nothing from his flock; what he wanted was the little ewe lamb that belonged to his neighbor, so he slaughtered that for his guest. What does he deserve?* (2 Sm 12:1-4). Angrily David pronounced sentence. Obviously the king was unaware of the trap into which he had fallen, and he decreed that the rich man deserved to die, and must make fourfold restitution for the sheep. It was a very severe view, and entirely just. But his own sin was not yet before his eyes; what he had done was still behind his back. He did not yet admit his own iniquity, and hence would not remit another's. But the prophet had been sent to him for this purpose. He brought the sin out from behind David's back and held it before his eyes, so that he might see that the severe sentence had been passed on himself. To cut away diseased tissue in David's heart and heal the wound there, Nathan used David's tongue as a knife.

This is what the Lord did to the Jews who brought before him an adulteress, setting a trap to catch him but falling into it themselves. *This woman was caught committing adultery*, they said. *Now Moses ordered that such women should be*

12. *Peto ut ignoscas, quia ego agnosco.*
13. See Mt 7:3.

stoned. What is your judgment concerning her? (Jn 8:4-5). They thought to catch the Wisdom of God between the two jaws of their trap, for if he ordered her to be executed, he would lose his reputation for gentleness, but if he ordered her to be released, he would be open to the accusation that he was subverting[14] the law. So how did he reply? He did not say, "Execute her"; neither did he say, "Let her go." What he said was, *"Anyone who knows himself to be without sin shall be the first to thrown a stone at her.* It is a just law that orders an adulteress to be executed, but this just law demands innocent administrators. Take note of this woman you are bringing to me, and take note who you are." On hearing this they departed, one by one. The adulteress remained, and so did the Lord; the wounded woman remained with the doctor; great misery remained with great mercy. Those who had brought her were ashamed, but did not ask forgiveness; she whom they had brought was covered with confusion, but healed. *The Lord said to her, "Woman, has no one condemned you?" She answered, "No one, sir." And he said, "Neither will I condemn you. Go, and sin no more*" (Jn 8:7.10-11). Did Christ act in opposition to his own law? Remember that the Father had not given the law apart from his Son. If heaven and earth and all things in them were made through him, do you suppose the law was written without the Word of God? No, God does not contradict his own law, any more than an emperor acts in opposition to his laws when he pardons someone. Moses was a minister of the law, but Christ the lawgiver; Moses acts as judge in passing sentence of stoning, but Christ grants pardon as king. God had mercy on the woman in accordance with his great mercy, just as David here asks, and begs, and tearfully implores him on his own account. That was what the Jews who brought the woman refused to do. They recognized their wounds when the doctor pointed them out, but they did not seek healing from the doctor.

And the same is true of many people who are not ashamed to sin, but ashamed to do penance. What incredible foolishness! If you are not ashamed of the wound itself, how can you be ashamed of the bandage on your wound? Isn't it more smelly and disgusting uncovered? Flee to the doctor, then, do penance and say, *I admit my wrongdoing, and my offense confronts me all the time.*

Verse 6. The sinless Christ, himself judged, alone judges justly

9. *Against you alone have I sinned, and in your sight I have acted wickedly.* How can he say that? Were not his sins of adultery and murdering the woman's husband committed in the sight of human beings as well? Didn't everyone know what David had done? How then can he say, *Against you alone have I sinned, and in your sight I have acted wickedly*? Because you alone, Lord, are without sin. The only one who can justly inflict punishment is the one who has nothing in

14. Variant: "would incur the charge of blasphemy as one who subverted."

himself that deserves punishment; the only one who justly rebukes is he who has nothing in him that could merit rebuke. So the psalm confesses, *Against you alone have I sinned, and in your sight I have acted wickedly. So will you be justified in your verdict, and prevail when you are judged.* This is difficult, brothers and sisters, because it is hard to see to whom that could be said. Obviously he is addressing God, and still more obviously God the Father has never been judged. What does it mean, then, *against you alone have I sinned, and in your sight I have acted wickedly. So will you be justified in your verdict, and prevail when you are judged*? He sees our future judge being subjected to judgment,[15] the just one subjected to judgment by sinners, and victorious because there was nothing in him that could be judged. Alone among all human beings the Man-God could truly say,[16] "If you have found any sin in me, name it."[17] But perhaps there was some sin hidden from human eyes, and they simply failed to find what was indeed there, but not manifest? No, for in another place he said, *Now the prince of this world is coming*, that sharp-eyed detector of all sins, *now the prince of this world is coming*, inflicting death on sinners because he is the lord of death,[18] for *through the devil's envy death entered the world* (Wis 2:24). Now, said the Lord on the brink of his passion, *Now the prince of this world is coming, and he will find nothing in me*, nothing of sin, nothing that deserves death, nothing that merits damnation. And then, as though one of them had asked him, "Why should you die, then?" he went on to say, *But so that all may know that I am doing my Father's will, rise, let us leave here* (Jn 14:30,31). "I am suffering undeservedly," he says, "for those who deserve to suffer; I am suffering their death, which I do not deserve, so that I may bring them to deserve my life."

To this sinless sufferer the prophet David says in our psalm, *Against you alone have I sinned, and in your sight I have acted wickedly. So will you be justified in your verdict, and prevail when you are judged.* You vanquish men and women, and all judges; every self-styled just person is unjust in your sight. You alone judge justly, unjustly judged as you have been, you who have power to lay down your life, and power to take it up again.[19] Therefore you prevail when you are judged. You vanquish all human beings, because you are greater than all of them, and all men and women were made through you.

15. Variant: "Behold our future judge, judged by sinners."
16. Variant: ". . . nothing in him, or in the Father who sent him, that could be judged. He alone was true, and therefore could truly say. . . ."
17. See Jn 8:46.
18. See Heb 2:14.
19. See Jn 10:18.

Verse 7. Original sin

10. *Against you alone have I sinned, and in your sight I have acted wickedly. So will you be justified in your verdict, and prevail when you are judged. Lo, I was conceived in iniquity.* What it seems to suggest is this: "All those who committed sins like yours, David, are certainly convicted, for adultery and murder are no small evils, no slight sins. But what about those who have never done anything of the kind, from the time they left their mothers' wombs? Are you imputing sins to them as well, so that Christ may be said to prevail over absolutely everyone, as soon as he is judged?"

David spoke in the person of the whole human race, and had regard to the chains that bind us all. He had regard to the propagation of death and the origin of iniquity, and he said, *Lo, I was conceived in iniquity.* But surely David was not born of adultery? Was he not the son of Jesse, a righteous man, and his wife? How then can he say he was conceived in iniquity, unless iniquity is derived from Adam? And with iniquity, indissolubly linked, comes the chain of death. Each of us is born dragging punishment along with us, or at any rate dragging our liability to punishment. In another place a prophet declares, *No one is pure in your sight, not even an infant whose life on earth has been but one day* (Jb 14:4-5, LXX). We know that sins are canceled by baptism in Christ; Christ's baptism has power to forgive sins. Well, then, if infants are completely innocent, why do mothers come running to church when their babies are ill? What does that baptism effect, what is there to be forgiven? What I see is an innocent crying, not someone getting angry! What has baptism washed away? What is destroyed by it? The inheritance of sin is destroyed. If the baby could speak, if he had David's reasoning power,[20] he would answer your question, "Why do you regard me simply as an infant? Admittedly you cannot see the load of sin I carry, but I was conceived in iniquity, *and in sins did my mother nourish me in the womb.*" Christ was born outside this bond of carnal concupiscence,[21] without male intervention, for he was conceived by a virgin of the Holy Spirit. He cannot be said to have been conceived in iniquity; nor could it be said of his mother that she nourished him with sins in her womb, for to her it had been promised, *The Holy Spirit will come upon you, and the power of the Most High will overshadow you* (Lk 1:35).

Human beings are conceived in iniquity, and nourished on sins by their mothers while still in the womb, not because sexual intercourse between husband and wife is sinful, but because the sexual act is performed by flesh subject to punishment. The punishment due to the flesh is death. Mortality is plainly inherent in the flesh. This is why the apostle spoke of the body not as

20. The editors of the CCL refer this to David's baby, who died (see 2 Sm 12:15-24), but it seems better to understand it in a general sense.

21. Reading *concupiscentiae carnalis* with the CCL editors. Most codices have "mortal concupiscence."

something doomed to die, but as dead already: *The body indeed is a dead thing by reason of sin, but the spirit is life through righteousness* (Rom 8:10). How could anything conceived and begotten from bodies dead because of sin be born free of the bond of sin? The sexual act is chaste in a married person and incurs no guilt, but its sinful source drags condign punishment along with it. A married person is no less mortal because married, and his or her mortality springs from sin, and only from sin. The Lord too was mortal, but not as a consequence of sin; he took upon him our penalty, and thereby canceled our guilt. That is why though all die in Adam, all shall be brought to life in Christ.[22] As the apostle teaches, *Through one man sin entered this world, and through sin death, and thus it spread to all, as in him all have sinned.*[23] The verdict has been solemnly given: in Adam all have sinned. The only new-born baby who could be born innocent is one not born from the work of Adam.

Verse 8. Repentance entails a risk

11. *Lo, you have loved truth; the unseen, hidden secrets of your wisdom you have revealed to me.* He says, *You have loved truth*, which implies that you have not left sins unpunished, even in people whom you forgive. *You have loved truth*, for you have dispensed mercy first, but in such a way as to leave room for truth as well. You forgive sinners who confess; yes, you forgive them, but only when the sinners punish themselves. In this way both mercy and truth have their say: mercy, for the man or woman is set free; truth, for the sin has been punished. *Lo, you have loved truth; the unseen, hidden secrets of your wisdom you have revealed to me.* What are these *hidden secrets*? What are the *unseen* things? They are hidden and unseen because though God forgives even serious sinners, nothing is as hidden, nothing as unseen, as his forgiveness. At this uncertain prospect the Ninevites did penance; for even after the prophet's threats, even after his edict, *Only three more days, and Nineveh will be overthrown*, they debated among themselves the possibility of asking for mercy, saying to each other, *Who knows whether God may change his sentence for the better, and have mercy?* (Jon 3:9). It was uncertain, as they acknowledged by asking, *Who knows?* All the same, they did penance with uncertain prospects, and deserved certain mercy. They prostrated themselves in tears, in fasting, in sackcloth and

22. See 1 Cor 15:22.
23. Rom 5:12. *In quo omnes peccaverunt* is a crucial and controversial phrase. Modern biblical scholarship generally understands it in accordance with the underlying Greek to mean "inasmuch as . . ." or "in view of the fact that, all have sinned." However, Augustine took it to mean "in whom [Adam] all have sinned," as the next sentence shows. See his work *The Merits and Forgiveness of Sins and the Baptism of Infants* I, 10-11, where his argument (like that of St Paul in the relevant passage) hinges on the typology Adam-Christ. We are in Christ not because we imitate him but by regeneration and sharing his life; similarly we are one with Adam by more than mere imitation.

ashes; they knelt and wept; and God spared them. Nineveh remained standing. It did, didn't it? Was Nineveh toppled? One outcome may seem good to human judgment, but God judges otherwise.

Yet I think the prophet's prediction was verified. Consider what Nineveh was, and how what it was was overthrown. It was overthrown in respect of its evil ways, and built up in goodness, as Saul the persecutor was overthrown, and Paul the preacher built up. Wouldn't we all agree that this city where we are now would be overthrown to good purpose, if all those crazy people would abandon their silly entertainments and flock to church with compunction in their hearts, begging God's mercy for their past deeds? Would we not say then, "Whatever became of Carthage? It's not what it was, so it has been overthrown in a sense; but now it is something that is wasn't formerly, so it has been built anew." Jeremiah was told something similar: *See, I will give you authority to uproot and undermine, to overthrow and demolish, and then to build up and plant* (Jer 1:10). The voice of the Lord is heard there, the Lord who said, *I will strike, and I will heal* (Dt 32:39). He strikes the rotten area of our misdeeds, and heals the pain of the wound. That is what doctors do when they cut, and strike, and heal: they arm themselves to inflict the blow, they carry a weapon because they come to cure. But the sins of the Ninevites were very grievous, so they said, *Who knows?*

God had given his servant David deep insight into this uncertain matter; for when the prophet confronted him and rebuked him, David cried, *I have sinned*; but immediately he heard from the prophet, or rather from the Spirit of God who was in the prophet, *Your sin is forgiven*. You revealed to him the unseen, hidden secrets of your wisdom.

Verse 9. Hyssop

12. *You will sprinkle me with hyssop, and I shall be cleansed*, he says. We know hyssop: it is a humble plant, but has healing properties; it is said to cling to rock by its roots. That gives us a mysterious image of a heart that needs to be cleansed. You too must grip your rock, grip the root of deliberate love.[24] Be humble in your humble God, that you may grow tall in your glorified God. You will be sprinkled with hyssop, because the humility of Christ will cleanse you. Do not despise this plant; have regard for its medicinal virtue. I will add something else, which we often hear doctors say, and is verified by the experience of sick people: they tell us that hyssop is efficacious for purging the lungs. Now the lung symbolizes pride, because in the lung we find inflation, and also panting. It was said of Saul when he was a persecutor—of Saul in his pride, that is—that he was on his way to arrest Christians breathing out murderous threats.[25] He was

24. *Radicem dilectionis.*
25. See Acts 9:1.

panting out slaughter, panting out bloodshed, because his lungs were not yet cleared. But now listen to someone in the psalm who has been humbled, because purged by hyssop: *You will sprinkle me with hyssop, and I shall be cleansed; you will wash me* (which means cleansing), *and I shall be made whiter than snow*. So too God promises through a prophet: *Though your sins be brilliant scarlet, I will make you as white as snow* (Is 1:18). From people so cleansed Christ provides himself with a garment free from any stain or crease;[26] for the robe he wore on the mountain, which shone gleaming white like snow,[27] symbolized the Church, cleansed from every stain of sin.

Verse 10. The humility of one who listens

13. So the speaker has been sprinkled with hyssop; where is his humility? Listen to the next verse: *As I listen you will give me delight and gladness, and my humbled bones will dance for joy*. "I will find my joy in listening to you, not in speaking against you." You have sinned; why try to defend yourself? You want to do the talking; but let it be, listen, allow God to get a word in, in case you wound yourself still more seriously by thrashing about. You have committed the sin; there is no point in trying to defend it. Let it come out as confession, not as self-justification. If you engage yourself as counsel for the defense you will lose your case, for the advocate you have brought in lacks integrity, and your defence of yourself is worthless. Who are you, to defend yourself? You are better qualified to accuse yourself. Do not plead, "I didn't do anything," or "What did it amount to anyway, what I did?" or "Other people have done the same." If in committing your sin you did nothing, as you claim, you will be nothing yourself and you will receive nothing. God is prepared to grant you forgiveness, but you are shutting the door in your own face; he is prepared to give, so do not put up a barrier of defense, but open your whole self by confession.

As I listen you will give me delight and gladness. May God himself enable me to say what I feel about this. Those who hear are more fortunate than those who speak. The learner is humble, but the teacher has to work hard not to be proud, in case a dishonorable desire to curry favor insinuates itself, and in wishing to curry favor with men and women he loses favor with God. Great peril is to be feared in teaching, my brothers and sisters, and I am sorely afraid as I speak to you. Believe what my heart is telling you, though you cannot see it. God knows how great is the fear that oppresses me as I talk to you—God who will, I hope, be gentle with me and ready to show mercy. But when we listen inside ourselves as he makes some suggestion and teaches us, we are safe, and being safe we rejoice, for we are subject to our teacher; we seek his glory and praise him as he schools

26. See Eph 5:27.
27. See Mk 9:2; Mt 17:2.

us. His truth delights us deep within, where nobody makes a din or has to listen to it. There, within, the psalmist testifies that he found his delight and gladness: *As I listen you will give me delight and gladness*, he says. And the reason why he listens is that he is humble. Anyone who hears, who truly hears and hears correctly, hears humbly, for all the honor belongs to the one from whom he hears whatever it is. After saying, *As I listen you will give me delight and gladness*, the psalmist immediately indicated the effect this listening had upon him: *My humbled bones will dance for joy*. His bones had been humbled. The bones of a listener keep no trace of haughtiness in them, no self-importance, though the speaker finds it hard to overcome these faults in himself.

This truth is exemplified in a great and humble man, a man than whom no one greater had arisen among all those born of women.[28] So deeply did he humble himself that he claimed to be unworthy to unbuckle his Lord's sandal.[29] He was reputed to be the Messiah, and he could have taken advantage of this false opinion to give himself airs and extend his influence; for he had not set himself up as the Messiah, but he could have acquiesced in the mistake of those who thought he was and spontaneously tried to confer the honor upon him. However, he rejected a usurped honor in order to win true glory.[30] Look at the humility of John the Baptist who listened, and ascribed glory to the one who was his teacher and therefore his friend. *The bride is for the Bridegroom*, he said, *but the Bridegroom's friend, who stands and hears him* . . . he resolved to be one who stood and heard, you see, not one who fell down through talking: *who stands and hears him*, said John. So you have heard about his listening, so what about his delight and gladness? He promptly continues, *The friend who stands and hears him rejoices intensely at the Bridegroom's voice* (Jn 3:29). *As I listen you will give me delight and gladness, and my humbled bones will dance for joy.*

Verse 11. "Look away from my sins"

14. *Turn your face away from my sins, and blot out all my iniquities*. Already my humbled bones are dancing for joy, already I am cleansed with hyssop and have been made humble. Now *turn your face away*, not from me, but *from my sins*. He prayed in another psalm, *Do not turn your face away from me* (Ps 26(27):9). He does not want God's face averted from him, but he does want it averted from his sins; for if God does not avert his face from a sin, that means he turns toward it, and if he turns toward it, he punishes it.[31] *Turn your face away from my sins, and blot out all my guilt*. He is preoccupied about his grievous sin,

28. See Mt 11:11; Lk 7:28.
29. See Mk 1:7.
30. Variant: "true grace."
31. There is an untranslatable play on three similar-sounding verbs: *Peccatum ... unde se Deus non avertit, advertit; si advertit, animadvertit.*

but now he goes further and makes bold to ask that all his iniquities be blotted out. He is taking the doctor's skill for granted, and presuming on the immense mercy that he invoked at the beginning of the psalm: *blot out all my iniquities*. God averts his face and this of itself blots them out, for by turning his face away from sins he effaces them, whereas if he turns his face toward them, he is keeping the score. So now that you have heard how he blots out sin by turning away, listen to what he does if he turns toward it: *the Lord frowns on evildoers, to blot out their memory from the earth* (Ps 33:17(34:16)), and this because he does not delete their sins. But what is the psalmist's prayer? *Turn your face away from my sins*. That is a wise prayer, for he is not turning his own face away from his sins; certainly not, for he prayed earlier, *I admit my wrongdoing*. If you do not turn your own face away from your sin, you can ask God to turn his away from it; you are right to make that prayer. But if you thrust your sin behind your back, God fixes his gaze upon it. Switch your sin to a position before your face, if you want God to turn his face away from it. Then you may pray to him without anxiety, and he will hear you.

Verse 12. David's patience in adversity

15. *Create a clean heart in me, O God*. He prayed, *Create*, as though meaning, "Bring something new into being."[32] But because he was praying as a penitent, less innocent now than before committing his sin, he showed what he meant by *create* in the next line: *Implant a new and upright spirit within me*. "In consequence of what I did," he says, "my former upright spirit has grown old and bent." Another psalm laments, *They bent my soul down* (Ps 56:7(57:6)). When a person lies down amid earthly desires he is in a sense bent over, but when he stretches upward to heavenly things his heart becomes upright, and then God can be good to him, for the God of Israel is very good to those of upright heart.[33]

Let me have your attention now, brothers and sisters. Sometimes when God means to forgive someone in the world to come, he corrects that person in this world. Remember David's case. He had been told through the prophet, *Your sin is forgiven* (2 Sm 12:13), yet the calamities with which God had threatened him because of that sin still fell upon him. His son Absalom[34] waged a bloody war against him, and humiliated his father in many ways. David walked in sorrow,[35] humiliated and distressed; and so submissive was he to God that he regarded all his woes as just punishments from God, confessing that no part of what he suffered was undeserved. Already he had an upright heart, with which God was

32. The CCL editors insert *non* after *crea*, "not as though . . . "; but the *quasi* that follows seems to render the emendation unnecessary.
33. See Ps 72(73):1.
34. *Abessalon*, as in Augustine's Exposition of Psalm 3.
35. See 2 Sm 15:30.

not displeased. When an abusive fellow, one of the soldiers on the other side who supported the king's rebellious son, flung insults into David's face, he listened without rancor. One of David's companions was angry, and wished to go and strike down this man who was hurling curses at the king, but David would not allow him. What did he say, as he forbade it? *God has sent him to curse me* (2 Sm 16:10). He recognized his guilt and embraced his punishment, seeking God's glory and not his own. He praised the Lord for whatever good fortune he had, and he praised the Lord for what he was suffering. He blessed the Lord at all times, and the Lord's praise was in his mouth always.[36]

This is how all those of upright heart conduct themselves. Very different are the crooked who consider themselves upright and God perverse: when they do anything bad they rejoice, and when they have to endure anything bad they blaspheme. What is more, when they find themselves in trouble and under the lash, they say from their misshapen hearts, "God, what have I done to you?" The truth is that they have done nothing to God; all the harm they have done is to themselves. *Implant a new and upright spirit within me.*

Verses 13-14. The Holy Spirit

16. *Do not cast me away from your face.* Just now he prayed, *Turn your face away from my sins*, and now he says, *Do not cast me away from your face.* He fears God's face, but also invokes it. *Do not cast me away from your face, nor take your Holy Spirit from me.* There is a holy spirit in everyone who confesses, for it is already due to a gift of the Holy Spirit that you are disgusted by what you have done. Sins are pleasing to an unclean spirit, displeasing to a holy spirit.[37] So although you are still imploring pardon, from another point of view you are already united with God, because you are disgusted with the evil thing you have done; and so what is displeasing to him is displeasing to you as well. That makes two fighting against your illness—you and the doctor. Confession of sin and the will to punish sin cannot be present in any of us by our own doing; and so when we are angry with ourselves and find ourselves displeasing, it can happen only by the gift of the Holy Spirit. This is why the psalm does not say, "Give me your Holy Spirit," but "Do not take it from me." *Do not take your Holy Spirit from me.*

---

36. See Ps 33:2(34:1).
37. Or "to the Holy Spirit." In this and the following paragraph two questions arise: 1) Where should we read "spirit" and where "Spirit"? That is, does Augustine mean the created spirit of a human being, whether "unclean" as here, or so closely united with the indwelling uncreated Holy Spirit that the whole human being, both material and non-material elements, is "spirit" in the Pauline sense? Or does he mean the uncreated Spirit of God directly? 2) If he does mean God, should we understand it as God without distinction of Persons (since "God is spirit" as Augustine quotes), or as a reference to the third Person, the Holy Spirit? This question is directly addressed in the next paragraph.

17. *Give back to me the gladness of your salvation.* Give back to me what I used to have, before I lost it by sinning. *Give back to me the gladness of your salvation*: that must mean "of your Christ." Who could ever be healed without him? It must mean Christ, because before he was born from Mary he was the Word in the beginning, the Word who was with God, the Word who was God; and accordingly the mystery of the incarnation was believed in by the holy fathers as something future, just as we believe in it as something accomplished. There is a difference in the epochs, not in the faith. *Give back to me the gladness of your salvation, and strengthen me by your original spirit.*[38] Some have understood this to be a reference to the Trinity in God, to God himself, apart from the incarnation; for scripture also says, *God is spirit* (Jn 4:24). If something is not material, and yet exists, it must be spirit. This is why some interpreters[39] think that the Trinity is mentioned here: the upright spirit is the Son, the holy spirit is the Holy Spirit, and the original spirit is the Father. This may be correct. Alternatively the psalmist may have meant the upright spirit in a human being, so that he was saying, "Implant a new and upright spirit within me, for by sin I have bent and distorted my spirit." In that case the Holy Spirit himself would be the original spirit whom the psalmist did not want taken away from him, and by whom he asked to be strengthened. Neither opinion is heretical.

Verse 15. An ex-sinner teaches sinners

18. But notice the next petition: *Strengthen me by your original spirit.* Strengthen me in what respect? You have forgiven me, and I am certain that what you have forgiven will not be imputed to me. Therefore I am free from anxiety, and being strengthened by this grace I will not be ungrateful. What shall I do, then? *Let me teach your ways to sinners.* I am myself an ex-sinner, and as an ex-sinner let me teach sinners. That is to say, I am no longer a sinner: you have not taken a holy spirit away from me, but have strengthened me in the original spirit, so *let me teach your ways to sinners.* "And what ways will you teach to sinners?" *The impious will be converted to you.* If David's sin is reckoned to have been impiety, let the impious not despair on their own account, provided they are converted to God and learn his ways, for they see that God forgave David for his impious deeds. However, it may be that David's actions should not be classed as impiety, for properly speaking impiety is apostasy from God. It means not worshiping the one God, either because one never has worshiped him, or because having formerly done so one has left him. On this understanding, the prediction that *the impious will be converted to you* envisages an extreme case. You are so full of rich mercy that no sinners who turn to you need despair, and

38. *Spiritu principali.*
39. For example, Jerome, in his *Commentary on the Letter to the Galatians* IV, 6.

this is true not just for sinners in general but even for the impious. *The impious will be converted to you.* To what end? That they may believe in him who justifies the impious, so that their faith may be counted as righteousness.

Verse 16. The prospect of ultimate incorruptibility

19. *Deliver me from bloods,*[40] *O God, God of my salvation.* The Latin translator used an un-Latin expression here to convey the sense of the Greek. We all know that Latin does not put the word "blood" into the plural; but the Greek did so with good reason, because it had found a plural in the original Hebrew, so the trustworthy Latin translator opted for unidiomatic Latin rather than inaccuracy of meaning.

So why does it use the plural, *from bloods*? Because by "many bloods" it wanted us to understand many sins; it pointed to their origin in sinful flesh. When the apostle was considering sins that proceed from corruptible flesh and blood, he said, *Flesh and blood will not possess the kingdom of God.* Yet according to the true faith taught by the same apostle, our flesh will rise again, and will merit incorruption. He tells us this himself: *This corruptible body must put on incorruption, and this mortal body be clothed in immortality* (1 Cor 15:53). But the corruption is the consequence of sin, and therefore can itself be called "sin." We use a similar idiom with the word "tongue": it can mean a little piece of flesh, the member that moves in the mouth as we pronounce different words; but it can also mean the result that this member achieves, namely language. So we speak of the Greek tongue being different from the Latin tongue, but it is not the fleshly member that is different, only the sounds it produces. So just as we can call speech uttered by our tongue a "tongue," so too we can give the name "blood" to the iniquity that comes about through blood.

The psalmist is therefore considering his very many iniquities, those concerning which he earlier prayed, *Blot out all my iniquities*, and he attributes them to corruptible flesh and blood. This is why he now pleads, *Deliver me from bloods*; that is to say, "Set me free from my iniquities, cleanse me of all corruption." In praying, "Set me free from bloods," he is voicing a desire for incorruption, for *flesh and blood will not possess the kingdom of God, nor will corruption possess incorruption* (1 Cor 15:50). So he begs, *Deliver me from bloods, O God, God of my salvation.* He is showing us that when salvation is perfectly accomplished in these bodies of ours there will remain none of that corruption which goes by the name, "flesh and blood." And that salvation will mean perfect health for our bodies. How can the body be considered healthy now, when it declines, and has needs, and suffers from the perpetual illness of hunger and thirst? Hereafter these things will not be found in it. Food is for the

40. *De sanguinibus.*

stomach, and the stomach for food, but one day God will do away with both.[41] The form of our bodies will be rendered perfect by God. When death has been swallowed up in victory[42] no proneness to decay will remain, no weakness will creep up on us. Our bodies will be affected by no process of aging; they will not be so wearied by labor as to need the support of food, or any refreshment to revive them. But we shall not be without food and drink, because God himself will be our food and our drink. He alone is the food that restores us and never fails.

Deliver me from bloods, O God, God of my salvation. He can address God in this way because we are already within that salvation. Listen to the teaching of the apostle: *In hope we have been saved.* And notice that he was speaking precisely of bodily salvation: *We groan inwardly as we await our adoption as God's children, the redemption of our bodies, for in hope we have been saved. But if hope is seen, it is hope no longer, for when someone sees what he hopes for, why should he hope for it? But if we hope for what we do not see, we wait for it in patience* (Rom 8:23-25). This patience is characteristic of all who persevere to the end.[43] They will be saved with the salvation which is not yet ours, but which we will have one day. We do not yet possess the reality, but our hope is sure.[44] And then *my tongue shall shout with joy of your justice.*

Verses 17-19. Praise and true sacrifice

20. *O Lord, you will open my lips, and my mouth will proclaim your praise.* Your praise, because I have been created; your praise, because when I sinned I was not abandoned; your praise, because I was warned to confess; your praise, because I have been cleansed, so that I may not fret and fear.[45] *You will open my lips, and my mouth will proclaim your praise.*

21. *If you had wanted a sacrifice I would certainly have offered it.* David lived at a time when animal sacrifices were customarily offered to God, but he foresaw the future. Do we not recognize ourselves in these words of his? Those former sacrifices were symbolic; they prefigured the one saving sacrifice. We have not been left without any sacrifice to offer to God, for listen to what this man says as he takes thought for his sin, and wants forgiveness for the evil thing he has done: *If you had wanted a sacrifice I would certainly have offered it; but you take no pleasure in holocausts.* Are we to offer nothing, then? Are we to approach God like that? How shall we propitiate him? Offer sacrifice, yes; but what you must offer you have within yourself. Do not purchase incense from somewhere else,

41. See 1 Cor 6:13.
42. See 1 Cor 15:54.
43. See Mt 10:22; 24:13.
44. *Nondum est res, sed certa spes.*
45. Some codices have "by which [praise]" instead of "because" throughout this sentence.

but say, *The good things I have vowed to give you are within me, O God* (Ps 55(56):12). Do not seek outside yourself some animal you can slay, for you have something to kill inside yourself. *A sacrifice to God is a troubled spirit. A contrite and humbled heart God does not scorn.*[46] Bulls, he-goats and rams he does indeed scorn, for it is no longer the right time for these to be offered. They were presented as sacrifices when they prefigured something, when they promised something; but now that what was promised has come, the promises themselves are obsolete. *A contrite and humbled heart God does not scorn.* You know that God is on high, but if you lift yourself high he will withdraw far away from you; if you humble yourself, he will come near to you.

Verse 20. Zion the lookout post, Jerusalem the vision of peace

22. Now see who it is who has been speaking. At first it seemed to be one individual, David, who was praying, but now recognize in him an image of ourselves and a type of the Church. *In your good will, O Lord, deal kindly with Zion.* Deal kindly with this Zion. For what is Zion? The holy city. And what is the holy city? The city founded on a mountain, that cannot be hidden.[47] Zion is the lookout post gazing toward something it longs for; the name Zion means "Lookout Post," as Jerusalem means "Vision of Peace." If you are awaiting our future hope in full confidence, and if you are at peace with God, you recognize yourselves in Zion and in Jerusalem. *And let the walls of Jerusalem be rebuilt*, it continues. *In your good will, O Lord, deal kindly with Zion, and let the walls of Jerusalem be rebuilt.* Let Zion not attribute to herself any merits she may have; do you deal kindly with her. *Let the walls of Jerusalem be rebuilt.* May the ramparts of our immortality be built up in faith, and hope, and charity.

Verse 21. God's fire

23. *Then you will accept a sacrifice of righteousness.* The sacrifice you offer now is offered for sin; it consists of a troubled spirit and a contrite heart; but on that future day you will offer a sacrifice of righteousness, an offering of pure praise. *Blessed are they who dwell in your house, Lord; they will praise you for ever and ever* (Ps 83:5(84:4)). That is a sacrifice of righteousness. *Oblations and holocausts.* What are holocausts? Victims entirely consumed by fire. When the animal was placed whole on the altar to be burnt, it was called a holocaust. May the divine fire consume us entirely, may that heat seize the whole of us. What heat do I mean? *No one can hide from his heat* (Ps 18:7(19:6)). What heat is that? The heat mentioned by the apostle when he says, *Ardent in spirit* (Rom 12:11).

46. Variants: "he will not despise;" "do not despise."
47. See Mt 5:14.

May it not be our souls alone that are consumed by that divine flame of wisdom, but our bodies too, that they may gain immortality through it. Let our holocaust be so raised up to God that death may be swallowed up in victory.[48] *Oblations and holocausts. Then will they lay calves upon your altar.* Why calves? Why will he choose them? Perhaps they suggest the innocence of youth, or necks not subjected to the yoke of the law?

Concluding exhortations on family discipline

24. In Christ's name this psalm has now been fully dealt with, as best I could, even though not as well as I would have liked. It remains for me to say a few words to you, brothers and sisters, in view of the rampant evils among which we live. As long as we must live in these human circumstances, there is no escaping from them. We must live tolerantly among bad people, because when we were bad ourselves, good people lived tolerantly among us. If we remember what we were, we shall not despair of those who are now what we were then.

All the same, dearest friends, at a time when there is so much variation in moral standards and such appalling decadence, keep strict control over your homes. Rule your children, rule your households.[49] Just as it is our responsibility to talk to you in church, so it is yours to dispose matters in your homes in such a way that you may give a good account of those under you. God loves discipline. It is a perverse and misguided innocence that loosens the reins in favor of sins. It is very unhelpful, indeed extremely harmful, for a son to take advantage of an easy-going father, only to find God's severity later; and he will not be alone when he finds it, but will have his dissolute father for company. Why? If the father does not commit the sins, and does not behave like his son, does that mean he has no duty to restrain his son from that wicked conduct? Suppose the son thinks that his father would behave likewise, were he not past it? The sin that you do not object to in your son gives you vicarious pleasure. All you lack is youth, not lust.

Above all, brothers and sisters, take care that your children grow up in the faith, those children for whom you went surety so that they might be baptized. It may be that a bad child has ignored a parent's advice, or reproof, or severity. Never mind; you fulfill your role, and leave God to fulfill his in the child's regard.

---

48. See 1 Cor 15:54.
49. Some codices read, ". . . your sons . . . your daughters."

Index of Scripture

(prepared by Michael Dolan)

(The numbers after the scriptural reference refer to the section of the work)

Old Testament

Genesis

1:20 49,18
1:26 38,11
2:17 37,5; 37,26; 41,14
2:24 II,34,1; 37,6; 40,1
3:5 35,17
3:19 40,6; 41,14; 46,13
4:10 39,13
4:15 39,13
22:12 I,36,1; 43,19-20
24:2-3 44,13
25:23 40,14; 46,6
25:27 44,20
32:28 49,14
49:10 44,13

Exodus

3:14 38,7; 38,22; 49,14
12:46 II,33,24
23:7, LXX II,36,20

Deuteronomy

13:3 I,36,1
25:5 44,23
32:39 50,11

1 Samuel

21:11 I,33,2
21:12-15 I,33,2; II,33,2

2 Samuel

12:1-4 50,8
12:13 50,15
16:10 50,15

1 Kings

19:8 49,9

2 Kings

2:23 46,2

Tobit

4:16 35,1

Job

1:11 I,34,7
1:21 II,33,4; II,36,10; 37,24
2:10 I,34,7
9:24 III,36,13
14:4-5, LXX 50,10
15:26 45,13
37:22, LXX 47,3

Psalms

1:1 35,6
1:1-2 39,14
1:2 III,36,5
1:4 I,34,9; 43,23-24
1:6 I,36,9
2:6-9 47,5
2:9 44,18; 47,15
2:10-11 47,5
2:11 50,4
3:1 I,33,2
3:2-3(1-2) I,34,5
3:5(4) 42,4; 44,33; 47,2
3:6(5) 40,10
5:13(12) I,34,2
6:8(7) 39,4
8:5(4) 35,12
10:2(11:1) 35,9
12:5(13:4) 37,22

14(15):5 III,36,6
15(16):2 I,34,12; 49,19
15(16):5 I,34,12; I,36,4
16(17):13-14 I,34,2
17:4(18:3) 39,4
17:26-27
(18:25-26) 44,17
17:45
(18:43-44) 44,25
17:45(18:44) 45,6; 47,7
18:2,5(19:1.4) 49,11
18:5(19:4) 39,10
18:6(19:5) 44,3
18:7(19:6) 45,13; 50,23
18:13-14
(19:12-13) 35,17; 37,16; 39,20
18:15(19:14) I,34,15
21:2(22:1) II,34,5; 37,6; 37,27; 40,6; 41,17
21:2-3(22:1-2) 43,2
21:5.7(22:4.6) 43,3
21:8(22:7) 43,14
21:14(22:13) 40,12
21:17-19
(22:16-18) I,34,6; 43,8
21:19(22:18) 37,6
21:23(22:22) 44,23
21:27(22:26) I,48,3
21:28(22:27) 47,7
21:30(22:29) I,48,3
22(23):5 35,14
22:9(63:8) 43,25
23(24):3-4 47,2
23(24):7.9 47,1
24(25):1 41,12
24(25):7 35,3
24(25):9 II,36,7
25(26):9 47,11; 49,13
26(27):4 38,6; 41,5
26(27):9 44,18; 50,14
26(27):10 45,11
26(27):12 40,8
26(27):14 II,36,4; 41,11
30:23(31:22) II,34,6; 37,12; 41,18
31(32):1 44,7
31(32):9 II,33,5; 42,6; 46,9; I,48,16
32(33):5 35,7
33:2(34:1) 35,16; II,48,10
33:16(34:15) 39,2
33:17(34:16) 39,2; 50,14
34(35):3 38,20
35:7(36:6) 41,13; 41,14
35:10(36:9) 41,2
35:12(36:11) 38,2
36(37):2 II,48,4
36(37):23 49,30
36(37):37 I,36,12
38:7(39:5-6) II,48,11
39:5(40:4) 38,11
39:18(40:17) 40,1
40:5(41:4) 42,7
42(43):1 49,13
42(43):5 II,33,19
43:7(44:6) 45,13
43(44):23 I,34,3
44:3(45:2) 43,16
44:11(45:10) 47,7
45:2(46:1) 49,22
49(50):16 III,36,20
49(50):21 II34,12; 39,4
49(50):23 39,4
50:5(51:3) 44,18; 49,28
50:10(51:8) 38,4
50:11(51:9) 44,18
50:18-21
(51:16-19) 49,15
50:19(51:17) 41,17
51:4(52:2) I,34,11
54:7(55:6) 38,2
54:23(55:22) 39,27
55(56):12 49,21; 50,21
56:7(57:6) 50,15
60:3(61:2) 39,28; 49,13
61:12(62:11) 44,5
63:7-8(64:6) 41,13
66:2-3(67:1-2) 39,18
69:6(70:5) 49,30
71(72):11 45,10; 47,7
72(73):1 44,17
72(73):16-17 41,9
72(73):26 I,34,12; I,36,5
72(73):28 43,25
76:3(77:2) II,48,3
77(78):24-25 I,33,6
79:17(80:16) 38,2
81(82):1 49,2
81(82):6-7 49,2
83:11(84:10) I,48,2
83:5(84:4) 41,11; 42,4; 43,9; 50,23
84:9(85:8) 38,16; 49,23
84:18(85:7) 39,18
86(87):4 44,33
90(91):13 39,1
91:15(92:14) III,36,4
93(94):20 38,17
94(95):2 44,10
95(96):4-5 49,2
95(96):5 47,15
100(101):5 II,34,13
101:38
(102:27) 38,7
107:6(108:5) 47,7
109(110):4 I,33,5
111(112):7 35,5
113B(115):8 46,11
114(116):3-4 45,4; 49,22; 50,4
114(116):6 38,17

115(116):10 39,16
115(116):
12-13 35,14; II,36,8 44,7
115(116):13 39,16
115(116):15 39,16; 40,1
117(118):22 39,1; 44,20; 47,3
118(119):57 I,34,12; I,36,4
118(119):71 38,17; 42,342,3
119(120):2-5 44,8
120(121):1 35,9
120(121):1-2 39,6
120(121):2 35,9
121(122):7 47,13
123(124):1,3 II,34,15
125(126):6 III,36,7
129(130):1 39,3
129(130):3 42,7
138(139):8 49,18
138(139):16 43,26
139:9(140:8) III,36,13
141:5(142:4) 37,18; 39,24
141:5(142:6) I,34,6
141:6(142:5) II,36,14; III,36,11
142(143):2 42,7
143(144):
8,12-15 37,25
143(144):15 37,25
147:15 44,6

Proverbs

2:11 III,36,5
3:11-12 37,23
10:26, LXX II,48,8
17:6, LXX I,48,3
18:3 35,10; 39,3
19:17 III,36,6
21:20 III,36,5

Song of Songs

1:3 37,9; 44,22
2:2 47,8
2:5 LXX 37,5
4:8 LXX I,33,10
6:9.5 44,26
8:6 47,13

Wisdom

2:15 III,36,12
2:20,18 I,48,11
2:24 50,9
5:3-4 II,48,4
5:8-9 III,36,10
9:15 35,1; 37,10

Sirach

10:14 37,8
15:9 47,2; 49,29
35:26 41,16

Isaiah

1:18 50,12
2:2 45,6
2:3 45,12; 47,5
3:14 49,11
5:3 46,13
5:4.7 35,8
5:6 35,8; 45,10
6:3 49,4
14:13-14 47,3
23:1, LXX 47,6
26:13 39,28
26:18 47,5
29:13 III,36,12; 37,17; 39,15; 45,6;
II,48,1
42:14, LXX II,34,12; 49,6
48:22 38,16
52:5 II,34,10
52:15 47,7
53:2 43,16; 44,3
53:7 37,20
53:7,5 40,13
53:9 37,19
54:5 46,9
57:16-17 42,3
58:1 46,7
58:7 42,8; 49,13
58:9,10,7 42,8
65:24 42,8

Jeremiah

1:10 50,11
2:29 42,7
9:1 38,20
10:11 47,15
17:16 III,36,13
23:24 39,27; 49,18
31:33 45,6

Baruch

3:38 47,15

Ezekiel

36:20 II,34,10

Daniel

2:35 45,12

Hosea

6:6 44,27; 49,12

Jonah

3:9 50,11

Micah

4:1 45,6
4:2 45,12; 47,5

New Testament

Matthew

3:7-9 46,11
4:3,4 III,36,5
5:5 II,34,7
5:6 II,33,15; 35,14; II,48,8
5:8 35,15; I,36,5; 39,21; 42,4; 44,25
5:10 II,34,13; 43,1
5:14 44,33
5:16 44,29
5:35 39,5
5:44 II,36,1
5:48,45 39,4; 49,28
6:1 44,29
6:1.2 49,12
6:6 II,33,8; 35,5
6:19-21 44,27
6:20 38,12
6:21 II,48,2
6:24 40,3
7:7 I,33,1
7:13-14 43,18
7:23 II,34,2
8:2 39,23
8:8 38,18
8:10 38,18
8:11 46,12
8:11-12 38,18
8:12 I,36,11; 46,12
9:12 38,18
9:13 44,27; 49,12
10:22 41,11; 42,3
10:24-25 40,8
10:28 II,36,3; III,36,13; 40,2
10:30 III,36,13
10:34 44,11
11:10 49,11
11:15 II,33,16; I,48,2
12:7 44,27
12:48 44,12
13:28 40,4
14:28 39,9
15:8 45,6
15:22 44,27
15:26 37,1
15:28 44,27
16:16 49,2
16:16-23 II,34,6
16:18 39,25
16:22 39,25
16:22,23 I,34,8
16:23 39,25
17:19 45,6
18:3 44,1
18:10 43,16
19:4-6 37,6
19:6 44,3
19:14 46,2
19:17 44,3
19:21 43,25
19:21.28 49,8
19:28 44,23
20:22 II,36,8; 37,16; 39,16
21:9 II,33,5
21:38 40,1; 40,10
22:16 37,17
22:16-17 II,34,11
22:18 II,34,11; 37,17
22:29-30 43,16
22:42-46 I,33,6
23:2-3 III,36,20
23:3 39,15; I,48,5; 49,23
23:13 37,20
24:12 37,14; 39,1
24:13 I,36,7; 39,1; 39,3; 41,11; 42,3
24:19 39,28
24:22 39,28
24:23 39,1; 49,3
24:35 III,36,11
24:40 I,36,2
25:21 38,5
25:26-27,30 38,5
25:34 35,5; I,36,10; III,36,9; 44,24; I,48,6; II,48,4
25:34,35 49,13
25:34,41 39,19
25:34,41,46 III,36,6
25:34-35.37.40 49,11
25:34-38 44,27
25:35 I,36,2; 49,11; 49,20
25:35-36 40,2
25:35,37,40 III,36,6
25:40 38,12; 40,11; I,48,16
25:41 35,5; I,36,11; 37,3; 44,24; I,48,6; II,48,4
25:41.34.46 I,48,5
25:42 I,36,2; 37,3
25:42-43 37,6
25:44-45 37,6
26:26 I,33,10
26:28 II,34,11; 40,6; 42,7
27:37 46,4
27:42 II,34,11; 44,1
27:46 II,34,5; 37,6; 37,27; 41,17; 49,5
28:10 44,23

28:13 II,36,17; 37,19
28:20 II,34,12; 46,7; 47,14

Mark

1:2 49,11
1:7 35,9
2:11 40,5
3:33 44,12
8:38 39,16
10:18 44,4
13:21 47,7
14:34 42,7
15:26 46,4
15:34 49,5

Luke

1:32 I,33,6
1:35 50,10
2:30 I,34,12; 39,18
5:21 III,36,3
7:27 49,11
7:6-9 46,12
8:25 45,5
10:27.29.
30.34-37 I,48,14
11:26 II,48,1
11:41 44,27
12:20 II,48,1; II,48,7
12:33 III,36,8 ;I,48,9
12:49 45,13
12:52-53 44,11
14:11 41,12
15:24-32 44,9
16:2.3 I,48,12
16:9 I,48,9; I,48,12
16:24 38,22
16:28 I,48,14; 49,9
18:11,13 39,27
18:13 49,30
18:14 41,12
20:18 45,12
20:35-36 43,16
20:36 43,16
23:21 II,34,11; 40,12
23:28,31 40,12
23:34 39,25; 44,14
23:38 46,4
23:42 39,15
23:43 II,33,24; I,34,14; 39,15
24:18-21 II,34,4
24:46-47 49,4

John

1:1 I,33,6; 35,1; 44,3; 49,1
1:1-3 46,8
1:1,14 44,20
1:3-4 44,5
1:5 I,34,4
1:10 I,34,4
1:11 I,48,5
1:12 49,2
1:14 I,33,6; 44,3; 49,5
1:16,9 35,9
1:17 44,7
1:20 35,9
1:47 44,20
1:47-51 44,20
2:19,21 40,12
3:29 35,9; 50,13
4:7 II,34,4
4:24 50,17
5:22.27 I,48,5
6:41 II,33,15; II,48,8
6:53 I,33,8; II,33,12
6:54 II,33,12
6:54.56 I,33,8
6:71 40,11
7:37-38 45,8
7:39 45,8
8:4-5 50,8
8:7,10-11 50,8
8:12 42,4
8:33 46,11
8:34 40,6
8:39 46,11
8:44 44,12
8:48 35,17; II,36,17; II,48,4
9:27-28 39,26
10:18 II,33,7; 40,10; 42,7
10:20,21 II,48,4
10:30 49,5
11:25 III,36,15
11:48.50 40,1
11:51 40,1
12:19 40,1
14:6 39,18; 42,4; I,48,6
14:8 37,11; 38,6
14:8-9 45,1
14:9 37,11; 44,3
14:10 II,34,5
14:21 37,11; 37,15; 43,16; I,48,5
14:30,31 50,9
15:20 40,8
16:12 I,36,1; 38,3
17:20 47,14
18:36 47,5
19:6 40,12
19:11 49,5
19:19 46,4
19:28 II,34,4
20:17 I,48,8
20:28 49,5
20:29 II,48,5; 49,5
21:15-17 37,17
21:17 II,36,8

Acts

1:8 49,5
1:11 46,7; 49,5
2:37-38 45,4
7:39 46,6
9:4 I,34,1; 37,6; 39,5; 44,20
9:6 44,16
9:13-16 II,36,5
10:13 II,34,15
12:7 II,33,22
13:46 35,8; 45,6; 45,10
17:18 45,7
17:28 II,34,6
19:28 45,7
21:11 II,36,6
21:13 II,36,6

Romans

1:21 35,10; 35,18
1:22 35,10
1:24 35,10; 35,18
1:31 I,33,9
2:5 49,28
2:24 II,34,10
2:28-29 47,11
3:23 44,3
5:3-4 42,5
5:3-5 II,36,6; II,36,9
5:6 37,26; 44,3
6:12 35,6; 50,3
7:22-23 42,7
7:22-25 44,7
7:23-25 35,6
7:24-25 I,36,6; 42,7
8:3 II,34,3
8:10 50,10
8:10-11 40,3
8:18 II,36,8; II,48,9
8:23 37,5
8:23-25 50,19
8:24-25 37,5; 38,13
8:25 37,15
8:32 45,11
8:35 II,36,6
9:5 46,8
9:27 I,33,7; 47,3
10:4 38,14; 45,1
10:10 I,34,14; 39,15
11:4 49,9
11:25 45,15; 46,3
11:26 45,15
12:11 50,23
12:21 II,36,1
13:8 II,33,1
15:1 47,1

1 Corinthians

1:10 40,9
1:12 35,9
1:13 35,9; 44,23; 46,5
1:22-25 II,33,4
2:6 44,20
2:8 47,1
2:15,14 49,27
3:1-2 I,36,1; 38,3; 49,27
3:2 44,20
3:6-7 35,9
3:9,10,6 I,36,2
3:15 37,3
4:1 35,9
4:3 III,36,19; 41,13
4:7 47,4
4:9 39,9
4:15 44,23
4:16 III,36,2; III,36,20; 39,6
5:7 39,13
5:8 39,13
6:1 II,36,20
6:3 49,10
9:24 39,11
10:1-2 I,33,3
10:3 I,33,3
10:4 I,33,3
10:11 I,33,3
10:12 41,12
13:3 43,21; 47,13
13:12 I,33,10; 35,14; I,48,5
14:20 44,1; 46,2
15:22 35,12
15:50 50,19
15:53 50,19
15:53-54 35,6

2 Corinthians

2:15 37,9; 44,22
4:16 38,9
4:17-18 II,48,9
5:1 38,21
5:6 I,48,5
5:6-7 37,15
5:6,9 38,21
5:10 III,36,13
5:13 44,20
5:17 38,9
6:1 47,8
6:10 I,48,3; II,48,5
8:9 39,28; 40,1
9:6 III,36,7
9:7 42,8
10:10 49,27
10:12 II,34,10
11:2 49,9
11:2-3 39,1

11:27 II,33,17; III,36,2
12:9-10 45,13
12:10 38,18
12:11 III,36,18
12:15 II,36,6

Galatians

2:4 40,8
2:20 49,31
3:13 37,26
4:14 49,11
4:19 49,27
4:24 I,33,3
5:17 I,36,6
6:1 37,22
6:2 41,4
6:9-10 III,36,7
6:14 44,3

Ephesians

2:3 37,5
2:14 47,3
4:17-18 41,2
5:8 I,34,4
5:14 45,12; II,48,4
5:28-29 I,48,6
5:30 37,6
5:31 II,34,1; 40,1
5:32 37,6; 44,12
6:12 I,34,4

Philippians

1:18 49,23
1:23-24 44,32
2:6-7 44,12
2:6-8 I,33,6
2:7 40,1
3:12-13 39,3
3:12,14 38,8
3:12-14 38,6; 38,14
3:13-14 39,3
3:15 38,14
3:20 II,48,2
4:5-6 46,7
4:17,10 49,11

Colossians

2:3 40,2
3:1-3 39,28
3:3-4 I,36,3; 43,5; II,48,3
3:4 I,36,7
3:5 39,8

1 Thessalonians

2:7 49,27
5:17 37,14

2 Thessalonians

3:6 II,36,20

1 Timothy

1:13 39,3; 50,6
1:13,16 45,13
1:15 49,31
3:15 47,1
4:8 40,3
4:12 III,36,20; 39,6
6:17 I,48,3
6:17-19 44,28; I,48,9

2 Timothy

2:12-13 39,1
3:2 44,9
3:5 47,8
3:8 II,36,12
3:9 II,36,12
4:7 39,3
4:8 39,3

Titus

2:8 I,34,4

Hebrews

12:5-6 37,23
12:6 II,36,4
8:10 45,6

1 Peter

2:4 44,20
5:8 49,29
21:23 37,26

2 Peter

2:20 II,48,1

1 John

1:8 38,14
2:1-2 II,36,20
3:1-2 49,2
3:2 I,33,10; II,36,8; 37,15; 43,5
5:19 I,34,4

Revelation

5:5 49,29
10:10 43,25
19:16 44,23

Index

(prepared by Joseph Sprug)

The first number in the Index is the Psalm number.
More than one Exposition is cited by the number in parentheses, for example (2)
The number after the colon is a paragraph number.

Aaron, 33(1):5,6,7; 33(2):2
abandon (-ed; -ment)
  God's apparent decision, 43:3
  Lord has taken me up, 45:11
Abessalon, 33(1):2; 50:15
Abimelech, 33(1):3,4,6,7; 33(2):2,2
Abraham, 33(2):17,25; 34(1):10; 36(3):1,2; 39:15; 42:7; 44:13,15; 46:13
  his children imitate his faith, 46:11
  Lazarus and the rich man, 48(1):10; 48(2):1
  promised offspring, 46:11
  self-knowledge, 43:19-20
  tested by God, 36(1):1
  two sons (=covenants) , 33(1):3
Absalom, *See* Abessalon.
abyss, 35:10,18; 41:15
accusation: false, 34(1):11; 38:3
Achis, King of Gath, 33(1):2,4,7,8,11; 33(2):2,2 ??? ,12
acrobat, 39:9
actor, 39:9
Adam and Eve, 34(2):3; 35:12,17; 36(1):10; 37:5,15,33; 38:9; 44:10; 47:9; 48(1):3,6; 48(2):2,11
  iniquity derived from, 50:10
  sleep; figure of Christ's death, 40:10
adoption, 41:11
adultery, 49:25; 50:2,10
adultress; Jews try to trap Jesus, 50:8
adversity, 50:4
affection, 33(1):9; 33(2):2,16
  for sin, 35:1
  subordinate to the will, 44:23
affliction, 36(3):7
Agabus, 36(2):6
alms, 36(3):6,7; 44:27,28; 48(1):9,16; 49:12
  fasting; good will, 42:8
  pride and, 44:29
altar: *I will go in to God's altar*, 42:5
Amalek, 43:10
Ananias, 36(2):5
ancestors, 48(2):11
angel(-s), 33(1):6; 33(2):3,9,19,22; 34(1):9,13; 35:12; 36(1):10; 36(2):16; 36(3):4; 38:15; 41:9; 42:4,5; 44:4,20; 45:11; 46:2,7; 49:11,12
  source of joy, 43:16
  those who fear God and, 33(2):11
  Why stand here gazing up . . ., 49:5
anger, 33(2):5; 36(1):9; 36(2):2; 37:7
animal(-s), 46:1
  all belong to God, 49:17
  gentle, 33(2):5
  good things given to by God, 35:13
  privileges of human beings and, 35:12
  sacrifice prefigured the one s. , 50:21
  salvation, 35:11,12
  subject to human beings, 48(1):16
anointing: kings and priests; locality, 44:19
  oil poured on stone by Jacob, 44:20
  your God has anointed you, O God, 44:19
ants, 36(2):11
  industry: summer and winter, 41:16; 48(1):12
anxiety, 36(3):12; 37:3; 41:12; 45:3; 50:18
Apocalypse, 49:9
apostasy, 50:18
apostles, 35:8; 36(2):20; 44:32; 45:4,7,8; 46:4; 47:14
  Christ shouted through, 48(1):2
  Christ's neighbors, 37:17
  churches begotten by, 44:23
  fearful at Christ's passion, 37:17
  first Christian community, 44:28
  friends of the Bridegroom, 35:9
  Lord, show us the Father, 38:6
  raised offspring for Christ, 44:23
  their sound went forth throughout . . ., 39:10
  twelve thrones, 49:9
Arius, 35:9
armies, 43:10

armor: spiritual and invisible, 34(1):2
arrogance, 45:13
arrow(-s), 37:5; 39:16; 44:16
art: lapses of taste, 34(2):2
as if (usage) , 48(2):5
astrology, 40:3
Athenians, 45:7
attitude: called "foot", 35:18
Augustine, Saint:
  confesses his bad life, 36(3):19
  slander against, 36(3):19
avarice, 36(3):11; 38:12

Babylon, 44:25
baby-talk, 33(1):11
Bagai, 36(2):20,22
bald man, 44:1
baptism, 36(3):19; 41:1; 43:15; 44:23; 47:8
  forgiveness of sins, 41:12; 45:4; 50:10
  life after, 50:1
  repetition of, 36(2):23; 39:1; 44:11
  sins after, 48(2):1
Barnabas, 33(2):19
Bathsheba, 50:2
battle, 35:6
beard: saliva dribbling down, 33(1):11
  strength, 33(1):11; 33(2):4
beatific vision: face-to-face clarity, 43:5
beauty, 36(2):13; 39:8; 49:4
  inner face: conscience, 44:29
  justice as supreme b. , 44:3
  of creation, 41:7
  of justice, 41:7; 44:14
  Word made flesh, 44:3
bedding, 40:5
beggars, 36(3):1,2,5; 42:8; 48(1):3; 48(2):5
being:
  I AM WHO AM, 38:7,22
  non-being and, 38:22
  when to say something "is", 38:7
believer, 41:5
  God knows my heart, 39:17
  Lord, who is like you, 34(1):14
  righteous, 39:6
belly, 43:23-24,25
Bible:
  opening roofed-over texts, 36(3):3
  ruminating on, 36(3):5
  sudden changes of speakers in, 44:8
  two Testaments in agreement, 49:4
  words laden with mystery, 46:1
birds:
  born from water at God's command, 49:18
  knowledge about all birds, 49:18
bishops: successors of apostles, 44:32
blasphemy, 34(2):2; 36(1):9; 36(3):3; 44:9; 50:15
blessed: on earth and in heaven, 40:3
blessing, 48(1):17
  good will, 36(2):14
  harvest, 36(3):7
  temporal goods, 48(2):8
blind(-ness), 36(1):5; 36(2):8; 40:9; 43:14
  carnally-minded persons and, 38:3
  healed man cursed by Jews, 39:26
  spiritual; eyes clogged by many sins, 39:21
blood: Cain, 39:13
  plural usage (Greek) , 50:19
  shedding, 44:27
boasting, 38:18; 43:9; 49:31
  What have you that you did not receive, 47:4
body and soul:
  See also human body; soul
  ruled and ruler, 41:7
  soul weighed down by body, 37:10; 38:3; 41:10
  whole human person, 37:11
body of Christ, *See* Church.
bones, 37:6; 41:18
  humbled bones will dance for joy, 50:13,14
  Lord, who is like you, 34(1):13,14
  safeguarded, 33(2):24
  term = the righteous of the Lord's body, 34(1):14
bow (as ambush) , 45:13
bow: *broken to pieces*, 36(2):3
bread, 48(2):10
  righteousness, 48(2):8
  word of God, 36(3):5
breast, 33(1):6; 38:3; 49:27
  praying and, 34(2):5
  symbol of secrecy, 34(2):5
bride:
  beauty (Song of Songs) , 44:26
  Queen has taken her place . . ., 44:24
Bridegroom:
  beauty of, 44:3
  children of Korah, 41:2; 46:2
  friend of, 50:13
  synagogue as mother of, 44:12
  Word of God, 44:7
brother: slandering his brother, 49:27
bruises, 37:9
building:
  inspection of trees used for, 45:3
  plan, 44:4
business, 35:5; 36(1):2; 38:3

Caecilian, 36(2):19,21,22
Caiaphas, 40:1
Cain, 40:14; 48(2):11
  cursed and banished from earth, 39:13
calf, golden, 34(2):15
Calvary, 46:2,3
  Korah, 41:2; 43:1; 44:1; 45:1
calves, sacrifice of, 50:23
Canaanite woman, 37:1; 44:27

Carthage, 36(2):19,20; 44:23; 47:6
cataracts, 41:13,14
catechumens, 41:1
Catholic Church, 36(2):11,20; 36(3):20; 39:16; 43:21; 44:32
celebration, 41:9; 43:13
centurion:
  asks Christ to heal his servant, 46:12
  I am not worthy, 38:18
certainty: prophets and future events, 43:8
  human condition beset with uncertainties, 38:19
chaff, 34(2):10; 36(3):19; 40:8; 47:8; 49:13
chance, 36(1):3
change, 38:22; 41:12; 44:2
charioteer, 33(2):6; 39:9,11
charity, 33(2):1; 36(1):3; 36(2):1,13; 44:33; 46:10,13; 48(2):3
  always still owing, 36(3):18
  Bear one another's burdens, 41:4
  chilling; blazing, 37:14
  Christ receives when given to the poor, 36(3):6
  help for least of Christ's brothers, 37:6; 48(1):16
  I was hungry and you fed me, 44:27
  law and growing cold, 38:5
  running to Christ with, 33(2):10
chastening, 37:3
chastisement, 38:17,18
chastity, 33(2):6; 50:5
cheating, 49:26
  making friends from sinful mammon, 48(1):12
childlikeness, 44:1; 46:2
children:
  follow parents' example, 48(1):14
  growing up in faith, 50:24
  heirs, 48(1):14
  mourning over death of, 37:24
  storing up wealth for, 38:12
children of God, 33(1):10; 43:5; 47:8; 49:2
  inheritance of, 36(2):8
  key: God as lovable, 49:2
  whips used by God on, 36(3):9; 40:6
choice: ceases on judgment day, 36(1):1
chrism, 44:20
Christ (the word)
  meaning = anointed, 44:19
Christian life:
  brothers of Christ, 48(1):8
  Christ, the end of our journey, 45:1
  Christ's way, 36(2):16
  falling occurs in the heart, 44:16
  hidden with Christ in God, 36(1):3; 39:28; 48(2):3
  I live my own life no longer, 49:31
  love and fear as guides, 39:20
  made new by imitating his passion, 37:27
  narrow path, 43:17
  not I, but Christ lives in me, 39:27
  obey the commandments, 36(1):8
  ourselves as weapons in, 34(1):2
  paths of the undefiled, 36(2):7
  proclaim; suffer; glorify, 39:15
  seeking: imitate Christ's sufferings, 37:18
  sell all you possess . . ., 49:8
  sufferings of Christ and, 36(2):16,17
  traveler and lodger, 38:21
  Wait for the Lord, 36(3):14
Christians, 45:7,8; 47:8
  begotten children, 44:23
  children of Korah, 41:2
  elder shall serve the younger, 46:6
  enemies of Christianity, 43:6-7
  fear of proclaiming aloud, 39:16
  Gentile origin, 44:12
  good seed, 42:2
  persecuted, 34(2):8
  subordinate to apostles, 46:5
  taunted, 43:10
Church, 33(1):6; 34(1):10; 35:9; 39:8,28; 42:4; 46:5; 49:11,27
  See also Catholic Church; persecution
  almsgiving, 44:28
  apostles and, 44:32
  ascension of Christ and, 49:5
  betrothed to one husband, 49:9
  beware the foot of pride, 35:18
  bones = the righteous, 34(1):14
  bride of Christ the Bridegroom, 44:3,33
  bride: *I am wounded with love*, 37:5
  Christ speaks in person of his body, 37:6; 40:1
  Christ: Head and body, 34(2):1
  Christ's voice in his members, 34(1):1; 39:5; 40:6
  city founded upon a mountain, 44:33
  creation: the second day, 47:1
  cursing, 48(2):10
  daughters of Tyre, 44:28
  earth where blood has been received, 39:13
  enemies ask: *When will his name disappear*, 40:1,7
  Eve, mother of the living, 40:10
  everyone magnify the Lord, 33(2):6
  gleaming white robe of Transfiguration, 50:12
  good and evil mingled in, 34(1):10
  growing/filling the entire world, 47:2
  holy milk at breast of, 38:3
  integrity, 49:9
  Jacob's ladder and, 44:20
  land of the Lord, 36(1):4
  leaders, 39:6
  lesson learned from its Head, 44:15
  love the unity of, 33(2):6
  lying witnesses against, 36(2):18

members, hold fast to the Head, 40:8
members: all the righteous since world began, 36(3):4
mouth and belly, 43:25
one body, one voice: Christ, 34(2):1
persecuted, 34(1):14
saints as garments of, 44:22
Saul, why are you persecuting me, 37:6
single voice with Christ, 37:6
sins of Christ's body, 37:6
sleek old age, 36(3):4
sound gone forth through all the earth, 39:15
speaker, as a single body, 41:1
spread through the nations, 36(3):4; 44:30
suffering in Head and body, 37:16
suffering of Christ as example for, 34(2):1
suffers what Christ suffered, 40:8
temple of the King, 44:31
temptations, 41:19
tent, 41:9
two in one flesh (with Christ) , 37:6; 40:1; 44:12
voice of Christ's body, 34(1):1
weakness of Christ's body, 37:22
widespread through all nations, 36(3):4
circumcision, 33(1):7; 44:12; 47:3,11
city of God, 45:10; 47:2,3,4,7
cleanliness, 33(2):8
clothe the naked, 36(3):8
clothing: sweet scents, 44:22
cloud, 35:8,12; 36(2):12; 45:15
God thundered from, 45:10,13
come (the word): meaning: believe, 45:12
commandment, 39:21; 40:4; 41:3; 45:6; 47:9; 49:6,9
earthly promises, 34(1):7
harmony with, 42:5
pain as God's precept, 38:17
compassion, 33(1):9; 49:22
complacency, 50:4
compunction, 50:11
conduct, 38:3; 50:15
confession:
everlasting, 44:33
gift of the Spirit, 50:16
praise of God, 34(2):10
secret sins, 37:16
shame, 39:16
sins purged by, 42:7
conscience, 33(2):8; 34(2):2; 35:5; 36(2):10,11; 38:22; 45:11; 49:1,9; 28
beauty of, 44:29
consolation, 36(2):10
dare to approach God, 33(2):11
guilty, 45:3
nothing more interior than, 45:3
sin and God's absence from, 45:3
witness, when God is judge, 37:21
consolation: comfort from material things, 36(2):10
conspiracy, 40:9
contemplation, 38:6; 43:16
to live in the Lord's house, 41:5
conversion (moral), 36(2):11; 49:28
dishonesty in searching, 35:3
Forgetting what lies behind, 39:3
God's word and correcting life, 49:1
impious people, 50:18
name of Christ, 40:13
numbers beyond reckoning, 39:10
old self into a new self, 44:2
opportunity for, 39:28
persecution and, 34(1):8
praise God for, 39:26
converts, 43:22; 44:23
cornerstone, 47:3,5
correction, 48(2):9; 49:30
covenant:
Abraham's two sons, 33(1):3
new, 45:6,10
Old and New, 35:12
coveting, 39:7,28; 41:3; 48(1):3
creation:
absolutely gratis, 43:15
all good found in Creator, 44:4
all present in Word of God, 44:5
all things belong to Creator, 49:17
birds, 49:18
Church as work of the second day, 47:1
Come and see the deeds of the Lord, 45:12
God's wisdom in the Word, 49:18
in God we have all that was made, 34(1):12
love Creator in creature, 39:8
Maker is to remake his work, 38:17
second day: the firmament, 47:1
signs of things to come, 47:1
Take your scourges away, 38:16
Creator: finding God, 41:7
cross:
boasting of, 44:3
instrument of healing, 43:14
insults to, 46:2
new sacrifice, 33(1):6
tree of salvation, 39:15
crowds: not to be imitated, 39:7
crucifixion:
See also under Jesus Christ
abolished as human punishment, 36(2):4
abomination, 37:26
drummed, 33(1):9
legs of the two thieves broken, 33(2):7
old nature crucified with Christ, 40:6
three men on crosses, 34(2):1
cruelty: mothers; doctors, 33(2):20
curse, 34(2):2; 39:26; 40:9; 43:14; 48(1):17; 48(2):10
Cyprian, Saint, 36(3):13

damnation, 43:18; 48(1):6,7; 50:5
dance, 47:11
Daniel (prophet) , 42:4; 44:33; 45:12; 47:2
darkness, 33(2):10; 36(1):6; 47:1; 48(2):4
David, King, 33(1):2,4,6; 33(2):2; 33(2):2; 34(1):1,4,9; 37:2; 46:8; 50:2,3,6
  See also Saul, King
  Against you alone have I sinned, 50:9
  animal sacrifices, 50:21
  conceived in iniquity, 50:10
  cursed, 50:15
  feigned insanity, 33(1):2,3,8; 33(2):4,12
  just punishment of, 50:15
  Nathan's parable, 50:8
  type of the Church, 50:22
  Your sin is forgiven, 50:11,15,18
day(-light), 47:1
  as prosperity, 41:6,16
dead:
  bodily concerns, 48(2):7
  sleeper, rise from the dead, 45:12
  spirits; grave-cults, 48(1):15
deaf, 38:16
  carnally-minded persons and, 38:3
  fear of speaking, 38:4
  humiliated, 38:4
death, 34(1):1; 39:20; 41:13; 43:18,21; 47:13; 50:19
  bowed down to the very end, 37:10
  called 'sin', 34(2):3
  certainty of, 38:19
  corporal and spiritual, 48(2):2
  curse inflicted on first parents, 37:26
  day of, is hidden, 34(1):14
  devil, lord of, 50:9
  Earth you are . . ., 46:13
  fear of, 48(1):6
  making-alive is promised us, 40:3
  mortal body carried with us, 37:5
  nearness of your own last day, 36(1):10
  pain: sinners and the righteous, 33(2):25,26
  punishment due to flesh, 50:10
  shepherd of unbelievers, 48(2):2,3,4
  soul troubled by imminence of, 42:7
  temporal goods left behind, 48(2):7
  untimely extinction, 48(1):11
  when he sees the wise dying, 48(1):11
  when you die, you will not be dead, 36(3):15
  You fool . . . this very night . . ., 48(2):1,7
debt: anxiety, 45:3
  condign punishment for debtor, 45:3
decadence, 50:24
deceit, 39:26
deer:
  longs for springs of water, 41:1,10
  rest their heads on each other, 41:4
  snakes killed by, 41:3
delight, 36(1):4,12; 39:3; 41:3,10; 50:13
deliverance, 48(2):5
demon, 34(1):6; 42:4; 46:2,11; 47:3
  Christ accused of having, 48(2):4
  gods of the heathen, 49:2,6
  You are the Son of God, 49:2
depth (the word) , 41:13
desire, 34(1):12; 34(2):4,6; 36(1):4; 36(3):13; 38:6; 39:3; 41:3,5,6; 42:2
  all is before God, 37:14
  earthly, 50:15
  eternal, not temporal, goods, 43:2
  for incorruption, 50:19
  humans and animals, 35:12
  Make known to me my end, 38:10
despair, 36(2):11; 50:5,7
devil, 33(1):4; 33(2):14; 34(1):7,15; 35:17; 36(3):5,13,15; 37:3; 38:15,18,21,22; 39:3; 40:9; 41:10,18; 44:1,25; 45:7; 47:3,9; 50:4
  See also demon; Satan; serpent
  children of, 44:12
  corrupting the mind, 39:1
  death and, 48(2):2
  deceives by praising Christ, 40:4
  earthly needs and, 40:4
  human enemy, 40:4
  lord of death, 50:9
  persecutions of the Church, 40:1
  roaring lion, 49:29
  ruler of this world, 34(1):4
  temporal prosperity and, 40:4
  worship in present life, 40:3
Diana, 45:7
Dido, 47:6
dignity, 48(1):16
  Head and body of the Church, 37:6
disciples:
  crucifixion and loss of hope, 46:7
  man whose sight was restored, 39:26
discipline, 49:24; 50:24
disease, 47:4
dishonesty, 33(2):14
dissimilarity, 34(2):6
distress, 36(2):16; 37:13
divinization, 35:14
doctor, *See* physician.
Donatists, 33(2):7,19,22; 36(3):18,19,20
Donatus, 33(2):7; 35:9; 36(2):22,23
donkey: gentleness, 33(2):5
dream, 48(2):5,7
drum: crucifixion, 33(1):9; 33(2):2
drunkenness, 35:14
dust, 34(1):9; 43:25
dwelling, 48(1):2

ears: *Let anyone . . . listen*, 48(1):2
earth, 45:15
  hands of the ungodly, 36(3):13
earthlings, 48(1):3
  he has summoned all the earth, 49:3

land of the dying, 36(3):11
righteous will possess, 36(3):11
trembled with rising of Christ, 36(2):17
eat, 48(1):3
ecstasy, 34(2):6; 37:12
Egypt, 43:2; 46:6
elect: numerous, 47:9
Elijah, 33(2):17
Elisha: children jeered at, 44:1; 46:2
emptiness, 38:10,11
end of the world: *Woe betide those* . . ., 39:28
endurance, 33(2):24; 39:28; 42:3,5; 43:1,17; 45:1
people who hate, 36(2):1
suffering and, 36(2):6
enemies, 40:13; 41:18; 42:4; 43:10,11,13; 44:16; 49:26
commanded to love, 39:21
confounded and awed, 34(1):8
curse, 43:14
empty accusations by, 37:25
enjoined to pray for, 34(1):8; 37:4
gloating, 37:22,23
God will toss them like straw, 43:6-7
hate without reason, 37:25
invisible warfare, 34(1):4
Let them be thrust back . . ., 39:26
loving to limit of strength, 39:1
of truth, 36(2):12
prayer of praise to God for, 39:4
some flatter, some insult, 39:26
united in conspiracy, 40:9
enigma, 48(1):5
enlightenment:
Arise, sleeper, rise from the dead, 48(2):4
entertainments, 39:9
envy, 49:30
of the prosperous, 36(1):9
secret, 36(1):9
wicked people, 36(1):3
Esau, 46:6
eternal fire
threats of, 49:7
eternal life, 33(1):9; 34(1):1; 36(3):8,11,13; 37:23; 41:13; 42:4; 43:17; 44:12; 45:13
beatitude, 36(2):4
kingdom we are to receive, 36(3):6
One thing I have begged . . ., 41:5
promise: *May the Lord keep him safe*, 40:3
eternal punishment:
weeping and gnashing of teeth, 36(1):11
eucharist:
bread of angels, 33(1):6
How can this man give his flesh to eat, 33(2):12
humility; salvation, 33(1):6,10
scandal, 33(1):8
Eve, 40:10; 47:9; 48(1):6
See also Adam and Eve
evil-doer: does harm to self, 34(1):11
example:
children and parents, 48(1):14
lapse of the great, 50:3,5
preachers, 36(3):20
existence: true being, 38:7
extinction: death seen as, 48(1):11
eye, 41:7
disease, 39:21
sight, 36(3):15
wanton glances, 50:3

faith, 33(1):10; 33(2):2,10,25; 35:1; 36(1):1; 36(2):3; 36(3):8,14; 37:15; 38:9,18; 39:9,15; 41:5,13; 43:16; 44:13; 49:7
anger and, 36(1):9
believing we shall come to see, 44:25
brought to life by, 49:5
centurion's trust, 46:12
children growing up in, 50:24
children of Abraham, 46:11
Christ dwells in heart through, 45:5
cleansing the heart, 44:25
diversity of languages, 44:24
embarrassed to proclaim in public, 39:16
forgetting: Christ goes to sleep, 34(1):3
heading for a fall, 38:14
healing, before Christ, 36(3):4
heaven and, 48(2):2
inheritance to last forever, 36(2):8
interior eyes, 36(2):8
invisible, 38:10
jeering at believers, 48(2):3
Jesus and the stormy sea, 34(1):3
justice hidden in my heart, 39:17
listen first, see later, 47:7
made new by, 39:18
moving mountains, 45:6
righteousness and, 36(1):6; 39:27; 50:18
seeing good in others, 33(2):15
Show us the Father, 37:11
spiritual armor, 34(1):2
support for the heart, 33(2):24
united with God, 33(2):9
wavering: too difficult, 40:4
you see if you believe, 45:12
faithful, the:
God's tent on earth, 41:9
living stones, 44:31
numbers beyond reckoning, 39:10
sons of men, 48(1):3
false accusations, 40:8
by enemies, 37:25
made against Christ, 36(2):17; 37:19
family: oppositions in household, 44:11
famine, 33(2):17
fantasies, 37:11
fasting, 43:16
almsgiving related to, 42:8
lunching on prayers, 42:8

temptation of Christ, 34(2):3
fate, 40:6
father:
household opposition, 44:11
son and, 50:24
fear, 41:14,18; 47:6; 50:13
chaste, 38:10
face of God, 50:16
justice; guide, 39:20
of proclaiming, 39:16
of saying something bad, 38:4
Peter's heart, 39:23
righteous will fear and be afraid, 39:6
source of sin, 38:2
suffering, 36(2):17
those who kill body, not the soul, 36(3):13
fear of God:
Christ teaches, 33(2):18
lacking in sinners, 35:2
Lord's angel will deliver, 33(2):11
nothing lacking to those who fear, 33(2):14
feast day, 41:9
feet, 38:2
charity, 33(2):10
Felician of Musti, 36(2):20,22
fight, 35:6
finished (the word) , 45:1
fire, 34(1):11; 37:3; 40:12; 49:7
I have come to set fire . . ., 45:13
firmament
children of, 47:1
people worthy to be named, 47:1,8
first-born: rights of, 46:6
fish: one hundred and fifty-three, 49:9
flattery, 39:26; 49:1,26
fleece, 45:10
flesh:
cravings of, 36(1):5
infirmity, 40:5
no power to speak, 42:6
persecutors, 36(3):13
thigh as, 44:13
Two in one flesh (Church) , 40:1
Florentius of Hadrumetum, 36(2):20
food, 50:19
foolishness, 33(2):4; 39:8
foot of pride, 35:17,18
forbearance, 36(2):1
forgiveness: *cool refreshment*, 38:22
forgiveness of sin, 41:12
bad conscience, 45:3
catechumens, 41:1
Christ as blasphemer, 36(3):3
hidden; unseen, 50:11
hope, 50:5
praise God for, 39:26
trust in God, 33(2):26
fortitude, 42:3
Fortunatus, 36(2):20
fountain of life, 41:2
fraud, 33(2):14
freedom, 34(1):15
frogs, 45:10
fruit(-s), 48(2):4
funeral: grandiose, for rich man, 48(1):13; 48(2):1
furnace, 36(3):9
the three young men in, 33(2):22
future:
all things are present with God, 49:18
certainty of outcomes, 43:10
meaning of *in store*, 36(3):15
prophets refer to as if past, 43:8
prudent provision for, 48(1):12
speaker sees as present, 49:12
future life:
See also eternal life; heaven
bodily needs in, 50:19
face-to-face with God, 43:5
glory; inheritance, 36(2):8
God correcting a person in this life, 50:15
God's promise, 40:3
reward, 36(2):16

Gaius Seius, 33(2):13
generations: ancestors and children, 48(1):15
generosity, 36(2):13
Gentiles, 33(1):7; 33(2):2,10; 35:8: 43:12; 44:16,25; 45:6,8,10,15: 46:3,5,9; 47:3,6,14
companions of the north, 47:3
first to understand the prophets, 47:7
Tyre as symbol of, 44:27
gentle people, 36(1):12
gentleness, 33(2):5; 44:15
gifts:
from Christ, 36(2):14
God has given what you are to return to him, 44:9
God the author of all, 45:15
temporal and eternal, 35:7
treasures in heaven, 44:27
what was not received from God, 44:7
withdrawn by God, 34(1):6
glory, 36(1):3; 44:29; 48(2):7; 49:22; 50:15
future; inheritance, 36(2):8
hope, 37:5
sufferings, 36(2):9
way of Christ's lowliness, 37:16
gluttony: Esau, 46:6
goal: future life, 38:6
God:
See also Holy Spirit; Jesus Christ; Trinity; ungodly
acknowledged in her houses, 47:4
all things past and future are with God, 49:18
anger, 37:3,5
armor of, 34(1):2
attributes, 34(1):7; 35:13

author of all his gifts, 45:15
avenger, 49:28
Be still and see that I am God, 45:14
cares for all equally, 45:9
coming near to, 34(2):6
confinement in place, 45:9
everything found in Him, 36(1):12
face of, 50:16
faithful in his promises, 39:3
finding fault with, 44:17
finding God, 41:7
forgetting, 49:29
glory, 39:4
God's anointing of God, 44:19
goodness of, 41:12
gracious countenance, 45:9
hearts far from, 48(2):1
his speaking is eternal, 44:5
hunger, 49:19
invisible realities of, 41:2,8
judgment(-s), 47:11
deep, 41:13,14
just, 36(3):9
justice and mercy, 35:10; 44:18
justice of his wrath, 37:7
unerring judgment, 34(1):9
unfathomable abyss, 41:14
of wrongdoing, 42:7
king has desired your beauty, 44:26,27
king you are marrying, 44:26
knowledge:
knows us; yet he tests us, 36(1):1
of things before they were created, 49:18
secret and supreme, 49:18
light and spring, 41:2
love for us, 34(1):12
I will show myself to him, 37:11
loyalty required by, 49:15
mercy, *See* mercy.
miraculous interventions, 43:4
no beginning; new for us, 39:4
nothing comparable to, 34(1):13
omnipresence, 34(2):6; 39:27; 44:20; 49:18
our food and drink, 50:19
petitions for temporal goods, 43:2
possessed for our enrichment, 34(1):12
possession; possessed, 36(1):4
power manifested, 45:9; 49:18
praising God by doing all things well, 34(2):16
prayer to, *See* prayer.
promises deferred, 39:2
refuge and strength, 45:2-3,4,7,13
reign over all nations, 46:10
seeking a reality above the soul, 41:8
seeking Him in material creatures, 41:8
seen by the pure of heart, 42:4
seen only with the mind, 41:7
silence of, 34(2):12
soul athirst for, 41:5
spoke only one Word, 44:5
strikes and heals, 50:11
supporter, 45:11,13,15
taunt: *Where is your God*, 41:6,10,19
testimony: *I am your God*, 49:14
the true "is", 38:7
thinking of, as depraved, 44:17
throne in human hearts, 45:9;, 46:10
tongue and scribe's pen, 44:6,10
united with, in faith, 33(2):9
watching the wicked, 33(2):21; 35:3
godless, 47:3
persecution of the righteous, 34(1):14
seed will perish, 36(3):10
gods, 46:9,13
distinction among them, 49:2
God as maker of, 49:1
God as source of terror to, 49:2
shall die as mortals die, 49:2
stone, 41:6
gold, 36(1):12; 44:24
refined from straw, 36(1):11
Goliath, 33(1):2,3,4,10
good and evil:
See also sin; wickedness
fear of finding one's own iniquity, 35:3
found in all worldly activities, 36(1):2
God's bounty shared by all people, 42:2
innocence of evil, 46:2
intention related to, 39:26
mingled in the Church, 34(1):10
paths: broad or narrow, 39:6,7
people: just and unjust, 36(2):1
restrain tongue from evil, 33(2):18
threshing-floor, 47:9
turn from evil; do good, 33(2):19; 36(3):8
good example: good lives, 50:1
good fortune: praise God for, 48(2):9; 50:15
good thief, 34(1):14; 39:15
good will, 35:1
ladders and wings, 38:2
treasure of the poor, 36(2):13
good works, 36(1):8; 41:9; 46:10; 48(1):9,16; 48(2):3; 49:22,31
All nations, clap your hands, 46:3
Do good, and live in the land, 36(1):4
honor of God; in public, 44:29
pride, 44:29
rich in, 44:28
weary of doing, 36(3):2,7
works of the godless will perish, 36(3):10
goodness
fallen silent even for good words, 38:4
imitation of the good, 39:6
thank God for, 49:30

gospel: beauty of, 49:4
governing: lowly status as subject to, 48(1):2
grace, 35:10; 36(1):3; 38:2; 42:7; 43:26; 44:7,17; 45:10,11,13; 47:3,4,8; 49:9,31; 50:18
  bedews your lips, 44:7,8,10,17
  confessing weakness, 38:18
  deified by, 49:2
  given gratis, 49:31
  gratuitous worship, 43:15,16
  heaven = the concern of, 44:8
  punishment as, 38:17
grass, 48(2):3
gratitude, 36(2):13; 39:3
grave-cults, 48(1):15
greatness, 38:8; 39:6
greed, 34(1):12; 38:11; 48(1):2
  loves unity, 39:28
  source of sin, 38:2
  unchecked, 39:7
grief: death of a child, 37:24
groaning, 34(2):6; 37:13,14; 43:2
grumbling, 48(1):1
guile, 49:26,27
guilt, 36(2):3,22; 44:18; 50:13

hair, 38:12
hands: *Clap your hands . . .*, 46:3,9,12
happiness, 33(2):3; 35:7; 41:9; 49:22
  earthly; non-worshipers, 48(1):1
  earthly; true, 36(3):14
  eternal, 36(2):16
  everlasting confession, 44:33
  God went up amid shouts of joy, 46:7
  love of good days, 33(2):17
  prayers heard, 33(2):8
  resurrection and, 36(1):9
  temporal, 48(2):1
  ungodly people, 36(1):3,9; 36(3):14
happy day (expression), 43:19-20
harmony, 49:30
  tongues confessing; hands at work, 46:3
hate, 33(2):8
  bad person hates the good, 36(2):1
  God's friend hates what He hates, 44:18
  shared; common cause, 36(2):1
  without reason, 37:25
head-wagging, 43:14
healing, 39:8,20; 40:5
  hyssop, 50:12
  persecutors and the cross, 43:14
health, 37:5
  boasting, 42:7
  perfect; future life, 50:19
hearing, *See* listen,
heart:
  abyss, 41:13
  bellowing its groans, 37:13
  blessed are the pure . . ., 39:22
  circumcision of, 47:11
  clean; see God, 33(2):8
  cleansing, 44:25; 50:12
  contrite and humble, 50:21
  Create a clean heart in me . . ., 50:15
  cross in, 50:1
  cursing in, 48(1):17
  ears of the, 48(1):2
  eyes of the, 33(2):15
  faith awakened in, 45:5
  faith hidden in, 39:17
  fixed on this earth, 37:10
  God knows the heart, 36(1):2
  God's innermost being, 44:5
  God's throne in, 45:9
  home on this earth, 39:28
  honoring with the lips, 36(3):12
  humble: God will not scorn, 49:15
  incapable of knowing itself, 39:23
  insincerity, 39:16
  name of God on lips only, 48(2):1
  overflows with a good word, 44:4,8
  peace: bedroom of the heart, 35:5
  petitions of, 36(1):5
  precious jewels of virtue in, 33(2):15
  proclaiming with the lips only, 39:15
  rumination in, 46:1
  secrets of, 43:19-20,21
  serpent's word, or word of God, 48(1):1
  throbbing, 37:15
  throne of Christ in, 46:10
  treasure and, 48(2):2
  true wealth in, 37:24
  uplifted, 39:28
  upright, 35:16; 50:15
  virginity of, 39:1
heat, 50:23
heathens, 49:6
heaven, 35:12; 36(3):6; 38:18,21; 43:15; 44:8; 49:5,13,22
  beg to live in Lord's house forever, 38:6
  dwelling fixed in, 48(2):3
  faith and, 48(2):2
  God has blessed you, 44:8
  how to put money in, 38:12
  Lay up for yourselves treasure in, 38:12
  meaning: all saints, 49:11
  New Testament promise, 34(1):7
  treasure in, never fails, 36(3):8; 44:27
heavens, 41:7
  proclaiming justice, 49:13
  word = 'peoples', 49:11
heel, 48(1):6
heirs: include extra brother in heaven, 48(1):14
hell, 33(2):25; 41:14; 48(2):2,4,7,8
help: from direction of mountains, 35:9
heretical nuns, 44:31
heretics, 35:9; 39:1; 45:12; 47:10; 49:3,9
Hermon, 41:12
Herod, 47:5
hidden things, 45:1

holocaust, 49:15,16; 50:21,23
  definition, 49:15
  sacrifices done away with, 39:12,13
Holy Spirit, 33(1):7; 33(2):1,21; 36(2):6,9,14; 37:9; 40:3; 41:11; 45:8; 48(2):1; 48(2):11; 49:4,5; 50:10,16,17
  miracles and, 45:4
  sevenfold gifts of, 49:9
homes: tents and, 48(1):15
honor, 48(2):11
hope, 33(1):1; 35:12,14; 36(1):4; 36(2):6; 37:5,15,28; 38:9; 39:6,15; 41:10,19; 42:2; 43:8,16; 46:7; 48(2):5; 48(2):5; 49:1; 50:19
  children of God, 49:2
  disconcerted in bad times, 36(2):9
  for what we do not see, 38:13
  future happenings, 43:15
  pregnant woman as symbol of, 39:28
  present and future, 40:3
  simply ask for God himself, 39:7
  illusion, 36(2):9
  lodged in God, 36(2):9
  set in human beings, 36(3):20
  shelter of God's wings, 35:13 uncertainty, 38:19
horse, 33(2):5
house: *Distribute its houses*, 47:14
household: oppositions within, 44:11
human being(-s):
  becoming like foolish beasts, 48(2):11
  called "gods" (deified) , 49:2
  called angels, 49:11
  Christ as only a human, 40:1
  conceived in iniquity, 50:10
  deep abyss, 41:13
  duty: live according to God's will, 48(1):1
  gifts given to, 36(2):13
  humility re gifts, 38:18
  live on word of God, 36(3):5
  nature; sin, 44:18
  nothing compared with HIM WHO IS, 38:9
  privileges; and animals, 35:12
  two types: Adam and Christ, 35:12
human body:
endued with health, 37:11
  dead because of sin, 39:20; 42:7; 50:10
  redemption of, 37:5
human condition, 42:2
  displeasing things as self-made, 44:9
  living in uncertainty, 38:19
  suffering; strength from the Lord, 36(2):17
humiliation, 42:3
  belly sticking to the ground, 43:23-24,25
  both punishment and grace, 38:17
  deaf, 38:4
  fallen silent, 38:4
humility, 36(2):1; 41:12; 46:2,13; 48(1):3; 50:13
  blessing the Lord, 33(2):3,4
  Christ slays the devil (Goliath), 33(1):4
  Christian's business to be lowly, 33(2):23
  confessing one's sins, 34(2):3
  disciplined by, 38:18
  God comes down to the humble, 33(2):23; 39:20; 50:21
  hearing with, 44:25
  holding fast to Christ, 33(1):10
  meekness, 33(2):5
  unwilling to be praised, 33(2):5
  wholeness, 35:17
hunger, 33(2):19; 42:1; 49:19
hymn, 43:13
  good word from the heart, 44:9
  song of praise, 39:4
hypocrites, 34(2):11; 37:17; 40:8; 48(1):17
hyssop, 50:12

identity: discover who we are, 46:2
Idithun, 38:12,3,4,6,10,11,13,17,18,22
idolaters, 34(2):15; 45:6
idols, 34(1):13; 35:13; 39:28; 40:1,4; 44:2; 45:10
ignorance, 33(1):8; 33(2):2,12; 34(1):9
  bad will, 35:4
  pardon and, 35:3
  sin; mercy, 50:6,7
illiteracy: book of the world, 45:7
illusions, 37:11
image of God, 38:11
  coming close to God, 34(2):6
  humans and animals, 48(1):16
  mind or reason, 42:6
  not neglected on earth, 40:3
  sons of men, 35:12
  within; spiritual, 48(2):11
imitation:
  crowds on broad road, 39:7
  Do what they tell you . . ., 49:23
immortality, 33(2):8,9,19; 35:6; 37:5,11; 40:1; 44:15, 44:21; 47:1; 48(2):2; 49:19; 50:19,22,23
impiety: David's sin, 50:18
  war against God, 45:13
imposters, 36(1):2
Incarnation:
  flesh from Abraham's stock, 47:15
  flesh to die for us, 39:5
  future; accomplished, 50:17
  God with flesh, 46:8
  God-Man, human for our sake, 36(2):15
  likeness of sinful flesh, 49:5
  Son leaving Father, 44:12
  Word united with flesh, 44:3
incest, 36(2):20
incorruption, 50:19
infant baptism, 50:10
infinity, 36(2):16
inheritance: coheirs, 49:2

kingdom prepared for you, 36(3):14
inheritance, 36(2):8; 46:6; 48(2):9
iniquity, 39:1,21; 40:8; 42:3; 44:18; 48(1):6
attachment to, 35:1
blood (usage of term) , 50:19
blot out my iniquity, 50:6,14
derived from Adam, 50:10
eating, 48(2):8
self-destroying, 34(1):11
innocence, 36(1):12; 36(3):15; 37:21; 40:5; 50:23
insanity, 33(1):8
instruction: hated, 49:24
insult, 34(2):8,9,11; 39:26; 43:15; 48(1):11
integrity, 36(1):2
intention:
good works, 44:29
liability for punishment, 40:9
morality of spoken words and, 39:26
people not good, but with good intentions, 39:26
preparing self to sin, 50:3
interest on loans, 36(3):6; 38:5
interpretation, 36(1):2
invisibility, 38:10
invoke (the word) , 41:13
is (the word) , 38:7
Isaac, 36(1):1; 36(3):1; 46:13
Israel, 33(1):6; 36(3):12; 46:3; 49:11,14,19
crippling of, 44:20
God's plan for, 43:2
land given to, 34(1):7
one who guards, 43:22
ivory palaces, 44:23

Jacob, 43:5; 46:13; 49:14
elder shall serve the younger, 46:6
man without guile, 44:20
name changed to Israel, 44:20
oil poured on stone by, 44:20
thigh, 44:20
Jacob's ladder, 38:2; 44:20
jealousy, 33(1):2; 33(2):6; 44:22
Jerusalem, 33(1):5; 36(1):9,12; 36(3):4; 47:3
beauty of Christ's gospel, 49:4
Let the walls be rebuilt, 50:22
Vision of Peace, 50:22
witnesses to Christ in, 49:5
Jesus Christ, 34(1):1; 35:9,12; 38:9; 42:5; 44:10,18; 48(1):2
See also Bridegroom; Christian life; Church; Incarnation; Second Coming; Son of God; Son of Man; Word of God
accept *the needy and poor man*, 40:1,2
all nations are his subjects, 44:14
Angel of Great Counsel, 33(2):11
Anyone who knows himself to be without sin, 50:8
apostles and, 35:9
Arise, Lord, help us, 43:26
ascension, 45:1; 46:7,10
Church entrusted to us, 49:5
asleep; arise, 43:22; 45:5
beautiful [fifteen descriptors] , 44:3
beauty of, 43:16; 49:5
came to save sinners, 49:31
carried in his own hands . . ., 33(2):2
centurion and, 38:18
chrism (the word) , 44:19
Church and, *See* Church.
claims all sin as his own, 37:16
Come, children, and hear me, 33(2):16
compassion; affection, 33(1):9
confessing the name of, 43:21
cornerstone, 47:3
crucifixion, 33(2):24; 39:15
bones not broken, 34(1):14
come down from the cross, 49:5
Jews and, 48(1):5
Jews did not recognize Christ, 49:5
King of the Jews, 46:4
mocking the cross, 46:2,7; 48(1):11
scandal to the Jews, 44:3
why have you forsaken me, 49:5
David prefigured, 33(1):4
David's Lord, 33(1):6
death, *See below:* passion and death
deceitful praise by devil, 40:4
Destroy this temple . . ., 40:12
divine deliverer, 40:2
divinity:
contemplation of, 40:2
godhead lies hidden in, 40:1
hidden God of gods, 49:5
same as the Father, 44:15
Do not weep over me, 40:12
drawing near to the light, 33(2):10
dwells in hearts through faith, 45:5
empty accusations against him, 37:19
enemies ask: *When will his name disappear*, 40:1,7
enemies plan killing him, 40:10
enemy seeking his life, 39:24
ennobled in God's presence, 45:4
false witnesses against him, 36(2):17
Father, forgive them . . ., 39:25
feigned friends of, 37:17
following Christ, 39:6
foremost place in the book, 39:14
foundation, 47:4
fount of life, 35:15
future judge subjected to judgment, 50:9
Gentiles and, 33(1):7
gifts to humans, 36(2):14
God and man, 44:19
God born from the human race, 44:13
God of gods, 49:1
God of the whole earth, 46:9

gods, if any, were made through, 49:1
Good Teacher, 44:4
He [Moses] *wrote about me*, 47:1
Head of all the righteous of all time, 36(3):4
headstone of the corner, 39:1
hold fast to his body and blood, 39:13
Hosanna, Son of David, 33(2):5
humanity:
  death and, 34(2):3
  his death was no sham, 37:26
  ignorance of Christ, 34(2):2
  phantom flesh, 37:26
  praying as proper to, 34(2):5
  raised the human up to heaven, 40:2
  seed of David, 46:8
  surpassing all other humans, 44:7
  true flesh inherited from Adam, 37:27
humility, 33(2):7; 50:12
obedience unto death, 33(1):9
this is my body, 33(1):10; 33(2):2
hunger and thirst, 34(2):4
hungry for our sake, 49:19
I am needy and poor, 39:27
I am the light, 42:4
I am the living bread, 33(2):15
I am the truth, 39:18
I am thirsty, 34(2):4
I am with you throughout all days, 46:7; 47:14
I announced the news . . ., 39:10,11
immolated as our passover, 39:13
innocence, 40:14
jeered at, 46:8
judge, 44:29
King of glory, 47:1
kingship not of this world, 47:5,15
knowledge of last day, 36(1):1
Korah, 41:2
lawgiver, 50:8
leader and his followers, 39:25
leaving his mother, the Jewish race, 44:12
led like a sheep to the slaughter, 44:15
life through, 48(2):2
lion, 49:29
Lord most high and terrible, 46:4
mediator between God and man, 36(2):20
members in him: *My God, my God, why . . .*, 40:6
miracles, 39:15; 47:5
mountain in prophecy, 45:6
name: Anointed God, 44:21
new Adam; life-giving Spirit, 37:15
not put to shame, 33(2):10
our eternal life with, 48(1):10
passion and death
  bones not broken, 33(2):24
  Christ's 'ignorance' of, 34(2):2
  come down from the cross, 34(2):11; 40:13; 44:1
  crucified in weakness, 37:27
  disciples lose hope, 46:7
  Father, forgive them . . ., 44:15
  glory of martyrs, 40:1
  godhead did not die, 40:2
  green wood, 40:12
  guards claim disciples removed his body, 36(2):17
  Head and his body, 37:6
  imitation of, 48(1):3
  Jews and, 37:11
  led like sheep to slaughter, 38:3
  My God, my God, why . . . 34(2):5; 37:6,27
  My soul is sorrowful, 40:6
  Peter's denial, 37:17
  proof: he is only human, 40:1
  psalm 37, and gospel accounts, 37:6
  scourged, 40:6
  silence at his trial, 37:20
Peoples will fall under your assault, 44:16
power and wisdom of God, 46:10
power of, 40:13
  to come down from cross, 34(2):11
  to lay down his life, 33(2):7
  to raise his own flesh, 40:12
  to take up life again, 40:10
  Whom do you seek . . . 34(2):3
praying, 34(2):5
present in his members, 40:11
priest, 36(2):20
proclaims, suffers, is glorified, 39:15
promises kept by, 44:15; 47:7
prophecies made by, 39:1
propitiation for our sins, 33(2):26
psalms = voice of Christ, 37:6
resurrection, 40:12; 43:26; 47:1
  earth trembled, 36(2):17
  flesh arose, 49:5
  soldiers guarding his tomb, 37:19
risen among the pagans, 43:22
robe gleaming white like snow, 50:12
rock, 39:3
sackcloth; fasting, 34(2):3
salvation comes from the Jews, 47:11
seen today as only a man, 40:1
sharing in his suffering, 36(1):9
sheep voiceless before its shearer, 37:20
silence of, 49:6
sinless, 34(2):2,3; 37:19; 37:6; 40:6; 43:2; 44:7; 50:9
sinners and, 48(2):1
sleeps when faith is forgotten, 34(1):3
speaking in person of his body (Church), 37:6

stone rejected by the builders, 44:20
suffering and, 49:5
suffering undeservedly, 50:9
suffering: as example, 36(2):4
teacher, 33(2):16; 36(1):1
Tell my brothers . . ., 44:23
There was no one to seek my soul, 39:24
This is our God, 47:15
touching, restraining, inspiring us, 49:3
trust in, 38:12
trusting in the least of his followers, 40:11
truth, 37:11
Unto the end, 45:1
Way, Truth, and Life, 42:4
weakened (for a time) , 40:14
what Christ did for us, 36(2):15
Whoever has seen me, Philip, 45:1
whole life as beautiful, 44:3
why have you forsaken me, 41:17; 43:2
will come as judge with mighty power, 37:20
You [Christ] have a demon, 35:17; 48(2):4
Jews, 33(1):6,9; 33(2):10; 37:11; 38:18; 40:9; 44:25; 45:6,10,12; 46:5,6,7; 47:2,3; 48(2):4
See also circumcision; Israel
Christ as, 44:12
Christ's kinfolk, 37:17
converts, 45:6
crucifixion of Christ and, 33(2):10; 40:1,13; 46:2; 48(1):5;
defeated by their own evil, 34(1):11
did not recognize Christ, 45:12
faithlessness, 46:12
gave Christ evil for good, 44:7
hate for Christ, 37:25
kill Christ for sake of national place, 40:12
loss of kingdom, 39:28
promised land, 44:8
rooted out from city, 40:12
salvation (Christ) comes from, 47:11
saw no beauty in Messiah, 44:3
signs: circumcision and unleavened bread, 39:13
try to trap Jesus, 50:8
victories over powerful forces, 43:2
Job, 33(2):4; 34(1):7,11; 36(1):11; 37:5; 45:13; 47:9; 48(2):9
John the Baptist, 35:9,18; 46:11; 49:11; 50:13
Jordan (river) , 41:12
journey, 34(1):6
joy, 33(2):9; 35:14; 36(2):8; 38:2; 39:11; 43:16,19-20; 45:8; 48(2):5
bones will dance for joy, 47:11; 50:13
Clap your hands . . ., 46:3
eternally present face of God, 41:9
God gladdens my newness, 42:5
in prayer, 34(2):6
leaping for joy, carrying their sheaves, 36(3):7
Judah: name means "confession" , 47:11
Judas, 34(1):10; 36(2):2; 40:8,9,11; 49:9
judge: appointment of, 36(2):22
attention to punishment, 44:18
judgment day, 36(1):3,7,10; 36(3):6; 43:15; 44:24; 47:9; 48(1):5
abyss, 35:10
certain people will share in judging, 49:8
certainty as fact; uncertainty as time, 36(1):1
choice ceases, 36(1):1
Come, you whom my Father has blessed, 49:13
confident waiting for, 36(1):10
conscience as witness, 37:21
distinguishing good people, 49:11
evil; last day, 48(1):6
Fire will go before him, 49:7,8
fruitful earth, 49:11
future judge (Christ) subjected to, 50:9
Gather his just ones to him, 49:12
God's anger and the sinner, 36(2):2
God's silence, 34(2):12; 49:6
hear my case, 36(3):13
heaven above and earth below will be called, 49:11
ignorance re last day, 36(1):1
intermingling of just and unjust, 36(3):17
nets cast to the right, 49:9
people invited to participate, 49:11
placed on left or right, 35:5
prophecy, 39:28
right hand filled with justice, 47:10
sheep and goats, 39:19
spiritual person judges everything, 49:27
swift arrival of, 44:10
thrones at, 49:9
Julian: apostasy, 36(2):18
just man: seed will be blessed, 36(3):7
just people: hands of the persecutor, 36(3):13
just person: destitute, 36(3):1,5
justice, 35:9; 44:18
beauty of, 41:7; 44:14
Christ will come as judge, 44:15
doing injustice to others, 35:1
God's unerring judgment, 34(1):9
hating sin, 50:7
heavens will proclaim, 49:13
mercy now; judgment later, 36(1):2
pursuit of, 37:26
righteousness, 39:19
supreme beauty, 44:3
two types of people, 36(2):1
works of mercy, 49:12
justice, 35:9; 44:18
justification, 49:2

kindness, 49:30
king(-s), 47:5
anointing, 44:19
kingdom of God, 50:19

See also heaven.
kingdoms, 45:10,13
knock(-ing), 33(1):1,4,7; 39:27
knowledge:
ability to bear, 36(1):1
divine and human, 49:18
tests: God causes us to know, 36(1):1
Korah:
children of, 41:2; 43:1,2,6-7,10,16,17,19-20; 44:1; 45:1,4,7; 46:2,7; 47:1
the name, 46:2
ladder, 38:2
angels ascending and descending, 44:20
lamb, 38:3; 44:6
land:
Church as Lord's land, 36(1):4
eternal, 36(3):11
inheritance of the gentle, 36(1):12
Jewish people, 44:8
language(-s), 50:19
tongues express one faith, 44:24
last day, *See* judgment day.
law, 38:10; 40:14
charity growing cold, 38:5
Christ brings law to perfection, 45:1
experience the sweetness of, 38:6
keeping with one's own strength, 40:4
mind vs. members, 44:7
promised land and, 44:8
put into hearts, 45:6
reflecting night and day, 36(3):5
Word of God and, 50:8
Lazarus and the rich man, 33(2):25; 38:22; 48(1):10; 48(2):1,7
laziness, 38:5
leaping across, 38:1,23,5,6
learning: learner is humble, 50:13
leaven, 39:13
leisure, 36(1):2
lentils, 46:6
letter and spirit, 33(1):7
life:
Christ's power over death, 40:10
daily pleasures, 48(1):10
human = just a few days, 36(2):16
longing for good days, 33(2):17
make known to me the number of my days, 38:5-7,9,10,22
promised in present and in future, 40:3,5
shortness of, 35:13; 36(3):1
successive stages of, 38:9
travel; no settling down, 34(1):6
light, 34(1):4; 34(2):6; 35:15; 36(1):6,7; 37:12,15; 38:6; 41:2
creation of, 47:1
drawing near to Christ, 33(2):10
one reality with truth, 42:4
lily, 47:8
lion, 39:1,21; 40:4; 44:6; 49:29
lips, 48(1):17; 49:23; 50:20
listen(-ing}, 33(1):1,4; 33(2):16; 48(1):2,3,5; 49:14,23; 50:5
delight and gladness, 50:13
hear first, then see, 44:25
only when you are God's people, 49:14
rumination in the heart, 46:1
loans: interest on, 36(3):6
righteous persons, 36(3):6
lodger, 38:21
longing, 38:6
As a deer longs . . ., 41:1,10
contemplation of the Lord forever, 41:5
for invisible realities of God, 41:8
Lord's Prayer:
brothers to Christ, 48(1):8
Forgive us our debts, 38:14
Lot (and wife), 33(1):5; 36(3):14
love, 37:11; 39:20; 44:28
appropriate, 39:28
bride of Christ *wounded with*, 37:5
carnal; jealousy, 33(2):6
Creator in the creature, 39:8
debased, 33(2):6
enemies, 39:1
God's saving help postponed, 34(2):9
grown cold = silence of the heart, 37:14; 39:1
holocaust = wholly on fire, 49:15
I am wounded by love, 44:16
paired commandments: God and neighbor, 33(2):10
runners' course, 39:11
strong as death, 47:13
within, 44:29
loyalty: all that God requires of us, 49:15
Lucilla, 36(2):19
lung: as pride, 50:12
lust, 33(2):6; 35:10; 39:3; 41:3; 50:3,5,24
lying, 38:4
lyre: and psaltery, 42:5

Maccabees, 33(2):22; 36(3):9
Majorinus, 36(2):19
malediction, 40:9
malevolence, 39:26
malice, 34(1):11; 49:26
manna, 33(1):3
manure, 49:7
Marratius, 36(2):20
marriage, 35:5; 44:1
martyrdom: motive or pain, 34(2):13
martyrs, 34(1):1; 35:14; 36(2):3; 36(3):13; 37:3; 39:1; 40:4; 41:19; 43:1; 47:13
celebrate birthdays of, 39:16
confessing the name of Christ, 43:21
falling asleep they arouse Christ, 43:22
growth of the Church, 40:1
mighty gentleness, 44:15
number of, 49:9

passion of Christ and, 40:1
soul does not die, 40:2
swallowed up alive, 34(2):15
unconquered souls, 36(3):13
Mary, Blessed Virgin, 34(2):3; 47:15; 50:10
Massa Candida, 49:9
material goods: longing for, 35:13
materialism: things of the spirit and, 38:3
Matthias, Apostle, 49:9
Maximian (-ists), 35:9; 36(2):19,22,23
condemnation of, 36(2):20,21,22
council proceedings against, 36(2):20
medicine, 37:5
meditation, 36(3):5
meekness, 33(2):5
Melchizedek, 33(1):5,6,7; 33(2):2
mercy, 33(1):9; 35:12,14; 36(3):6; 39:2,19,20; 40:6; 41:15,16; 42:2; 43:15; 45:13; 46:13; 49:7,28; 50:1,6,11
Christ's wounded members, 39:20
Do not sit in judgment . . ., 42:7
God postpones the last day, 36(1):1
God's justice in this world, 36(1):2
God's manifold mercies, 35:11
heaven and earth, 35:7,8
immense, 50:14
love God for his mercy, 44:18
recipient of, as neighbor, 48(1):14
sacrifice and, 44:27
sinning knowingly and, 50:6
merit, 36(3):6; 48(2):3; 49:9,31
Messiah, 35:13; 44:3; 50:13
metaphor: tongue and pen of a scribe, 44:6,10
midday, 36(1):7
milk, 33(1):6; 38:3
millstone, 36(1):2
mind, 44:6; 49:28
childish cast of, 46:2
devil corrupting, 39:1
fixed on God alone, 48(2):4
gift, 36(2):13
governs body, 41:7
image of God, 42:6; 48(2):11
understanding and, 42:6
miracles, 35:8; 43:4; 45:4,15
miser, 38:11
misery, 39:3
misfortune, 41:6,9; 49:22
mockery, 46:2,7; 48(1)11; 48(2):4
money, 48(2):4
See also wealth
good use = lending to Christ, 48(1):9
keeping it safe, 48(1):12
money-lenders, 36(3):6; 38:11
moral standards, 50:24
mortality, 37:5; 42:2; 50:10
Moses, 36(2):12; 36(3):20; 40:13,14; 47:1; 48(1):5; 49:9,14; 50:8
mother:
apparent cruelty of, 33(2):20
breast milk, 33(1):6
giving babies to nurses, 49:27
oppositions in household, 44:11,12
motives, 43:21
mountain (-s), 42:4
abyss and, 35:10
authorities of this world, 45:7
city of God on, 47:2,3
clouds as, 45:10
Come, let us go up, 45:12
friend of the Bridegroom, 35:9
metaphor, 35:10
my voice heard from, 47:2
people called clouds, 35:9
people who are great, 39:6
shifted out to sea, 45:6,7,10
stone grown to be mighty, 45:12
mourn: beatitude, 34(2):6,7; 37:2
mousetrap, 34(1):10
mule, 33(2):5
murder, 50:2,10
murmuring, 36(3):8
music, 41:10
mustard seed, 45:6
mystery, 46:1
invisible sacramental oil, 44:19
queenly apparel, 44:24
touching God, 33(2):23
mystical body of Christ:
I was hungry and you fed me, 39:5
single person asking God's help, 39:28
Why are you persecuting me, 39:5

name(-s):
meanings of personal names, 33(1):4
mysterious change of, 33(1):2-3,7; 33(2):2
Nathan, 50:2,5,8
Nathanael, 44:20
nation(-s), 48(2):4
he summoned all the earth, 49:4
Hear these things . . ., 48(1):2
Jesus as king of, 46:9
subjected peoples, 46:5
neighbor, 37:17
Good Samaritan, 48(1):14
person to whom we show mercy, 48(1):14
nets: one hundred and fifty-three fish, 49:9
New Covenant, 38:9; 49:16
New Testament:
elder (O.T.) will serve the new, 40:14
promise: kingdom of heaven, 34(1):7
night, 41:6,16; 47:1; 48(2):3,4
Nineveh, 49:28; 50:11
noise, 45:14
numbers, 39:10
five (senses) , 49:9
one hundred and fifty-three, 49:9
representing crowds, 49:9
ten plus seven, 49:9
Numidia (-ns), 36(2):19,20
nurse fostering her children, 49:27

obedience, 41:9; 49:23
occasions of sin, 50:3
oil: visible and invisible, 44:19
old age, 36(2):16; 36(3):1,9
Old Covenant, 38:9
Old Testament:
  earthly blessings desired in, 35:13
  promise re temporal goods, 34(1):7
  prophecies, 40:14
olive, 46:13
original sin: forbidden fruit, 47:9
  Through one man sin entered . . ., 50:10
overcoming: two kinds of people, 34(1):8
ownership: God as owner, 49:18
  greed, 39:7
pagans, 39:16; 40:1,14; 41:2,6; 43:12,22; 48(2):1
pain, 34(2):13; 37:4; 42:5
  body's distress, 42:6
  corrective, 40:6
  God's precept, 38:17
  keeping silent from good words, 38:4
  love and, 37:5
  relief on bed of, 40:5
  scourging, 37:24
  silence from good words, 38:4
Pancratius of Badias, 36(2):20
parable, 48(1):5
paradise: *today you will be with me*, 39:15
paralysis: inner person, 36(3):3
pardon, 35:3; 50:8
party, 41:9
passions: control, 39:9
pastimes, 40:5
path: narrow or broad, 39:6,7; 43:17
patience, 34(1):10; 37:5; 40:13; 50:19
Paul, apostle, Saint, 35:8,9; 39:3; 43:1,21; 44:20,22,32; 45:7; 46:5; 47:6,14; 48(1):3
  Barnabas and, 33(2):19
  bound in Jerusalem, 36(2):6
  glorious in his preaching, 44:22
  good days, 33(2):17
  slandered, 49:27
  taken up to third heaven, 37:12
  throne on judgment day, 49:9
peace, 34(2):6; 35:6; 38:16; 39:16,28; 48(2):6; 49:23
  bedroom of the heart, 35:5
  delight in abundance of, 36(1):12
  everlasting, 33(2):23
  husband and wife, 33(2):8
  none in my bones, 37:6
  seek; pursue, 33(2):19
  sin and, 45:3
  Why do you disquiet me, 33(2):19
peacemakers, 36(3):16
penance: ashamed of, 50:8
penitent, 47:5; 50:15
penitential psalm, 44:18
Pentecost, 45:8; 49:4
perfection:
  being: *I AM WHO AM*, 38:22
  knowing one cannot be perfect, 38:14
  like your Father in heaven, 49:28
  not reached in this life, 38:13,14
perish, 44:22; 48(1):12,13; 48(2):4
  unjust will perish entirely, 36(3):16
  works of the godless, 36(3):10
Perpetua, Passion of, 47:13
persecution, 34(1):6; 34(2):1; 40:8; 43:13,14,17,22,23-24,26
  being heard in time of, 33(2):22
  bones not broken, 34(1):14
  cause of right, 43:1
  cause of the right, 34(2):13
  Church: Head and body, 34(2):8
  conversion and, 34(1):8
  devil and the Church, 40:1
  God as our ally, 34(1):4
  God's help is slow in coming, 34(2):9
  God's love and, 34(2):9
  guilt, 36(2):3
  never ceases, 39:1
  ongoing, 34(2):8
persecutors, 36(3):13
  swallowed up by, 34(2):15
perseverance, 36(1):7; 39:1,11; 41:11; 44:25; 50:19
Perseverantius of Theveste, 36(2):20
personification, 43:19-20
perversity, 48(1):1
Peter, Apostle, Saint, 34(2):4,6,15; 36(1):1; 36(2):8; 43:19-20; 44:23,32; 45:4; 49:13
  Do you love me, 37:17
  fear in his heart, 39:23
  fear; denial of Christ, 37:17
  hidden weakness, 41:13
  rescue by angel, 33(2):22
  walking on water, 39:9
  would run ahead of Christ, 39:25
petition: carnal, 36(1):5
  for temporal goods, 43:2
Pharaoh, 33(1):3
Pharisee, 39:20,27; 48(1):5; 49:30
physician, 34(1):7; 35:17; 39:8; 40:6; 45:4,11; 47:3; 49:31; 50:7,8,11
  apparent cruelty of, 33(2):20
  does what he sees is necessary, 34(2):13
  love for the sick person, 47:4
piety, 46:13
pilgrim(-age), 38:21; 41:9,10; 42:2; 49:22
pit of misery, 39:3
pity, 50:6
plan (building) , 44:4
planter (Paul) , 35:9
pleasure, 34(1):12; 35:6; 38:2,3,6,15; 39:8; 40:5; 43:16,17; 47:9; 49:7,27; 50:1,3
Pomponius of Macri, 36(2):20
poor:

animal sacrifice and, 49:20
generosity of the, 36(2):13
prayers (borrowed money), 36(3):6
promises for present labors, 48(1):10
shall eat and be satisfied, 48(1):3
sons of men, 48(1):3
possessions, 48(2):5
choosing God = having all, 34(1):12
content with the necessary, 39:28
Go and sell all you possess, 43:25
master of or mastered by, 48(1):2
pain of not possessing, 37:5
potter, 38:17
poverty: bless the Lord, 33(2):3
cry out as a poor person, 33(2):11
help for the needy, 36(1):2
power: God, *stretch out your hand*, 34(1):7
Praetextatus, bishop of Assuras, 36(2):20
praise, 44:33
bless the Lord at all times, 33(2):3,4; 35:16; 48(2):10
confession as, 34(2):10
doing everything well, 34(2):16
extends to ends of earth, 47:10
forever and ever, 41:11; forever, 43:9
glory to God, 39:4
God *extremely worthy of*, 47:2
God's house, 41:9
leading good lives as, 47:10
mercenary, 48(2):9,10
mouth of a sinner, 47:2; 49:29
open my lips . . ., 50:20
righteousness, 50:23
sacrifice of, 49:21,22,23,30,31
seeking, 35:5
sing a new song to the Lord, 39:4,13
situations negate praise of God, 49:30
spurious, 39:26
thanksgiving, 44:9
times of good fortune, 48(2):9
when benefits are received, 48(2):10
prayer, 36(1):8; 36(2):13; 44:33; 49:21
See also praise
crying out from a deep place, 39:3
desire is continuous, 37:14
Do not turn your face away, 50:14,16
fallen silent when love stops, 37:14
Go into your private room . . . 35:5
grown slack, 49:22
happiness, when heard, 33(2):8
the heart as private room for, 33(2):8
interior desire never ceases, 37:14
joy in, 34(2):6
listen for my weeping, 38:20
manipulating God, 39:4
necessary petition: *Send forth your light . . .*, 42:4
not heard, 33(2):9
poor persons, 36(3):6
profit to us, not to God, 39:4
seeking things extraneous from God, 33(2):9
temptation and, 34(2):3
two wings: fasting and almsdeeds, 42:8
waited and waited for the Lord, 39:2
within me, 33(2):8; 34(2):5; 41:17
preach(-er; -ing), 35:8
begetting children by, 44:23
example to the faithful, 36(3):20
pregnancy: symbol of hope, 39:28
prelates: workers in the field, 36(1):2
presence: of Abimelech, 33(1):7
of God: keeping guard over conduct, 38:3
pride, 33(1):4,9,10; 33(2):5,10; 35:10,17,18; 37:8,10; 38:18; 39:6,20,25; 41:12; 44:29; 46:13; 47:6; 48(1):3,9; 48(2):2; 50:4,12
priest(-hood) Jewish, 39:13
Levitical, 36(2):20
order of Melchizedek, 33(1):5
Primian, 36(2):19,20,21,23
prize, 38:6,8,14; 39:11
probation, 36(1):11
proclamation: lips in opposition to heart, 39:15,17
procreation: sexual union required, 44:4
prodigal son, 47:3
professions: integrity in, 36(1):2
profit (money-lenders, 36(3):6
promise:
bones of Christians guarded, 33(2):24
God delivers, 39:12
not abandoned on earth, 40:3
only what gospel promises, 39:28
perfect accomplishment of, 39:12
prophecies in scripture, 39:28
property: all belongs to Creator, 49:17
sold; proceeds given to apostles, 46:4
prophecy(-ies; -ets), 33(1):7; 44:2
banishing of wars, 45:13
Church heard the promises, 47:7
future as if already past, 43:8
Nathan's purpose, 50:8
promises in scripture, 39:28
requests phrased as desires, 34(1):8
salvation, 37:28
prosperity, 36(2):16; 41:6,16; 43:2,17
danger to the soul, 50:4
devil and, 40:4
envy and, 36(1):9
protection, 33(2):13
providence:
care, comforting, correcting, 39:27
created beings as medium for, 43:5
God does not abandon on earth, 40:3
God helps through human agency, 34(1):6
God's plan for Israel, 43:2
hear God in good words, 49:23
purpose in Israel's history, 43:2

steps directed by the Lord, 36(2):15
temporal needs and, 34(1):7
provocation, 34(1):11
prudence, 36(2):11; 48(1):12
psalms:
Christ speaks in, 39:5
listening to Christ in, 34(1):1
opening page of the book, 39:14
resurrection of Christ, 47:1
Songs of Ascents, 38:2
who is speaker in, 37:6
psaltery, 42:5; 48(1):5
punishment, 34(1):10; 37:5
banished from the face of God, 49:7
God turning toward sins, 50:14
as grace, 38:17
justice, 50:7
liability related to intention, 40:9
owing to us, 49:31
sin demands p. , 44:18
purity, 39:21; 42:4,7; 44:25

Quintasius of Capsa, 36(2):20

rain, 39:27; 42:2; 45:10; 46:13
reality, 35:14,15
rebuke, 37:3,25; 38:2; 49:24,28
redemption, 33(2):26
bodies and, 50:19
by Christ alone, 48(1):8
cost of redeeming one's soul, 48(1):9,13
seeking God, 34(1):15
reflection, 35:14
mind sees itself through itself, 41:7
refuges, 45:2,4
relaxation, 40:5
religion:
God as our allotted portion, 34(1):12
having appearance only, 47:13
honoring God with lips; heart far away, 37:17
remembering, 35:12; 37:2,11
repentance, 33(2):11; 36(1):2; 39:19,23; 48(2):4; 49:6,7,28; 50:1
rest, 36(1):2; 37:2,14; 48(2):6; 49:22
resurrection of the body, 34(2):1
equality with an angel, 36(1):10
hope for bodily pleasures, 43:16
vision reserved for, 43:5
retention: holding on to today, syllable, etc., 38:7
retirement, 36(2):16
retribution: judgment day, 36(2):2
reward, 36(3):9
doing bad things and, 33(2):18
earthly, 35:13
goal of following Christ's way, 36(2):16
intention and, 40:9
rich, 33(2):14; 48(1):9
See also Lazarus and the rich man
blessed in this life, 48(2):8
death and Lazarus, 33(2):25
earthlings, 48(1):3
grandiose funerals for, 48(1):13; 48(2):1
poor and rich neighbors, 39:28
poor man who lay at rich man's gate, 36(2):7
truly needy, 33(2):15
trust in God, not wealth, 44:28
righteous(-ness), 33(2):15,21,22; 35:5; 38:5,8,18; 39:3,9; 42:3,7; 43:25; 44:17; 46:6; 48(2):3,4
believers, 39:6
bread as, 48(2):8
child of righteous parents, 36(3):1,2
Christ the Head of all since world began, 36(3):4
dominion over the wicked, 48(2):4,11
faith and, 36(1):6; 39:7; 50:18
heart, 35:16; 39:15
hunger and thirst for, 48(2):8
invisible enemies, 34(1):5
justice and, 39:19
measure of, 33(2):26
nothing derogatory in our lives, 34(1):4
pain of losing, 37:24
painful death, 33(2):25
persecuted, 34(1):14
person as God's sword, 34(1):2
praise God always, 34(2):16
sacrifice, 50:23
scepter of righteous rule, 44:18
semblance of, 49:30
spirit is life through, 40:3
strengthened, 36(2):4,6
throne of Wisdom, 46:10
troubles of the, 33(2):23
usury, 36(3):6
vindication, 34(2):14
will possess the earth, 36(3):11
wisdom, 36(3):12
river: *joy to God's city*, 45:8
rock, 39:9,25; 44:6
Roman law, 39:13
Rome, 44:23
Romulus, 44:23
root, 48(2):4
ruler(-s), 44:17
running, 33(2):10; 38:6,8; 39:11; 41:2,3

Sabbath, 37:2,5,10
never ceasing to pray, 37:14
remembering, 37:5,9,10,12,13,15
sackcloth, 34(2):3,4,5
sacraments, 33(1):8
flowing from Christ asleep on the cross, 40:10
good lives and receiving, 47:8
sacred scriptures, *See* Bible.

sacrifice, 39:12,13; 50:7
Aaron (animals); 33(1):5
animal as symbolic, 50:21
Christ (his body and blood) ,33(1):5
cross, 33(1):6
good things are within (spiritual) , 50:21
inner; within me, 41:17
mercy and covenant, 44:27; 49:12
myself as victim to immolate, 49:21
New Covenant, 49:16
no fault found with, 49:15
of praise, 49:21,22,23,30.31
old superseded by the new, 39:13
prefigured in Old Covenant, 49:16
slaughter animals for the poor, 49:20
troubled spirit, 49:15
Sadducees, 43:16
sadness, 39:2; 41:18; 48(2):5
sin as cause, 42:3
wicked people and, 36(1):3
saint(-s), 36(3):9,11; 47:10; 49:11
Church of Christ, 47:1
garments of the Church, 44:22
God speaks through, 44:5
heaven: word = all saints, 49:11
mocked, 48(2):4
tabernacles of God, 44:23
Your right hand will conduct you . . ., 44:15
Salem (later Jerusalem) , 33(1):5
saliva, 33(1):11; 33(2):4; 38:3
salvation, 33(1):10; 33(2):13; 34(1):5,6,7,12; 36(2):8,11; 37:3,5; 38:20; 39:6,15,16,18,26; 40:9,14; 44:7,22; 47:5; 48(2):5; 50:3,19
animals, 35:11,12
body and blood of Christ, 33(1):6
certain as if already accomplished, 43:8
confession of the Good Thief, 34(1):14
given birth to spirit of, 39:28
gladness of, 50:17
good person is pitted against evil, 36(2):1
hope and, 41:11
Jacob, 43:5
prophets, 37:28
remnant, 33(1):7
Samaritan: man who fell among robbers, 48(1):14
sanctification, 45:8
Satan: the word, 39:25
Saul, King, 33(1):2; 33(2):2; 50:4
Saul (later Paul) , 36(2):2,5; 50:11,12
arrow (word) turned him into Paul, 44:16
Why are you persecuting me, 44:20
scandal, 33(2):14
schism(-atics), 40:9; 49:9
scourging, 37:23,24
sea, 45:6,15
seasons: changing, 41:16
second coming of Christ, 45:12
Christ will not come in silence, 49:28
Our God will come openly, 49:6,11
seed: good seed, 42:2
sowing, 36(3):7,14
seeking, 39:24,26
self: soul is troubled when turned to, 41:12
self-control, 50:3
self-indulgence, 38:5
self-love, 44:9
senses, 36(2):13; 38:16; 41:7; 49:9
sensuality, 34(1):9
serpent, 47:9; 48(1):1
servant: parable of lazy steward, 38:5
serving fellow-servants, 38:4
sexual intercourse, 50:10
shame, 33(2):10,11; 43:10
doing penance, 50:8
face to face with yourself, 49:28
sheep, 48(2):2,3: 50:8
shield, 34(1):2; 45:13
shows (entertainment), 39:9,10
Christian martyrs, 39:16
sick, 50:1
disarranged all his bedding, 40:5
time passes slowly for, 36(1):10
sign: miraculous, 45:12
Peter walking on water, 39:9
silence, 33(2):8; 49:6,26
fear of committing sin, 38:4
God will come openly, 49:6
quiet re something I should have said, 38:4
sins with the tongue, 38:3
soft sound from above, 42:7
vacillation, 38:5
Simeon, 39:18
similarity, 34(2):6
sin(-s), 35:10; 37:1,9,10; 41:18
See also confession; conversion; forgiveness of sin; repentance; sinner
acting in ignorance, 50:6,7
affection for, 35:1
all spring from greed or fear, 38:2
attachment to, 36(1):1
bodily members at disposal of, 41:9
chastisement for, 38:17
choosing to be bitten by snake, 41:3
Christ seems to take all as his own, 37:16
concur simply by approving, 49:25
consent, 50:3
corruption a result of, 50:19
death and, 34(2):3; 50:10
deceiving ourselves, 38:14
deep calls to deep, 41:14
defending, 35:10
despair, 50:5
doing wrong knowingly; great mercy, 50:6
enslaved for law of sin, 35:6
falling; rising again, 50:3
fear of committing; silence, 38:4

God turning toward = punishment, 50:14
God's absence from conscience, 45:3
great sins guarded against, 39:22
grieving for, 37:24
harm to self, not to God, 50:15
hate for, 35:6; 50:7
human nature, 44:18
humble confession of, 34(2):3
intention, 50:3
Jesus and propitiation for, 33(2):26
Jesus asked to judge adultress, 50:8
lesser folk and the great, 50:3,5
many bloods (plural) , 50:19
more numerous than hairs of my head, 39:22
myself punishing my sin, 50:7
Nathan's parable, 50:8
no peace in my bones, 37:6
occasions of, 50:3
only thing not received from God, 44:7
patron saint for, 50:3
peace and, 45:3
perseverance in, 35:6
pleasing to unclean spirit, 50:16
punishment by God, 44:18
sadness caused by, 42:3
secret, 35:17
self-justification, 50:13
slaves to, 40:6
spiritual blindness, 39:21
suffering for, 40:6
take serious thought for, 37:24
Turn your face away . . ., 44:18; 50:16
unconcern about small sins, 39:22
unwitting; small mercy, 50:6
Wash me more and more . . ., 50:7
weighed down by number of, 39:20
whip = medicine against, 37:24
with open eyes, 50:1
sincerity, 39:13,16
sinner(-s), 34(1):11; 35:1; 36(1):10; 36(3):20; 39:3,20; 47:2
arms crushed, 36(2):4
borrows on interest, 36(2):13
commended; supported, 49:25
conscience; cure, 45:3
determination to do wrong, 35:2
earthlings, 48(1):3
elder shall serve the younger, 46:6
fallen; foot of pride, 35:18
fear of being rebuked, 35:2
God foresees judgment day, 36(2):2
God strikes and heals, 50:11
God will blot out their memory from earth, 50:14
I will make you as white as snow, 50:12
imitation of, 35:18
perishing, 36(3):14
praise in mouth of, 49:29
proud head held high, 37:8
receives praise, 39:26
seeks to kill the just, 36(3):12,13
strangers to God, 47:8
sword piercing their own heart, 36(2):3
taking stand against God, 38:3
teaching, by ex-sinner, 50:18
tents of, 48(1):2
tolerating, 36(3):17
unaware of God watching, 35:3
uses in present world, 36(1):11
washed white as snow, 44:26
will perish, 36(2):10
wretched death of, 33(2):25,26
sky, 47:1
slander, 36(3):19; 49:27
slave: property of master, 49:17
ugly but faithful, 33(2):15
sleep, 40:10
smoke, 36(2):12; 36(3):14
snake, 39:1; 40:4; 41:3
snow, 50:12
sojourning, 38:21
son: severed from father, 44:12
Son of God:
See also Jesus Christ; Word of God
begetting of, 44:5
equal to the Father, 35:1
Nathanael's confession, 44:20
once rich, became poor, 39:28
one nature with the Father, 49:2
Word and, 44:5
Son of Man:
body is on earth, 44:20
judgment through, 48(1):5
our immortality and, 44:21
sons of men belong to, 48(1):3
song: epithalamia, 44:3
new hymn to our God, 39:13
Songs of Ascents, 38:2
sons of men (biblical usage) , 35:12; 48(1):3
soothsayers, 40:1
sorrow: pain of the soul, 42:3,6
soul:
See also body and soul; spiritual life
blessed during lifetime, 48(2):8
caring for, 34(1):6
disquiet in, 33(2):19
God's weapon, 34(1):2
king's daughters, 44:23
made by God, does not die, 40:2
My soul is sorrowful . . ., 42:7
poured out above myself, 41:8,10
power to kill one's own soul, 36(2):3
price of redemption, 48(1):9,13
rewards and punishments, 37:11
righteous; chair for Wisdom, 46:10
salvation, 48(2):5
seeking Christ's life (good way; bad way) , 37:18

separation from God = death, 48(2):2
servant of God, 46:10
sorrowful, 41:10,19
sword to defeat the devil, 34(1):7
troubled when it turns on self, 41:12
Why are you sorrowful, 42:6,7
sounding-chamber, 42:5
sour grapes, 48(2):8
sovereignty, 44:17; 48(1):2
speak(-er; -ing), 48(1):5
changes in sacred scripture, 44:8
fallen silent because of fear, 38:4
mouth to speak with, 38:16
wait to hear from God before s. , 38:4
spectacle (shows), 39:9
speech:
sound; fading away, 44:6
tongue, 50:19
spider, 38:18
spirit:
carnally-minded persons and, 38:3
existing, but not material, 50:17
good things of the, 33(2):15
heat; ardent in s. , 50:23
new and upright, 50:15
spiritual wealth, 33(2):15
troubled, 41:17; 49:15; 50:21
spiritual life:
ascetical practices, 41:9
beginning to live for God, 48(2):4
danger in prosperity, 50:4
inner thirst, 41:2
inward paralysis, 36(3):3
nourishment for the soul, 35:1; 38:3
running, 38:9
soul close to God, 34(2):6
weary of well-doing, 36(3):2
springs, 41:5
stealing, 36(1):12
steps: *directed by the Lord*, 36(2):15
Songs of Ascents, 38:2
steward: parable: entrusted with master's money, 38:5
still: *Be still and see that I am God*, 45:14
stone (-s), 39:1
anyone who trips over, 45:12
grew to be a mighty mountain, 45:12
pagan god, 41:6
worship of, 46:9,11
storm, 45:5; 49:13
strangers: children of wicked people, 48(1):14
leave their wealth to strangers, 48(1):14,15
parents and children, 48(1):14
straw: gold refined from, 36(1):11
strength, 37:15
beard as symbol of, 33(1):11; 33(2):4
from God or self, 45:3
refusal to be strong, 38:18
relying on one's own, 34(1):15; 48(1):7,8,9; 49:22
vicious, 38:18
stumbling-block, 49:27
suffering, 36(1):6; 39:16; 42:5; 44:15
acceptance of, 42:8
call upon God in, 49:22
Christ came to suffer, 49:5
Christ's life; Christian life, 36(2):16,17
Church suffers what Christ suffers, 40:8
done to death all the day long, 43:1
drinking the bitter cup of, 48(1):11
glory in, 36(2):9
Head and body, the Church, 37:16
imitating sufferings of Christ, 37:18
inflicted by Saul (later Paul) , 36(2):5
inner person, 37:15,16
inward from self; outward from others, 37:16
motive of martyrs, 34(2):13
must will Christ's suffering to be ours, 37:16
promised share with Christ, 36(1):9
renown as motive for, 43:21
sin; corrective pain, 40:6
temporal, 36(2):16; 48(2):9
voluntary, 34(2):1
summer, 41:16
sun, 34(1):13; 38:10; 39:27; 41:6; 42:2
Susanna: prayer by, 34(2):5
swallowing, 34(2):15
swiftly (the word) , 44:6
sword, 36(2):3
God loosening his sword, 34(1):4
made from servant's soul, 34(1):7
word as, 44:11
syllable: holding on to, 38:7
synagogue: as mother of Christ, 44:12

tabernacle, 41:9
Tarshish (Tarsus), 47:6
taste (in art) , 34(2):2
tax, 49:29
tax-collector, 39:20,27; 49:31
teacher, 36(1):1; 50:13
tears: daily diet, 41:7
delicious, 41:6
temple: living stones, 44:31
one stone formed from many, 39:1
veil rent asunder, 45:1
temporal goods, 48(1):17; 48(2):9
as blessings, 48(2):8
bless the Lord, 33(2):3
craving for, 36(3):13
death and, 48(2):7
desire for blessings (O.T.), 35:13
desire for gains, 38:3
entire concern for, 48(2):2
food that will perish, 33(2):14
gifts of God, 35:7

God and temporal needs, 34(1):7
happiness, 48(2):1
Old Testament promises, 34(1):7
petitioning God for, 35;12; 43:2
uncertainty of wealth, 45:2
wallowing in, 34(1):12
wicked people flourishing, 36(1):3
worship and, 43:16
temptation, 33(2):8; 34(1):3,14; 34(2):10; 36(1):1; 36(3):19; 38:10; 39:21; 41:18; 42:3
devil's evil suggestions, 48(1):6
Get behind me, Satan, 34(1):8
God as disinterested in us, 48(2):6
law too hard to keep, 40:4
prayer in, 34(2):3
tense (verbs):
prophets and future events, 43:9
tent (-s), 41:9,10,17; 42:4; 44:3; 45:10; 48(1):2,15
test (-s):
coming to know oneself, 43:19-20
disinterested worship, 43:15
God tests in order that we know, 36(1):1
sinners used to test the just, 36(1):11
thanksgiving: praise as, 44:9; 49:21
thigh, 44:13,20
thirst, 41:6
Thomas, Apostle:
Because you have seen . . ., 49:5
My Lord and my God, 48(2):5; 49:5
thorns, 47:8
threat, 41:15
threshing-floor, 34(1):10; 36(3):19; 45:10; 47:8,9,14; 49:8
threshold, 33(1):10; 33(2):2
throne: of Wisdom, 46:10
stands for ever and ever, 44:17
time:
holding on: today; yesterday, 38:7
number of my days, 38:7,9,10,22
present days as true being, 38:7
quick passage of, 44:10
slow passage of, 36(1):10
Timothy: advice against pride, 48(1):9
title, 33(1):2
Tobit, 41:7
tolerance, 50:24
tombs, 48(1):15,16
tongue:
My tongue is the pen of a scribe, 44:6,10
restrain from evil, 33(2):18
sinning with, 38:3
words, 34(2):3; 50:19
torrent, 35:14,15
tortuousness, 44:17
torture, 39:16; 49:7
bones remain unbroken, 33(2):24
trap, 34(1):11; 50:8
treasure: heart and, 48(2):2
storing in heaven, 38:12
tree, 34(2):2; 36(3):9; 48(2):3,4; 49:11
tribulation, 34(1):1; 39:28; 41:16; 45:3,4; 49:22; 50:4
Trinity, 35:1; 49:1,2; 50:17
trouble(-s), 33(2):23; 36(3):17; 42:5; 43:2,3,17; 49:22
trust, 48(1):3,8
blessed trust, 33(2):13
defense: trust in God, 37:21
deliverance by God, 43:3
human agents, 35:9
in God, not self, 41:12
in Truth, 35:13
in wealth or in God, 48(1):9
truth, 33(2):6; 34(2):6; 35:14; 37:11; 38:3; 39:13;18; 40:8; 41:3,18; 42:2; 44:15,19; 45:13; 46:13; 50:11
Christ speaks through us, 34(2):12
enemies of, 36(2):12
gods and, 49:2
must hear before speaking, 38:4
one reality with light, 42:4
promised; given, 39:12
soundness of mind, 39:8
trust in, 35:13
unutterable reality, 35:14
witness to, and child of, 38:3
Tyre:
daughters of, as Church, 44:28
symbol of Gentiles, 44:27
Tyrian maidens, 44:27,28

ugliness, 44:3
unbelief (-ievers), 47:3
children of the devil, 44:12
prophecies of Christ and, 39:1
understanding, 41:2,9,13,18; 47:7; 48(1):16; 49:22
children of Korah, 43:2,6-7,10,16,17,19-20
failure; refusing, 35:1,4
image of God, 48(2):11
like a horse or mule, 42:6; 48(1):16
meditation of my heart, 48(1):4
Sing psalms with, 46:9
spiritual, 33(1):7,8
Whoever sees me sees the Father, 44:3
ungodly, 36(1):9,11; 36(2):2; 36(3):13; 47:11; 49:13
union with God:
misery: not yet one with God, 49:22
unity, 33(2):6; 36(2):19; 39:1; 47:7
body of Christ as one single person, 39:28
charity and, 33(2):19
cornerstone, 47:5
gown as symbol of, 44:24
Head and body (Church) , 40:1
King's temple, 44:31

one in saying *My God, my God* . . ., 40:6
promote: magnify the Lord, 33(2):7
two Testaments in agreement, 49:4
Unto the end (term), 45:1
usury, 36(3):6

values, 48(2):11
earthly, 36(3):9
false, 48(1):13
vice, 41:3
Victorinus of Leptis Magna, 36(2):20
Victorinus of Munatiana, 36(2):20
vindication, 34(2):13,14
vineyard, 35:8; 36(1):8; 37:28; 46:13
virgins:
five wise, five foolish, 49:9
innumerable, 49:9
long to please the king, 44:30
pleasing the Bridegroom, 44:32
virtue, 41:9
power of charity, 47:13
Set your hearts on, 47:13-14
vision: face-to-face, 48(1):5

wages, 35:13
parable of vineyard, 37:28
war, 42:4; 45:13
warped beam, 44:17
warriors, 43:4; 44:13
waste: of God's gifts, 44:9
water:
longing for a drop from Lazarus, 48(1):10
rivers of living water, 45:8
way: *salvation among the nations*, 39:18
weakness, 33(2):4,8; 38:18; 41:13; 45:13; 49:5; 50:3
body of Christ, 37:22
donkey of the Lord, 33(2):5
wealth, 33(2):14; 48(1):7,8,9
despise riches in Christ's name, 48(1):17
give away; claim eternal interest, 36(3):6
leave their wealth to strangers, 48(1):14,15
riches taken away as test, 34(1):6
sinfulness and, 48(1):12
spiritual, 33(2):15
storing up, for children, 38:12
weapons, 38:15; 45:13,14
evangelical, 45:13
ourselves as, 34(1):2
wedding: clothes, 44:1,23
invited guests as the bride, 44:3
weeds, 42:3
weeping, 38:20
well-spring: fountain of life, 41:2
wheat, 34(2):10
whips, 36(3):9; 37:24; 40:6
wicked (-ness), 42:2
ancestors, 48(2):11
following behind, 34(1):8
good fortune, 41:9
happy; flourishing, 36(1):3
hate for, 35:6
seen as prospering, 48(2):6
will: human affections and, 44:23
will of God:
Christ's example, 39:14
cling to God, 43:25
conformity with, 35:16; 44:17
discerning, 36(3):2
duty of humans is to obey, 48(1):1
just persons, 36(3):5
living and dying, 34(1):14
peoples seek to bend to their own lusts, 44:17
power of the enemy and, 36(2):4
rightly directed, 36(1):12
wills (law): testator and adjudicator, 36(3):18
wind, 34(1):9
wings like a dove's, 38:2
winter, 41:16
day of tribulation, 48(1):12
present time as, 36(1):3
wisdom, 41:3,13; 44:25; 50:23
Christ as Wisdom of the Father, 36(1):1
divine, 33(2):6
God's throne, 34(1):2
Let those who are perfect be wise . . ., 38:14
My mouth shall speak wisdom, 48(1):4
righteous person as throne of, 46:10
righteous will muse on, 36(3):12
soul as weapon, 34(1):2
unseen, hidden secrets of, 50:11
when he sees the wise dying, 48(1):11
wives: cross-grained, 33(2):8
woman: bent over for eighteen years, 37:10
wondrous feats, 39:9
Word of God:
all of past, present, future are in Word, 44:5
all works of God are in the Word, 44:5
Bridegroom, 44:7
creation and, 49:18
In the beginning . . ., 33(1):6; 44:3,20; 46:8; 49:1; 50:17
never ceases to be spoken, 44:5
seeing face to face, 33(1):10
words:
arrows *sharp and very powerful*, 44:16
blurting or belching, 44:9
good words by one leading bad life, 49:30
morality related to intent, 39:26
sword, 44:11
You have thrown my words behind you, 49:24
words of God (scripture):
arrows, 37:5
bread as, 36(3):5
effective in conversion of life, 49:1
in the heart, 36(3):12

works: praise offered to God, 44:9
works of mercy: justice and, 49:12
world (-liness), 40:5
  active involvement in, 36(1):2
  as meaning 'sinners', 34(1):4
  chosen way, 48(2):4
  illiterate can read book of, 45:7
  swallowing, 34(2):15
  universality, 36(2):19
worship, 43:15,16; 45:10; 48(1):1,3; 50:18
  gifts as motive for, 35:7
  idols and the world's Creator, 34(1):13
  put right in matter of, 46:9
  reward for, 35:7; 43:16
wound: love and pain, 37:5
writing, 34(2):3
written word: abiding, 44:6
wrongdoer(-s; -ing), 49:26
  enslaved to, 33(2):14
  failure to understand, 35:1,4
  God sees what he must reproach, 42:7
  wound themselves, 36(2):3

years, 38:7
youth: symbol of newness, 42:5

Zacchaeus, 49:13,21
zeal, 47:2
Zion, 47:3,6,7,12,13; 49:4; 50:22